Understanding Children's Development
Third Edition

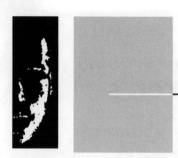

Basic Psychology

This series offers those new to the study of psychology comprehensive, systematic and accessible introductions to the core areas of the subject. Written by specialists in their fields, they are designed to convey something of the flavour and excitement of psychological research today.

Understanding Children's Development
Third Edition
Peter K. Smith, Helen Cowie and Mark Blades

Understanding Neuropsychology
J. Graham Beaumont

Understanding Cognition
Peter J. Hampson and Peter E. Morris

Understanding Abnormal Psychology
Neil Frude

Understanding Children's Development

Third Edition

Peter K. Smith,
Helen Cowie
and Mark Blades

First published 1988
Reprinted 1988, 1989
Second edition 1991
Reprinted 1991, 1992, 1993, 1994, 1995, 1996
Third edition 1998

2 4 6 8 10 9 7 5 3 1

Blackwell Publishers Ltd
108 Cowley Road
Oxford OX4 1JF
UK

Blackwell Publishers Inc.
350 Main Street
Malden, Massachusetts 02148
USA

British Library Cataloguing in Publication Data

A CIP catalogue record for this book is available from the British Library.

Library of Congress Cataloging-in-Publication Data

Smith, Peter K.
Understanding children's development / Peter K. Smith, Helen Cowie, and Mark Blades. – 3rd ed.
p. cm. – (Basic psychology)
Includes bibliographical references and index.
ISBN 0-631-19412-6 (pbk. : alk. paper)
1. Child psychology. 2. Child development. I. Cowie, Helen.
II. Blades, Mark. III. Title. IV. Series: Basic psychology
(Oxford, England)
BF721.S57325 1998
155.4 –dc21 97-19079
CIP

Typeset in 10 on 12 pt Palatino
by Best-set Typesetter Ltd, Hong Kong
Printed in Great Britain by T. J. International, Padstow, Cornwall

This book is printed on acid-free paper.

Contents

Plates and
Box Plates

Plates

Box Plates

Figures and Box Figures

Figures

Box Figures

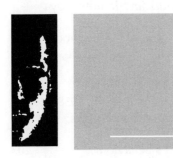

Tables and Box Tables

Tables

Box Tables

Series Preface

Psychology is a relatively new science which has already made notable achievements; yet its methods are constantly being questioned and redefined. This book is one of a series of introductory psychology texts, designed to convey the fast-moving and relevant nature of contemporary research while at the same time encouraging the reader to develop a critical perspective on the methodology and data presented. The format of the book is intended to aid such independent inquiry, as is shown in particular by the boxes at the end of each chapter that concentrate on individual studies as 'worked examples'.

The books in the Basic Psychology series should be accessible to those who have no previous knowledge of the discipline. *Understanding Children's Development* can profitably be used by students on their own without a teacher, but resources aimed at group work, for example as part of social work or teacher training courses, are also included: a further reading section, discussion points and practical exercises follow each chapter.

Peter K. Smith

Preface

We are bombarded by opinions on child development. Everyone has a view of how children should be brought up, and explanations for why people have turned out the way they have.

Even if you have not studied psychology before, you no doubt already have views on how children develop. You may agree or disagree with the following statements, but you will probably have heard them or opinions very much like them:

1 'Animal behaviour is instinctive; human behaviour is learned. That's the difference.'
2 'She gave me a lovely smile. I'm sure she recognized me even though she's only two months old.'
3 'I wouldn't leave my child at a nursery. If you have a baby you should look after it yourself.'
4 'A good smack never did a child any harm. That's how they learn what is right and what is wrong.'
5 'If things go wrong in the early years of a child's life there's not much you can do about it.'
6 'Parents shouldn't try to teach their children to read. That's best left to the school.'
7 'They don't do any work at Paul's school. They just play all day.'
8 'You can't understand how a child's mind works. They just think differently from us, and that's all there is to it.'
9 'Children see far too much violence on television these days.'
10 'Just wait until they are teenagers. That's when the trouble starts.'
11 'IQ tests don't tell us anything about real intelligence. They're a means of social control.'
12 'Psychologists can't teach us much. What they say is just common sense.'

In this book we don't aim to provide absolute answers to the many questions which arise in the course of rearing children. But we do aim to provide up-to-date accounts of research in this area. We hope to present controversies and to outline the various ways in which child psychologists' research findings enhance our understanding of the developmental process.

The material is arranged in three major sections. In Part One an introductory chapter describes to the reader the ways in which psychologists study developmental processes. It also raises issues about the specific status of psychology, its methods of inquiry and ethical questions in research. This chapter, or parts of it, could profitably be re-read after the rest of the book or taught course has been completed. Chapter 2 surveys the biological and evolutionary background of behavioural development. It introduces conceptual terms such as 'instinct', 'learning' and 'canalization', which are used later in the book.

Part Two deals with social and moral development in childhood, up to and including adolescence. Topics include parent–child attachment, sex differences, peer relationships, the influence of television on social behaviour, play and prosocial behaviour. Part Three covers perceptual, linguistic and cognitive development in children. The contribution of Jean Piaget is given particular attention, as are psychometric and other more recent approaches to assessing intelligence and attainment. Part Three concludes with a consideration of how disadvantage and deprivation affect children from different social classes and ethnic minority groups. Appendices give details of ethical guidelines in carrying out research, resources for teachers and careers in psychology.

We have tried to emphasize the variety, strengths and weaknesses of different kinds of psychological investigation. To bring this out more vividly, each chapter (after the first) concludes with two 'boxes'. Each box consists of a detailed description of one particular study, discussing its aims, design, results, analysis, and strengths and limitations. Study of these boxes should be useful not only in terms of the content of the studies themselves, but also in helping the reader get a feel for how psychological research is carried out. More advanced students may wish to pursue the references to original work given throughout the text, while beginners should read the book without being distracted by them. The references are provided primarily for use by teachers, and also because we feel that acknowledgement should be made to those psychologists who have put forward certain theories or carried out particular studies.

Each chapter offers suggestions for further reading, giving indications of level and content. There are also ideas for discussion points which might be taken up as essay titles or topics for debate in class; and examples are given of practical exercises that might be carried out by students on the basis of the material in the foregoing chapter.

Peter K. Smith and Helen Cowie

Preface to the Second Edition

For this second edition we have sought feedback from users of the book, to expand the coverage as well as bring material fully up to date. As a result the book has increased from twelve chapters to fourteen.

Part One has remained largely unchanged; but the opportunity has been taken in chapter 2 to review the recent work on 'mindreading' in primates, which links to similar work on 'theory of mind' in children and strengthens the relevance of this chapter to the rest of the book.

In Part Two, some reorganization has taken place. Chapter 3 has a number of additional sections, to cover topics such as: the role of fathers; siblings; grandparents; divorce and step-parenting; and child abuse. The material on attachment, and day care, also includes more recent research. Chapter 4 is expanded to include material on aggression in childhood, and bully/victim problems in schools.

There is a completely new chapter 5. Much of this is devoted to recent work on emotional development in children, 'theory of mind', and hypothesized deficits in autistic children. This is supplemented by material from the previous chapter 3 on gender identity, together with new material on ethnic identity, and material from the previous chapter 4 on television/mass media, to make a new chapter which seems still most appropriately titled 'Becoming Socially Aware'. Chapters 6, 7 (retitled) and 8 are not changed substantially.

In Part Three, the major change is the introduction of a new chapter 12, 'Learning in a Social Context', which considers alternative approaches to Piaget's theory in some detail. It reviews the work of the Russian psychologist Lev Vygotsky, and the American psychologist Jerome Bruner, emphasizing their views on the social and cultural context of learning and thinking. The remaining changes in Part Three are, again, general updating of material, including some more material on preverbal communication in chapter 10.

We have kept to the original plan of having practical exercises, discussion points, and boxes at the end of each chapter, which readers generally seem to find helpful. In particular, the boxes highlight the advantages and disadvantages of different research designs. There are four new boxes; two reflect experimental design, one is a questionnaire study featuring cohort-sequential design and one features a pioneering study of Vygotsky form the 1930s.

Appendix A has been changed to provide the revised Ethical Principles for Conducting Research with Human Participants, approved by the British Psychological Society in February 1990. In line with BPS guidelines, we have largely removed the term 'subjects' from our text and replaced it by the term 'participants'.

We hope that this new edition will not only broaden the coverage beyond the first edition, but also reflect some of the exciting new developments occurring in child development research over the last few years.

Peter K. Smith and Helen Cowie

Preface to the Third Edition

Substantial changes have been made in the third edition, to keep pace with changes in the discipline, and in response to user feedback.

The most substantial change is the addition of a third author, Mark Blades. The first two authors were aware of shortcomings in the second edition in the areas of information processing and memory development in children; also, the area of children's understanding of mind has grown tremendously in the years since the second edition. Mark Blades is expert in both these areas, and his joining us gives a welcoming strengthening and expansion to Part Three of the book.

In Part One, only small changes have been made to chapter 1. Chapter 2 has changed considerably, however; the material on animal behaviour has been considerably reduced, while keeping sufficient to make clear the evolutionary background to child development. Material on prenatal development, previously absent, has been added to this chapter.

In Part Two, chapter 3 has been expanded to take more account of recent developments in attachment theory, and includes more on parenting styles. Material on siblings has been moved into chapter 4, which now focuses mainly on peer relationships and friendships, with some deletion of older material on teachers and pupils. Chapter 5 has lost its theory of mind material to a new chapter 13, but is updated in other areas. Chapters 6 and 7 have also been brought up to date without major changes; as has chapter 8, with two new boxes.

In Part Three, chapter 9 has been substantially revised. Chapter 10 incorporates some new material. Chapter 11 has been updated, and chapter 12 on the information processing approach is entirely new. Chapter 13, on children's understanding of mind, is also new, although it does take some material from the second edition's old chapter 5. Chapter 14 is an updated version of the old chapter 12, and chapter 15 is a more substantially revised version of the old chapter 13. Finally, chapter 16 (old chapter 14) contains more material on cultural context and a new box on political violence as it affects children.

Each chapter continues to have two boxes featuring a study in detail (with the exception of chapter 1), and also further reading and discussion points. However, the practical exercises have been removed; they will be assimilated into an Instructor's Manual to accompany the text.

We hope that this new and enlarged coverage of important developmental issues will continue to provide a useful source for readers.

Peter K. Smith, Helen Cowie and Mark Blades

Acknowledgements

Peter Hepper and Angelas Fawcett kindly provided photographs which have been used in this edition. We would like to thank Kevin Riggs for helpful comments on chapter 13, and Siobhan Hughes-Jones, Shu Shu and Caroline Oates for reading parts of the manuscript.

The editors and publisher wish to thank the following for permission to use copyright material:

Fig. 1.1 Baltes et al., 'Life Span Developmental Psychology', *Annual Review of Psychology*, 31, 1980. Fig. 1.3 Bronfenbrenner, *The Ecology of Human Development* (Harvard University Press, 1979).

Fig. 2.1 Seifert, K. and Hoffning, R., *Child and Adolescent Development* (3rd edn) (copyright © 1994 by Houghton Mifflin Company. Used with permission). Fig. 2.2 Bronson, *Human Birth: An Evolutionary Perspective* (Aldine de Grutyer, 1987, copyright © Appleton-Century-Crofts). Fig. 2.4 Arey, *Developmental Anatomy: A Textbook and Laboratory Manual of Embryology* (7th edn) (W. B. Saunders, 1965). Fig. 2.5 Reprinted with permission from Plomin, Owen and McGuffin, 'The genetic basis of complex human behaviours', *Science*, 264, fig. 3 (copyright © 1994 American Association for the Advancement of Science). Fig. 2.7 Fishbein, H., *Education, Development and Children's Learning* (Goodyear Publishing Company, Pacific Palisades, California, 1976). Fig. 2.8 Tinbergen, 'Young blackbirds gaping at a model parent', *Study of Instinct* (Oxford University Press, 1951). Fig. 2.9 Tinbergen, 'An oyster catcher reacting to a giant egg in preference to a normal egg', *Study of Instinct* (Oxford University Press, 1951). Fig. 2.10 Lorenz, K. 'Results of an experiment showing that ducklings follow a model more readily 9–17 hours after hatching than at any other time', *On Aggression* (Methuen, London, 1966). Fig. 2.13 Sternglanz et al., 'Facial stimuli in adult preference for infantile facial features: an ethological approach and the stimulus noted as most effective', *Animal Behaviour*, 25 (Academic Press, 1977).

Fig. 3.1 Belsky, 'Belsky's process model of the determinants in parenting', in 'The determinants of parenting: a process model', *Child Development*, 55 (copyright © Society for Research in Child Development, University of Michigan, 1984). Box fig. 3.1.1 Watson, John S. and Ramey, Craig T., 'Apparatus used as a contingency mobile', in 'Reactions to response-contingent stimulation in early infancy', *Merrill-Palmer Quarterly*, 18, 3, pp. 219–27 (Wayne State University Press, 1972). Box fig. 3.1.2 Watson, John S. and Ramey, Craig T., 'Apparatus used as a contingency mobile', in 'Reactions to response-contingent stimulation in early infancy', *Merrill-Palmer Quarterly*, 18, 3, pp. 219–27 (Wayne State University Press, 1972).

Fig. 4.1 Lewis et al., 'The beginning of friendship', *Friendship and Peer Relations* (John Wiley & Sons, Inc., New York, 1975, copyright © Professors Michael Lewis and Leonard Rosenblum). Fig. 4.2 Clark et al., 'Sociograms of association networks in two classes of preschool children', *Journal of Child Psychology and Psychiatry*, 10 (Cambridge University Press, 1969). Fig. 4.3 Dodge et al., 'A model of social skills and social exchange in peer interaction', in 'Social competence in children', *Monographs of the Society for Research in Child Development*, 51, 2 (Society for Research in Child Development, University of Michigan, 1986). Fig. 4.4 Parker and Asher, 'Two models of the role of peer acceptance in leading to maladjusted outcomes', in 'Peer relations and later personal adjustment: are low accepted children at risk?', *Psychological Bulletin*, 102 (American Psychological Association, Washington, DC, 1987). Fig. 4.5 Patterson et al., 'A developmental progression for antisocial behaviour', in 'A developmental perspective on antisocial behaviour', *American Psychologist*, 44 (American Psychological Association, Washington, DC, 1989). Box fig. 4.1.1 Coie, Dodge and Coppotelli, 'Five types of sociometric status', *Developmental Psychology*, 18 (American Psychological Association, Washington, DC, 1982). Box fig. 4.2.1 Olweus et al. (eds) *The Development and Treatment of Childhood Aggression* (Erlbaum, 1989). Box table 4.1.1 Coie and Dodge, 'Five types of sociometric status', *Developmental Psychology*, 18 (American Psychological Association, Washington, DC, 1982). Box table 4.1.2 Coie and Dodge, 'Five types of sociometric status', *Developmental Psychology*, 18 (American Psychological Association, Washington, DC, 1982).

Fig. 5.1 Emmerich et al., 'Development of gender constancy in disadvantaged children', unpublished report (copyright © Educational Testing Service. All rights reserved. Adapted and reproduced under license). Fig. 5.3 Lefkowitz et al., *Growing Up to be Violent*, with kind permission from Elsevier Science – NL, Sara Burgerhartstraat 25, 1055 KV Amsterdam, The Netherlands (Pergamon, 1977). Table 5.1 Lewis and Brooks-Gunn, *Social Cognition and the Acquisition of Self* (Plenum Publishing Corporation, New York, 1979). Table 5.2 Kuhn et al., 'Sex role concepts of 2 and 3 year olds', *Child Development*, 49 (Society for Research in Child Development, University of Michigan, 1978). Table 5.3 Barry et al., 'A cross cultural survey of same sex differences in socialization', *Journal of Abnormal and Social Psychology*, 55 (American Psychological Association, Washington, DC, 1957). Table 5.4 Boulton and Smith, 'Ethnic and gender partner and activity preferences in mixed race schools in the UK; playground observations', in Hart, C. H. (ed.), *Children in Playgrounds* (State University of New York Press, 1991). Table 5.5 Greenberg, 'Viewing and listening: parameters among British youngsters', in Brown (ed.), *Children and Television* (Collier Macmillan, London, 1976). Table 5.6 Friedrich and Stein, 'Aggressive and prosocial television programs and the natural behaviour of pre-school children', *Monographs of the Society for Research in Child Development* 38, 4 (Society for Research in Child Development, University of Michigan, 1986). Table 5.7 Himmelweit et al., *Television and the Child: An Empirical Study of the Effect of Television and the Young*.

Fig. 6.1(a) Hooff, 'A comparative approach to the phylogeny of laughter and smiling', in Hinde (ed.), *Non-Verbal Communication* (Cambridge University Press, 1972). Fig. 6.1(b) Smith, 'Ethological methods', in Foss (ed.), *New Perspectives in Child Development* (Penguin, Harmondsworth, 1974). Fig. 6.2 Krasnor and Pepler, 'The study of children's play – some suggested future directions', in Rubin (ed.), *Children's Play* (Jossey Bass, San Francisco, 1980). Box fig. 6.1.1 Hutt, 'Exploration and play in children', *Symposia of the Zoological Society of London*, 18 (The Royal Zoological Society, London, 1966). Box fig. 6.1.2 Hutt, 'Exploration and play in children', *Symposia of the Zoological Society of London*, 18 (The Royal Zoological Society, London, 1966).

Fig. 7.1 Colby et al., 'A longitundinal study of moral judgement', *Monographs of the Society for Research in Child Development* (Society for Research in Child Development, University of Michigan, 1983). Box fig. 7.1.1 Zahn-Waxler et al., 'Child-rearing and children's prosocial limitations towards victims of distress', *Child Development*, 50 (Society for Research in Child Development, University of Michigan, 1979). Table 7.1 Grisec, 'The socialisation of altruism', in Eisenberg, W. (ed.), *The Development of Prosocial Behaviour* (Academic Press, New York, 1982). Table 7.2 Hoffman, 'Moral development', in Mussen, P. H. (ed.), *Manual of Child Psychology*, 2 (© 1970; reprinted by permission of John Wiley & Sons, Inc). Table 7.3 Piaget, 1932, *The Moral Judgement of the Child* (Penguin, Harmondsworth, 1977). Table 7.4 Colby et al., 'A longitudinal study of moral judgement', *Monographs of the Society for Research in Child Development* (Society for Research in Child Development, University of Michigan, 1983). Box table 7.2.1 Damon, W. and Killen, M., 'Peer interaction and the process of change in children's moral reasoning', *Merrill-Palmer Quarterly*, 28, 3, pp. 347–67 (Wayne State University Press, 1982).

Fig. 8.1 Katchadourian, *The Biology of Adolescence* (W. H. Freeman and Co., 1977). Fig. 8.3 Tanner, J. M., 'Growing up', *Scientific American*, 229, September 1973 (copyright © 1973 by Scientific American, Inc. All rights reserved). Fig. 8.4 Tanner, J. M., 'Growing up', *Scientific American*, 229, September 1973 (copyright © 1973 by Scientific American, Inc. All rights reserved). Fig. 8.6 Meilman, 'Cross sectional age changes in ego identity status during adolescence', *Developmental Psychology*, 15 (American Psychological Association, Washington, DC, 1979). Fig. 8.7 Schofield, *The Sexual Behaviour of Young People* (Longman, 1965). Table 8.1 Katchadourian, *The*

Biology of Adolescence (W. H. Freeman and Co., 1977). Table 8.2 Erikson, E., *Identity, Youth and Crisis* (Faber and Faber Ltd, 1968). Table 8.3 Montmayor and Eisen, 'The development of self-conceptions from childhood to adolescence', *Developmental Psychology*, 13 (American Psychological Association, Washington, DC, 1977). Table 8.4 Goldman and Goldman, *Children's Understanding of Sexual Terms* (Routledge, 1982). Table 8.6 Reiss, I., *The Social Context of Premarital Sexual Permissiveness* (Holt, Rinehart & Winston Inc., Orlando, 1967, copyright © Dr Ira Reiss). Table 8.8 Rutter et al., 'Adolescent turmoil: fact or fiction?', *Journal of Child Psychology and Psychiatry*, 17 (Cambridge University Press, 1976).

Fig. 9.1 Fantz, 'The origin of form perception', *Scientific American*, 204 (copyright © 1961 by Scientific American, Inc. All rights reserved). Fig. 9.2 Fantz and Miranda, 'Newborn infant attention to form of contour', *Child Development*, 46 (Society for Research in Child Development, University of Michigan, 1975). Fig. 9.4 Shaffer, *Developmental Psychology: Theory, Research and Applications* (copyright © 1985 by permission of Brooks/Cole Publishing Company, Pacific Grove, CA 93950). Fig. 9.5 Maurer and Barrera, 'Infants' perceptions of natural and distorted arrangements of a schematic face', *Child Development*, 52 (Society for Research in Child Development, University of Michigan, 1981). Fig. 9.6 Maurer and Barrera, 'Infants' perceptions of natural and distorted arrangements of a schematic face', *Child Development*, 52 (Society for Research in Child Development, University of Michigan, 1981). Fig. 9.7 Eimas, Peter D., 'The perception of speech in early infancy', *Scientific American* (copyright © 1985 by Scientific American, Inc. All rights reserved). Fig. 9.8 Mitchell, 'Effects of early visual experience on the development of certain perceptual abilities in animals and man', in Walk, R. D. and Pick, H. L., Jr (eds), *Perception and Experience* (Plenum Publishing Corp., New York, 1978). Fig. 9.9 Held, 'Plasticity in sensory-motor systems', *Scientific American*, 213 (copyright © 1965 Eric Mose, Jr). Box fig. 9.1.1 From: *Development in Infancy* (2nd edn) by Bower (copyright © 1982 by W. H. Freeman and Company. Used with permission). Box fig. 9.2.1 Blakemore and Cooper, 'A kitten in a cylinder with vertical black and white stripes', *Nature*, 228 (reprinted with permission from *Nature*, copyright © 1970 Macmillan Magazines Limited).

Fig. 10.1 Ferreiro, 'Literacy development: a psychogenic perspective', in Olsen, D. et al. (eds), *Literacy, Learning and Language* (Cambridge University Press, 1985). Box fig. 10.1 Nelson, in *Developmental Psychology*, 13 (American Psychological Association, Washington, DC, 1977). Table 10.1 Scarlet and Woolf, 'When it's only make believe – the construction of a boundary between fantasy and reality in story-telling', in Winner, E. and Gardner, H. (eds), *Fact, Fiction and Fantasy in Childhood* (Jossey Bass, San Francisco, 1979). Table 10.2 McNeill, *The Acquisition of Language* (Harper & Row, New York, 1970). Table 10.3 Cazden, C. B., *Child Language and Education* (Holt, Rinehart & Winston Inc., New York, copyright © 1972 Dr Courtney B. Cazden). Box table 10.1.1 Bradley and Bryan, in *Nature*, 301 (reprinted with permission from *Nature*, copyright © 1983 Macmillan Magazines Limited).

Fig. 11.5 Inhelder and Piaget, *The Growth of Logical Thinking from Childhood to Adolescence* (Routledge & Kegan Paul, London, 1955/1958). Fig. 11.6

Shayer and Wylam, 'The distribution of Piagetian stages of thinking in British middle and secondary school children: II', *British Journal of Educational Psychology*, 48 (copyright © 1978 Dr M. Shayer). Fig. 11.7 Danner and Day, 'Eliciting formal operations', *Child Development*, 48 (Society for Research in Child Development, University of Michigan, 1977). Box fig. 11.1.1 Borke, in *Developmental Psychology*, 11 (American Psychological Association, Washington, DC, 1975). Box fig. 11.2.1 McGarrigle and Donaldson, in *Cognition*, 3 (reprinted copyright © 1974 with kind permission of Elsevier Science – NL, Sara Burgerhartstraat 25, 1055 KV Amsterdam, The Netherlands).

Fig. 12.1 Atkinson and Shiffrin, 'Human memory: a proposed system and its control processes', in Spence, K. W. and Spence, J. T. (eds), *Advances in the Psychology of Learning and Motivation*, vol. 2 (Academic Press, New York, 1968). Fig. 12.3 Vurpillot, 'The development of scanning strategies and their relation to visual differentiation', *Journal of Experimental Child Psychology*, 6, 1968. Box fig. 12.1.1 Siegler, 'Three aspects of cognitive development', *Cognitive Psychology*, 8 (Academic Press, 1976). Box fig. 12.1.2 Siegler, 'Three aspects of cognitive development', *Cognitive Psychology*, 8 (Academic Press, 1976). Box fig. 12.1.3 Siegler, 'Three aspects of cognitive development', *Cognitive Psychology*, 8 (Academic Press, 1976).

Fig. 14.1 Haste, 'Growing into rules', in Bruner, J. S. and Haste, H. (eds), *Making Sense* (Methuen, London, 1987). Box table 14.1.1 Vygotsky, 'The development of scientific concepts in childhood', in Rieber and Carlton (eds), *The Collected Works of L. S. Vygotsky*, vol. 1 (Plenum Publishing Corp., New York, 1987).

Fig. 15.1 Raven, *Standard Progressive Matrices* (H. K. Lewis & Co., London, 1958). Fig. 15.2 Sternberg, R. J. and Rifian, B., 'The development of analogical reasoning processes', *Journal of Experimental Psychology*, 27, 1978. Table 15.1 Gregory, *Psychological Testing: History, Principles and Applications* (copyright © 1992 by Allyn and Bacon. Reprinted by permission).

Fig. 16.1 Davie et al., *From Birth to Seven* (Second Report of the National Child Development Study) (Longman and National Children's Bureau, London, 1972). Fig. 16.2 Davie et al., *From Birth to Seven* (Second Report of the National Child Development Study) (Longman and National Children's Bureau, London, 1972). Fig. 16.3 Davie et al., *From Birth to Seven* (Second Report of the National Child Development Study) (Longman and National Children's Bureau, London, 1972). Fig. 16.7 Wedge and Essen, *Children in Adversity* (Pan Books, London, 1982). Fig. 16.8 Wedge and Essen, *Children in Adversity* (Pan Books, London, 1982). Fig. 16.9 Wedge and Essen, *Children in Adversity* (Pan Books, London, 1982). Table 16.1 Coleman Report (copyright © HMSO). Table 16.2 Rampton Report (copyright © HMSO). Table 16.5 Lazar and Darlington, 'Lasting effects of early education', *Monographs of the Society for Research in Child Development*, 47 (Society for Research in Child Development, University of Michigan, 1982). Box table 16.2.1 Lazar and Darlington, 'Lasting effects of early education', *Monographs of the Society for Research in Child Development*, 47 (Society for Research in Child Development, University of Michigan, 1982). Box table 16.2.2 Lazar and Darlington, 'Lasting effects of early education', *Monographs of the Society for Research in Child

Development, 47 (Society for Research in Child Development, University of Michigan, 1982).

Every effort has been made to trace the copyright holders but if any have been inadvertently overlooked the publishers will be pleased to make the necessary arrangement at the first opportunity.

Part One

Theories and Methods

Studying
Development

The study of how behaviour develops forms part of the science of psychology. But what do we mean by terms such as 'science', 'psychology' and 'development'? This chapter aims to supply the answer, but although it comes first in the book, it may not necessarily be best to read it thoroughly at the outset. Especially if you have not studied psychology before, it might be useful to read it through quickly at this stage, and return to it later, even after finishing the rest of the book, for a more thorough understanding. The issues raised in this chapter are important, but understanding them fully will be easier if you already know something of psychological theories and methods of investigation.

In an important sense, we are all psychologists. We are all interested in understanding behaviour, both our own and that of our parents, children, family and friends. We try to understand why we feel the way we do about other people, why we find certain tasks easy or difficult, or how certain situations affect us; and we try to understand and predict how other people behave, or how their present behaviour and situation may affect their future development. Will a child settle well with a childminder, or do well at school? Will watching violent films on television be harmful? What level of moral reasoning can we expect a child to understand? And so on.

In an interesting and perceptive book, Nicholas Humphrey (1984) has described us as 'nature's psychologists', or *homo psychologicus*. By this he means that, as intelligent social beings, we use our knowledge of our own thoughts and feelings – 'introspection' – as a guide for understanding how others are likely to think, feel and therefore behave. Indeed, Humphrey goes further and argues that we are conscious, that is, we have self-awareness, precisely because this is so useful to us in this process of understanding others and thus having a successful social existence. He argues that consciousness is a biological adaptation to enable us to perform this intro-spective psychology. Whether this is right or not (and you might like to think about this again after you have read chapter 2), we do know that the process of understanding others' thoughts, feelings and behaviour is something that develops through childhood and probably throughout our lives. According to one of the greatest child psychologists, Jean Piaget, a crucial phase of this process occurs in middle childhood (see chapter 11); though more recent research has revealed how much has developed before this.

If we are already nature's psychologists, then why do we need an organ-ized study of the science of psychology? A professional psychologist would probably answer that by systematically gathering knowledge and by carry-ing out controlled experiments, we can develop a greater understanding and awareness of ourselves than would otherwise be possible. There is still much progress to be made in psychology and in the psychological study of devel-opment. We are still struggling to understand areas such as the role of play in development, the causes of delinquency, the nature of stages in cognitive development. Most psychologists would argue, however, that the discipline of child development has made some progress and even in the most difficult areas knowledge has now become more systematic, with theories being put forward. Our understanding has clearly advanced in some areas. We now know more, for example, about the importance of social attachments in infancy (chapter 3), or the process by which a child learns its native language (chapter 10), or how our understanding of others' minds develops (chapter 13), than previous generations ever did or could have done without organized study. Common beliefs are not always correct. An example offered by Tizard and Phoenix (1993, p. 1) gives a graphic illustration. In the course of researching the lives of children of mixed parentage, one of these authors reported to a group of journalists that many of the young people in their sample saw advantages in their family situation through the meeting of two distinctive cultures. The journalists responded with incre-dulity since the findings ran contrary to the popular belief that these children inevitably suffered from identity problems, low self-esteem and problem behaviour!

We have much to learn about cultural and social influences on the ways in which we think about children and about the impact which psychologists and other social scientists have on policies to ensure that children the world over are given at least basic provision for their needs. It is clear that we are a long way from achieving this goal. In a thought-provoking article on the issue of children's rights, Burman (1996) explores the notion of advocacy on behalf of all children which was proposed by the United Nations Convention on the Rights of the Child (United Nations, 1989), which placed emphasis on non-discrimination, acting in the best interests of the child, and listening to the views of the child.

The Convention built on earlier legislation by specifying children's rights not only to protection and provision, but also to participation – so giving some political rights to children (we look at the impact of political violence on children's development in box 16.1). In the context of participation, it addressed such contentious issues as child labour and children's rights to freedom of thought and speech. Its recommendations are binding to those countries which ratify it (including the UK, which signed it in 1991). Lopatka (1992), the chairman of the United Nations working group which drafted the Convention, argued that the rights of the child are universal, yet he also asserted the need to take into account the cultural values of the child's community. However, as Burman indicates, a major criticism of the Convention concerns difficulties in implementing it in societies where families are very poor or where civil liberties are severely constrained or where a country is at war. The tension between the child's supposedly universal developmental needs and the realities of his or her social situation may be nearly impossible to resolve.

There are similar controversies with the England and Wales Children Act which came into effect in the UK in 1991. The Children Act states that the child's welfare must be paramount and that adults must ascertain what the wishes and feelings of the child are; in legal cases, courts should take into account the emotional needs of the child. The Children Act requires all local authority agencies to work together in the best interests of protecting the child. This means, amongst other things, that teachers are legally obliged to share their knowledge of abuse or significant harm to the child with other agencies, most frequently social services. The Children Act appears to be enlightened in shifting the emphasis from parents' rights over their children to their responsibilities towards the young people in their care. When parents divorce, the local authorities have a duty to protect and promote the welfare of the children involved, and the courts must now pay due attention to the wishes of the child. A process of conciliation is now more common because of the Children Act, in line with its intention to benefit children in this situation. At the same time, in practice courts have the right to judge the child's competence to make autonomous decisions, and may as a result disregard children's wishes in the wider context of 'the best interests of the child'. You can see that it is extremely difficult to achieve the balance between what the child thinks he or she wants at the time against what in the view of adults may be in the longer term best for the child. And who is right – the adult or the child?

◀Development Observed▶▶▶

The biologist Charles Darwin, famous for his theory of evolution, made one of the earliest contributions to child psychology in his article 'A biographical sketch of an infant' (1877), which was based on observations of his own son's development. By the early twentieth century, however, most of our understanding of psychological development could still not have been described as 'scientific' knowledge; much was still at the level of anecdote and opinion. Nevertheless, knowledge was soon being organized through both observation and experiment and during the 1920s and 1930s the study of child development got seriously under way in the USA with the founding of Institutes of Child Study or Child Welfare in university centres such as Iowa and Minnesota. Careful observations were made of development in young children and of normal and abnormal behaviour and adjustment. In the 1920s Jean Piaget started out on his long career as a child psychologist, blending observation and experiment in his studies of children's thinking (see chapter 11). Observation of behaviour in natural settings fell out of favour with psychologists in the 1940s and 1950s (though it continued in the study of animal behaviour by zoologists, chapter 2). Perhaps as a reaction against the absence of experimental rigour in philosophy and early psychology, and the reliance on introspection (that is, trying to understand behaviour by thinking about one's own mental processes), many psychologists moved to doing experiments under laboratory conditions. As we will discuss later, such experiments do have advantages, but they also have drawbacks. Much of the laboratory work carried out in child development in the 1950s and 1960s has been described by Urie Bronfenbrenner (1979) as 'the science of the behavior of children in strange situations with strange adults'.

Schaffer (1996, pp. xiv–xvii) also notes the profound changes in the ways in which psychologists now approach child development. He points out that there is now much more value attached to the study of children in real-life settings despite the methodological challenges which such contexts place on the social scientist. Furthermore, there is a growing recognition of the need on the part of social scientists to understand the processes of how children grow and develop rather than simply the outcomes, and to integrate findings from a range of sources and at different levels of analysis – for example, family, community, culture. A brief overview of recent texts on child development reveals a consistent shift in perspective away from viewing aspects of the child's emotional, cognitive and social development in isolation, each separate from the other. Durkin (1995, chapter 1) challenges the idea that the best way to understand how a child develops is to remove him or her from his or her usual environment and conduct experiments in laboratory conditions. He argues that development is intimately related to the social context provided by other people and by the wider social structure within which the child grows. Furthermore, individuals themselves also affect their social environment.

We hope that in the course of reading this text you begin the process of integrating perspectives – for example, by reflecting on the links to be made by psychologists between the concept of the child's 'internal working model of relationships' (chapter 3) and recent discoveries about 'theory of mind' (chapter 4). We hope too that you find the opportunity to recognize the complementary virtues of various different methods of investigation and gain a sense that the child's developmental processes and the social context in which they exist are closely intertwined, each having an influence on the other.

◄What Is 'Development'?►►

The term 'development' refers to the process by which a child, or foetus and more generally an organism (human or animal), grows and changes through its life-span. In humans the most dramatic devel[opment occurs] in prenatal development, infancy and childhood, [as the individual develops] into a young adult capable of becoming a parent [himself or herself. From] its origins much of developmental psychology h[as thus been concerned] with child psychology, and with the change[s from conception and] infancy through to adolescence. These are the prim[ary areas covered in this] book.

Generally, developmental processes have been r[elated to age. A typical 3-] year-old has, for example, a particular mastery [of spoken language (see] chapter 10), and a 4-year-old has typically pr[ogressed further. A de-] velopmental psychologist may then wish to find [out, and theorize about,] the processes involved in this progression. Wh[at experiences, rewards,] interactions, feedback, have helped the child devel[op in this way?]

Two important but different research strategies have commonly been used in this endeavour. These are 'cross-sectional' and 'longitudinal' de- signs. In a cross-sectional design an investigator might look at several age groups simultaneously. For example, she might record language ability in 3- year-olds and 4-year-olds, at the same point in time. In a longitudinal design, the investigator follows certain subjects over a given time period, measuring change. For example, our investigator might have recorded the language ability for a sample of 3-year-olds and a year later visited the same children to get a sample of what they can do as 4-year-olds.

Each method has advantages and disadvantages. The cross-sectional de- sign is quick to do, and is appropriate if the main interest is in what abilities or behaviours are typical at certain ages. Because of the convenience of the method, the majority of developmental studies have been cross-sectional. Longitudinal designs are generally preferable if the focus of interest is the process of change, and the relationship between earlier and later behaviour. In our example above, it is longitudinal data which give us the most ready access to information on what kinds of experience foster language develop- ment, and whether individual differences at 3 years of age predict anything about individual differences a year later, at age 4.

Although longitudinal studies are more powerful in this way they have a number of drawbacks. One is simply the possibility of subject attrition – some participants may move away, lose contact, or refuse or be unable to participate by the next time of testing. This could influence the generality of conclusions, especially if the reason for participant loss may be related to the dependent variables of the study.

Another problem with longitudinal designs is that they are time-consum- ing! In our example a wait of one year may not be too off-putting. But, if you wanted to see whether friendships in childhood related to happiness as an adult (see chapter 4), you might find yourself having to wait 20 years! Some longitudinal studies have now in fact proceeded for this length of time and longer. A few major studies which originated in the USA in the 1930s, as well as some nation-wide surveys starting in Britain during the years after the Second World War, have provided or are providing longitudinal data span- ning 20, 30 or 40 years (see box 8.1 for an example in New Zealand). Such long-term studies give us some of our most powerful evidence on the nature of development, so far available. However, when a study goes on for so long, another problem may arise. When the study was initially designed decades ago, it may not have asked the sort of questions that we now find most interesting. Any long-term longitudinal study will be dated in its conception. It will also be dated in its conclusions, which will refer to developmental outcomes for people born decades ago. Such conclusions may not always be applicable to today's children. For example, the effects of parental divorce on a child's later adjustment may be different now, when divorce is more frequent and socially acceptable, than 30 or 40 years ago when the social stigma attached to divorce in Western societies was much greater (see pp. 82–4).

Baltes's conceptualization of life-span development

Paul Baltes, a German psychologist, has been influential in emphasizing the life-span nature of development and the importance of historical influences (see Baltes et al., 1980). Baltes points out that age-related trends, the traditional staple of developmental psychology, constitute only one of three important influences on development throughout the life-span (figure 1.1). Each of these influences is determined by an interaction of biological and environmental factors (cf. chapter 2), though one or the other may predominate in particular cases.

Of the three kinds of influence, 'normative age-graded' is one that has a fairly strong relationship with chronological age. The advent of puberty at adolescence (see chapter 8) would be an example of a normative age-graded influence with a strong biological component, while entering school at 5 years (in Britain) would be a normative age-graded influence with little biological determination.

'Normative history-graded' influences are those associated with historical time for most members of a given generation (or 'cohort', see below). A famine, for example the Ethiopian famine of the 1980s, would be an example

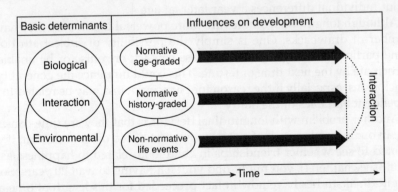

Figure 1.1   Three major influence systems on life-span development: normative age-graded, normative history-graded and non-normative life events. These influence systems interact and differ in their combinational profile for different individuals and for different behaviours (adapted from Baltes et al., 1980).

of strong biological determinants on development. The advent of television (see box 5.2), or historical changes in family size (for example the 'one-child' policy in China since the early 1980s) are examples with little biological determination.

Finally, 'non-normative life events' are those which do not occur in any normative age-graded or history-graded manner for most individuals. The effects of brain damage in an accident would be an example with strong biological determinants; the effects of job loss, or moving house, or divorce, examples with less strong biological determinants. All are significant events that can occur in the life-span of an individual at many age points and at many historical times.

This sort of conceptualization leads to further consideration of designs for studying development, apart from the cross-sectional and longitudinal ones already mentioned. One of these is cohort design, in which different cohorts (i.e. samples of children born in different years) are compared at the same ages. The characteristics of the three designs mentioned so far are thus:

Cross-sectional design
Different participants   Different ages   Same historical time

Longitudinal design
Same participants   Different ages   Different historical times

Cohort design
Different participants   Same ages   Different historical times

Yet another design is a combination called cohort-sequential design. As an example of this, we might look at the effects of compensatory preschool programmes (see chapter 16) on children born in 1970, 1975 and 1980, following each cohort longitudinally through from age 3 years to, say, age 18 years. As well as several sets of cross-sectional and longitudinal data, this hypothetical design (figure 1.2) would let us see whether historical change over the last decade or so (for example in educational policy, or the relative position of minority groups in society) had an impact on whatever long-term effects of the programmes might be detected. Obviously, this would be immensely time-consuming, and indeed such a study has not been carried out! Even one set of actual longitudinal studies originating in the 1970s has proved a major research undertaking (see chapter 16). So far, cohort sequential designs have been rarely used, and only on a smaller scale. An example is given in box 4.2.

A different approach is to examine the effects of a particular kind of non-normative life event when it happens, perhaps irrespective of age, or with age as another factor. The effects of divorce on children, mentioned earlier, is one example. Investigators of this topic typically record the adjustment of children, often of a range of ages, over a period of time from when the parental separation occurred. Other examples would be the study of bereavement, or the effects of sudden unemployment.

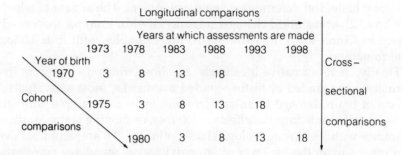

Figure 1.2   A hypothetical study design, combining cross-sectional, longitudinal and cohort comparisons, to examine the effects of compensatory preschool programmes at different ages and different historical periods. If started in 1973, the study would continue until 1998. The ages of each sample of children from each cohort and at each year of study are shown in years.

Bronfenbrenner's ecological model of human development

The American psychologist Urie Bronfenbrenner has proposed another influential conceptualization of development (1979). He emphasizes the importance of studying 'development-in-context', or the ecology of development. 'Ecology' refers here to the environmental settings which the person or organism is experiencing, or is linked to directly or indirectly. Bronfenbrenner conceives of this ecological environment as a set of four nested systems (see figure 1.3). Most familiar to the psychologist is the 'microsystem' – what an individual experiences in a given setting. For a young child, one microsystem may comprise the home environment with parents and siblings.

Another microsystem may be the school environment, with teachers and peers. Most psychological research is carried out at the level of one microsystem, for example looking at mother's talk and child's speech in the home (chapter 10), or peer popularity and aggression at school (chapter 4).

At the next level is the 'mesosystem'. This refers to links amongst settings which the individual directly participates in. For example, the quality of the child's home environment might affect his or her school performance or confidence with peers.

The third level is the 'exosystem'. This refers to links to settings which the individual does not participate in directly, but which do affect the individual. For example, the mother's or father's work environment may affect their behaviour at home, and hence the quality of parental care. The child does not directly experience the parent's work environment, but he or she experiences the effects indirectly.

The fourth and final level is the 'macrosystem'. This refers to the general pattern of ideology and organization of social institutions in the society or subculture the individual is in. Thus, the effects of parental stress at work, or unemployment, will be affected by such factors as working hours in that

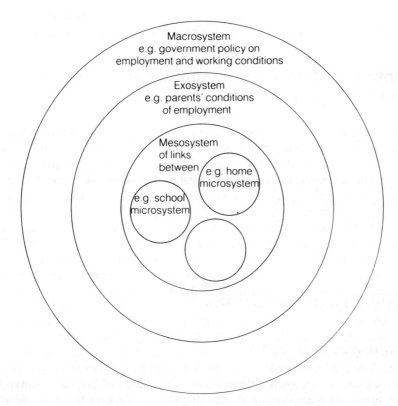

Figure 1.3 The nested circles of macro-, exo-, meso- and microsystems proposed by Bronfenbrenner (1979), with examples relevant to a school-age child.

society, rates of pay, holiday and leave entitlement, occupational status, or the degree of social stigma attached to unemployment.

Bronfenbrenner's model illustrates how a decision or change in the macrosystem (e.g. change in employment conditions) may affect the exosystem (parent's work experience) and hence a child's mesosystem and microsystem. This is not controversial in itself. However, recognizing these links does suggest the importance of trying to conceptualize and design psychological investigations extending beyond just the microsystem level.

Bronfenbrenner proposes that we view human development as the process of understanding and restructuring our ecological environment at successively greater levels of complexity. The child first comes to understand its primary caregivers (chapter 3), then its home and nursery or school environment, then wider aspects of society. Changes in the ecological environment (or 'ecological transitions') are especially important in development. Examples might be: having a new sibling; entering school; getting a job; being promoted; getting married; taking a holiday. (Note the similarity to Baltes's ideas of life events.) At such times the person is faced with a challenge, has to adapt, and thus development takes place. Indeed, Bronfenbrenner feels that seeing how a person copes with change is essential to understanding that person: 'If you want to understand something, try to change it.'

Obtaining Information about Behaviour and Development

As you read through this book, you will see that psychologists have used a wide variety of means to obtain useful information, whatever their theoretical or conceptual orientation has been. Some form of experimental study is perhaps the most common form of investigation reported in psychological books and journals. Nevertheless, non-experimental methods, such as naturalistic observation or field surveys, are also respectable procedures provided there is a clear aim to the research. The crucial variable is the degree of control the investigator has over what is happening. We shall discuss this variable in some detail, together with two other aspects of project design – the way behaviour is recorded and the selection of participants. These aspects are also highlighted in the boxes that follow all the subsequent chapters.

What degree of control?

A great deal can be learned from recording behaviour in natural situations or settings. Suppose we were interested in what kinds of help are shown by preschool children to others in distress (chapter 7). Perhaps the most suitable approach here is for the investigator simply to observe children in natural settings such as the home, or ask parents or adults to keep diary records of events. Or, we might try to save time simply by interviewing parents, or giving a questionnaire. The investigator interferes as little as possible, only to the extent of making sure he or she gets reliable data. This kind of approach is most suitable when we do not yet have much systematic knowledge about the phenomenon, and need to gather this descriptive data.

From this kind of study we can learn what kinds of behaviour occur, and how frequently. But do we advance our understanding of the processes involved? To some extent, the answer is yes. For instance, we can carry out 'correlational analyses' of various kinds. In a correlation we examine whether a certain behaviour occurs systematically or more frequently together with some other particular behaviour or in some particular situation. For example, we may find that helpful behaviour by children is correlated with clear communications by the mother (p. 228). Such findings certainly suggest explanations as to the processes involved. Parents who communicate clearly may have children who are more helpful because the communications bring this about. However, can we be confident that this explanation is better than some other, different explanation? Not really. The relation between cause and effect might be reversed: for example, children who are for other reasons helpful may have better relationships with parents, who are thus more willing to take time to explain things to them.

Or, some other factor may account for both aspects separately. Perhaps parents who are less stressed and more happy have both more time to communicate to children and less stressed children who are therefore more helpful. In that case, stress would be the crucial factor and not parental communication.

This weakness of correlational evidence is a most important concept to grasp. If you find it difficult, think of this example. Suppose you correlated, from day to day through the year, the number of people wearing shorts and the number of people eating ice-creams. You would probably get a positive association or correlation. This does not mean that wearing shorts causes people to eat ice-creams, or vice versa; we know that in this case the daily variation in temperature, a third variable, is the likely cause of both.

At several points in this book we will draw out these limitations of correlational methods. The way psychologists have tried to proceed further is to use some form of experiment. In an experiment we focus on one or a small number of variables of interest which we think are important: then we try to exclude other variables from our possible explanations. Three kinds of experiment will be described.

The weakest form of experiment is the 'quasi-experiment' (see Cook and Campbell, 1979, for extended discussion). In a quasi-experiment the variable which the investigator thinks is important is changed naturally, and the investigator watches what happens. For example, in box 5.2 we refer to a before-and-after study in 1955 of the effects on children's behaviour of introducing a new television transmitter in Norwich. The investigators felt that the introduction of the opportunity to watch TV was an important variable and they took the opportunity to measure its effects.

Unfortunately quasi-experiments are not much more powerful than correlational studies at excluding alternative explanations. Usually, we know too little about (i.e. have too little control over) the characteristics of our participants and the circumstances of the variable which is changing. For example, in the situation just described, which parents first acquired television sets when they were available? They would almost certainly be different in many ways from those who did not acquire television sets (and indeed the study identified some such differences). Also, children might differentially view programmes of certain types, depending on personality and interest. How can we tell whether changes in behaviour are due to watching the programmes, or whether the programme-watching is just a by-product of these changes?

The most powerful way to answer such cause–effect questions is to carry out a 'true' or 'controlled' experiment. We can distinguish field experiments and laboratory experiments, but both share two important features. The first is that there are two or more well-specified 'conditions' which participants can experience. The second is that participants are assigned to conditions in a systematic fashion. In these ways the experimenter seeks to ascribe an outcome definitely to differences between certain conditions. Alternative explanations in terms of other uncontrolled differences between conditions, or between the participants in different conditions, can be excluded.

Let us take further the idea that television viewing may affect children's social behaviour. Suppose we invite children in small groups to a laboratory, where we randomly assign them to one of three conditions. In one condition they see several violent cartoon programmes; in another they see several non-violent cartoons; in the third (called a control condition) they do not watch television at all but do something else, like drawing. Afterwards they go to a playroom and are filmed by the experimenter, who records their social behaviour.

Suppose the experimenter finds a significant difference. Children who watched the violent cartoons are more aggressive to each other in the playroom than those who watched non-violent cartoons, or did drawing. This difference in aggressiveness can confidently be ascribed to watching the violent cartoons. It cannot be explained by systematic differences in the participants (we assigned them randomly) and it cannot be explained by unknown variations in the children's experiences (we chose the cartoons, and made the children sit through all of them).

Sometimes the investigator compares the effects of two or more conditions he or she is interested in (for example, violent and non-violent cartoon films). Sometimes it is appropriate to include a 'control group', which is a condition including all the same experiences except that which the investigator is particularly interested in. The children who experienced drawing, above, were a control group for the general experience of coming to the laboratory and meeting the experimenters. Any differences between the control group and the two experimental groups showed the effects of watching cartoons. Any difference between the two experimental groups further showed the effects of whether the cartoons were violent, or non-violent.

In all experiments we can identify 'independent variables' and 'dependent variables'. Independent variables are those controlled or manipulated by the experimenter: in our example, the experience of watching cartoons, and whether the cartoons were violent or not. The dependent variables are those we choose to examine for possible effects: in our example, social behaviour in the playroom.

The laboratory experiment allows tight control of assignment of participants and of the independent variables; but is it rather artificial? What do the participants feel about coming to the laboratory? Would they normally choose to watch such cartoons? Can we expect a reasonable range of normal behaviour in this environment? Perhaps not. To some extent we can try to overcome these objections in a 'field experiment'. For example, we might try showing different kinds of television cartoons to different groups of children at a school, or at a summer camp. The children would normally be at the school, or camp, and watching some television might be part of their expected programme.

In general in a field experiment the investigator attempts to combine the rigorous control of experimental design with the advantages of a naturalistic setting (see box 5.1 for an example). This can, at its best, be a very powerful method. However, it is difficult to maintain both experimental control and naturalness, and the field experiment may slip either into becoming a quasi-experiment, or into becoming more constrained and unnatural, like the laboratory experiment.

Thus, in all investigations the naturalness of the setting needs to be balanced against the degree of knowledge and control we have over the setting. Where the balance is best struck depends very much on the kind of behaviour or skill we are interested in. We do want to be reasonably sure that the conclusions we draw from our study apply to the 'real world'. This concern has been labelled as the need for 'ecological validity'. Bronfenbrenner (1979) has defined ecological validity as 'the extent to which the environment experienced by the participants in a scientific investigation has the properties it is supposed or assumed to have by the investigator'. In other words, is it reasonably representative as regards the conclusions we wish to draw from the study? If we felt that the results of a laboratory experiment on cartoon watching were not representative of the effects of real-life television watching, then we would say this experiment lacked ecological validity.

Recording data

Whatever design of investigation we are using, we also have to decide how to record the data. A variety of methods is available and whether the choice is obvious or requires some deliberation depends on the topic of investigation. Sometimes several types of data may be gathered in one study.

One method is to make observational records of behaviour (e.g. box 2.2) whereby the investigator watches the participant(s) and makes systematic records of whether certain behaviours occur. Usually the investigator defines certain 'behaviour categories' in advance, and then scores when they occur. Some method of 'time sampling' is often employed to assist in quantifying the scoring (see Martin and Bateson, 1991, for extended discussion). Sometimes the investigator asks the participant(s) to keep his or her own records, perhaps a diary of occurrences (e.g. box 7.1). Again, the participants will probably need some training in what and what not to record in this way.

Another set of methods involves interviews and questionnaires. In an interview, the investigator asks participants about a topic and explores their thoughts, feelings or attitudes with them. Often some degree of structure is imposed on the kinds of questions asked in the interview (e.g. box 14.2). A still more structured approach is to give participants a questionnaire in which they fill in replies to preset questions (e.g., box 8.2). A questionnaire is often given individually, but can be given in groups. A questionnaire sent to large numbers of people is called a 'survey' (e.g. pp. 251–3). Tests can also be given individually or (in some cases) in groups. In a test the participant may be asked certain questions and also perhaps be asked to carry out certain actions, e.g. solve certain puzzles. The test differs from the interview in that it is designed to measure a particular ability or trait, and it is scored in a strictly defined way that can be compared with normative values obtained earlier in the process of test design (see chapter 15).

Reliability and validity

Whatever measuring instrument or method we use, we need to be sure of its 'reliability'. Basically, a reliable method is one that would give the same answer if you, or another investigator, were to repeat the measurement in the same conditions. A straight, firm ruler is reliable, a crooked or floppy one is not. Similarly, if we recorded 'aggressive behaviour' in children, but did not define our behaviour categories or method of time sampling, this would be unreliable; someone else might have a different idea of what is aggressive, and get different results even if watching the same behaviour. Methods need to be carefully specified and tried out if they are to be reliable.

The term 'reliability' is often confused with 'validity': both are very important in any investigation. We have just seen that reliability refers to the recording of data. Validity, in contrast, refers to whether the data we obtain are actually meaningful. Remember the concept of 'ecological validity' we discussed above. Our measurements in a laboratory experiment might be very reliable (well specified and repeatable) but this does not guarantee that they are valid in the sense of meaningful in the 'real world'.

Problems of validity actually arise in all kinds of investigation. If we are making records in a natural setting, we have to beware that the presence of an observer does not change the behaviour being observed. If you stand in a playground recording aggressive behaviour, will less aggression occur than usual because you are there? This is a problem of 'observer effects'. Similarly, in experiments there are 'experimenter effects'. The experimenter may unwittingly help some participants more than others, or score some participants more leniently. One type of experimenter effect is known as the 'Clever Hans' effect. Clever Hans was a horse which apparently could count. If his trainer asked 'what is three and four' Hans would tap with his front foot seven times. However, the German psychologist Oskar Pfungst (1911) discovered that Hans actually relied on subtle non-verbal (and unintentional) cues from his trainer, who inclined his head slightly forward after Hans had tapped the correct number of times. Hans was clever, but not in the way originally thought. The demonstration was a reliable one, but the conclusions drawn initially were not valid.

Participant characteristics

One aspect of validity concerns the representativeness of the participants investigated. If we do a survey of young men's attitudes to sexual relationships, they may not be representative of the views of young women (chapter 8). Or, we may not have enough participants to give us even a reliable source of data.

A data set obtained from one person is called a 'case study'. Normally a case study tells us little about the general population but, if we can obtain very extensive records (for example, the records Piaget obtained of his own children described in chapter 11) or if the person is especially interesting (for example, the case studies of extreme deprivation described in chapter 14) then this method may be very valuable. A case study may often serve as a source of ideas or hypotheses for later study (e.g. p. 309).

Many psychological investigations are done on small samples of some 10–50 individuals, who can be brought to a laboratory or observed in a single setting. Usually statistical tests are then carried out to see whether the results are sufficiently stable or characteristic that it is likely they would be true of larger samples. The means of carrying out simple statistical tests (such as correlation, t test, and chi-square) are described in introductory texts such as Robson (1983, 1993), together with the meaning of probability or p values. Examples of the results of such tests are given in many of the boxes in this book.

Sometimes a survey or other investigation is carried out on a large sample of hundreds of participants. Such a sample may be regarded as normative, or representative, of some section of the population. For example, one longitudinal study in Britain included all the children born in one week of March 1946. These could reasonably be taken as representative of children born in Britain in the later 1940s. Again, statistical tests are usually employed to look at correlations, or at differences between subgroups in the sample.

Ethical issues

Whenever an investigation is made with human or animal participants, investigators should have due respect for their rights and welfare. Investigations with animals kept for experimental purposes are in fact controlled by strict Home Office guidelines. In addition, societies such as the British Psychological Society have issued ethical guidelines for the planning of investigations. Many investigations involve some disturbance of privacy, or inconvenience to participants. Some may involve temporary deception, or even some distress or pain in the case of animal experiments. Even when legally permissible, any such outcomes should be balanced very carefully against the likely benefits from carrying out the investigations. Needless to say, any negative outcomes to participants must be carefully justified and only accepted under the most unusual circumstances; they should never be a feature of student experiments or investigations. The ethical principles approved by the British Psychological Society, and revised in 1990, are reprinted in appendix A and should be consulted in case of any uncertainty on this issue.

Another ethical issue relates to the accurate reporting of results. It is clearly the duty of investigators to report their results in as accurate and unbiased a way as possible, but there have been occasions when this principle is known to have been violated. The British psychologist Sir Cyril Burt reported data on twins which he claimed to have gathered for many years, in order to prove that intelligence was largely inherited. His results were published in numerous articles as his sample of twins accumulated. However, it has now been shown beyond reasonable doubt that in the latter part of his life Burt did not gather more data, but invented it (Hearnshaw, 1979). Thus a great deal of his twin data set is believed by most psychologists to be fraudulent, and the conclusions drawn from it unwarranted. Much attention has been drawn to this deception, partly because of the social implications of the theory of hereditary intelligence, and partly because fraud on this scale is believed to be rare. Drawing attention to such misdemeanours hopefully serves to make future occurrences less probable.

Objectivity and bias

Scientific investigation is supposed to be objective, not biased by the personal beliefs or values of the individual investigator or the wider society. In practice, this is not entirely the case. The kinds of problems chosen for study, and the way they are tackled, are inevitably affected by personal or societal ideas of what is important. This may be especially so in certain areas of psychology. Stephen Gould (1981), in a compelling book entitled *The Mismeasure of Man*, demonstrates this in the instance of the study of intelligence testing and the view held by some psychologists that there were innate racial differences in intelligence. The kinds of study carried out earlier in the century, and the way those studies were interpreted, clearly reflected bias (for example, racial prejudice) in some investigators. At times this involved misconceived inferences from results, or observer bias in scoring or testing. At extremes it bordered on fraudulence similar to the Burt example. Gould takes an optimistic view, in the sense that biases can be recognized and exposed, at least after the event. Indeed much more sophisticated studies of the issues involved in race and intelligence have now been carried out.

◀The Scientific Status of Psychology▶▶▶

This chapter began by briefly considering the nature of psychology as a scientific discipline. We shall conclude by discussing briefly what is meant by the term 'science', and whether this is what psychologists practise. The nature of scientific inquiry has been written about by philosophers of science: we shall summarize the views of two – Popper and Kuhn.

For a long time it was generally held that science proceeded by gathering factual data, by observation and experiment, and by deriving general laws from these facts. This has been called the 'traditional' or 'inductivist' view. However, throughout the twentieth century, scientists and philosophers of science have put more emphasis on the role of hypotheses or theories in science. A hypothesis, or theory, is a proposition that some relationship holds amongst certain phenomena. For example, some psychological hypotheses discussed in this book include: that the fetus can learn characteristics of the mother's voice (pp. 61–3); that the first hours of birth are critically important for mother–infant bonding (pp. 72–3); that viewing violent television pro-grammes makes children behave more aggressively (pp. 166–7); that children are attracted to a level of moral reasoning just above their current level (pp. 229–30); that infants aged 6 weeks can perceive the depth (distance) of an object (pp. 294–6); that children cannot understand another's point of view until about 7 years of age (p. 344); that preschool 'Head start' programmes can benefit a child educationally throughout the school years (p. 502).

The 'traditional' view would be that hypotheses such as these are derived from facts we have gathered, and that if we get enough factual support then the theory will have been 'proved' correct. However, this view is not now generally held. Instead, most scientists and philosophers believe that the role of theory is a primary one, and that theories cannot be proved, only dis-proved. A most articulate proponent of this viewpoint is Sir Karl Popper (1902–94), who argues that our ideas about the world, or 'common-sense beliefs', serve as the starting point for organizing knowledge from which scientific investigation proceeds. Thus, theory serves a primary role and indeed structures what and how we observe or categorize 'facts', or observa-tions about the world. Psychologists are in a good position to appreciate this argument, as part of their discipline (and part of this book, e.g. chapters 9, 10 and 11) is concerned with how children construct hypotheses about percep-tual data and how they gain greater knowledge about the world through forming hypotheses to test against experience. Indeed, we started this chap-ter by considering how people are 'nature's psychologists' in this sense (see also chapter 13).

Popper considers that science and knowledge progress by advancing hypotheses, making deductions from them, and continuing to do so until some deductions are proved wrong or 'falsified'. The hypothesis is then changed to cope with this. A hypothesis can thus never be finally proved correct, as there is always the possibility that some further observation or experiment might discredit it. A hypothesis can, however, be falsified and it is through this process that science progresses.

You can think about this by examining the hypotheses we have just listed. Have any been falsified (some have)? Did the falsifying lead to better hypotheses (sometimes)? Could any be 'proved' beyond question?

Popper's notion of falsification has been a powerful one, and he uses it to distinguish 'science' from 'non-science'. If propositions, hypotheses or theo-ries cannot actually be falsified, then according to Popper, this is not science. It may be interesting and enlightening, like a novel, but it is not science. Not all philosophers of science agree with Popper's approach. At least, not many believe that scientists spend most of their time trying to disprove their theories. A different view was put by Thomas Kuhn (1922–96), who saw a mature branch of any science as having an accepted 'paradigm'. A paradigm is a basic set of assumptions, or way of trying to solve problems. Atomic theory provided a paradigm in the natural sciences, for example.

Psychology, 'psychoanalysis', 'behaviourism', 'sociobiology' (see chapter 2) and the 'information processing' approach (viewing the brain as a com-puter) could be taken as paradigms in this sense. However, the most influen-tial paradigm informing the present book is the 'cognitive-developmental' paradigm. This links behaviour to the kind of cognitive development or thinking ability expected at the age or level of development the individual is at. Piaget's theory of cognitive development is often taken as a reference point here (chapter 11), though the approach is not necessarily tied to Piaget's ideas.

Kuhn described how a branch of science might develop; it starts in a 'pre-paradigmatic stage' where it would be characterized by rather random fact-gathering, and many schools of thought which quarrel about fundamental issues. With maturity, one paradigm is accepted and directs the way observations and experiments are made. Kuhn called this phase 'normal science'. Scientists work within the paradigm, extending and defending it. The paradigm is not rejected unless many difficulties or falsifications accumulate, and in addition a superior paradigm appears. A period of 'revolutionary science' with competing paradigms then emerges, with eventually one proving superior, when 'normal science' resumes.

Kuhn characterizes science as having a fruitful paradigm which can unify the efforts and direction of study of many scientists. Falsification has a relatively minor role to play, he argues, since all theories have some anomalies (phenomena which cannot yet be well explained). Only the appearance of another paradigm can really upset things.

Kuhn's ideas have been criticized, and modified, but his idea of a paradigm, while rather vague in practice, has had considerable impact. Psychologists in particular often seem to be claiming that a particular approach or theory is setting up a 'new paradigm'! Kuhn himself seems to have thought that psychology and other social sciences may well still be at a pre-paradigmatic stage. It is indeed true that no single paradigm as yet unites the whole of psychology. Still, certain paradigms (e.g. the cognitive-developmental approach) do seem to be fruitful and capable of bringing together several areas of psychology. Perhaps, after working through this book, the reader may decide for himself or herself what kind of scientific status the study of psychological development has, what it has achieved, and what it may reasonably hope to achieve in the foreseeable future.

Further Reading ▶ ▶

A very readable introductory text on methods of studying behaviour is P. Martin and P. Bateson 1991 (2nd edn): *Measuring Behaviour: an Introductory Guide*, Cambridge: Cambridge University Press; it has most detail on observational methods, and on studying animals. A more advanced sourcebook for research methodology and experimental design in psychology is provided by C. Robson 1993: *Real World Research*, published by Blackwell Publishers.

There are many good statistics texts available for psychology and the social/behavioural sciences. Amongst the most suitable for introductory psychology courses is C. Robson 1983 (2nd edn): *Experiment, Design and Statistics in Psychology*, Harmondsworth: Penguin. An excellent, thorough and broader text is H. Coolican 1990: *Research Methods and Statistics in Psychology*, London: Hodder & Stoughton.

The way in which psychologists can be affected by the social climate of the time, and the ethical issues involved in doing research with social policy implications, is well exemplified in S. J. Gould 1981: *The Mismeasure of Man*, Harmondsworth: Penguin, and by B. Tizard and A. Phoenix 1993:

Black, White or Mixed Race? Race and Racism in the Lives of Young People of Mixed Parentage, London: Routledge. The journal *Childhood* gives up-to-date debates on the construction of childhood and the family, children's rights and cross-cultural perspectives on society's responsibilities towards children.

H. R. Schaffer 1996: *Social Development,* Oxford: Blackwell Publishers, explores the ways in which current models of child socialization have implications for policies in such areas as day care, dealing with antisocial behaviour in young people, and addressing family conflict and breakdown. K. Durkin 1995: *Developmental Social Psychology,* also published by Blackwell, gives thorough coverage on gender issues, the influence of culture and the impact of research in the social sciences on policy-making around families and young people.

An introduction to Popper's ideas on scientific method can be found in B. Magee 1973: *Popper,* Glasgow: Fontana. Kuhn's ideas are best expressed in T. Kuhn 1962: *The Structure of Scientific Revolutions,* London: University of Chicago Press (2nd edn, 1970). An accessible general overview is A. F. Chalmers 1982 (2nd edn): *What is this Thing called Science?* Milton Keynes: Open University Press.

◀Discussion Points▶ ▶ ▶

1   Has our knowledge of psychological development advanced beyond 'common sense'?
2   What is meant by 'development' and how can we study it?
3   What are the advantages and disadvantages of carrying out experiments in psychology?
4   What ethical issues are involved in psychological investigation?
5   In what ways can psychology be considered to be, or not to be, a science?

2 The Biological Perspective

In this chapter we look at the way behaviour develops – the importance of our genetic inheritance and how this genetic blueprint interacts with our environment to channel growth and development along a particular pathway. We then examine these issues in two ways – ontogenetically and phylogenetically. Ontogenesis refers to the development of behaviour in the individual. Most of the book is concerned with this! In this chapter, we start examining the process from conception to birth, a period when genetic determination of development is at its strongest. Phylogenesis refers to the evolution of behaviour; we examine briefly issues of instinct, maturation and learning in birds and mammals – including our closest non-human relatives, the monkeys and apes. This evolutionary perspective continues with an overview of sociobiology and behavioural ecology, which many biologists believe provides the most successful approach to explaining why animals behave as they do, and which some researchers have tried to apply to human behaviour.

◄From Conception to Birth►►►

This period of about nine months constitutes the first stage in human development – itself divided into three substages, illustrated in figure 2.1.

Germinal stage

The baby is conceived when a sperm cell from the father unites with an egg cell or ovum from the mother. The fertilized egg is called a *zygote*. The zygote starts dividing, and dividing again, with cells rapidly differentiating. After

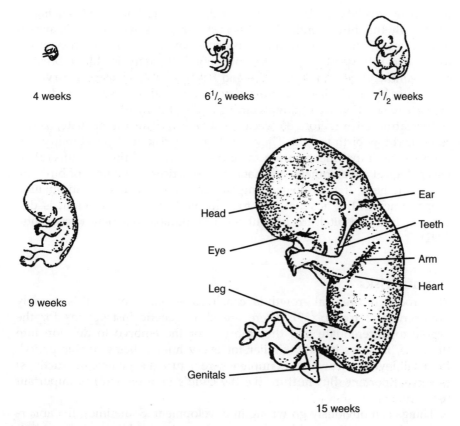

4 weeks   6$^1/_2$ weeks   7$^1/_2$ weeks

9 weeks

Head

Ear

Teeth

Eye

Arm

Leg

Heart

Genitals

15 weeks

Figure 2.1 Stages of prenatal growth.

about a week, it starts to implant onto the wall of the mother's uterus. This is complete after two weeks, at which point it is called an *embryo*.

Embryonic stage
This lasts from about the third to the eighth week after conception. By the end of this time, although only an inch long, the embryo has the basic plan of a human body, with head, arms, legs, hands and feet. It connects to the *placenta*, by means of the umbilical cord. The placenta is a special area on the wall of the uterus. Here, the blood supply from the mother meets that of the embryo and they intermingle through thousands of tiny blood vessels. By this means, the mother supplies oxygen and nutrients to the growing embryo. By the eighth week, the embryo is also safely cushioned in a kind of water bed – the amniotic sac – which surrounds it and keeps it at a constant temperature.

Fetal stage
By now, the major structures of the body have differentiated, and bone cells develop, marking the stage of the fetus. Relatively small features develop –

fingernails, eyelids, eyebrows; and cartilage in the bones are starting to harden. By the third month, the fetus is starting to move, and its heartbeat can be heard; and the movements become obvious to the mother by the fourth and fifth month. By the seventh month the fetus is able to breathe, cry, swallow, digest, and excrete – and has a realistic chance of surviving premature birth. The last 2 months of normal conception see a considerable increase in size and weight, with birth usually at 9 months.

Premature birth (before 36 weeks) can be a risk for the neonate, as can associated low birth weight. They are at greater risk of physical injury and neurological impairment during the birth process, and this can affect their psychological development. Neonatal care practices at the time of birth are important here. If neurological impairment is avoided, then stimulation programmes in the hospital and to help mothers after the infant is discharged from hospital are helpful for a favourable outcome (Rosenblith, 1992).

Prenatal risks

The process of prenatal growth is 'canalized' – that is to say, it is strongly predetermined (see p. 39). There are clear genetic instructions for the zygote to differentiate into the embryo, for the embryo to develop into the fetus, in ways broadly similar for every human being at this period. Prenatal development is an example where nature (i.e. genetic instructions) is very important. But nurture (i.e the child's environment) is important too.

Things can obviously go wrong in development. Sometimes, the abnormalities are genetic, as with Down's syndrome, a condition arising from a chromosomal abnormality which we discuss later (p. 34). Sometimes, they are environmentally caused. One class of environmental hazards are called *teratogens*. Teratogen is an ancient Greek work meaning 'creating a monster' – a reference to the marked abnormalities that can sometimes occur in prenatal development. This is especially so in the embryonic period – this is when the basic ground plan of the body is being formed, with differentiation of major organs including arms and legs. Drugs and other harmful substances can reach the embryo through the mother's blood stream, and if they do so in the embryonic period, some can cause gross body or limb abnormalities. For example, the drug thalidomide, prescribed to prevent recurrent miscarriages in the 1950s, led to babies being born with severe limb deformities – but only when the drug was taken during the first two months of pregnancy. Thalidomide is no longer prescribed in these cases. But other drugs such as cocaine, heavy consumption of alcohol during pregnancy and heavy cigarette smoking are among risk factors for healthy prenatal development. Other risk factors include poor maternal nutrition, infectious diseases such as rubella (German measles), exposure to radiation and possibly maternal stress. A risk factor means that later problems are not inevitable, but they are more likely, especially if other risk factors or adverse circumstances are present.

Pregnancy sickness

Many mothers experience pregnancy sickness in the early stages of pregnancy; they may feel nausea at the sight and smell of foods they previously enjoyed, vomit easily, and especially feel 'morning sickness' on rising in the morning. Profet (1992) has argued that pregnancy sickness has been selected for in evolution, as an adaptive mechanism to protect the embryo against teratogens, especially toxic chemicals from foods. She argues that certain foods, including certain plant foods, contain toxins which would not harm the mother but could harm the embryo, notably during the period when major organs are being formed. Her argument is supported by the fact that pregnancy sickness appears to coincide with the period of maximum vulnerability to teratogens, with a peak at around 6 to 8 weeks; that it is found cross-culturally; and that women who experience nausea and vomiting have lower rates of spontaneous abortion than those women who do not.

Fetal learning

Just as the fetus can be affected by toxic environmental stimuli, it is also capable of learning from the environment. This is especially so during the last 3 months in the womb. During this period, the fetus responds to sounds (auditory stimuli), which are filtered through the amniotic fluid. Sounds can reliably affect fetal heart rate and motor responses from as early as 20 weeks of gestational age (indeed, congenital deafness can now be diagnosed during the prenatal period; Shahidullah and Hepper, 1993b). A number of experiments have shown that the fetus actively processes this auditory input, and distinguishes between music, language and other sounds (Karmiloff-Smith, 1995). Box 2.1 describes a study showing how the neonate's discrimination of the mother's voice is linked to audiory experience *in utero*.

◀The Nature of Birth▶▶

A full-term pregnancy lasts about 9 months, and then the infant is born. Nine months may seem like a long time to be pregnant. But in fact, from the point of view of our position compared with other primates, including the great apes, 9 months is short. We can compare humans with other primates on the basis of general growth, gestation period and brain size at birth:

growth: complete at age 11 for chimpanzees and gorillas, at age 20 for humans;
average gestation period: 228 days in chimpanzees, 256 days in gorillas, 267 days in humans;
brain size at birth as a per cent of adult size: 41% for chimpanzees, 25% for humans.

On the basis of general growth rates, we might expect the gestation period in humans to be about twice that in the great apes, but it is not – it is quite similar. But it seems as a consequence that human neonates are, in a comparative sense, quite immature, with only one-quarter of brain size achieved at birth compared with about one-half in primates generally. The human infant's brain size only reaches one-half adult size by 1 year (and three-quarters of adult size by 3 years).

The probable explanation for this has its origins in our evolutionary history (see p. 53). A significant development in hominid evolution was bipedalism – being able habitually and easily to walk around on two legs, with an erect posture; the apes can only do this rather awkwardly and for shorter periods, often going on all fours or brachiating – climbing in trees. This shift to bipedalism seems to have gone along with a change in climate and an opportunity for early hominids to gather, scavenge and hunt for food on more open, savanna grasslands (Lovejoy, 1981). Bipedalism also freed up the hands; instead of walking on hands and knuckles, humans could use the hands for carrying, and also for making tools – something incipient in chimpanzees (box 2.2) but a hallmark of human evolution.

But bipedalism seems to have had a price. To be energetically efficient, the pelvic bones and hip joints had to be refashioned; and this in turn meant a restriction on the pelvic opening through which the infant is born – a greater restriction than in the brachiating great apes. According to Leutenegger (1981), there were therefore two competing trends occurring in our evolutionary history – increased efficiency of bipedal locomotion, but also increasing brain size (taking advantage of the manual opportunities of bipedalism and the social opportunities of group living on the savanna). Each was vital; but increased brain size means larger heads, whereas the constraints on size from the birth canal were becoming more restrictive. The inevitable consequence was earlier birth – birth when the neonatal brain was only one-quarter adult size, not one-half. Instead of a gestation period of about 18 months (which one might expect by extrapolation from other primates), gestation period is 9 months. The 'additional' 9 months after birth results in a very helpless infant, and this condition is sometimes referred to as *exterogestation* or *secondary altriciality* (Montagu, 1961; Trevathan, 1987).

This might seem a disadvantage; human infants do indeed need a lot of care and attention for the first year, if they are to survive. But, it has been argued that this actually reinforced the trend to increasing sociality and cooperative group living in early hominids. Basically, mothers needed help with their infants (Lovejoy, 1981; Trevarthan, 1987). This help is often needed in parturition (the actual birth process), as well as subsequently. The help can come from the mother's own mother, the father of the infant, other relatives, or friends. In traditional societies, some older women would be experienced in assisting at births; in modern societies, some nurses are trained as midwives for this purpose.

Figure 2.2 shows the usual position in which the infant is born – head first, and with the head facing away from the mother's face. Because of the size of the infant, especially the head, the birth process is not easy; most women find it quite painful. As birth approaches, the mother feels contractions of the uterus (the largest muscle in the human female, it can exert a force of up

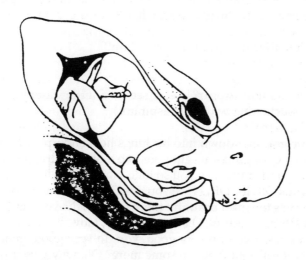

Figure 2.2   Typical birth position.

to 60 pounds during labour). Irregular contractions can occur before, but with the onset of true labour these become regular; there may be difficulties in sleeping, and persistent backache. After some hours these contractions become more forceful and occur around every five minutes. By this time the mother has usually sought out assistance or (in modern societies) gone into hospital. She may be lying on a bed, although the more usual position in traditional societies is to be in a semi-reclining or squatting position.

Contractions become stronger and closer together. The cervix (through which the infant must pass) has softened and dilated. Experiences of pain may actually lessen here, but effort increases – the woman is straining and pushing (hence the term 'labour'). The fetal membranes rupture now, if they have not already done so. The infant's head starts to emerge, often accompanied by a cry from the mother. The midwife, or perhaps the mother herself, helps rotate the head to get the shoulders in the best position to come out. The infant is born, attached still by the umbilical cord. The cord is still pulsating, and for a few minutes the infant is 'cushioned' by the maternal blood supply as its lungs start to fill and it takes its first breaths, and cries. The cord is cut; and within 30 minutes the placenta is also expelled.

This moment of birth is something totally new for the infant, and its cry is a sign of health as it adapts to its new, extrauterine environment. It is often a climactic experience for the mother, and one of joy for the father and other relatives. Here is a transcript of a birth conversation, recorded by Trevathan in Texas, USA, with a bilingual Hispanic mother:

Midwife: Push, Karen. The baby's coming out now. Push hard. Good. Coming down. Grab the baby! Grab the whole thing! There you go.

Mother: Oh, my love. Oh, my baby. Oh, I love you.

Father: It's a boy?

Midwife: Is it really? (laughs) I told you, huh!

Mother: It's a boy?

Father: It's a boy.

Midwife: One minute Apgar? Let's see . . . a little floppy . . . pink feet . . . (suctioning with bulb aspirator).

Mother: What's that?

Midwife: If he gets that down into his lungs he'll end up with pneumonia.

Mother: (Baby crying.) It's alright poor baby, oh, it's alright. Oh my baby, yes, yes. I waited for you so long, now you're here. Oh, my baby, oh, it's OK, it's OK, I love you. It's OK. (To father.) You wanna see it? He's the most beautiful thing (laughs). Never, never, ever seen a baby so beautiful. Oh God, oh baby, I love you. (Baby cries.) No, no, no. Oh you do very good, you do very good, good, yes, yes, yes. It's alright. You cry some more? Oh, why you cry? Why you cry, oh yes. Shshshshshshsh. No, noooooo.

Midwife: Give her [mother] some orange juice.

Mother: (To midwife in normal pitch voice.) Can I sit up so I can breastfeed the baby? (Baby cries, mother continues to talk, but hard to hear.) Oh, my baby, don't cry, I'm sorry, I love you. Yes, it's alright.

Midwife: What are you spitting up, fellow?

Father: He's big, huh?

Mother: He's the strongest little thing.

Midwife: Got a good grip, huh?

In the above, the midwife refers to the '1-minute Apgar'. The Apgar score (Apgar, 1953) is a simple and quick way of evaluating an infant's well-being immediately after birth (often, at 1 minute, and 5 minutes). The scoring is shown in table 2.1. A score of 7–10 is healthy, 4–6 somewhat depressed, and below 4 cause for serious concern, especially at 5 minutes. Although in modern societies women have often been given medication during labour, to relieve pain, these can result in lower Apgar scores and a less immediately responsive infant; hence many women now prefer a more natural labour where possible.

Delivery of the baby is not always straightforward. Some 3 to 4 per cent are 'breech' deliveries; here, the baby is not in the usual, head-first position for coming out, and instead the buttocks, knees or feet may come first with the head last. This prolongs the delivery process, since the buttocks, knees or feet do not dilate the cervix so well as the head. The baby may attempt to breathe before its head is delivered. Even in modern societies mortality is 10–20 per cent in breech deliveries. This again suggests that help at birth has a long evolutionary history (Trevathan, 1987).

Interaction after birth

Behaviour after birth is strongly influenced by cultural practices and expectations; and indeed, if the infant is taken away soon after birth in a hospital

Table 2.1 The Apgar scoring technique

SCORE	0	1	2
COLOUR	Blue, pale	Body pink, extremities blue	Completely pink
HEART RATE	Absent	Slow, <100	Over 100
REFLEX IRRITABILITY	No response	Grimace	Cry
MUSCLE TONE	Flaccid	Some flexion of extremities	Active motion
RESPIRATORY EFFORT	Absent	Slow, irregular	Good, crying

delivery, mother–infant interaction is obviously curtailed! This is discussed further on pp. 72–3. The usual pattern however is that the mother will stimulate the infant in a variety of ways: touching, stroking and rubbing its body, making eye contact while facing it, and bringing it up to her chest, and talking to it. Usually within the first hour she will breastfeed the infant. Characteristically, mothers will comment on the appearance of the baby, and often on how it resembles the father – perhaps to reassure the father of his paternity (Daly and Wilson, 1982).

Breastfeeding

In traditional societies, breastfeeding was essential for the infant's survival. Breastfeeding is normally done by the mother, but in some societies and in some historical periods (early modern Europe is an example) wet-nursing, or breastfeeding of someone else's infant by a mother who is already breastfeeding, has been quite common. In modern societies, mothers can dispense with breastfeeding and use bottle feeding if they wish. An advantage of this is that fathers can participate equally! However, human milk is particularly well suited to the needs of human infants.

The primary constituents of milk are fat, protein and carbohydrate. D. M. Ben Shaul (1962) surveyed the milk composition of a range of mammals, and found that it depends on lifestyle. Mammals which live in cold, wet environments, such as dolphins, produce large amounts of fat in their milk so as to help maintain body warmth. Those mammals which leave their infants in a nest or den site for a long time (such as lions, rabbits, many rodents and carnivores) have relatively large amounts of protein and fat in the milk to sustain the infants between feeding periods. Mammals which carry their young with them (marsupials like kangaroos; species with precocial young such as deer and antelope; and most primates) have milk lower in fat and protein and higher in carbohydrates. Primates have milk especially high in carbohydrates, including lactose, which is a key nutrient for brain growth.

Human milk follows the primate pattern closely. The milk composition is typical for a species where feeding would be on demand (as it would be in traditional societies where mothers carried their infants with them) and where brain growth continues rapidly after birth.

Actually, the very first milk produced by the mother after birth is not typical. It is called the colostrum, and is yellowish or bluish and different from the 'true milk' that appears within about 3 days. The colostrum appears to be useful in providing the infant with a high concentration of a variety of antibodies, providing early immunological protection; it also contains vitamin K, which is essential for blood clotting (and this may prevent blood loss at the site of the umbilical cord). Given these advantages, it is surprising that quite a number of societies, including traditional societies, practise 'colostrum-denial'; the infant is nursed by another mother, or fed a substitute such as sweetened water, for the first 3 days. There appear to be no advantages and some disadvantages to this practice, and the reason why these beliefs are held in some societies is not clear (Barkow, 1989).

◀Genetics and the Groundplan for Development▶▶▶

Our bodies are made up of cells – brain cells, blood cells, muscle cells, bone cells and so on. But as we have seen, we all started life as just one cell – the 'zygote' formed by the union of mother's egg and father's sperm, which develops through various stages. Now, let's look at the code for this development, the instructions that enable this development to take place.

If we look at a cell under powerful microscopes, we find that each cell has a nucleus containing thread-like structures called chromosomes (see figure 2.3). These chromosomes are typically arranged in pairs; 4 pairs in fruit flies, 24 pairs in chimpanzees – and 23 pairs for humans. Each chromosome in turn consists of a chain of genes; the genes are strung along the chromosomes like beads on a necklace. The whole collection of genes is called the 'genotype'. It is the genes that provide instructions for the production of materials in the body for growth and development. These instructions will lead to an organism having basic body organs – having wings, or not; legs, or not; and also what kind of wings, legs, etc. As humans, we owe our basic body plan to our genes. Also, as individuals, such aspects as the colour of our hair, or of our eyes, whether our hair is curly, depend on particular genes we may or may not have.

In sexual reproduction, the egg cells (ova) of the mother and the sperm cells of the father contain only a half-set of chromosomes – one from each pair, following some reassortment of genes between each pair. After mating and fertilization, the zygote (fertilized egg) now has a new set of chromosome pairs, with one set of each pair from the mother and one set from the father. The offspring thus receives a mixture of the genes of each parent, approximately half from each, reassembled into new combinations.

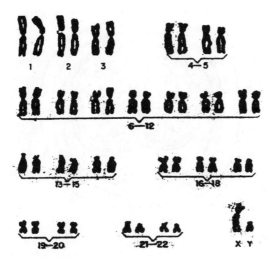

Figure 2.3 Human chromosome complement arranged into a standard karyotype, numbered as shown. The sex chromosomes, labelled X and Y, are at the lower right. (Original furnished by Dr J. J. Biesele, from H. E. Sutton, *An Introduction to Human Genetics*. New York: Holt, Rinehart & Winston, 1965).

Many genes simply ensure the basic groundplan of the species – in our case, that we have two eyes, a nose, mouth, two arms, two legs, etc. Others vary more between individuals, so that some of us have black hair, some brown, some red. Some genes affect one particular characteristic strongly, others affect several more weakly or in interactive combination. Geneticists study these influences. The Human Genome Project, started in 1990, aims to look in detail at the structure and nature of the human genotype – what genes we have and how they are laid out along our chromosomes. Since we have some 50,000 to 100,000 genes, this is an ambitious task!

Besides affecting the physical development of the organism, the genotype also influences behavioural development – a topic known as behaviour genetics (Plomin, DeFries, McClearn and Rutter 1997). The area is contentious, as it relates to the extent to which the genes ('nature') or the environment ('nurture') are responsible for our behaviour – a topic we start to look at in the evolutionary perspective, in the next section. However, there is no doubt that features of the genotype can affect behavioural development in the human species.

Twin studies

One source of evidence comes from twin studies. Although mothers usually conceive only one infant at a time, about 1 in every 80 pregnancies involves twins. Twins can be monozygotic, or dizygotic:

monozygotic: identical twins, who come from a single fertilized egg cell which has split into two early in development. Usually, the twins share the

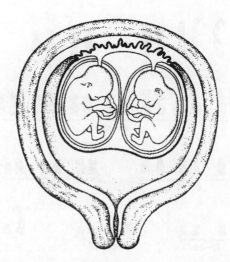

Figure 2.4   Twins in utero. These identical twins have a single placenta but individual amniotic sacs. (Adapted with permission from L. B. Arey, *Developmental Anatomy: A Textbook and Laboratory Manual of Embryology* [7th edn]. Copyright 1965 by W. B. Saunders Company).

placenta and surrounding membrane, but have their own umbilical cord to the mother's blood supply, and amniotic sac (see figure 2.4). They are genetically identical and hence of the same sex.

dizygotic: fraternal twins, who come from two separately fertilized egg cells, each of which develops totally separately in the womb with its own placenta. They may be of the same or different sex. They are siblings, and share 50 per cent of genes in common like other full siblings (although it is possible, and has been documented, for fraternal twins to be half-siblings; Rosenblith, 1992).

Twins can be considered as being reared in very similar environments – normally by the same parents, at the same time and in the same circumstances. But identical and fraternal twins differ in genetic similarity (100% versus 50%). Thus, it can be argued, if identical twins grow up to be more similar in certain respects than fraternal twins, then this should be due to heredity or genetic factors (which differ) rather than environmental factors (which are in common).

In fact, identical twins do often show greater similarity than fraternal twins; see figure 2.5. The extent to which this is so, is taken by behaviour geneticists as a measure of the heritability of the trait in question. So for example, figure 2.5 suggests higher heritability for verbal reasoning than for memory.

There are of course some questionable assumptions here; in particular, it is possible that identical twins are treated in more similar ways by parents than fraternal twins are, so that their environment is more similar as well as their genetic inheritance. Behaviour geneticists have attempted to avoid this

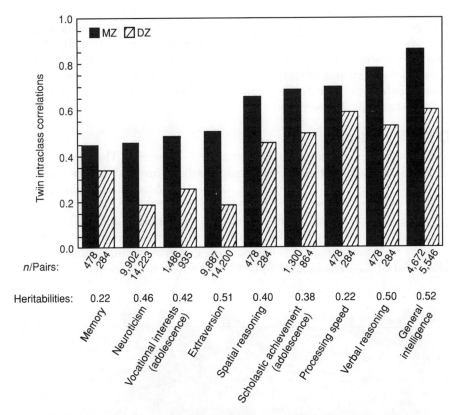

Figure 2.5   MZ and DZ twin intraclass correlations for personality (neuroticism and extraversion), interests in adolescence, scholastic achievement in adolescence, specific cognitive abilities in adolescence (memory, spatial reasoning, processing speed, verbal reasoning), and general intelligence. (Adapted with permission from R. Plaomin, M. J. Owen and P. McGuffin 1994: The genetic basis of complex human behaviours. *Science*, 264, 1733–9.)

confusion by obtaining data on identical twins reared apart (rather few in number, however); and by using other methods such as comparing adopted and non-adopted siblings (Plomin, DeFries, McClearn and Rutter 1997).

Chromosomal abnormalities

Another source of evidence for genetic effects on behaviour comes from changes at the level of chromosomes. Of the 23 pairs of chromosomes in humans, 22 pairs (the 'autosomes') are basically matched pairs similar in structure. The 23rd pair, the 'sex chromosomes', is different. One type called the X chromosome is considerably longer and more complex than the alternative called the Y chromosome (see figure 2.3). If you receive two X chromosomes, you will normally develop as a female; if you receive one X and one Y chromosome, you will normally develop as a male. This of course has very definite implications for development, and is discussed further in chapter 5.

Occasionally some mistake is made in genetic transmission, often a change or 'mutation' at the gene level. Sometimes the mistake can take place at a whole chromosome level. The most well-known example relates to the 21st chromosome pair; occasionally this pair may fail to separate in forming the egg or sperm, and the offspring may end up having three chromosomes – a trio instead of a pair at this location. This Trisomy 21 condition is usually referred to as Down's syndrome.

Down's syndrome

Down's syndrome occurs in approximately $\frac{1}{800}$ live births. The chromosomal abnormality usually originates in damage to the ovum prior to conception. A woman's ova are present from birth so they are increasingly vulnerable to damage over time; hence, older mothers are more likely than younger mothers to have a baby with Down's syndrome. Mothers aged 20–24 have a $\frac{1}{9000}$ chance of having a baby with Down's syndrome; whereas in mothers aged 45 or more the chances rise to $\frac{1}{30}$. Paternal age is also associated with increased likelihood of having a baby with Down's syndrome.

Plate 2.1   A child with Down's syndrome.

A photograph of a person with Down's syndrome is shown in plate 2.1. There are specific physical characteristics in Down's syndrome, including a flat appearance to the face, with a low bridge to the nose and high cheek-bones; and upward and outward slanting eyes with a conspicuous upper eye-lid fold. In addition muscles may be floppy, contributing to poor motor co-ordination.

So far as behavioural development is concerned, persons with Down's syndrome vary greatly but the chromosomal abnormality is a disability. There is likely to be mental retardation, with particular difficulty taking in visual, auditory and other sensory information at speed, and slow reaction times; particularly poor memory for heard speech, leading to poor speech comprehension; poor speech pronunciation; and poor number ability. Young children with Down's syndrome are usually sociable and friendly, though frustration and temper tantrums may occur. The child with Down's syndrome is likely to have better visual skills than hearing and speech skills, so they may find it easier to sign or even to read than to acquire intelligible speech. Their level of spontaneous activity is low, and they need extra encouragement to explore, experiment and learn. Programmes designed to develop play and communication at an early age can be helpful. However, the rate of development of children with Down's syndrome often slows down from infancy onwards; adults commonly show a deterioration of mental abilities and sometimes difficult behaviour. On the positive side, home-rearing can sometimes lead to greater IQ gains than institutional rearing, and some people with Down's syndrome do continue intellectual development beyond adolescence (Rauh, Rudinger, Bowman, Berry, Gunn and Hayes, 1991).

How Behaviour Develops: Nature and Nurture ▶▶

The genes regulate the production of amino acids and thus determine the first stages in cell growth and differentiation in the body and in the brain and nervous system. They thus are often thought of as providing a blueprint for growth and also for behaviour. The actual course of growth and of behavioural development, however, depends upon, and is influenced by, the external environment. Not only does the environment provide the 'building materials' such as food and water but the particular environmental experiences of the organism also interact with the genetic instructions to determine in detail which exact course of development is followed.

Figure 2.6 depicts in very simple form the interaction of information from the genotype and information from the environment in determining behaviour. Both genotype and environment are obviously essential for any behaviour. Thus, we cannot say that a particular behaviour is genetic and another behaviour environmental; nor can we sensibly say that a behaviour comprises some percentage of each.

The diagram in figure 2.6 is a simple one – some psychologists might say too simple. (For example, the information in the genotype may influence the choice of environment, so the two influences are not as independent as they seem.) However, it may help in conceptualizing terms such as 'instinct', 'maturation' and 'learning', and the issue of the rigidity or flexibility of behavioural development.

Although we cannot say that a behaviour is mostly genetic or environmental, we can say that the difference in behaviour between two individuals is mostly genetic or environmental. In humans, for example, differences in eye colour can usually be ascribed to genetic differences (although both genotype and environment are necessary for the development of eye colour); whereas differences in spoken language can usually be ascribed to environmental differences (although both genotype and environment are necessary for the development of language).

Many writers have used the terms 'instinct', 'maturation' and 'learning' in discussing the development of behaviour. There are problems with the definition of these terms, and some psychologists prefer not to use the term 'instinct' at all. However, in order to understand discussion on these matters we need to know what writers who use such terms intend. Representative definitions are given below.

Instinct   Instinctive behaviour is observed in all normal healthy members of a species. Thus, it is little influenced by the environment. The genetic instructions provide detailed information for the development of instinctive behaviour, and only quite general environmental input (such as is necessary for healthy growth) is needed for its expression.

Maturation   Maturation refers to the emergence of instinctive behaviour patterns at a particular point in development. The genetic instructions facilitate the expression of certain behaviour patterns when a certain growth point is reached or a certain time period has elapsed.

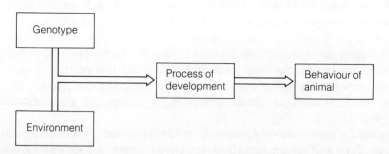

Figure 2.6   Simple model of how both information from the genotype and information from the environment combine and interact to determine the course of behaviour development.

Learning Learning refers to the influence of specific environmental information on behaviour. Within a wide range of variation, the way an animal behaves depends on what it learns from the environment. Thus, individuals of a species may differ considerably in their learnt behaviour patterns.

Issues of instinct, maturation and learning will recur throughout this book. Here, pursuing the evolutionary perspective, we give some examples from animal behaviour.

Bird song: an example of behavioural development

There are many species of song bird, each of which has a characteristic song, or song repertoire, though individuals may differ in the details of their song. We can use the development of bird song in different species to illustrate our discussion of behavioural development. Many ingenious experiments have been performed on this topic (see Thorpe, 1972, for a review).

For some species of bird the song might be described as 'instinctive'. Some birds have been reared experimentally in isolation, or deafened, or fostered by another species, so that they cannot hear the songs of birds of their own kind. In some species, such as doves, hens and song sparrows, the song develops quite normally in such circumstances. This is also true of cuckoos, which are of course regularly reared by foster parents. In such cases there is little environmentally caused variation between healthy individuals, and all members of the species sing much the same song.

Even if 'instinctive', however, the song may not appear fully formed. For example, in whitethroat, the male develops its song first as a continuous reiteration of one note, with other notes being added gradually. This occurs whether the bird is isolated, or not. Thus, this is an example of maturation.

The situation is different in chaffinches, whose song has been studied intensively by Thorpe (1972). Chaffinches sing a song consisting of three main phrases, followed by a terminal flourish. If a chaffinch is reared in isolation, it will not produce a proper chaffinch song. It will produce a much simpler song, of the right length and frequency but not divided into phrases, and without the terminal flourish. The full song is therefore not instinctive and some more specific environmental input is needed for its development. The song is more complex if chaffinches are reared in groups, but in isolation from adult chaffinches. Presumably, the experience of countersinging with other chaffinches is a helpful environmental input. Even so, the song is not perfect, and only the experience of hearing the adult chaffinch song produces a fully formed song in the young chaffinch. Clearly, learning is important in this species.

However, let us note two constraints on this learning of chaffinch song. One is that the young chaffinch will only learn its song from adult chaffinches. If fostered by another species, it will not learn that species' song. In other words, the type of learning is limited to songs that are within a narrow range characteristic of adult chaffinches. The second point to bear in mind is that this learning can only occur within a certain period. Learning capacity is at its maximum in the first spring, when the bird is 8 months old, and ceases after about 14 months, when the bird's singing behaviour becomes fixed or unalterable.

Chaffinch song provides an excellent example of how genotype and environment interact in constraining development. Some learning occurs in chaffinch song, but it is highly constrained in time and duration. As a result, chaffinch song is stable. Chaffinches introduced into New Zealand in 1862, and South Africa in 1900, still sing very much the same song as European chaffinches.

The situation is different again in other species, where learning of the adult song is much more flexible. In bullfinches, for example, the song is learned and there are few constraints on the type of song; if fostered by canaries, a young bullfinch will adopt canary song and ignore the songs of other bullfinches.

Rigidity and flexibility

As you can see from the bird song example, it can often be rather simplistic to say that a behaviour is either 'instinctive' or 'learned'. Many

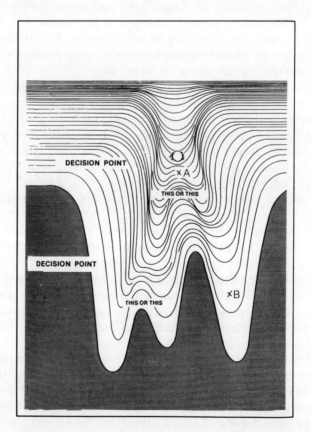

Figure 2.7   Waddington's 'epigenetic landscape' (adapted from Fishbein, 1976).

psychologists now prefer to talk in terms of the 'rigidity' or 'flexibility' of behaviour, or of how 'modifiable' or 'canalized' behavioural development is. Rigid behaviour is less susceptible to environmental modification, flexible behaviour is more so. In the examples above we can see successive increases in flexibility in the adult song of doves, chaffinches and bullfinches, respectively.

A helpful way of conceptualizing this issue is shown in figure 2.7. This type of figure, produced by Waddington (1957), is called an 'epigenetic landscape'. The ball represents the organism while the landscape represents the possibilities for development constrained by the genotype. The movement of the ball down the slope represents development. The direction of travel (development) is influenced by the shape of the landscape, as it is easier for the ball to roll down the troughs, or canals. However, environmental influences can also influence the direction of travel, pushing the ball in certain directions.

At certain times there are choice or decision points in development, and environmental influences may easily affect the direction of development at such points (for example, the point marked A in figure 2.7). At other times, environmental influence, unless extreme, will have little effect (the point marked B, for instance). The development of chaffinch song could easily be interpreted within this framework.

Waddington, and others since, talk of the 'canalization' of behaviour. This is another way of referring to the rigidity as against flexibility of behaviour. We talk of canalized behaviour when the troughs or canals in the epigenetic landscape are deep and environmental variations have little effect. If the canals are shallow, the environment produces much greater variation.

◄The Evolution of Behaviour►►►

Although as humans we are very different from non-human species, we have an evolutionary history being primates (the taxonomic group including monkeys and the great apes). We share the basic principles of genetic transmission and the interaction of genes with environment in determining behaviour. In this section we look at some relevant aspects of mammalian and avian behaviour – especially parent–offspring interaction, and communication – and then further at the concepts of instinct, maturation and learning, in this evolutionary context.

Parent–offspring relations, peers and play

The mother mammal or bird must look after offspring if they are to survive, and the father may also help in some species (see p. 57). The main ways in which the mother, sometimes the father, and sometimes older siblings, may help offspring is in providing warmth and shelter, food, transport, and protection from predators. This kind of help is often called 'parental investment'.

The young are usually distinguished as being of one of two types:

Altricial young   The young are helpless at birth, often blind and unable to move. Examples are mice, pups, kittens, and many bird fledglings. Brood or litter size is often large. The young are fed periodically when mother returns to the nest or den. The young take some time to learn the characteristics of the mother, and vice versa. Rapid bonding is not necessary, as the mother will find the young in the den or nest when she returns. As a result, experimental fostering is often relatively easy.

Precocial young   The young are relatively independent at or soon after birth, and able to move around often within a few hours. Examples are deer, cattle, sheep and some birds such as hens and ducks. In precocial mammals the mother often has just one young in a litter, and it is fed when it wishes, or 'on demand'. The young very rapidly learn to follow the mother around, and a bond of recognition and attachment is formed between mother and young, so that the latter will not get separated or lost. As a consequence, experimental fostering is very difficult in these species.

The primates (monkeys and apes) do not fit too well into this scheme, as they carry their young around (as distinct from putting them in a den, or having them follow). The young are usually quite helpless or altricial, and, being carried around, do not need to bond as rapidly with the mother as do precocial young. However, there is usually only one young in a litter (it would be too much for a mother monkey to carry two offspring), and suckling is 'on demand'.

Young mammals and birds, after a period of high initial dependence on the mother or parents, go through a period during which they become less dependent but do not leave the mother completely. In mammals the young may range further away before returning, and may get more interested in same-age peers (e.g. littermates) than in parents. Much social interaction between littermates involves play, or grooming. Social play usually consists of wrestling or chasing, the non-serious intent being signalled by a playful face or approach (see also chapter 6). It is believed that this kind of play is useful, perhaps for exercise, developing later fighting or hunting skills, or forming social bonds or hierarchies, though the extent to which it is necessary or essential for this is controversial (see Smith, 1982; Martin and Caro, 1985). Littermates may co-operate in later life, especially if they stay in the same social group. This is true of lions and elephants for example, and also of baboons and macaques, and of chimpanzees (box 2.2). They may learn to recognize each other and behave in a more co-operative way than with strangers (see discussion of kin selection). Experience together as young animals is probably important for this.

Communication systems in mammals and birds
Animals often communicate with one another. In communication some sort of signal is sent from one individual to another, which may influence the latter's behaviour. Recent research on mammalian calls suggests that they are more complex and sophisticated than originally thought. For example, a

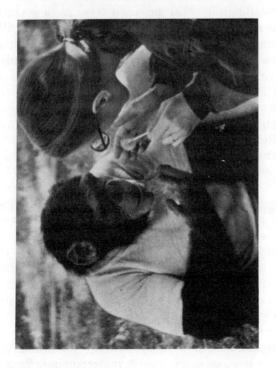

Plate 2.2 Washoe, a young female chimpanzee taught to use sign language, signs 'sweet' for lollipop (left) and 'hat' for woollen cap (on right) (from Atkinson, Atkinson and Hilgard, 1981).

study of ground squirrels in Canada (Davis, 1984) has found that these animals give at least two kinds of alarm call. A short chirp is given in the presence of hawks, and squirrels hearing this immediately run to their burrow. A long whistle is given to weasels, and squirrels then stand erect, watch and flee (they do not go direct to the burrow, as the weasel might follow them in).

Signals used by monkeys and apes seem especially complex (see Seyfarth and Cheney, 1984). For example, vervet monkeys (a ground-living, social species) have three kinds of alarm call, with corresponding responses. 'Leopard alarms' cause other monkeys to run to trees; 'eagle alarms' cause them to look up in the air or run into bushes; while 'snake alarms' cause monkeys to rise on their hind legs and look into the grass around them. These conclusions, based first on observation, have been confirmed by controlled experiments involving playback of tape-recorded calls. Vervet monkeys also 'grunt' at other monkeys, and the same methods have shown that grunts which sound the same to a human observer, differ in spectrographic analysis according to whether the grunt is directed to a dominant animal a subordinate animal, or a monkey from another group.

The most dramatic studies of animal communication have been made with captive apes, usually chimpanzees. A husband and wife team, Gardner and Gardner (1969), taught American Sign Language (ASL) to Washoe, a young female chimpanzee who lived with them. Washoe acquired a large number of signs, and could convey messages such as 'please tickle' and 'give drink' (plate 2.2). The Gardners claimed that Washoe could use several signs strung together meaningfully, that she used signs in new situations (e.g. 'water bird' when she first saw a swan), and that altogether Washoe had language competence not dissimilar to that of a 2-year-old human child. Similar methods have been used successfully with other chimpanzees, with a female gorilla called Koko (Patterson, 1978), and with an orang-utan, Princess (Shapiro, 1982).

Other methods have also been used. Premack (1971) taught a female chimpanzee, Sarah, to communicate using plastic shapes, and Savage-Rumbaugh and Rumbaugh (1978) used a computer keyboard to similar effect, teaching Lana (another female chimpanzee) to communicate with the experimenter in verb–object phrases.

Criticisms have been made of these studies, for example that only rote-learning is taking place, or that the experimenter, as with 'Clever Hans' (see chapter 1), is giving unintentional cues to the animal as to the right response. Terrace et al. (1979), working with a chimpanzee called Nim, strongly criticized some of the Gardners' more ambitious claims, and the selective way in which they reported their data. The Gardners have defended their position, pointing out that their claims and methods of data reporting are no worse, and often better, than the methods used by those studying child language (van Cantfort and Rimpau, 1982; Drumm et al., 1986).

Human language is much more flexible than any non-human communication system, but it too has a biological underpinning; Steven Pinker's book *The Language Instinct* (1994) strongly expresses this viewpoint. We discuss this perspective, and human language development generally, in chapter 10.

◀Instinct, Maturation and Learning▶▶▶

'Instinctive' behaviour: early studies

The study of species-typical or 'instinctive' behaviour was first put on a scientific footing by Konrad Lorenz and Niko Tinbergen in the 1940s and 1950s. For this work they shared the Nobel Prize for Physiology or Medicine in 1973 (together with Karl Von Frisch for his work on dance language in honey bees). In his book *The Study of Instinct*, Tinbergen (1951) put forward a set of influential ideas about the organization of behaviour. He postulated that many sequences of behaviour were largely uninfluenced by environmental variation. He called such sequences 'fixed action patterns' or FAPs. The FAP was set off by a particular stimulus called a 'sign stimulus'. The sign stimulus was detected by an 'innate releasing mechanism' or IRM, which then activated the FAP.

An example is illustrated in figure 2.8, which shows young blackbirds in a nest. When the mother arrives, the hatchlings stretch their necks and gape for food. This is a fixed action pattern. The sign stimulus which releases

Figure 2.8 Young blackbirds gaping at a model 'parent'.

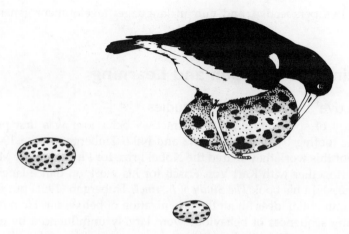

Figure 2.9   An oyster catcher reacting to a giant egg in preference to a normal egg (foreground) and a herring gull egg (left) (from Tinbergen, 1951).

this does not need to be an actual blackbird; it is simpler. Any close moving object which is larger than 3 cm in diameter and above the level of the nestlings will do.

Sometimes an artificial or unusual stimulus can release a fixed action pattern even more strongly or effectively than the natural stimulus. This is called a 'supernormal stimulus'. Figure 2.9 shows an example where an oyster catcher has chosen to try to incubate an oversized egg. The FAP is incubation, and the oversized egg is a supernormal stimulus. Another example is the FAP of feeding by parent birds in response to the gape of the hatchlings. A young cuckoo in the nest will give a large, bright orange gape which often provides a supernormal stimulus and means that the young cuckoo gets most of the food brought to the nest.

In the foregoing discussion we have looked at birds, but many of the examples from Tinbergen's and Lorenz's work were from fishes, amphibia and insects. 'Instinctive' behaviour, or as we might now prefer to say, 'species-typical' behaviour of a strongly canalized or rigid nature, is in fact most characteristic of these simpler species. So far as birds are concerned, and mammals especially, some of the early ideas now seem too simple. For example, Lorenz supposed that specific energy built up for each FAP, so that eventually it would find an outlet even without being released by a sign stimulus; or, he conjectured, the energy would be 'displaced' into another activity. In his book *On Aggression* (1966) he applied such ideas to mammalian and even human behaviour, but no clear evidence for a 'buildup' of aggressive energy has been found, and these ideas are not now given much credence.

Imprinting and the concept of sensitive periods

One of Lorenz's ideas, which has remained influential, is that of 'imprinting'. We saw earlier how the young in precocial species (such as ducks,

Plate 2.3 Young ducklings 'imprinted' on Konrad Lorenz follow him wherever he goes (from Atkinson, Atkinson and Hilgard, 1981).

hens, deer) may learn to follow their mother around very soon after birth. But how do they learn whom to follow? Lorenz discovered that while the following mechanism is highly canalized ('instinctive'), there is some flexibility in learning what (or whom) is to be followed. Generally, the young bird or mammal learns the characteristics of a conspicuous moving object nearby during a period soon after birth or hatching; it then follows this object around. It is this process of learning which object to follow that is known as imprinting. Usually imprinting occurs to the mother, since she is the main figure the offspring encounters during the critical, or sensitive, period after birth. But imprinting to other objects can occur. Lorenz imprinted some ducklings on himself, so that they then followed him everywhere (plate 2.3). This is easy to do with sheep as well (as in the nursery song, where 'everywhere that Mary went, the lamb was sure to go').

Lorenz introduced the term 'critical period' to describe the restricted period of time in which he believed imprinting took place. In ducklings this period is from about 9 hours to 17 hours after hatching (see figure 2.10). Lorenz also believed that imprinting was irreversible after this period. Subsequent research has suggested that the learning which takes place in imprinting is not quite as rigid as this, but that nevertheless it is the case that such learning occurs most readily within a restricted period. Usually researchers now refer to this as a 'sensitive period'. We have seen another example of a sensitive period already, in the instance of chaffinch song. Another example might be the development of kin recognition in littermates.

Imprinting in which the young learn the characteristics of the parent is known as 'filial imprinting'. It is important in precocial species in order to ensure that the young follow the correct animal (unless an experimenter such as Lorenz intervenes!). Lorenz also believed that at the same time the young learned the characteristics of their species, so that they would ultimately choose a member of their own species to mate with. This is called 'sexual imprinting' and the evidence for it is less well established. However, Bateson (1982) has shown that early experience is important for mating preference in Japanese quail. Bateson found that Japanese quail prefer as mating partners other quail that differ in appearance slightly, but not a lot, from quail they were reared with. If quail are reared normally with siblings, then as adults they prefer to mate with cousins, rather than with either siblings or unrelated birds. However, such choices can be altered if they are reared with non-sibling quail of different appearance. This species imprinting seems normally to involve learning the appearance of kin, and then later selecting as a mate an individual who would be related, but not too closely, thus achieving a balance between the costs of inbreeding and outbreeding.

Learning processes

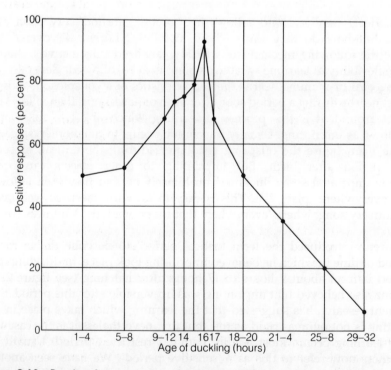

Figure 2.10   Results of an experiment showing that ducklings follow a model more readily 9–17 hours after hatching than at other times.

Imprinting is often presented as a special form of learning, highly constrained in what is learned and when it is learned. Many forms of learning are more flexible, especially in mammals, though the idea that there are some constraints on learning (some degree of canalization in development, see figure 2.7) seems to apply widely (Hinde and Stevenson-Hinde, 1973). Learning may occur through observation and imitation of others, for example in much bird song acquisition and in the learning of food preferences and tool use in chimpanzees (box 2.2). Some learning occurs through 'trial-and-error'. The degree to which the individual is rewarded or 'reinforced' in its behaviour is also important in learning. For example, rats will learn not to eat food that produces nausea, even if the nausea occurs an hour later (Garcia et al., 1966). In the more advanced mammals, especially the monkeys and apes, it seems as though we are encountering the beginnings of mental activity ('thinking') as we are familiar with it. This involves a kind of internal, symbolic representation of the world in the brain. Thinking consists of the internal manipulation of these symbols.

Some examples of behaviour seen in monkeys certainly suggest this kind of thinking. In species such as macaques and baboons, individuals will sometimes form cliques against a rival (for example, Packer's observations on p. 58); or will give different vocalizations to animals of different social status or relatedness (Seyfarth and Cheney, 1984). It appears as though monkeys are thinking in quite complex ways about their social relationships. This goes along with a relatively larger cerebral cortex in these species. With this sort of brain, behaviour becomes much more flexible, and learning during development much more important.

Thinking in primates

Researchers who have studied primates (monkeys and apes) have often been impressed by their thinking abilities; and this is especially true of the great apes the chimpanzee, the gorilla, and the orang-utan. Studies have been made both in the wild, and in laboratories; an example of a naturalistic study of chimpanzees is provided in box 2.2. Let's look at some examples of advanced intelligence in the great apes:

Tool use and making   Tool use has been observed in a number of species, but tool-making – deliberately altering a natural object to a specific end – was long thought to be uniquely characteristic of humans. However, it has been observed in chimpanzees in natural conditions (see p. 64) and in other great apes in experimental situations. Related to this is an ability to use objects in insightful ways – for example stacking boxes on top of each other to reach an out-of-reach clump of bananas; or using poles as ladders to get over fences.

Pretence   There are some observations of chimpanzees using objects in 'pretend' ways (for a discussion of pretend play in children see chapter 6). A classic example is of a chimpanzee called Viki, home-reared by two psychologists. Viki was observed at times to be acting as if she had an imaginary pull-toy:

Very slowly and deliberately she was marching around the toilet, trailing the fingertips of one hand on the floor. Now and then she paused,
glanced back at the hand, and then resumed her progress . . . she interrupted the sport one day to make a series of tugging motions . . . She
moved her hands over and around the plumbing knob in a very mys-
terious fashion; then placing both fists one above the other in line with
the knob, she strained backwards as in tug of war. Eventually there was
a little jerk and off she went again, trailing what to my mind could only
be an imaginary pulltoy. (Hayes, 1952)

Self-recognition   Chimpanzees and orang-utans can recognize themselves
in a mirror. This has been shown by so-called 'mirror image stimulation' or
MIS studies (Gallup, 1982). An animal is first accustomed to a mirror. Then,
while anaesthetized, it is marked conspicuously (for example with red dye)
on an ear, nose or eyebrow in a way which it cannot see directly. Its reaction
on seeing its mirror reflection is noted. Monkeys will reach for the mirror
image as if it was another animal. However (after a few days of prior mirror
exposure), a chimpanzee or orang-utan will reach for its own body part,
strongly suggesting it recognizes itself in the image. Surprisingly, gorillas
have not yet been found to have this ability.

Learnt symbolic communication   All three species of great ape have been
trained to communicate using non-verbal signals (see p. 42); this is at least a
rudimentary kind of learnt language. These instances are based on laboratory
studies, but there is an example of learnt communication in natural surroundings too. Nishida (1980) has described a 'leaf-clipping display' amongst wild
chimpanzees in Tanzania. A chimpanzee picks several stiff leaves and repeat-
edly pulls them from side to side between its teeth; this makes a distinctive
and conspicuous ripping sound. It is used as possessive behaviour or court-
ship display by a male to a female, or a female in oestrus to a male. This
display has not been seen to be used in this way in other chimpanzee
populations, and may be a social custom of this particular group.

Deception   Deception is involved when an individual sends a signal to
another individual, who then acts appropriately towards the signal according to its obvious meaning, which is, however, untrue. Deception is well-
known in many animal species, but is particularly complex in primates.
    As an example, consider an observation made on chimpanzees by Plooij
(in Byrne and Whiten, 1987).

An adult male (A) was about to eat some bananas that only he knew
about, when a second male (T) came into view at the edge of the
feeding area. The first quickly walked several metres away from the
food, sat down and looked around as though nothing had happened
(see figure 2.11a).

Here A is deceiving T by giving signals that 'there is nothing of interest
around here' (untrue!). If A looked at the bananas, then T (being more
dominant) would take them instead.

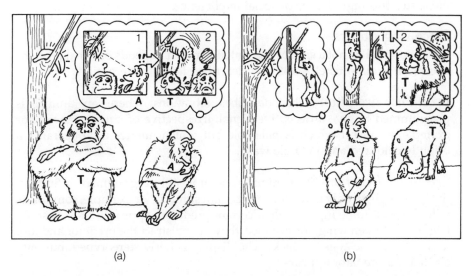

Figure 2.11   Tactical deception in chimpanzees (after Byrne and Whiten, 1987).

However, the observation continues:

The newcomer (T) left the feeding area (see figure 2.11b) but as soon as he was out of sight he hid behind a tree and peered at the male who remained (A). As soon as A approached the food and took it, T returned, displaced the other and ate the bananas.

This is actually counter-deception by the second chimpanzee, who seems to have realized that the first was hiding something!

The evolution of high intelligence

Why has such high intelligence evolved in the primates and especially the great apes? There is a cost to high intelligence – large brains use up more energy for maintenance, and a longer developmental period entails greater risks. So there must be benefits to counterbalance these.

The traditional view has been that high intelligence helps animals cope with the physical environment. Parker and Gibson (1979) suggested that high intelligence evolved as a means of better obtaining food. For example, tool use, tool making and imitative learning are all involved in food gathering in chimpanzees (see box 2.2).

An alternative argument is that high intelligence has been selected for because of its advantages in social interaction (Byrne and Whiten, 1988). As we have seen, primates are clever in social contexts – recognizing and deceiving others, forming alliances, achieving dominant status. Being socially clever could have considerable advantages for an animal's reproductive success. Byrne and Whiten (1988) call this 'Machiavellian intelligence', or tactical deception. The example of the two chimpanzees described above illustrates this high degree of social intelligence.

Deceiving others

Deception itself is not a sign of high intelligence; it depends on what level the deception is at. Mitchell (1986) has described levels of deception.

Level-one deception This describes situations where an animal is programmed to give a deceptive signal, irrespective of circumstances. For example, an insect which is palatable but which mimics in appearance a brightly coloured and inedible wasp.

Level-two deception The animal's signal is still programmed or 'instinctive', but is given only in response to certain stimuli. For example, some birds will 'pretend' to be injured when certain predators approach their nest. By feigning a broken wing, for instance, they may distract the predator and lure it away from the eggs or chicks. The display is fairly stereotyped, but only elicited if a predator appears.

Level-three deception Here the animal's signal can be modified by learning. An example might be a dog which by limping (even though not injured) gets more petting and attention; this differs from the bird's feigned injury in that it has been learnt in ontogeny as a successful strategy. However, it may be no more than stimulus-response learning of the type 'lifting my paw in a certain way results in my being petted'. Many cases of tactical deception (Whiten and Byrne, 1988) are likely to be of this kind.

Level-four deception Here the animal deliberately corrects or changes its signals so as to encourage the receiver to act in certain ways. It is as if the animal doing the deceiving knows, and calculates, the effects on the recipient. The chimpanzee example described in the last section would come at this level. Here it appears there is an understanding of deceptive intent, and a flexibility of response, which Whiten and Byrne (1988) highlight in their analysis of tactical deception as evidence that the animal understands the tactic it uses.

The evolution of 'mindreading' and of metarepresentations

At these higher levels of intelligence and intentional action, it would seem as though an animal has some idea of what is going on in another animal's mind – it is, as it were, 'mindreading'. Other researchers talk of a 'theory of mind' – implying that an individual can hypothesize about what is going on in another's mind (it might be thinking 'that animal is hungry' or 'that animal is hiding food', for example). Level-four tactical deception is a good indicator of this. Somewhat similar skills can be seen developing in children (see chapter 5; Whiten, 1991). More generally, mindreading skills, and also the other aspects of high intelligence mentioned previously, can be taken as examples of 'second-order representation', or 'metarepresentation'. A first-order, representation is symbolizing something in your mind – for example an object such as a table, or a banana; or a state such as being hungry. In a second-order or metarepresentation, one or more first-order representations are themselves represented.

For example, in tool-making the first-order representation of the actual action is manipulated relative to the representation of the desired object; this process involves second-order representation. In pretence, the representation of the actual object co-exists with the representation of it as having pretend characteristics (Leslie, 1987). In self-recognition, the representation of the mirror image is related to the representation of one's own self, or body. In symbolic communication, symbols (non-verbal or verbal) stand for or represent other objects or actions. And in level-four deception, the intentionality of deceit implies that the sender can represent both the true and the falsely signalled state of affairs (somewhat analogous to pretence).

Some researchers argue that these abilities all represent a metarepresentational capacity which is found in the great apes, and which is also an important aspect of children's development (Whiten and Byrne, 1991). However, other researchers point out the distinctive differences which remain between the great apes and the human species. Povinelli and Eddy (1996) have reported a series of studies on chimpanzees, in which they examined what young chimpanzees (up to 7 years) know about seeing. They trained chimpanzees to gesture for food, and then gave them a choice of two persons to beg from; one could see them, one could not. Could the chimpanzee 'mindread', or at least understand that one person could see their gesture while another was unable to do so?

Plate 2.4 shows one condition in which they succeeded. If one person was facing the chimpanzee and the other had their back to the chimpanzee, the chimpanzee would beg from the person facing them. Not surprising, perhaps! But what was surprising was the failure of the chimpanzees in the other conditions. Here, both persons would face the chimpanzee, but one might be blindfolded; or have a bucket over his/her head. The chimpanzees begged to the blindfolded person, or the person with the bucket over their head, as much as to the other person. In another study, the chimpanzees could not discriminate between two persons with their backs to them, even when one person had his/her head turned round looking over their shoulder at the chimpanzee.

This seems to suggest a lack of mindreading abilities in chimpanzees and pushes us back to a more behaviourist interpretation of the anecdotal and naturalistic evidence cited earlier. There are caveats to the work by Povinelli and Eddy. Are the experiments ecologically valid, for example (Smith, 1996)? A chimpanzee persistently begging from someone who is not looking at them might seem stupid, but in the wild it could make sense – another chimpanzee is likely to respond to the grunts or at least see the outstretched hand; who is being stupid, a chimpanzee begging from a person with a bucket over their head, or the person with the bucket over their head who fails to respond to the begging grunts of the chimpanzee? This general issue about ecological validity has occurred also with work on children, see chapter 11.

(a)

(b)

Plate 2.4   (a) The stimulus configuration for bucket probe trials. (b) The stimulus configuration for back-versus-front probe trials.

There seems little doubt that chimpanzees are at least very clever behaviourists – very adept at learning links between stimulus situations and behaviour, and more so than monkeys, for example. But maybe they lack the kind of motivation to understand others' mental states that humans, and even human infants, seem to have. As Tomasello (1996) points out, 'in their natural habitats, chimpanzees do not spontaneously point for others to distal entities in their environments, either with or without finger extension. They also do not hold objects up to show them to others, or try to bring others to locations so that they can observe things there, or actively offer objects to other individuals by holding them out to them. Chimpanzees and other apes also do not engage in the intentional teaching of offspring' (p. 165).

What would happen if chimpanzee infants were raised in a human environment where they *did* receive intentional teaching? There are a number of studies now of such 'human-raised' or 'enculturated' apes – indeed Washoe was an early example. More recent studies have focused more on indices of mindreading and intentionality, such as imitating, and pointing. In a review, Call and Tomasello (1996) conclude that enculturated apes do show more human-like skills of social cognition; they are more likely to share deferred imitation of a human action, for example. But there remain differences, and so far it looks as though even human-raised apes lack the motivation for sharing experiences with other intentional beings, which human infants seem to develop in a canalized way; we shall look more at the related work on children in several chapters, especially chapters 3, 10 and 12.

◀An Evolutionary Perspective on Human Behaviour▶ ▶ ▶

As humans, we are primates – members of the same order of animals as the monkeys and apes. Our closest animal relatives are the great apes, the chimpanzee, gorilla and orang-utan. We know that early humans, or 'hominids', had become different from the early apes by 5 million years ago. In East Africa scientists such as Richard Leakey and Donald Johanson have unearthed fossil remains of hominids which are 3–4 million years old (Leakey and Lewin, 1977; Johanson and Edey, 1981). These very early hominids, called australopithecines, were smaller than us (about 4-foot tall) and had smaller brains (about 500–600 cubic centimetres), but had already walked erect and had moved from the ape habitat of forest to the hominid habitat of open grassland. Over the next few million years fossil remains document the increasing body size and especially brain size of the hominids and their increasing technological and cultural sophistication as evidenced by stone-tool manufacture and later by shelter construction, use of fire and cave art. By some 50,000 years ago early humans were physically much like us today: *Homo sapiens* had arrived. Changes over the past 50,000 years have been largely cultural, not biological, as people learned to domesticate animals, cultivate plants, build cities, pursue the systematic advance of knowledge and develop modern technology.

Does our primate ancestry tell us anything useful about ourselves now? This has been a very controversial issue. Some scientists studying animal behaviour have tried to make links to human behaviour. This is true of some of the ethologists, such as Konrad Lorenz and Irenaus Eibl-Eibesfeldt; and of some recent sociobiologists, such as E. O. Wilson at Harvard University in the USA. Let us look first at some of their suggestions, and then at some of the limitations of 'human ethology' or 'human sociobiology'.

Figure 2.12   The 'eyebrow flash': the right-hand photograph shows the raising of eyebrows during greeting in a Frenchman (after Eibl-Eibesfeldt, 1972).

Lorenz (1966) and Eibl-Eibesfeldt (1971) have made use of the concepts of fixed action pattern (FAP) and sign stimulus to explain some kinds of human behaviour. An example of a human FAP is claimed to be the facial expression involved in greeting – a smile, widening of the eyes and flash (rapid raising and lowering) of the eyebrows (figure 2.12). This has been found to be very similar in a wide variety of human societies. An example of a sign stimulus is claimed to be the 'cute' facial and bodily appearance of babies, which elicits caring and parental behaviour. In an experimental study Sternglanz et al. (1977) presented the stimuli shown in figure 2.13 to a number of young adults. They rated the one shown at (b) as being most attractive. It has quite large eyes and a moderately large forehead. Dolls and 'cute' animals in film cartoons have similar facial proportions (c).

◀Sociobiology: Why Do Animals Behave as They Do?▶▶

Most readers will probably have some idea of evolutionary theory, stemming from the work of Charles Darwin in the nineteenth century. A detailed knowledge of this theory is not necessary for our purposes, but a very brief summary will be useful for some understanding of recent developments in

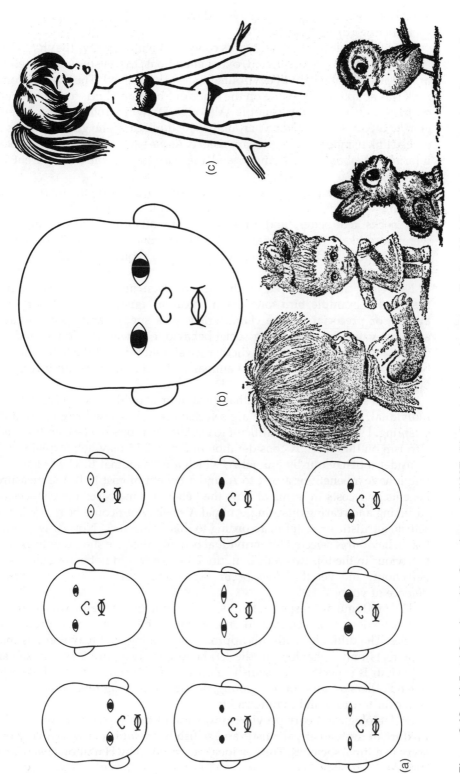

Figure 2.13 (a) Facial Stimuli used by Sternglanz et al. (1997); (b) the stimulus noted as most effective; (c) dolls and cartoon animals with similar facial proportions (from Eibl-Eibesfeldt, 1971).

what has been called 'sociobiology' and the way in which it explains animal social behaviour.

Darwin's evolutionary theory was concerned with the ways the characteristics of an animal were selected, over generations, to be especially suited to or 'adapted' for the kind of environment in which it lived. The giraffe's long neck was adapted for feeding on the kinds of leaves and buds found high up on trees and bushes, for example. Although Darwin wrote before modern genetic theory was developed around 1900, the idea of the gene provides a crucial link in modern evolutionary theory. As we saw earlier, the genes code information about development, and they are passed on from parent to offspring.

Giraffes, for example, have genes for long neck growth. In the past, as giraffes were evolving, those individuals which had genes for especially long necks fed better, and thus had more offspring, who themselves were more likely than average to have genes for long necks. Thus, genes for long necks, and actual long necks, came to typify the modern giraffe species.

Behaviour can be selected for during evolution, just as body characteristics can. For example, bird song, communication signals, whether young are altricial or precocial, all are characteristic of a species and seem to have adaptive value. In considering social behaviour, however, a long-standing controversy has existed about whether we should think of the behaviour as being adaptive for the individual animal, or for the social group it is in, or even for the entire species.

Darwin's approach implied that behaviour should be adaptive for the individual, as the genes which are selected are only passed from parent to offspring. However, it was difficult to explain examples of co-operation and altruism on this basis. A consideration of figure 2.14 may help explain this. Consider a behaviour by animal A, which affects animal B. The behaviour might have a benefit or a cost to A, and a benefit or cost to B. We measure benefits and costs in terms of how the behaviour increases the chances of surviving and rearing offspring. Animal A's behaviour could be mutualistic, selfish, altruistic or spiteful, according to this framework. Now, if we argue that behaviour is selected for individual benefits, then we should only expect behaviour in the top two cells in figure 2.14. We would not expect altruistic behaviour, and yet this does occur (e.g. communal suckling; communal defence of young).

The predominant response to this, until about 25 years ago, was to argue that behaviour was selected for the good of the whole social group, or species. The difficulty with this approach, appealing as it may seem, is that it predicts only behaviour in the left-hand cells of figure 2.14. No selfish behaviour is expected. Yet, selfish behaviour is also common (e.g. failure to defend others or nurse others' young; deceit in bird song repertoire; aggression over territory and mating rights).

Sociobiological theory provides a way out of this impasse. It predicts the mixture of mutualistic, altruistic and selfish behaviour that we actually observe in animal societies. The key idea, put forward by Hamilton (1964), and

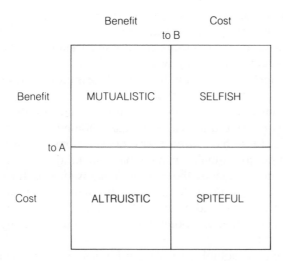

Benefit   Cost
to B

	Benefit to B	Cost to B
Benefit to A	MUTUALISTIC	SELFISH
Cost to A	ALTRUISTIC	SPITEFUL

Figure 2.14   Cost and benefit to two animals, A and B, of a social interaction between A and B.

a central idea in modern sociobiology, is that of 'kin selection'. This is the hypothesis that an animal will behave altruistically towards its kin, especially those closely related. This was always taken for granted for an individual's offspring, as it was only through offspring that genes were directly passed on. Hamilton's insight was that an animal would share a greater than average proportion of genes with relatives too, especially close relatives such as siblings and cousins. Helping relatives is another way in which particular genes get passed on to the next generation, admittedly only an indirect way compared with having offspring oneself.

Kin selection theory then predicts that helpful or altruistic behaviour may be directed towards relatives, provided that it is not too harmful to the animal giving the help, and provided that the other animal is closely enough related to make it worthwhile. Close relatives will be helped more. Much evidence supports this theory. Examples include communal suckling in lions and elephants, and communal defence; see also box 2.2.

Another prediction of kin selection theory is that males will only assist females and offspring if it is likely that they are the genetic father (or close relative). The likelihood that a male is the genetic father is referred to as *paternity certainty*. Paternity certainty will be higher in monogamous species, and it is indeed in such species that males help most in rearing the young (e.g. many nesting birds; a few mammals such as hunting dogs, marmosets). For implications of this for human behaviour, see pp. 29 and 101.

In an interesting extension of kin selection theory, Trivers (1974) postulated that we should expect to see *parent–offspring conflict*. This is because the genetic interests of parent and offspring are not identical. The mother is related to all her offspring equally, and would be selected (other things being equal) to provide each with the same amount of parental investment or help. However, an individual offspring would be selected to favour itself over its siblings, with whom it shares only half its genes; thus, according to Trivers, it should seek more than its fair share of parental investment. This should lead to conflict with the mother, over the amount and duration of parental investment, and also to conflict with siblings, or sibling rivalry. Since Trivers wrote his article, there have been many observations of parent–offspring and sibling conflict in animals. In mammals, suckling is a very important form of parental investment by the mother. In many species, the infant seems to try to continue suckling for longer than the mother wishes; the mother may reject the attempts of older infants to suckle, quite forcefully. Siblings may also compete with each other for access to the mother, in feeding situations.

There is more to sociobiology than just kin selection, however. Another way of explaining altruistic behaviour is through what is called 'reciprocal altruism' (Trivers, 1971). The hypothesis is that one individual will help another, at some smaller cost to itself, if it can expect similar help back from the other animal in the future. This is the old adage 'if you scratch my back, I'll scratch yours'. There is some evidence of reciprocal altruism, the most convincing being in monkeys and apes where it is clear that individuals do recognize each other and could thus stop helping individuals who failed to reciprocate ('cheats'). In a study of baboons, Packer (1977) found that pairs of unrelated males would help each other in challenging a dominant male. Individuals that gave such help to a particular male often received help back from the same male. As the males were unrelated, kin selection could not explain this.

Sociobiology has become the prevailing theoretical paradigm for explaining why animals behave towards others in the way they do, in terms of the evolutionary advantages of such behaviour. (A related theoretical area is that of 'behavioural ecology', which puts more emphasis on the animal in the non-social environment, for example on how animals should most efficiently forage for food.) These theories have encountered problems and have severe critics. Nevertheless, they have changed the study of animal social behaviour away from being primarily an observational and descriptive science. Sociobiology makes specific predictions, and field observations are now guided towards the testing of these.

Sociobiologists such as E. O. Wilson (1978) are less interested in instinctive mechanisms of behaviour; rather, they wonder whether human behaviour, like animal behaviour, seems to maximize the survival and reproductive success of individuals. For example, do the predictions of kin selection apply to humans? It does seem to be the case that people are most generous or altruistic to close kin, even when it is not socially sanctioned. In agricultural and tribal societies (i.e. people not yet living in large cities) kinship is a very important organizing framework, affecting expectations about whom you shall marry as well as expectations for help and alliance in warfare.

There are other parallels to be drawn. For example, almost all human societies are either monogamous or polygynous (though a few tribes are polyandrous, notably in Sri Lanka and Tibet). Sociobiology can explain this, especially when it is also noted that monogamous societies tend to be those where fathers can help directly in child-rearing, whereas in polygynous societies men compete for status, for example by acquiring wealth or cattle, and do little to help their wives directly. As another example, what seem to be characteristic sex differences in men and women, for example in abilities, in aggression and in attitudes to sexual behaviour, have been given a sociobiological explanation (Wilson, 1978; Symons, 1979; Buss and Schmitt, 1993). There has been strong reaction against these views. Some scientists believe that even to attempt such explanations is misplaced, because of the dangers of, for example, making sex differences seem natural and inevitable. These scientists believe that the flexibility of human learning is so great that nothing useful is learnt from evolutionary theorizing (e.g. Sahlins, 1977; Rose et al., 1984). At times the debate has become more personal than scientific.

◀Human Behaviour Is Modifiable▶▶▶

A real problem for such extrapolations from sociobiology is that human behaviour seems to be of an order of magnitude more flexible even than that of other advanced mammals. There are enormous cultural variations in the behaviour of people in different societies: for example in the language spoken, technology used, moral or religious beliefs held, and methods of child-rearing used. These are learned variations. A Chinese baby brought up in China learns Chinese, and Chinese manners; brought up in the USA, it learns American English and American manners. In addition to this flexibility of learning, humans can cumulatively pass on and build up knowledge and beliefs through cultural traditions (e.g. the development of the idea of democracy; the development of electronic and computer technology). While there are some examples of traditions among animals (e.g. dialects in bird song; patterns of tool use in chimpanzees), no animal species has been found cumulatively to build up traditions of technology or behaviour in this way.

If human behaviour is so flexible, is there any scope for theorizing based on our evolutionary past? There may be, but perhaps only in limited ways. Human cultural variation is enormous, but there are still some apparent cultural universals. Examples are:

The pattern of sensori-motor development in the first 12–18 months of
    life.
The attachment relationship which develops between infant and caregiver.
Forms of play in children, especially rough-and-tumble play.
The structure of human language, and the way it is acquired.
Human non-verbal signals and emotional expressions.

Some sex differences in behaviour, and patterns of marriage.
Situations in which aggressive behaviour is elicited.

Of course, these could be similar simply for cultural reasons – societies just happen to have passed on the same learned tradition. However, this does seem implausible in some cases. There is little that parental treatment can do to alter the pattern of sensori-motor development in infancy; and facial expressions of emotion, such as smiling and crying, appear in blind children who cannot see such expressions in other humans.

It would certainly be misleading to call these types of behaviour 'instinctive'. To do so leads to a quagmire of misunderstanding whereby it is inferred that some behaviours are inevitable and unalterable. It may, however, be justified to think of some human behaviour development as reasonably canalized. Thus, the development of human language, from babbling to one-word utterances to syntax, may be fairly strongly canalized (see chapter 10), whereas the actual language learned is weakly canalized, if at all. Possibly some sex differences are somewhat canalized, such that they will develop unless positive steps are taken to prevent them, whereas other sex differences may not be canalized at all and could easily be changed. Whether substantiated or not, this at least is a language of reasoned debate. The metaphor of canalization, or of the modifiability of behaviour, enables us to get away from the instinctive/learned dichotomy. We can consider the possibility of there being some limited links to our evolutionary past, without having to defend the innateness, desirability or complete inevitability of certain human characteristics.

◀Further Reading▶ ▶ ▶

The development of the fetus, and of the young infant, are covered in greater detail in J. F. Rosenblith 1992: *In the Beginning: Development from Conception to Age Two*, Newbury Park and London: Sage. The birth process and comparisons of humans with other species are discussed by W. R. Trevathan in *Human Birth: an Evolutionary Perspective*, New York: Aldine de Gruyter, 1987. For a readable account of behaviour genetics with special relevance to human behaviour, see R. Plomin, J. C. DeFries, G. E. McClearn and M. Rutter 1997 (3rd edn): *Behavioral Genetics: a Primer*, New York: W. H. Freeman.

The work on chimpanzees described in box 2.2 can also be found in J. van Lawick-Goodall 1971: *In the Shadow of Man*, Glasgow: Collins. A general account of how useful it is to apply animal models to human development is provided by J. Archer 1992: *Ethology and Human Development*, Hemel Hempstead: Harvester Wheatsheaf. R. Byrne 1995: *The Thinking Ape: Evolutionary Origins of Intelligence*, Oxford: Oxford University Press, covers many aspects of ape cognition and has two specific chapters on theory of mind research with non-human primates; another good chapter on this topic is in P. Mitchell 1997: *Introduction to Theory of Mind*, London: Arnold.

◄Discussion Points►►►

1   To what extent is the birth process affected by cultural practices?
2   How relevant is behaviour genetics for understanding human behaviour?
3   Is the distinction between instinctive and learned behaviour a useful one?
4   Can studies of animals tell us anything useful about human behaviour?
5   Can chimpanzees engage in mindreading?

Box 2.1
Newborn and fetal response to the human voice

Research in the 1980s (see chapters 3 and 9) had shown that newborn infants could distinguish between the voice of their own mother, and that of an unfamiliar female. DeCasper and Fifer (1980) established this for infants only 1 to 3 days old; and Querleu, Lefebvre, Renard, Titran, Morillion and Crepin (1984) found a similar result for infants only 2 hours after birth, largely ruling out the possibility of rapid learning of the mother's voice postnatally. Studies had also found that the fetus could respond to auditory stimuli, with head and body movements. For example, Shahidullah and Hepper (1993a) demonstrated this using an ultrasound scanner, which produces a visual picture of the fetus, in this case showing the head, upper body and arms (see box plate 2.1.1). A headphone for the auditory signals was placed on the mother's abdomen. As early as 20 weeks of gestational age the fetus would show a slow, diffuse bodily response to auditory stimuli presented in this way; and by 25 weeks gestational age, an immediate startle-type response was seen.

It thus seemed likely that learning of the mother's voice occurred *in utero*; however, the fetus would not hear the mother's voice in the same way as the newborn infant, since the sound would be transmitted internally, through the body, as well as externally. Interestingly, a study by Fifer and Moon (1989) had found that 2-day-old newborns preferred the sound of their mother's voice filtered to sound as it would have done in the womb, to the mother's natural voice!

The aim of this series of three studies was to examine further the origins of learning the mother's voice, in the fetus. Two of the three studies were carried out with fetuses in the mother's womb, and using the ultrasound equip-

ment described earlier. In each of the two studies, ten fetuses of gestational age 36 weeks participated. All of the fetuses were subsequently born at 39–40 weeks, without complications, and with healthy Apgar scores (over 8, at 1 and 5 minutes; see table 2.1).

In one of these, two conditions were compared: the mother speaking normally, and a tape recording of the mother's voice (played through the speaker on the mother's abdomen). This was the independent variable; each fetus experienced both conditions, with order being counterbalanced. The dependent variable was the mean number of movements elicited in the fetus (recorded on video). This averaged 5.2 for the mother speaking normally, and 6.7 for the tape of the mother's voice, the difference being just significant at $p < .05$ on a matched pairs t test. The fetuses responded more to the tape of the mother's voice, which the researchers argued would be a more novel stimulus, lacking some components of the mother's voice which would come internally through the body to the fetus when the mother spoke normally. The researchers reported no obvious differences in mother's heartrate or general physical activity between the two conditions, which if present would confound the results.

In the second study of ten fetuses, two tapes were presented to each; of the mother's voice speaking normally, and of a strange female (in fact, another fetus's mother) speaking normally. Again, order was counterbalanced. The mean number of movements elicited in the fetus was 7.2 for the mother's voice, and 6.0 for the strange female's voice. This difference did not approach statistical significance on a matched pairs t test. The researchers concluded that the fetus could

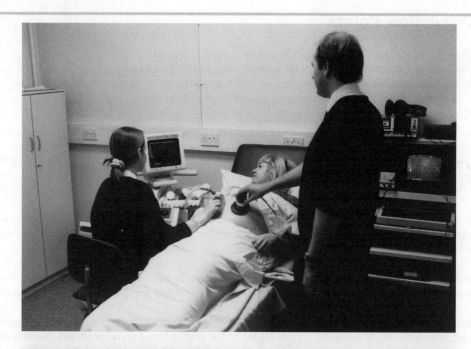

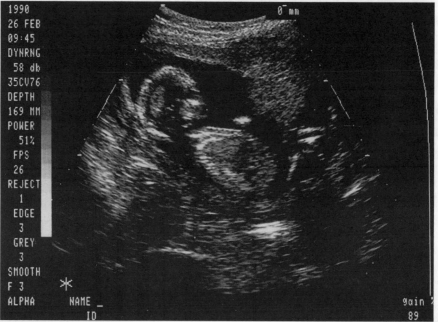

1990
26 FEB
09:45
DYNRNG
 58 db
35CV76
DEPTH
169 MM
POWER
 51%
FPS
 26
REJECT
 1
EDGE
 3
GREY
 3
SMOOTH
F 3
ALPHA   NAME _
             ID
0¯ mm

gain
89

Box Plate 2.1.1   An ultrasound scanner on the mother (above) produces an image of the fetus.

not distinguish the mother's voice from a strange female's voice when both were heard externally.

In a third study, the same researchers worked with 35 newborn infants aged 2 to 4 days. They compared the movement responses of the newborns to tape recordings of the mother's voice, and that of a strange female. For half the infants, the voices were normal; for the other half, the voices were in 'motherese' (see chapter 10). An analysis of variance found a significant interaction ($p < .01$); basically, the mother's normal voice elicited fewer movements than did the mother's motherese voice, or either version of the strange female's voice.

In looking at these studies, it seems as though the fetus and newborn infant are going through stages in familiarizing themselves with the auditory stimulus they are most often encountering, the mother's voice. First, the fetus is familiar with the mother's voice as experienced in utero; all other voices, even a tape of the mother's voice, appear different. A few hours and days after birth, newborns still prefer the mother's voice as they heard it in the womb (Fifer and Moon, 1989), but they can now discriminate the mother's normal voice from that of other females. However, the mother's 'motherese' voice still seems as strange as an adult female's voice, and recognition of this will come later.

These experiments are ingenious, and carried out in difficult circumstances. Careful precautions were followed in having standard testing conditions and presentation of stimuli. It would be reassuring to have the experiments with the fetuses replicated, since the sample sizes were small and a crucial finding in the first study only just reached statistical significance. Also, no direct statistical comparison was made for fetal response to the mother's actual speech and a tape of a strange female, even though the mean movement scores were closer than for the comparison with the tape of the mother's voice. Finally, it would be important that the videotapes of fetal movements were scored blind to condition, to avoid experimenter effects (see chapter 1).

As Karmiloff-Smith (1995) puts it, 'prior to any ex utero experience, newborns show that they have already extracted information about some of the invariant, abstract features of mother's voice during their period in the womb'. Research such as this forms part of a variety of studies indicating that human development is strongly canalized in the early stages, and that the newborn infant is far from being the 'blank slate' postulated by some earlier theorists.

Based on material in Hepper, P. G., Scott, D. and Shahidullah, S. 1993: Journal of Reproductive and Infant Psychology 11(3), 147–53.

Box 2.2
The behaviour of free-living chimpanzees in the Gombe Stream Reserve

This study concerns the behaviour of chimpanzees in their natural habitat. Jane Goodall spent 5 years observing chimpanzees in the Gombe Stream area of Tanzania, in Africa. She spent much time approaching and following groups of chimpanzees, and letting them get used to her presence. She then made systematic observations and notes about what she observed. She established a base camp and at later stages in the project put out bananas at a feeding area near the camp to attract the chimpanzees and make observations easier.

She found that chimpanzees moved around singly or in small groups, looking for food such as fruits and leaves within a large home-range area. Group composition varied. Infants (0–3 years) were carried by their mothers or followed them closely, and juveniles (3–7 years) usually travelled with their mothers as well. Subadults (8–12 years) and adults (12 up to around 40 years), however, seemed to join up or disperse quite freely. Chimpanzees live in forested areas and move around both on the ground and in trees. At night, they sleep in nests made from tree branches.

The newborn infant is dependent on its mother

for food, transport and protection, but after 6 months or so begins to crawl around on its own while staying in the mother's vicinity. Soon it engages in play, with both mother, siblings and peers – tickling, wrestling and chasing play. Infants and juveniles watch and imitate when they see mother obtaining food, or making tree nests, and this is hypothesized to be important for their own acquisition of these skills. When the juvenile becomes a subadult, the frequency of play decreases and mutual grooming increases (box plate 2.2.1). Later observations have established that subadult females often leave their home range and may join a more distant group. Males, however, usually stay in the home range they were born in. Although older males do not stay with the mother all the time, they may still associate with her frequently. An older sibling may 'adopt' and care for an infant sibling if the mother dies.

There is a dominance hierarchy amongst the mature chimpanzees within a local group. Though most interactions are peaceful and friendly, long-term observations have shown how, at certain times, the dominance order is challenged and considerable conflict may ensue. Goodall and her co-workers documented how a 20-year-old chimpanzee called Figan came to dominate a 22-year-old, Evered, who was his main rival for being the most dominant, or alpha, male. Figan sought out fights with Evered when circumstances favoured him – especially when he was with his brother, Faben. Faben, a 25-year-old, had a paralysed right arm; he thus was not a serious contender for alpha

male himself, but could help his brother. This example illustrates both the importance of dominance for individuals and the way kinship (in this case, a sibling tie) can persist into adulthood. Dominance conflicts are usually between males, and the main benefit of being the alpha male is probably increased opportunity to mate with females.

Goodall's observations also revealed several instances of tool use in chimpanzees, and the first records of actual tool-making in a non-human species. Examples of tool use are: leaves for wiping the body; rocks to crack nuts; sticks to prise open the banana boxes; sticks and stones for throwing at baboons or other animals. Two examples of tool-making were documented; each involves some deliberate change in a tool to make it more suitable for its purpose. In one the chimpanzee wishes to drink water out of a crack or hollow. It gets some leaves, chews them in its mouth to make a spongy wad, then uses this to soak up the water and puts it back in its mouth again. In the other, the chimpanzee wishes to eat termites. This is difficult because they are in a termite nest, but it obtains them by poking slender branches or twigs down the entrance holes to the nest, pulling out the twigs with termites attached and licking them off (box plate 2.2.2). Chimpanzees prepare twigs for this by picking suitable small branches and breaking off the accessory stems, which can be inserted readily (this is watched with fascination by younger chimpanzees, who then imitate the process).

Although primarily vegetarian, chimpanzees will eat insects (such as termites), birds' eggs, and will

Box Plate 2.2.1   Chimpanzees grooming.

Box Plate 2.2.2   A chimpanzee pokes a twig into a termite nest.

even hunt and kill small mammals such as young bushpigs or baby baboons. Several chimpanzees may co-operate in such a hunt. The kill is divided up rapidly amongst them, and other chimpanzees may then come up and form 'sharing clusters' around them, requesting a portion of the food.

Goodall's observations provided the first really substantial data on the natural behaviour of chimpanzees. Later research broadly confirmed her findings, with some minor changes. Territorial behaviour between local groups of chimpanzees has now been established, with some violent conflicts between groups and occasional instances of cannibalism. Further instances of tool use and tool-making have been found, with indications of 'cultural' differences amongst chimpanzees living in different parts of Africa.

This study did not have any prior hypothesis. It is thus not an experiment and there are no dependent or independent variables. It is an observational study, designed to obtain basic data. Studies of a species based on observation in its natural habitat are often called 'ethological studies', and this is an example. Such studies can discover things not expected, such as chimpanzee tool-making. However, they cannot establish cause and effect. The hypothesis that infants watching adults leads to learning, for example, would benefit from some more experimental confirmation. Ethological observation is also difficult and time-consuming – this is why Goodall started putting out bananas, even at the risk of changing the animals' behaviour.

Based on material in J. Van Lawick-Goodall 1968: *Animal Behaviour Monographs* 1(8), 161–311.

Part Two

The Social World of the Child

3   Parents and Families

The newborn baby has a lot to find out about the social world. If you pick her up, she will respond no differently to you than to anyone else. Yet some 9 months later the infant will discriminate familiar and unfamiliar persons, and will probably have developed one or more selective attachments. If you pick her up now she may well look anxious or cry; whereas if her mother or father picks her up, she will be reassured and pacified.

In this chapter we look first at the development of social interactions and attachment relationships between infants, parents, and other family members. The importance of such attachments for later development is considered, with its implications for policy issues such as institutional rearing, day care and childminding for young children. Finally we examine some of the factors affecting successful and less successful parenting.

◀Early Social Behaviour and Social Interactions▶▶

The human infant is fairly helpless (or altricial) at birth. He or she depends on parents, or caregivers, for food, warmth, shelter and protection. For these reasons alone it is important for human infants, as for any other young mammal, that an attachment develops between the infant and the mother (or father, or other caregiver; we will use the term caregiver generically). In addition, human infants acquire something from this relationship that is largely absent in other mammals, the beginnings of symbolic communication and cultural meaning. The particular relevance of early caregiver–infant interaction for language development is considered in chapter 10. Although fairly helpless, the human infant does have some reflexive (instinctive or highly canalized) abilities which assist the development of social interactions with caregivers. These are: (1) behaviours which operate primarily in social situations; (2) behaviours to which social responses are given; (3) an enjoyment of contingent responding by others; (4) an ability to learn, including discriminating social stimuli and attempting to imitate certain observed behaviours. Let us consider these in turn.

1   Behaviours that operate primarily in social situations. The types of auditory and visual stimulation which adults provide are especially attractive to infants at or soon after birth (see also chapter 9). For example, infants orientate to (i.e. turn their head towards) patterned sounds rather than monotones, and especially to patterned sounds within the frequency range of human speech. They are interested in visual stimuli which move around, and which have a lot of contour information. The human face provides moving stimulation with much contour information, often at just the right distance for the infant to fixate easily. Infant reflexes, such as grasping, and rooting and sucking at the breast, are also used primarily with caregivers. None of these reflexive behaviours is directed only to adults, but all are well designed to operate with adults and to give the infant an initial orientation to social situations.

2   Behaviours to which social responses are given. Newborn babies will both smile and cry. In both cases this behaviour has no social meaning to the baby at first. She smiles apparently randomly from time to time, and cries if hungry or uncomfortable. However, caregivers respond to these signals as if they were social. They tend to smile and talk back if the infant smiles; and to pick up an infant and talk to her if she is crying (plate 3.1: one study found that picking up an infant reduced crying on 88 per cent of occasions, which is very rewarding for the adult). Gradually the infant will learn the social consequences of smiling, and crying, because of the social meaning and social responses which caregivers give to them. It is similar with babbling, which begins around 2 months of age.

3   An enjoyment of contingent responding by others. From quite early on it seems as though infants like to get 'contingent' stimulation – that is, stimulation which appropriately follows quickly on some action of their own; as it were, a 'reply' to their own action. An experiment which demonstrated this very neatly is described in box 3.1: usually caregivers provide contingent responding in a rapid and appropriate fashion when they react to the infant's smiling, crying, cooing or babbling, or a bit later on engage in games such as peek-a-boo. Many studies of mother–infant interaction in the home have found that maternal 'sensitivity' (which is largely synonymous with contingent responsiveness) is correlated with good social development and attachment in the infant. Enjoyment of contingent responsiveness can develop into turn-taking and into proper interactions such as conversations, or games. A game such as peek-a-boo is initially structured solely by the adult, who takes advantage of the infant's pleasure at the surprise generated by the sudden appearance and disappearance of the adult's face, or a teddy-bear; it becomes a more genuine turn-taking sequence as the infant comes to expect the next repetition of the game and thus

take a more active part itself in the exchange (see Bruner and Sherwood, 1976).

4   An ability to learn. The development of perceptual abilities in infancy is discussed in detail in chapter 9. We saw in chapter 2 (box 2.1) how some aspects of the mother's voice are learnt even before birth; infants learn to discriminate the sound of the mother's voice from that of a stranger within a few days of birth (p. 285), and learn to prefer pictures of faces to similar but scrambled up pictures by 2 months of age (p. 276; figure 9.4). Throughout the first months of life, infants are discriminating social stimuli and learning the consequences of social actions. By around 6 months of age they quite clearly discriminate between familiar and unfamiliar adults, for example in orienting and in ease of being comforted.

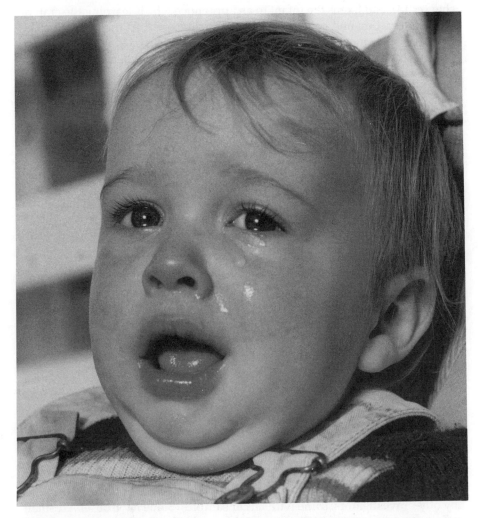

Plate 3.1 Crying is a very powerful message to adults about babies' needs; picking up a crying baby usually reduces the crying.

Another aspect of infant learning is imitation. Research by Kaye and Marcus (1978, 1981) shows that imitation of social stimuli is occurring between 6 months and 12 months of age. These investigators tried presenting infants with certain actions each time they got their attention. For example, they might open and close their mouth five times, like a goldfish; or clap hands in front of the infant, four times. Each action sequence was contingent on the infant re-establishing eye contact with the experimenter. Besides often establishing eye contact, the infants also tried to imitate the actions themselves, often trying to copy one feature at a time; the imitations improved over trials, and as the infants got older.

To summarize, these various features of infant behaviour assist in getting into social interaction sequences with adult caregivers. However, you can see that the adult has a vital role to play in this, by responding in appropriate ways and at appropriate times. Kaye (1982) calls this 'scaffolding' (see also chapter 14), and likens the infant to an apprentice who is learning the craft of social interaction and communication from an expert. At the beginning the adult has to do most of the work to keep things going: picking the infant up, putting their face at the right distance, responding whenever the infant makes a signal, perhaps having the 'illusion' that the infant is replying when it smiles or grimaces. Things get less one-sided as the infant develops her own social repertoire and begins to learn to take turns in social interaction. Even so, gearing one's behaviour at an appropriate pace and level to the child remains important through infancy and beyond.

Very early bonding: the work of Klaus and Kennell

Although infants only gradually learn about their parents or caregivers, it has been claimed that the mother very quickly forms a bond with the infant, in the first hours or days after birth. In its strongest form it is claimed that the first 6–12 hours after birth are a sensitive period for the mother to form a strong emotional bond with her infant through physical contact. If she is absent, the bond is less strong, and later maltreatment or abuse more likely. This 'early bonding' hypothesis, if true, has profound implications for practices in maternity hospitals where, especially a decade or so ago, mothers were often separated from their infants with little contact for the first day or so.

The hypothesis was proposed by Klaus and Kennell (1976), on the basis of a study of 28 mothers in an American maternity hospital. Fourteen had the traditional treatment – 5 minutes' contact at delivery, then separation for some 6–12 hours followed by half-hour feeding sessions every 4 hours. The other 14 had extra contact – an hour of cuddling after birth, and then an extra 5 hours each day. One month later, and also one year later, there appeared to be some differences favouring the extra contact group. For example, the mothers were more likely to soothe the baby if it cried. This suggests that the extra contact in the first day or so makes a difference.

During the 1980s however, a number of similar studies were carried out by other investigators, some with larger samples. Some have observed small effects, some none at all. Reviews of this evidence (Goldberg, 1983; Myers, 1984) suggest that while early contact is pleasurable for the mother and may have some short-term effects, the long-term effects are very small or non-existent. The positive results of the early studies are flawed by methodological drawbacks, small samples and focusing attention on a small number of significant results out of a very large number of measurements. Thus, the existence of this sensitive period is now thought to be very questionable; many other influences are important in the mother's relationship to the infant, and over a longer time period. The changes in hospital practice are probably beneficial; but parents who miss the first few hours or so of contact (some mothers, most fathers, and all adoptive parents) need not feel that they have lost out on a period crucial for later relationships with the baby.

Temperament

Even from soon after birth, infants seem to vary considerably in their behavioural characteristics. Some will cry a lot, others will be equable; some will be active, others less so; and so on. In a longitudinal study in New York, Thomas and Chess (1977) interviewed mothers of young children at regular 3-month intervals, and found considerable consistency in what they call characteristics of temperament. Based largely on questionnaires, they identified nine main dimensions of temperament, shown in table 3.1. On the basis of these dimensions, the researchers distinguished difficult babies (negative, irregular, and unadaptable), and easy babies (positive, regular and adaptable). Temperamentally difficult babies are more of a challenge for parents to cope with, and seem to be more at risk for later behaviour problems. The best outcome is if parents respond in a way suited to the baby or toddler – providing extra motor opportunities for active babies, for example, or specially encouraging approach in shy babies.

Thomas and Chess tend to see temperamental characteristics as inherent in the child; an alternative view is that since temperament is based on mother (or caregiver) ratings, it is a dyadic characteristic which much more reflects

Table 3.1   Temperament dimensions from the work of Thomas and Chess

Activity level – the amount of physical activity during sleep, feeding, play, dressing, etc.

Regularity – of bodily functioning in sleep, hunger, bowel movements, etc.

Adaptability to change in routine – the ease or difficulty with which initial response can be modified in socially desirable ways.

Response to new situations – initial reaction to new stimuli, to food, people, places, toys, or procedures.

Level of sensory threshold – the amount of external stimulation, such as sounds or changes in food or people, necessary to produce a response in the child.

Intensity of response – the energy content of responses regardless of their quality.

Positive or negative mood – amount of pleasant or unpleasant behaviour throughout day.

Distractability – the effectiveness of external stimuli (sounds, toys, people, etc.) in interfering with ongoing behaviour.

Persistence and attention span – duration of maintaining specific activities with or without external obstacles.

the mother's own psychological state and how she understands her child's behaviour (St. James-Roberts and Wolke, 1984). Bornstein, Gaughran and Segui (1991) have devised an *Infant Temperament Measure* (ITM) which looks at ten infant behaviours (such as: smiles and laughs to a stranger; fusses/ cries) and combines mothers' global ratings, and both mothers' and observers' ratings during a 30-minute session. This multi-method assessment is intentionally designed to assess different perspectives on the infant's temperament. Temperament may be an important aspect to consider in parenting outcomes (see p. 102 and fig. 3.1).

◄The Development of Attachment Relationships►►►

Suppose you are watching a 1- or 2-year-old infant with his mother in a park. This is what you might observe. The mother sits down on a bench, and the infant runs off. Every now and then he will stop to look around, point to objects or events, and examine things on the ground such as leaves, stones, bits of paper, or crawl or jump over grass verges. The infant periodically stops and looks back at the mother, and now and then may return close to her, or make physical contact, staying close for a while before venturing off again. Usually the infant does not go further than about 200 feet from the mother, who may however have to retrieve him if the distance gets too great or if she wants to move off herself.

The infant seems to be exploring the environment, using the mother as a secure base to which to return periodically for reassurance. This is one of the hallmarks of an 'attachment relationship'. The development of attachment has been described in detail by John Bowlby (1969). The observations of children in parks were made in London by J. W. Anderson (1972), a student of Bowlby's.

Bowlby described four phases in the development of attachment, subsequently extended to a fifth:

1 The infant orientates and signals without discriminating different people. We have already described this as characteristic of the infant in the first few months of life (excepting unusual laboratory situations).
2 The infant preferentially orientates to and signals at one or more discriminated persons. This marks the beginning of attachment. The infant is more likely to smile at the mother or important caregivers, for example, or to be comforted by them if distressed. Exactly when this occurs depends on the measures used, but it is commonly observed at around 5–7 months of age.
3 The infant maintains proximity preferentially to a discriminated person by means of locomotion and signals. For example, the infant crawls after the person, or returns periodically for contact, or cries or protests if the person leaves ('separation protest'). This is often taken as the definition of

attachment to a caregiver. From 7–9 months usually brings the onset of attachment, in this sense. An important related criterion is that the infant becomes wary or even fearful of unfamiliar persons ('fear of strangers').

4 The formation of a goal-corrected partnership occurs between child and caregiver. Until now the mother has served as a resource for the child, being available when needed. The goal-corrected partnership refers to the idea that the child also begins to accommodate to the mother's needs, for example being prepared to wait alone if requested until mother returns. Bowlby saw this as characterizing the child from 3 years of age, though there is evidence that 2-year-olds can partly accommodate to verbal requests by the mother to await her return (Weinraub and Lewis, 1977).

5 Lessening of attachment as measured by the child maintaining proximity. Characteristic of the school-age child, and older, is the idea of a relationship based more on abstract considerations such as affection, trust and approval, exemplified by an internal working model of the relationship (p. 79).

Bowlby and other psychologists in an ethological tradition see attachment as a canalized developmental process, whose primary function is to provide the infant with protection, as in other mammals. Others put more emphasis on processes of learning in attachment development, and on the symbolic communication which occurs in its context. As we have seen, both the largely instinctive repertoire of the newborn and certain perhaps constrained forms of learning are important in early social interactions. Some aspects of cognitive sensori-motor development (chapters 9, 11) are also essential for attachment; until the infant has some idea of cause–effect relations, and of the continued existence of objects or persons when out of sight, he cannot consistently protest at separation and attempt to maintain proximity. Sensori-motor development is also a canalized process, and an ethological and a cognitive-learning approach to attachment development need not be in opposition.

Many of the characteristic behaviours in attachment have been described by Mary Ainsworth (1967, 1973). She observed babies both in the Ganda people of Uganda, and in Baltimore in the USA. She described behaviours such as smiling and vocalizing preferentially to the mother, and being comforted; crying when the mother leaves, following her and greeting her by smiling, lifting arms, hugging or scrambling over her and burying the face in her lap; using the mother as a secure base for exploration, and as a haven of safety if frightened.

Who are attachments made with?

In many articles and textbooks the attachment relationship is defined as attachment to the mother (e.g. Sylva and Lunt, 1981), thus assuming that it is only or primarily the mother with whom a baby forms an attachment. How true is this? Some studies suggest that early attachments are usually multiple, and although often the strongest attachment is to the mother, this need not always be so (see Smith, 1980, for a review).

One study was done in Scotland, interviewing mothers and asking to whom their babies showed separation protest (Schaffer and Emerson, 1964). The proportion of babies having more than one attachment figure increased from 29 per cent when separation protest first appeared, to 87 per cent at 18 months. Furthermore, for about one-third of the babies the strongest attachment seemed to be to someone other than the mother, such as father, grandparent or an older sibling. Generally attachments were formed to responsive persons who interacted and played a lot with the infant; simple caretaking such as nappy changing was not in itself such an important factor. Cohen and Campos (1974) obtained similar results in a study in the USA.

Studies in other cultures bear out these conclusions. In the Israeli kibbutzim, for example, young children spend the majority of their waking hours in small communal nurseries, in the charge of a nurse or *metapelet*. A study of 1- and 2-year-olds reared in this way used a modified version of the 'strange situation' to measure attachment to the mother, and the *metapelet*. It was found that the infants were strongly attached to both; either could serve as a base for exploration, and provide reassurance when the infant felt insecure (Fox, 1977). In many agricultural societies mothers work in the fields, and often leave young infants in the village, in the care of grandparents, or older siblings, returning periodically to breastfeed. In a survey of data on 186 non-industrial societies, it was found that the mother was rated as the 'almost exclusive' caretaker in infancy in only five of them. Other persons had important caretaking roles in 40 per cent of societies during the infancy period, and in 80 per cent of societies during early childhood (Weisner and Gallimore, 1977).

The security of attachment

Ainsworth and her colleagues developed a method for assessing how well attached an individual infant is to her mother or caregiver (Ainsworth et al., 1978). This method is known as the *Strange Situation*, and has been used extensively with 12–24-month-old infants in the USA, and also in many other countries including Britain, Germany, Holland, Israel and Japan. Essentially it is a method of checking out, in a standardized way, how well the infant uses the caregiver as a secure base for exploration, and is comforted by the caregiver after a mildly stressful experience.

The Strange Situation The experiment involves seven short episodes, which take place in a comfortably equipped room, usually at a research centre where the episodes can be filmed. Besides caregiver or mother (M) and infant (I), there is a stranger (S) whom the infant has not seen before. The episodes are: (1) M and I in room, I explores for 3 minutes; (2) S enters, sits for 1 minute, talks to M for 1 minute, and gets down on the floor to play with I, 1 minute; (3) M leaves, S plays with I then withdraws if possible, up to 3 minutes; (4) M returns, S leaves unobtrusively, M settles I and then sits down for 3 minutes; (5) M leaves, I is alone for up to 3 minutes; (6) S comes in, attempts to settle I then withdraws if possible, up to 3 minutes; (7) M returns, S leaves unobtrusively, M settles I and sits down (session ends, after about 20 minutes).

In a well-functioning attachment relationship, it is postulated that the infant will use the mother as a base to explore (episodes 1, 2 and end of episode 4), but be stressed by the mother's absence (episodes 3, 5 and 6; these episodes are curtailed if the infant is very upset or the mother wants to return sooner). Especial attention is paid to the infant's behaviour in the reunion episodes (4 and 7), to see if he or she is effectively comforted by the mother. On the basis of such measures, Ainsworth and others distinguished a number of different attachment types. The primary ones are type A (Anxious/Avoidant), type B (Secure) and type C (Anxious/Resistant); later, type D (Disorganized) was added.

Type A These babies are characterized by conspicuous avoidance of proximity to or interaction with the mother in the reunion episodes. Either the baby ignores the mother on her return, greeting her casually if at all, or he mingles his welcome with avoidance responses such as turning away, moving past or averting gaze. During separation, the baby is not distressed, or distress seems due to being left alone rather than to mother's absence.

Type B These babies are characterized by actively seeking and maintaining proximity, contact or interaction with the mother, especially in the reunion episodes. He may or may not be distressed during the separation episodes, but any distress is related to mother's absence.

Type C These babies are characterized by conspicuous contact- and interaction-resisting behaviour in the reunion episodes. Rather than ignoring the mother, this is combined with some seeking of proximity and contact, thus giving the impression of being ambivalent.

Type D These babies show a very disorganized or disoriented pattern of behaviour in the Strange Situation; Main and her colleagues (1985) believe this type to be a useful extension of the original Ainsworth classification.

An important test of the utility of attachment security types is that they should predict to other aspects of development. There is now considerable evidence for this. For example, secure attachment at 12 months has been correlated with the quality and sensitivity of mother–infant face-to-face interaction at 6–15 weeks, with curiosity and problem-solving at age 2, with social confidence at nursery school at age 3, with empathy and independence at age 5 (Oppenheim et al., 1988) and with lack of behaviour problems (in boys) at age 6 (Lewis et al., 1984). Anxious/resistant attachment has been related to the likelihood of infant maltreatment or abuse (p. 100), and changes in attachment type have been related to changes in life events (such as financial or marital changes) of the mother (see Bretherton and Waters, 1985, and Waters, Vaughn, Posada and Kondo-Ikemura, 1995, for reviews of this area of research).

Van IJzendoorn and Kroonenberg (1988) provided a cross-cultural comparison of Strange Situation studies in a variety of different countries. In American studies, some 70 per cent of babies were classified as securely attached to their mothers (type B), some 20 per cent as type A and some 10 per cent as type C. However, some German investigators found that some 40–50 per cent of infants were type A (Grossman et al., 1981), while a Japanese study found 35 per cent type C (Miyake et al., 1985). Such percentages must raise a question about the nature of 'anxious attachment'. Is it a less satisfactory mode of development, as Ainsworth and others allege, or are these just different styles of interaction?

Takahashi (1990) argues that the Strange Situation must be interpreted carefully when used across cultures. He found that Japanese infants were excessively distressed by the infant alone episode (episode 5), because normally in Japanese culture they are never left alone at 12 months. Hence, fewer Japanese infants scored B. Also, there was no chance for them to show avoidance (and score as A), since mothers characteristically went straight and without hesitation to pick up the baby. This may explain why so many Japanese babies were type C at 12 months (yet they are not at 24 months, nor are adverse consequences apparent). This distortion might be avoided by virtually omitting episode 5 for such babies.

Criticisms of the attachment construct

Attachment theory is currently an important and vigorous approach to early social development (see Ainsworth and Bowlby, 1991, or Bretherton, 1992, for an account of its development). However, criticisms have been made of it. Some feminist psychologists have objected to implications they see coming from attachment theory, for example, that women's identity is expected to be tied to child-rearing; they see a high price being paid for maternal sensitivity, in other areas such as careers and self-esteem (Singer, 1992; Woollett and Phoenix, 1991). A mother who stays at home to look after young children full time can feel frustrated or isolated, particularly if she has little support from her husband or relatives. Research on the causes of depression in women has identified a number of contributory factors, one of which is being at home full time with two or more children under five if other stresses are present (Brown and Harris, 1978).

Criticisms have also been made of the attachment typing resulting from the Strange Situation procedure (Lamb et al., 1984). The typology was originally based on only 26 American infants (although since used with larger samples), and it has been suggested that the classification has been derived prematurely, on an inadequate sample base. The suggestion that type B attachment is 'normal' has been criticized, especially bearing in mind the cultural variations we saw earlier. It has also been pointed out that the procedure measures the relationship between mother and infant, not characteristics of the infant. When father–infant attachment has been assessed, several studies have found that the attachment type is not related to that with the mother (in fact there is a moderate relationship between the two, as shown by Fox, Kimmerly and Schafer, 1991).

Despite these criticisms and reservations, however, the Strange Situation procedure remains a commonly and internationally used technique. For 3- up to 6-year-olds, variants of the Strange Situation, such as Reunion episodes after separation, have been used with some success (Main and Cassidy, 1988).

Attachment beyond infancy and internal working models

Research in the last decade has seen attachment become a life-span construct, with corresponding attempts to measure it at different developmental stages (see Melhuish, 1993, for a review). We have seen how, as the infant becomes older, attachment relationships become less dependent on physical proximity and more dependent on abstract qualities of the relationship such as affection, trust, approval, internalized in the child and also of course in the adult. Researchers have found it useful to think of internal representations of the relationship in the child's mind; the child is thought of as having an *internal working model* of his or her relationship with the mother (and similarly with other attachment figures) (Bowlby, 1988; Main, Kaplan and Cassidy, 1985). These are described as cognitive structures embodying the memories of day-to-day interactions with the attachment figure. They may be 'schemas' or 'event scripts' which guide the child's actions with the attachment figure, based on their previous interactions and the expectations and affective experiences associated with them.

Dyads of differing attachment type would be expected to have differing working models of the relationship. Secure attachment would be based on models of trust and affection. By contrast, a boy with a type A anxious/avoidant relationship with his mother may have an internal working model of her which leads him not to expect secure comforting from her when he is distressed. She may in fact reject his approaches. His action rules then become focused on avoiding her, thus inhibiting approaches to her which could be ineffective and lead to further distress. This in turn can be problematic, as there is less open communication between mother and son, and their respective internal working models of each other are not being accurately updated.

Several studies have attempted to measure attachment quality in older children, by trying to tap in to their internal working models. One method has been the *Separation Anxiety Test*, in which children or adolescents respond to photographs showing separation experiences; an example is shown in plate 3.2. The child is asked how the child in the picture would feel and act, and then how he/she would feel and act if in that situation (Main et al., 1985). Wright, Binney and Smith (1995) found this test to have good rater reliability and consistency for 8- to 12-year-olds. They found large differences in responses between children having clinical treatment for behaviour disturbance and a normal control group (see table 3.2). Securely attached children generally acknowledge the anxiety due to the separation but come up with feasible coping responses; insecurely attached children generally either deny the anxiety, or give inappropriate or bizarre coping responses.

Internal working models of relationships can normally be updated, or modified, as new interactions develop. It may be that for younger children, such change must be based on actual physical encounters. However, Main et al. (1985) suggest that in older children or adults who have achieved formal operational thinking (chapter 11), it is possible to alter internal working models without having such direct interaction. To measure attachment in older adolescents and adults, they developed the *Adult Attachment Interview*. This is a semi-structured interview which probes memories of one's own early childhood experiences. The transcripts are coded, not on the basis of the experiences themselves, so much as on how the person reflects on and evaluates them, and how coherent the total account is.

Main et al. (1985) reported that the Adult Attachment Interview (AAI) yielded four main patterns:

1   Autonomous: persons who can recall their own earlier attachment-related experiences objectively and openly, even if these were not favourable.
2   Dismissive: persons who dismiss attachment relationships as of little concern, value or influence.
3   Enmeshed/preoccupied: persons who seem preoccupie with dependency on their own parents and still actively struggle to please them.

Plate 3.2   Boy by Landrover; a picture from the Separation Anxiety Test.

Table 3.2   Two protocols from the Separation Anxiety Test

From control sample:

Child: Mum is going shopping and the boy is staying at home alone.
Interviewer: How would you feel?
Child: A bit scared and try to have some fun.
Interviewer: Why?
Child: Because someone can break in and kidnap me.
Interviewer: What would you do?
Child: Try and have fun and think mum and dad are in the house and no-one can kidnap me.

From clinical sample:

Child: Mum is going shopping and the boy is staying at home alone.
Interviewer: How would he feel?
Child: Bad.
Interviewer: Why?
Child: Cause he's often seen the video Home Alone and get burglars.
Interviewer: What would he do?
Child: So he sets booby traps and ends up hitting mum in the face with iron bars and blow torches. So he sits and watches TV but he gets burnt by the fire and goes to hospital, his mum visits him and he's dead.

4   Unresolved: persons who have experienced a trauma, or the early death of an attachment figure, and have not come to terms with this or worked through the mourning process.

Van IJzendoorn (1995) has summarized work using the AAI, which he argues has satisfactory coding reliability. In terms of validity, he examines links between the parent's AAI coding and (if they are a parent) their infant's Strange Situation coding. Main et al. (1985) had reported some evidence for such a link, and indeed the AAI coding system is premissed on it; it was argued that Autonomous adults would have Secure infants; Dismissing adults would have Avoidant infants; Enmeshed adults would have Ambivalent infants; and Unresolved adults would have Disorganized infants. Van IJzendoorn looked at a large number of available studies in the decade since Main's work; the results for parent–infant concordance are shown in table 3.3. There is clearly considerable linkage between adult AAI and infant Strange Situation coding; Van IJzendoorn argues this 'intergenerational transmission' of attachment may be via parental responsiveness, though other factors such as temperament may also be influential (see comments by Fox, 1995, for a critique of this work).

Van IJzendoorn and Bakermans-Kranenburg (1996) have looked at the distribution of AAI codings across different groups of people, from 33 separate studies, as summarized in table 3.4. Mothers, fathers and older adolescents do not differ significantly in their distribution across the three main

Table 3.3   Concordance between infant Strange Situation coding and parental AAI coding

3-way; 18 studies	Dismissing	Autonomous	Enmeshed	
Avoidant	116	46	27	
Secure	53	304	46	
Ambivalent	10	19	40	
4-way; 9 studies	**Dismissing**	**Autonomous**	**Enmeshed**	**Unresolved**
Avoidant	62	29	14	11
Secure	24	210	14	39
Ambivalent	3	9	10	6
Disorganized	19	26	10	62

Table 3.4   Normative data on AAI codings (percentages)

33 studies	Dismissing	Autonomous	Enmeshed
Mothers	24	58	18
Fathers	22	62	16
Adolescents	27	56	17
Lower SES	33	48	18
Clinical patients	41	13	46

categories. People from lower socioeconomic groups are slightly more likely to score as Dismissing. However, the large difference is in persons having clinical treatment, the great majority of whom do not score as Autonomous on the AAI.

Does security of attachment change through life, or does infant–parent attachment set the pattern not only for later relationships, but even for one's own future parenting? Some mothers who had had very negative experiences with their own parents seemed to have come to terms with this, and ascribed rational reasons for it (for example marital stress, or overwork). These mothers were more likely to have secure infants themselves; perhaps they had succeeded in updating their own working models of attachment relationships, even in retrospect, to the benefit of their relationships with their own children.

◀Relationships with Other Family Members▶▶▶

Although earlier researchers tended to focus rather exclusively on the mother when discussing the child's early social relationships and attachment, more recently attention has been paid to the child's relationships with other family members: father and grandparents (we discuss siblings in chapter 4).

Fathers

How important is the other parent – the father? And has the role of the father changed in recent years, as is often suggested? Research in a number of societies has shown that fathers can fulfil a parenting role just as much as mothers, for example in single-parent father families; but that typically, fathers do not have such a large part in child-rearing and domestic tasks as do mothers (Lamb, 1987).

So far, the highest degree of father involvement in any human society seems to be amongst the Aka pygmies, a hunter-gatherer people in the Central African Republic. Fathers were found to be present with an infant or child for 88 per cent of the time, and to be holding an infant for 22 per cent of the time. This high degree of physical intimacy by fathers seems to be encouraged by the overlapping subsistence activities of men and women. Men don't just leave women in the campsite to look after children, while they go hunting with nets; women often assist in hunting, and men often carry infants back after the hunt. Nevertheless, even in this society mothers still engage in more child care than fathers (Hewlett, 1987). Another society where paternal care is encouraged is Sweden. Equality between the sexes has been encouraged since the 1960s, including legislation about work opportunities and parental leave, and an advertising campaign (see plate 3.3) to encourage fathers to take child-care responsibilities seriously. While this has had some impact, it is still true that Swedish mothers do most of the housework and provide most child care, even when both parents are working (Hwang, 1987).

In *Becoming a Father* (1986), Charlie Lewis carried out an interview study of 100 fathers of 1-year-old children in Nottingham, UK. One aspect which Lewis documented was that the majority of fathers (65 per cent) now attended all stages of the birth of their child. Many fathers were anxious about it, and had been encouraged to attend by their wives; but most found it a positive experience. As one father put it:

> I found it hard work and much more traumatic than I thought it would be . . . I felt by the end of the experience that I had done a full day's work and was absolutely washed out, but nevertheless I wouldn't miss being there a second time. (Lewis, 1986, p. 70)

This is undoubtedly a change since three decades earlier fathers were discouraged from attending hospital deliveries (it is also worth noting that up to the 1950s and 1960s many more deliveries took place at home anyway). However, it was not the case that fathers who were present at the birth were also much more involved with child care after the baby was home; Lewis found no correlation between these two. Mothers predominantly did the child care, feeding, nappy changing and getting up at night if the baby was fretting. At least two factors seem to contribute to this. Firstly, the father will

Plate 3.3   A Swedish father cradles his young son. Photographs such as this were used in campaigns directed to increasing paternal involvement in child care (from the Department of Information, Stockholm).

more often be in longer hours of employment. Lewis did find that fathers contributed more when the mother was also working. Secondly, it is easy for fathers to feel marginalized in baby care; mothers are seen as the 'experts' at this. Indeed it is only mothers who can breastfeed! However, mothers may contribute to keeping their own areas of expertise, as the following interview demonstrates:

Interviewer: How about changing him? Do you often change his nappies?

Father (to wife): Don't think I've done that, have I?

Wife: In the first week when I weren't well.

Interviewer: Is there any reason why you haven't?

Wife: Only 'cos I've always been there. They don't bother me in the slightest, you know.

Father: Nappies don't bother me, you know. If Jan [wife] turned round to me and said, 'Could you do it for me, then?' . . . Like I say, she's a very competent mother.

(Lewis, 1986, p. 100)

Lewis was able to compare his data, obtained in 1980, with similar data obtained by the Newsons in interviews in 1960. Some results are shown in table 3.5. The most dramatic and significant changes are in the husband helping in the period after birth, and getting up for the baby at night; the changes for bathing and nappy changing are less clear-cut and not significant. In the USA, Lamb (1987) similarly concludes that there have been some modest increases in paternal involvement over the last decade or so. The idea of the new, nurturant father is not entirely mythical, but it would be easy to exaggerate the changes that have taken place.

Grandparents

About 70 per cent of middle-aged and older people become grandparents. Since the average age of becoming a grandparent, in Western societies, is about 50 years for women, and a couple of years older for men, they are likely to remain grandparents for some 25 years or more; about a third of their life-span. Grandparenthood is thus an important part of the life cycle for most people.

Only a small proportion of grandparents live in the same house as grandchildren, but many live fairly close, while those who are more distant characteristically keep contact via letters, phone calls and visits. Grandparents can have considerable influence on their grandchildren's behaviour. Tinsley and Parke (1984) described both indirect and direct influences. Indirect influence has its effect via some other person or agency, without there necessarily being any direct interaction. For example, the parent–child interaction will be influenced by the way the parent has been brought up and the experiences of child-rearing which the parent has had modelled by his or her parent, i.e. the grandparent. Grandparents can also provide emotional and financial support for parents, which will be especially valuable at times of emotional or financial stress.

Table 3.5 Changes in father involvement in child care, 1960 to 1980

	1960 (N = 100)	1980 (N = 100)
Husband helps in the period after birth? (Yes)	30	77 $p < 0.001$
Husband gets up to baby at night? (Yes)	49	87 $p < 0.001$
Husband involved in putting baby to bed/getting to sleep?		
little/never	29	26
occasional	35	24
often	35	48 n.s.
Husband involved in bathing baby?		
little/never	54	62
occasional	26	9
often	20	29 n.s.
Husband involved in nappy changing?		
little/never	37	40
occasional	43	32
often	20	28 n.s.

Source: Lewis, 1986

Direct influences can also take many forms. Perhaps the strongest case is when a grandparent acts as a surrogate parent when the child is young (for example in a single-parent family, or with a teenage pregnancy, or as a caregiver while both parents work). It is most often the maternal grandmother who fills this role. However, grandfathers can be important too; Radin, Oyserman and Benn (1991) found that grandfathers can have a direct positive influence on young grandchildren of teen mothers, especially for grandsons.

Even if not acting as a surrogate parent, a grandparent who has contact with a grandchild can act as a companion and be an important part of the child's social network. Many grandparents enjoy conversations with grandchildren, asking them to run errands, and giving them small gifts. They can also act directly as a source of emotional support, acting as a 'buffer' in cases where a grandchild is in conflict with parents, or where the parents are in conflict with each other.

For example, Johnson (1983) analysed the responses of 58 US grandmothers to the divorce of one of their children. The younger grandmothers (below 65 years of age) generally maintained their level of contact with the grandchildren (usually weekly or more), and half of them actually increased their level of contact. One grandmother described how she filled a gap in the custody arrangements:

> I pick them up on Friday after work. We go to the Pizza Hut for dinner
> – then home to watch TV. I keep lots of goodies around for them. They

fight, I shush them. Then they zonk out. The next morning, I fix breakfast – they watch TV. Then I take them to their dad's and dump them.
It's kinda nice. (Johnson, 1983, pp. 553–4)

The older (over 65) grandmothers also usually maintained or increased
contact after parental divorce, but the level of contact was noticeably less.

It is not easy in all situations for grandparents to see grandchildren after
parental divorce. The issue of rights of access of grandparents of a non-
custodial parent has been of recent concern in the UK and other countries. In
the USA, all 50 states have passed statutes allowing grandparents to petition
for legally enforceable visitation rights to see their grandchildren
(Thompson, Tinsley, Scalora and Parke, 1989), and the 1989 Children Act in
the UK should also facilitate this.

Another role of grandparents is to pass on information and values directly
to grandchildren. They are particularly well placed to pass on the family
history, and knowledge of times past. Sometimes the values of grandparents
may conflict with those of the parental generation; for example, in an
interview study of older people in London, Townsend (1957, pp. 106–7)
remarked that 'the grandparents were notably lenient towards grandchildren'. As one informant put it, 'the grandmother can be free and easy.
She [her daughter] has to be fairly strict with them.' At other times grandmothers have been thought of as being too strict and punitive. Indeed in the
1930s and 1940s, some psychiatrists and social workers regarded the grandmother's influence very negatively. Vollmer, an American doctor, remarked
(1937, pp. 378, 382) that 'every pediatrician . . . will have made this discovery: grandmothers exert an extraordinarily pernicious influence on their
grandchildren' and that 'the practical conclusion is that the grandmother is
not a suitable custodian of the care and rearing of her grandchild'! Whatever
grandmothers were really like in the 1930s, most present-day grandparents
appear sensitive to the need not to interfere too much with parental-rearing
methods, and as we have seen, the consensus of research is that the balance
of their influence is overwhelmingly positive. Some negative stereotypes of
grandparents still persist, however; many children's books portray grandparents as somewhat inactive persons in their eighties or nineties, rather
than (as many grandparents are) actively employed and in their fifties or
early sixties.

▸Care Outside the Family: Day Care and Childminding▸ ▸ ▸

In many Western societies the standard expectation, at least until recently,
has been that mothers of young children should stay at home to look after
them until they are old enough to go to nursery or infant school, that is 3–5
years of age. Nevertheless, it has always been the case that many mothers
of young children have gone out to work, either through preference or
through financial necessity. During the mid-1970s some 600,000 mothers of

preschool children in the UK were in paid employment (and at that period most fathers were working full time). Some parents manage to share care in their own home with grandparents, older siblings or neighbours; for example, a study of London working-class homes found an average of more than four caregivers including parents (Tizard and Tizard, 1971). The alternatives are to place the child in a day nursery or creche, or with a childminder. Day nursery places have long been inadequate to demand, and it is difficult to know the numbers of children placed with childminders, as many childminders do not register. There are some 50,000 registered childminders in the UK, but the number of unregistered (illegal) childminders has been estimated at two to three times as many (Jackson and Jackson, 1979).

There has been considerable controversy over both nursery-based day care and childminding (which Americans call 'home-based day care'). Some research in the 1950s and 1960s (including the writings of Bowlby) led to cautions about day care. Subsequently, a large body of research (much of it carried out in the USA) suggested that day care does not have adverse effects provided that it is of high quality; that is, there are good staff–child ratios, low staff turnover and a stimulating, well-provided environment. In such circumstances, it was concluded that day care had no overall effects on intellectual development, and did not disrupt the child's attachment relationship with the mother (Belsky and Steinberg, 1978; Clarke-Stewart, 1982). It does increase the degree to which the child interacts, both positively and negatively, with peers.

The controversy over day care was reopened in the late 1980s by Belsky (1988) and others. Belsky (1988) pointed out that about half of US mothers with 1-year-olds were in employment. However, an analysis he made of some recent studies led him to conclude that 'a rather robust association emerges between extensive non-maternal care experience initiated in the first year of life and insecure infant–mother attachment assessed in the Strange Situation (Belsky, 1988, p. 401). Belsky concluded that initiating day care of more than 20 hours per week before the child is one year of age may be a risk factor for mother–infant relationships. Combining data from five studies, the risk of having insecure attachment to the mother was 43 per cent for infants experiencing high day care, but only 26 per cent for infants experiencing low (or no) day care.

Not everyone agreed with Belsky's conclusion. Clarke-Stewart (1989) queried whether the Strange Situation is a valid procedure for infants of working mothers (who experience many more routine separations); whether insecure attachment to mothers can be generalized to general emotional security; and whether the differences may be due to other factors (e.g. differences between mothers who choose to work and those who do not). In an empirical study, Clarke-Stewart (1991) assessed 150 children aged 2 to 4 years who had experienced different child-care arrangements, in the USA. She found that children in day-care centres had *better* social and intellectual development than those in home care (with either mother or childminder).

However, a survey by Baydar and Brooks-Gunn (1991) of 1,181 children in the USA, based on longitudinal data, gave findings more in support of

Belsky's views. They reported that maternal employment starting in the first year of the infant's life had 'significant negative effects on cognitive and behavioral outcomes', but not if maternal employment was deferred to the child's second or third year. (Of alternative arrangements to mother care, grandmother care had the best outcome.)

Another study, of 1,100 Bermudan children by Scarr and Thompson (1994), gave yet another result. They compared infants placed in non-maternal care either before, or after, one year of age, and for more, or less, than 20 hours per week; and made assessments when the children were 2 years, and 4 years old. This was a very definite test of Belsky's hypothesis, but the researchers found no differences in cognitive or socio-emotional measures.

Issues of day care are clearly complex, and influenced by many variables; for a review, see McGurk et al. (1993). In any event, the new controversy and evidence do not affect the previous conclusions about day care starting after the first year. Interestingly, in Sweden either parent can take the first 12 months off on full pay, to look after a new baby (on average, fathers take $1\frac{1}{2}$ months of this). Thus, the concern about day care starting in the first year does not worry the Swedes (Hwang, Broberg and Lamb, 1990).

Ideally, childminding (or in the USA, home-based day care) could provide an economic form of day care with high adult to child ratios; and perhaps best of all is when such care is provided by relatives, such as grandparents. There has been relatively little research on childminding, but such as there is has mostly been carried out in the UK. Several studies have been very critical of the effects of childminding, including one conducted in London (Mayall and Petrie, 1977, 1983) and one in Oxfordshire (Bryant et al., 1980). Both found that children often appeared insecure in the minder's home, and scored below expectations on tests of language or cognitive ability. These studies did not have proper control groups for comparison, however, so it is not clear that the children's problems were due to the minding, rather than home circumstances (Raven, 1981).

There are certainly problems to be expected with some unregistered minders. Jackson and Jackson (1979) carried out a 'dawn watch' in Hudders-field, tracking down where mothers took their children to be minded before the early morning shifts in the factories. They found that some of the unregistered childminders provided a very poor emotional and material environment. Much can be done here by improving facilities for childminders, providing training courses and encouraging registration and resource back-up (Moss, 1987).

Melhuish (1990) and his colleagues compared the progress of children in London, who (starting before 9 months of age) experienced either care with relatives, childminding or private nursery care. The adult–child ratio was best for care by a relative, next for childminders and lowest for nursery care. At 18 months, communication to children, and also some aspects of the children's language development, were highest for children cared for by relatives and lowest in the nursery group. (Contrary to Belsky's worries there were no apparent differences in attachment to mothers.) By 3 years of age the children in nurseries continued to receive less language stimulation; their naming vocabulary was the least developed, though they did not differ on other language measures. There were no significant differences in cognitive development, however, and the nursery children did show more prosocial behaviour such as sharing, co-operation and empathy with others. These differences held even after controlling for measures of social class (such as mothers' education) which discriminated between the three groups.

◀Bowlby's 'Maternal Deprivation' Hypothesis▶ ▶

There has been concern over day care and childminding for young children partly because of the hypothesis that children should not be 'deprived' of contact with the mother during a critical period when the primary attachment relationship is being formed. This hypothesis, which has come to be known as the 'maternal deprivation' hypothesis, was proposed by John Bowlby (1953, 1969). It carries strong practical policy implications. Many aspects of it have been strongly criticized, however (see Rutter, 1981). We review both the hypothesis and the critiques in this discussion.

Bowlby first put forward his views publicly in a 1951 report to the World Health Organisation, published in paperback in 1953 as *Child Care and the Growth of Love*. The report was inspired by the needs of refugee or homeless children, separated from or without parents in the aftermath of the Second World War. At that time, as in the inter-war years, institutional care focused on the physical needs of the child, good food and a clean environment – but little on the child's emotional needs, which were poorly recognized. On the basis of psychoanalytic beliefs, contemporary ethological work and his own evidence, Bowlby proposed (1953) that 'mother love in infancy and childhood is as important for mental health as are vitamins and proteins for physical health'. This viewpoint provided a most important, indeed vital, corrective to the prevailing current of opinion. Bowlby went further, however. In a now notorious passage, he stated:

> What is believed to be essential for mental health is that the infant and young child should experience a warm, intimate and continuous relationship with his mother (or permanent mother-substitute – one person who steadily 'mothers' him) in which both find satisfaction and enjoyment.

This statement, that the infant should have a continuous, unbroken relationship with one person (normally the mother), is backed up elsewhere in Bowlby's writings by assertions that mothers should not be separated from their young children, for example by work (even part-time), or hospitalization, and that if such separations do occur, there is a poor prognosis for social and cognitive development. The period of from about 6 months to 3 years was regarded as especially crucial. Even if not universally believed, this statement had a profound effect on a generation of mothers.

Why did Bowlby hold this belief? We can identify a number of sources of evidence which led him to these views:

1   The idea of a critical period for attachment formation came from the early work on imprinting and the following response (see chapter 2). The 9-month 'fear of strangers' was supposed to prevent subsequent attachment bonds being formed.

2   Observations of young children separated from parents when placed for short-term stays in a hospital or institution, for example, showed that the children went through a characteristic sequence: first protesting, but able to be comforted; secondly despair, and being inconsolable; thirdly denial and detachment, with the child superficially unconcerned at the separation, but denying any affection or response to the mother on eventual reunion. These stages were vividly shown in a series of films made by J. and J. Robertson (1967–73), entitled *Young Children in Brief Separation*.

3   Much research evidence suggested that children in long-term institutional care were retarded in social, language and cognitive development; presumably as a result of the effects of maternal separation. Studies by researchers such as Goldfarb and Spitz, documented the extreme retardation often found in orphanages and foundling homes, and the adverse long-term effects of institutional rearing (e.g. Goldfarb, 1947; and see chapter 16).

4   The adverse effects of long-term maternal separation were soon apparently further confirmed by research carried out with rhesus monkeys in the USA. Harry and Margaret Harlow (1958, 1969) reported a series of studies in which young rhesus monkeys were separated from their mothers and raised in isolation. Either they were placed in total isolation, in steel cages with diffused light and filtered sound, or they were placed in partial isolation, in wire cages where they could see and hear, but could not contact other monkeys. Either way, when such an isolation-reared monkey was released and placed with other monkeys, it showed complete social maladjustment, usually being terrified of other monkeys, crouching, rocking and biting itself, and occasionally being hyper-aggressive even to a play invitation. If isolated for only the first 3 months, a young monkey could recover, but isolation for 6 or 12 months seemed to produce irreversible effects. At adolescence these animals were unable to mate satisfactorily, and if a female did have a baby, she abused it rather than cared for it.

5   There was evidence which linked delinquency or behaviour problems in adolescence to some form of separation experience in childhood, such as hospitalization, or a 'broken home' brought about by parental separation or divorce. The evidence came from retrospective studies; that is, those which started with adolescent children to obtain certain data on their childhood experiences. Bowlby's interpretation was that the separation experience caused the later behaviour problems.

Criticisms of the hypothesis

Much further evidence has accumulated on the matters Bowlby addressed. As a result, the maternal deprivation hypothesis, at least in its strong form, has become largely discredited, although the debate continues (see Rutter, 1981). Let us consider the main reasons why the evidence cited above does not necessarily lead to the conclusions which Bowlby reached.

1   The ethological evidence for critical periods is not so strongly stated now as in the 1950s; furthermore, the 'imprinting' characteristic of precocial birds and some mammals is not characteristic of primates (see chapter 2). The 'fear of strangers', which was thought to emerge as the primary attachment bond was formed, is also now seen as overstated. Recent evidence suggests that 1- and 2-year-olds can form new social relationships with adults and we have already seen how children at this age characteristically form several strong attachment relationships.

2   We have seen that Bowlby's idea of attachment to just one caregiver ('monotropism') seems incorrect. It follows from this that separation from the mother could be compensated for by the presence of another attachment figure. This does seem to be the case. Indeed, the Robertsons' work referred to above found just this. Here, children were being placed in short-term care while the mother had a second baby and was to be in hospital for about a week. The Robertsons showed that institutional care led to the phases of protest, despair and denial, but that short-term foster care in a family, especially if the foster-mother got to know the child beforehand, very greatly alleviated the child's distress. Similarly, if a young child is in hospital, regular visits or stays by mother, father and/or other attachment figures can prevent obvious distress.

3   The early work on the effects of institutional rearing has been re-evaluated (see also chapter 16). No one denies the terrible effects of the pre-war orphanages, which were poorly equipped and staffed by persons with little understanding of the psychological needs of the child. However, any effects of separation from the mother were confounded with the generally unstimulating environment provided. It is not surprising that children become linguistically and cognitively retarded if they are hardly spoken to and given few toys and little sensory stimulation. It is not surprising that they are socially immature, if they receive little social contact and few socially contingent responses. Such was often the case (see also chapter 16), but these are not necessary concomitants of institutional care. More recent research has found that improved institutional care has fewer dramatically harmful effects (see box 3.2).

4   The Harlows' monkey research apparently gave experimental backing for the long-term and irreversible effects of maternal deprivation in another primate species. Yet these studies also confounded maternal deprivation with general social and sensory deprivation. Moreover, later research in this programme has shown how severe deficits can be ameliorated (Suomi and Harlow, 1972; Novak, 1979). The breakthrough came when the isolation-reared monkeys, instead of being released directly into a peer group, were first placed individually with a younger monkey. For example,

6-month isolates were paired with 3-month-old 'therapist' monkeys. The younger monkey approaches and clings to the older one, rather than attacking it, and seems to help it catch up on the sort of physical contact experiences it has missed. Even 12-month isolates can be helped by this method. This research has shown that deprivation effects may not be irreversible, if the right corrective treatment is used. It also shows that in many respects, peers can be as effective as mothers in reducing the effects of social isolation.

   5   The retrospective evidence linking adolescent behaviour problems to early separation experience is open to various interpretations. No clear causal link can be inferred. For example, suppose a correlational link has been found between delinquency and a 'broken home' in early childhood. Parental separation may mean that there is increased discord at the time, or later, or perhaps less supervision of the child is given by a single parent. These might be the real causes of the delinquency, not the separation itself. Rutter (1981) argued that it is the discord often present in separating or divorcing families which leads to later behaviour problems. It is not separation as such, since death of a parent, while obviously affecting the child, does not usually lead to the outcomes which were being ascribed to maternal deprivation.

In the long term Bowlby's work had some markedly beneficial effects. Together with other research it led to a marked improvement in the standard of institutional care (see box 3.2) and in many areas the phasing out of institutional care in favour of fostering arrangements. It also led to much easier access of parents to a child in hospital care. In general, a greater awareness of the child's emotional needs was stimulated. However, there were some effects which many people now see as detrimental, particularly a feeling of guilt amongst mothers who, perhaps out of necessity, went out to work while their children were young.

   There is some evidence that repeated hospital admissions before 5 years of age can lead to later behaviour problems in adolescence. Two large-scale survey studies (Douglas, 1975; Quinton and Rutter, 1976) have found such a correlation. Does this also support the critical period idea? The opposite view is put by Clarke and Clarke (1976), who argue that repeated hospital admission is probably a symptom of inadequate parental care over a sustained period, with the latter being the causative factor. Nevertheless, the original studies did control for factors such as social class and parental interest in education, and the independent replication means that the findings cannot be dismissed lightly.

   Moderate shared care of young children seems to be very common, harmless and even perhaps beneficial. However, it does seem that extreme shared care, with tens of adults involved, can lead to immediate and long-term problems. A study by Tizard (box 3.2) best documents this, but it is supported by independent research (see Rutter, 1981). The Tizard study also hints at the possibility that an early attachment bond is important for later adjustment, as the later adopted children in this study tended to share the same school problems as those who remained in institutional care.

A quite different source of evidence about effects of shared care of young children comes from the Israeli kibbutzim. These communities have had a strong egalitarian philosophy which led to children being raised communally, sleeping in large dormitories away from their parents, and being educated by nurses or *metaplot* (Sing: *metapelet*); children would see their parents for an hour or two each day, but were otherwise raised in a group environment. A comprehensive review of the effects of this system has been made by Aviezer et al. (1994). They concluded that collective sleeping arrangements were a problematic aspect of the kibbutz system; in fact, many kibbutzim have now reverted to children sleeping with their parents. Collective sleeping arrangements were associated with a greater incidence of insecure (ambivalent) attachment, as assessed by the Strange Situation; the authors conclude that in this respect, the traditional kibbutzim deviated too far from what is natural for human infants and their parents. In other respects however the communal child-rearing environment did foster group-oriented skills and close peer relationships.

An overall assessment is that many of Bowlby's ideas on maternal deprivation are discredited. Nevertheless, it is a normal process for 1- and 2-year-olds to form strong attachments to a few persons, characterized by proximity seeking and separation protest. Bonds can be formed later, as studies of late adoption show, and many of the apparent adverse effects of maternal deprivation are now seen as due to other factors, perhaps not specific to the first 2 or 3 years of life. But, in certain more limited senses than Bowlby first proposed, it may be that this early period is more crucial for social adjustment than are later years.

◀Styles of Parenting▶▶

Independent of the body of research on attachment security, studies have been made of how parents may vary in their styles of child-rearing. Some parents believe in strong discipline, others do not, for example. An American psychologist, Diana Baumrind, tried to conceptualize three global styles of child-rearing in the USA (Baumrind, 1967, 1980). Her styles were:

Authoritarian – parents who have strict ideas about discipline and behaviour which are not open to discussion.
Authoritative – parents who have ideas about behaviour and discipline, which they are willing to explain and discuss with children and at times adapt.
Permissive – parents who have relaxed ideas about behaviour and discipline.

Maccoby and Martin (1983) felt that it would be best to separate out two dimensions of parenting style – how demanding or undemanding parents are about their children's behaviour, on the one hand, and how responsive or unresponsive they are to their children on the other. They therefore produced the four-fold classification shown in table 3.6. This approach to parenting

Table 3.6 Styles of parenting from Maccoby and Martin (1983)

	Responsive	Unresponsive
Demanding	Authoritative	Authoritarian
Undemanding	Permissive	Uninvolved

styles, typically measured by questionnaires given to parents, has been widely used and does predict to aspects of children's development. Let's look at a couple of examples.

Dekovic and Janssens (1992) had a sample of 112 children aged 6 to 11 years. They ascertained their sociometric status in school (see chapter 4), and their prosocial behaviour from ratings by teachers and classmates (see chapter 7). They estimated parenting style from observations at home in the evenings when both parents were present (time-consuming, but probably more valid than self-report questionnaires). They found that authoritative parents tended to have popular, prosocial children; authoritarian parents tended to have sociometrically rejected children.

Steinberg, Lamborn, Dornbusch and Darling (1992) carried out a larger, longitudinal study, of 6,400 adolescents aged 14 to 18. For this size sample they obviously had to rely on questionnaire measures of parenting style. They also asked the adolescents to report on parental involvement in their schooling, and obtained their school grades for achievement. They found that authoritative parenting was related to better school performance. Interestingly, there was a mediating effect of parental involvement, usually thought of as helpful in this context. The parent's involvement in the adolescent's school work was especially helpful when it came from authoritative parents, but not so much when it came from authoritarian parents – maybe the latter can be too critical and not so supportive as authoritative parents can be (with *laissez-faire* or undemanding parents not being involved very much with school anyway).

Steinberg et al. characterized authoritative parenting in their study as having three components – parental acceptance and warmth; behavioural supervision and strictness; and psychological autonomy granting or democracy. However, this highlights difficulty with the Maccoby and Martin scheme (table 3.6), which includes the last two components, but does not explicitly include warmth – nor, indeed, other possibly important dimensions such as parental punitiveness. Baumrind's original global approach does include more components (Baumrind identified authoritative parents as being warm and accepting of their children, in contrast to authoritarian parents), but confounds them so that one does not know which type is responsible for the effects obtained. These difficulties are discussed in a review by Darling and Steinberg (1993), who also point out the possible cultural specificity of this work. There is evidence, for example, that these parenting-style schemes have greater predictiveness for Euro-American families than they do for African-American families.

Types of families

The stereotypical family is of a heterosexual married couple with their bio-logical children (usually, two of them!). But in reality there is much variation in types of families. In Great Britain for example, about 80 per cent of children under 16 are with both natural parents (Clarke, 1992). About 10 per cent are in lone-parent families (usually, but not always, the mother), about 9 per cent are with one natural parent and one step-parent, and about 1 per cent are in other arrangements. These figures apply to one moment of time; it is estimated that through their entire childhood, only about one-half of British children (53%) will stay with both married natural parents.

A small number of children are brought up, not by a heterosexual couple, but by gay or lesbian parents of the same sex. What are the effects of this on children? Patterson (1992) reviewed a number of relevant studies. She concluded that gender identity, gender role behaviour and sexual preferences of children of gay and lesbian parents fall within the normal range of variation; peer relationships were found to be satisfactory. To date, this research does not suggest that children of gay or lesbian parents develop differently in any significant sense.

Much more research has been done on one-parent families, divorced and remarried (or reconstituted) families with step-parents. Here, the outcome can be more problematic.

◄Divorce and Step-parenting►►

Divorce has become more common in modern Western societies (Clarke, 1992). It can be distressing for children when the apparently secure base of the family is broken in this way. There is likely to be conflict between spouses, uncertainty for the future, effects on family income, possible relocation, and possible loss of contact with one parent and related kin (Richards, 1994). Wallerstein (1985) has described three phases in the divorce process. First is the acute phase, typically lasting about 2 years, in which the emotional and physical separation takes place. Second is a transitional phase, in which each parent experiences marked ups and downs while they establish separate lives. Third is a post-divorce phase, in which each parent has established a new lifestyle, either as a single parent or remarried.

What are the consequences of this for the child's development? The effects of divorce have been found to vary considerably with the child's age when the separation occurs (Hetherington, 1988). Preschool children, although upset, are least able to understand what is going on. By middle childhood the changes are better understood, but there may be persistent wishes or fantasies of the parents reuniting. For early adolescents, the reaction may more often be one of shame or anger, perhaps siding with one parent or the other. The impact on children varies over time as well; clearly longitudinal studies are vital to get any real understanding of the impact of divorce on children. Several such studies have been made.

One study commenced with 144 middle-class white families in Virginia, USA (Hetherington, Cox and Cox, 1982). Half the children were from divorced, mother-custody families, and half from non-divorced families; their average age at separation was 4 years. After 1 year, most children from divorced families (and many parents) experienced emotional distress and behaviour problems associated with the disruptions in family functioning. This was much improved after 2 years; the main exception being that some boys had poor relations with their custodial mothers and showed more antisocial and non-compliant behaviour than boys from non-divorced families.

A follow-up was made after 6 years, when the children had an average age of 10 years, of 124 of the original 144 families. By now, 42 out of 60 divorced mothers had remarried (and 2 of these had redivorced); also 11 of 64 originally non-divorced families had divorced. A general finding was that children of divorced parents experienced more independence and power in decision making at an earlier age, and their activities were less closely monitored by parents. They 'grew up faster'. Mother–daughter relationships were generally not much different from those in non-divorced families. However, mother–son relations continued to be rather tense for divorced mothers who had not remarried; even despite warmth in the relationship, sons were often non-compliant and mothers ineffective in their attempts at control.

Remarriage and the presence of a stepfather seemed to improve matters for sons, who perhaps responded well to a male figure to identify with; however, the stepfamily situation often made matters worse for daughters, with the stepfather–stepdaughter relationship being a particularly difficult one. Step-parents are almost inevitably seen as intruders by stepchildren, and often try to tread an uneasy path between assisting their spouse in discipline problems (which may lead to their rejection by stepchildren), and disengagement. The difficulties facing some stepfamilies were also documented by a study in London by Ferri (1984), which still pointed out that many such families had successfully met the challenge. Remarriage does generally increase the life satisfaction of the adults, but forming strong relationships in the reconstituted family is often a gradual and difficult process.

Another study, starting in 1971, was of 131 children from 60 divorcing families in Northern California (Wallerstein, 1987). The children were between $2\frac{1}{2}$ and 18 years at the time of decisive parental separation. Initially, virtually all the children were very distressed at the separation. Things were not much better after 18 months; some of the younger girls had recovered somewhat, but some of the younger boys showed significantly more disturbance. A follow-up after five years showed a more complex picture. What was most important now was the overall quality of life within the post-divorce or remarried family. About one-third of the children, however, still showed moderate to severe depression.

At a follow-up after 10 years, some 90 per cent of the original sample could still be located. Interviews with children now 16- to 18-years-old, who had perhaps experienced the separation at the most vulnerable time, showed that many still felt sad and wistful about what had happened, while often accepting its inevitability. As one girl said:

> I don't know if divorce is ever a good thing, but if it is going to happen, it is going to happen. If one person wants out, he wants out. It can't be changed. I get depressed when I think about it. I get sad and angry when I think about what happened to me. (Wallerstein, 1987, p. 205)

All the children had been in the legal and physical custody of their mothers; about 40 per cent had moved in for a while with their fathers during adolescence, but most had returned; visits to father varied greatly, but were not usually more than weekly due in part to geographical separation. However, the quality of the father–child relationship was an important determinant of adjustment.

Although traditionally custody is given to one parent, usually the mother, joint custody is being increasingly advocated where possible (i.e. where both parents live fairly close and maintain a reasonable relationship). Luepnitz (1986) compared children who were in sole custody with the mother, sole custody with the father, or joint custody, 2 years or more after final separation. In fact, measures of child adjustment were found to be independent of custody type. Joint custody has the advantages of the child being able to develop two independent relationships, and of reducing financial and parenting pressures on a single parent. Luepnitz reported that 'the vast majority of children in joint custody were pleased and comfortable with the arrangement'. Single custody can however protect wives from possible abuse, and give more flexibility to relocation and remarriage.

Interestingly, Luepnitz found that only 11 per cent of her sample of children showed signs of maladjustment. This is less than one-third the level reported in Wallerstein's study, and may be due to sample differences. Wallerstein recruited subjects by promising counselling, and thus may have recruited particularly distressed families; whereas Luepnitz may have recruited rather non-distressed families who were willing to discuss custody arrangements and their outcome. Whatever the extent of maladjustment, however, all the major studies agree that experiencing good relationships with both parents and an absence of continuing conflict are generally conducive to the most positive outcome for the children involved. Hetherington (1989) describes 'winners, losers, and survivors' of parental divorce. Depending on circumstances, some children may continue to be damaged and insecure through to adulthood; others recover and 'survive'; yet others may develop particularly caring and competent ways of behaving as a result of coping with the experience.

Some of the ill-effects of divorce are probably attributable to conflicts between partners which predate the actual separation of the parents. A longitudinal analysis was made by Cherlin et al. (1991) of 7- to 11-year-olds in Britain, using the National Child Development Study (a survey of mothers of all children born in one week in 1958), and 7- to 11- and 11- to 16-year-olds in the USA, using the National Survey of Children which began in 1976. These analyses looked at children's school achievement and behaviour problems before, as well as after, divorce. Generally, the apparent effects of divorce (compared with children in non-divorcing families) were considerably reduced when the situation pre-divorce was taken into account. As the authors put it, 'at least as much attention needs to be paid to the processes that occur in troubled, intact families as to the trauma that children suffer after their parents separate'.

Conflict between parents

There is considerable research evidence that conflict between parents can in itself be distressing for children – whether it precedes marital separation and divorce, or not. A study by Gottman and Katz (1989) in Illinois, USA, of 56 families with a 4- to 5-year-old child, used both laboratory observations and home interviews. The researchers found that more maritally distressed couples had more stressed children who showed more negative peer interactions, and more illness. A follow-up of the same families was made when the children were 8 years old (Katz and Gottman, 1993). Teacher ratings of the children's internalizing and externalizing behaviour problems were made. Earlier marital mutual hostility predicted later externalizing (antisocial) behaviour in the children, and earlier husband angry-withdrawn behaviour predicted later internalizing (self-blame) behaviour in children. These and other studies are reviewed by Davies and Cummings (1994); parental conflict clearly has adverse effects on children, and this contributes to the effects found in studies of separation and divorce (though it does not appear to be the only factor involved).

◀ Child Neglect and Abuse ▶ ▶

Usually, parents love and care for their children. No parent is perfect, but most provide 'good enough' parenting. Some conflict between parents and their offspring is inevitable (and indeed is predicted from evolutionary theory, see chapter 2), but generally such disagreements are kept within reasonable bounds.

In some cases, however, parents or other caregivers may neglect a child, failing to give him or her the love, care and attention necessary for normal healthy development. Even more drastically, some may subject a child or children to physical or sexual abuse. Abuse can result in severe injuries, long-lasting psychological trauma and even death. The extent of child abuse is very difficult to determine, as naturally parents are secretive about it, and children are often too young or too frightened to seek help. It also depends on the definition of abuse. Physical abuse has been defined as 'the intentional, non-accidental use of force on the part of the parent or other caretaker interacting with a child in his or her care aimed at hurting, injuring or destroying that child' (Gil, 1970). Sexual abuse has been defined as 'the involvement of dependent, sexually immature children and adolescents in sexual activities that they do not fully comprehend, to which they are unable to give informed consent or that violate the social taboos of family roles' (Kempe, 1980).

In the UK the National Society for Prevention of Cruelty to Children (NSPCC) has reported some 9,000 cases of physical abuse and 6,000 cases of sexual abuse per year (Creighton and Noyes, 1989). Some 200 children may die each year as a result of direct or indirect maltreatment by their parents; child abuse is in fact the fourth commonest cause of death in preschool children (Browne, 1989). The peak of physical abuse is in early childhood, with boys being more at risk than girls; the peak for sexual abuse appears to be later in middle childhood, with girls primarily at risk.

Diagnosis of abuse has its own set of problems. Questioning of young children has to be done carefully to maximize the accuracy and usefulness of children's testimony (Fundudis, 1989). In the case of sexual abuse, observation of unstructured play with anatomically correct dolls may be useful. Unlike conventional dolls, these dolls have sexual organs and characteristics. Some studies suggest that most children, while noticing the characteristics of the dolls, do not show sexually explicit play with them; when it is observed, such explicit play (for example, sucking a doll's penis) may well arise from the child's preoccupations based on pre-vious exposure to explicit sexual information or activity (Glaser and Collins, 1989). However, the use of these dolls remains controversial (Westcott et al., 1989).

It can also be very difficult and distressing for victims of child abuse to speak out. At times they may not be believed and interviews by police and judges can seem very intimidating. In the USA and the UK it is increasingly possible to allow children to give evidence by means of a closed circuit television 'video link', so that they need not directly face their abuser (Davies, 1988). Psychologists are closely involved in this work, and in at-tempts to help victims of abuse recover from their experiences (British Psy-chological Society, 1990).

The statistics we have indicate that child abuse tends to be more common in lone-parent and low-income families. In cases of physical abuse, mothers and fathers are about equally likely to be involved (though there are obvious questions about who is willing to admit abuse – a mother may 'shelter' an abusing father or cohabitee). In cases of sexual abuse, some 95 per cent involve males as the perpetrators.

What leads a parent to abuse a child? Abusing parents have been found very often to have insecure attachment relationships with their children. In one study, 70 per cent of maltreated infants were found to have insecure attachments to their caregivers, compared with only 26 per cent of infants with no record of maltreatment (Browne, 1989).

Crittenden (1988) has examined the representations of relationships in abusing parents, using the idea of internal working models discussed earlier. She interviewed 124 mothers in Virginia, USA, many of whom had abused or maltreated their children, and gave them the Separation Anxiety Test (p. 79). She reported that adequate mothers generally had warm and secure relationships with both their children and their partner. By contrast, abusing mothers appeared to conceptualize relationships in terms of power struggles. They tended to be controlling and hostile with anxiously attached children, and to have angry and unstable adult relationships. Another group, of neglecting mothers, appeared to conceive of relationships as emotionally empty. They were unresponsive to their anxiously attached children, and were involved in stable but affectless relationships with partners. These findings have implications for working with these families. Crittenden argues that 'the problem for those offering treatment to abused and abusing individuals is to find ways both to change their experience and also to change their conceptualization of it. Without a change in the representational model, the new experience will be encoded in terms of the old model and will be rendered useless' (Crittenden, 1988, p. 197).

The above work generally refers to abuse by natural parents. Another risk factor, for young children, is abuse by step-parents. Studies in Canada, the UK and elsewhere show quite clearly that the risk of abuse, including fatal abuse, is much greater for children with stepfathers; the increase in risk (compared with being with the natural father) is between around 7, and around 100 (Daly and Wilson, 1996). Daly and Wilson take an evolutionary perspective on this data, arguing that it is not in the stepfather's genetic interest to divert parental investment to children not related to him (cf. p. 57, chapter 2); in terms of proximal mechanisms, some stepfathers may just not develop any attachment to their new stepchildren. This finding needs to be kept in the perspective that most step-parents do not abuse their stepchildren, and genuinely attempt to form good relationships; but as discussed earlier, this is not always easy, and especially when there are additional stresses, young children may be more at risk than when with both natural parents.

The effects of child abuse can be wide-ranging and long-lasting. Malinosky-Rummell and Hansen (1993) have reviewed the evidence, and find links between childhood physical abuse and adolescent criminal behaviour, adult family violence, and non-familial violence. Spaccerelli (1994) has reviewed effects of childhood sexual abuse, which is a risk factor for long-term effects on mental health. Both reviews point out that other factors can moderate the effects – for example, the kinds of coping strategies used by the individual, the nature of support which they have, and the way in which they are able to appraise and understand what has happened to them.

◄Models of Parenting►►►

We've looked at aspects of parenting where there are difficulties – where parents separate or divorce, or where there is actual abuse of children. But what about the more normal range of parenting? There is still a lot of variation in how different parents carry out the task.

Belsky (1984) has advocated a model of parental functioning which distinguishes three main influences on the quality of parental functioning. In order of suggested importance, these are:

1   personal psychological resources of the parent: this will include parental mental health, the quality of internal representations of relationships and their development history;
2   contextual sources of support: including the social network of support from partner, relatives and friends, and job conditions and financial circumstances;
3   characteristics of the child: in particular easy or difficult temperament (see p. 73).

Belsky's actual process model of factors influencing parenting is illustrated in figure 3.1. The model is also useful for understanding how variations in family functioning, satisfactory as well as unsatisfactory, may come about.

Belsky's model can be useful in thinking of ways to help parents with difficult or disruptive children. There has been considerable interest in the area of parenting skills, and ways of helping parents change, improve their coping and child-management skills, or develop a more secure relationship with their child. These approaches have mainly focused on the first area of Belsky's model, that of personal psychological resources of the parent.

Van IJzendoorn, Juffer and Duyvesteyn (1995) reviewed 16 studies which involved working with parents to improve parental sensitivity and attachment security. Interventions were varied but covered increased support from home visitors, use of videos, parent education, and individual (mother) and joint (mother–child) psychotherapy. Generally, short-term

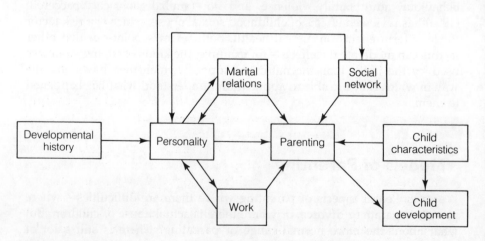

Figure 3.1   Belsky's process model of the determinants of parenting.

preventive interventions seemed more effective than long-term therapy-based interventions. There were appreciable improvements in many studies in maternal sensitivity to the child, but only small improvements in attachment security.

This review suggests that it is easier to produce changes at the behavioural level, than at the representational level. This need not be surprising; changes at the representational level may be deeper and need more sustained effort to bring about. Some insight into this comes from a study reported by Fonagy, Steele, Steele, Higgitt and Target (1994). They carried out a longitudinal study with 100 mothers and 100 fathers, in London, who were given the AAI and other measures shortly before their child was born. The Strange Situation was used subsequently to measure security of attachment, to mother at 12 months and to father at 18 months. As other studies have found (table 3.2), the parent's AAI scores predicted the infant's Strange Situation scores. The researchers also obtained estimates of the amount of deprivation and disrupted parenting which the parents had themselves experienced. They looked to see if this too influenced infant attachment. Interestingly, it did, but it interacted strongly with the way in which the parents had dealt with their own representations of their experiences of being parented. Coding the AAI, the researchers developed a *reflective self-function* scale to assess the ability parents had to reflect on conscious and unconscious psychological states, and conflicting beliefs and desires. Of 17 mothers with deprived parenting and low reflective self scores, 16 had insecurely attached infants, as might be expected. By contrast, of 10 mothers who had experienced deprived parenting but had high reflective self scores, all had securely attached infants. The researchers argued that reflective self-function may be a way to change internal working models, and demonstrate resilience to adversity and a way of breaking the intergenerational transmission of insecure attachment.

It is a continuing challenge to see how parents of difficult or disruptive children can be helped. The studies cited here have used theoretical models based on attachment theory; others have used models based more on social skills and behavioural approaches. Belsky's model also draws attention to the wider social context; the employment status of parents, housing conditions and social support.

The extent to which parents make a difference to childen's development has, however, been disputed. Scarr (1992) argues that by and large, parents need only provide a basically warm, supportive and nurturant environment for their children to develop their innate potential. She supports her argument by reference to studies in behaviour genetics (see chapter 2). Using twin and adoption studies, behaviour geneticists have shown that what is called the shared family environment – the aspects of the family environment common to all siblings – contributes very little to understanding individual differences. For example, children adopted into the same family, show very little similarity as they grow up (Plomin and Daniels, 1987). If this conclusion is accepted, then most individual differences are due to heredity, plus non-shared family environment; the latter referring to the particular rearing environment each child has.

Even the non-shared family environment can be influenced by what is called genotype–environment interaction. In other words, to some extent children help create their own rearing environment. A child's temperament for example (which appears to be strongly genetically influenced), influences the ways parents behave towards that child and the expectations they have of them.

Of course, no one denies that extremes of environment can adversely affect development; studies of children reared in profoundly non-stimulating environments, and studies of environmental enrichment, show that children can be held back if they do not receive a basic minimum of language and intellectual stimulation, and love and affection (see chapter 16). Scarr accepts this, and says that children require this average expectable environment for normal development; but that beyond this, individual variation in development is mainly due to inherited individual potential, finding expression in a reasonably good environment that is partly created by the person for themselves.

Scarr's views give greater prominence to genetic factors than some psychologists think is justified; and they appear to downplay the importance of parenting, beyond the basic minimum or good enough parenting. They also imply that many parent–child similarities are due to genetic rather than environmental factors. These issues are controversial and hotly debated (Baumrind, 1993).

◄Further Reading►►►

Useful general texts are J. G. Bremner 1994 (2nd edn): *Infancy*, Oxford: Blackwell Publishers; A. Fogel 1994 (2nd edn): *Infancy*, St Paul: West Pub. Co., and J. F. Rosenblith 1992 (2nd edn): *In the Beginning: Development from Conception to Age Two*, Newbury Park and London: Sage. K. Kaye 1982: *The Mental and Social Life of Babies*, London: Harvester Press, is a more argumentative text on early social development.

M. Rutter 1981 (2nd edn): *Maternal Deprivation Reassessed*, Harmondsworth: Penguin, is a thorough review of the controversy and later evidence bearing on Bowlby's views. J. Holmes 1993: *John Bowlby and Attachment Theory*, London: Routledge, provides a readable biography and assessment of Bowlby's work. J. Bowlby 1979: *The Making and Breaking of Affectional Bonds*, London: Tavistock Publications, is a collection of a number of Bowlby's articles, and his last book was published in 1988: *A Secure Base: Clinical Applications of Attachment Theory*, London: Tavistock/Routledge. S. Scarr and J. Dunn 1987: *Mother Care/Other Care*, Harmondsworth: Penguin, is a review of the evidence on this issue which needs supplementing by more recent research. K. Browne, C. Davies and P. Stratton (eds) 1988: *Early Prediction and Prevention of Child Abuse*, Chichester and New York: John Wiley & Sons, gives a comprehensive review of these topics; and H. R. Schaffer 1990: *Making Decisions about Children*, Oxford: Blackwell, explores the ways in which our psychological knowledge can influence crucial decisions about children in matters such as custody, adoption and fostering.

◀Discussion Points▶▶▶

1   How do infants become social?
2   What is meant by 'secure' and 'insecure' attachment? Are these culturally biased terms?
3   Do mothers, fathers and grandparents have different influences on a child's behaviour?
4   What did Bowlby mean by 'maternal deprivation'? How useful or valid has this concept proved to be?
5   What are the problems in diagnosing, and treating, child abuse?

Box 3.1
Reactions to response-contingent stimulation in early infancy

The objective of this study was to examine the importance of contingent responsiveness on behaviour in 8-week-old infants. Forty infants were recruited from the San Francisco area in the USA and the study was carried out in the infants' homes.

A special apparatus, the 'contingency mobile', was designed for the study. It is shown schematically in box figure 3.1.1. The mobile was attached to the infant's cot so that it hung about 18 inches above the infant's head. The display consisted of three spheres or rectangles painted in different colours. An electric motor, when activated, caused the display to rotate for one second, through 90 degrees. There were three conditions:

1   The 'contingency' condition (18 infants). A pressure-sensing pillow was put in the cot. Small changes in pressure on the pillow activated the electric motor and caused the display to rotate. When the infant was lying with her head on the pillow she could cause the display to rotate by making small head movements.
2   The 'non-contingency' condition (11 infants). The pressure-sensing pillow was disconnected from the motor. The display rotated once every 3 or 4 seconds, independent of the infant's actions.
3   The 'stable' condition (11 infants). The pressure-sensing pillow was disconnected from the motor. The display did not rotate at all.

In all conditions the mothers were asked to hang the display and activate the system for 10 minutes a day, for 14 consecutive days, at times when the infant was peaceful but alert. The number of times the infant activated the pressure sensor in the pillow was recorded on an automatic counter.

The results are shown in box figure 3.1.2. The infants with the contingency mobile increased the number of pillow activations they made per session from about 90 (days 1 and 2) to 135 (days 13 and 14) (significant at $p < 0.01$ on a matched pairs t test). For the non-contingency mobile and the stable condition the changes were not significant. This showed that, as early as 8 weeks, infants can learn a simple response to produce contingent stimulation.

However, the investigators obtained another interesting result when they went to collect the equipment. One mother in the condition (1) group apologized that she had used the mobile additionally to the specified times, as a baby-sitter device to keep the baby happy. It turned out that almost all the mothers in this condition reported that their infants smiled and cooed at the mobile, after a few sessions. As one mother said, 'You have to see it, when he's with his mobile, you can't distract him, he loves it.' Almost none of the mothers in the other two conditions reported this kind of strong positive emotional response.

This second result shows that contingent stimulation is enjoyed by the 8-week-old infant and produces or 'releases' socio-emotional behaviour such as smiling and cooing. These infant behaviours are normally used in social interactions with caregivers, and usually it is caregivers who provide response-

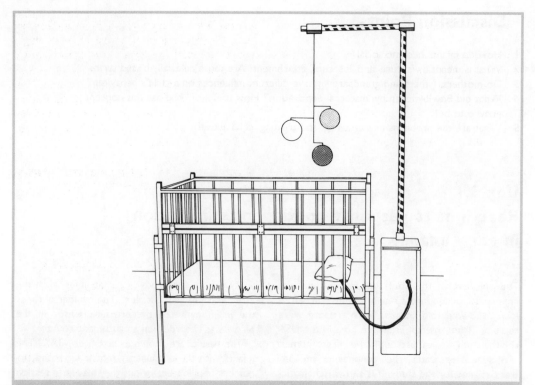

Box Figure 3.1.1   Apparatus used as a 'contingency mobile' (adapted from Watson and Ramey, 1972) (based on material in J. S. Watson and C. T. Ramey 1972: *Merrill-Palmer Quarterly*, 18, 219–27).

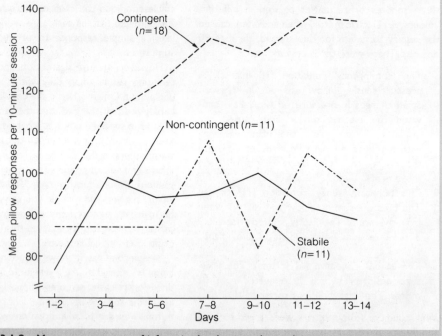

Box Figure 3.1.2   Mean response rate of infants in the three study conditions.

contingent stimulation at this age. Watson and Ramey suggest that playful, game-like interactions are especially suitable for providing rapid contingent responses to infants, and thus eliciting positive social behaviours.

The independent variable in this study is the mobile condition; there is an experimental condition, a control for display movement and a control just for the presence of the display. The dependent variables are pillow activations and mothers' reports on socio-emotional behaviour. Obtaining the mothers' reports was not planned in advance,

and the authors report that these were recorded 'less systematically and objectively than would have been desirable'. Nevertheless, it would have been a pity not to have reported this information, which, serendipitously, adds much to the interest of the results. The technique of this study is likely to be less useful in older infants, where the nature of the contingent stimulus and the infant's attempts at imitation are of more interest.

Based on material in J. S. Watson and C. T. Ramey 1972: *Merrill-Palmer Quarterly*, 18, 219–27.

Box 3.2
The effect of early institutional rearing on the behaviour problems and affectional relationships of 4-year-old children

The objective of this study was to see whether institutional rearing in early life resulted in behaviour problems and disturbances in affectional relationships. The research was carried out in London, and focused on 26 children aged 4 years who had been admitted to a residential nursery before 4 months of age and were still there. (In 17 cases the mother or putative father still spoke of reclaiming the child; the remaining 9 had not been adopted, for various other reasons.) There were two comparison groups. One consisted of 39 children who had also been admitted to a residential nursery before 4 months, but had either been adopted (24 children) or restored to their mothers (15 children) before 4 years of age. The other group comprised 30 children from local working-class homes who had not experienced any residential care. All the children were assessed at age 4.

The residential nurseries contained around 15–25 children, in small mixed-age groups. They were well provided with books and toys. Owing to rota systems and high staff turnover, the average number of staff who had worked with each child for at least a week over the previous 2 years was 26 (range 4–45).

Each child was interviewed individually, usually with a familiar nurse or the mother present. An intelligence test was given, ratings made of the

child's observed behaviour, and questionnaires given to the parent or nurse about the child's behaviour problems and attachments. Most comparisons of the three groups employed chi-squared tests of significance. On the ratings of the child's behaviour, the main differences were between the adopted/restored children, and the other two groups. The adopted/restored children were more friendly to the interviewer, and more co-operative and talkative during testing.

The institutional children had the highest score for behaviour problems, but only marginally. Their scores were significantly higher for 'poor concentration', 'problems with peers', 'temper tantrums' and 'clinging'. However, the home-reared children scored significantly higher for 'poor appetite or food fads', 'over-activity' and 'disobedience'. In the answers to the attachment questionnaire, the nurses reported that many of the institutional children (18 of the 26) did 'not care deeply about anyone'. While sometimes clinging and following, their attachments seemed shallow. Some of them, and some of the adopted/restored children (who otherwise had good attachments to natural or adoptive parents), were also described as being 'overfriendly' to strangers.

The independent variable in this study is the early rearing experience; the dependent variables are measures of behaviour problems and social behaviour. The encouraging findings of the study are that the children who had experienced institutional rearing did not have very marked or severe behaviour problems (and a related study found quite good linguistic and cognitive development in this group, see chapter 16). Also, the adopted children generally did well and formed good relations with foster parents. However, most of the children still in institutional care had failed to form any strong attachments; this is not surprising as staff turnover was high and staff tended to discourage strong specific relationships from developing.

A real-life study such as this cannot be as neatly designed as a laboratory experiment. The children in the three groups differed in some respects (including sex and racial background), so rearing experience is confounded by these other factors. Ideally, also, the investigator would not know the background of each child interviewed, but this was not possible. Finally, the interview material relies on nurses' or mothers' reports, which may be less objective than actual observations of the child's behaviour.

A follow-up of the same children at 8 years of age was subsequently reported (Tizard and Hodges, 1978). Only 8 of the 26 children now remained in institutions. The late adopted children generally had good relations with their adoptive parents. The children all had reasonably good scores on IQ tests, and the early adopted children especially had high IQ and reading test scores. However, the long-term effects of institutional-rearing experience did show up in teachers' ratings. Compared with the home-reared controls, the children who had experienced some institutional rearing were rated as more attention-seeking, restless, disobedient and not getting on well with other children. Teachers' ratings, however, could be biased by negative stereotyping (i.e. if the teachers had negative beliefs about the effects of having been brought up in an institution, irrespective of the child's actual behaviour).

A further follow-up of the same children was made when they were 16 years of age (Hodges and Tizard, 1989). The sample available was now only about two-thirds of the original one, and a new comparison group of home-reared children was used, matched for sex, social class and family position. The findings were fairly clear. IQ scores were similar to those at 8 years, and the small variations were with family placement (adoptive/restored) rather than whether the child had or had not experienced early institutional care. However, both parents and teachers rated the ex-institutional children higher on emotional and behavioural problems than the home-reared children. Ex-institutional children had more problems with social relationships, both inside the family (mainly for children restored to natural parents), and outside the family, with peers (for both adopted and restored children). The adopted children tended to score higher on symptoms of anxiety, while those who had been restored to natural families tended to score higher on antisocial behaviour and school problems. These findings were supported by interviews with the young people themselves, suggesting they were not just due to stereotyped judgements by adults.

The careful follow-up of these children is an excellent example of the power of a longitudinal study, even with a relatively small sample size. The findings do indicate that experiencing extreme multiple caretaking in the first few years of life can be a noticeable risk factor for developing satisfactory social relationships, even by adolescence.

Based on material in B. Tizard and J. Rees 1975: *Journal of Child Psychology and Psychiatry*, 16, 61–73.

4 Friends and School

In this chapter we look at children's relationships with other children – with siblings, and with peers. A 'peer' is someone who is about the same age as yourself; for children, this is usually someone in the same year, class or age grade. We examine the concept of friendship; what is a friend? How do we measure friendship? We also consider the concept of 'sociometric status'. We then examine the nature of aggression between children, and its relationship to friendship and popularity; concluding with an examination of school bullying.

◄Early Peer Relationships►►►

From an early age, peers seem to be especially interesting to children. In one study of 12–18-month-old infants, two mother–infant pairs who had not previously met shared a playroom together. The investigations observed whom the infants touched, and whom they looked at. The results are shown in figure 4.1. The infants touched their mothers a lot (thus remaining in proximity to them, as we would expect from attachment theory, chapter 3). However, they looked most at the peer, who was clearly interesting to them (Lewis et al., 1975).

The interactions between under-2s have been examined using video film. Video is very useful, since at this age range peer interactions are short, subtle and easy to miss. They often consist of just looking at another child and perhaps smiling, or showing a toy, or making a noise. In toddler groups an infant might make such overtures to another child once every minute or so, and each may last only a matter of seconds (Mueller and Brenner, 1977). This rather low level of peer interaction is probably because infants are not yet very accomplished at the skills of social interaction, such as knowing what are appropriate behaviours in certain situations, what behaviour to expect back, and waiting to take one's turn. As we saw in chapter 3, adults can 'scaffold' social interactions with infants; but it takes young children some 2 or 3 years to become really competent at interacting socially with age-mates. There is some evidence that early peer experience (e.g. in toddler groups or day nurseries) can help this along (Mueller and Brenner, 1977: Rubin, 1980). There is also some evidence that infants who are 'securely attached' to their mothers are more confident and better able to explore both objects and peers, and to make new social relationships over the next year or so (Bretherton and Waters, 1985). Nevertheless, under-2s do have some abilities which assist peer interaction. One is imitation, which we also discussed in chapter 3. A study in France by Nadel-Brulfert and Baudonniere (1982) observed 2-year-olds in a laboratory playroom equipped with pairs of identical objects. It was found that when one child picked up or played with an object, the other child was very likely to pick up the corresponding identical object; these imitations had a definite social function, helping to maintain communication and play between the children.

Another study of French children showed evidence of a different range of abilities at 11 months and at 23 months (Tremblay-Leveau and Nadel, 1996). Here, pairs of toddlers from the same day-care centre were observed with a familiar experimenter and some toys; so, this was a 'triadic' situation. Both dyadic and triadic interactions were observed, with some degree of turn-taking even by the younger, 11-month-old children. The particularly interesting feature of the results from this study was the differing reactions

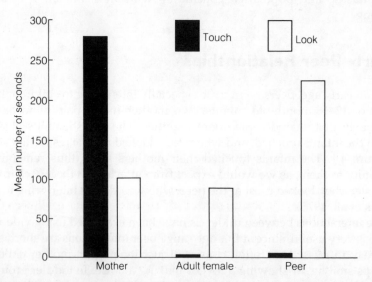

Figure 4.1 Amount of time during a 15-minute period in which children aged 12–18 months touched and looked at mother, an unfamiliar adult female and an unfamiliar peer (from Lewis et al., 1975).

of infants when they were 'included' within an ongoing interaction with the adult, or 'excluded'. When temporarily out of the interaction, the other child made many more attempts to interact with the peer; perhaps by 'showing-off' or interposing their body between the adult and peer, or by naming the toy being played with, or another toy, and smiling. At 11 months they were 5 times more likely to attempt interactions with the peer when excluded, and 8 times more likely at 23 months. The researchers conclude that this shows an early awareness of one's social position and an active attempt to overcome loneliness when excluded; and also of attention to others and, perhaps, some awareness of their mental states. If so, this would be a precursor of the kinds of theory of mind abilities which we consider further in chapter 13.

It was probably important in this study that the toddlers knew each other. However, the situation in which young children will know each other best of all is when they are raised in the same family; typically, siblings aged a year or so apart.

◀Siblings▶ ▶ ▶

Eighty per cent of us have siblings – brothers or sisters. Usually, siblings only differ in age by a few years. Thus, while not exactly 'peers', they are generally close enough in age, and similar enough in interests and developmental stages, to be important social partners for each other in the home and family environment. Characteristically, older siblings can show great tolerance for younger ones, and can act as an important model for more competent behaviour. They can also show hostility and ambivalence, and this has been observed in many different societies (Eibl-Eibesfeldt, 1989).

A study by Stewart (1983) in the USA showed that older siblings can act as attachment figures in the Strange Situation. Stewart used an extended version of the procedure, with 54 family groups. At one point the older sibling (who was aged from 30 to 58 months) was left alone with the infant (who was aged from 10 to 20 months). Every infant responded to the mother's departure with some degree of distress. Within 10 seconds of the mother's departure, 28 of the older siblings had responded by showing some form of caregiving behaviour; for example approaching and hugging the infant, offering verbal reassurance of the mother's return, or carrying the infant to the centre of the room to distract him or her with toys. These actions were quite effective. The other 26 older siblings, however, ignored or moved away from the infant and did not show caregiving responses. This pattern of pronounced variation in the quality of sibling relationships is in fact a recurrent one in studies of siblings.

The Strange Situation is of course just that – a strange situation! What is found in actual sibling relationships in the home? Extensive research of this kind has been carried out by Judy Dunn and her colleagues (Dunn and Kendrick, 1982; Dunn, 1984; Dunn, Brown and Beardsall, 1991). Dunn and Kendrick (1982) started making observations in the homes of 40 firstborn children living with both parents in or near Cambridge, UK. At first visit, a new sibling was due in a month or so, and the first child was in most cases nearing their second birthday. Subsequent visits were made after the birth of the sibling, when the second child was about 1 month old, and again at 8 months and at 14 months. Besides interviewing the parents, the natural behaviour between the siblings and with their parents was observed.

Naturally enough, many firstborns showed some signs of jealousy when the new sibling arrived. Previously they had been the centre of attention from mother, father or grandparents; now, the new brother or sister got the most attention. Parents do of course make some efforts to involve the firstborn in this, for example in feeding sessions, but inevitably rates of interaction with firstborns do decline overall (at times, fathers can play a more important role with the older child while the mother is undertaking primary caregiving responsibilities with the new baby). At this point, much of the jealousy and ambivalence of the firstborn is directed towards parents:

Mother: He keeps having tantrums and misery. Anything sets him off. He's just terrible. (Dunn and Kendrick, 1982, p. 31)

Not many firstborns show much overt hostility to the infant, but some do; and some behaviour can be ambivalent. In the following example it is difficult to know if the behaviour is friendly, hostile, or more probably a mixture of both:

Mother: He wants to play with her but he's so rough. Lies on top of her. Then she cries. He wants to roll all over her. I have to keep her away from him 'cause I can't let her be bashed about yet. (p. 36)

Other children may express hostility in conversation, as the following extract shows:

Child: Baby, baby (caressing her). Monster. Monster.
Mother: She's not a monster.
Child: Monster. (p. 68)

However, such hostility really is ambivalent. The great majority of the firstborns do show much interest and affection towards their new sibling:

Mother: He asks where she is first thing in the morning. He's happy when he can see her. (p. 34)

They may also show empathy and prosocial behaviour (see also chapter 7):

Mother: When she cries he's very concerned. Gets her dummy [pacifier], then comes and tells me. (p. 32)

There was considerable variation in the typical response when the infant was upset. Fourteen of the firstborns were themselves upset, like the boy just mentioned. Ten were neutral. Five were sometimes gleeful, while ten children actually increased their younger sibling's upset. Overall, Dunn and Kendrick feel that the sibling relationship is one in which considerable emotions may be aroused – both of love and of envy. (Incidentally, evolutionary psychologists would not be surprised at finding sibling rivalry – see chapter 2.) However, the title of Dunn and Kendrick's book, *Siblings – Love, Envy, and Understanding*, brings out another important feature; that of the enhanced understanding which this close and emotionally powerful relationship may generate. This may be an optimal situation in which to learn how to understand and hence influence others. Very early on (under 2 years of age) siblings seem to be learning how to frustrate, tease, placate, comfort or get their own way with their brother or sister. This is true not only of the older siblings, but of the younger ones as they grow up; consider the following observation of Callum, now 14 months, with his older sister Laura, aged 3 years:

> Callum repeatedly reaches for and manipulates the magnetic letters Laura is playing with. Laura repeatedly says NO gently. Callum continues trying to reach the letters. Finally, Laura picks up the tray containing the letters and carries it to a high table that Callum cannot reach. Callum is furious and starts to cry. He turns and goes straight to the sofa where Laura's comfort objects, a rag doll and a pacifier, are lying. He takes the doll and holds tight, looking at Laura. Laura for the first time is very upset, starts crying, and runs to take the doll. (p. 116)

The obvious interpretation here is that Callum has figured out how to annoy Laura so as to get his own back on her. These are interesting observations to consider in the light of ideas about children's 'theory of mind' (see chapter 13), and the critique of Piaget's ideas about egocentrism (chapter 11). Nevertheless it is also worth bearing in mind that children can learn these social cognitive skills with adults and peers, as well as with siblings. The study by Tremblay-Leveau and Nadel on triads, discussed earlier, indicated early awareness of others in non-siblings; and research on children with no siblings (only children) appears to suggest that they show no deficits in sociability or adjustment and do well on achievement and intelligence scores (Falbo and Polit, 1986). This, and other research on family-size effects, does suggest that the adult–child relationship is still the most powerful so far as many aspects of development are concerned.

Also important, is the way mothers talk to one sibling about the other sibling, or discuss feelings within the family. In a follow-up at middle childhood, Dunn, Brown and Beardsall (1991) found that these did relate to later understanding and emotional quality of relationships. And in early adolescence, someone who had grown up with an unfriendly or hostile sibling was more likely to be anxious, depressed or aggressive.

◀Peer Relationships in Preschool and School▶▶▶

By 2 or 3 years of age a child is usually thought ready for nursery school. Certainly the period from 2 to 4 years sees a great increase in the skills children have interacting with peers. As we shall see in chapter 6, socio-dramatic play and rough-and-tumble play with one or more partners become frequent in this age range. Parallel with this, the child is beginning to develop concrete operational thought and to be able to take the perspective of others in simple ways (chapters 11 and 13).

The increase in social behaviour in preschool children was documented by Mildred Parten at the Institute of Child Development in Minnesota in the late 1920s. She observed 2–4-year-olds and described how they might be 'unoccupied', an 'onlooker' on other's activities, or, if engaged in an activity, they could be 'solitary', in 'parallel' activity with others or in 'associative' or 'co-operative' activity with others. Parallel activity is when children play near each other with the same materials, but do not interact much – playing independently at the same sandpit for example. Associative activity is when children interact together at an activity, doing similar things, perhaps each adding building blocks to the same tower. Co-operative activity is when children interact together in complementary ways; for example, one child gets blocks out of a box and hands them to another child, who builds the tower. Parten (1932) found that the first four categories declined with age, whereas associative and co-operative activity, the only ones involving much interaction with peers, increased with age.

Subsequent researchers have frequently used Parten's categories, though often simplified to 'solitary' (including unoccupied and onlooker), 'parallel' and 'group' (comprising associative and co-operative). Studies in the UK and the USA have found that, very approximately, preschool children in free play divide their time equally amongst these three categories, with the balance shifting more towards 'group' activity as they get older (Smith, 1978). Most group activity involves just two or three children playing together, though the size of groups does tend to increase in older preschoolers. These trends continue in the early school years. According to a study of more than 400 Israeli children, group activity rises to about 57 per cent of the time in outdoor free play, while parallel activity falls to about 6 per cent; the number of groups comprised of more than five children increased from about 12 per cent to 16 per cent between 5 and 6 years of age (Hertz-Lazarowitz et al., 1981). The size of children's groups continues to increase through the middle school years, especially in boys, as team games such as football become more popular (Eifermann, 1970).

By the middle school years, sex segregation of children's groups is becoming very marked. In fact, children tend to choose same-sex partners even in nursery school, but by no means exclusively; typically, some two-thirds of partner choices may be same-sex, though this is influenced by such factors as the class size, toys available and the role of teachers in encouraging (or not) cross-sex play (Smith, 1986). However, by the time children are getting into

Plate 4.1 The beginnings of social relations and friendship between peers can be seen in toddler groups and nursery schools; these 3-year-olds are very much aware of each other's behaviour.

team games, from about 6 or 7 years onward, sex segregation in the play-ground is very much greater.

In a study of 10–11-year-old children in American playgrounds, Lever (1978) found that there were distinct differences between boys' and girls' activities and friendships. Boys more often played in larger mixed-age groups, while girls were more often in smaller groups or same-age pairs. Boys tended to play competitive team games that were more complex in their rules and role-structure, and seemed to emphasize 'political' skills of co-operation, competition and leadership in their social relations. Girls seem to put more emphasis on intimacy and exclusiveness in their friendships (Berndt, 1982).

The nature of children's groups changes again as adolescence is reached. Large same-sex 'cliques' or 'gangs' become common in early adolescence, changing as heterosexual relationships become more important in later ado-lescence. A study of Australian adolescents aged 13–21 years (Dunphy, 1963) presents a picture of this process. Natural observations were supplemented by questionnaires, diaries and interviews in this study. At the younger end of this age range many teenagers went around in cliques comprising some three to nine individuals of the same sex. They would interact little outside

their own clique. A few years later, however, adolescents would be partici-
pating in larger groups or 'crowds', made up of several interacting cliques.
These would still be same-sex groups, but the more mature or higher-status
members of the crowds would start to initiate contacts with members of the
opposite sex. Gradually, other members of the crowd would follow their
lead. This led to a stage where heterosexual crowds were made up of male
and female cliques in loose association. Finally, young people associated
most in heterosexual couples, going on dates, and loosely associated with
other couples, prior to engagement and marriage.

◀Friendship▶▶▶

Friendship is related to social participation, but it is not the same thing.
While a solitary child obviously does not have friends, a child who interacts
a lot with others may or may not have friends. Usually we take friendship to
mean some close association between two particular people, as indicated by
their association together or their psychological attachment and trust. It is
quite possible to interact a lot with others generally, but not have any close
friends.

The measurement of friendship: sociometry

How can we record children's actual friendships? This has been done in
three main ways: by direct observation of behaviour; by asking another
person, such as a teacher or parent; or by asking the child.

If you watch a class of children, you can record which children are interacting together. If you do this at regular intervals, it is possible to build up a
picture of the social structure in the class. For example, in a study of two
classes in a nursery school, Clark, Wyon and Richards (1969) observed a
child for 10 seconds to see whom he was playing with, then they observed
another child, and so on through the class; this was continued over a 5-week
period. From this data the authors constructed a 'sociogram' for each class,
as shown in figure 4.2. Each symbol represents a child; the number of lines
joining two children represents the percentage of observations on which they
were seen playing together. The concentric circles show the number of play
partners a child has: if many, that child's symbol is towards the middle, if
none, at the periphery. This enables us to see at a glance that in class A, for
example, there is one very popular girl who links two large subgroups; one
boy and one girl have no clear partners. In class B there are several subgroups, and, unlike class A, there is almost complete segregation by sex; two
boys have no clear partners. This is a very neat way of illustrating social
structure, provided the class is not very large.

Observation gives a valid measure of who associates with whom, but this
may not be quite the same thing as friendship. An alternative is to ask a
teacher, for example, 'who are John's best friends in the class?', or to ask John
himself, 'who are your best friends?' These nomination methods also give
data that can be plotted on a sociogram. If John chooses Richard as a 'best

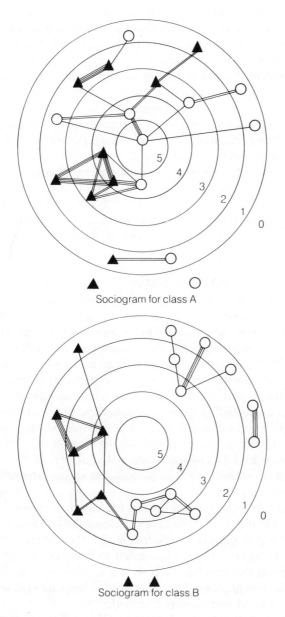

Sociogram for class A

Sociogram for class B

Figure 4.2 Sociograms of association networks in two classes of preschool children; circles represent girls, triangles boys (from Clark et al., 1969).

friend', but Richard does not choose John, this can be indicated by an arrow from John to Richard; if the choice is reciprocated, the arrow would point both ways on the sociogram.

A common nomination method is to ask each child to name their three best friends. Other methods are to ask children to rate each child for liking (e.g. asking them to sort names into three pairs of 'like', 'neutral' and 'don't like'), or to ask them which they prefer of all possible pairs of children. For younger children who cannot read well, photographs of classmates can be used (see Hymel, 1983, for a review).

For older children – approaching or in adolescence – Robert Cairns has developed a method for examining the more complex cliques or groups which characterize this period. Besides asking for friendship nominations, Cairns and his colleagues get information on social groups and networks by asking questions like 'are there people who hang around together a lot at school? Who are they?' By combining information from different informants, it is possible to develop a 'social-cognitive map' of the friendship structure in these adolescent groups. Besides looking at the position of an individual in the group (as in traditional sociometry, e.g. figure 4.2), it is then also possible to look at the centrality of a group or clique in the wider peer group network of the school (Cairns, Leung, Buchanan and Cairns, 1995).

The concept of sociometric status

Some investigators have also asked children to say whom they do not like. There may be ethical objections to this; for example, such questions actually might bring about increased negative behaviour to unliked peers. So far such effects have not been found (Hayvren and Hymel, 1984). Researchers who have obtained both positive and negative nominations have not constructed sociograms (which would then look very complicated), but have rather categorized children into 'sociometric status types': as 'popular', 'controversial', 'rejected', 'neglected' or 'average', according to whether they are high or low on positive and on negative nominations (see box 4.1, and especially box figure 4.1.1).

In a study of 8- and 11-year-olds over a 4-year period, Coie and Dodge (1983) looked at the stability of these sociometric status categories on a year-to-year basis. Was a child still in the same category after a 4-year interval? They found that this stability was highest for 'rejected' children; 30 per cent of those rejected at the start of the investigation were still rejected four years later, and another 30 per cent were 'neglected'. By contrast, those merely 'neglected' at the start of the study tended to become 'average'. Thus, the researchers argued that children who were positively rejected in the middle school years were perhaps much more in need of help than those who simply kept a low profile and were ignored or neglected.

Other studies have found that 'rejected' children differ in their behaviour in what seem to be maladaptive ways. For example, Ladd (1983) observed 8- and 9-year-olds in playground breaks. Rejected children, compared with average or popular children, spent less time in co-operative play and social conversation, and more time in arguing and fighting; they tended to play in smaller groups, and with younger or with less popular companions. In another study, Dodge et al. (1983) looked at how 5-year-olds attempted to get into ongoing play between two other peers. They suggested that whereas popular children first waited and watched, then gradually got themselves incorporated by making group-orientated statements, and neglected children tended to stay at the waiting and watching stage, rejected children tended to escalate to disruptive actions such as interrupting the play.

A social skills model

These sorts of findings can be taken to suggest that rejected children are lacking in some social skills. This is a widely held view, and has been developed by Dodge et al. (1986).

Dodge and his colleagues suggest that the social skills of peer interaction can be envisaged as an exchange model (see figure 4.3). Suppose child A is interacting with child B. According to this model she has to (1) encode the incoming information to perceive what child B is doing, (2) interpret this information, (3) search for appropriate responses, (4) evaluate these responses and select the best, and (5) enact that response. For example, suppose child B is running forward with arms raised, shouting and smiling. Child A needs to perceive all these actions, interpret their meaning (is this friendly or aggressive?), search for appropriate responses (run away? ignore? play fight?), select what seems best, and then do it effectively. Child B, of course, will be engaged in a similar process with respect to child A.

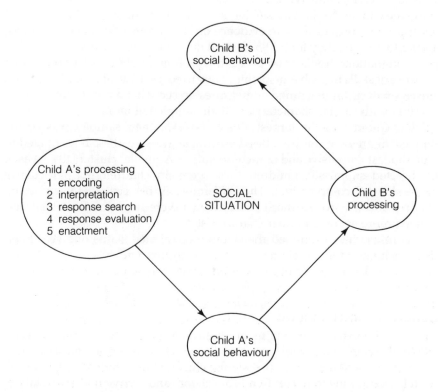

Figure 4.3 A model of social skills and social exchange in peer interaction (adapted from Dodge et al., 1986).

This model may be helpful in making the term 'social skills' more explicit. If a child has a social skills deficit, where is this located? Does an over-aggressive child misinterpret others' behaviour (stage 2), or just too readily select aggressive responses (stage 4), for example? There is some evidence for both of these; Crick and Dodge (1994) summarize evidence relating to this model, together with some reformulation of its details.

However, not all behaviour labelled as maladjusted may be due to lack of social skills. As we discuss later, some aggressive children may be quite skilled at manipulating others. And some rejected children may be simply reacting to exclusion by the popular cliques and would not necessarily be rejected or lacking in social skills in other situations outside the classroom.

Types of rejected children

Why do some children become rejected by peers? And is there one common reason? In fact, the situation appears quite complicated (Asher and Coie, 1990). There appear to be several subtypes of rejected children, and different reasons for peer rejection. In particular, there appears to be a major distinction between some children who are rejected because they are aggressive, and others who are rejected because they are submissive – a distinction between externalizing and internalizing problems in behaviour (Asher, Parkhurst, Hymel and Williams, 1990).

A study in the Netherlands (Cillessen, van IJzendoorn, van Lieshout and Hartup, 1992) provided more evidence on this. From a sample of 784 boys, aged 5 to 7 years, they found 98 rejected children. The researchers gathered peer nominations, teacher and peer ratings, observations of behaviour, and a measure of skills in problem-solving. They used a statistical procedure called cluster analysis on this range of measures, to see what natural groupings of children with similar characteristics their sample fell into.

They found that the largest cluster (48% of their sample) was of the rejected–aggressive children. Besides being aggressive, these boys tended to be dishonest, impulsive and non-co-operative. A smaller cluster (13%) was of the rejected–submissive children; these were shy children, not particularly aggressive (or co-operative). The remaining 39 per cent of their rejected children formed two further clusters which were not so well defined and seemed more average in their characteristics.

The researchers examined the stability of rejected status one year later; this was highest for the rejected–aggressive groups, with 58 per cent of these children still being rejected; it was only true for 34 per cent of the other children.

Loneliness in childhood

Do rejected or neglected status children feel lonely? Asher and Wheeler (1985) developed a Loneliness and Social Dissatisfaction questionnaire, which is a 24-item self-report scale for children. It includes 16 items such as 'It's hard for me to make friends at school', and 'I have nobody to talk to in class', as well as eight 'filler' items about hobbies and interests. This and subsequent work (Asher et al., 1990) found that rejected children do score significantly higher on self-reported loneliness; interestingly, neglected children (who lack friends but are not actively disliked) do not score particularly highly. However, of the subtypes of rejected children, it is the rejected–submissive who get the highest loneliness scores (Asher et al., 1990).

One factor in experiencing loneliness may be an awareness of who dislikes who. MacDonald and Cohen (1995) used traditional sociometric procedures with 429 pupils aged 7 to 12 years. In addition, they asked pupils to guess which other pupils would have said they liked, or disliked, them. They found that rejected children were least accurate at predicting who liked them, but did well at predicting who disliked them (conversely, popular children were less good at predicting who disliked them). This is an interesting set of findings; not least, it suggests that to say that rejected children 'lack social skills' is an over-simplification. Rather, they seem good at knowing who dislikes them – better than popular children, in fact! But, this very saliency of being disliked may, the researchers suggest, be a factor in experiencing loneliness. If they are correct, then rejected–submissive children would be particularly accurate at identifying children who disliked them, more than rejected–aggressive children; but subtypes of rejected children were not analysed in this study.

What characterizes friendships?

It seems as though peer rejection and loneliness are important factors in the lives of many children. So, what are such children missing out on? What actually characterizes friendship? It may seem an obvious question, but it deserves looking at in some detail. Only if we know what friendship involves, can we start seriously examining what a lack of friendships is likely to lead to.

A considerable body of research over the last 20 years has been summarized by Newcomb and Bagwell (1995), and by Hartup (1996). Newcomb and Bagwell conclude that relations between friends, compared with non-friends, exhibit four particular features: reciprocity and intimacy; more intense social activity; more frequent conflict resolution; and more effective task performance.

Let's look at a couple of the many studies which illustrate these characteristics. One is by Howes, Droege and Matheson (1994). It was carried out with pairs of 4-year-olds, who were videotaped in a room at a child-care centre. Altogether, 24 dyads were observed; 6 had been long-term friends, for about 3 years; 12 had been short-term friends, for about 6 months; and 6 had never been friends (based on observation, and nomination). The levels of communication and play between the dyads were recorded over a 20-minute session.

Two main findings emerged from the analysis. First, friends (whether long- or short-term) engaged in more complex levels of pretend play than did non-friends (for Howes' work on levels of pretend play, see chapter 6). Secondly, there were differences in the amount of high-level co-operative pretend play, and in the communications which served to extend such play; here, friends did more than non-friends, but in addition long-term friends did more than short-term friends. These differences were substantial, as shown in table 4.1, and statistically significant despite the small sample.

This finding illustrates two of the main characteristics of friendship; there is more intense social activity between friends, and this goes along with more intimacy and reciprocity, as in the co-operative forms of pretend play in this study.

As another example, let's look at a study of older children, by Azmitia and Montgomery (1993). This was carried out with 11-year-olds, in schools in California. Same-sex pairs of pupils were given scientific reasoning tasks (these were tasks of formal operational thinking, as is discussed in chapter 11). There were 18 pairs of friends (who had each nominated the other as a friend, so they were mutual friends); and 18 pairs of acquaintances (who had not nominated the other as a friend, but who did not dislike them either). The problem-solving efforts were recorded on videotape and audiotape.

The researchers found that friends achieved higher problem-solving accuracy, especially in the harder problems, than did the non-friends. This seemed to be related to greater transaction between them in evaluating possible solutions. Friends appeared more willing to elaborate and critique each other's reasoning; even if they disagreed, they could handle this constructively to take things further.

This study illustrates most of the characteristics of friendship. In particular, besides the more effective task performance, friends appeared better able to handle disagreements or conflict of view. More generally, as Newcomb and Bagwell (1995) found over many studies, friends may well have conflicts, but they differ from non-friends in that they are better able to resolve these conflicts. A conflict with a friend is more likely to be made up than a conflict with a non-friend.

Conceptions of friendship

How do children themselves conceive of friendship? In one research programme (Bigelow and La Gaipa, 1980), children aged 6-14 years were asked to write an essay in class about their expectations of best friends. Essays were obtained from 480 Scottish children and also from 480 Canadian children, and analysed for their content. Results were similar in Scotland and Canada.

Table 4.1 Differences in behaviour in dyads of differing friendship status, adapted from Howes, Droege and Matheson (1994)

	Long-term friends	Short-term friends	Never friends
Parallel play	3.2	4.1	11.5
Simple social play	24.7	24.2	13.0
Complex pretend	11.5	12.8	4.3
Co-operative pretend	2.0	0.7	0.0

At the earlier ages children mentioned sharing common activities, receiving help and living nearby; later, admiring and being accepted by the partner; and later still, such aspects as loyalty and commitment, genuineness and potential for intimacy. These last were found to be especially important in adolescence. Bigelow and La Gaipa have suggested a three-stage model for friendship expectations (table 4.2).

In similar research, Selman and Jaquette (1977) interviewed 225 persons aged from 4 to 32 years on their understanding and awareness of friendship relations. They documented five stages of understanding, also outlined in table 4.2, linked to stages in perspective-taking abilities (chapter 11). Although different in detail, there are considerable correspondences between the two schemes. There clearly seems to be a shift towards more psychologically complex and mutually reciprocal ideas of friendship during the middle school years, with intimacy and commitment becoming especially important later in adolescence (Berndt, 1982). Older children are obviously aware of one of the characteristics of friendship – reciprocity and intimacy.

Table 4.2 Two analyses of stages of understanding friendship

Bigelow and La Gaipa (1980)	Reward–cost stage Common activities, living nearby, similar expectations	Around 7–8 years
	Normative stage Shared values, rules and sanctions	Around 9–10 years
	Empathic stage Understanding, self-disclosure, shared interests	Around 11–12 years
Selman and Jaquette (1997)	Momentary physical playmate Playing together, being in proximity	Around 3–7 years
	One-way assistance A friend helps you, but no notion of reciprocation	Around 4–9 years
	Fairweather co-operation Reciprocity focused on specific incidents rather than the friendship itself; conflicts may sever the relationship	Around 6–12 years
	Intimate; mutual sharing Awareness of intimacy and mutuality in a relationship which continues despite minor setbacks	Around 9–15 years
	Autonomous interdependence Awareness that relationships grow and change; reliance on friends but acceptance of their need for other relationships	Around 12–adult

Quality of friendship

Bukowski, Hoza and Boivin (1994) used some of the suggested characteristics of friendship to develop a Friendship Qualities Scale. This is an instrument in which children can rate friends and peers on several subscales, as indicated in table 4.3. Bukowski et al. used this Scale with 10–12-year-olds. They found that the subscales of Companionship, Help, Security and Closeness were related – that is, someone rated high on one of these tended to be rated highly on the others. Reciprocated friends rated higher on these subscales than non-reciprocated friends; and in a longitudinal sample, friends who had remained friends after 6 months scored higher than those who had not stayed friends.

The remaining Conflict subscale related negatively to the others. Reciprocated friends scored lower on Conflict than non-reciprocated friends; however, stable friends did not differ on Conflict from non-stable friends. Note that the Conflict items here refer mainly to frequency of conflict. Items to do with resolving conflicts successfully appear in the Security subscale (table 4.3), again illustrating how conflict resolution is an important aspect of friendship, and one which predicts to stability of friendship more than does simple frequency of conflict.

The importance of friendship

We have seen that there are immediate benefits to having friends; you can avoid feelings of loneliness, engage in more intense and reciprocal social activities, and with their help, solve tasks more effectively. So, is having close friends an important developmental milestone? What other effects are there of having, or not having, friends? This is a difficult question to answer, since it is not something one can test experimentally. However, several sources of evidence support the general idea that friendship has a wider importance, both at the time and for later development (Hartup, 1996).

An interesting small-scale study at the preschool age range was carried out by Field (1984) in a US kindergarten. This class of 28 children had been together from the age of 6–12 months and half the children were now due to leave the kindergarten. Field noted in the 2-week period prior to leaving that these children showed increased rates of fussiness, negative affect, aggressive behaviour, physical contact and fantasy play – possibly signs of anticipation and attempted coping with the separation from peers and their

Table 4.3 Sample items from the Friendship Qualities Scale

COMPANIONSHIP	My friend and I spend all our free time together.
HELP	My friend helps me when I am having trouble with something.
SECURITY	If I have a problem at school, I can talk to my friend about it.
	If my friend and I have a fight or argument, we can say 'I'm sorry' and everything will be alright.
CLOSENESS	If my friend had to move away, I would miss him.
CONFLICT	My friend and I disagree about many things.

familiar environment. Also, this could be due to anxiety about attending a new school. However, in observing the children who stayed behind, Field found these children showed similarly increased agitated behaviour after the other children had left. This could have been, on a small scale, a 'grief' response to the friends they had lost.

This suggests that friendships are affectively important to a child, even at 3 or 4 years of age. Do they have other consequences? In a study of pre-adolescents, Mannarino (1980) identified those who had 'chums' – close, stable best friendships – and compared them with those who did not, on measures of altruism and self-concept. Pre-adolescents with chums had higher levels of altruism, and higher levels of self-concept, than those who lacked chums. This is further support for the importance of friendship, though being a correlational study, it does not prove that having a chum in itself caused the greater altruism or self-concept (rather than, for example, the other way round).

Is friendship in childhood important for later development? In one US study data were gathered on a large number of 8-year-olds in school, including IQ scores, school grades, attendance records, teachers' ratings and peer ratings. Eleven years later, when the subjects were nearly adult, the researchers checked mental health registers to see who had needed any psychiatric help during this period. Those who had were two-and-a-half times more likely to have had negative peer ratings at 8 years; indeed, the peer ratings were the best of all the earlier measures at predicting appearance in the mental health registers (Cowen et al., 1973).

A large-scale review of all available studies was undertaken by Parker and Asher (1987); similar findings were later obtained by Kupersmidt, Coie and Dodge (1990). Parker and Asher looked at three measures of peer relationships: peer acceptance/rejection (basically, number and quality of friendships); aggressiveness to peers; and shyness or withdrawal from peers. They examined the relationship of these to three main kinds of later outcome: dropping out of school early; being involved in juvenile and adult crime; and adult psychopathology (mental health ratings, or needing psychiatric help of any kind). Most, but not all, of the studies they reviewed were carried out in the USA (the study by Cowen et al. was one of these).

They found that the different studies were very consistent in linking low peer acceptance (or high peer rejection) with dropping out of school; and suggestive but not so consistent in linking it with juvenile/adult crime. Conversely, the studies were very consistent in linking aggressiveness at school with juvenile/adult crime; and suggestive but not so consistent in linking it with dropping out of school. The data on effects of shyness/withdrawal, and on predictors of adult psychopathology, were less consistent; while some studies found significant effects, others did not, and thus any links or effects remain unproven at present.

Most of the studies were 'follow-back' designs; that is, retrospective data on peer relations was sought for people who were currently dropping out of school, getting in trouble with the law or seeking psychiatric help. A smaller number were 'follow-up' designs – taking a large sample of schoolchildren,

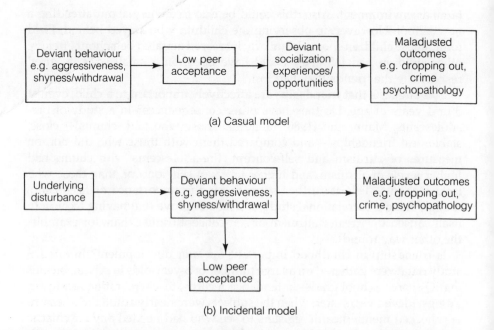

(a) Casual model

(b) Incidental model

Figure 4.4 Two models of the role of peer acceptance in leading to maladjusted outcomes (from Parker and Asher, 1987).

obtaining data on peer relations, and seeing what happens later. The latter, while more costly to organize, are likely to provide more valid data for establishing predictive links. However, whichever design is used, the data is correlational in nature. We cannot be certain that low peer acceptance, for example, is a causal predictor of later problems. Two somewhat different causal models, discussed by Parker and Asher, are shown in figure 4.4. In (a) the low peer acceptance has a direct causal role; in (b), it is an outcome of more enduring traits such as aggressiveness, or shyness, rather than a cause in itself. (In both models, the original reasons for the deviant behaviour are not spelt out; you might consider whether some of the factors discussed in chapter 3 would be relevant in making the models more complete.)

Most psychologists probably favour a version of model (a) over model (b), whatever the difficulties of proof are. Either way, many psychologists also believe that social skills training may be useful for those children who lack friends; this training is anyway usually directed to changing behaviours which are the correlates of peer rejection (such as high aggression, or high withdrawal).

Social skills training

Several attempts have been made by American psychologists to help improve social skills in neglected children and rejected children. In one study (Furman et al., 1979), 4- and 5-year-olds who seldom played with other children were identified by observation. Some were given special play sessions with a younger partner, to see if this might give them more confidence in social interaction. This did seem to help, and more so than play sessions with a same-age peer, or no intervention at all. However, this study only used levels of social interaction as the measure of adjustment, so it does not directly address the issue of friendship and rejection.

Other researchers, working with middle-school children, have used more direct means of encouraging social skills – modelling techniques, for example. A child might watch a film showing an initially withdrawn child engaged in a series of increasingly complex peer interactions. Watching such films has been shown to increase social interaction subsequently (O'Connor, 1972). A more instructional approach was used by Oden and Asher (1977). They coached 8- and 9-year-old children identified as socially isolated (neglected or rejected) on skills such as how to participate in groups, co-operate and communicate with peers; they did this in special play sessions with the target child and one other peer. These children improved in sociometric status more than those who had special play sessions without the coaching. This effect was present a year later at a follow-up assessment, and was also replicated by an independent study (Ladd, 1981). However, another study with 9-year-olds found that academic skill training was even more effective than social skill training (Coie and Krehbiel, 1984). Thus, the hypothesis that rejected children are lacking in social skills, while promising, may not be the whole story. Malik and Furman (1993) provide an overview of clinical interventions to help children's social skills in peer relationships.

◀Factors Affecting Popularity in Children▶▶▶

We have seen how children differ in popularity and have discussed the theory that less popular children have less adequate social skills. We have also seen, however, that this theory is partly but not wholly confirmed by the available evidence; we need to take account of other factors that may predict popularity.

One such factor is physical attractiveness. Children, like adults, differ in how physically attractive they are rated by persons who know them. In one study (Vaughn and Langlois, 1983) ratings of physical attractiveness were obtained for 59 preschool children. The correlation with sociometric preference using a paired-comparison method was 0.42 ($p < 0.01$); the correlation was higher for girls (0.66, $p < 0.01$) than for boys (0.22, n.s). Several other studies have found that ratings of physical attractiveness correlate with sociometric status (e.g. box 4.1). Around puberty, early physical maturation is also a variable affecting popularity and status (chapter 8).

Popularity may also be influenced by the composition of the peer group a child is in. Children tend to choose as friends, peers similar to themselves (Hartup, 1996). We have noted already how, through the middle-school years, children choose predominantly same-sex partners. Also children tend to choose friends of the same race or ethnic background as themselves, and children of similar intelligence or academic achievement. Thus, a child might tend to appear sociometrically 'neglected' or 'rejected' simply because he or she differs in such respects from most others in the class.

The factors affecting popularity may thus vary in different classes and different schools. That this was so was shown in a large-scale investigation by J. S. Coleman (1961), who looked at the factors influencing social status in teenagers in ten different schools in varying locations in the state of Chicago, USA. Coleman identified teenagers who were in the 'leading crowd' or high-status clique in different classes. He found that prowess in sporting activities was usually the major factor affecting popularity in boys, though in one school having a car was very important, especially for popularity with girls. For girls, being a leader in activities and having nice clothes were important. For both boys and girls popularity with the opposite sex seemed an important component of being in the 'leading crowd'. Coleman argued that beauty was more important than brains for popularity in most high schools, and voiced concern that 'the adolescent subcultures in these schools exert a rather strong deterrent to academic achievement'. Given the individually competitive nature of academic achievement in the conventional school system, Coleman argued, it was difficult for a teenager to get social status and respect by intellectual achievement; whereas sporting or athletic achievement was displayed publicly and for the benefit of the whole class or school.

Critics have accused Coleman of exaggerating his case (Rutter et al., 1976). For example, even though athletic students were more popular than academic ones, the most popular of all were students who were both good scholars and good athletes. However, the issue was taken further by David Hargreaves (1967) in a study of social relations in a British secondary modern school for boys. This school had five streams in the fourth-year classes, of which Hargreaves observed all but the bottom, remedial stream. The A stream contained boys who would take academic exams. They had largely positive views of the teachers, and popularity in this class correlated positively with academic achievement. In the lower streams, however, views of teachers and also of A stream 'swots' became increasingly negative. Popularity was not correlated with academic success, and the leaders of these cliques had anti-school values and were prone to delinquent behaviour. Hargreaves concluded that there were 'two subcultures' in the school, with radically different values. He thought the situation typical of many secondary schools among children approaching school-leaving age, and one exacerbated by streaming for academic ability.

◄Aggression in Children►►

We have mentioned children's aggressive behaviour several times, and its links to peer rejection. In this section, we look at the development of aggressive behaviour, and its causes.

As with Parten's study of social participation, some of the early studies on aggressive behaviour in children were based on observational studies in nurseries and child-care centres. For example, Jersild and Markey (1935) observed conflicts in 54 children at three nursery schools. Many kinds of conflict behaviour were defined: for example, *snatches* as 'takes or grabs toys or objects held, used, or occupied by another child; uses, tugs at, or pushes material away with hands or feet; all contacts with material which, if completed, would deprive the other child of the use and possession of material'; and *unfavourable remarks about persons* as comments like 'you're no good at it'; 'you don't do it right'; 'I don't like you'. Jersild and Markey recorded who was the aggressor and who the victim, what the outcome of the struggle was, and the role of the teacher. They found some decline in conflicts with age, and overall boys took part in more conflicts than girls. A follow-up was made of 24 children, after about 9 months. Conflicts had become more verbal, but individual differences between children in types and frequencies of conflict tended to be maintained. Very similar results were found in an observational study by Cummings et al. (1989); they reported that aggressive boys tended to stay aggressive between 2 and 5 years of age, even though the overall level of physical aggression declined over this period.

In another early study, Appel (1942) made observations in 14 different nursery schools. She delineated 15 kinds of adult responses to children's aggression. Five are 'ending techniques': diverting; separating or removing; restraining; arbitrary decision making; enforcing a rule. Ten are 'teaching techniques': explaining property rights; urging self-defence; suggesting a solution; suggesting the child find a solution; interpreting; encouraging friendly acts; making light of troubles or hurts; requiring good manners; disapproval; retaliation. An evaluation of the effectiveness of these different techniques was made, by deciding whether the conflict continued or ended after the adult intervention. Some techniques were much more effective than others at ending the immediate conflict. Least effective was suggesting to the children that they find a solution themselves. Appel concluded that 'teachers should not intervene too readily in children's conflicts. Children will teach each other a great deal. Too much interference prevents self-reliance.'

Through the 1950s and early 1960s direct observation was neglected, and more constrained investigations in laboratories, often experimental in nature, were seen as the preferred method (see p. 6). Aggression was assessed by means of observing children punching inflatable dolls, and pressing buttons to supposedly deliver punishment to another child. These studies have subsequently been criticized as lacking ecological validity (p. 15). By the late 1960s, direct observation had started to make a comeback. For example, Blurton Jones (1967) observed the social behaviour of children in an English nursery school. Most aggressive behaviour occurred in the context of property fights. Blurton Jones drew a clear distinction between aggressive behaviour, evidenced by beating or hitting at another with a frown or angry face, and rough-and-tumble play, where children chased and tackled each other, often smiling or laughing (see also chapter 6). These two kinds of behaviour can be confused because of their superficial similarity.

Types and typologies of aggressive behaviour

As observations of aggressive behaviour accumulated, researchers started distinguishing the main categories. Some long-standing distinctions have been between verbal and non-verbal aggression (based on the presence or absence of verbal threats or insults); between instrumental and hostile aggression (based on whether the distress or harm is inferred to be the primary intent of the act); and between individual and group aggression (depending on whether more than one child attacks another).

The distinction based on intent was elaborated by Manning, Heron and Marshall (1978). They proposed a three-way classification. They defined 'specific hostility' as that which occurs in a specific situation which annoys or frustrates the aggressor: defending one's own rights, or keeping a toy, for example. The victim is almost incidental to the situation. In contrast, 'harassment' is more unprovoked, and is directed at a person. The aggressor gains nothing tangible from the act; the reward appears to be the victim's reaction. Finally, 'games hostility' is seen as rough, intimidating or restrictive activities which occur in a rough-and-tumble or fantasy game; for example, very rough variants of rough-and-tumble, or bullying, intimidating or imprisoning against the victim's will in a fantasy game.

The distinction between verbal and non-verbal aggression has been elaborated by Bjorkqvist and colleagues, based primarily on data from nominations and ratings of peers in a study in Finland (Bjorkqvist, Lagerspetz and Kaukainen, 1992); they add a third category of indirect aggression, which is aggression not aimed directly at someone but via a third party. Thus, examples of 'physical aggression' would be: hits, kicks, pushes; of 'direct verbal aggression': insults, calls the other names; and of 'indirect aggression': tells bad or false stories, becomes friends with another as revenge. Physical aggression falls off rapidly in adolescence, but verbal and indirect aggression increase, as can be seen from table 4.4. As is also clear from table 4.4, girls may show less physical aggression, but there is not much difference in verbal aggression, and girls appear to show more indirect aggression. This sex difference has been confirmed by subsequent studies, including Crick and

Table 4.4 Peer-estimated aggression of different types, at different ages, for boys (B) and girls (G); adapted from Bjorkqvist et al., 1992

		8 yrs	11 yrs	15 yrs	18 yrs
Physical aggression	B	0.61	0.82	0.50	0.15
e.g. kicking	G	0.15	0.22	0.07	0.07
Verbal aggression	B	0.44	0.96	0.95	0.75
e.g. verbal abuse	G	0.15	1.09	0.98	0.90
Indirect aggression	B	0.32	0.83	0.81	0.60
e.g. gossip	G	0.40	1.30	1.14	1.06

Grotpeter (1995) in the USA, who use the term 'relational aggression' for indirect aggression.

Causes of high aggression

For most children, while a certain amount of aggressive and assertive behaviour is normal, it is kept within reasonable bounds such that they are not disruptive of peer group activities and hence rejected by peers. However, some children show high levels of aggression, often of a hostile or harassing nature, which can be quite stable over time and for which some adult intervention seems justified. If not dealt with at the time, such children who show persistent high aggressiveness through the school years are at greatly increased risk for later delinquency, antisocial and violent behaviour (Farrington, 1990).

Genetic factors have been implicated in high aggressiveness. Mason and Frick (1994) summarized 12 twin studies and 3 adoption studies (see also chapter 2); they found there was a moderate degree of heritability for measures of antisocial behaviour, especially severe (violent or criminal) behaviour. Of course, it is unlikely that a propensity for specific criminal acts is inherited; what may be inherited are certain temperamental characteristics (see p. 73). In a longitudinal study in New Zealand, Caspi et al. (1995) assessed temperament on a sample of 800 children at ages 3, 5, 7 and 9 years; and behaviour problems at 9, 11, 13 and 15 years. They found that early 'lack of control' (emotional lability, restlessness, short attention span, and negativism) correlated with later externalizing problems (such as aggressiveness).

There is considerable evidence that home circumstances can be important influences leading to aggressive and later antisocial behaviour. In a review, Patterson, DeBaryshe and Ramsey (1989) suggest that certain key aspects of parenting are involved. They argue that children who experience irritable and ineffective discipline at home, and poor parental monitoring of their activities, together with a lack of parental warmth, are particularly likely to become aggressive in peer groups and at school. Such children are experienc-

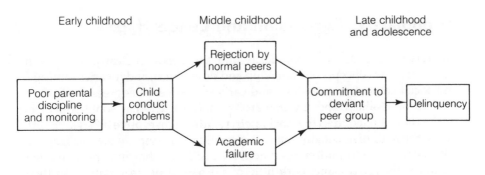

Figure 4.5 A developmental progression for anti-social behaviour (from Patterson et al., 1989).

ing aggressive means of solving disputes at home, and are not being given clear and effective guidance to do otherwise. Antisocial behaviour at school is likely to be linked to academic failure and peer rejection, according to this view (cf. box table 4.1.1); and in adolescence, especially if parental monitoring is lax, these young people are likely to be involved in deviant and delinquent peer groups. This hypothesis is shown in figure 4.5. (You may find it interesting to compare figure 4.5 with figure 3.1 and figure 4.4; all relate to different linked aspects of parenting and peer relations. Do you feel they can be linked together, or are some aspects in disagreement?)

Patterson's approach suggests that the social skills of parenting are very important in early prevention of antisocial behaviour; and his interventions focus on helping parents improve their child-management skills, for example via manuals and videotaped materials (cf. chapter 3).

Another component of this model is the importance of the deviant peer group in adolescence. Although, in early and middle childhood, aggressive behaviour leads often to peer rejection, the picture becomes more complex in adolescence. Studies by Cairns on social networks of US adolescents confirm that aggressive pupils tend to associate with other aggressive pupils (Cairns et al., 1988). Dishion et al. (1995) also found that, in 13–14-year-olds, highly antisocial boys had more antisocial friends; these friendships were more coercive and of shorter duration than those between less antisocial pupils, but were still seen as satisfying by those involved. It seems that at this age, an aggressive child may not necessarily be rejected but may congregate with others of a similar antisocial tendency in ways which they can find rewarding. A longitudinal study of 13–14-year-olds, by Berndt and Keefe (1995), found that pupils with disruptive friends tended to become more disruptive themselves over a half-year period. Although pupils with high-quality friendships (intimate, reciprocal) were generally less likely to be disruptive, those whose friends were both of high quality *and* disruptive were particularly at risk of becoming more disruptive themselves. These findings do seem to support that aspect of Patterson's model which suggests that friendship with antisocial peers can help maintain antisocial behaviour.

◄Popularity, Aggression and Leadership►►►

The relationship between popularity and aggression is clearly complex. It ties in with the concepts of leadership and dominance; and it varies with age, and social context. In preschool and early school years, aggressive children tend to be disliked and unpopular. We saw earlier that some American studies have linked 'rejected' sociometric status to disruptive behaviour with peers. Such studies usually make it clear that it is unprovoked aggression which causes such children to be actively disliked – they may push another child, or disrupt a game, with little or no reason or provocation. In their research Manning et al. (1978) found that specific hostility seemed to be characteristic of well-adjusted children (perhaps equivalent to 'popular' children in box figure 4.1.1), whereas the other forms of aggression were more characteristic of children who had poor peer relationships (perhaps similar to 'rejected' children in box figure 4.1.1).

Some children, however, are quite aggressive but not clearly disliked. These are the 'controversial' children in box figure 4.1.1. According to American researchers, such children are highly socially skilful and highly aggressive (box 4.1). Peers describe them as good leaders, but also as starting fights – a pattern of behaviour which appeals to some peers but not to others. In other words, some children may use aggressive behaviour as a means of acquiring status in the peer group.

Some British studies confirm some aspects of this picture. One intensive study of playground behaviour in an Oxford first school and a middle school was made by Sluckin (1981). In the first school he describes how a boy called 'Neill' was known by his peers as the 'boss' of the playground. Neill was often observed in conflicts, although usually these were not overt fights (Neill was not particularly strong physically) but verbal conflicts by which Neill sought to enhance his prestige and manipulate social situations. Neill disliked losing, and would try to redefine or reinterpret situations so that it appeared he had won. For example, in a race with Ginny, where they finished at the same time, Neill cried out 'yes yes' (I'm the winner). Ginny called out 'draw', to which Neill replied 'no, it wasn't, you're just trying to make trouble'. In another example, playing football, Neill says 'I'm in goal, bagsee'. Nick replies 'no, I'm in goal'. Neill retorts 'no, John's in goal' and John goes in the goal. Here (perhaps avoiding a fight) Neill has kept the initiative and given the impression of being 'in charge' even though he did not get his own way entirely. Neill had a high dominance status in the playground, and was clearly a leader of sorts, but he does not seem to have been especially popular. His leadership was often disruptive, since he always insisted on winning games.

Another example comes from Hargreaves' (1967) work, discussed earlier. In the delinquent clique of the lower streams a boy called 'Clint' was the best fighter and was described as the 'cock of the school'. Although an intelligent boy, he had rebelled against the academic values of the school and become the dominant member of the delinquent subgroup. He had done so by his reputation as a fighter. As his peers reported, 'he beat up a prefect last year . . . Clint was hurt an' all, but he won'. His reputation was maintained because no-one challenged him: 'Clint must be the best 'cos Don won't have him a scrap. Clint's the best fighter. Then Don comes next. They've never had a fight, but Clint's the best fighter 'cos Don won't have him.' Also, Clint's confidence was displayed publicly: 'People are afraid of you if you go swaggering around the playground threatening everybody.' However, although the leader of this clique, Clint was apparently too bigheaded and indiscriminately aggressive to be really popular: 'Everyone knows Clint 'cos he's cock, but he's not popular, 'cos no one likes him, you know what I mean? I don't see why he should go round bullying people like he does just 'cos you can fight them. Taking money off them and all that. He's bigheaded.' In fact, on a sociometric test of friendship, Clint received six choices, but Don, the second-ranking 'cock', received 11. Don was more popular because he did not abuse his power: 'Don's smashing to get on with. You've no need to be frightened of him 'cos he won't touch you.' Whereas Clint would seem to be 'controversial' by the typology of box figure 4.1.1, Don would be 'popular'. Both are high on dominance status.

Dominance

The quotes from the playground observations of Sluckin and Hargreaves suggest that school children can rank others for 'dominance' or 'fighting strength' in a consistent way. Several psychologists have confirmed that this can be done reliably from about 4 or 5 years of age onwards (Sluckin and Smith, 1977). They have used the concept of a 'dominance hierarchy' in children's groups, just as it has been used in the study of animal social groups. Winning fights is one criterion of dominance, but more generally it is taken as getting one's own way or influencing others. Thus, the concept is close to that of 'leadership'.

While some of this research has involved asking children for their rankings of peers, other researchers have used direct observation of which individuals win conflicts. Strayer and Strayer (1976), observing children in a Canadian preschool, separated out three kinds of conflict behaviours: 'threat-gesture', 'physical attack' and 'objection/position struggles'. They then examined the usefulness of a dominance hierarchy for each of these three kinds of behaviour, separately, whenever there was a clear winner or loser. Strayer and Strayer looked at the linearity of the hierarchies (basically, how many reversals of expected position there were) to assess how descriptively useful the concept of a hierarchy was in each case. The values were very high, though slightly lower for 'object/position struggles' than for the other two behaviours.

Savin-Williams made studies of dominance formation in groups of American teenagers (aged 10–16 years), mostly previously unacquainted, who came together in 5-week summer camps. In one report (Savin-Williams, 1976) he studied intensively one cabin group of six boys aged 12 and 13. It took about 3 days for a stable, ordered hierarchy to emerge; it then remained very consistent throughout the duration of the camp. Observational measures of dominance correlated highly ($r = 0.90$) with a sociometric measure from the children themselves. The most frequently observed dominance behaviours were verbal ridicule (seen 235 times), giving a verbal command which was obeyed (seen 190 times) and ignoring or refusing to comply with another's command (seen 158 times). The most dominant boy also was usually the leader in hiking and athletics, and was well liked. However, the least dominant boy, quiet, serious, but friendly, was also popular.

Another study (Savin-Williams, 1980) was of four groups of five girls (aged 12–14) at summer camp. Again dominance hierarchies formed, although they did not seem as clear-cut as in boys' groups, perhaps because girls more often formed smaller groups (pairs or threesomes). Verbal ridicule was again the most frequently observed indicator of dominance. The position in the dominance heirarchy correlated significantly with ratings of leadership. However, Savin-Williams distinguished between 'maternal leaders' who were perceived by peers as a source of security and support, and 'antagonists' who imposed themselves on others.

Summary

A number of studies seem to present converging findings. Children are often popular, and some are leaders, because they are socially skilled and mature and, although they stand up for themselves, are not gratuitously aggressive. Another way of being a leader, or achieving high dominance status, is to be a good fighter. This is a more 'controversial' way, which may not bring true popularity with all one's peers. High aggression without the social skill to go with it, however, leads to unpopularity and 'rejection'. As children move into adolescence, social networks enlarge; aggressive, dominant children will tend to become leaders of gangs of antisocial peers. Such children will have status and some popularity in their own networks; even if their friendships are in some respects less satisfying, it is no longer adequate to consider them as rejected, lacking friends or lacking social skills in a straightforward way.

◀ Bullying in Schools ▶ ▶

Bullying or harassment emerged as one of the three types of aggressive behaviour defined by Manning et al. (1978). Bullying can be carried out by one child, or a group. It is usually a repeated action against a particular victim. Also, the child(ren) doing the bullying is generally thought of as being stronger, or perceived as stronger; at least, the victim does not feel him/herself to be in a position to retaliate effectively. While some bullying takes the form of hitting, pushing and taking money, it can also involve teasing, telling stories and social exclusion.

Bullying and victimization in schools has become a topic of considerable public concern in many countries. Research in western Europe suggests that bullying is quite pervasive in schools, and probably to a greater extent than most teachers and parents realize, since many victims keep quiet about it. It is difficult to observe bullying, for obvious reasons. It is often assessed by means of an anonymous questionnaire, which children or young people can fill in confidentially (Smith, 1991).

The occurrence of bully/victim problems

A study of pupils in the South Yorkshire area of England found that some 27 per cent of primary school pupils reported being bullied 'sometimes', and some 10 per cent in secondary schools (Whitney and Smith, 1993). These and other studies suggest that bully/victim problems in English schools are considerable, and similar figures have been reported from Dublin in Eire (O'Moore, 1989), in Italy (Genta et al., 1996), Australia (Rigby, 1996) and other countries. The incidence seems to be somewhat less in Scandinavian countries such as Norway (see box 4.2), but still considerable enough to justify remedial action.

Most of the children or young people who report being bullied say that it takes the form of teasing; but about a third report other forms such as hitting or kicking, or (more occasionally) extortion of money. These latter may seem the more serious forms, but some 'teasing', especially that related to some disability, or which takes the form of racial or sexual harassment, can be very hurtful to the victim.

It is a fairly consistent finding that boys report, and are reported as, bullying more than girls; whereas boys and girls report being bullied about equally. Girls' bullying more usually takes the form of behaviours such as social exclusion, or spreading nasty rumours, rather than the physical behaviours used more by boys. Victims are more likely to report being alone at break time, and to feel less well liked at school; having some good friends can be a strong protective factor against being bullied. Only a minority of victims report that they have talked to a teacher or anyone at home about it, or that a teacher or parent has talked to them about it (Whitney and Smith, 1993).

The more serious forms of bullying, at least, can have very serious consequences. For children being bullied, their lives are made miserable often for some considerable period of time. Kochenderfer and Ladd (1996) found that in 5–6-year-olds, continued victimization led to loneliness and school avoidance. Already probably lacking close friends at school, victims of bullying are likely to lose confidence and self-esteem even further. Boulton and Smith (1994) found that in middle school, victims scored significantly lower on athletic competence, social acceptance and global self-worth, on Harter's self-esteem scale (see p. 165). Research by Gilmartin (1987), using retrospective data, suggests that these children and young people are at increased risk for relationship difficulties later in life, especially intimate heterosexual relationships.

Such long-term effects can be brought out by in-depth case-study interviews. The following extract, from a woman aged 28 who experienced being bullied throughout much of her school career, and was now engaged to be married, illustrates such long-term effects:

Do you feel that it's left a residue with you . . . what do you feel the effects are? . . .

I'm quite insecure, even now . . . I won't believe that people like me . . . and also I'm frightened of children . . . and this is a problem. He [fiance] would like a family. I would not and I don't want a family because I'm frightened of children and suppose they don't like me? . . . those are things that have stayed with me. It's a very unreasonable fear but it is there and it's very real.

Those who bully others are learning that power-assertive and sometimes violent behaviour can be used to get their own way. We saw earlier how children who are aggressive at school are more likely to be involved in criminal activity later. A follow-up by Olweus (1991) of Norwegian secondary-school pupils up to age 24, found that former school bullies were nearly four times more likely than non-bullies to have had three or more court convictions.

Intervention strategies

A lot can be done to reduce bully/victim problems in schools. The most extensive intervention has been carried out in Norway, and is described in box 4.2. In the UK, a large intervention study was carried out in Sheffield, in 16 primary and 7 secondary schools (Smith and Sharp, 1994). Results were generally encouraging; rates of bullying fell in most schools, quite sharply in primary schools; and in secondary schools there was an increase in willingness to seek help from teachers. The main intervention was the development of a school anti-bullying policy, involving consultation between teachers, pupils, parents and other school personnel. This could be backed up by curriculum work, playground improvements, assertiveness training for victims, and peer support services such as peer counselling (Cowie and Sharp, 1996). A pack, 'Don't Suffer in Silence', was circulated to many schools as a result of this intervention. Other countries, notably the USA, Canada, Australia and Japan, are developing programmes about bullying in school.

◄Further Reading►►►

For sibling relationships see J. Dunn 1984: *Sisters and Brothers*, Glasgow: Fontana/Open Books; and more generally, J. Dunn 1993: *Young Children's Close Relationships: Beyond Attachment*, Newbury Park and London: Sage.

For a collection of work on children's friendships, see W. M. Bukowski, A. F. Newcomb and W. W. Hartup (eds) 1996: *The Company They Keep: Friendship in Childhood and Adolescence*, Cambridge and New York: Cambridge University Press.

S. Asher and J. D. Coie (eds) (1990): *Peer Rejection in Childhood*, Cambridge: Cambridge University Press, discuss the evidence on peer rejection, loneliness and consequences of lacking friends. A classic ethnographic account of the social life of a school playground is in A. Sluckin 1981: *Growing Up in the Playground*, London: Routledge & Kegan Paul.

R. B. and B. D. Cairns 1994: *Lifelines and Risks: Pathways of Youth in Our Time*, New York and London: Harvester Wheatsheaf, provide a fascinating longitudinal account of changes in friendship networks and developmental pathways of 695 American children through adolescence. D. Pepler and K. Rubin (eds) 1991: *The Development and Treatment of Childhood Aggression*, Hillsdale, NJ: Erlbaum, covers a wide range of topics.

D. Olweus 1993: *Bullying in School: What We Know and What We Can Do*, Oxford: Blackwell Publishers, describes the Norwegian intervention campaign; P. K. Smith and S. Sharp (eds) 1994: *School Bullying: Insights and Perspectives*, London: Routledge, describes the English intervention. Both, together with K. Rigby 1996: *Bullying in Schools and What to Do About It*, Melbourne: ACER, cover a lot of general material on school bullying.

◀**Discussion Points**▶▶▶

1   How special are sibling relationships compared with peer relationships?
2   Are friendships important for children? How can we find out?
3   Why are some children popular, and others not?
4   Why are some children more aggressive than others?
5   What would be the best ways of tackling bullying in schools?

Box 4.1
Dimensions and types of social status:
a cross-age perspective

Two studies were carried out in in this investigation of the types of social status in children's
groups, and the kinds of behaviours which correlated with them.

In the first study approximately 100 children at
each of three age levels (8,11 and 14 years) were
interviewed at two schools in North Carolina,
USA. Each child was seen individually, and asked to
name the three classmates whom he or she liked
most, and the three classmates whom he or she
liked least. Then, he or she was asked to name the
three children who best fitted each of 24 behavioural descriptions, such as 'disrupts the group' or

'attractive physically'. The interview was repeated
12 weeks later to check that the data were reliable.

The scores used were the total nominations
each child received for each of the 26 questions
(liked most, liked least, and 24 behavioural descriptions). The correlations between the liked most
and liked least scores, and some of the behavioural
descriptions, are shown in box table 4.1.1. (The
results were similar when each age group was
treated separately.) The interesting thing about
these results is that different behavioural descriptions correlate significantly with the 'liked most'
and 'liked least' ratings. The two measures are not

Box Table 4.1.1   Correlations between nominations for
'most-liked' and 'least-liked' and behavioural descriptions for
311 children aged 8 to 14

	Liked most	Liked least
Supports peers	−0.63*	−0.24*
Leads peers	−0.51*	−0.08*
Co-operates with peers	−0.51*	−0.31*
Attractive physically	−0.57*	−0.25*
Remains calm	−0.43*	−0.28*
Defends self in arguments	−0.37*	−0.03
Acts shy	−0.12	−0.05
Gets rejected by peers	−0.28*	−0.30*
Acts snobbish	−0.04	−0.66*
Starts fights	−0.02	−0.70*
Gets into trouble with teacher	−0.03	−0.71*
Disrupts the group	−0.07	−0.78*

*$p < 0.001$

simply opposites of each other. 'Liked most' children tend to be supportive, co-operative leaders and attractive physically; 'liked least' children tend to be disruptive, aggressive and snobbish.

If 'liked most' is not just the opposite of 'liked least', the researchers argued that it made sense to think of them as independent measures (in fact the correlation between them was 4.21, which is quite a small value). In that case, there are four possible status outcomes shown in box figure 4.1.1 and mentioned in the text above (see p. 118), with a fifth if 'average' children are included.

In the second study the differences between these five status groups were examined more closely. More children of the same ages were interviewed at the same schools over the next 2 years. They were asked to nominate the three peers whom they liked most, liked least and who best fitted the descriptions 'co-operates', 'disrupts', 'shy', 'fights', 'seeks help' and 'leader'. Out of a total of 848 children, 486 were selected who clearly fitted one of the five social status groups. It was then possible to calculate the average 'behavioural profile' for children of each social status in terms of the six behavioural descriptions obtained from peers. Box table 4.1.2 shows the results. Children who lead in a co-operative way are 'popular'. Children who lead but fight and are disruptive are 'controversial', liked by some but disliked by others. Disruptive children who lack any co-operative or leadership skills are 'rejected'. Children who lack co-operative or leadership skills and are not aggressive either are 'neglected'. The pattern of results was similar across the three ages, for both sexes, and for different ethnic groups.

The strengths of this study are the large pool of participants and the attempt to make important distinctions in types of sociometric status. The authors speculate, for example, that 'controversial' children, high on both leadership and aggression, may become leaders of delinquent peer groups in adolescence. A weakness is that no direct observational measures were taken; we do not know that 'rejected' children really fight a lot, for example,

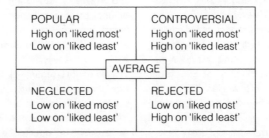

Box Figure 4.1.1   Five types of sociometric status (based on material in J. D. Coie, K. A. Dodge and H. Coppotelli 1982: *Development Psychology*, 18).

Box Table 4.1.2   Behavioural profiles associated with five types of sociometric status in 486 children

	Leads peers	Co-operates	Acts shy	Seeks help	Fights	Disrupts group
Popular	HIGH	HIGH		Low	Low	Low
Controversial	HIGH		Low	High	HIGH	HIGH
Rejected	Low	LOW		HIGH	HIGH	HIGH
Neglected	Low	Low		Low	Low	Low
Average						

Note: Use of upper case denotes a stronger difference than lower case; a blank cell implies the score was near the average for all the children.

only that other children (who do not like them) say they do. Some subsequent work (see p. 118) has linked the status groups to more direct behavioural measures.

Based on material in J. D. Coie, K. A. Dodge and H. Coppotelli 1982: *Development Psychology*, 18, 557–70.

Box 4.2
Bully/victim problems among schoolchildren:
basic facts and effects of a school-based intervention
programme

Norway has been very active in researching and intervening in problems of school bullying. Local and then nationwide surveys of the extent of the problem revealed that some 9 per cent of the school population were fairly regular victims of bullying, and some 7–8 per cent engaged in bullying others. Often, these children and young people did not tell teachers or parents about their involvement in bullying. In 1982 two young people in Norway took their own lives because of bullying at school. This and the associated media interest and public concern, combined with the previous research findings, led to the Ministry of Education supporting a nationwide Norwegian Campaign Against Bullying. This commenced on 1 October 1983.

The intervention programme, aimed at students, teachers and parents, had a number of components:

- a 32-page booklet for school personnel, giving detailed suggestions about what teachers and school can do to counteract bullying.
- a 4-page folder with information and advice for parents.
- a 25-minute video cassette showing episodes from everyday lives of two bullied children, a 10-year-old boy and a 14-year-old girl. Child actors were used in making this video, which could be used as a basis for class discussion.
- a short inventory or survey given to pupils, to ascertain the level and nature of bully/victim problems in each school.

In an evaluation carried out by Dan Olweus in the Bergen area of Norway, the effects of this interven-

tion programme were assessed in 42 primary and junior high schools, with some 2,500 students. Children only start school at 7 years in Norway; these students were aged around 11 and 14 years. A cohort-sequential design was used (cf. pp. 9–10 and figure 1.2), and is illustrated in box figure 4.2.1. The four grade (age) cohorts started at grades 4, 5, 6 and 7 (ages 11, 12, 13 and 14) in May 1983, shortly before the intervention campaign was started. Measurements were taken at this point (time 1), and again in May 1984 (time 2), and May 1985 (time 3).

This cohort-sequential design was important for interpreting any results. Suppose that there was some improvement in bullying problems with time. This could be due to the intervention programme; or it could be due to age or historical changes. Usually in a study of this kind we would control for these by comparing the results for other children who did not experience the intervention, or 'treatment'. However, as the intervention campaign was on a national basis, there could not be any 'no-treatment' control groups. What could be done was to make 'time-lagged contrasts between age-equivalent groups'. For example, the children who were grade 6 at time 2, and had experienced one year of intervention, could be compared with those who were grade 6 at time 1, before the intervention started. Later, the same comparison could be made with children who were grade 6 at time 3, after 2 years of intervention. Altogether, five such time-lagged comparisons can be made (see box figure 4.2.1).

These comparisons are matched for age, obviously an important factor. The children are differ-

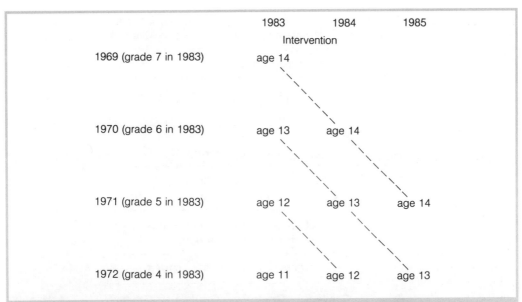

Box Figure 4.2.1   Design of cohort-sequential study of effects of an intervention programme against school bullying. Year of assessment is shown horizontally, and cohort (year of birth/initial grade level) vertically. The approximate ages of each sample of children from each cohort and at each year of study are shown in years.

ent, but in the same schools, and given the large sample size this should not matter. Also, you will be able to see from the design that the same children, starting in grades 5 and 6, serve as both baseline groups and treatment groups in different comparisons.

The measurements made at the three time points were based on anonymously filled-in questionnaires from the students. These indicated the frequency of being bullied and bullying others, and of spending playtime alone; self-ratings of antisocial behaviour; ratings of satisfaction with school life; and ratings of the number of peers in the class being bullied or bullying others.

The results were encouraging. There were substantial reductions in the levels of both being bullied, and bullying others, reported by both boys and girls. Box table 4.2.1 shows the changes for the two time 1–time 3 comparisons (shown in box figure 4.2.1), on the questionnaire scores for 'How often have you been bullied in school?', and 'How often have you taken part in bullying other students in school?' Similar reductions were found for ratings of peers involved in being bullied or bullying. The bullying was not just displaced elsewhere; there

were no changes in reports of bullying on the way to and from school. There were some decreases in the self-reports of antisocial behaviour, and some increases in student satisfaction with school life, such as liking playground time.

This research programme provides a convincing account of the application of psychological research to diagnosing a social problem, helping devise an intervention programme, and then assessing the results of such an intervention. The independent variable is time of assessment, while the dependent variables are the questionnaire measures. The data do depend largely on self-reports, which could be open to distortion or to effects of repeated testing; but are supported by ratings of peers.

The cohort-sequential design overcomes the absence of conventional no-treatment control groups. However, the comparisons do not control for historical effects. For example, suppose some other events had happened in 1984, such as severe economic depression, or increased racial tension such as the Rushdie affair in the UK in 1989; these might influence the comparisons. In effect, the comparisons are measuring the effects of the intervention programme (itself an historical effect!) and any

Box Table 4.2.1   Effects of intervention programme: questionnaire scores for (a) being bullied, and (b) for bullying others, for boys and girls, for each of the two time 1-time 3 comparisons (at grade 6, and grade 7)

How often have you been bullied in school?

(a)	BOYS		GIRLS	
	Grade 6	Grade 7	Grade 6	Grade 7
Time 1	0.36	0.47	0.46	0.19
Time 3	0.19	0.18	0.11	0.07

How often have you taken part in bullying other students in school?

(b)	BOYS		GIRLS	
	Grade 6	Grade 7	Grade 6	Grade 7
Time 1	0.49	0.47	0.26	0.23
Time 3	0.33	0.31	0.10	0.04

other large-scale effects felt in 1983–5. Nevertheless, there were no other such obviously important effects in Norway in the period concerned.

Another study, carried out on 37 schools in the Rogaland area of Norway around Stavanger, did not obtain such encouraging findings (Roland, 1989). Here assessments were made in 1986; preliminary results showed that levels of bullying had remained largely stable for girls, but had actually increased for boys. Nevertheless the schools that had implemented the intervention programme most thoroughly did have better results. The discrepancy between this study and the one based in Bergen remains to be explained.

Based on material in D. Olweus, in K. Rubin and D. Pepler (eds) (1991): *The Development and Treatment of Childhood Aggression*. Hillsdale, NJ: Erlbaum.

5 Becoming Socially Aware

So far, we have looked at the child developing in the context of the family, the peer group and the school. In this chapter we shall look at how the child develops an understanding of him- or herself, and of others; and discuss various influences on this process. There is an important body of research which makes links between the child's social world (the focus of part two of this book) and the child's thinking and language abilities (the focus of part three). We will start by considering children's developing sense of self; their understanding of their own emotions; and how the child learns to categorize others and understand their emotional expressions. (This further relates to the developing awareness of others' mental states, beliefs and desires: what has been called a 'theory of mind', or skills in 'mindreading', discussed in chapter 13.)

The second part of the chapter examines the development of gender and ethnic differences – how children understand these, as well as what behavioural differences are found. Finally, we shall look at the effects of television on sex stereotyping and on social behaviour.

◄How Children Begin to Understand Self and Others►►►

One basic step the infant must take in understanding about others is to realize that he or she is distinct from other people, who have a separate continuing existence. In other words, they must acquire a sense of self as distinct from others.

One early landmark of this is referred to as 'person permanence'. It has been assessed in terms of infants' recognition of particular others, and search for them when that person disappears from view. Person permanence implies an internal representation of a social being, corresponding to that person's continuity in time and space. Closely related to the concept of person permanence is that of 'object permanence', applied to non-social objects, and discussed in chapter 11. Both are achieved during the sensori-motor period (up to about 18 months of age), with major progress in the degree of permanence achieved (measured by the success of the infant's search strategies) towards the end of the first year.

The infant's recognition of self

While person permanence experiments show that an infant can recognize particular others and expect them to continue existing, they do not tell us specifically about the infant's own sense of self. The development of self-recognition has been discussed in detail by Lewis and Brooks-Gunn (1979). They found that infants aged as early as 9 to 12 months were capable of some differentiation between pictorial representation of themselves, and others; for example, they would smile more and look longer at pictures of themselves than at pictures of other same-age babies. By 15 to 18 months, children are using verbal labels such as 'baby', or their own name, to distinguish pictures of themselves and others. One ingenious technique to assess self-recognition has been the 'Mirror test', also used with primates (chapter 2). In a study of this kind, Lewis and Brooks-Gunn (1979) used 16 infants at each of six age groups – 9, 12, 15, 18, 21 and 24 months. Each infant was first placed by the mother in front of a fairly large mirror, and their behaviour observed for about 90 seconds. Then, the infant's nose was wiped with rouge discreetly, on the pretence of wiping the infant's face (only one of the 96 infants immediately felt for his nose after this). The infant was subsequently placed in front of the mirror again and observed for another 90 seconds. How would the infant react?

At all ages, most of the infants smiled at their image in the mirror (see table 5.1), and many pointed to the mirror or reached out to touch it. However, in the first, 'no rouge' condition, very few touched their own nose, and not many touched their own body at all. When the rouge had been applied, the effect depended markedly on the infant's age. The 9- and 12-month-old infants never touched their own nose, despite being able to see their unusually red nose in the mirror; a minority of 15- and 18-month-olds, and most 21- and 24-month-olds, did reach for their own noses. This suggests that after

Table 5.1   Percentages of infants smiling, and touching own nose, on viewing their reflection in a mirror

Infants' behaviour	Age (months)	9	12	15	18	21	24
Smiling	No rouge	86	94	88	56	63	60
	Rouge	99	74	88	75	82	60
Touching own nose	No rouge	0	0	0	6	7	7
	Rouge	0	0	19	25	70	73

Source: Lewis and Brooks-Gunn, 1979

about 18 months, an infant has a pretty good idea that the reflection in the mirror is a representation of him- or herself.

How children categorize others

We have seen how infants achieve person permanence through the sensori-motor period, often ahead of object permanence. As concepts of particular persons become more stable, persons can begin to be categorized along social dimensions. Lewis and Brooks-Gunn (1979) argued that the three earliest social dimensions learned are familiarity, age and gender. They argue that these are concurrently developed in relation to oneself and to other persons.

The importance of familiarity is apparent from the research which shows that infants behave differently to familiar and to strange adults by around 7 to 9 months of age (when attachment relationships have usually formed), if not earlier (see chapter 3; and Sroufe, 1977). A bit later, infants respond differently to familiar and unfamiliar peers. Jacobson (1980) found that wari-ness of an unfamiliar peer (compared with a familiar peer) developed be-tween 10 and 12 months. Greater previous experience with the familiar peer predicted an earlier onset of wariness of the unfamiliar peer.

Age and gender are also used very early on in a categorical way. Infants aged 6 to 9 months of age discriminate in their behaviour between the approach of a child and of an adult, and infants aged 9 to 12 months can differentiate between photographs of baby and adult faces. Lewis and Brooks-Gunn (1979) suggest that height, movement, voice, and extreme dif-ferences in facial and hair characteristics (in baby and adult photographs) are the cues which infants use to catagorize by age. Verbal age labels (e.g. baby, mummy, daddy) begin to be used correctly by 18 to 24 months of age. By the preschool years, age can be used as an explicit criterion for classification. Edwards and Lewis (1979) found that $3\frac{1}{2}$-year-olds could successfully sort head-and-shoulders photographs of persons into four categories: little chil-dren, big children, parents and grandparents.

Differentiation of people by gender also occurs early. Nine- to 12-month-olds respond differentially both to photographs of female and male strangers (Brooks-Gunn and Lewis, 1981) and to direct approach by male and female strangers (Smith and Sloboda, 1986). Verbal gender labels (e.g. mummy, daddy, boy, girl) begin to be used correctly after 18 months of age. The development of gender identity is considered further, later in this chapter.

◀ Emotional Development ▶ ▶ ▶

Producing emotions

From birth onwards, babies start signalling their emotional state (see also chapter 3, p. 70; chapter 10, p. 302). Perhaps the earliest distinction one can make for babies is between positive and negative affect – whether they are contented and happy, as indicated by smiling; or discontented and dis-tressed, as indicated by pursing the lips and crying. A study by Ganchrow,

Steiner and Daher (1983) showed that at the time of the very first feed, newborns would produce distinct facial expressions to a sweet liquid (slight smile) or bitter liquid (mouth corners down, pursed lips). Observers who watched the babies without knowing which liquid was being given, could judge whether the babies liked or disliked the liquid, and also the intensity of response.

Interviews with mothers suggest that they can distinguish a variety of emotions in their infants in the first few months of life (Campos et al., 1983). Some basic or 'primary' emotions, which may be discernible from the first few weeks onwards, are happiness, interest, surprise, sadness, fear, anger and pain. For example, surprise is indicated by wide-open eyes and mouth, together with a startle response by the trunk and limbs. Fear responses increase considerably after about 7 months of age, when infants become wary and fearful of unfamiliar persons and objects (see chapter 3, p. 75); and sadness can occur in periods of separation from a familiar caregiver. (The balance of different emotional expressions is crucial in scoring the 'Strange Situation' procedure, see chapter 3, p. 76, where anger as well as happiness may occur in reunion episodes).

Anger and pain also become increasingly easily distinguished from each other, especially after about 7 months. This was shown in a study by Izard et al. (1987). They looked at babies' facial expressions when they were given routine inoculations. The babies were aged from 2 to 8 months. For younger babies the reaction was one of generalized distress, but for older babies a distinctly angry expression (brows compressed together, eyelids tensed, mouth compressed or squared) became progressively more frequent.

One of the earliest descriptions of emotional development comes from Charles Darwin (1877), who published an article about the early development of one of his own children. Here is his description of the development of anger:

It was difficult to decide at how early an age anger was felt; on his eighth day he frowned and wrinkled the skin round his eyes before a crying fit, but this may have been due to pain or distress, and not to anger. When about ten weeks old, he was given some rather cold milk and he kept a slight frown on his forehead all the time that he was sucking, so that he looked like a grown-up person made cross from being compelled to do something which he did not like. When nearly four months old, and perhaps much earlier, there was no doubt, from the manner in which the blood gushed into his whole face and scalp, that he easily got into a violent passion. A small cause sufficed; thus, when a little over seven months old, he screamed with rage because a lemon slipped away and he could not seize it with his hands. When eleven months old, if a wrong plaything was given him, he would push it away and beat it: I presume that the beating was an instinctive sign of anger, like the snapping of the jaws by a young crocodile just out of the egg, and not that he imagined he could hurt the plaything.

Darwin's account is interesting for several reasons. It brings out clearly both his skill as an observer, and also the difficulty in interpreting emotions especially at younger ages. Darwin's account is an example of the diary method (p. 15); though in this case Darwin actually wrote up the article 37 years after keeping the diary on which it is based! Finally, you will see that Darwin suggests that some emotional displays are 'instinctive', in children as well as in animals. The very early development of emotional display in infants does seem to suggest that some of the mechanisms for producing emotion are 'innate', or strongly canalized in development (p. 39). The main alternative view would be that infants learn emotional expression from others, through observation and imitation; this seems less plausible in early infancy, but more plausible later, for example in explaining cultural differences in emotional expression.

Recognizing emotions in others

If infants were to learn aspects of emotional expression from others, they would have to understand something of their meaning. How early does this occur? We will look at two kinds of evidence, both suggesting that during the first year infants can distinguish and react appropriately to different emotional expressions by caregivers. Some studies have looked at dialogues between mother and baby (cf. pp. 72, 302). Usually mother and baby are interacting happily. What would happen if the mother adopted a sad face, or an angry face? Haviland and Lelwica (1987) asked mothers to do this for a short while with their 10-week-old babies, adopting appropriate facial expressions and tone of voice. The babies did react differently. If the mother appeared happy, so did the baby. If the mother appeared angry, so did the baby. If the mother appeared sad, the baby did not particularly look sad, but did engage in chewing, mouthing and sucking.

These studies show that babies can discriminate emotions in others early on. Their reactions seem broadly appropriate, but it could be misleading to say that the baby 'understands' the mother's angry emotion; they might for example simply find the angry tone of voice (loud and harsh) unpleasurable in itself. However, evidence that infants can sensibly interpret the emotional expression of their mother comes from studies of 'social referencing'.

Social referencing

Sometimes, an infant will look carefully at his or her mother (or familiar caregiver), as if to gauge their emotional expression, before as it were deciding how to react themselves to a situation. This kind of behaviour is referred to as 'social referencing', and has been defined as a 'process characterized by the use of one's perception of other persons' interpretation of this situation to form one's own understanding of the situation' (Feinman, 1982, p. 445). Not surprisingly, it is more likely in ambiguous situations, where some extra 'advice' is needed by the infant. Two well-studied examples are: reactions to strangers and behaviour on the 'visual cliff'.

From about 7 months of age, we have seen that infants do tend to be wary of strangers, even if overt fear is rare except in unusual laboratory situations (p. 92). The infant's reaction to the stranger is known to be quite strongly affected by context, and part of this context is now known to be the mother's reaction to the stranger. Feiring, Lewis and Starr (1984) observed how 15-month-olds would respond to a stranger. They would often turn to the mother when the stranger entered, as if to ascertain her reaction. The experimenters asked the mother to either interact positively with the stranger, or ignore the stranger. The reaction of the infants to the stranger was less positive when the mother ignored the stranger. Similar results have been obtained with the reactions of 12-month-old infants to toys, depending on the facial expression of the mother (Klinnert, 1984).

Another experiment was carried out using the 'visual cliff' (illustrated on p. 283). In the visual cliff, infants generally refuse to move onto a glass surface when it appears that there is a large drop at the boundary (see p. 284). The situation can be made more ambiguous by making the apparent drop smaller. This was done by Sorce et al. (1985) with a sample of 12-month-olds. The mother was opposite the baby (see the right-hand photo on p. 283) and some mothers were asked to adopt a happy face, others a fearful face.

The results were clear. Of 19 infants whose mother had a happy face, 14 crossed the visual cliff; of 17 whose mother had a fearful face, none crossed. This strongly suggests that the infants are interpreting the mother's expression appropriately, as a commentary on the situation. This is particularly well illustrated by this experiment, as a mother's fearful expression would normally cause an infant to approach the mother for safety; but in this experiment, the mother's fearful expression actually prevents approach across the apparent cause of danger, the visual cliff.

The relationship between sense of self, and understanding others

We saw earlier how a sense of self develops by around 18 months. A sense of self can be used as a reference point for understanding others, and some psychologists regard the two as inextricably linked. The idea goes back to an American child psychologist, J. M. Baldwin (1861–1934). It is supported by Lewis and Brooks-Gunn (1979), who advanced three principles regarding early social awareness:

1 Any knowledge gained about the other also must be gained about the self.
2 What can be demonstrated to be known about the self can be said to be known about the other and what is known about the other can be said to be known about the self.
3 Social dimensions are those attributes of others and self which can be used to describe people. Related ideas are developed by Paul Harris (1989) in his theory of how children come to understand others, which we shall discuss shortly.

The link between knowledge of self and of others is also supported by empirical work. Bischof-Kohler (cited in Perner, 1991) carried out the mirror test on infants aged 16 to 24 months; she also assessed their level of empathy when playing with an experimenter who is 'sad' when the arm of a teddy bear falls off. There was a high correlation between a child's level of self-recognition, and their level of empathic behaviour, irrespective of the child's age. In general, it seems as if the beginnings of a truly empathic understanding of others emerges at around 20 months (see also chapter 7), at the same time as other aspects of understanding others (for example, jealousy and deception; chapter 3) and as self-recognition as assessed by the mirror test emerge.

This awareness of others *vis-à-vis* oneself also seems to be a prerequisite for the 'secondary' emotions such as pride, guilt or shame, which develop after the 'primary' emotions such as happiness, fear, anger and surprise. The secondary emotions depend on some understanding of how others perceive your situation; they are self-conscious emotions. A study of the development of embarrassment in children, a secondary emotion of this kind, is given in box 5.1.

Talking about mental states

From about 18 months, further insight can be obtained into emotional development by looking at how infants talk about emotions – how they use 'emotion words' in natural conversation (Bretherton et al., 1986). Both diaries of child speech and observations in the home show that use of words which label emotions (such as 'have fun', 'surprised', 'scared', 'yucky', 'sad'), while rare at 18 months, are common by 24 months. Interestingly, although these words are used somewhat more frequently by children to refer to themselves than to refer to others, the use of these words for self and others goes very much in parallel; this supports the ideas discussed above of the interdependence of concepts of self and other.

By 28 months, children are using language to comment on and explain their own feelings, for example:

'I see tiger. That too scary.'
'Me fall down. Me cry.'

And the feelings of others, for example:

'Grandma mad. I wrote on wall.'
'You sad Mommy. What Daddy do?'

They can also use them to guide or influence someone else's behaviour, for example:

'No not angry. Not nice.' (age 19 months; parents are quarrelling.)
'Baby crying. Kiss. Make it better.' (age 22 months; to mother, in shop where
    child noticed other child crying.)
'I hurt your hair. Please don't cry.' (age 24 months; to child victim, after being
    scolded for hair-pulling.)

(from Bretherton et al., 1986)

Emotional deception

When can children deliberately manipulate emotions to achieve a certain effect on others? For example, can they deceive others by hiding or changing a facial expression of emotion? It looks as though they can do this by 3 or 4 years of age.

In one study, Cole (1986) looked at how 3- and 4-year-old girls would react when given a disappointing present. The girls were given picture-story tasks to do. Before the tasks, each girl had rated ten possible gifts from best to worst. After the first set of tasks, the children were given their 'best' present; but after the second set of tasks, they were given their 'worst' present (a broken toy, or some raisins). How would they react? Cole found that when the interviewer was not present, the children (filmed by a videocamera) would show disappointment to the 'worst' toy, but that when the interviewer stayed present, many would hide their disappointment with a half-smile. (The children were subsequently given the opportunity to trade in their 'worst' toy for another one.)

Another study (Lewis et al., 1989) was done with children who were just 3 years of age (33–37 months). The child sat at a table with the experimenter (and the mother in the background), and was told that the experimenter was going to put out a surprise toy (actually, a Fisher-Price zoo), but that they must not peek while the experimenter left the room; they could play with the toy when the experimenter returned. The experimenter then left the room, and the children were observed and filmed through a one-way mirror. The experimenter returned and asked 'did you peek?' before playing with the child and reassuring them that it was alright if they did peek.

Of 33 children taking part, 29 did peek at the toy when the experimenter left! Of these, 11 admitted to peeking, 11 denied it and 7 gave no answer to the question. Besides the verbal deception of many children, there was evidence of facial deception. The children who peeked tended to put on a smile when the experimenter re-entered and looked at them (unlike the few children who did not peek, who did not smile), and when questioned, these children continued smiling; those who denied peeking had the most relaxed and positive facial expression!

As we saw in chapter 2 (p. 50), there can be different levels of deception. The above examples would seem to indicate level-four deception, that is a deliberate intent to deceive. In the Lewis et al. (1989) study, it could admittedly be argued that the child's response 'no', to 'did you peek?' may have been just an avoidance reaction, or a stereotyped denial strategy; but this would hardly explain the manipulation of facial expression which occurred as well.

◄Understanding Others' Emotions, Desires and Beliefs▶▶▶

We have seen that there is considerable evidence that children can understand other people's emotions, desires and beliefs by 3 or 4 years of age, and indeed that the beginnings of this can be seen by 2 years of age. How does this understanding come about? One theory has been put forward by Paul Harris in his book *Children and Emotion* (1989). Harris believes that it is a child's awareness of his or her own mental state which allows them to project mental states on to other people using an 'as if' or pretence mechanism; understanding someone else results from imagining yourself in their position. (This is in fact similar to the argument by Humphrey, chapter 1, p. 3.) On this basis, Harris argues that there are three important precursors, or preconditions, for the child to be able to understand another person's mind. These are (1) self-awareness; (2) the capacity for pretence; and (3) being able to distinguish reality from pretence.

1   *Self-awareness*: as we saw earlier, children are aware of themselves by about 18–20 months of age and can verbally express their own emotional states by 2 years.

2   *The capacity for pretence*: in chapter 6 (pp. 181–3) we see that the ability to pretend that something in the world is something else emerges in pretend play during the second year. Specifically, children start acting out scenes with dolls or stuffed animals, for example feeding teddy 'as if' he were hungry. By 2 and 3 years of age, children are conjuring up animate beings in their pretend play, with emotions and desires of their own.

3   *Distinguishing reality from pretence*: when children are in pretend play, they do not usually confuse this with reality. Admittedly this can happen sometimes. When an adult joins in with a 1- or 2-year-old's play, the child can be confused as to whether the adult is in 'pretend' or 'real' mode; for example, if a child knocks an empty cup over in play and mother says 'you spilled your tea, better wipe it up', the child may actually pick up a cloth to wipe it. However, more usually, and especially by 3 or 4 years, the pretence–reality distinction is a stable one. Things would be difficult if it was not! Suppose a child pretends a wooden block is a cake, for a tea party. If they confused pretence and reality, they would actually try to eat the wooden block. By 3 years, children often signal the pretend mode in their play, for example 'let's pretend to be families. You be daddy...'. Direct interviews with 3-year-olds also confirm that they can distinguish real from imaginary situations, and understand the use of the words 'real' and 'pretend'.

How do all these precursors come together in Harris's theory? He supposes that once a child is aware of his or her own emotional state, he or she can use the ability to pretend in order to project this emotional state on to inanimate beings (in pretend play), or on other people; and to realize that the other person's imagined reality may differ from their own reality. Let's take as an example the child who said 'You sad Mommy. What Daddy do?', cited earlier. We can suppose that previously this child has experienced sadness herself; and perhaps has experienced sadness because her Daddy was nasty to her. Her ability to imagine things in an 'as if' or pretend mode enables her to suppose that Mummy too may be sad, because Daddy was nasty to her also. Furthermore, she does not confuse this with her own emotional state;

the child does not have to be sad herself, in order to imagine that Mummy is sad, for a certain reason.

There is one obvious alternative interpretation which would dispense with Harris's 'as if' mechanism. That is that young children learn to link common situations with common emotions (compare the discussion of Borke's results in chapter 11, pp. 361–3). Perhaps they just have learnt that mummies are usually sad because daddies have been nasty to them, and it doesn't require any imaginative projection of one's own emotional state.

One way to distinguish this alternative explanation from Harris's theory is to see whether children can understand that someone else's emotion in a given situation depends on what they desire or want. To ascertain this, Harris and his colleagues asked children to listen to stories about animal characters, for example, Ellie the elephant and Mickey the monkey. Ellie the elephant is choosy about what she likes to drink. Some children were told that she likes milk to drink and nothing else; others that she likes coke to drink and nothing else. Mickey the monkey is mischievous and mixes up the drink containers; for example, he might pour all the coke out of a coke can, fill it with milk, and offer it to Ellie. How would she feel when she tastes the drink? Four-year-olds are able to answer correctly that (if she likes milk) she will be pleased, or that (if she likes coke) she will be sad, and explain why in terms of Ellie's desires.

This does tend to suggest that, at least by 4 years, children are taking account of someone's desires in predicting their emotional state; they are not just basing their judgement on a stereotyped situation–emotion link (such as: you are pleased if you are given a drink). In a subsequent study, the experimenters also asked children how Ellie would feel before she tasted the drink. How would she feel if she likes coke, and is given a coke can (which Mickey has secretly filled with milk). By 6 years (though in this study, not at 4 years), children correctly judge that Ellie would be happy when given the can, though sad when she tasted the contents. Here, belief and desire of another are being successfully linked in the prediction of emotion, even when the belief is different from the child's own belief (the child knows the coke can has milk, but Ellie has a 'false belief'), and the desire may be different from the child's desire; not all children like coke (or milk).

From the above account, we might say that children are developing hypotheses about other persons' emotions, desires and beliefs. This could be described as developing a 'theory of mind' or skills in 'mindreading'. As we saw at the end of chapter 2, there are similar ideas about the evolutionary origins of intelligence in the higher primates. Further research on development of 'theory of mind' in children is considered in chapter 13.

By 6 or 7 years children seem able to understand and manipulate emotions in a more complex way. It would appear that, as well as being able to understand that someone else can feel a different emotion (meta-representation), they can begin to operate recursively on such understanding (Harris, 1989). Consider, for example, how children might respond to the following story:

Diana falls over and hurts herself. She knows that the other children will laugh if she shows how she feels. So she tries to hide how she feels.

What will Diana do, and why? Many 6-year-olds (but not 4-year-olds) are able to say that Diana will look happy, and explain why; for example, 'she didn't want the other children to know that she's sad that she fell over'. This is an embedded sentence with a recursive structure of the form 'I may not want you to know how I feel'. We've seen that 4-year-olds can cope with 'I know how you feel', but only by 6 years does this further recursion seem to become possible (see also discussion of higher-order false belief tasks in chapter 13).

◀ Early Sex Differences ▶ ▶ ▶

We saw earlier how infants use sex, or gender, as one way of categorizing people. We will now look further at sex differences in behaviour and the development of children's awareness of these differences. Then some hypotheses about why sex differences develop are compared. Incidentally, some authors prefer to use the term 'gender' rather than 'sex' when referring to differences which may have been produced by upbringing, reserving 'sex' for purely biological differences. In practice, the distinction is not always that easy. Here we refer to 'sex differences', but to 'gender identity', these being the most common usages.

Sex differences among children in Western societies
Many studies have been carried out in the UK and the USA on sex differences in infants and young children, most involving observations of behaviour in the home or in nursery classes. Individual studies often have rather small samples, say 20 children or so, and measure a large number of behavioural categories; so even by chance one or two measures may give apparently 'significant' differences. (Remember a result significant at the 0.05 level occurs by chance 1 in 20 times.) Thus, it is important to look for replication of findings over a number of studies. There are many reviews of this subject area in the literature (e.g. Archer and Lloyd, 1986; Hargreaves and Colley, 1986).

The results of research in the infancy period (up to 2 years) do not reveal many consistent differences between boys and girls. The similarities certainly outweigh the dissimilarities. However, the replicated findings include: girl infants may be more responsive to people, staying closer to adults, whereas boy infants may be more distressed by stressful situations which they cannot control (such as the 'Strange Situation' separations discussed on p. 76). Girls also seem to talk earlier.

Among 2-year-olds and in older children some sex differences in toy choice are apparent. Observations of 2-year-olds at home, and of 3- and 4-year-olds in nursery classes, show that boys tend to prefer transportation toys, blocks and activities involving gross motor activity such as throwing or kicking balls, or rough-and-tumbling; girls tend to prefer dolls, and dressing-up or domestic play. Many activities, however, do not show a sex preference at this age.

School-age children tend to select same-sex partners for play, and more so as they get older. Also, boys tend to prefer outdoor play and, later, team games; whereas girls prefer indoor, more sedentary activities, and often play in pairs. Boys more frequently engage both in play-fighting and in actual aggressive behaviour. Girls tend to be more empathic, and remain more orientated towards adults (parents and teacher) longer into childhood. All these differences refer to overall trends, with much overlap between boys and girls in general. Many differences, while statistically significant when tests are carried out on large samples, are actually quite small in magnitude.

Awareness of gender identity and sex differences

If you ask a 2-year-old 'are you a boy or a girl?', quite a few will not know the answer or will be easily confused, although many will answer correctly. The easiest task seems to be to show pictures of a male and female of stereotyped appearance (such as figure 5.1). In one such study, Thompson (1975) found that 24-month-old children gave 76 per cent correct identification of sex; this rose to 83 per cent by 30 months and 90 per cent by 36 months. By 3 years most children can correctly label their own, or another person's sex or gender, and are said to have achieved 'gender identity'.

The next stage, called 'gender stability', is achieved by 4 or 5 years. This is when a child realizes that gender is normally constant; for example, a girl will answer that she will be a mummy when she grows up. A bit later the child reaches 'gender constancy', a mature awareness that biological sex is unchanging, despite changes in appearance. This is tested by questions such as 'could you be a girl if you want to be?' (to a boy), or 'suppose this child (picture of boy) lets their hair grow very long; is it a boy or a girl?' This is reported to be achieved around 7 years of age, at or soon after the child can conserve physical quantity (see chapter 11), but may be achieved earlier if children understand the genital difference between the sexes (Bem, 1989).

Sex-role stereotypes are also acquired early; these are beliefs about what is most appropriate for one sex, or the other. In one study (Kuhn et al., 1978), preschool children were shown a male doll and a female doll, and asked which doll would do each of 72 activities, such as cooking, sewing, playing with trains, talking a lot, giving kisses, fighting or climbing trees. Even $2\frac{1}{2}$-year-olds had some knowledge of sex-role stereotypes (see table 5.2). This sex-stereotyping increases with age and is well established by the middle school years. In a study of 5- and 8-year-old children in England, Ireland and the USA (Best et al., 1977), the majority of boys and girls, of both ages and in all countries, agreed that females were soft-hearted whereas males were strong, aggressive, cruel and coarse. Many more characteristics were stereotyped in the 8-year-olds study only.

By 8 years of age children's stereotypes are very similar to those obtained with adults. Several studies have shown that adult stereotypes are quite

Figure 5.1   Stereotyped female and male figures (adapted from Emmerich et al., 1976).

Table 5.2   Beliefs about boys and girls, held by both boys and girls aged $2\frac{1}{2}$ and $3\frac{1}{2}$[a]

Beliefs about girls	play with dolls
	like to help mother
	like to cook dinner
	like to clean house
	talk a lot
	never hit
	say 'I need some help'
Beliefs about boys	like to help father
	say 'I can hit you'

[a] Only results at or approaching statistical significance are recorded.
Source: Kuhn et al., 1978

consistent across a variety of ages and social backgrounds. They are also reflected in the mass media, such as books, comics, films and TV programmes (see later in this chapter). By and large, of course, such stereotypes correspond to actual differences in behaviour. Nevertheless, they often seem to exaggerate such differences, especially at a time when sex roles may be changing quite rapidly. For example, few children's books have depicted working mothers, even though about one-third of mothers of young children have been in employment for decades.

Cross-cultural studies

The sex differences in behaviour and sex-role stereotypes so far discussed apply to Western urban societies such as the UK and the USA. But how widely do they apply in other societies? Much of what we know here comes from the work of anthropologists. One study made a survey of the anthropological literature on child-rearing in 110, mostly non-literate, societies (Barry et al., 1957). They found that in more than 80 per cent of those societies where accurate ratings could be made, girls more than boys were encouraged to be nurturant, whereas boys more than girls were subject to training for self-reliance and achievement. In many societies responsibility and obedience were also encouraged in girls more than boys (table 5.3). The degree of pressure for sex-typing does vary with the type of society, and appears to be especially strong in societies where male strength is important for hunting or herding, and less strong in societies with small family groups, where sharing of tasks is inevitable.

A more detailed study of child-rearing was made in the 'Six Cultures Study' (Whiting and Edwards, 1973; Whiting and Whiting, 1975), in which direct observations were made on samples of children in Kenya, Japan, India, the Philippines, Mexico and the USA. In the majority of these societies girls were more nurturant and made more physical contacts while boys were more aggressive, dominant and engaged in more rough-and-tumble play. Differences among the six cultures could often be related to differences in socialization pressures, e.g. the extent to which older girls were required to do 'nurturant' tasks such as looking after younger siblings.

◀Theories of Sex-role Identification▶▶▶

Why do boys and girls come to behave in different ways, and to have certain beliefs about sex-appropriate behaviour? There are several theories about this process of acquiring a sex-role, or 'sex-role identification'. Here we consider biological factors, social learning theory and the cognitive-developmental approach.

Table 5.3 Incidence among different cultures of training girls or boys more strongly for certain characteristics

	Girls trained more %	Boys trained more %	No difference %
Nurturance (n = 33)	82	0	18
Responsibility (n = 84)	61	11	28
Obedience (n = 69)	35	3	62
Self-reliance (n = 82)	0	85	15
Achievement (n = 31)	3	87	10

n = number of cultures rated
Source: Barry et al., 1957

Biological factors

Boys and girls differ in one chromosome pair; girls have two linked X chromosomes, whereas boys have one X and one Y chromosome. This genetic difference normally leads to differential production of hormones, both in the fetus and later in adolescence (chapter 8). These hormones lead to differentiation of bodily characteristics, such as the genital organs, and may also influence brain growth and hence behaviour patterns.

Much of the evidence linking sex hormones to behaviour comes from animal studies, but there have now been a number of studies on human children who have received unusual amounts of sex hormone early in life, for example while in the uterus. The most common syndrome is called Congenital Adrenal Hyperplasia (CAH), in which due to a lack of certain enzymes, the adrenal glands produce excessive androgens (a male sex hormone).

A pioneering study of this kind was reported by Money and Ehrhardt (1972). They examined girls who had been exposed to unusually high levels of androgen before birth, in this case because of a hormone treatment given to some mothers for problems such as repeated miscarriages (subsequently discontinued). Any malformation of the genitals was corrected surgically and the children were reared as girls. Compared with a matched group of girls who had not been exposed to excess androgen, these girls and their mothers reported themselves as being more tomboyish and less likely to play with other girls and like feminine clothes. In evaluating this study the parents' knowledge of the hormonal abnormalities must be borne in mind; this could have affected their behaviour towards the children. However, it may seem unlikely that the parents actually encouraged these girls to be tomboyish, for example.

In a comprehensive review, Collaer and Hines (1995) reviewed the evidence for the effects of sex hormone abnormalities on behaviour over a range of outcome variables. They conclude that the evidence is strongest for childhood play behaviour; in normal fetal development male sex hormones seem to predispose boys to become more physically active and interested in rough-and-tumble play. They also argue that the evidence is relatively strong in two other areas: aggression (see chapter 4), and sexual orientation (for an overview of work on development of sexual orientation, see Patterson, 1995). Such effects are consistent with evidence that some sex differences appear early in life, and in most human societies (such as boys' preference for rough-and-tumble).

However, while biological factors are probably important in any comprehensive explanation of sex differences, they do not in themselves explain the process of sex-role identification, and they do not explain the variations in sex roles in different societies. Nor did Money and Ehrhardt (1972) ignore the influence of social learning. In related studies they looked at what happens when a child's sex is reassigned at some point after birth (for example, if a girl exposed to excess androgens is raised first as a boy, before the mistake is realized). Whatever the biological sex, the child can normally be raised according to the assigned sex without major difficulties; the major aspects of sex-role identification are acquired by learning. However, as might be expected, reassignment of sex becomes very difficult once a child has got some way in establishing its own gender identity, as has happened by 3 years of age. Money and Ehrhardt (1972) concluded that there is a critical period between 18 months and 3 years when gender identity is being established. Before this period, gender reassignment is easy; after it, it is very problematical.

Social learning theory

One approach to the learning of sex-role identification, espoused by psychologists such as Bandura (1969) and Mischel (1970), is that children are moulded into sex-roles by the behaviour of adults, especially parents and teachers – the social learning theory approach. The idea of reinforcement is particularly important in this theory, which postulates that parents and others reward (or 'reinforce') sex-appropriate behaviour in children. Parents might encourage nurturant behaviour in girls, and discourage it in boys, for example. This theory also supposes that children observe the behaviour of same-sex models, and imitate them; for example, boys might observe and imitate the behaviour of male figures in TV films, in their playful and aggressive behaviour.

Do parents behave differently towards boys and girls? The answer seems often to be yes. For example, Fagot (1978) studied children aged 20–24 months in American homes. She found that girls were encouraged by their parents to dance, dress up, follow them around, and play with dolls, but were discouraged from jumping and climbing; boys, however, were encouraged to play with blocks and trucks, but discouraged from playing with dolls or seeking help. Thus, even many of the earliest sex differences could be explained by parental reinforcement. In a similar study of 35-year-olds (Langlois and Downs, 1980), mothers, fathers and also same-age peers reinforced sex-appropriate behaviour and discouraged sex-inappropriate behaviour in children. Other studies have found direct evidence that reinforcements or punishments by same-age peers can affect the child's behaviour (Lamb et al., 1980).

The role of observation and imitation in sex-role identification is less clear-cut. If observation in itself were important, we would expect most children to acquire a female sex-role identity, as the great majority of caregivers of young children, and nursery and infant school teachers, are female. Imitation of same-sex models may be important, but probably only by middle childhood, by which time gender constancy is achieved. In fact, it is the influence of the child's own gender awareness that many psychologists now consider to be the missing element in the social-learning approach to sex-role identification.

Cognitive-developmental theory

The cognitive-development approach in this area stems from the writings of Kohlberg (1966, 1969). He argued that the child's growing sense of gender identity is crucial to sex-role identification. Children tend to imitate same-sex models and follow sex-appropriate activities, because they realize that this is what a child of their own sex usually does. This process has been termed 'self-socialization' by Maccoby and Jacklin (1974), since it does not depend directly on external reinforcement. The difference between the cognitive-developmental and social-learning viewpoints is summarized in figure 5.2.

What evidence is there for the cognitive-developmental view? In a number of studies the development of gender identity and constancy has been found to correlate with the degree of sex-typed behaviour. For example, in a study of 2- and 3-year-olds by Weinraub et al. (1984), it was found that the children who had achieved gender identity more securely were also the ones who were observed to make more sex-stereotyped toy preferences. In another study of 4–6-year-olds (Ruble et al., 1981), the level of gender constancy was measured, and each child was shown a film of either same- or opposite-sex children playing with a new toy. Only children high on gender constancy were influenced by the film; if a child high on gender constancy saw opposite-sex children playing with the toy, that child avoided playing with it subsequently.

A second source of support is that reinforcement theory in itself seems insufficient to explain sex-role development. For example, several studies have found that nursery school teachers tend to reward 'feminine' type behaviours (e.g. quiet, sedentary activities near an adult) in both boys and girls equally, yet this does not prevent boys engaging more in noisy, rough-and-tumble play. The limited importance of reinforcement by teachers is also brought out in a study by Serbin et al. (1977). They asked teachers in two

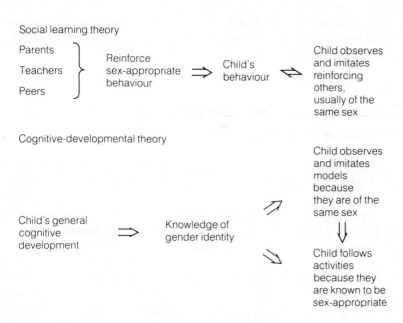

Figure 5.2 Summary of two approaches to sex-role development: social learning theory and cognitive-developmental theory.

preschool classes to praise and encourage co-operative play between boys and girls for a 2-week period. This did increase the level of co-operative cross-sex play, but as soon as the special reinforcement was discontinued, cross-sex play declined to just as low a level as before.

A detailed study by Fagot (1985) has shown how reinforcement theory must be augmented by other considerations. She observed 40 children aged 21–25 months in playgroups, looking at what activities were reinforced (e.g. by praise or joining in) and by whom. As in other studies, she found that the teachers reinforced 'feminine' activities in both boys and girls. She also looked at the effectiveness of the reinforcement (in terms of continuation of the activity). This varied with who was reinforcing, and with what was being reinforced. Girls were influenced by teachers and by other girls, but not much by boys. Boys were influenced by other boys, but not much by girls or teachers. Furthermore, boys were not influenced at all by girls or teachers during 'masculine' activities such as rough-and-tumble or transportation toys.

In summary, while reinforcement does seem to have some effect, it looks as though its effects are being 'filtered' through other factors. From some studies it seems that the child's own gender identity is important here. In Fagot's (1985) study, however, the children were so young that gender identity was unlikely to have been achieved. The effects of reinforcement must have been mediated either by some early, non-verbal awareness of gender not tapped by the usual tests (figure 5.2), or by some canalized processes of activity preference and behavioural compatibility between the sexes. It appears that any complete understanding of sex-role development will require an integration of biological factors, reinforcement and social learning provided by others, with the cognitive-developmental view which provides an active role for the child himself or herself. Recent work on the way children grow into gender roles is considered by Archer (1989) and Golombok and Fivush (1994).

◄Ethnic Awareness, Identity, Preference and Prejudice►►►

Besides differing by gender, people differ in terms of their racial or ethnic group; both are usually obvious from physical characteristics such as hair and skin colour, and facial appearance. There is not universal agreement on how people should be classified by ethnic group. In the UK, for example, some people whose (grand)parents come from the Indian subcontinent might wish to be called by the general term of British Asian, others might wish to be called Indian, Pakistani or Bangladeshi from the country of origin of their (grand)parents, while yet others might wish to be called Black, in common with Afro-Caribbeans and other ethnic minority groups seen as being in an underprivileged position in a predominantly white society. The UK government census of 1991 asks people to identify themselves into one of nine ethnic groups: white, black (African), black (Caribbean), black (other),

Indian, Pakistani, Bangladeshi, Chinese, and other. In North America, main ethnic groups would include white, black, American Indian, Chinese. An inclusive group such as white could be broken down into finer ones, e.g. Anglo-Saxon, Celtic, Hispanic. Other important dimensions are language (e.g. English Canadian and French Canadian) and religion (e.g. Muslim Indian and Hindu Indian). In this section we will look at how children become aware of ethnic differences and identify with an ethnic group; and how this affects their behaviour.

Ethnic awareness

As a child grows up he or she will become aware that people differ by ethnic origin. This ethnic awareness can be assessed by, for example, showing a child photographs of different persons and saying 'show me the Afro-Caribbean person', 'show me the Chinese person', and so on. By the age of 4 or 5 years children seem able to make basic discriminations, for example, between black and white; and during the next few years more difficult ones, such as Anglo-American and Hispanic.

A bit later, at around 8 or 9 years, children understand that ethnic identity remains constant despite changes in age, or superficial attributes such as clothing. For example, in one study children were shown a series of photos of an Italian-Canadian boy, labelled as such, putting on native-Indian clothes (plate 5.1). When asked to identify the boy in the final photo, half the 6-year-olds thought that he was different from the boy in the first photo and that he really was Indian. By 8 years, none made this mistake (Aboud, 1988). This development is similar to that of gender awareness and gender constancy (p. 154), though it seems to occur a year or so later.

Ethnic identity

Ethnic identity can be thought of as awareness of one's ethnicity. It closely parallels the developing awareness of ethnicity in others. It is usually assessed by using dolls, or photographs, and asking the child to point to one that looks most like them. Generally, children of 4 years and above choose the doll or photograph of someone from their own ethnic group, though there are variations in different studies (Aboud, 1988). Of course, a child might quite well use other (non-ethnic) criteria to decide which is most like them, such as facial expression; so it is best to provide several examples for each ethnic group, for the child to choose from.

Ethnic preference

How do children react to, and evaluate, the ethnic differences which they become aware of from about 4 years? We can look at this in several different ways.

First, we could use similar test situations to those used in assessing ethnic awareness and identity, with dolls or photographs representing different ethnic groups. This time, however, we could ask the child which they would like to be themselves; or which they would like to play with.

Plate 5.1   Part of test for understanding that a child's ethnic identity does not change with superficial attributes such as clothes (from Aboud, 1988).

A number of studies of this kind have found that most white children choose or prefer the white doll (or photo) from 4 years, whereas black and other ethnic minority children are more divided, with (in some of the earlier studies) most of them choosing the white doll too. These preferences strengthen up to about 7 years. Beyond 7 years, black children tend to choose the black doll or photo more frequently. These studies were mostly carried out in North America or the UK, where whites form the dominant and more privileged social group; and this probably influences the results. Effects of historical period are likely to be very important here (cf. p. 8). With the rise of ethnic minority group consciousness and pride in their own culture which has characterized recent decades in North America and the UK, the extent to which minority group children choose their own group has increased, at least among 7- to 11-year-olds (Davey, 1983; Milner, 1983).

Another way of looking at ethnic preference is more naturalistic; we could observe whom children actually choose as play partners, in playgroup or playground situations. We saw earlier (p. 114) that children tend to segregate by sex; do they segregate by race?

The answer from available studies seems to be a definite 'yes'. For example, Finkelstein and Haskins (1983) observed black and white kindergarten children in the USA. They found that even these 5-year-olds showed marked segregation by race, and that this increased over the kindergarten year. However, neither black nor white children behaved differently to other-race peers than to same-race peers.

In older children too, segregation by race is noticeable, whether in the US (e.g. Schofield and Francis, 1982), or in the UK (e.g. Boulton and Smith, 1991).

However, segregation by race seems to be less marked than segregation by sex, at least in the middle-school period. Table 5.4 shows choice of playground partners from two UK middle schools with a mixture of white and British Asian children. Amongst these 8- to 9-year-old children, segregation is marked by both sex and race, in that order of priority. It may be noticed that segregation by race is less marked amongst boys than amongst girls, a finding consistent with that of Schofield and Francis (1982). This may be because boys play in larger groups than girls; when playing football, for example, ethnic group may be ignored in order to fill up a team with the requisite number of good players.

Ethnic prejudice

Preference is not in itself the same as prejudice. One might choose to play with same-sex or same-race partners, but still regard other-sex and other-race children as being just as good or able as oneself and one's friends. Indeed, the limited evidence from Finkelstein and Haskins' (1983) study is that their kindergarten children showed preference, but not necessarily prejudice; when a white child played with a black child his or her behaviour did not change (and vice versa).

Prejudice implies a negative evaluation of another person, on the basis of some general attribute (which could be for example sex, race or disability). Thus, racial prejudice means a negative evaluation of someone as a consequence of their being in a certain racial or ethnic group. If a white child dislikes a black child because of some individual attribute, this is not prejudice. But if a white child dislikes a black child (and black children) because of his or her colour, this is racial prejudice. It may not always be easy to be sure whether an action is racial prejudice in individual cases, but the experience of prejudice can be very damaging and at times tragic. The disastrous effects of racial prejudice in the school system is illuminated in a case study of a British school, *Murder in the Playground* (MacDonald, 1989; see also chapter 16).

Many children do seem to show racial prejudice from 4 or 5 years of age, as they become aware of ethnic differences. For example, children can be asked to put photos of children from different ethnic groups along a scale of

Table 5.4 Mean percentage of White and Asian play-mates, by gender, summed for 8- and 9-year-olds in two UK middle schools

	White playmates	Asian playmates
White boys	62.9	19.9
White girls	84.4	7.0
Asian boys	16.2	79.9
Asian girls	9.4	89.6

Source: Boulton and Smith, 1991

liking (Aboud, 1988). Or, children can be asked to assign positive descriptions such as 'work hard' and 'truthful', or negative adjectives such as 'stupid' or 'dirty', to all, some, one or none of the photos representing different ethnic groups (Davey, 1983). The results are rather similar to those of ethnic identity; prejudice seems to increase from 4 to 7 years, mainly at the expense of minority ethnic groups. During middle childhood, white children tend to remain prejudiced against black or minority-group children, while the latter show a more mixed pattern but often become more positive towards their own group.

Aboud (1988) argues that there are definite stages in children's development of prejudice. Before about 3 or 4 years of age, ethnic awareness is largely absent and prejudice is not an issue. From 4 to 7 years, she argues, children perceive other ethnic groups as dissimilar to themselves, and because of this tend to have negative evaluations of them. From 8 years onwards, children can think more flexibly about ethnic differences, and in terms of individuals rather than groups. Thus, the rather natural prejudice of the younger child against dissimilar others can be modified especially from around 7–8 years onwards. (This theory however has some difficulty in explaining why some minority-group children prefer the majority group up to 7 years of age.)

Schools have been a focus for work to reduce racial prejudice in children. This can be assisted by a multi-racial curriculum approach which emphasizes the diversity of racial and cultural beliefs and practices and gives them equal evaluation. Procedures such as Co-operative Group Work (Cowie et al., 1994) may help to bring children of different race (and sex) together in common activities, and thus reduce ethnic preference and prejudice in the classroom.

The rationale for such efforts finds support from Boulton and Smith (1996). A study was made of liking and disliking between white and Asian students aged 8–10 years in racially mixed classes (following procedures similar to those in box 4.1). It was found that generally, 'liked most' nominations were given to own-race classmates; but 'liked-least' nominations were not so strongly biased by race. Nominations for 'co-operates' also tended to follow same-race lines. However, racial bias in liking was not strongly correlated with general racial prejudice as measured by a traditional photo task. In a follow-up study, it was found that the most common reason given for liking other children was that they co-operated and played together; the most common reason for liking someone least was that they were a bully. Race was hardly ever mentioned as a reason for liking or disliking a classmate.

These results present an apparent paradox; children prefer own-race classmates, and rate them as more co-operative; but this is not related to general racial prejudice, and is not consciously based on race. Boulton and Smith hypothesize that it stems from a 'developmental legacy' of playing more with same-race classmates, following the sequence Aboud (1988) proposed. Playing together leads to perceptions of co-operation, and to liking, which will then tend to follow same-race lines unless children are brought into appreciable, close contact with other-race children.

Boulton and Smith also hypothesize that perceptions of bullying are less dependent on actual contact; it is quite possible for peers to see bullying going on, without being involved themselves. Thus, disliking based on perceptions of bullying might be less biased by own-race perception, as indeed was found. On this basis, the authors argue that co-operative group work activities could help improve inter-racial liking, but only if they really do enhance co-operation and are carried out in an environment free from bullying and disruption (Cowie et al., 1994).

Self-concept and Self-esteem

A general term for how people think about themselves is self-concept, or identity. This can refer to all aspects of the self – appearance, personality, ability, as well as gender, nationality, ethnic group. Some aspects of one's self-concept are evaluative; we all compare ourselves with others and think that we are good at some things and not so good at other things. These evaluations we make are called by psychologists self-esteem.

It is possible to measure self-esteem by means of questionnaires. For example, in the Harter Self-Perception Profile for Children (Harter, 1985), designed for 8–13-year-olds, children read a series of paired items such as:

some kids find it hard to make friends BUT some kids find it's pretty easy to make friends

They decide which statement is true for them, and whether it is 'sort of true' or 'really true'. There are 36 such statements, and the answers give scores for the child's own perception of their 'global self-worth', as well as for more specific aspects of self-esteem such as scholastic competence, social acceptance, athletic competence, physical appearance, and behavioural conduct.

The Influence of Television

The mass media exert an important influence on children's awareness of their world, and their behaviour (Clifford, Gunter and McAleer, 1995). The influence of television has attracted most attention among the mass media over the past 20 or 30 years. This is probably because of the relative newness of television, compared with radio, books and magazines, and also because of the degree of exposure that the average child receives. More recently still, the influence of computer and video games has received considerable attention. Patricia Greenfield's *Mind and Media* (1984) is a useful study which looks at and compares the impact of these various media forms. However, most research has been done on television, and it is this we will discuss in this section.

Television has only been available since the late 1940s, but the television set is now commonplace in the great majority of homes. We also know that children watch a great deal of television. When it was first introduced, children in Britain watched about 2 hours a day (box 5.2). This has tended to increase, perhaps as transmission hours have been extended. A survey in Britain made in 1971 (Greenberg, 1976) found a peak of exposure in working-class boys aged 12–14 years (table 5.5). A survey by Cullingford (1984) found that most children (well over 80 per cent at all ages from 7 to 12) reported watching television the previous evening, and typically watching three to six programmes each evening. Many 9-year-olds and almost all older children had watched television after midnight, at some time. Thus, children do not only watch children's programmes. Even from the early surveys (e.g. box 5.2) evidence is that crime thrillers, dramas and comedies have been popular from middle childhood onwards.

Children, then, spend a great deal of time watching television. So how does it affect them? In Britain an early report by Himmelweit et al. (1958) looked for changes in children's behaviour as television started coming into most people's homes (see box 5.2). Much research has also been carried out in the USA. The effect of television probably depends on many factors, such as the child's age, sex and background, and of course the nature of the programmes shown. There has been considerable concern in the USA at the use of children's television advertising to promote 'war toys' such as GIG Joe, Transformers, or Teenage Mutant Ninja Turtles, linked to corresponding programmes (Carlsson-Paige and Levin, 1987; see chapter 6). There is also concern that violence on television may make children more aggressive, and that many programmes portray stereotyped images of sex roles, or of ethnic minorities. Conversely, some social scientists think that television can be used to encourage prosocial and co-operative behaviour, or reduce stereotyped views (Greenfield, 1984). Other researchers think that television does not have nearly as much effect, either way, as most people fear (Cullingford, 1984).

There are different theoretical perspectives on this issue. One point of view is that watching violence on television might be 'cathartic' – a Greek word referring to the purging of emotions which was supposed to result

Table 5.5 Daily amount of television viewing (in hours and minutes) by British adolescents in 1971

| | 12–14 years | | 15–19 years | |
	Middle class	Working class	Middle class	Working class
Male	3.01	3.22	2.01	2.06
Female	2.48	2.48	1.56	2.13

Source: Greenberg, 1976

from watching classical drama. Perhaps children watching James Bond films or any programmes featuring violence have their emotions purged or drained in a similar way. A more prevalent view is that watching television violence may encourage aggression. This could be so because the child may imitate actions seen on television, especially if they are associated with admired figures, or if aggression seems to have successful outcomes. The issue is certainly an important one: it has been estimated that the average child in the USA, by the age of 16, will have spent more time watching television than being in school, and will have seen 13,000 killings on television!

There is certainly some evidence favouring the latter theory rather than the former. For example, one study looked at how young children respond to actual violence between others (Cummings et al., 1985). Two 2-year-old children and their mothers were brought to an apartment-type room in a research laboratory. After settling in, two actors entered a kitchenette area at the far end of the room. Following a script, they simulated first a friendly exchange, then a period of angry verbal conflict, then a reconciliation of their differences. It was observed that the children typically responded to the conflict episodes with signs of distress, and also increased aggression to the other child. Furthermore, some of the children who experienced the simulation the second time, a month later, showed still higher levels of aggression and distress. The witnessing of anger on the part of others seemed to arouse emotion in these children and release aggression, rather than purge it vicariously.

The children in Cumming's study were 2 years old. At that age children do not watch much television, rather paying attention to actual people. But from 3 years of age onwards children seem to watch and imitate people on television as much as actual persons. Do we have direct evidence that television violence produces aggression?

There have been a number of laboratory studies which have suggested this. Typically, children would be shown aggressive or non-aggressive films, and then placed in situations where they could hit a punch bag or inflatable doll, or push buttons which supposedly 'helped' or 'hurt' another child. Children who watched aggressive films punched the bag or doll, or pushed the 'hurt' button, more. However, these experiments have been criticized as very artificial. Hitting the punch bag might have been playful, not aggressive; and some of the experiments seem so contrived that the main effect being measured may be obedience to the experimenter (Cullingford, 1984). We will look in detail at two more naturalistic studies: one is a 'field experiment', while the other has a correlational, longitudinal design.

A field experiment on nursery-school children

Friedrich and Stein (1973) studied 4-year-old children enrolled in a 9-week summer nursery-school programme. After 3 weeks of baseline observations, the 100 children were assigned to 'aggressive' ($n = 30$), 'prosocial' ($n = 30$), or 'neutral' ($n = 40$) conditions. For the next 4 weeks, children saw a total of 12 television programmes. The children in the aggressive condition were taken as a group to see 'Batman' or 'Superman' cartoons; those in the prosocial condition saw *Mr Rogers' Neighbourhood*, which prompted themes of co-operation, sympathy and friendship; while those in the neutral condition saw factual films with little aggressive or prosocial content. During the 4-week period, and also the final 2 weeks, the children's behaviour was closely observed.

Some of the results are shown in table 5.6. It seems that the children who watched the prosocial programmes were scored as more patient ('tolerance of delay') than the children who watched the aggressive programmes, and tended to be more persistent at tasks and more spontaneously helpful or obedient ('rule obedience'). However, the findings on aggressive and prosocial behaviour were complicated. Aggressive behaviour decreased amongst those children who were initially high in aggression, and watched the prosocial or neutral programmes, but there was no significant effect for children initially low in aggression. For prosocial behaviour, it was found that this increased in children from lower-social-class families who watched the prosocial programmes; but it also increased in children from higher-social-class families who watched the aggressive programmes!

The results of this study are rather mixed. They do suggest some positive effects from watching programmes with prosocial rather than aggressive content, but some effects are not statistically significant or even go in the opposite direction. The researchers carried out many analyses and clearly tried to emphasize the 'desired' findings in their report, which is often cited. Nevertheless, the results of these and similar studies leave scope for sceptics.

A longitudinal, correlational study on adolescents

Quite a different research strategy is exemplified in a study by Lefkowitz et al. (1977). These researchers interviewed the parents of 8–9-year-old children (184 boys, 175 girls) to find out their favourite television programmes, and

Table 5.6 Mean changes in rates of behaviour (per minute) in preschool children exposed to television programmes with aggressive, neutral or prosocial content

	Aggressive	Neutral	Prosocial	
Aggression				
initially low	0.039	0.079	0.046	n.s.
initially high	−0.019	−0.123	−0.088	$p < 0.05$
Prosocial				
lower social class	−0.007	−0.026	0.093	$p < 0.05$
higher social class	0.071	0.047	−0.017	$p < 0.05$
Tolerance of delay	−0.016	0.036	0.019	$p < 0.05$
Task persistence	−0.039	−0.068	0.014	n.s.
Rule obedience	−0.039	−0.014	0.014	n.s.

Source: Friedrich and Stein, 1973

hence constructed a measure of exposure to television violence. This score was higher for boys than for girls. The children were also asked to rate the others in their class for aggressiveness. They found that the correlation between the two measures was 0.21 for boys, but only 0.02 for girls. The correlation for boys, while small, was significant ($p < 0.01$); but this correlation could mean either that viewing television violence caused aggression, or that aggressive boys liked watching violent television programmes. Yet another explanation could be that some other factor, parental discord in the home for example, led a child both to watch violent television programmes and also to be aggressive himself.

The same measures were taken 10 years later, when the children were 19-years-old. The correlations between the same two measures at this time, and the correlations between the two time periods, are shown for both boys and girls in figure 5.3. The results for the boys are the most interesting and the most quoted. They show that watching a lot of violent television at age 9 is significantly correlated ($r = 0.31$) with peer-rated aggression at age 19; however, peer-rated aggression at age 9 is not correlated ($r = 0.01$) with watching violent television at age 19. This certainly suggests that watching violent television leads to aggression, rather than vice versa. A similar, though less strong, association was found when aggression was measured by self-ratings, or personality questionnaires. Some other factor or factors might still be responsible for the associations, but this technique (known as 'cross-lagged correlations') does give more weight to the findings than a simple correlation would do. The researchers felt they had identified a small but statistically reliable influence of television violence on aggressive behaviour in boys.

The findings for girls (figure 5.3) are much weaker, and tend to go in the opposite direction. The researchers attempted to explain this by arguing, first that there were few aggressive females portrayed on television (this was in the 1960s), and secondly, that since female aggression was less socially approved of, then 'for girls, television violence viewing may actually be a positively sanctioned social activity in which aggressive girls may express aggression vicariously since they cannot express aggression directly in social interactions' (Lefkowitz et al., 1977, p. 122). It seems that the researchers have resorted here to a 'cathartic' explanation, despite there being no direct evidence to support it.

This longitudinal study was continued until the participants were 30 years of age (Eron, 1987); throughout, there was significant continuity of aggressive tendencies; aggressive youngsters were more likely to have criminal convictions as adults. However, as we saw in chapter 4, there could be many causal factors producing such continuity, independently of watching violent TV programmes.

A continuing controversy

The influence of violent television continues to be debated, and has expanded to the influence of war toys (chapter 6), and of violent videos. In the UK, there was particular concern about violent videos following the murder of a 2-year-old child, Jamie Bulger, in February 1993 by two 10-year-old

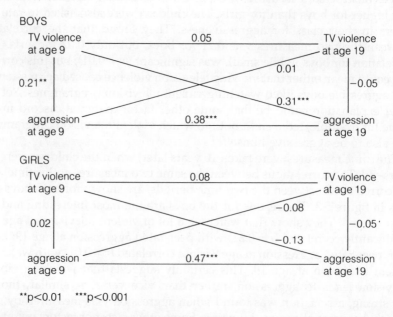

Figure 5.3 Cross-lagged correlations between amount of television violence viewed at ages 9 and 19 and peer-related aggression at ages 9 and 19, for 184 boys and 175 girls (from Lefkowitz et al., 1977).

children; according to Elizabeth Newson, in a widely circulated report *Video Violence and the Protection of Children* (1994), there has been an increase in these kinds of crimes; the new factor which she implicates as the cause of this 'has to be recognised as the easy availability to children of gross images of violence on video' (p. 273). Although the studies we have looked at, and others, do tend to support the hypothesis that television can affect social behaviour, the evidence is not clear-cut. Some findings are small, or not significant. Some are present only for certain measures, or for one sex or for children initially high in aggression.

Some reviewers feel the case is not proved (e.g. Freedman, 1984; Gunten and McAleen, 1997). After all, they would argue, much television violence involves fantasy figures (such as Batman and Superman films in the Friedrich and Stein study), which older children certainly distinguish from real violence. Also children may be 'desensitized' to violence in serials which are viewed basically as entertainment. Cullingford (1984) found that many children could not remember much of what they had viewed the evening before, and that the more programmes they had watched, the fewer details they could remember. He argued that children 'see that television is not to be taken seriously, that the murders are there as stunts, that shooting is a part of entertainment. Thus the violence on television passes them by.' This may seem a bland and complacent view, but the research evidence so far, while suggestive that television does have some effects on aggression or prosocial behaviour, is not of sufficient weight for us to be really certain how important the effect is. We know from case studies of a few abnormal individuals that television violence can on occasion provide a stimulus or model for some violent crime. But it may be that for most children, most of the time, the impact of television is rather small.

If we are considering aggression, then other influences may be much more important. For example, actual aggression in the home between parents might be a more potent influence than fictitious aggression on television. Parental discord has been consistently found to predict later conduct disorders (Rutter, 1981; and chapter 3). We saw the impact of actual (though simulated) aggression on young children in the study by Cummings et al. (1985). The latter state that viewing actual discord in the home could be a powerful influence on aggression in the home, an influence that is not so easily turned off as a television set (cf. p. 99).

◀Television Programmes as a Source of Social Stereotypes▶▶▶

The other major concern of social scientists in connection with the content of television programmes is that they may present a stereotyped picture of real life which may encourage undesirable prejudices. These might be, for example, about female roles (in what is arguably still a male-dominated society), about minority ethnic groups or other nationalities, and about people with disabilities.

Television programmes, like many children's books, do seem to present a one-sided view of sex-roles. Researchers in both the UK and the USA have carried out 'content analyses' of television programmes, seeing how many male and female characters there are, and what sort of roles they have. These studies have found that there are two or three times as many male as female characters, and that the males are usually portrayed as more powerful, dominant, rational and intelligent. Females are often depicted as weak and passive, watching admiringly while the males have most of the action (Sternglanz and Serbin, 1974; Durkin, 1985). There has been increasing awareness of the imbalance, and some attempt to redress it with programmes such as *Wonder Woman* to parallel *Superman* and other popular male-dominated programmes. Nevertheless, many programmes present a stereotyped and sometimes prejudiced or 'sexist' view of sex roles.

We saw earlier how parents, and later peers, are probably very important in sex-role learning, so how important is television viewing in this process? In *Television, Sex Roles and Children* (1985), Kevin Durkin has reviewed the evidence. He concludes that there is little to suggest that the more television children watch, the more sex-stereotyped are their views. The few studies which did report this seem to have been methodologically unsound (as with some of the work on television violence and aggression). Durkin emphasizes that the child or young person is an active agent in interpreting television programmes, not just a passive recipient of a 'dose' of sex-role stereotyping. Thus, it is important to consider the age of the child, his or her understanding of gender, as well as the family and sociocultural context.

A related topic is whether television programmes can be used effectively in 'counter-stereotyping' – presenting sex roles of a deliberately non-traditional kind. This has been attempted in the British children's programme *Rainbow*, and in an American programme called *Freestyle*. There is some evidence that 9- to 12-year-olds who watched *Freestyle* did have less stereotyped views of sex roles, especially when viewing at school was followed by teacher-led discussion. There are, however, important ethical issues to consider in such attempts to 'manipulate' attitudes, which are discussed in Durkin's book.

Other ethnic groups or nationalities may also be portrayed adversely in the mass media. Table 5.7, taken from Himmelweit et al. (1958) (see box 5.2), shows how 'villains' were much more often foreigners than 'heroes' and 'heroines' were (and also of lower social class, though the upper/middle-class bias of British television programmes in the 1950s may have lessened somewhat and does not now get so much attention). Until recently there were few programmes which showed people from ethnic minorities, such as people of Asian or Afro-Caribbean origin, in ordinary roles, or which presented their cultural background. There are now some programmes for young children, such as *You and Me* in Britain, or *Sesame Street* (first made in the USA), which have tried to remedy this. Some research has indicated that these programmes do have positive effects on inter-racial attitudes and encourage greater cultural pride and self-confidence among ethnic minority children (Greenfield, 1984). Similar findings have also been made concerning the portrayal of disabled persons in a more realistic and positive light, for example in *Sesame Street* (Greenfield, 1984; Clifford et al., 1995).

Most reviewers agree that parents have an important role to play in the effects television may have on their children. Besides encouraging responsible viewing habits, parents can talk about programmes with their children, discussing information or attitudes which are being transmitted. From the beginning (e.g. box 5.2) research has indicated that children are influenced most by television portrayals which are not counteracted or put in perspec-

Table 5.7 Percentage of heroes/heroines and villains having certain characteristics in 13 television plays (Himmelweit et al., 1958)

	Heroes/heroines (n = 27)	Villains (n = 11)
British nationality	60	37
Upper or upper/middle class	93	55
Glamorous and high-powered occupations	70	55

Source: Himmelweit et al., 1958

tive by anything in their immediate environment. Thus besides influencing the educational value of television programmes, parents and teachers can probably have an appreciable effect on how programmes influence children's social attitudes and behaviour (Greenfield, 1984; Collins et al., 1981).

◀Further Reading▶▶▶

The best introduction to emotional development in children is P. Harris 1989: *Children and Emotion*, Oxford: Blackwell. Also useful is J. Dunn 1988: *The Beginnings of Social Understanding*, Oxford: Blackwell.

A review of sex differences in children (and adults) is provided by J. Archer and B. Lloyd 1986 (2nd edn): *Sex and Gender*, Harmondsworth: Penguin. A more advanced collection is D. Hargreaves and A. Colley (eds) 1986: *The Psychology of Sex Roles*, London: Harper and Row. S. Golombok and R. Fivush 1994: *Gender Development*, Cambridge: Cambridge University Press, is another useful source.

The development of racial awareness in children is reviewed by F. Aboud 1988: *Children and Prejudice*, Oxford: Basil Blackwell.

A readable review of the effects of television and other mass media on behaviour is in P. M. Greenfield 1984: *Mind and Media: the Effects of Television, Computers and Video Games*, Aylesbury: Fontana. More sceptical views of the impact of television are in D. Howitt 1982: *Mass Media and Social Problems*, Oxford: Pergamon; and C. Cullingford 1984: *Children and Television*, Aldershot: Gower. The impact of television on sex roles is reviewed by K. Durkin 1985: *Television, Sex Roles and Children*, Milton Keynes: Open University Press. Another good source on this is B. Gunter and J. McAleer 1997 (2nd edn): *Children and Television: The One-eyed Monster?* London: Routledge.

◀Discussion Points▶▶▶

1 When does a child develop a sense of self?
2 When can a child understand someone else's emotional state?
3 What causes sex differences in behaviour?
4 How does awareness of race develop?
5 How good is the evidence relating television violence to aggressive behaviour in children?

Box 5.1
Changes in embarrassment as a function of age, sex and situation

This research aimed to examine the origins of a secondary emotion, embarrassment. Some researchers had treated shame and embarrassment as identical emotions. The present researchers argued that whereas shame results from unfavourable comparison of oneself relative to a standard, embarrassment can have a wider meaning and can result from a simple awareness of being observed. Embarrassment was operationalized as a smiling facial expression, combined with or followed by gaze aversion and nervous touching (hand movements to touch hair, clothing, face or other body parts).

How early does embarrassment appear? The researchers worked with 44 children who were around 22 months old; 30 of these were seen again at 35 months. About half the children were boys, half girls. Visits were made to the child's home, and video recordings made, in the mother's presence, of four standard situations.

The four situations were:

1 dance (mother): the mother took a small tambourine and asked the child to dance;
2 overpraise: the experimenter interacted with the child and praised him/her effusively about clothes, appearance, etc.;
3 mirror: the mother called the child to a mirror to see their reflection (the camera was positioned to see the reflection in the mirror;
4 dance (experimenter): the experimenter asked the child to dance.

Altogether 52 per cent of the children showed embarrassment (using the above definition) in at least one situation at 22 months; and 82 per cent at 35 months (a significant increase). The percentage of children who showed embarrassment in each situation is shown in box table 5.1.1. At 2 years, this shows percentages for the cross-sectional analysis (all children) and for the longitudinal analysis (only the 30 children also seen at 3 years).

At 22 months there was no significant difference, statistically, between the four situations. At 35 months, the most embarrassment was observed in the dance (experimenter) and mirror conditions, with the dance (experimenter) condition showing a significant increase with age.

There was some indication that more girls showed embarrassment at 22 months, with no sex difference at 35 months; however, the sample size may be rather small to establish sex differences. As it is, one can see some appreciable differences at 2 years between the cross-sectional and longitudinal data (especially for dance/mother), which probably reflect sample size variations. Children do vary individually in how much embarrassment they show; and in this study, significant consistency in likelihood of showing embarrassment was obtained from the longitudinal data.

The researchers took their findings to indicate that embarrassment could emerge following self-referential behaviour. Referring to other data on the latter (as in the mirror task, see table 5.1), they reported that the 2-year-olds who did not show

Box Table 5.1.1   Percentage of children showing embarrassment in different situations

AGE	Dance/M	Mirror	Overpraise	Dance/E
2 yrs/C–S	27.7	25.0	29.5	29.5
2 yrs/LONG	16.7	26.7	30.0	33.3
3 yrs/LONG	20.0	35.3	26.7	56.7

Source: Adapted from Lewis et al., 1991

self-referential behaviour, did not show embarrass-ment. However, some 2- and 3-year-olds who did show self-referential behaviour, did not show em-barrassment; thus, self-referential behaviour was a necessary but not a sufficient condition for this self-conscious emotion to be displayed.

This study is an attempt to do a naturalistic experiment; the child is in the home with the mother, the mother is asked to act as naturally as possible, but there are standardized procedures to follow, and a videocamera is present. The report does not give any details of how intrusive the pro-cedure was, or what familiarization procedures (if any) were followed. Some of the sample variability in responses (box table 5.1.1) might be attributed to these factors. There was a high dropout rate in the longitudinal study (14 out of 44) due to 'family moves and family unwillingness to participate in the follow-up visit' (p. 7), suggesting that intrusiveness was a problem for some families. However, re-search of this kind is likely to be difficult and have drawbacks, whatever procedures are followed.

Based on material in M. Lewis, C. Stanger, M. W. Sullivan and P. Barone (1991), *British Journal of Devel-opmental Psychology*, 9, 485–92.

Box 5.2
Television and the child: an empirical study of the effect of television on the young

The objective of this research study was to assess the impact of television on children and young people. The study was funded by the Nuffield Foun-dation, at the suggestion of the Audience Research Department of the BBC. Television sets were only just becoming common in households during the 1950s, thus there was considerable interest and concern about what the effects might be. At this time there was also still the opportunity to com-pare large numbers of children who both did, and did not, have a television set in their home.

The researchers carried out both a 'main survey' and some subsidiary studies, in particular a 'before-and-after study'. The main survey was carried out in London, Portsmouth, Sunderland and Bristol, from May to July 1955. Questionnaires were given to children aged 10–11 and 13–14 years. In addition, children filled in diaries of their activities after school for one week, and measures of personality and teachers' ratings were obtained.

The design compared children who had televi-sion at home ('viewers') with those who did not, and were not regular guest viewers ('controls'). Viewers and controls were matched individually for age, sex, intelligence score and social class; alto-gether 1,854 matched viewers and controls were tested. The results of this comparison could give an indication of how television viewing affected chil-dren; but a critic might still raise objections. The design is not tightly controlled (for which partici-pants should be assigned randomly to conditions) but is correlational in design, taking advantage of the fact that many homes did not yet have tele-vision. Despite the matching on some criteria, viewer children and their families might differ from controls in other respects – as they clearly did in so far as viewers' parents had chosen to acquire a television set while control families had not, despite having similar incomes. In other words, there might be pre-existing differences between children from homes which bought a television set early, and those which did not. These, rather than the effects of television *per se*, might be responsible for any findings from the main study.

As a check on this, the researchers carried out a before-and-after study (a quasi-experiment, p. 13) in Norwich, where a new television transmitter was being introduced. They gave questionnaires to 10–11- and 13–14-year-olds both before the instal-lation (when hardly any family there had a television set) and one year later (when many, but not all, had). At the later point in time they matched view-ers and controls as in the main study, with 370 children in all. They could then see whether differ-ences found later were already present in families before a television set had been acquired. In some cases this was so: for example, the main study found that viewers attended Sunday School less regularly. The before-and-after study revealed that this, and a generally lower level of religious interest and observance, was a characteristic of families who bought television sets early and not an effect of television as such.

The main findings were that both age groups watched television for about two hours a day; more than any other single leisure activity. There were no sex or social class differences in this, but more intelligent children did spend less time viewing. Also, more active, outgoing and sociable children spent less time watching. Children settled down to a routine within about 3 months of their family acquiring a set. Many children watched, and preferred, 'adult' programmes, particularly crime thrillers, comedies, variety programmes and family serials. Viewers spent less time than controls listening to the radio, going to the cinema and reading. The findings for reading were complex, however; acquisition of a television caused an initial decline in the time spent reading books and comics, but book-reading tended to recover, especially as some television programmes such as serials encouraged children to read the books on which they were based.

There were small but consistent differences in values and outlook. Viewers were more ambitious about jobs and more 'middle class' in their values. Adolescent girl viewers were more concerned about growing up and marrying than controls. Viewers made fewer value judgements about foreigners, though where stereotypes were given, they tended to reflect those offered by television. In general, television had most impact where the child could not turn for information to parents, friends and the immediate environment. Effects tended to be greatest in older children of least intelligence.

Many children spoke of being frightened by certain programmes, and sometimes of how these caused nightmares or difficulties in falling asleep. Such reactions seemed accentuated by viewing in the dark. Children enjoyed exciting programmes and being a little frightened, but not being really scared. Aggression on television upset them if they could identify themselves with the situation; the sheer amount of physical violence was less important. Viewers were no more aggressive or maladjusted than controls.

There was little difference in general knowledge between viewers and controls, except for less intelligent or younger children unable to read well, where the stimulus of television did give them an advantage. Viewing seemed to have little effect on school performance, or teachers' rating of concentration; teachers did say that they felt television viewing was a cause of tiredness in the morning, but this stereotype was not borne out by the comparison of viewers and controls.

This research has strengths in its scope and its large number of subjects. It is in some ways of historical interest, as both the nature of television programmes and children's behaviour may have changed in the 30 intervening years. At the time there were no programme transmissions between 6.00 pm and 7.30 pm; only one or two channels were available; programmes were in black and white; and the content was probably more 'middle class' and certainly contained less for ethnic minorities than at present. Probably levels of violence on television were lower than now, although it was already a cause for concern. It is also possible that 'second generation' television-viewing families have adapted to television in a way that affects its impact on their children. However, the study is virtually unrepeatable in that it took advantage of a time when genuine comparisons of viewers and non-viewers in Britain could still be carried out.

Based on material in H. T. Himmelweit, A. N. Oppenheim and P. Vince 1958: *Television and the Child: An Empirical Study of the Effect of Television on the Young*, London: Oxford University Press.

6 Play

Three sequences of behaviour are described below. Study them and think what they have in common.

Example 1 A 2-year-old lies in his cot, babbling to himself: 'Big Bob. Big Bob. Big Bob. Big and little. Little Bobby. Little Nancy. Little Nancy. Big Bob and Nancy and Bobby. And Bob. And two three Bobbys. Three Bobbys. Four Bobbys. Six.' (All with giggles and exaggerated pronunciation.)

Example 2 Helen, a 4-year-old, is sitting in a play house, by a table with a plastic cup, saucer and teapot. She calls out 'I'm just getting tea ready! Come on, it's dinner time now!' Charlotte, also 4, answers 'Wait!'; she wraps up a teddy in a cloth in a pram, comes in and sits opposite Helen, who says 'I made it on my own! I want a drink.' (She picks up the teapot.) 'There's only one cup – for me!' (pretends to pour tea into only one cup). Charlotte pretends to pour from the teapot into an imaginary cup, which she then pretends to drink from. Darren, a 3-year-old, approaches. Charlotte goes and closes the door, shutting a pretend bolt and turning a pretend key; but Helen says 'No, he's daddy; you're daddy aren't you?' (to Darren). Charlotte 'unbolts' and 'unlocks' the door, and Darren comes in.

Example 3 Some 6- and 7-year olds are in a school playground. A boy runs up to another, laughing, and grabs his shoulders, turns and runs off. The second boy chases the first, catches him by the waist and pulls him round. They tussle and swing around, then fall and roll over on the ground, grappling. They get up and run off, laughing and chasing again.

Most observers would agree in saying that, despite their differences, all three are examples of play, or playful behaviour. Respectively they could be described as language play, fantasy or pretend play and rough-and-tumble play. This chapter first discusses why we consider such behaviour sequences to be playful, what are the defining characteristics of play, and how it differs from the related behaviour of exploration. The next section examines the development of various kinds of play in childhood. The ideas of leading play theorists are then discussed, before the final section examines what empirical studies can tell us about the significance of play in children's development.

◄The Characteristics of Playful Behaviour►►►

There have been numerous attempts to characterize or define play; a concise definition seems almost impossible. Different authors tend to list different selections of criteria, or to give definitions which embody some of these criteria. There is probably less agreement between researchers as to the definition of play than there is between observers as to whether an episode of behaviour is playful or not!

Some generally agreed features of play are worth noting but fall short of being defining criteria. For example, play is often described as an 'active' behaviour (yet, not all play is physically active, see example 1 above); it is described as characteristic of infancy and childhood (yet adults play, even if it is often with children); and as behaviour which is easily suppressed by other motivations, such as hunger, fear or anxiety, curiosity, or fatigue.

The last feature is related to the idea that play does not have an end in itself, or external goal. Thus, if an external goal is present (such as a need to eat, or to seek comfort) then play ceases. This has led to a functional definition of play, that the behaviour has no clear immediate benefits or obvious goal. Symons (1978) advanced this sort of definition for monkey social play, but it can equally apply to human play (Smith, 1982). If you look at examples 1 to 3 above, it is not clear when an episode is completed, or obvious what the purpose of the behaviour is. In fact, some theorists believe the child gets benefits from playing, but they are not clear, immediate ones. Indeed, there is considerable disagreement about exactly what the benefits of play are (see pp. 195–9).

Fagan (1974) made a distinction between the functional approach just outlined, and a structural definition of play. The latter attempts to describe the sorts of behaviour that only occur in play, or the way in which behaviours are performed playfully.

The main examples of behaviours that only occur in play, are play signals. In mammals they often take the form of an open-mouthed play face (as in monkeys grappling), or a bouncy gambol (as in puppies or kittens initiating a chase). In children similarly laughter and the associated 'open mouth play face' (see figure 6.1) usually signals play. Such play signals are especially useful in rough-and-tumble play (example 3 on p. 177), where they can indicate that no aggressive intention is implied in a chase or wrestle.

Not all play is indexed by play signals, however. Often play is made up entirely of behaviours familiar in other contexts – running, manipulating objects, etc. According to the structural approach, we think of these behaviours as being done playfully if they are 'repeated', 'fragmented', 'exaggerated' or 're-ordered'. For example, a child just running up a slope may not be playing; but if she runs up and slides down several times (repetition), runs just half-way up (fragmentation), takes unusually large or small steps or jumps (exaggeration) or crawls up and then runs down (re-ordering), we would probably agree that it was playful.

This structural approach is not in opposition to the functional one. After all, the child running up and down the slope has no immediate purpose, apart from enjoyment. The two approaches are logically distinct, however.

Another approach, which can encompass both the previous ones, is to say that observers identify play or playfulness by a number of different play criteria. No one criterion is sufficient, but the more criteria are present, the more agreement we will have that the behaviour is play. A formal model along these lines, proposed by Krasnor and Pepler (1980), is shown in figure 6.2. 'Flexibility' sums up the structural characteristics of play – variation in form and content. 'Positive affect' refers to the enjoyment of play, especially indexed by signals such as laughter. 'Nonliterality' refers to the 'as if' or pretend element (see example 2 on p. 177 above). 'Intrinsic motivation' refers to the idea that play is not constrained by external rules or social demands, but is done for its own sake.

An empirical test of Krasnor and Pepler's model was made by Smith and Vollstedt (1985). They used the four criteria above, and a fifth – means/ends, i.e. the child is more interested in the performance of the behaviour than in its outcome. They made a video film of nursery-school children playing and

(a)

(b)

Figure 6.1   Play signals: (a) 'open mouth face' in a chimpanzee (from Hooff, 1972); (b) 'play face' in a human child (from Smith, 1974).

designated short, discrete episodes which they asked 70 adults to view. Some scored each episode as to whether it was playful or not, others as to the applicability of the play criteria. Analyses showed that the episodes seen as playful were often seen as nonliteral, flexible and showing positive affect. Furthermore, the more of these were present, the higher the ratings for playfulness. Means/ends also correlated with play, but did not add anything to the first three criteria. Interestingly, the intrinsic motivation criterion did not correlate with play judgements, despite its common occurrence in definitions of play. Observers often rated non-playful activities (such as watching others, or fighting) as intrinsically motivated; equally some play episodes were externally constrained, e.g. by the demands of others in social play.

The play criterion approach seems a promising one: it does not attempt a one-sentence definition – a seemingly hopeless task. It does acknowledge, however, the continuum from non-playful to playful behaviour, and seeks to identify how observers actually decide to call a behaviour sequence 'play'.

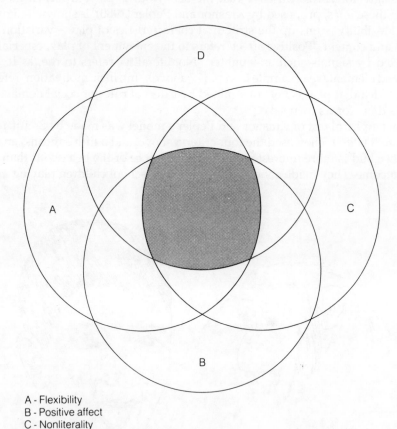

A - Flexibility
B - Positive affect
C - Nonliterality
D - Intrinsic motivation

Figure 6.2 A model of play criteria. The shaded area is that most likely to be considered as playful (from Krasnor and Pepler, 1980).

The main criteria so far identified for young children, as we have seen, are enjoyment, flexibility and pretence.

Exploration and play

A behaviour that is sometimes confused with play is exploration. These were often subsumed together in the 1950s and 1960s, perhaps because of the influence of behaviourism and learning theory. Both exploration and play were awkward for traditional learning theorists, as neither was obviously goal-seeking or under the control of reinforcers. It is also true that with very young children, during sensori-motor development (see chapter 11), the distinction between exploration and play is difficult to make, as for young infants, all objects are novel. By the preschool years, however, the distinction is clearer. An experiment illustrating this, by Hutt (1966), is detailed in box 6.1. Using a novel toy, Hutt suggested that children typically proceed from specific exploration of the object to more playful behaviour.

◀The Development of Play▶▶▶

Fantasy and sociodramatic play

The beginnings of fantasy play can be seen from about 12–15 months of age. In the course of his extensive observations of his own children, Piaget (1951) recorded the following behaviour on the part of his daughter Jacqueline (the numbers refer to Jacqueline's age, in years, months and days):

> every appearance of awareness of 'make-believe' first appeared at 1;3(12) in the following circumstances. She saw a cloth whose fringed edges vaguely recalled those of her pillow; she seized it, held a fold of it in her right hand, sucked the thumb of the same hand and lay down on her side, laughing hard. She kept her eyes open, but blinked from time to time as if she were alluding to closed eyes. Finally, laughing more and more she cried 'Nene' [Nono]. The same cloth started the same game on the following days. At 1;3(13) she treated the collar of her mother's coat in the same way. At 1;3(30) it was the tail of her rubber donkey which represented the pillow! And from 1;5 onwards she made her animals, a bear and a plush dog, also do 'nono'. (p. 69)

The development of pretend play is documented by Fenson and Schnell (1986), who distinguish three parallel trends: decentration, decontextualization and integration.

Decentration

(a) child pretends to drink from empty cup
(b) child pretends to feed doll from empty cup
(c) child makes doll feed itself from empty cup

Decontextualization

(a)   child uses empty cup to drink from
(b)   child uses object such as shell as pretend cup to drink from
(c)   child pretends to drink from imaginary cup

Integration

(a)   child pretends to feed doll
(b)   child feeds one doll, then another
(c)   child feeds doll, then washes it, and puts it to bed.

The earliest pretend play tends to involve the child directing actions towards herself – in Jacqueline's case, pretending to sleep on a cloth. It is clear from Piaget's records that a month or so later Jacqueline directed the same actions to a toy bear and a stuffed dog. This is what is meant by decentration – incorporating other participants into pretend activities. The others may be parents (e.g. the child tries to feed a parent with an empty cup), or stuffed animals or dolls. By around 24 months the child can get the doll itself to act as an agent, rather than have things done to it (see above).

Early pretend play also depends heavily on realistic objects – actual cups, combs, spoons, etc., or very realistic substitutes. Decontextualization refers to the ability to use less realistic substitute objects – for example, a wooden block as a 'cake', or a stick as a 'gun'. Experiments have shown that the more different the object from its referent, the more difficulty children have in using it in a pretend way. It has also been shown that adults can help the process, by modelling or prompting the pretend use. In one study (Fein, 1975), after modelling by an adult, some 93 per cent of 2-year-olds would imitate making a detailed horse model 'drink' from a plastic cup; however, only 33 per cent would imitate making a horsey shape 'drink' from a clam shell. The less realistic objects made the pretence more difficult, especially as two substitutions were needed (the horsey shape, and the clam shell). If the horse alone or the cup alone were realistic, 79 per cent and 61 per cent of the children respectively could imitate successfully.

By 3 years of age this kind of decontextualized pretence occurs much more spontaneously in children's play. Here we also begin to get quite imaginary objects or actions, without any real or substitute object being present (example 2 on p. 177 has several examples). While possible for 3- and 4-year-olds, this is easier still in middle childhood. When asked to pretend to brush their teeth, or comb their hair, one study (Overton and Jackson, 1973) found that 3- and 4-year-olds used a substitute body part, such as a finger, as the brush, or comb; whereas most 6–8-year-olds (and indeed, adults) imagined the brush or comb in their hand.

These studies have usually relied on laboratory situations, where infants have been provided with particular toys. A much more naturalistic study has been reported by Haight and Miller (1993), in a book *Pretending at Home*. They reported a longitudinal study of nine children (four girls and five boys), each observed in the home environment and videofilmed for 3 or 4 hours at 12, 16,

20, 24, 30, 36 and 48 months of age. An interesting finding was that three-quarters of pretend play was social; usually with mothers, though equally often other children by 48 months. Even the earliest pretend play episodes were more likely to be social, than solitary. The authors describe one characteristic of this mother–child social, pretend play as being mutual responsiveness, with neither partner initiating or dominating most episodes. Joint episodes were generally longer than episodes of solo pretend play. While

Table 6.1 Stages in social pretend play with mothers, and with peers; adapted from Howes and Matheson, 1992

Age period	Play with mother	Play with peers
12–15 months	Mother structures child's actions by commenting, suggesting, and demonstrating. Child is corrected when her pretend acts violate the real world	Isolated pretend acts within social play do not elicit a response; but children watch and imitate the partner's pretend
16–20 months	As above; and child imitates, watches and complies with mother	Children engage in similar or identical pretend acts; and attempt to recruit partner to joint pretend
21–24 months	Mother becomes an interested spectator who creates a context and provides support for the child's enactments	Children engage in similar pretend actions while they simultaneously engage in social exchange; join the pretend of the partner, attempt to recruit the partner to joint play, and organize materials for joint pretend.
25–30 months	Child offers storyline or script. Mother requests creation of new elements and prompts child to a more realistic or detailed enactment	Each partner's pretend reflects the same script but their actions show no within-pair integration. Partners inform each other of the script by comments on their own pretend and telling the other how to act
31–36 months	Mother praises and encourages independence; may pretend with child	Joint pretend with enactment of complementary roles. Children discriminate between speech used for enactment and speech about enactment; assign roles, and negotiate pretend themes and plans
37–48 months	As above	Children adopt relational roles, are willing to accept identity transformations and generate or accept instruction for appropriate role performance; they negotiate scripts and dominant roles and use metacommunication to establish the play script and clarify role enactment

nine children is a small sample on which to make generalizations, this study does make the point forcibly that laboratory studies looking at solo, pretend play can only give a very partial account of real-life pretence.

Reviewing both laboratory-based and more naturalistic studies, Howes and Matheson (1992) have developed a scheme for the development of social pretend play, with mothers, older siblings and peers. A slightly simplified version of this is shown in table 6.1. The work of Howes and others shows the change from predominantly adult-oriented to predominantly peer-oriented social pretend. You could look again at example 2 at the start of the chapter; match the role assignment and negotiation of the action at the end with the 37–48 months stage in table 6.1.

In table 6.1 the word 'script' appears from the 25–30-month stage onwards. Pretend play sequences become more integrated with age. Initially, one action is involved; then variations on a single theme, such as stirring the spoon in the cup; then drinking; or feeding two dolls in succession. By 2 years of age multischeme combinations are in evidence. Mini-stories begin to be acted out, following 'scripts' such as shopping, or bedtime (plate 6.1). Language plays an increasing role in maintaining the play structure. All these developments come together in sociodramatic play, prominent in 3- to 6-year-olds. Here, two or more children act out definite roles, such as mummy and daddy, spacemen and monsters, doctors and patients (Singer and Singer, 1991).

The ultimate in imagination in the preschool/early school years is perhaps the imaginary companion, who may follow the child around, or need to be fed at mealtimes, or tucked up in bed with the child. Some one-quarter to one-third of children have some form of imaginary companion, judging from parents' reports (Partington and Grant, 1984).

Plate 6.1   Preschool children acting out a pretend sequence of preparing a meal.

Language play

The most well-known examples of language play come from Weir's book *Language in the Crib* (1962). Weir left a tape recorder on under her 2-year-old son's crib at night-time. At this age toddlers often talk to themselves a lot before going to sleep, or waking up. Sample extracts are shown on p. 177 and p. 305. A similar study (Keenan and Klein, 1975) recorded social play, with syllables and words, between twins aged 21 months. Children appear to use these presleep monologues or dialogues to play with and practise linguistic forms they are in the process of acquiring (Kuczaj II, 1986; and p. 305).

The humorous use of language becomes very prominent in the older preschool child. Chukovsky (1963) reports examples of rhyming poems created by 3- and 4-year-old children:

> I'm a whale
> This is my tail
> I'm a flamingo. Look at my wingo.

Preschool children will spontaneously express a whole range of humorous responses, including interactive 'pre-riddles', conventional riddles and joking behaviours. However, what they find amusing changes with age and cognitive development. By about age 2, incongruous language and labelling of objects and events appear humorous:

> J., aged 3 years, while drawing a picture of her mother, put hair all round the circle face and then called it 'Mommy porcupine' with shouts of glee.

By about age 4 conceptual incongruity appears humorous:

> C., aged 5, said to her mother 'I can play a piano by ear'. Then she banged her ear on the piano keyboard and laughed.

By about age 6, children begin to understand and enjoy humour with multiple meanings (McGhee, 1979); however, they usually cannot do so when younger, and often laugh inappropriately or make up 'pre-riddles':

> L., aged 3 years, after her older sister told the riddle, 'Why does the turtle cross the road? To get to the Shell station', insisted on telling a 'riddle' also. Her riddle was 'Why does the dog cross the road? To get to the station' (she laughed at the 'riddle').

> B., aged 5 years, asked 'What's red and white? A newspaper' and laughed at his 'riddle'.

> S., aged 6, asked his uncle and father this riddle, 'Why was 6 afraid of 7? Because 7, 8, 9!' Everyone laughed at this joke. (Examples adapted from Bergen, 1990)

Language is often used playfully in sociodramatic play episodes. Several examples have been given by Garvey (1977): 'Hello, my name is Mr Elephant!'; 'Hello, my name is Mr Donkey!' In school-age children rhymes and word play are common, and have been documented by Opie and Opie (1959). The repetition of well-known verses, with variations, has more in common with the rule-governed games common by the age of 6 or 7 years (see below and also chapter 10).

Rough-and-tumble play

The origins of play fighting and chasing may lie in the vigorous physical play which parents often engage in with toddlers – tickling, throwing and crawling after them, for example. Actual play fighting between peers is common from 3 years on through to adolescence. Wrestling generally involves some struggle for superior position, one child trying to get on top of another and pin him or her down; though roles quickly reverse themselves. More fragmentary episodes involve pushing, clasping, leg play and kicking. Chasing play is generally included in rough-and-tumble as well (example 3, p. 177).

The friendly intent in play of this kind is typically signalled by smiling and laughter. Up to adolescence play fighting seems distinct from serious fighting, at least in the majority of cases. The former is carried out with friends, who often stay together after the episode. The latter is often not between friends, involves different facial expressions and the participants usually do not stay together after the encounter. Play fights tend to be shorter, are not watched by others (plate 6.2) and participants do not hit hard. Young children themselves are aware of these differences. One study (Costabile et al., 1991) used videofilms of play fighting and real fighting made in Italy, and England. They showed the films to children aged 8 and 11 years, and asked them to say whether each episode was playful or real fighting, and why. Children were very good at this, and gave reasons such as:

'it didn't last long enough to be a [real] fight'
'it was only a play fight because he didn't hit him hard'
'it was a real fight because they were both angry'
'that was a play fight as the other boys didn't watch them'.

Interestingly, children from both countries were just as good at recognizing play fighting in the videofilm from the other country, as their own; the evidence to date suggests that the forms of play fighting are very similar across cultures.

Although play fighting and real fighting are usually distinct, they sometimes get confused. Pellegrini (1988, 1994) has shown that in boys, sociometrically rejected children (see p. 118) are much more likely than other children to be involved in play fights which turn into real fights; whether deliberately or through a lack of social skills, these children may respond inappropriately to the usual play signals. Primary school teachers often say that a lot of play fighting becomes real fighting, and it is possible that they are basing this judgement on the minority of children for whom this is true

Plate 6.2   Children play fighting.

(Schafer and Smith, 1996). For most children, only around 1 per cent of play fights turns into real fights. However, there is evidence that by adolescence, strength and dominance become more important in the choice of partners in play fighting, and deliberate manipulation of play conventions may then become more common (Boulton, 1992).

War toys and war play

Another kind of aggressive play is when children use toy guns or weapons, or combat figures, to engage in pretend fighting or warfare. This kind of play is banned in some nurseries and playgroups. Parents too have mixed views about it. Costabile et al. (1992) surveyed parents in Italy, and England. Some actively discouraged it:

'I do not like it. In fact children who do war play become less sensible and less obedient.'

Some were uncertain, or felt it should be allowed within limits:

'Unsure. We don't encourage it, but don't discourage it, either.'

Some allowed it unconditionally:

'A natural part of a child's development, just as they act out cooking etc. War/fighting is featured in so many things it would be difficult and unnatural to exclude it from a child's life.'

Researchers too are divided. Nancy Carlsson-Paige and Diane Levin have written two books on the issue, *The War Play Dilemma* (1987) and *Who's Calling the Shots?* (1990), in which they argue that war toys and combat figures encourage stereotyped good-versus-evil aggressive scripts, which impoverish the child's imagination and encourage actual aggressive behaviour. They recognize the difficulties in banning such play entirely (there are plenty of stories of children making toy guns out of lego, if replica guns are banned in the nursery); but advocate adults intervening to turn such play to more constructive, and less aggressive ends (a policy also favoured by most parents, in the survey by Costabile et al.). However, Brian Sutton-Smith (1988) argues that for children, war play is clearly pretend, and just reflects an aspect of real life. As one boy said when his father asked him not to use toy guns:

'But Dad, I don't want to shoot anybody, I just want to play.'

The developmental issues regarding war play have still to be resolved (see Smith, 1994; Goldstein, 1995; and also p. 170). The issue bears some similarity to the debate about violent videos and television (see chapter 5). On the one hand, for most children such activities are natural, separated from real life, and probably do little if any harm. But it is easy to feel uncomfortable when the activity becomes very prominent; and, although the evidence is uncertain, there is the possibility that for children who are already disturbed or have violent tendencies, sanctioning violent play (or violent videos) can make matters worse.

Video and computer games

Another area of concern in the 1990s has been the increased time children spend with computer games or in video arcades. As with war toys, much of this activity is engaged in by boys, and it is very popular in the 9–15-year age range (Goldstein, 1994). Many such games do have aggressive fantasy themes.

Playing video games may increase hand–eye co-ordination and skill at that particular game, but what are the other effects? Parents sometimes fear that video games lead to social isolation. However, a study of 300 French schoolchildren (Bonnafont, 1992, in Goldstein, 1994) found that while parent–child communication might be disrupted (since parents often did not understand the games), there was a lot of social contact with peers in the context of video games.

Games with rules

The play of preschool children often has some rule structure; for example, if someone is role-playing 'doctor' to a 'patient', there are some constraints on what he or she is expected to do, exerted by the other participants. Nevertheless, any rules or constraints are largely private to that particular play episode, and can be changed at any time ('I'm not the doctor now, I'm a policeman'). By the time children are 6 or 7 years old, rule-governed games like hopscotch, tig or football take up much more playground time. These are games with public rules, sometimes codified, with much less latitude for change. The transition from play to games is nevertheless a gradual one (see also chapter 7, and Piaget's study of the game of marbles).

Play sequences

Piaget (1951) described a developmental sequence from practice play, through symbolic play, to games with rules, while acknowledging that these were overlapping stages. By 'practice play', Piaget mainly meant early sensori-motor play in infants, and most animal play. As others have pointed out, if practice play means play that is neither symbolic nor rule-governed, then it can occur well beyond the sensori-motor period. Indeed rough-and-tumble would seem to count as practice play, unless it has symbolic elements (as in monster play), or is rule-governed (as in tig).

Smilansky (1968) postulated a four-fold sequence, from functional play (similar to practice play) to constructive play, then dramatic play and finally games with rules. She thus suggested that constructive play (making something, e.g. from Lego bricks) was intermediate between functional and dramatic play (plates 6.3, 6.4 and 6.5). Some American play researchers have used this scheme as a 'play hierarchy'. Piaget (1951), however, thought that 'constructive games are not a definite stage like the others, but occupy . . . a position halfway between play and intelligent work, or between play and

Plate 6.3 'Practice' or 'functional' play in a 1-year-old infant; simple actions like mouthing, banging or pushing are performed with one or two objects.

Plate 6.4　These 3-year-olds are engaged in 'constructive play' – making things from objects.

Plate 6.5　This child is engaged in a simple pretend sequence – putting a doll to sleep in a pram.

imitation'. The goal-directed nature of much constructive activity, for Piaget, made it more accommodative than purely playful behaviour (see later, and chapter 11). Either it was work-like, or some symbolic element might be present. The distinct, sequential nature of constructive play in Smilansky's scheme is thus questionable (Takhvar and Smith, 1990).

Factors affecting play

We have seen how parents often encourage play when it starts to appear in their young children. Some researchers think this early encouragement is very important. MacDonald (1992) argues that it is a form of parental investment (cf. p. 39) in children, which is of recent historical origin. He contrasts typical high levels of parent–child play in higher socioeconomic groups in urban societies with lower levels in lower socioeconomic groups and in tribal societies, where there is more emphasis on sibling rearing.

There does seem to be a social class difference in parents' attitudes to pretend play. Newson and Newson (1968), in a longitudinal interview study of child-rearing in Nottinghamshire families, found that for most social class groups more than 70 per cent of mothers reported that they sometimes joined in play with their 4-year-olds; this fell to under 50 per cent in social class V (labourers, cleaners, long-term unemployed). Similarly, there was a social class difference in whether children talked about their fantasies to their mothers. Social class differences have also been reported in children's sociodramatic play in nurseries and playgroups. Several studies have suggested that children from disadvantaged backgrounds and non-urban societies show less frequent and less complex fantasy and sociodramatic play, starting with a large-scale study by Smilansky (1968) in Israel.

These studies have been criticized by McLoyd (1982) for poor methodology. Some failed adequately to define social class, or confounded it with other variables such as race, or school setting. McLoyd claims that the general pattern is one of marginal and conflicting findings. Global statements about social class may be unwarranted, since any such effects will vary with historical time, cultural group and even location within a country. For example, the results of the Newsons' study may be valid for white children in the Nottinghamshire area around 25 years ago, but not for other groups, in other times and other places. If nothing else, the number and type of families placed in social class V (as 'persistently unemployed') would be different in a period of continuing high unemployment.

If children, for whatever reason, do not engage in much fantasy or sociodramatic play in nursery school, it does seem that nursery staff can encourage it by play tutoring. This technique was pioneered by Smilansky (1968), and has been summarized by Christie (1986). Such intervention at its least intrusive involves verbal guidance or suggestions; alternatively, more direct involvement in the play may be made by acting as a model for roles and actions, or by giving deliberate training in imaginative activities or fantasy themes. Play tutoring can be made even more effective if appropriate toys are provided (e.g. dressing-up clothes, hospital props), and if children are taken on visits (e.g. to a zoo, hospital or factory).

Several investigators have studied sex differences in children's play. Differences in the frequency of fantasy play are inconsistent, but there are sex differences in the choice of roles in sociodramatic play. Naturally enough, girls tend to act out domestic scenes – shopping, washing the baby, etc. Boys less often imitate male roles, as they have usually not been able to observe their father at work; rather, they rely on roles familiar from books (e.g. police, fireman), or act out film or television characters such as Spiderman.

There does appear to be a reliable sex difference in rough-and-tumble play; this has almost always been found to be preferred by boys. A predisposition for boys to engage more in this activity may be related to the influence of sex hormones during the period of fetal growth, as indicated by Collaer and Hines (1995). However, social factors are likely to be very important too; fathers engage in more rough-and-tumble play with boys, even by 2 years of age, and this kind of play is very much socially stereotyped as a male activity (Goldstein, 1994; see also chapter 5).

◀ Play Theorists ▶ ▶

Theoretical perspectives on the nature of play and on its role in development cover a wide range. Several influential ideas can be traced back to the late nineteenth century and early twentieth century. The views of a number of earlier play theorists and educators are summarized here.

Friedrich Froebel   The ideas of Froebel, as expounded in *The Education of Man* (published posthumously in 1906), were influential in the start of the kindergarten and nursery school movement. 'Kindergarten' translates from German as 'child-garden', and this aptly sums up Froebel's ideas about play and development: 'Play, truly recognized and rightly fostered, unites the germinating life of the child attentively with the ripe life of experiences of the adult and thus fosters the one through the other.' On this view play exemplifies development from within the child, but can be nurtured by adult guidance and the provision of appropriate materials. Froebel's influence, following that of Pestalozzi (with whom he studied for two years), encouraged a positive evaluation of the educational significance of play, as compared with the rote-learning approach which nevertheless became characteristic of many infant schools at the end of the nineteenth century (Whitbread, 1972).

Herbert Spencer   In his book *The Principles of Psychology* (1878, final edition 1898), Spencer proposed a less enthusiastic view of play. He believed play is carried out 'for the sake of the immediate gratifications involved, without reference to ulterior benefits'. He suggested that the higher animals are better able to deal with the immediate necessities of life, and that the nervous system, rather than remaining inactive for long periods, stimulates play. 'Thus it happens that in the more evolved creatures, there often recurs an energy somewhat in excess of immediate needs . . . Hence play of all kinds – hence this tendency to superfluous and useless exercise of faculties that have been quiescent.' Spencer's approach has been labelled the 'surplus energy' theory by subsequent writers, who have noted that the idea can be traced back further to the eighteenth-century philosopher Friedrich von Schiller.

Karl Groos   At the turn of the century, Groos published two influential works, *The Play of Animals* (1898), and *The Play of Man* (1901). Groos criticized Spencer's theory on a number of grounds. He thought that surplus energy might provide 'a particularly favourable condition for play', but was not essential. He also thought play had a much more definite function than in Spencer's theory. Groos argued that a main reason for childhood was so that play could occur: 'perhaps the very existence of youth is largely for the sake of play'. This was because play provided exercise and elaboration of skills needed for survival. This has been called the 'exercise' or 'practice' theory of play, and in its modern form it has many adherents.

G. Stanley Hall   In his book *Adolescence* (1908) and elsewhere, Hall argued that Groos's practice theory was 'very partial, superficial, and perverse'. This was because Groos saw play as practice for contemporary activities. By contrast, Hall thought that play was a means for children to work through primitive atavisms, reflecting our evolutionary past. For example, 'the sports of boys chasing one another, wrestling, making prisoners, obviously gratify in a partial way the predatory instincts'. The function of play was thus cathartic in nature, and allowed the 'playing out' of those instincts that characterized earlier human history. This became known as the 'recapitulation theory' of play. In the form proposed by Hall, it has had little or no recent support.

Maria Montessori   The work of Montessori has been another major influence in the education of young children (see Kramer, 1976). Like Froebel, Montessori saw the value of self-initiated activity for young children, under adult guidance. She put more emphasis on the importance of learning about real life, however, and hence on constructive play materials which helped in sensory discrimination and in colour and shape matching. She did not value pretend or sociodramatic play, seeing pretence as primitive and an escape from reality. She preferred to encourage children actually to serve meals, for example, and to clear up around the house themselves, rather than play at mealtimes in a 'play house'. This particular aspect of her philosophy, however, did not find favour in Britain in the 1920s and 1930s.

Jean Piaget   The place of play in Piaget's theory of cognitive development has often been misunderstood (see Sutton-Smith, 1966; Piaget, 1966; and Rubin and Pepler, 1982 for reviews). Piaget saw adaptation as depending on the two processes of accommodation and assimilation (see chapter 11). Play 'manifests the peculiarity of a primacy of assimilation over accommodation'. Children acted out their already established behaviours, or schemata, in play, and adapted reality to fit these. For example, referring to episodes such as his daughter Jacqueline's pretending to sleep (p. 181), Piaget wrote:

> It is clearly impossible to explain this symbolic practice as being pre-exercise; the child certainly does not play like this in order to learn to wash or sleep. All that he is trying to do is to use freely his individual

powers, to reproduce his own actions for the pleasure of seeing himself do them and showing them off to others, in a word to express himself, to assimilate without being hampered by the need to accommodate at the same time.

Here is a criticism both of some aspects of Groos's approach (play as pre-exercise), and of play as being important in learning. For Piaget learning was related more to accommodation to reality. This emphasis may be linked to Montessori's influence, for Piaget carried out his early research at a modified Montessori school, and for many years was president of the Swiss Montessori Society. The functions of play in Piaget's framework are two-fold. Play can consolidate existing skills by repeated execution of known schemas, with minor variations. Also, it can give a child a sense of 'ego continuity', that is, confidence and a sense of mastery. It does this because failure is largely circumvented in fantasy play, where the real properties of the materials are not at issue, and no external goal is aimed for.

Sigmund Freud   Freud himself did not write a great deal about play, but it has come to have an important role within the psychoanalytic movement, and especially in play therapy. Freud thought that play provided children with an avenue for wish fulfilment and mastery of traumatic events. As Peller (1954) put it, 'play ... is an attempt to compensate for anxieties and depression, to obtain pleasure at a minimum risk of danger and/or irreversible consequences'. Thus play provided a safe context for expressing aggressive or sexual impulses which it would be too dangerous to express in reality. In addition play could, within limits, help achieve mastery of traumatic events; 'Small quantities of anxiety are mastered in play, but anxiety of high intensity inhibits play.' Both aspects are important in play therapy. First, play expresses the child's wishes and anxieties (Peller relates the development of fantasy play themes to Freud's psychosexual stages). Second, play can help overcome such anxieties, by catharsis or by working through them.

Susan Isaacs   The view of play as essential to both emotional and cognitive growth of young children, strong in the British educational tradition, owes much to Susan Isaacs and to her successor at the Institute of Education at London University, Dorothy Gardner. Isaacs combined a belief in the emotional benefits of play (deriving from the psychoanalytic tradition) with a wider view of its benefits for physical, social and cognitive development generally, echoing the evolutionary perspective that animals that learn more, also play more: 'Play is indeed the child's work, and the means whereby he grows and develops. Active play can be looked upon as a sign of mental health; and its absence, either of some inborn defect, or of mental illness' (Isaacs, 1929).

Lev Vygotsky   Another combination of the affective and cognitive aspects of development occurs in Vygotsky's approach to play (1966; from a lecture given in 1933). Like psychoanalysts, Vygotsky saw the affective drive behind play as being 'the imaginary, illusory realisation of unrealisable desires'; not with very specific or sexual impulses, but in a much more general sense, to do with the child's confidence and mastery (for example, in attitudes to authority in general): 'Play is essentially wish fulfilment, not, however, isolated wishes but generalized affects.' Furthermore, Vygotsky saw play as being 'the leading source of development in the preschool years'. Essentially, this was because the nature of pretend play meant that the child was liberating itself from the immediate constraints of the situation (e.g. the actual object), and getting into the world of ideas (e.g. what that object might become): 'The child is liberated from situational constraints through his activity in an imaginary situation.'

Recent theorists In recent decades, theorists have tended to argue the benefits of play for cognitive development and creative thinking. Jerome Bruner (1972) suggested that play in the advanced mammals, and especially in human children, serves both as practice for mastery in skills, and as an opportunity for trying out new combinations of behaviour in a safe context. Sara Smilansky (1968; Smilansky and Shefatya, 1990) and Dorothy and Jerome Singer (1991) have advanced the value of fantasy and sociodramatic play in particular. Brian Sutton-Smith (1967) initially supported the importance of play for creative processes; but more recently (Sutton-Smith, 1986) has come to argue against what he sees as the 'idealization' of play. In sharp contrast to the other theorists we have considered, he now concludes that many theories about play, and even the way we define play, reflect the needs of adults in organizing and controlling children, rather than the actualities of children's behaviour. Stephen Kline (1995) has drawn attention to the 'global toy curriculum', the worldwide promotion and marketing of particular theme toys and play products, which must be taken account of when considering any benefits of play for children's development.

Empirical Studies ▶ ▶ ▶

Much theorizing about the importance of play was carried out in the absence of any real evidence that play does, or does not, have the effects or benefits postulated. Here we will review the evidence about the importance of play from three different perspectives: the forms of play, or 'design studies' – does the actual nature of play behaviour reveal something of its value?; correlational studies – what tends to go with playfulness in children?; and experimental studies – attempts to compare the value of play experiences in controlled conditions.

The forms of play If we look closely at what goes on in playful episodes we may form hypotheses as to what uses the behaviour has. Indeed, it is this approach that Piaget used, and which led him to his own theory of play (p. 193).

Some theorists have speculated on the importance of pretend play for theory of mind development (see chapter 13). Leslie (1987) has argued that pretend play is an indicator of metarepresentational abilities as early as 18 months, and is important in developing these latter abilities for understanding that someone else may represent things differently (have different knowledge, or beliefs) from yourself. Lillard (1993) and Jarrold et al. (1994) have reviewed the evidence on pretend-play skills and theory of mind, and each conclude that the evidence is not strong. Much early pretend play appears to be largely imitative, as is shown in table 6.1. On the basis of Howes' model, there is little reason to suppose that social pretend implies metarepresentational abilities on the part of the child until 37–48 months, which is when theory of mind abilities emerge by most criteria; so, there is little reason to postulate that it has a leading role in theory of mind development.

Observations of the flexibility present in play led Bruner (1972) to postulate its role in problem-solving and creativity. Working with Bruner, an extensive study of Oxfordshire nursery schools was made by Sylva, Roy and Painter (1980). They documented which activities of nursery-school children resulted in what they considered to be complex or challenging activities. They concluded that activities with some sort of goal, and the means to achieve it, were the most challenging – activities such as building, drawing, doing puzzles. They called these 'high-yield' activities. Depending on one's exact definition, these might be considered less playful (i.e. more constructive, or goal-directed) than what they thought of as 'medium-yield' activities – pretending, play with small-scale toys, manipulating sand or dough. Finally, 'low-yield' activities comprised informal and impromptu games, gross motor play and unstructured social playing and 'horsing around' (i.e. rough-and-tumble play).

The Sylva, Roy and Painter study actually suggests that the unstructured, free play kinds of activities may be less cognitively useful than more structured activities. A similar philosophy lies behind the 'structuring play in the early years at school' programme (Manning and Sharp, 1977). It would seem though that the emphasis in Sylva and colleagues' study is on cognitive, rather than social, challenge or complexity. Observations of sociodramatic play suggest there is considerable negotiation about social roles (cf. table 6.1). Observations of rough-and-tumble show that co-ordination with a large number of partners is often involved, and suggest it may have social functions in terms of making friends, or practising fighting or dominance skills.

Studies on the forms of play are suggestive of functional hypotheses, and may rule some hypotheses out; are these conclusions supported by other forms of evidence?

Correlational studies If playful behaviour has useful developmental consequences, then we would expect that children who practise a lot of a certain type of play should also be more advanced in other areas of development for which play is supposed to be beneficial.

One study, by Hutt and Bhavnani (1972), used data from the novel toy experiment we have mentioned earlier (see box 6.1 and p. 181). They traced 48 children who had been observed with the novel toy at around 4 years of age, when they were 4 years older. From the earlier data they had recorded those children who, after investigating the toy, used it in many imaginative ways (15 of the 48). Four years later they gave the children some tests designed to measure creativity (see also chapter 15). The imaginative players scored significantly higher on these tests than did the children who at 4 years had not played much with the novel object.

This is consistent with the idea that imaginative play fosters creativity; but no more than that. An alternative explanation would be that another factor (for example, shyness with adults) was responsible for the poor performance both with the novel object, and later in the tests. Or, perhaps the playfulness of the imaginative children is just a by-product of their creativity, not a cause of it. As discussed elsewhere (chapter 1), correlations may be due to extraneous factors, and we cannot infer causal relations from them.

Many other correlational studies have been reported in the literature. In one (Johnson et al., 1982), 34 4-year-olds were observed in play and also given cognitive and intelligence tests. The researchers found that constructive play, but not sociodramatic play, was positively and significantly correlated with intelligence scores. This finding would be congruent with the position of Sylva's group (above). In another study (Connolly and Doyle, 1984), 91 preschoolers were observed in social fantasy play, and measures of social competence were obtained from observation, role-taking tests (see chapter 11) and teacher ratings. It was found that the amount and complexity of fantasy play significantly correlated with several measures of social competence. This would be congruent with the point made above that the benefits of sociodramatic play may be social more than cognitive.

A study by Watson and Peng (1992) has been one of the few to look at effects of war-toy play. They coded for pretend aggression play and real aggression in 36 preschool children (taking care to distinguish these from rough-and-tumble play). Parents completed questionnaires saying how much toy-gun play the children did at home, and how aggressive were the TV programmes that they watched. There was an association for boys (but not for girls) between a history of toy-gun play (based on parents' ratings) and levels of real aggression in the day-care centre. However, this finding could simply reflect that temperamentally aggressive children also like playing with toy guns. Pretend aggression in the day-care centre did not correlate with real aggression. All these studies are subject to the same caveats about drawing conclusions from correlational evidence.

Experimental studies of play   In experimental studies of play, the benefits of some form of extra play experience are compared with the benefits of some non-play experience. If participants are randomly allocated to the play or non-play conditions, it should be more possible to make causal inferences than is the case in correlational studies.

Some experiments have used short sessions, often of about 10 minutes' duration. Children, usually of nursery-school age, are given some play experience with objects; others are given an instructional session, or an alternative materials condition (e.g. drawing), or are put in a no-treatment control group. After the session is over, they are then given an assessment, for example, of creativity (e.g. thinking of unusual uses for the objects they have played with), problem-solving (e.g. using the objects to make a long tool to retrieve a marble) or conservation. A number of such studies claimed some form of superiority for the play experience, but subsequent work has not always borne these claims out. In a review, Smith and Simon (1984) argued that the earlier studies were methodologically unsound due to the possibility of experimenter effects (see p. 16). When the same experimenter administers the conditions and tests the subjects immediately after, some unconscious bias may come in.

Some studies were criticized for inadequate control for familiarity with the experimenter. When these factors are properly taken account of, there is little evidence that the play experience helps, or indeed that such sessions have any real impact. Smith and Simon concluded that either the benefits of play in real life occur over a longer time period, or they are not substantial enough to measure by this sort of experimental procedure (for a critical reply, see Dansky, 1985). More recently, experiments on the effects of make-believe and imagery on deductive reasoning in 4- to 6-year-olds have been reported by Dias and Harris (1988, 1990). The results are suggestive for the role of pretence in theory of mind development; but unfortunately, full protection against experimenter effects was not taken.

A more ecologically valid approach is to look at the effects of play over periods of weeks, or perhaps a school term. This has been done in a number of studies, especially those that looked at the effects of play tutoring (see p. 191) in preschool classes. Several studies on disadvantaged preschool children in the USA found that play tutoring, besides increasing children's fantasy play, also had benefits in a variety of areas on cognitive, language and social development. The problem with these studies was that the play-tutored children were compared with children who received little or no extra adult intervention. Thus, general adult involvement and conversation might have caused the gains, rather than fantasy play *per se*. This alternative idea has become known as the 'verbal stimulation' hypothesis.

Some play-tutoring studies since then have embodied controls for 'verbal stimulation', or more generally, adult involvement. Box 6.2 discusses one in detail. This, and some similar studies, found little superiority for the play-tutoring condition. This does not mean that play tutoring is not worthwhile, but it does imply that it is of no more value than some other kinds of adult involvement.

Summary   Considerable empirical investigation has now been made into the benefits of play, but 'the jury is still out'. Most of the investigations have concentrated on the supposed cognitive benefits of play, and have been made in an explicitly educational framework. Yet as we have seen, the evidence for strong cognitive benefits, either from theory, observation, correlational or experimental studies, is not convincing. If anything, the evidence is better for the benefits of play for social competence. This has been less thoroughly studied, while the postulated benefits of play for emotional release and catharsis (see p. 166) have scarcely received any well-controlled experimental study at all.

According to a Department of Environment report in 1973, 'the realisation that play is essential for normal development has slowly but surely permeated our cultural heritage'. This, like the words of Isaacs quoted on p. 194, embodies a prevalent view which Sutton-Smith (1986) calls 'the idealisation of play'. Yet, in some societies children seem to play little but develop normally. As we have seen, the empirical evidence is mixed. Another view emerging from studies of both animal and human play is that, while play is likely to have benefits, it is unlikely that they are essential. Rather, these benefits could be achieved in a number of ways, of which play would be one: for example, children can acquire social competence by playing, but by other activities as well. Whatever the final verdict, it will not detract from the enjoyment of play, on the part of both the participant and the observer. This in itself gives an enduring value to play, whatever the extent of its developmental consequences may be.

◄Further Reading►►►

Two useful overviews, especially for those interested in education, are J. R. Moyles 1989: *Just Playing*, Milton Keynes: Open University Press; and J. R. Moyles (ed.) 1994: *The Excellence of Play*, Buckingham and Philadelphia: Open University Press. For social, pretend play see C. Howes 1992: *The Collaborative Construction of Pretend*, Albany, NY: SUNY Press; and for make-believe play generally, D. and J. Singer 1991: *The House of Make-Believe: Children's Play and the Developing Imagination*, Cambridge, MA: Harvard University Press.

J. Hellendoorn, R. van der Kooij and B. Sutton-Smith (eds) 1994: *Play and Intervention*, Albany, NY: SUNY Press, considers issues of play therapy, and play for children with special needs. J. H. Goldstein 1994: *Toys, Play and Child Development*, Cambridge: Cambridge University Press, considers a range of educational and policy issues in relation to research on play.

◄Discussion points►►►

1   How important is it to define play? Does play at different ages require different definitions?
2   Are exploration and play really distinct?
3   How useful is it to distinguish stages in the development of play?
4   Have theorists been too ready to speculate about the value of play, without sufficient evidence?
5   Are experimental studies of play worthwhile?

Box 6.1
Exploration and play in children

The aim of Hutt's study was to see how a novel object elicited exploratory behaviour in young children, and how this behaviour changed with repeated exposure. The main participants were 30 nursery-school children, aged 3–5 years. Each child had eight 10-minute sessions in a room in the nursery school. The first two sessions were for familiarization, and five toys were provided. For the ensuing six experimental sessions a novel toy was also available – a red metal box with a lever, whose movements could be registered on counters and could result in a buzzer sounding and a bell ringing (see box figure 6.1.1).

There were two independent variables. One was the complexity of the novel object; the other was exposure to the object, measured over the six successive sessions. The object complexity was varied through 'no sound or vision' (bell and buzzer switched off, counters covered up), 'vision only', 'sound only', to 'both sound and vision' available. The dependent variables were taken from counter readings (showing how much lever manipulation had taken place) and observations of the children, especially the amount of time spent exploring (visually or tactually) the novel object.

The results showed that children looked at the object immediately on entering, and often approached it or asked the observer what it was. They would then examine the object visually and manually, holding and manipulating the lever. For the 'no sound or vision' and 'vision only' conditions, this exploration and manipulation declined rapidly over sessions. However, for the 'sound only' and 'both sound and vision' conditions, manipulation of the lever increased over the first five sessions. More detailed analysis of the observations showed that in these conditions, although exploratory behaviour declined, more playful or game-like behaviours increased (see box figure 6.1.2), for example running around the object with a truck and ringing the bell each time, or using the object as a seat and pretending it was a car.

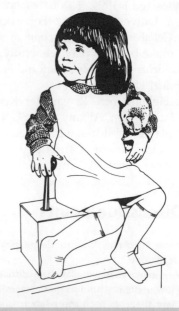

Box Figure 6.1.1   A child exploring and later playing with a novel object (based on material in C. Hutt 1966: *Symposia of the Zoological Society of London*, 18.

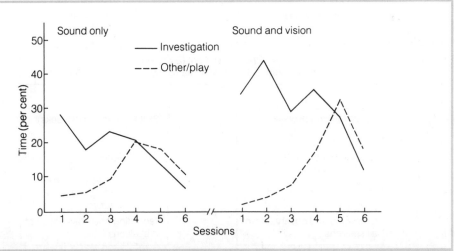

Box Figure 6.1.2 Proportions of time spent in investigating and in other activities, including play with the novel object, when sound, or sound and vision, were available.

These observations led Hutt to suggest that exploration could lead on to play, and to characterize the two behaviours distinctly. Exploration was characterized as relatively serious and focused, essentially asking 'what does this object do?' Play was characterized as relaxed, and by a diversity of activities essentially asking 'what can I do with this object?'

This study combined an experimental design with some degree of natural observation of the child's behaviour. Note that the less-structured observations allowed for the distinction between exploration and play to be made; an outcome not expected in the initial aims of the study. The results are shown as graphs of changes over sessions, as in box figure 6.1.2, and the exploration/play distinction is reported qualitatively. No statistical tests are used, though some might have been appropriate. No control group is really necessary for this study as exploration of the novel object could not occur in its absence.

The exploration/play distinction is considered further by Weisler and McCall (1976) and Wohlwill (1984). It has been noted that the particular novel object used in this study probably makes the distinction clearer than some situations might do. In other reports Hutt (1970) stated that boys were much more exploratory than girls in this setting, but this sex difference has not been well replicated in other studies of exploratory behaviour (McLoyd and Ratner, 1983).

Based on material in C. Hutt 1966: *Symposia of the Zoological Society of London*, 18, 188.

Box 6.2
A comparison of the effects of fantasy play tutoring and skills tutoring in nursery classes

This study was set up to discover whether fantasy play tutoring had any different, or more beneficial, effects than skills tutoring which involved an equal amount of extra adult involvement. The participants (mean age 4 years) were mainly from economically disadvantaged backgrounds. They comprised classes of about 20 children, two from each of two nursery schools.

At each school one class experienced extra 'play tutoring', the other extra 'skills tutoring'. Recordings of the tutoring sessions confirmed that the amount of verbal interaction by the tutor was simi-

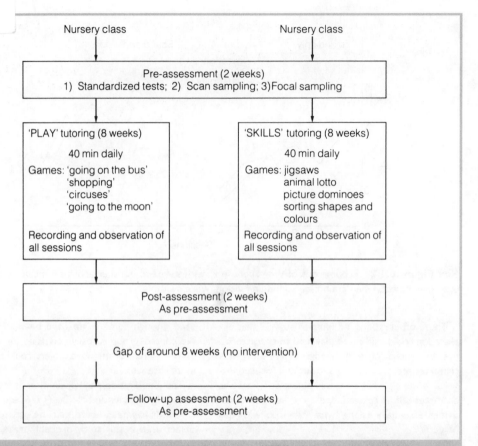

Box Figure 6.2.1 Design of study conducted by Smith et al. (1981) of play tutoring and skills tutoring.

lar in the two conditions but that a fantasy element was prominent only in the play tutoring. The research design is shown in box figure 6.2.1. The independent variables were tutoring condition and time when assessments were made (both before, and at two time points after, the intervention period). The dependent variables were scores on a variety of social, cognitive and language assessments, obtained by test and by observation.

Statistical analyses were made of the changes in scores on the various measures using a technique known as analysis of variance. In all classes the children improved on most of the measures, but with little difference between the two tutoring conditions. There were no differences between conditions for changes in play complexity, verbalizations, attention span, role-taking, creativity, or intelli-

gence test subscales. The only differences found consistently at both schools, and remaining at follow-up, were that the play-tutored children showed a greater interest in fantasy play, social participation, subgroup size and physical activity.

In most respects this study supported the 'verbal stimulation' hypothesis concerning the effects of play tutoring (see p. 198). It suggested that different forms of structured adult involvement had similar educational benefits. Play tutoring did, however, additionally foster social participation.

It may be noted that there was no 'no-treatment' control group in this study. Thus it is assumed that the interventions do have some effect, i.e. that they are to a significant degree responsible for the gains at post-assessment. The authors based this assumption on several previous studies which showed that play tutoring did have a greater effect compared with control groups with little or no extra adult involvement; in this study they wished only to compare play tutoring with a non-fantasy tutoring of equal intensity. Nevertheless, use of a no-treatment control group would have enabled stronger conclusions to be drawn about whether either kind of intervention was worthwhile from an educational viewpoint.

Based on material in P. K. Smith, M. Dalgleish and G. Herzmark 1981: *International Journal of Behavioural Development*, 4, 421–41.

7 Helping Others and Moral Development

◄The Development of Prosocial Behaviour►►

In a broad sense, prosocial behaviour can be taken to mean helping, comforting and sharing on the part of one person to another. In a standard text on the subject Mussen and Eisenberg-Berg (1977, pp. 3–4) define it as 'actions that are intended to aid or benefit another person or group of people without the actor's anticipation of external rewards. Such actions often entail some cost, self-sacrifice or risk on the part of the actor.' Children are capable of demonstrating prosocial behaviour from a very early age as we can see from the following examples, taken from mothers' reports.

1   Bobby, at 19 months   As I was vacuuming I began to feel a little faint and sick . . . I turned off the vacuum cleaner and went to the bathroom kind of coughing and gagging a little. Bobby followed me to the bathroom door, and the whole time that I was in there he was pounding on the bathroom door saying 'OK Mommie?' I finally came out and picked him up and he looked at me with a very concerned, worried look in his eyes, and I said 'Mommie OK'. Then he put his head on my shoulder and began to love me (Zahn-Waxler and Radke-Yarrow, 1982, p. 116).

2   Todd, almost 2 years   Today there was a little 4-year-old girl here, Susan. Todd and Susan were in the bedroom playing and all of a sudden Susan started to cry . . . I said 'What happened?' and she said 'He hit me'. I said 'Well, tell him not to hit you', and I said, 'Todd!' He didn't seem particularly upset, he was watching her cry. I said 'Did you hit Susan? You don't want to hurt people.' Then they went back in the bedroom and there was a second run-in and she came out. That's when I said sternly 'No, Todd. You musn't hit people'. He just watched her sniffle as she was being stroked

by her mum . . . on the table right by us were some fallen petals from a flower and he picked up one little petal and smiled and handed it to her and said 'Here'. She kind of reached out and took it and then he searched for other petals and gave them to her (Zahn-Waxler et al., 1979, p. 322).

3   Cynthia, at 4 years   We were getting ready to go to friends for the rest of the day and preparations were becoming rather frantic. Cynthia said to Richard (her younger brother) 'Come on, I'll read you a story and we'll stay out of Mum and Dad's way'. They sat together on the couch and Cynthia 'read' (memorized) two books to him. When they were finished I said 'It was great being able to get ready without any interruptions' (Grusec, 1982, p. 140).

Comforting occurs in example 1, helping in example 3 and a form of sharing in example 2. These behaviours occurred when the child saw someone else in difficulty or distress, either through some event to which the child was a bystander (e.g. examples 1 and 3), or because the child itself had caused the distress (e.g. example 2). Example 1, of a child only 19 months old, suggests that prosocial behaviour can occur very early on. However, we might question whether the action is intended to aid another person, as our initial definition stipulated. Did Bobby intend to help his mother, or was he just reacting to her behaviour? It is difficult to tell at such an early age, whereas it is clear from what she herself says that Cynthia, aged 4, did intend to help her parents. However, we can also see that Cynthia was rewarded (verbally at least) for her behaviour; did she anticipate this, and therefore was hers not prosocial behaviour after all?

Durkin (1995, p. 433) points out, however, that kindness towards others is not always motivated by selfless concern for others, and it may be useful to distinguish between *prosocial behaviour*, which can occur for both selfish and unselfish reasons, and *altruistic behaviour*, in which there is no intentional benefit to the helper and where in some cases there may even be disadvantage or danger. Some researchers are greatly concerned about such definitional matters, whereas others are happy to label helping and sharing behaviours as prosocial, largely irrespective of context, intent or reward. You may like to compare these definitions of prosocial and altruistic behaviour with the definitions of mutualism and altruism used by ethologists and given in chapter 2: they are similar.

Some psychologists have used the concept of costs and benefits in an attempt to explain why it is that apparently self-sacrificing behaviour – where the helper incurs a 'cost' – persists and is not eliminated through natural selection. McGuire (1994), for example, points out that helping often occurs between people who are known to one another, so helping has the benefit of enhancing one's reputation in the social group. Despite the costs, he argues, there are also likely to be benefits to those who act prosocially, such as enhanced self-esteem, the development of empathy and the internalization of socially acceptable norms of co-operation and support. Other researchers (for example, Trevarthen and Logotheti, 1989) have considered the *intrinsic* value of prosocial behaviour from the earliest years of life and argue that, as social beings, we have in-born motivation to form co-operative relationships with one another; strategies for reaching out to others in a spirit of mutual trust and giving are established and developed initially in the context of the family, and children learn about how to act towards others by engaging in shared activities and routines with those who are close to them. This human quality is universal, although the ways in which this is expressed will vary from culture to culture. And, as we have seen in chapter 3, when attachments within the family are insecure, the capacity to relate in a trusting, empathic way towards others may be impaired where the child has internalized a working model of relationships rooted in the experience of *not* being helped at times of need.

Foot, Morgan and Shute (1990) point out that our social practice in Western society has emphasized the role of children as recipients of help when the reality is that there is an enormous, often untapped, potential for harnessing children's capacity to respond prosocially towards peers. They argue that we are only at the threshold of realizing the range of ways in which children could be sources of practical help and emotional support towards one another, and so further influence their own and their peers' cognitive and social development. We argue in this chapter that we need to look at prosocial and altruistic behaviour in a wider social context if we are to understand it in all its complexity.

Observational studies

The origins of prosocial behaviour in the young child have been the subject of several studies. Zahn-Waxler and Radke-Yarrow (1982) have described a study of 24 children which used a combination of cross-sectional and longitudinal design to span the age range from around 12 to 30 months. These researchers relied on mothers' recordings. Mothers were asked to report on their children's response to events in which negative emotions were expressed (a subset of this investigation is highlighted in box 7.1, and examples 1 and 2 above are from their studies). Two noticeable changes were found between the younger children (aged up to about 20 months) and the older children (20–30 months). The younger children often orientated to someone's distress, and often cried, fretted or whimpered themselves, but only seldom acted prosocially. Such prosocial behaviour as there was usually took the form of simply touching or patting the victim, or presenting objects. Prosocial behaviour was much more likely in the older children, however, and occurred in about one-third of all incidents reported. It took a variety of forms, such as reassurance ('you'll be all right'), combative altruism (hitting an aggressor), giving objects (e.g. bandages, comfort objects) or getting help from a third party. This developmental pattern was similar whether the child was a bystander to the distress or had caused it. From this study it is clear that children below 3 years of age can show some forms of prosocial behaviour. This is especially so after about 20 months, which is when sensori-motor development is completed (chapter 11), and thus when children understand cause–effect relations and the distinction between themselves and other people (chapter 5). Before this age children often seek comfort as much for themselves as for the other person, but after about 20 months they are increasingly aware that the distress is in the other person (and, somewhat later, of whether they have caused it or not), and act more appropriately.

Other researchers have documented prosocial behaviour by children in nursery school. Eisenberg-Berg and Hand (1979), for example, watched 35 children aged 4 and 5 years in preschool classes. They found that a child showed sharing, helping or comforting behaviour about once every 10–12 minutes, on average. There were few age or sex differences. In an Israeli study, Bar-Tal, Raviv and Goldberg (1982) observed 156 children aged 18 months to 6 years. Prosocial behaviours made up some 10–20 per cent of all social contacts. Again, there were no sex differences and no very prominent age changes.

Grusec (1982) used the same technique as Zahn-Waxler and Radke-Yarrow (1982), namely mothers' reports, to examine prosocial behaviour in children aged 4 and 7 years (example 3, p. 206 above, is from her study). She asked mothers to record, over a 4-week period, any act in which their child intended to help another (excluding regular duties). Mothers recorded about one such act every day or so. No difference was found between boys and girls. Some interesting results from this study are shown in table 7.1. The top half of the table shows it was rare for mothers not to respond when they

Table 7.1   Mothers' reports of reactions to their child's behaviour

	Child spontaneously helpful (% of incidents)	
	4-yr-olds	7-yr-olds
Acknowledge, thank, express personal appreciation	33	37
Smile, thank warmly, hug	17	18
Praise act or child	19	16
No outward response	8	9
	Child fails to be helpful (% of incidents)	
	4-yr-olds	7-yr-olds
Moral exhortation	26	30
Request altruism	22	30
Scold, frown	18	15
Empathy training	6	5
Direct or force behaviour	6	5
Accept lack of altruism	8	5

Source: Grusec, 1982

observed an act of helpfulness by their child. The great majority of such acts were 'rewarded' verbally, by thanking or praising, or physically by smiling or hugging. Similarly, the lower half of the table shows that if a child was not helpful when the mother thought that help was appropriate, it was very rare for the mother to accept this. Usually she encouraged the child to be helpful, either directly ('altruism requested') or in general terms ('moral exhortation'), or by expressing disapproval ('scolding', 'frowning'). More rarely, she would explain to the child how his or her lack of helpfulness might affect others ('empathy training'), or directly instruct or coerce the child to behave appropriately.

Many researchers have been concerned with the consistency of prosocial behaviour. For example, are children who are prosocial in one way, also likely to be so in others? Are children who are helpful at one age, likely to remain so at a later age? By and large the evidence suggests moderate consistency in these respects (Underwood and Moore, 1982). Some quite striking age consistencies were reported in a longitudinal study on siblings (Dunn and Kendrick, 1982; see also chapter 4): for example, they found that children (aged 1–3 years) who showed friendly interest and concern for a new baby in the first 3 weeks after birth were also likely to respond with concern if their younger sibling was hurt or distressed at a follow-up 6 years later (the correlation was 0.42, significant at the 0.05 level). They also noticed an interplay between helping and rivalry. The help which children offered their siblings was not necessarily appreciated by the recipients! The giving of help by an older child could, for example, elicit anger from a younger sibling.

When Dunn, Brown and Beardsall (1991) followed up the siblings who had been observed as preschoolers, they found that there were links between the quality of the relationships between the siblings in the preschool period and the children's behaviour at a later stage. Those who had grown up with a sibling who was unfriendly or aggressive were more likely as adolescents to have emotional difficulties in their relationships with others than those whose siblings had been warm and affectionate towards them. Children who perceived that their sibling was receiving more attention and affection from the mother were more likely to show aggressive or difficult behaviour in childhood and adolescence. It appeared that relative differences in how loved a young person feels have an influence on how socially adjusted they are. Dunn and her colleagues suggest that the growth of social understanding develops out of the child's experience of balancing her preoccupation with self against responsiveness to the feelings and emotions of others. Dunn (1995) argues that participation in the moral discourse of the family begins very early on in the child's life and that prosocial behaviour can only be fully understood if we consider it in the context of the dynamic web of family relationships.

This has implications for, amongst others, aspects of social development, the emergence of sensitivity and empathy towards others. On the basis of her extensive observations of children and their families, Dunn is convinced that current theories of moral and sociocognitive development neglect key aspects of the ways in which children come to understand and relate to one another. It is her belief that the growth of understanding involves more than 'an unfolding of cognitive abilities', and that 'self-concern and affective experience play central roles in the interactions in which moral and social rules are articulated and fostered, and the development of the child's theory of mind (see chapter 13) (Dunn, 1995, p. 341).

◀Factors Influencing Prosocial Behaviour▶ ▶ ▶

We have seen that mothers do not stand by idly when their child does, or does not, show helpful or altruistic behaviour; the evidence is that they often intervene. Fathers, teachers and peers are also likely to respond to a child's prosocial behaviour. What effect do such interventions have? We have also seen that interventions may take the form of reinforcement (e.g. praise) or punishment for not being helpful, modelling of altruistic behaviour, or moral exhortation. Are some techniques more effective than others? And what does the child contribute to this process?

One attempt to look at the effectiveness of different parental techniques in a naturalistic way is documented in box 7.1. This study suggests that (for 2-year-olds) affective explanation as to the consequences of their action (moralizing or prohibition with reasons), perhaps combined with some power assertion by the mother, is associated with prosocial behaviour by the child. However, this being an uncontrolled correlational study, cause-and-effect relations cannot be deduced with confidence. Many researchers have attempted experimental studies to elucidate more clearly the causes of prosocial behaviour.

A technique that many researchers focused on in the 1970s was reinforcement (verbal or material reward). We have seen from Grusec's (1982) study that children do often receive reinforcement for prosocial behaviour, but has this actually been shown to be an effective technique? Let us look at a typical experimental study. Gelfand et al. (1975) reported a study with 21 children aged 5–6 years. The children came to a research caravan where they played a marble-drop game to earn pennies. The pennies accumulated could be spent on a prize at the end, but periodically the child was told that he or she could donate a penny earned to help another child in a nearby room win a prize (in fact there was no other child; this was simulated by a tape recording of an adult and child in conversation). Over a series of trials, the effects of both prompts by the experimenter ('maybe it would be nice if you helped the other boy/girl once or twice') and praise for donating ('very good! Think how that boy/girl must feel now') were evaluated in terms of the subsequent rate of donations. It was found that both prompts, and praise, were effective in increasing donation rates – temporarily for some children, more permanently for others. The authors concluded that this was a clear 'demonstration of reinforcement effects on donating' (p. 983). Other studies have suggested that material reinforcement may be more powerful than social reinforcement for young children, and that the nature of the person giving the reinforcement is an important factor.

Other experimental studies have attempted to see whether modelling is a useful technique. Here, an adult models a helpful or altruistic act, which the child observes. One study (Grusec et al., 1978) has compared this with moral exhortation (preaching) for its effectiveness as a technique. The participants were 96 boys and girls aged 8–10 years. Children came individually to a research caravan in a school yard to play a marble-bowling game in which they could win marbles (the game was fixed so that all the children won the same number of marbles). Nearby was a poster reading 'Help poor children: Marbles buy gifts' over a bowl with some marbles already in it. An adult (of the same sex as the child) played the game first; she then either exhorted the child to give half her marbles, or said nothing (two preaching conditions), and then either gave, or did not give, half her own marbles (two modelling or performance conditions). The child was then left alone to play, but was observed through a one-way mirror to see how many marbles she donated. It was found that most children who saw the adult give marbles did so themselves, irrespective of preaching; whereas few children who saw the adult not giving marbles did so, although preaching did have some effect here. The children were asked to play the game again three weeks later and, irrespective of previous condition, few of them donated any marbles. This, and other studies, suggest that the behaviour children actually observe in others may be more important than moral exhortations from them though both do have some effect.

The experimental design of these studies is such as to enable us to make fairly certain inferences; for example, that modelling (performance) by an adult does increase the likelihood of altruism in a child who is watching. However, one could criticize these experiments for being rather artificial. The experimenters are unfamiliar, the situations are contrived and some deception is involved. Is it really helpfulness and altruism that is being measured in these settings, or is it just some kind of conformity to adult demands? For instance, in the study by Grusec et al. (1978) is it the case that modelling (performance) causes altruism in the child, or is it simply that the child is trying to puzzle out what is going on, and that the more compliant children, or perhaps the more uncertain children, tend to go along with what the adult seems to be suggesting? The fact that there was no effect of modelling at the 3-week follow-up would be consistent with this explanation.

An experimental study on 6–10-year-olds suggests just this sort of interpretation as regards age differences in generosity. Several experimental studies (unlike some naturalistic studies, see above) have found that generosity or altruism increases with age. However, Zarbatany et al. (1985) found that older children were only affected by experimenter obtrusiveness, not by other factors such as whether peers would know how generous the child was. The authors concluded that 'the finding that older children were more generous than younger children only under conditions of experimenter obtrusiveness provides some justification for concerns that laboratory analogue investigations of age differences in children's generosity may assess age differences in conformity to adult expectations rather than age differences in altruism' (p. 753). This critique could apply to other inferences made from laboratory studies, too. Of course, it could be argued that such compliance is similar to, or involved in, altruistic behaviour; but if so, it does seem different from the kind of 'genuine' helpfulness envisaged in our original definition, or seen in very young children who have as yet little notion of what is socially expected of them.

Prosocial behaviour in peer groups and in the classroom

Extensive research in laboratory conditions and in classrooms into co-operative learning has consistently produced results giving support to the idea that, in order to foster prosocial behaviour in young people, teachers must incorporate values of trust and co-operation into the whole school community and not simply 'teach' prosocial behaviour as a series of separate lessons, for example a once-a-week discussion of social and moral issues (Cowie, Smith, Boulton and Laver, 1994; Hertz-Lazarowitz and Miller, 1992; Foot, Morgan and Shute, 1990). Methods based on co-operation and trust, such as co-operative group work, form a direct challenge to traditional didactic methods of instruction and can be viewed with deep suspicion by both pupils and teachers (Cowie and Rudduck, 1988). Attitudinal barriers need to be broken down for such approaches to become widespread. However, these studies add further confirmation to the view that the development and fostering of prosocial behaviour takes place within a social and cultural framework of moral values.

Cowie and Sharp (1996) investigated ways in which schools can create structures which facilitate the emergence of prosocial behaviour by observing peer support systems in a number of naturalistic settings. They distinguished among three broad types of peer support – those based on befriending approaches, those based on mediation and conflict resolution approaches, and those based on counselling approaches. They found that, with the right sort of support, training and supervision, teachers could build on the natural potential for helping others which most young people have. They found too that these systems flourished best in settings where there was an already-established system for working together co-operatively and where there was a strong emphasis on values of sharing, trust and mutuality. Given the right sort of training and supervision, peer helpers demonstrated that they were able to offer themselves as a resource to peers troubled by experiences of victimization, rejection, isolation, relationship difficulties and other problems common during childhood and adolescence. Other studies have confirmed that this prosocial behaviour has benefits for the helpers as well as for those who seek help, and for the school as a whole (Carr, 1994; James et al., 1991; Sprinthall et al., 1992).

Children's perceptions of prosocial behaviour

So far we have considered effects which other people or institutions such as schools can have on the child – reinforcing, punishing, modelling, exhorting or scaffolding. Can we ascertain what the child is thinking about all this? One study (Eisenberg, 1983) found that schoolchildren (aged 7–17 years) clearly differentiated among people whom they might help. When faced with hypo-thetical moral dilemmas, they indicated that they would be more likely to help family than non-family members; friends rather than non-friends; people they knew rather than people they did not know; people more similar to themselves in race or religion; and non-criminals rather than criminals. These are not surprising findings, but they do put helping behaviour in a social context. Similarly, other studies have suggested that techniques such as reinforcement, exhortation or modelling are most effective when done by an adult whom the child loves or respects, e.g. a parent.

Rogers and Tisak (1996) found that 2nd, 4th and 6th grade children, when asked to reason about peers' responses to aggression, reasoned out of a concern for the well-being of all peers involved in a conflict and showed awareness of the relationship between victim and perpetrator. The findings indicated that children were able to consider the logic of different responses to aggression.

Other studies have looked at whether the level of moral reasoning in a child relates to that child's helpfulness or altruistic behaviour. Moral reasoning, or moral judgement as it is often called, is discussed in the next section, which is concerned with what the child thinks about a moral issue rather than what a child does, but we might expect the two to be related. There does seem to be some connection, with children at higher moral reasoning levels tending to be more altruistic (see Underwood and Moore, 1982, for a review). Amongst the studies we have considered here, Eisenberg-Berg and Hand (1979) found that the frequency of spontaneous sharing in nursery school did correlate with measures of moral reasoning (though the frequency of helping/comforting did not); while Eisenberg (1983) found that children at higher levels of moral reasoning were more likely to say that they would be helpful to other people who were not immediate friends or relatives.

It may well be that some ways of promoting prosocial and altruistic behaviour are those which both provide some social reward or praise for the child, and also appeal to the child's developing sense of reasoning or justice. However, more recent thinking and research suggest that psychologists ignore the social context in which this takes place at their peril. Box 7.1 shows that affective explanation by mothers is associated with prosocial behaviour in 2-year-olds. So far as the more general topic of discipline is concerned, Hoffman (1970) reviewed a large number of correlational studies relating parental-rearing techniques with measures of either moral reasoning or moral behaviour. He categorized the dominant parental techniques into 'love-oriented discipline' (which threatened withdrawal of affection or ap-proval), 'power-assertive discipline' (physical punishment or withholding privileges) and 'induction' (explaining the consequences of actions). As can be seen from table 7.2 (based on many studies), it seems that 'induction' is associated with moral maturity, whereas 'power-assertive discipline' tends to be associated with moral immaturity. Is 'induction' similar to 'affective explanation' in box 7.1? Quite probably, as it is in the context of a close parental relationship. Thus the evidence suggests that providing cognitive explanations enhances positive exhortation or reward in inducing prosocial behaviour, and is also effective as a disciplinary technique. Similarly, experimental studies have suggested that the most effective way to induce resistance to temptation is to combine the threat of punishment with an explanation or cognitive rationale (Parke, 1977).

Cross-cultural differences in prosocial behaviour

We have discussed the important role played by the family in encouraging or dismissing emergent qualities of prosocial behaviour in the young. Cross-cultural studies add a new perspective since there are quite wide variations in the values which different cultural groups place on prosocial behaviour and altruism. Two cultures' different sets of values and consequent behaviour towards one another were studied by Robarchek and Robarchek (1992). The Waorani people of the Amazon are extremely warlike, fight constantly with their neighbours and have a strong philosophy of individualism. If there is a raid from a neighbouring tribe, each person will save themselves regardless of the fate of friends or members of their family. By contrast, the Semai of the Malaysian rainforest are an extremely co-operative society who place great emphasis on mutual support amongst family members and the community. The children in these two contrasting societies are exposed to different value systems and, not surprisingly, develop differently with regard to prosocial behaviour. Yet it would be mistaken to assume that these people differ in the extent to which they love their children. In everyday life, both the Waorani and the Semai adults are affectionate and non-punitive towards their children, so there is evidence of the caring, supportive patterns of behaviour which we expect to find in families and communities. How can we explain the contrasting ways in which prosocial behaviour is expressed in different social settings? Eisenberg and Mussen (1989), in a review of cross-cultural studies of co-operation amongst children, conclude that in societies where co-operation is rewarded, the children show high levels of prosocial behaviour; where it is not rewarded or valued it is less likely to appear. Trevarthen and Logotheti (1989) make a similar point when they contrast children from communities where there is a large amount of violence and conflict. In those circumstances, they argue, children are much more likely to develop relationships which are unsociable and manipulative, in which the emphasis is on individual survival rather than on mutual co-operation (but see box 16.1 for another perspective).

Table 7.2 Research studies reporting positive or negative correlations between disciplinary strategies and measures of children's moral reasoning or behaviour (from Hoffman, 1970)

Type of parental discipline	Positive correlation	Negative correlation
Power-assertive	7	32
Love-orientated	8	11
Induction	38	6

◄The Development of Moral Reasoning►►►

Moral reasoning refers to how we reason, or judge, whether an action is right or wrong: it is different from moral behaviour. Often, of course, we do follow our moral reasoning when we decide on a course of behaviour. For example, we might reason that it is right to give some money for overseas aid, and then do so. It is equally clear that we do not always follow our moral reasoning. For example, if we are incorrectly given extra change in a supermarket, we might reason that it is wrong to keep it, but still do so.

We are concerned here with the way in which moral reasoning (often referred to as moral judgement) develops. A key question concerns the age at which a child may be considered to be morally responsible. This question has been especially salient in recent years with public moral debate (often highly emotional) over the culpability of children who commit violent crimes. Focusing on recent cases where children have been killed by other children (for example, the killings in the UK of the toddler James Bulger by two 10-year-old boys and in Norway of 5-year-old Silje Marie Redergard by three boys, one aged 6 and the others aged 5), Asquith (1996) points out the radically different ways in which these tragic deaths were treated in the two countries. In the UK, the 10-year-olds were characterized as 'evil' and there were strong and vociferous public demands for them to receive severe punishments, including life sentences. By contrast, in Norway, no-one, not even Silje's mother, seemed to blame the boys. Silje's mother stated publicly that it was impossible for her to hate small children, despite what they had done to her own daughter. These reactions illustrate wide differences in the social construction of childhood in these two countries and have implications for the ways in which we begin to consider the development of moral reasoning in children and adolescents.

Asquith argues that these disturbing cases challenge a society to consider and reconsider its concept of moral development and moral reasoning in children. Any system of justice for children must, he claims, be viewed in the wider context of the social, political and economic climate in which it takes place. The moral development of children must also be viewed in the context of the family and the community. The harsh treatment of children who commit crimes may well be inappropriate if these are children who have been raised in homes which are poverty-stricken and by parents who are themselves inadequate or under severe stress. In this instance, the reason for the child's offending behaviour may lie in the adverse circumstances in which he or she was brought up (see also chapter 16).

One important strand in the study of moral reasoning by psychologists is closely linked to cognitive development. Such an approach is called 'cognitive developmental'. Work in this area was pioneered by Piaget, and this tradition has been carried on in the USA by Kohlberg and others.

Piaget's theory

Piaget turned his attention to moral reasoning in children early in his career. He spent time in the suburbs of Geneva watching children at play and also posing them moral dilemmas. The results of his investigations were reported in *The Moral Judgement of the Child* (first English publication in 1932). Piaget describes how he studied the boys' game of marbles. He was interested in how children acquired the rules of the game, where they thought the rules came from, and whether the rules could be altered. Here, the 'rules of the game' are taken as corresponding to the 'rules of society' for adults – you should follow the rules, you can break them, but there are sanctions if you do so. Piaget used four methods here: he asked the children directly ('teach me the rules'); he played with a child, pretending to be ignorant so that the child had to explain the rules – though not too ignorant in case the child gave up in frustration!; he watched the child play with others; and he interviewed children about where rules came from and whether they could be changed.

From his results Piaget distinguished three stages in children's awareness of rules. In the first (up to 4 to 5 years), rules were not understood. In the second stage (from 4–5 to 9–10 years) the rules were seen as coming from a higher authority (e.g. adults, God, the town council) and could not be changed. In the third (from 9–10 years onwards) rules were seen as mutually agreed by the players, and thus open to change if all the players agreed. (Piaget also distinguished corresponding stages in how the child's awareness of rules was put into practice. He also examined a girls' game, a version of hide-and-seek, in much less detail and described similar stages occurring somewhat earlier, perhaps as the game was simpler.)

Here are two protocols (slightly edited) from Piaget's book, which illustrate the second two stages, and also Piaget's method of interview (called the 'clinical method', see p. 358).

1   B. E. N. (10 years, but still at the second stage)
   Piaget: Invent a rule.
   B. E. N.:   I couldn't invent one straight away like that.
   Piaget: Yes you could. I can see that you are cleverer than you make yourself out to be.
   B. E. N.:   Well, let's say that you're not caught when you are in the square.
   Piaget: Good. Would that come off with the others?
   B. E. N.:   Oh, yes, they'd like to do that.
   Piaget: Then people could play that way?
   B. E. N.:   Oh, no, because it would be cheating.
   Piaget: But all your pals would like to, wouldn't they?
   B. E. N.:   Yes, they all would.
   Piaget: Then why would it be cheating?
   B. E. N.:   Because I invented it: it isn't a rule! It's a wrong rule because it's outside of the rules. A fair rule is one that is in the game.
   (Piaget, 1932, p. 58)

2   From G. R. O. S. (13 years, and at the third stage)
  Piaget: Are you allowed to change the rules at all?
  G. R. O. S.: Oh, yes. Some want to, and some don't. If the boys play that way you have to play like they do.
  Piaget: Do you think you could invent a new rule?
  G. R. O. S.: Oh, yes you could play with your feet.
  Piaget: Would it be fair?
  G. R. O. S.: I don't know. It's just my idea.
  Piaget: And if you showed it to the others would it work?
  G. R. O. S.: It would work all right. Some other boys would want to try. Some wouldn't, by Jove! They would stick to the old rules. They'd think they'd have less of a chance with this new game.
  Piaget: And if everyone played your way?
  G. R. O. S.: Then it would be a rule like the others.

(Piaget, 1932, p. 63)

The difference between these two stages was thought of by Piaget as being that between a 'heteronomous' morality of coercion or restraint, and an 'autonomous' morality of co-operation or reciprocity. As the child's conception of rules changes, from their being absolutely fixed to their being mutually agreed, so a unilateral respect for adult or higher authority changes towards an equality with peers. These are cognitive changes, which in Piaget's later theory can be linked to the decline in egocentrism and the growth of operational thought (chapter 11). Important other factors are the growing independence from parents, and especially interaction with same-aged peers. Different children may have acquired slightly different versions of the rules, and through playing together these discrepancies will come to light and have to be resolved. This contact with divergent viewpoints, Piaget thought, was a crucial element in evolving the autonomous morality of reciprocity.

It is surprising that this ingenious, semi-naturalistic study was not followed up for decades. Despite its impact, it was only based on an unspecified but small number of participants. A large-scale follow-up was made some 50 years later by a Spanish psychologist, Jose Linaza (1984). He interviewed several hundred children, in England and Spain, about a number of games. He confirmed the main aspects of Piaget's sequence, and elaborated it. No difference was found in the sequence between English and Spanish children, or between boys and girls playing the same game, though different games did vary in the age at which certain stages were usually attained.

Piaget also reported the results of another study in his 1932 book. In this he presented children with several pairs of short episodes or stories which posed a problem of moral judgement. An example is given below:

(A)   A little boy who is called John is in his room. He is called to dinner. He goes into the dining room. But behind the door there was a chair, and on the chair there was a tray with fifteen cups on it. John couldn't have known that there was all this behind the door. He goes in, the door knocks against the tray, bang go the fifteen cups and they all get broken!

(B)   Once there was a little boy whose name was Henry. One day when his mother was out he tried to get some jam out of the cupboard. He climbed up on the chair and stretched out his arm. But the jam was too high up and he couldn't reach it and have any. But while he was trying to get it he knocked over a cup. The cup fell down and broke.

Piaget would tell children this pair of stories, and get them to repeat each to make sure that they remembered them. Then he would ask them to make a judgement as to which child in the two stories was the naughtiest. He found that before 9 or 10 years children often judged on the basis of the amount of damage, whereas after this age the child judged by motive or intention. Here are two short extracts from the protocols:

1   From S. C. H. M. A. (aged 6)

Piaget:	Are those children both naughty, or is one not so naughty as the other?
S. C. H. M. A.:	Both just as naughty.
Piaget:	Would you punish them the same?
S. C. H. M. A.:	No. The one who broke fifteen plates.
Piaget:	And would you punish the other one more, or less?
S. C. H. M. A.:	The first broke lots of things, the other one fewer.
Piaget:	How would you punish them?
S. C. H. M. A.:	The one who broke the fifteen cups: two slaps. The other one, one slap.

(Piaget, 1932, p. 120)

2   From C.O.R.M. (aged 9)

C. O. R. M.:	Well, the one who broke them as he was coming isn't naughty, 'cos he didn't know there was any cups. The other one wanted to take the jam and caught his arm on a cup.'
Piaget:	Which one is the naughtiest?
C. O. R. M.:	The one who wanted to take the jam.
Piaget:	How many cups did he break?
C. O. R. M.:	One.
Piaget:	And the other boy?
C. O. R. M.:	Fifteen.
Piaget:	Which one would you punish the most?
C. O. R. M.:	The boy who wanted to take the jam. He knew, he did it on purpose.

(Piaget, 1932, pp. 123–4)

In the first of these stages, children judge by the objective amount of damage, and also tend to see punishment as inevitable and retributive.

Table 7.3   Summary of Piaget's stages of moral judgement

Up to 4 or 5 yr	From 4–5 yr to 9–10 yr	After 9–10 yr
Premoral judgement	*Moral realism* (Heteronomous morality of constraint)	*Moral subjectivism* (Autonomous morality of co-operation)
Rules not understood	Rules come from higher authority and cannot be changed	Rules are created by people and can be changed by mutual consent
	Evaluate actions by outcomes	Evaluate actions by intentions
	Punishment as inevitable retribution	Punishment as chosen to fit crime

Source: Based on Piaget, 1932

Piaget called this stage 'moral realism', as compared with the 'moral subjectivism' of the following stage, in which subjective intent is taken account of, and punishment is seen more as a lesson suited to the offence. Piaget related these stages to his idea of heteronomous and autonomous morality from the marbles study. A summary of his stages is given in table 7.3.

There are problems with Piaget's dilemma method, many are pointed out in a critique by Karniol (1978). Characteristically, Piaget makes it difficult for the child by having unequal consequences in the two stories (15 cups versus one cup broken), thus in effect tempting the child to ignore intention. The stories are badly designed: for example, it is not clear that Henry was being naughty in going to get the jam, and he probably didn't intend to break the cup, he was just careless. So the 'bad intention' in this story has to be inferred. There are also considerable memory demands made on young children (Kail, 1990). Several studies have shown that when methodological improvements are made (e.g. contrasting intent and accident when there is equal damage) children as young as 5 years will judge on the basis of intent.

Further research has shown that young children do not have a monolithic conception of rules as constraints. They distinguish between behaviours that violate purely social conventions (e.g. not putting your belongings in the right place), and those which violate moral conventions (e.g. not sharing a toy, hitting a child). A study by Smetana (1981) of children aged 2–5 in two American nursery schools found that children distinguished between these two kinds of behaviour in terms of whether it was dependent on context (home, or school), and on the amount of punishment it deserved.

Despite limitations, the approach of presenting children and young people verbally with moral dilemmas has been pursued by a number of psychologists in the USA. It has been used especially by Kohlberg, over a longer age span than Piaget and on a more ambitious scale.

Kohlberg's theory

Kohlberg researched on the development of moral reasoning for some 30 years, and his theory has proved influential in education and criminology, as well as psychology. The work started with, and extended from, research for his doctoral thesis, in which he commenced in 1955 a longitudinal study of 50 American males initially aged 10–26 years. These participants were re-interviewed every three years. Kohlberg asked them questions, such as 'why shouldn't you steal from a store?', and also posed them story dilemmas. Of a number of dilemmas, the most famous is that of Heinz and the druggist (Kohlberg, 1969, p. 379).

> In Europe, a woman was near death from a special kind of cancer. There was one drug that the doctor thought might save her. It was a form of radium that a druggist in the same town had recently discovered. The drug was expensive to make, but the druggist was charging ten times what the drug cost him to make. He paid $200 for the radium and charged $2,000 for a small dose of the drug. The sick woman's husband, Heinz, went to everyone he knew to borrow the money, but he could only get together about $1,000, which is half of what it cost. He told the druggist that his wife was dying, and asked him to sell it cheaper or let him pay later. But the druggist said 'No, I discovered the drug and I'm going to make money from it.' So Heinz got desperate and broke into the man's store to steal the drug for his wife.

> Should Heinz have done that? Why or why not?

On the basis of these questions and dilemmas, Kohlberg postulated three levels of moral reasoning, each subdivided to make six stages in all. These levels and stages are defined in table 7.4. We look briefly at each level in turn.

Level one: preconventional morality   This is similar to Piaget's morality of constraint. Kohlberg (1976) thinks of it as 'the level of most children under 9, some adolescents, and many adolescent and adult criminal offenders' (p. 33). On this level the individual reasons in relation to himself and has not yet come fully to understand and uphold conventional or societal rules and expectations. Here is a level-one response from Joe, aged 10 years, one of Kohlberg's original longitudinal sample:

Kohlberg: Why shouldn't you steal from a store?
Joe: It's not good to steal from a store. It's against the law. Someone could see you and call the police.

(Kohlberg, 1976, p. 36)

Level two: conventional morality   This is 'the level of most adolescents and adults in our society and in other societies' (p. 33). At this level the individual thinks of what is right as conforming to and upholding the rules, expectations and conventions of society. Here is a level-two response from Joe, now aged 17 years:

Table 7.4   Kohlberg's stages of moral judgement

Level	Stage	What is right
Preconventional	Stage 1 Heteronomous morality	To avoid breaking rules backed by punishment, obedience for its own sake, avoiding physical damage to persons and property
	Stage 2 Individualism, instrumental purpose, and exchange	Following rules only when it is to someone's immediate interest; acting to meet one's own interests and needs, and letting others do the same. Right is what's fair, an equal exchange, a deal, an agreement
Conventional	Stage 3 Mutual interpersonal expectations, relationships and interpersonal conformity	Living up to what is expected by people close to you or what people generally expect of people in your role. 'Being good' is important and means having good motives, showing concern about others and keeping mutual relationships, such as trust, loyalty, respect, and gratitude
	Stage 4 Social system and conscience	Fulfilling the actual duties to which you have agreed. Laws are to be upheld except in extreme cases where they conflict with other fixed social duties. Right is contributing to society, the group, or institution
Postconventional or principled	Stage 5 Social contract or utility and individual rights	Being aware that people hold a variety of values and opinions, that most values and rules are relative to your group but should usually be upheld in the interest of impartiality and because they are the social contract. Some non-relative values and rights like life and liberty, however, must be upheld in any society and regardless of majority opinion
	Stage 6 (hypothetical) Universal ethical principles	Following self-chosen ethical principles. Particular laws or social agreements are usually valid because they rest on such principles. When laws violate these principles, one acts in accordance with the principle. Principles are universal principles of justice: the equality of human rights and respect for the dignity of human beings as individual persons

Source: Adapted from Colby et al., 1983

Kohlberg: Why shouldn't you steal from a store?

Joe: It's a matter of law. It's one of our rules that we're trying to help protect everyone, protect property, not just to protect a store. It's something that's needed in our society. If we didn't have these laws, people would steal, they wouldn't have to work for a living, and our whole society would get out of kilter.

(Kohlberg, 1976, p. 36)

Level three: postconventional morality   This level 'is reached by a minority of adults and is usually reached after the age of 20' (p. 33). Someone at this level broadly understands and accepts the rules of society, but only because they accept some general moral principles underlying these rules. If such a principle comes in conflict with society's rules, then the individual judges by principle rather than by convention. Here is a level-three response from Joe, now aged 24 years:

Kohlberg: Why shouldn't you steal from a store?
Joe: It's violating another person's rights, in this case to property.
Kohlberg: Does the law enter in?
Joe: Well, the law in most cases is based on what is morally right so it's not a separate subject, it's a consideration.
Kohlberg: What does 'morality' or 'morally right' mean to you?
Joe: Recognising the rights of other individuals, first to life and then to do as he pleases as long as it doesn't interfere with somebody else's rights.

(Kohlberg, 1976, pp. 36–7)

As a cognitive-developmental theorist, Kohlberg supposed that the level of moral reasoning was dependent on having achieved a level of cognitive development, and also of social perspective or role-taking (chapter 11). He thought that someone still at the concrete operational stage would be limited to preconventional moral judgement (stages 1 and 2). Someone at early formal operations would be limited to conventional morality (stages 3 and 4). Postconventional morality would be dependent on late formal operations being achieved.

Kohlberg hypothesized that in all societies, individuals would progress upwards through these stages, in sequence (stages would not be skipped, and subjects would not regress). He also hypothesized that an individual would be attracted by reasoning just above their own on the scale, but would not understand reasoning more than one stage above; if true, this would have obvious implications for moral education.

Early criticisms

A substantial number of criticisms of Kohlberg's methodology were made by Kurtines and Greif (1974). They pointed out that the moral judgement score of an individual was assessed from his or her scores on a number of dilemmas, yet the different dilemmas were derived intuitively and did not intercorrelate very highly. The scale was criticized as being unreliable, and the 'clinical method' of interview (similar to Piaget's) as being subjective. The validity of the scale was also called into question, since the invariance of sequence could not be properly proved from Kohlberg's sample if that was the sample from which he derived the sequence in the first place.

Table 7.5 'Man tells police that he robbed bank to pay for wife's cancer treatment' (adapted from *Japan Times*, Friday, 25 November 1994)

A man told police he robbed a bank so he could afford cancer treatment for his terminally ill wife. Larry A., 22, was arrested at a police roadblock after a chase on Tuesday following a holdup at the Mid-South Bank.

Detective Rick E. said that Larry A's account of his wife's illness was true. A woman who answered the telephone at Larry A's home and identified herself as his mother said his wife has ovarian cancer.

Larry A. told police he decided to rob the bank after several banks turned him down for a loan.

In the hold-up, a man handed a teller a note demanding $10,000 and threatened to 'blow you up', Detective E. said. The robber had no weapons.

Larry A. was given $4,000, police said. He was jailed on charges of robbery. Bail was set at $200,000.

Damon (1977) elaborated the criticism that the original dilemmas were intuitive, and in many ways unrealistic. How does the 'Heinz' problem appear to a 10- or 17-year-old? Damon listened to actual moral debates among children, and made up a number of interview items, such as:

> All of these boys and girls are in the same class together. One day their teacher lets them spend the whole afternoon making paintings and crayon drawings. The teacher thought that these pictures were so good that the class could sell them at the fair. They sold the pictures to their parents, and together the whole class made a lot of money.
>
> Now all the children gathered the next day and tried to decide how to split up the money.
>
> What do you think they should do with it? Why?
>
> Kathy said that the kids in the class who made the most pictures should get most of the money. What do you think? [More probe questions follow.]

From using these more realistic items, Damon derived a six-step 'positive-justice sequence', which describes children's reasoning about sharing, fairness and distributive justice. Other scales and sequences have also been published.

Turiel (1983) has criticized Kohlberg's theory for failing to acknowledge the different ways in which children learn to distinguish between social rules and conventions on the one hand (for example, 'You shall not undress in public' is a social convention) and moral rules which apply to principles of justice, truth and right (for example, 'It is wrong to kill' is a moral rule). Social conventions can be negotiated and changed but moral rules have an intrinsic quality. Turiel observed that children as young as 4 years could understand the difference between these two domains and found that they saw moral rules as more binding than conventions. This finding challenges Kohlberg's view that the principles only outweigh the conventions at a later stage of development, that is during adolescence.

Another criticism has been that Kohlberg's original participants were all male, and that the consequent sequence of stages reflects the development of male morality and is male-biased. This viewpoint has been put most strongly by Carol Gilligan in her book *In a Different Voice: Psychological Theory and Women's Development* (1982). In fact, Gilligan argues quite widely for a 'female psychology' to complement the predominantly 'male psychology' so far developed. So far as moral reasoning is concerned, Gilligan described a short-term longitudinal study in which she interviewed 29 women, aged 15–33, who were attending abortion- and pregnancy-counselling services. These women were faced with a very real moral dilemma – whether to have an abortion or go through with the pregnancy. Gilligan found that these women considered their dilemma in somewhat different terms from what she calls the 'justice' orientation of Kohlberg; rather they focused more on 'responsibility'. Instead of abstract, principled judgements which are universally applicable, as in Kohlberg's stages 5 and 6, these women made rational, context-dependent judgements which were more concerned about the impact of behaviour on people's actual feelings. Put simply, it is a question of whether you put principles before people (a 'male' characteristic), or people before principles (a 'female' characteristic). On this basis, Gilligan suggested an alternative ethic of care and responsibility as being more representative of women's moral-reasoning development.

Later revisions

Kohlberg and his co-workers, especially Anne Colby, revised some aspects of the theory. This, and independent replications, go some way to answering earlier criticisms. A new scoring system, called Standard Issue Scoring, was published in 1978. This scores, separately and with clear referents, the responses to the issue chosen by the subject for each dilemma; in the Heinz dilemma, for example, this would be the law issue if the subject says Heinz should not steal, the life issue if Heinz should save his wife. High reliabilities are reported for this scoring method. A rescoring of the original American longitudinal sample produced the results shown in figure 7.1. The stage sequence model is well supported for the first four stages. The low incidence of stage 5 is noticeable. Stage 6 is absent. Kohlberg therefore considered this to be a hypothetical stage, which has not been established empirically (Colby et al., 1983).

This sequence of stages has now been broadly confirmed in many other societies. A review by Snarey (1985) lists studies in 27 different cultural areas; most are cross-sectional, but there have been longitudinal studies in the Bahamas, Canada, India, Indonesia, Israel, Turkey and the USA. Naturally the dilemmas are adapted slightly for different cultures; the Turkish version of the Heinz dilemma, for example, involves a man and his wife who have migrated from the mountains, and are running out of food so that the wife

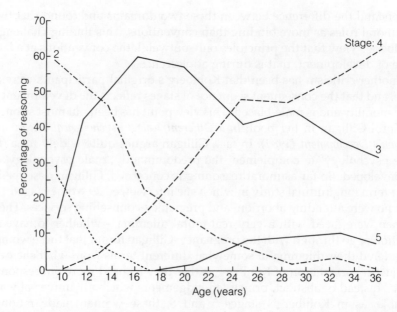

Figure 7.1 Mean percentage of moral reasoning at each stage for each age group (from Colby et al., 1983).

becomes sick; there is only one food store in the village, and the storekeeper charges so much that the man cannot pay. Here is an example of a level-one (stage two) response from Turkey (Snarey, 1985, p. 221):

Should the husband have stolen the food?

Yes. Because his wife was hungry . . . otherwise she will die.

Suppose it wasn't his wife who was starving but his best friend; should he steal for his friend?

Yes, because one day when he is hungry his friend would help.

What if he doesn't love his friend?

No, [then he should not steal] because when he doesn't love him it means that his friend will not help him later.

In his review Snarey found that almost all the studies in different societies agreed in finding a progression from stages 1 through to 4, at reasonably appropriate ages. There was some discordance about stage 5, however. Very few studies found true stage 5 reasoning, and even transitional stage 5 reasoning was only found in urban societies. It was not found at all in rural or village societies (e.g. Alaskan Eskimos, Guatemala, rural Kenya, New Guinea, rural Turkey). Rather than argue that individuals in these societies are in some sense inferior in moral reasoning, Snarey and other psychologists argue that Kohlberg's level three (stage 5) is significantly culturally biased. It reflects the individualistic, capitalistic orientation of middle-class

Western, urban society. Other religions, such as Hinduism, may put less value on individual human life than does the Christian religion. Other societies, socialist or rural, may put more emphasis on collectivist values based on reciprocity and on conflict resolution by interpersonal means. This is illustrated by an extract from an interview with an Israeli kibbutz male (Snarey, 1985, p. 222):

> Should Moshe steal the drug? Why or why not?
>
> Yes . . . I think that the community should be responsible for controlling this kind of situation. The medicine should be made available to all in need: the druggist should not have the right to decide on his own . . . the whole community or society should have the control of the drug.

In this example the person interviewed is somewhat at cross-purposes with the assumptions of the interviewer. Such responses may be difficult to score on Kohlberg's scheme, but (Snarey and others argue) should not therefore be devalued.

Can we teach moral values?

Kohlberg's research has encouraged psychologists and some educators to consider the social constructivist principles at the heart of moral reasoning. Although Piaget emphasized the role of peer interaction in the formation of moral judgements, he did not sufficiently explore the ways in which these kinds of social interaction promote further changes in the child's thinking. Doise (1990, p. 61) argues that 'in order to promote ethical behaviour, social representations of ideal relationships have to govern interaction patterns. Normative meta-systems such as the democratic conception of freedom and equality are necessary to further moral development in the Piagetian and Kohlbergian sense.' He proposes that:

- By co-ordinating their own actions with others, children are led to construct new cognitive co-ordinations which they are not capable of individually.
- Children who have participated in various social co-ordinations often become capable of executing these co-ordinations alone.
- Cognitive operations can be transposed from one setting to another.
- Social interaction becomes a source of cognitive progress through the sociocognitive conflict which it generates.
- Initial competencies are necessary for individuals to benefit from a specific interaction situation.

(adapted from Doise, 1990, p. 62)

The cognitive-developmental approach to moral reasoning has been very influential with definite implications for moral education. In becoming self-aware, children and young people are engaging in a process of learning about significant relationships and social roles. By co-operating with others in a social group that is significant to them, they can gain direct experience of learning about what is morally right for that group as well as the opportunity to learn that reciprocity is of greater value than the maximization of individual benefits. Schools are in a position to create this kind of context by actively promoting participative involvement in responsible action (involvement in school council; being a class representative; taking part in a peer support service would all be examples of this in practice) and democratic procedures. From this perspective, moral development cannot be effectively taught as a subject separate from the moral discourse and social life of the child's family and community.

Wright (1990) points out that teachers have always been important in engendering moral values in young people. However, he is critical of the idea that moral values can be taught didactically, since, in his view, a cooperative relationship between teacher and pupil provides a much deeper sense of morality and is at the heart of moral discourse as actively lived. The most effective context for enhancing and promoting moral development in children and young people is, he argues, based on a conception of equality, where the teacher's aim is to nurture amd strengthen the child's own moral 'voice'; it is one in which there is a fundamental respect for the person, where people listen to one another and where there is the opportunity for dialogue and debate. The child's moral sense will in these conditions arise out of his or her own experience and reflection, and not be based on the external authority of the adult.

◀ **Further Reading** ▶▶

N. Eisenberg and P. Mussen 1989: *The Roots of Prosocial Behaviour in Children*, Cambridge: Cambridge University Press, provides a useful introduction to the development of prosocial behaviour. K. Durkin 1995: *Developmental Social Psychology*, Oxford: Blackwell Publishers, has two useful chapters on the topic of prosocial behaviour and moral development.

For a cross-cultural perspective you may find it helpful to read C. A. Robarchek and C. J. Robarchek 1992: Cultures of war and peace: a comparative study of Waorani and Semai, in J. Silverberg and J. P. Gray (eds): *Aggression and Peacefulness in Humans and Other Primates*, New York: Oxford University Press.

J. Piaget 1977 [1932]: *The Moral Judgement of the Child*, Harmondsworth: Penguin, is worth reading for an insight into Piaget's style and methods; the theoretical excerpts are, however, rather dated and heavy going. Unfortunately, there is not a good, simple primer on Piaget's and Kohlberg's theories.

Good advanced collections are in E. Turiel (1983): *The Development of Social Knowledge: Morality and Convention*, Cambridge: Cambridge University Press; H. Foot, M. Morgan and R. Shute (eds) 1990: *Children Helping Children*, Chichester: John Wiley; H. Weinreich-Haste and D. Locke (eds) 1983: *Morality in the Making*, Chichester: John Wiley & Sons; and W. M. Kurtines and J. L. Gewirtz (eds) 1984: *Morality, Moral Behavior, and Moral Development*, New York: Wiley.

◄Discussion points►►►

1   How should we define prosocial behaviour? What implications does the definition have
    for the way in which prosocial behaviour is studied?
2   Contrast the use of naturalistic and experimental designs for studying what influences
    prosocial behaviour and altruism.
3   Compare Piaget's two methods of studying moral reasoning.
4   Is Kohlberg's way of obtaining levels of moral reasoning biased towards male, upper/
    middle-class, urban, Western-educated respondents?
5   How can either moral reasoning, or moral behaviour, be encouraged?

Box 7.1
Child-rearing and children's prosocial initiations towards victims of distress

The objective of this study was to examine the relationship between a mother's behaviour and her child's willingness to help others in distress. Particular attention was paid to mothers' reactions when their child observed or caused distress in another child. An intensive study of a small sample was used. Sixteen mothers of children aged between $1\frac{1}{2}$ and $2\frac{1}{2}$ years volunteered to take part. For a 9-month period they kept diary records of all incidents of distress in which someone in the child's presence expressed painful feelings, whether due to the child's own actions or not. The child's responses, and the mother's own behaviour, were recorded as soon as possible after the event, on a tape recorder. Mothers received initial training and an investigator visited the home every third week to check on the observations. At these visits the investigator also rated the mother on empathic caregiving (defined as anticipating difficulties, or responding promptly to the child's needs).

The analysis distinguished between those distress incidents which the child did not cause ('bystander incidents'), and those which the child did cause ('child-caused distress'). The children's prosocial behaviour took the form of physical or verbal sympathy ('All better now?'; hugs victim); providing objects such as food, toys or bandages; finding someone else to help; protecting the victim; or giving physical assistance. In bystander incidents children were altruistic on 34 per cent of occasions (range 5–70 per cent), and in child-caused distress they made reparations on 32 per cent of occasions

(range 0–60 per cent). There were clearly large individual differences between children, and these are fairly consistent over the two types of incident; the correlation between the two was 0.55, $p < 0.05$.

The mother's behaviour was categorized into various techniques, and the use of each technique calculated (more than one technique could be used in any incident). In bystander incidents, more frequent maternal techniques were 'no reaction' (56 per cent); 'reassurance' ('Don't worry, it's OK') (36 per cent); and 'modelling altruism to victim' (e.g. picks up and pats crying child) (21 per cent). In child-caused distress the most frequent maternal techniques were 'no reaction' (31 per cent); 'affective explanation' often involving moralizing ('You made Doug cry. It's not nice to bite') or verbal prohibition ('Can't you see Al's hurt? Don't push him') (22 per cent); 'neutral explanation' ('Tom's crying because you pushed him') (18 per cent); 'unexplained verbal prohibition' ('Stop that!') (15 per cent); 'suggestion of positive action' ('Why don't you give Jeffy your ball') (13 per cent); 'physical restraint' ('I just moved him away from the baby') (13 per cent); and 'physical punishment' ('I swatted her a good one') (9 per cent).

Was the way in which mothers reacted to child-caused distress related to the likelihood that a child behaved in a prosocial way in distress incidents? The investigators took the mothers scores for each technique, found the median and grouped mothers into those above or below the median (high or low

Box Table 7.1.1   Average percentage of incidents in which child shows altruism in bystander incidents and reparation for child-caused distress incidents when mothers are high or low in use of different techniques

Mother's technique	Altruism			Reparation		
	High use	Low use	t test	High use	Low use	t test
No reaction	29	40	n.s.	28	33	n.s.
Affective explanation	42	21	2.60 $p < 0.05$	44	13	4.77 $p < 0.01$
Neutral explanation	37	31	n.s.	37	23	n.s.
Unexplained verbal prohibition	24	42	2.41 $p < 0.05$	18	40	3.37 $p < 0.01$
Suggestion of positive action	32	37	n.s.	30	31	n.s.
Physical restraint	41	27	n.s.	31	29	n.s.
Physical punishment	29	28	n.s.	27	42	n.s.

on that technique). Then, the child's likelihood of prosocial behaviour was compared for 'high' and 'low' mothers on each technique, using independent groups t tests. The results are shown in box table 7.1.1, giving the analysis for the likelihood of children showing altruism in bystander incidents, and the corresponding analysis for the child showing reparation in child-caused distress incidents. It can be seen that mothers who gave affective explanations to their children when they caused distress are likely to have children who spontaneously show altruism to others, and also make reparation for distress they have caused themselves. On the other hand, mothers who gave more unexplained verbal prohibitions were likely to have children who showed less prosocial behaviour in both situations. Other techniques gave non-significant correlations. Physical methods (restraint, or punishment) were neither strongly effective nor ineffective, but they were positively correlated with some aspects of affective explanation; that is, many mothers combined affective explanation with some physical action.

The mothers' empathic caregiving ratings were also split into 'high' and 'low' groups. Mothers high in empathic caregiving had more prosocial children than did mothers low in empathic caregiving. For altruism in bystander incidents, the respective percentages were 46 per cent and 24 per cent; for reparation, the figures were 47 per cent and 17 per cent; both comparisons are significant at the 0.01 level on the t test.

The investigators conclude that 'the prototype of the mother whose child is reparative and altruistic is one whose communications when her child transgresses are of high intensity and clarity both cognitively and affectively . . . [it] is not calmly dispensed reasoning, carefully designed to enlighten the child, it is emotionally imposed, sometimes harshly and often forcefully. These techniques exist side by side with empathic caregiving.'

This study has noticeable strengths and weaknesses. The strengths are that it examines prosocial behaviour in real-life situations, and over some considerable time. One weakness is the small sample, composed only of volunteer mothers. It would certainly be problematic to generalize very widely, without a replicative study on a different sample. Another weakness might be the use of the mother's records: how objective were they? The training procedures, and investigators' recordings, went some way to alleviate this concern. Finally, the authors are tempted to infer causation from the correlations they discovered. They suggest that maternal techniques are influencing the child's behaviour. However, it could be that child characteristics influence the mother's behaviour. All we can be sure about is that, in this sample, empathic and affectively explaining mothers have prosocial children. We cannot be sure whether one causes the other, although we can generate plausible hypotheses from the data of this study.

Based on material in C. Zahn-Waxler, M. Radke-Yarrow and R. A. King 1979: *Child Development*, 50, 319–30.

Box 7.2
Peer interaction and the process of change in children's moral reasoning

Damon and Killen sought to discover, first, whether peer interaction in a moral debate would increase levels of moral reasoning; and secondly, whether certain kinds of peer interaction could be linked to such change. The study was carried out on 147 children, aged about 5–8 years, from public schools in an urban centre in the USA. The experimenters used Damon's positive-justice interview, rather than Kohlberg's scale, as a measure of moral reasoning. The interview was given both at pre-test and, about three and a half months later, at post-test.

About two months after the pre-test the children in the experimental condition participated in a peer debate, in groups of three. First, together with a fourth, younger child, they were given a task of making bracelets from beads and string. Then, the youngest child (who always made the fewest bracelets) was called away. After some further comments on the participants' efforts the experimenter then asked the three children to decide how ten sweet bars should be distributed between them and the fourth child. This peer debate was videotaped and scored for the content of discussion made by each participant.

The children in the first control group came individually to the laboratory and discussed a hypothetical justice problem of a similar nature. This controlled for the effect of practice in reasoning which was not in a peer context. The children in a second control group received no extra intervention; this controlled for changes in moral reasoning due to age and general experience over the three and a half months between pre-test and post-test.

A first analysis was done to see how many children had changed their modal level of moral reasoning. Very few had done so. However, many children had increased the proportion of their reasoning which was above their modal level, and these results are shown in box table 7.2.1. Here, the independent variable is the experimental condition, and the dependent variable is the change in moral reasoning. The experimental group display more change in moral reasoning than the control groups, ($X^2(2) = 144$, $p < 0.001$).

A second set of analyses considered only the children in the experimental condition. Whether or not there was a change in moral reasoning was now the independent variable, and the dependent variables examined were the kind of verbal interaction made in the peer debates. Chi-square analyses were used again. Children initially at low-reasoning levels, who both initiated and received a lot of statements indicating acceptance and clarification or elaboration, were especially likely to show a change in moral reasoning, $X^2(3) = 8.5$, $p < 0.05$, but this finding did not apply to children already at a high-reasoning level. However, many verbal con-

Box Table 7.2.1 Number of experimental and control participants whose percentage or reasoning above the modal value advanced from pre-test to post-test

	Advanced	Did not advance
Experimental group ($n = 78$)	32	46
Control group 1 ($n = 44$)	5	39
Control group 2 ($n = 25$)	4	21

tributions involving disagreements, rejection or ridicule predicted that moral reasoning would not change, $X^2(1) = 5.1$, $p < 0.05$).

A problem with small-scale intervention studies is that any convincing effects are likely to be small, and thus difficult to detect against general variation due to error and to random factors. In this study the peer debate only lasted about 10–11 minutes, so one might question what impact this could possibly have in a 3-month period. In fact, sufficient numbers of participants were employed that some increase in moral reasoning does seem to have been detected. While such changes were admittedly small, any larger changes would surely be suspect. The experimental design means that any change can be ascribed to the impact of peer interaction over a moral issue. The main objection would be that the peer debate was 'stage-managed' in an artificial situation (what did the children think was going on?) and might not be representative of real-life peer interaction.

Based on material in W. Damon and M. Killen 1982: *Merrill-Palmer Quarterly, 28*, 347–67.

8 Adolescence

Adolescence is the period of transition between childhood, and life as an adult; covering basically the teenage years. Biologically, it is marked by the onset of puberty. After puberty, a person is sexually mature and could potentially become a mother or father of a child. Socially, adolescence is marked by an increasing independence from parents as the young person prepares to leave home, to complete his or her education, to form sexual partnerships and to seek some vocation or employment.

Adolescence has been thought of as a difficult period, as indeed times of transition often are. The historian Philippe Aries (1962) actually argued that adolescence was a modern invention, and that in the Middle Ages 'children were mixed with adults as soon as they were considered capable of doing without their mothers or nannies' (p. 411). However, historians since then have criticized Aries' views as 'simplistic and inaccurate' (Hanawalt, 1992, p. 343); in medieval literature, adolescence was characterized in not unfamiliar ways, and potential conflict with the adult world was recognized. This conflict was perhaps overemphasized, by writers from both psychoanalytic and sociological traditions, during the 1950s and 1960s. Phrases, such as 'the identity crisis of adolescence', and the turmoil or 'storm and stress' of the adolescent period, have become familiar. In this chapter we will look at the nature of adolescence and examine how well the evidence supports these views. In doing so we shall note again the importance of the social and historical context in considering development. We need to keep a balance between the real cultural and historical variations, and the relatively invariant features which characterize adolescence. The most obvious universal feature is the onset of puberty, and we will start with an overview of the biological and physical changes which this involves.

◄The Biological and Physical Changes of Puberty►►

The precise timing of puberty depends on the measure taken, but in girls the onset of menstruation (menarche) provides a fairly definite marker, and in boys the time of first ejaculation (spermache). Puberty comes later for boys. The typical age sequence of physical changes is shown in table 8.1 (p. 241).

The physical differences between the boys and girls become much more obvious at puberty, due to hormonal changes. The reproductive organs become fully functional. In girls both the external genitalia (the vulva, including the clitoris) and the internal genitalia (the ovaries, fallopian tubes, uterus and vagina) become enlarged. The clitoris becomes more sensitive to stimulation, and the lining of the uterus and the vagina are strengthened.

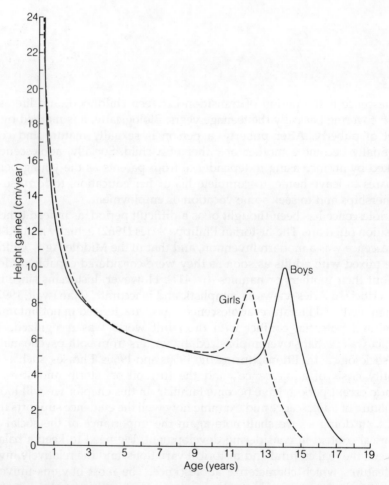

Figure 8.1 Typical individual curves showing velocity of growth in height for boys and girls (from Katchadourian, 1977).

Menarche follows these changes. In boys, the testes and penis become larger, and so does the prostate gland, which is important for the production of semen. This is followed by the first ejaculation.

Other changes are linked to these, but are not directly part of the reproductive system. In both sexes there is a growth of body hair, especially under the armpits and in the pubic areas. In boys there is more coarse body and facial hair, and the beginnings of beard growth. There are skin changes, and the sweat glands become more active, often leading to acne. The voice deepens, especially in boys. In girls, breast development occurs.

Another feature of the pubertal period is the adolescent growth spurt. Throughout the school years growth is fairly steady, averaging about 5 or 6 cm per year. This increases early on in puberty reaching about 9 cm per year in girls and 10 cm per year in boys before falling off sharply at adulthood (figure 8.1 shows these changes in growth velocity for an average boy and girl). The extent of this growth spurt is largely independent of the child's previous height and some 35 per cent of the variation in adult height is due to these rapid changes in adolescence.

All of the physical changes at puberty are linked to biological changes in the body. These are summarized in figure 8.2. The key role is played by the hypothalamus, as it controls the action of the pituitary gland which produces the necessary hormones. The action of the hypothalamus resembles that of a

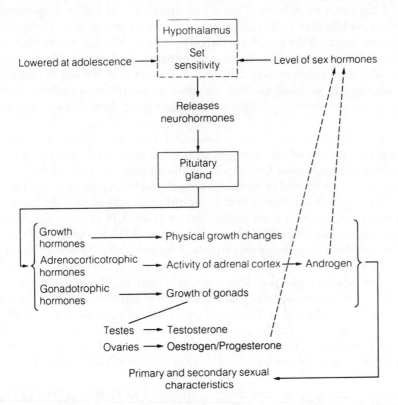

Figure 8.2   Summary of hormonal changes at puberty.

thermostat regulating temperature – it 'shuts down' when high enough levels of sex hormones are circulating in the body. These sex hormones (especially androgen, testosterone, oestrogen and progesterone) are produced by the adrenal cortex, and by the gonads (the testes and ovaries). The growth of the latter is in turn stimulated by hormones released by the pituitary gland. At puberty there is a change in the 'setting' or sensitivity of the hypothalamus. As a result, the pituitary gland works harder, and sex-hormone levels are raised.

Variations in physical maturation rates

The age of pubertal development can vary a great deal between individuals. This is dramatically shown in figure 8.3, which shows the growth and sexual development of three boys, each aged 14 years and 9 months, and of three girls, each aged 12 years 9 months. To some extent this variation may be genetic. For example, two randomly chosen girls will differ in age of menarche by, on average, 19 months; for two sisters, however, the average difference is only 13 months, and for identical twins, less than 3 months (Tanner, 1962). The variation is also linked to general body build. Children who are short and stocky tend to mature earlier than children who are slimmer and more linear in body shape (Katchadourian, 1977).

Environmental factors can also have very pronounced effects on maturation. Undernourishment or malnutrition can slow down growth and retard the onset of puberty. This is not surprising, as caloric requirements increase with puberty. Although it is difficult to prove, it is highly likely that nutritional differences are largely responsible for social-class and cultural differences in the timing of puberty. In less wealthy countries especially, social classes may differ by about a year in the age of menarche; the difference is less marked or absent in richer countries, where perhaps almost all young people get adequate nourishment (Katchadourian, 1977).

A fascinating phenomenon in western Europe and North America has been the secular trend in the age of menarche, illustrated in figure 8.4. This is based on records from the Scandinavian countries, going back to the mid-nineteenth century, and more recent records, including those in the UK and the USA. Figure 8.4 indicates that the age of menarche in girls declined over a hundred-year period from an average of around 16 or 17 in the 1860s to around 13 in the 1960s. The change averaged about 0.3 years per decade. There have been similar secular trends in height. Over the same period the average height of 12-year-olds increased by about 1.5 cm per decade; the trend for adult height was less – about 0.4 cm per decade – since some 'catching up' occurs in later maturers in early adulthood. Since the 1960s these changes in height and in age of menarche seem to have slowed down, as must happen eventually (Roche, 1979)! Nevertheless, a study in West Germany reported a continuing decrease in menarcheal age, from 13.3 years in 1979/80 (as in figure 8.4) to 13.0 years in 1989 (Ostersehlt and Danker-Hopfe, 1991).

Figure 8.4 has been extensively reproduced in textbooks, but in fact it seems that some of the earlier data is in error. Bullough (1981) re-examined

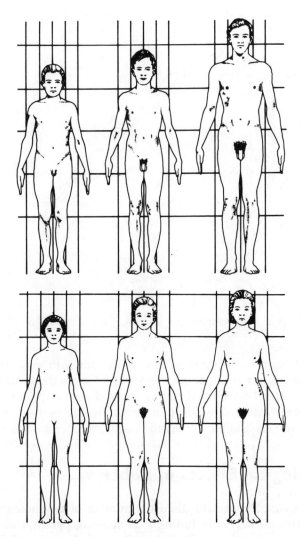

Figure 8.3 Individual variation in pubertal development: each of the 3 boys is 14 $\frac{3}{4}$ years old, and each of the 3 girls is 12 $\frac{3}{4}$ years old (from Tanner, 1973).

available data from the nineteenth century, which suggests that menarche occurred between 14 and 16 years of age. The data for the nineteenth century in figure 8.4 suggesting an age of 17 years are based on very small samples from Scandinavia which are not representative. Nevertheless no-one denies that there has been a secular trend. The historian Herbert Møller (1985, 1987) has looked at available evidence for still earlier periods, and for males. One source of evidence was records of Bach's choirboys in Leipzig for 1727–47. Their voices broke distinctly later, at around 17 years, than would be the case nowadays (14–15 years, table 8.1). An analysis of beard growth in males, from writings and portraits, suggests that before the nineteenth century many young men did not grow a beard until their twenties; for example, the

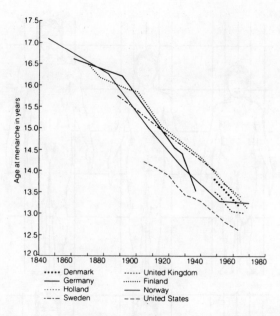

Figure 8.4 Changes in age of menarche over the past 120 years (from Tanner, 1973).

series of Rembrandt self-portraits only show him with a beard by age 24. Nowadays beard growth happens at around 17 years (table 8.1).

The secular trend is believed to have been due to improving nutritional and health standards. Decreases in mean family size may have been a contributing factor (see Malina, 1979, and Frisch, 1988, for a discussion).

◀Psychological Effects of Puberty▶▶▶

Through this chapter we will discuss a number of psychological changes associated with puberty – including a decrease in parent–child closeness. But how does puberty actually bring about such changes? Paikoff and Brooks-Gunn (1991) discuss a range of possible models; these cover direct and indirect effects of the physical changes themselves, of the increased level of sex hormones, and of the cognitive and self-definitional changes characteristic of this period.

Effects of physical changes

We have seen how the onset of puberty produces marked physical changes. These in their turn have psychological effects on the young person. The adolescent is becoming aware of his or her sexual development, and of associated changes in body size and shape, depth of voice, skin texture, and facial and body hair. Many writers on adolescence have ascribed the awkwardness or self-consciousness which is often thought to characterize this period to awareness of these changes.

A number of studies have examined the psychological impact of menarche on girls (Greif and Ulman, 1982). Retrospective studies, in which women are asked to recall their menarcheal experience, suggest that it remains a clear and vivid event in the memory; it is recalled in rather negative terms, as an unpleasant experience for which social support was lacking. These conclusions are limited by the samples (mainly middle-class American) and historical period studied (occurrence of menarche in the first half of the twentieth century).

A few studies have looked at attitudes in pre- and post-menarcheal girls. After menarche girls tended to report more negative emotions or experiences than they had expected, despite some educational preparation and support, usually from mothers. In a longitudinal study of 120 girls through menarche, Ruble and Brooks-Gunn (1982) confirmed that menarche did initially create some inconvenience, ambivalence and confusion, but that typically it did not seem to be a traumatic experience. The negative feelings were greater for early maturers, and also for girls who thought themselves poorly prepared for the experience. There can be positive features to menarche as well. Some studies have found that menarche can serve as a focal reference point, bringing a girl closer to her mother and heightening an awareness of and interest in her femininity. Menarche, or at least general changes associated with menarche, may be correlated with greater maturity on some personality characteristics (Greif and Ulman, 1982).

Some authors believe that the experience of menarche is better handled in other, traditional, cultures, in which there are well-defined rituals surrounding menstruation which give it a symbolic meaning and importance (Mead, 1928, 1949; Greif and Ulman, 1982). In the village of Lesu in Melanesia, for example, the focus of a well-known anthropological study by Powdermaker (1933), the onset of menstruation is an important ritual event for the women in the community. The girl is washed in the sea before sunrise by an old woman, who dips the leaves of a branch in the water and over the girl, saying:

> Leaf, leaf I wash her
> Soon her breasts will develop
> I take away sickness of blood.

The leaves are then mixed with white lime and rubbed over the girl's body. This ritual is thought necessary if the girl's breasts are to develop, and full womanhood achieved. A feast is held later the same day.

In many traditional societies boys also go through initiation ceremonies, often grouped together into an 'age set' spanning some 5 years. For example, in the Karimojong, a cattle-herding people of Uganda, boys to be initiated first have to spear an ox. Semi-digested food from the stomach sack of the slaughtered animal is smeared over the initiate's body, while the elders call out 'Be well. Become wealthy in stock. Grow old. Become an elder.' After further rituals, the boy has become a man and is allowed to grow his hair long in the fashion of men in the tribe (Dyson-Hudson, 1963).

These rituals are important in signalling the transition point from child to adult. Some anthropologists believe that they also reinforce the authority of the elders of the tribe, who perform the ceremonies. Another idea is that male initiation rites serve to break the close link children have with the mother. One study found that elaborate initiation rites were especially likely in societies where mothers nursed infants and shared the same bed with their child for a long period (Whiting et al., 1958). However, other explanations are possible. It may simply be that in male-dominated societies men may have several wives (so prolonged nursing and postpartum sex taboos are tolerated) and, independently, male initiation rites are important in forging male solidarity (Young, 1965).

Effects of hormones

Some researchers have argued that hormones may have a fairly direct effect on psychological functioning in adolescence, as well as any indirect effect through response to physical changes. Steinberg (1987) reported that pubertal maturation was associated with increased emotional distance from parents, in a US sample. Of course, this could just reflect an effect of chronological age; older adolescents being more mature, and less close to parents. However, utilizing individual variations in age of puberty, Steinberg showed that the effect of pubertal maturation was independent of chronological age. This was a cross-sectional study; further evidence that it is the pubertal maturation that causes the changes in parent–child relationships (rather than vice versa) came from a similar, longitudinal study (Steinberg, 1988; in fact Steinberg found influences in both directions). Puberty was associated with adolescent autonomy and parent–child conflict, and decreased closeness.

To what extent these and other studies can actually show that hormonal changes are in some way responsible is discussed by Buchanan et al. (1992). They also review a small number of studies which have actually measured hormone levels in relation to behavioural measures. They argue that there is some evidence to suppose that hormone levels affect such outcomes as moodiness and aggression, but that these effects interact in a complex way with the cognitive and self-evaluation changes occurring simultaneously. They conclude cautiously, quoting from a review 20 years earlier, that 'we have only begun to comprehend the many ways in which hormones affect and are affected by human emotions and behaviors' (p. 101).

Effects of cognitive changes

Entering the period of formal operational thought, adolescents are increasingly able to think about abstract issues and hypothetical situations (chapter 11). Thus, they may well reflect on how they are perceived by hypothetical others, and have problems adjusting to their changing physical appearance. David Elkind (1967) suggested that adolescents often imagine how their appearance or behaviour would seem to an 'imaginary audience' of others, hence their own self-consciousness. Elkind also argued that adolescents often thought that their own actions were very important in the eyes of others, and that they became bound up or obsessed with their own feelings, constructing a 'personal fable', an imaginary story of their own life, perhaps containing fantasies of omnipotence or immortality. These concepts of the 'imaginary audience' and the 'personal fable' led Elkind to postulate that a new kind of egocentrism appeared in adolescence (cf. chapter 11). In this 'adolescent egocentrism' young people are unable to differentiate their own feelings about themselves from what others might be feeling. Elkind was writing at a time when the 'storm and stress' view of adolescence was popular and empirical work on his concepts has yielded rather mixed results (Buis and Thompson, 1989).

Effects of early and late maturation

At 11 years a girl would be early in experiencing menarche; at 14 she would be late. Similarly a 12-year-old boy would be early, a 16-year-old late, in reaching puberty. Do these differences have important psychological consequences?

Early maturing boys tend to be at an advantage socially, as their growth spurt favours strength and sport achievement, usually highly valued in boys' groups (chapter 4). A boy who is late in reaching puberty may feel less confident socially and be rated as less mature, attractive or popular (Mussen and Jones, 1957).

A study in Sweden found a more complex picture for girls (Magnusson, Stattin and Allen, 1985). Data on 466 girls was obtained before puberty, after puberty at 14 years, and in a follow-up at 25 years. At 14 years it was clear that girls who had reached puberty early (before 11 years) were much more likely to be involved in drinking alcohol, smoking hashish, playing truant and generally breaking social norms more than girls who matured on time or late. However, this was found to be the case because these girls were more likely to mix with an older peer group who were more likely to engage in these activities. In other words, early maturation often led to associating with older peers, and if and when this happened the norm-breaking followed. This was a temporary effect; by age 25 the differences between early and late maturers in drinking alcohol had vanished. Nevertheless there was a more permanent effect of early maturation on education. Early maturing girls tended to engage in sexual activity earlier, get married and have children earlier, and were less likely to be in tertiary education than late maturers (2 per cent compared with 15 per cent). Another study, focusing on how early maturation relates to delinquency in girls, is featured in box 8.1.

Maturational timing may impact on academic achievement. A longitudinal study in the UK by Douglas and Ross (1964) was based on the National Survey of Health and Development, which followed 5,000 boys and girls born in one week in March, 1946. At secondary school, it emerged that both boys and girls who were early maturers scored higher than late maturers on tests of mental ability and performance while at school. Some other studies have reported similar results. However, the superior performance of early maturers might not be due to the physical changes of puberty and greater physical maturity. First, the effect seems to interact with social class, being larger in lower social class groups. Also, family size may explain much of the effect. Puberty tends to be later in large families, and being a member of a large family also tends to depress intelligence and school achievement in a slight but consistent fashion. When children of similar family size are compared, the differences between early and late maturers are small (Douglas and Ross, 1964).

A similar study in Sweden used a sample of 740 children followed from 9 to 14 years (Westin-Lindgren, 1982). In relation to achievement in Swedish, English and mathematics, the effects of social class were generally much greater than effects of early or late maturation. Thirteen- to 14-year-old early maturers did score better in Swedish and English if they came from families of manual workers, but there was little effect for children from families of salaried workers or employers. There were no effects of early or late maturation on mathematics scores. The possibly confounding effects of family size were not looked at in this study.

◀Identity Development and the 'Identity Crisis'▶▶▶

Who are you? What sort of a person are you? All of us have some sense of identity, of who or what we are. Try heading a blank sheet of paper 'Who am I?', and providing 20 short answers on the rest of the sheet. This 'Twenty Statement Test' is the kind of test some psychologists use in looking at identity development. Other methods are to see whether a person agrees with statements such as 'I take a positive attitude to myself', or to ask someone to rate his or her 'characteristic self' against adjective pairs such as relaxed–nervous, happy–sad or valuable–worthless. These latter assessments measure self-esteem (see also p. 165), or how one evaluates oneself, a very important aspect of overall identity.

In the earlier half of the twentieth century many theorists thought of adolescence as a time of acute identity crisis and turmoil. One influence here was that of psychoanalysis. Freud, at the turn of the century, was elaborating his views on human psychosexual development. On this view much of an individual's psychic energy was hypothesized as being taken up with trying to cope with unacceptable sexual impulses early in childhood. In the 'oral', 'anal' and 'oedipal' stages the very young child experiences frustration and anxiety at his or her developing sexual impulses, resulting in psychological defences and repression of these impulses during a 'latency period' from about 5 years of age to puberty. However, at puberty there was a renewed upsurge of sexual 'instincts' which reawakened old conflicts. The psychoanalytic approach was developed by Peter Blos (1962) in his book *On Adolescence*. Blos likened the adolescent transition to independence, to the earlier transition that the infant went through to become a self-reliant toddler; in both, ambivalence and regression were likely. Blos called adolescence a 'second individuation process', because of this parallel.

Freud's and Blos's theories have received much criticism. The 'instinct' model is outdated (chapter 2), and the emphasis on sexual concerns is generally felt to be exaggerated. However, a revision of the psychoanalytic approach made by Erik Erikson (1902–94) has attracted a lot of support.

Table 8.1   Approximate age and sequence of appearance of sexual characteristics during puberty

Age (yr)	Boys	Girls
9–10		Growth of bony pelvis Budding of nipples
10–11	First growth of testes and penis	Budding of breasts Pubic hair
11–12	Activity of prostate gland producing semen	Changes in lining of vagina Growth of external and internal genitalia
12–13	Pubic hair	Pigmentation of nipples Breasts fill out
13–14	Rapid growth of testes and penis	Axillary hair (under armpits) Menarche (average: 13.5 years; range 9–17 years). Menstruation may be anovulatory for first few years
14–15	Axillary hair (under armpits) Down on upper lip Voice change	Earliest normal pregnancies
15–16	Mature spermatozoa (average: 15 years; range: 11.25–17 years)	Acne Deepening of voice
16–17	Facial and body hair Acne	Skeletal growth stops
21	Skeletal growth stops	

Source: Adapted from Katchadourian, 1977

Erikson realized that Freud emphasized innate impulses too strongly; he gave a much larger role to cultural influences in personality formation. He accepted Freud's insight into the importance of sexual desires, but regarded other concerns as equally, or more, strong at various stages of the life cycle; he therefore described 'psychosocial' rather than 'sexual' stages of development. Finally, he thought that adolescence (rather than early childhood) was the most decisive period in the formation of adult personality. A summary of Erikson's eight stages in the life cycle is shown in table 8.2. In each stage there is a 'normative crisis' – the area in which Erikson considered conflict to be most characteristic.

Erikson elaborated his ideas about role confusion and identity in adolescence in an influential book *Identity: Youth and Crisis* (1968). He argued that while identity was important throughout the life cycle, it was in adolescence that the most turmoil in this area could normally be expected. He thought that adolescents typically went through a psychological or psychosocial 'moratorium', in which they could try out different aspects of identity without finally committing themselves. For example, a young person might

Table 8.2   The eight developmental stages proposed by Erikson (1968)

Normative crisis	Age (yr)	Major characteristics
Trust vs. mistrust	0–1	Primary social interaction with mothering caretaker; oral concerns; trust in life-sustaining care, including feeding
Autonomy vs. shame and doubt	1–2	Primary social interaction with parents; toilet training; 'holding on' and 'letting go' and the beginnings of autonomous will
Initiative vs. guilt	3–5	Primary social interaction with nuclear family; beginnings of 'oedipal' feelings; development of language and locomotion; development of conscience as governor of initiative
Industry vs. inferiority	6–puberty	Primary social interaction outside home among peers and teachers; school age assessment of task ability
Identity vs. role confusion	Adolescence	Primary social interaction with peers, culminating in heterosexual friendship; psychological moratorium from adult commitments; identity crisis; consolidation of resolutions of previous four stages into coherent sense of self
Intimacy vs. isolation	Early adulthood	Primary social interaction in intimate relationship with member of opposite sex; adult role commitments accepted, including commitment to another person
Generativity vs. stagnation	Middle age	Primary social concern in establishing and guiding future generation; productivity and creativity
Integrity vs. despair	Old age	Primary social concern is a reflective one: coming to terms with one's place in the (now nearly complete) life cycle, and with one's relationship with others; 'I am what survives of me'

temporarily adopt different religious beliefs, or changed views about their vocation, without adults expecting this necessarily to be a final choice. After this period of crisis, a more stable, consolidated sense of identity would be achieved.

There are of course good reasons why one's sense of identity might change considerably through adolescence. We have seen how marked physical changes occur, which will affect one's body image or sense of physical self. At this time also a pattern of sexual relationships needs to be decided upon. Society expects a young person to make some choice of vocation by around 18 years, and in many countries they also get the vote at this age and have to decide on their political preferences. Nevertheless, Erikson's ideas were not obtained from any large-scale survey; they were based on his own observations, and on his clinical practice. They certainly needed to be tested against empirical findings.

An interesting longitudinal case study which tested Erikson's ideas was reported by Espin, Stewart and Gomez (1990). They carried out a content analysis of 71 letters written by a Latin-American girl to her former teacher, over a 9-year period, between the ages of 13 and 22. Besides her adolescence, this was a traumatic period for her, since she and her parents were imprisoned for political reasons.

According to the content analysis, themes to do with Identity predominated in the earlier letters. These increased from 13 to 18 years, then declined. Themes to do with Intimacy increased steadily through the period and became predominant after age 19. Themes to do with Generativity were very low at first, but did start to increase after age 19. This single case study does support the notion of three successive overlapping stages from Erikson's model (table 8.2), but clearly more normative studies are needed.

The most thorough attempt to do this was made by James Marcia (1966, 1980). Marcia developed an interview technique to assess 'identity status' in certain areas, notably those of occupation, religion, political belief and attitudes to sexual behaviour. He would ask questions such as 'Have you ever had any doubts about your religious beliefs?' Depending on the answer to these and other questions, a subject would be characterized as in 'diffusion' (or 'confusion'), 'foreclosure', 'moratorium', or 'achievement of identity' (Marcia, 1966).

Someone in diffusion (confusion) status has not really started thinking about the issues seriously, let alone made any commitment. Thus in answer to the above question, they might answer 'Oh, I don't know. I guess so. Everyone goes through some sort of stage like that. But it really doesn't bother me much. I figure one's about as good as the other!' By contrast, someone in foreclosure status has formed a commitment, but without ever having gone through a crisis or seriously considered alternatives. They probably accept unquestioningly parental or conventional beliefs. They might answer 'No, not really, our family is pretty much in agreement on these things' to the question about religious doubts.

Someone in moratorium status is going through the crisis predicted by Erikson. They are going to form a commitment, but at present are still considering various alternatives. They might answer 'Yes, I guess I'm going through that now. I just don't see how there can be a god and yet so much evil in the world or . . .'.

Finally, someone in achievement status has been through the crisis and has reached a resolution. They have consolidated their identity in this respect. Thus, they might answer 'Yeah, I even started wondering whether or not there was a god. I've pretty much resolved that now, though. The way it seems to me is . . .'.

In this scheme diffusion is seen as the least mature status, and achievement as the most mature. The most likely transitions in identity status are shown in figure 8.5. The results of a cross-sectional study (Meilman, 1979) on

12- to 24-year-old males are shown in figure 8.6. It can be seen that only just over half the subjects interviewed had reached identity achievement at 24 years. Thus, identity achievement may go on well into adulthood. This is borne out by a study by O'Connell (1976), who carried out retrospective interviews with married women who had school-aged children. Most of the women said that they had experienced an increasingly strong sense of identity as they moved from adolescence through to when they married, then had their first child, then had their children going to school. Such findings suggest that identity development is not so strongly focused in adolescence as Erikson suggested.

Another study (Waterman and Waterman, 1975) compared identity status in a number of male college students and their fathers. The students were mainly of diffusion or moratorium status, while the fathers (aged 40–65) were mainly in the foreclosure status and had not reached identity achievement. These men had grown up in the 1930s to 1950s, and it could be that social expectations favoured a more conforming, 'foreclosure' kind of identity development at that time.

The best evidence on identity development would come from longitudinal studies, following the same participants. One, by Waterman, Geary and Waterman (1974), used American college students (as with the great majority of the studies in this area). Over a 3-year period, there was a decrease in foreclosure and an increase in achievement, although many students remained in diffusion status. However, college students are not typical of the whole population.

We can have more confidence in identity status measures if they correlate with, or predict, other variables. Persons in moratorium for vocation are indeed more likely to change their academic plans. Students in identity achievement have a wider range of cultural interests and express more interest in expressive writing and poetry (Waterman, 1982). Sex differences in identity status are not very marked (Archer, 1982), except in the area of sexual attitudes (which we shall discuss shortly). Identity status has been related to family background. Those in foreclosure report close relationships to parents, those in moratorium and achievement more distant or critical ones. Children from divorced families tend to score higher on identity status than those from intact families (cf. p. 98).

The work on identity status is an interesting attempt to try to pin down Erikson's ideas, but criticism has been made of how useful the status categories are and how adequately they assess identity (Cote and Levine, 1988). Also, the idea of an 'identity crisis' seems suspect on at least three counts. First, adolescents do not experience the moratorium status in different topic

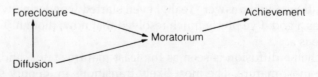

Figure 8.5   Most likely predicted changes in identity status.

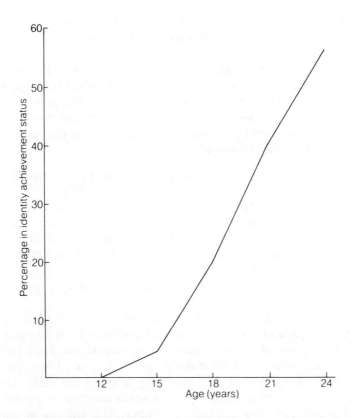

Figure 8.6   Percentage of males who were in identity achievement status at five age levels (from Meilman, 1979).

areas at the same time; at one particular time one content area may be stable while another area of life decisions is in crisis. A second point is that crisis can occur throughout adult life, and identity development can be quite prominent in the early adult years. Finally, we have a lot of evidence that for most young people, most of the time, changes in identity and self-esteem are gradual. We will conclude this section by looking at a couple of studies which show this, neither making use of the Marcia identity status categories.

Montemayor and Eisen (1977) used the Twenty Statements Test on about 50 young people each in the ages 10, 12, 14, 16 and 18. They found that there were significant age changes, but without any dramatic crisis at say 14 or 16 years. Many of the changes were from a more concrete to a more abstract way of describing oneself: for example, responses in terms of one's address or citizenship (e.g. 'I live in the High Street'), possessions ('I own a bike') or physical self ('I am 5-feet high') declined with age. Responses in terms of occupation ('I hope to be a doctor'), ideological beliefs ('I am a pacifist'), sense of self-determination ('I want to succeed in life') and interpersonal style ('I am a friendly person') increased with age. Some kinds of response showed a curvilinear trend, for example one's name ('I am called Fred'), or judgements and likes ('I like swimming'). Two sample answers from Montemayor and Eisen's study illustrate some of them:

> Boy, nearly 10: My name is Bruce C. I have brown eyes. I have brown hair. I love! sports. I have seven people in my family. I have great! eye sight. I have lots! of friends. I live at Pinecrest Dr. I'm going on 10 in September ... I have an uncle who is almost 7-feet tall. My teacher is Mrs V. I play hockey! I'm almost the smartest boy in the class. I love! food. I love fresh air. I love! school.

> Girl, nearly 18: I am a human being. I am a girl. I am an individual. I don't know who I am. I am a Pisces. I am a moody person. I am an indecisive person. I am an ambitious person. I am a very curious person. I am not an individual. I am a loner. I am an American (God help me). I am a Democrat. I am a liberal person. I am a radical. I am a conservative. I am a pseudoliberal. I am an atheist. I am not a classifiable person (i.e. I don't want to be).
>
> (Montemayor and Eisen, 1977, pp. 317–18)

Savin-Williams and Demo (1984) examined changes in self-esteem in a longitudinal sample of about 40 young people from 12 to 15 years of age. They used a variety of different measures of self-esteem. They found that changes were gradual, both on a daily and on a yearly basis. Feelings of self-esteem increased slowly but gradually through the early adolescent years. There were a few exceptions – a small number of young people who did experience very fluctuating feelings. The authors' general conclusion however is that there is 'a gradual process whereby adolescents' developing cognitive abilities permit greater self-awareness ... adolescence appears more to be a stage of development, in the true sense, than of disruption'.

The transition to work

For school leavers one of the main areas of identity achievement has traditionally been through the normal transition from school to work. But in the wake of widespread economic recession in many developed countries the majority of early school leavers experience unemployment at some stage in the 16- to 19-year age period. A number of studies now point to the personal consequences of youth unemployment in terms of psychological distress, anxiety, unhappiness, dissatisfaction, stigma and lowered self-esteem (for a review see Banks and Ullah, 1986). One study attempted to apply Erikson's developmental model to the experience of employment or unemployment (Gurney, 1980). Students were interviewed just before, and four months after, leaving school. Obtaining a job was a significant factor in perception of identity for females only. This research did not find unemployment to have traumatic effects, perhaps because of the short period of unemployment. However, later research does suggest that for most young people continued unemployment is a particularly distressing experience.

◀Sex-role Identity▶▶▶

We examined the development of gender identity in children in chapter 5, where we saw that this referred primarily to the awareness of oneself as a boy or girl. Many writers use the term 'sex-role identity' to refer to the acquisition of a set of standards for appropriate masculine or feminine behaviour, in a particular culture. This develops through middle childhood, but many aspects are likely to become much more significant at adolescence.

According to Douvan (1979), the development of sex-role identity is most difficult for adolescent females in modern urban societies. This is because schools encourage girls (like boys) to be independent, competitive and achieving, but on leaving school these traits are not valued for girls as they are for boys. Young women are conventionally expected to be non-assertive, and to give up any financial independence by assuming a domestic and motherly role on marriage. This conclusion is largely based on an extensive interview study carried out in the 1950s (Douvan and Adelson, 1966). This study has been criticized, however, for bias in the way the interviews were conducted (Hopkins, 1983). For example, boys were asked more questions about jobs, and girls were asked more questions about marriage. Furthermore, social attitudes have undoubtedly changed over the past 40 years, and greater assertiveness, independence and job-orientation in younger women is now relatively more accepted.

It could be argued that young men have less choice of different routes to establish sex-role identity (Conger, 1977). Female roles may at present be more changeable and varied (i.e. a young woman can readily choose to be either career-orientated, or a mother). Also, research has generally found that cross-sex interests or behaviour (e.g. boys doing needlework; girls doing metalwork) are tolerated in girls more than in boys. Overall, it is difficult to draw conclusions about whether boys or girls find sex-role identity a more difficult process.

Many young men and women develop attitudes and behaviours conforming to conventional stereotypes of masculine and feminine behaviour. For example, the majority of caring for young children is still done by women; the majority of car repair tasks are done by men. Using questionnaires it is easy to obtain measures of sex-role orientation in terms of tasks such as these. In the USA, especially, there has been interest in the concept of 'androgyny' – an androgynous person is someone, male or female, who scores fairly equally on both masculine and feminine items of sex-role orientation. For example, an androgynous person might enjoy both baby-minding and car-repairing. Some researchers have argued that androgyny is more psychologically healthy, and leads to higher levels of self-esteem (Bem, 1975; Spence and Helmreich, 1978). In part such arguments and findings may reflect a current questioning of conventional sex-roles, and the restrictions of choice and inequality of opportunity which they are thought by some to embody.

Sex-role conventions, besides changing with time, also vary between different societies (see also chapter 5). Margaret Mead documented many instances of such cultural variations. For example, from studies of three tribes living close to each other in New Guinea (Mead, 1935), she reported that amongst the Arapesh, both men and women were sensitive and non-aggressive and had 'feminine' personalities; amongst the Mundugamor, both men and women were ruthless, unpleasant and 'masculine'; amongst the Tchambuli, women were dominant and men more emotional and concerned about personal appearance, an apparent reversal of our own conventions. The pattern seems almost too neat to be believed, and indeed Mead has been criticized for being selective in her presentation of results (Harris, 1968; Blurton Jones and Konner, 1973). For example, in all three tribes men seem to have shown the most violent behaviour, and in all three societies men did the hunting. In her later writing Mead did recognize a possibly greater importance of biological factors in sex roles (Mead, 1949). However, her demonstration of cultural differences, while perhaps exaggerated, is in many respects a valid indication of how society can powerfully influence sex-role development, which has been borne out by many other studies (Archer and Lloyd, 1986).

◀Sexual Knowledge, Attitudes and Behaviour▶▶▶

Sexual knowledge

Adolescence is a time when knowledge of the processes of reproduction and of sexual intercourse assumes great importance. We have seen earlier how an understanding of menarche, for example, can ease the pubertal transition in adolescent girls. But how much do adolescents know about these matters? A large-scale study of children's sexual thinking was carried out, in four different countries, by Goldman and Goldman (1982), and their results showed that knowledge of sexual matters did increase greatly in early adolescence, but that surprising areas of ignorance remained.

The Goldmans interviewed children aged 5–15 in schools in Australia, England, North America (Canadian/US border area) and Sweden. About 30–40 children were interviewed in each country, at each age. Amongst many other items, the children were asked to explain the meaning of certain words such as 'pregnancy' and 'puberty'. Some of the results, for the three older age bands, are shown in table 8.3. This shows the percentage of participants who gave 'fully appropriate' answers (for example for 'puberty', some understanding that having children became possible).

It can be seen that early adolescence saw a rapid increase in understanding of terms such as 'rape' and 'virgin'. Some terms remained poorly understood at 15, however, notably 'venereal disease' and 'puberty' itself. This is taken by the Goldmans to point to the importance of increased sex education in schools. They consider this argument strengthened by the greater understanding shown by the Swedish children (e.g. for 'pregnancy', and 'puberty'). Sweden does have compulsory courses in sex education and personal relationships for 7–16-year-olds; in the other countries studied, sex

Table 8.3 Children's understanding of sexual terms: percentages of 'fully appropriate' responses at 11, 13 and 15 years of age in four different countries

	Age	Australia	England	N. America	Sweden
Rape	11	25	38	10	47
	13	73	65	64	87
	15	100	87	87	86
Virgin	11	8	15	0	13
	13	48	38	39	70
	15	83	63	61	93
Pregnancy	11	20	18	13	50
	13	27	45	30	77
	15	38	50	52	87
Venereal disease	11	0	0	0	0
	13	3	0	0	3
	15	20	10	20	20
Puberty	11	0	0	0	17
	13	3	3	9	20
	15	5	3	3	43

Source: Goldman and Goldman, 1982

education is largely confined to late in the secondary school. In all countries most children said they would have liked more sex education in school, and at an earlier age. The home remained the most cited source of information on sexual matters.

Sexual attitudes

An interesting feature of the Goldmans' study is that they had difficulty gaining access to many North American schools, simply because they wanted to ask questions with a sexual content. For many people sex is still a 'taboo' area. However, the Goldmans might have encountered even more difficulties if they had been doing their research 50 years earlier. Attitudes to sexual matters generally seem to have been much more restrictive then, and to have changed markedly through the 1960s and 1970s.

This shift in attitudes can be gauged from such sources as parents' manuals on how children should be brought up and educated; teachings of the churches on sexual matters; articles in the mass media; and direct attitudinal surveys by social scientists. As an example from parents' manuals, consider the following extract on masturbation from *What a Boy Should Know*, published in 1909:

The results on the mind are the more severe and more easily recognised ... A boy who practises this habit can never be the best that Nature intended him to be. His wits are not so sharp. His memory is not so good. His power of fixing his attention on whatever he is doing is lessened . . . The effect of self-abuse on a boy's character always tends to weaken it, and in fact, to make him untrustworthy, unreliable, untruthful, and probably even dishonest.

These stern warnings have scarcely lessened in the *Mothercraft Manual* of 1928 (Liddiard, 1928):

This is a bad habit . . . The habit, if left unchecked, may develop into a serious vice. The child's moral nature becomes perverted; one such child has been known to upset a whole school.

Current medical opinion, however, is that masturbation is normally harmless, and we also know that it is the usual way in which young males first reach orgasm following puberty. Masturbation has become much more socially acceptable, especially in adolescents. Dr Spock's 1976 manual stated that:

Some conscientious adolescents feel excessively guilty and worried about masturbation . . . If a child seems to be generally happy and successful, doing well in school, getting along with his friends, he can be told that all normal young people have these desires and that a great majority do masturbate. This won't take away all his feeling of guilt, but it will help. (p. 413)

Attitudes to premarital sexual intercourse have also changed. Over the 1960s and 1970s surveys showed that older generations had less permissive attitudes on such matters than younger people. This is not just a matter of age – it is not the case that everyone gets less permissive as they get older. Rather, it seems to reflect a genuine historical trend which has been working its way through the population as people socialized in earlier decades get older and eventually die. For example, in a general survey in the USA in 1969, only 21 per cent of Americans judged premarital sex to be 'not wrong'; yet by 1979, this had risen to 55 per cent (Reinhold, 1979). Similar changes occurred in the UK and other Western societies.

Attitudes to sex clearly vary with the nature of the relationship with one's partner. Most people, including adolescents, regard intercourse as more acceptable if there is affection for and emotional commitment to one's partner – if it is a 'steady' relationship. Reiss (1967) identified four standards of sexual behaviour in the USA, shown in table 8.4. Some form of the 'single standard' or 'double standard' seems to have been most common up to the 1950s, but the 'permissiveness with affection' standard seems most common now. The figures in table 8.5 show how 'permissiveness with affection' has been endorsed by a majority of American college students since the late 1960s, while 'permissiveness without affection', although more tolerated recently, remains less approved of. The double standard of attitudes to premarital intercourse in males and females is not so strong in recent surveys, as can be seen by comparing the attitudes to males and females in table 8.5. However, there is still a lot of cultural variation in such matters. Ma (1989) reported a comparison of attitudes to premarital sex in university students in the USA, and in Taiwan. This study confirmed that 'permissiveness with affection' was the most common standard for students in the USA; but that the 'single standard' of no sexual intercourse before marriage was most common amongst the Chinese students in Taiwan – but with some indication of a 'double standard', as women were less permissive than men.

Sexual behaviour

How have these general changes in attitudes affected the sexual behaviour of adolescents? What we know of sexual behaviour in young people, and adults also, comes from questionnaire and interview studies. The first modern large-scale survey was by Kinsey and his co-workers in the USA (Kinsey et al., 1948, 1953). There have been a number of other studies in the USA, and three notable studies in the UK by Schofield (1965), Farrell (1978), and Breakwell and Fife-Schaw (1992). A lot of this work was done in the late 1960s and early 1970s; the interest shown by social scientists in sexual attitudes and behaviour at this time probably reflects the considerable change attitudes and behaviour were undergoing. There was then less interest up to the mid-1980s but this has changed again as the spread of AIDS has its impact on sexual attitudes and behaviour (Cowan and Johnson, 1993).

Table 8.4 Four standards concerning premarital sexual intercourse, according to Reiss (1967)

Single standard:	no sexual intercourse before marriage
Double standard:	no sexual intercourse before marriage, for women; permitted for men
Permissiveness with affection:	premarital sexual intercourse allowed if partners have some emotional commitment to each other
Permissiveness without affection:	premarital sexual intercourse allowed or encouraged even without emotional commitment

Table 8.5 Percentage approval of premarital sexual intercourse by college students in the USA for different levels of affection between partners

	Early 1960s	Later 1960s	Early/mid-1970s
If no strong affection for partner			
approved for males	21	51	50
approved for females	11	28	38
If strong affection for partner			
approved for males	37	65	73
approved for females	27	50	70
If engaged to partner			
approved for males	52	76	85
approved for females	44	70	75

Obviously there are problems with interview or questionnaire studies in which adolescents are asked questions about their attitudes to sexual behaviour, whether they have had sexual intercourse, if so how many partners they have had, and so forth. These are usually considered very personal matters only to be revealed to a close confidant, if at all. Problems of truthful responding, which will always qualify interview studies, are likely to be particularly strong for sexual matters. There may also be problems in understanding terms (see table 8.3), as illustrated by the question and answer 'Are you a virgin?' 'Not yet' obtained in one study! The interviewer must obviously try to obtain rapport with the person being interviewed, stress the confidentiality with which the answers will be treated, make sure questions are properly understood, and make clear the reasons for carrying out the survey. Some assurance that replies are reasonably truthful can be obtained when systematic trends are found in the results, for example an increase in sexual experience with age. Finally, if results are to be generalized, a representative or random sample must be obtained, and not too many participants should refuse to answer or drop out of the survey.

In the UK, the Schofield report of 1965 was based on a sample of 2,000 unmarried adolescents aged 15–19. The sample was a random one across different parts of the country. Interviews took about an hour. The main qualification to the results of this thorough survey is that about 15 per cent of teenagers approached refused to take part. Young people reported going through successive stages of sexual experience. Dating was usually the first form of independent contact with a member of the opposite sex, often leading to kissing. This was usually lip kissing; deep kissing or 'French kissing' (where one partner's tongue enters the mouth of the other) was less common at this stage, and was usually preceded by breast stimulation over clothes. Further forms of petting included breast stimulation under clothes, and direct touching or stimulation of the partner's genitals. These heavier forms of 'petting' usually preceded full sexual intercourse, which only a minority of the sample reported having had (table 8.6).

A similar survey in the UK was reported by Farrell in 1978. This showed that the increased permissiveness in sexual attitudes had been reflected by an increased incidence of sexual behaviour in young people. Table 8.6 shows how the proportion of teenagers reporting having had sexual intercourse at 17 and 19 years of age approximately doubled in males and tripled in females over the period between the two studies.

Breakwell and Fife-Schaw (1992) surveyed sexual behaviour in 16–20-year-olds, but using questionnaires rather than interviews. They obtained 2,171 replies, a response rate of 37 per cent (45% for females, 30% for males); while these response rates are quite good for surveys of this kind, they are much lower than in the Schofield study and this puts some limits on the reliability of the figures obtained. Nevertheless, the pattern of results for sexual intercourse, shown in table 8.6, suggests a continuing trend to earlier sexual activity; and, a disappearance of the 'double standard' of greater permissiveness for males than females.

A similar change between the mid-1960s and mid-1970s has been found in

American studies, as figure 8.7 shows, for incidence of premarital intercourse. Again, the increase in sexual experience has been more marked in
females.

Another approach to documenting these historical trends has been to
send short questionnaires to people of differing ages, asking at what age
they first had sexual intercourse; this is something one might usually remember quite accurately. In a study of this kind in Norway, by Sundet et al.
(1992), short anonymous questionnaires were sent to 10,000 people aged 18
to 60, in 1987. The response rate was 63 per cent. Answers to the question
'How old were you (in years) when you had your first intercourse' are
shown in table 8.7. Younger persons report an earlier age than do older
persons. Note that the main drop occurs between persons born in the 1940s
and 1950s, that is, those who would be 18 in the 1960s and 1970s. Note also
the change from a later age for females, to an earlier age in more recent
samples. In a similar study in Sweden in 1967, people in their 50s recalled an
average age of 18.6 years; this fell to an average of 17.0 years in people in
their early 20s. A study ten years later found that this had fallen further, to
16.0 years.

What do we know of the factors influencing whether a young person
engages in sexual behaviour and sexual intercourse? In the Schofield report
there was little effect of social class, religious background or family
background. However, lack of discipline or restraint from parents was
associated with early sexual experience, especially in girls. Early physical
development, conformity to teenage rather than adult norms, and a lively
gregariousness were also associated with early sexual experience. Studies in
the USA have confirmed the influences of the peer group and of physical
attractiveness on sexual behaviour. They also suggest that sexually inexperi-
enced adolescents are more likely to describe themselves as religious. Social-
class effects seem to be complicated and to vary with historical epoch. The
Kinsey report of the late 1940s indicated greater sexual experience in lower
social-class groups, but this was not found in the 1960s. Some studies suggest

Table 8.6 Percentage of participants reporting having had
sexual intercourse in three UK studies of adolescents

	at 17 years		at 19 years	
	males	females	males	females
Schofield 1965	25	11	37	23
Farrell 1978	50	39	74	67
Breakwell & Fife-Schaw 1992	60	60	77	80

Note: Figures from Breakwell and Fife-Schaw (1992) are an average of
their 16–17/17–18 and 18–19/19–20 percentages

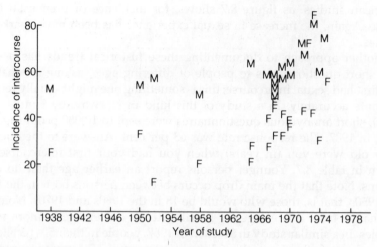

Figure 8.7 Incidence of premarital intercourse in American college men (M) and women (F) from 1938 to 1975 (from Hopkins, 1983).

greater sexual experience in students from higher social-class groups (Hopkins, 1983). However, the Norwegian study of Sundet et al. (1992) found a later age of first intercourse in more educated, and higher social class, persons.

No doubt many factors contributed to the changes in attitudes and behaviour in the 1960s and 1970s. Probably increased affluence and also a greater availability of effective contraceptives played a part. Sexual attitudes and behaviour will continue to change. The possibility of contracting venereal disease has always been some deterrent to more permissive or promiscuous sexual behaviour, and considerable publicity has been given to the risks of new strains of sexually transmitted diseases, especially the AIDS virus, in the 1990s. Nevertheless, many young people continue with sexual practices which are risky. Breakwell and Fife-Schaw (1992) found that between 16 to 20 years, rates of reported heterosexual anal penetration increased from around 4 per cent to 14 per cent; and homosexual anal penetration to about 1 per cent of male respondents. This tends to be a high-risk activity for infection. This research and other surveys (Meyrick and Harris, 1994) also suggest that only a minority of young people use effective contraception. Research such as this continues to feed in to public debates about necessary and desirable levels of sex education and availability of contraception.

◄Relations with Parents and Peers►►►

As adolescents become independent from their parents, they may spend more time with peers and turn to peers more for social support and identity. We saw in chapter 4 how researchers such as J. S. Coleman in the USA and

Table 8.7 Age of first intercourse in different cohorts of Norwegian adults (adapted from Sundet et al., 1992)

Birth years	Age in 1987	Males	Females
1963–9	18–24	18.3	17.2
1956–62	25–31	18.0	17.2
1949–55	32–38	18.2	17.9
1942–8	39–45	18.6	18.9
1935–41	46–52	18.8	18.8
1927–34	53–60	19.3	19.6

David Hargreaves in the UK documented the importance of peer groups or cliques in secondary schools, and how the values of such peer groups might diverge greatly from those of teachers and parents. Also, some evidence suggests that conformity with peers, especially in antisocial situations, does increase up to early adolescence before declining again. Anxieties about friendships with peers also peak at about this age, according to a study by J. C. Coleman (1980). Coleman asked adolescents to complete unfinished sentences about friendships in a small group, and analysed the results for their emotional content. Themes of anxiety and fear of rejection by friends increased from 11 to 13 and then to 15 years, but declined by 17 years (the effect being stronger for girls than boys).

One view of adolescent social development has been that there is a transition from 'parent orientation' to 'peer orientation'. During the 1960s and early 1970s, a number of studies attempted to compare the relative importance of parents and peers to the adolescent by placing them in opposition. For example, the adolescent might be asked to agree or disagree with statements such as 'I prefer to wear the kind and style of clothing that my parents suggest, regardless of what types of clothing my friends and schoolmates think are best.' Such research tended to support the view that adolescents become more peer-orientated and less parent-orientated as they get older, though with the qualification that the content area or situation is of great importance. For instance, parents were found to remain more influential than peers in areas such as educational plans and future life goals. However, peers were more influential in everyday and peer-status-linked issues such as choice of clothes and use of leisure time (Hopkins, 1983; Coleman and Hendry, 1990).

However, if parents and peers do have distinctively different styles of social influence, it may be rather meaningless directly to oppose them in strength, as some of this earlier research did. In fact, the nature of an adolescent's social relationships with his or her parents may be substantially different from that with peers. Through childhood the parental relationship is often characterized as one of 'unilateral authority', in which parents strive to impart an already constructed set of knowledge and attitudes to their children. Friendship, however, is a form of mutually reciprocal relationship in which divergent opinions may be expressed and new ideas discussed. We have come across these conceptions previously, in discussing the development of friendship (chapter 4) and Piaget's views of the development of moral reasoning (chapter 7). While parent–child relations may become more mutual during adolescence, it is thought that they do not become as truly mutual or reciprocal as peer relationships (Youniss, 1980).

In one study in the USA, 180 adolescents aged 12–20 years were asked to check on a questionnaire how father, mother or friend might react when a disagreement arose, or when they were being consulted about an important decision (Hunter, 1984). Responses such as 'he points out where I'm wrong for my own good', or 'he tells me that I would realize his ideas are right when I get more experience', were considered representative of unilateral influence, while responses such as 'he tries to figure out with me whether or not I'm right', or 'he tells me he wonders about the same thing' were considered representative of mutual influence. It was confirmed that parents were seen as more unilateral, and friends as more mutual, in their influence. This difference was greater for females than for males. There was not much effect of age, although parents were at their most unilateral with the 14–15-year age group.

A number of studies have suggested that parents and their adolescent children actually agree on many things, and that areas of disagreement can be exaggerated (Coleman and Hendry, 1990). In a longitudinal study of 112 young adolescents, from 11 to 13 years of age, Galambos and Almeida (1992) measured parent–adolescent conflict in five domains: chores, appearance, politeness, finance and substance use. Generally, parents and adolescents agreed that there was a decrease in conflicts over chores, appearance and politeness, though there was an increase in conflicts over finance. The influence that parents retain over adolescents may vary appreciably with the kind of parenting style adopted (cf. chapter 3). In another US study of early adolescents, Fuligni and Eccles (1993) gave self-report questionnaires to 1,771 11-year-olds. Peer orientation was higher in those adolescents who saw their parents as more authoritarian; and peer orientation and advice seeking was higher when parents gave few opportunities to be involved in decision making.

These two studies were of quite early adolescents; many 11–13-year-olds will not have reached puberty. It does seem likely that parent–offspring conflict increases, and parent–child closeness decreases, as puberty is passed, and we discussed some evidence for this earlier in the chapter. Larsen and Ham (1993) carried out an ingenious study with 483 10–14-year-olds in the USA. Students carried an electronic pager for 1 week, and recorded their emotional affect in response to randomized signals. They also filled in a life-events questionnaire. The 12–14-year-olds experienced significantly more negative affect than the 10–11-year-olds, and this was related to negative life events connected with family, school and peers; this seems to provide some support for a 'storm and stress' model of adolescence.

Laursen and Collins (1994) review a number of studies (such as Steinberg's, p. 238) which suggest a peak in parent–adolescent conflict in the mid-adolescent years. Another example, relating to affective closeness, is drawn from a large-scale study by Rossi and Rossi (1991) in the USA; figure 8.8 shows ratings for closeness to parents, at ages 10, 16 and 25; for different parent–child dyads; and for two birth cohorts, those born in 1925–39 who were adolescents in the 1940s–50s, and those born during 1950–9 who were adolescents in the 1960s-70s. What is apparent is that in every case, rated closeness is lower at 16 than at 10 years, though it recovers by 25. It is also clear that this dip in closeness is more pronounced (and rates of closeness generally are lower) in the later cohort.

A major British study made a further contribution to examining the 'storm and stress' hypothesis of adolescence. This is the 'Isle of Wight' study carried out by Michael Rutter and his colleagues, which we consider in detail.

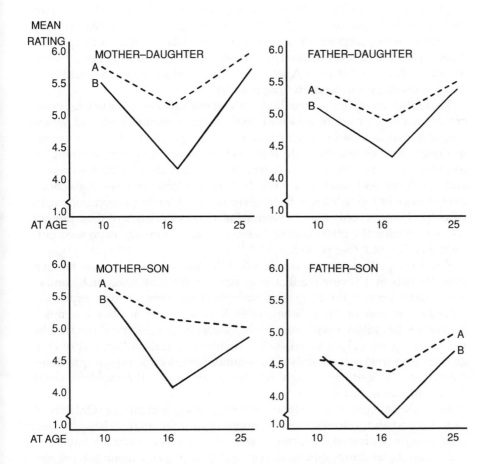

A Birth cohort 1925–1939, whose adolescence was during 1941–1955 (aged 46–60 in 1985).
B Birth cohort 1950–1959, whose adolescence was during 1966–1975 (aged 26–35 in 1985).

Figure 8.8 Affective closeness of children and their parents: cohorts whose adolescence was in 1941–1955 (dotted lines) vs. 1966–1975 (full lines). (Mean rating on 1–7 closeness scale.)

◄Conflict and Turmoil – the 'Isle of Wight' Study►►►

This study attempted to avoid problems of selective sampling. The Isle of Wight, in the English Channel off the coast of Hampshire, provided a bounded area of population living in small towns and villages. Behavioural questionnaires were completed by parents and teachers for all the 14- to 15-year-olds on the island, numbering 2,303. The most detailed results, however, were obtained from two subsamples. One, of 200 teenagers, was a random sample of the total population; the other, of 304 teenagers, was of those with extreme scores from the parent and teacher questionnaires which pointed to 'deviant' behaviour. The adolescents in both these subgroups were given further questionnaires and tests, and were interviewed individually by psychiatrists. Their parents and teachers were also interviewed. Two main areas are explored in the report (Rutter et al., 1976): one is the extent of conflict between adolescents and their parents (the 'generation gap'); the other, the extent of inner turmoil and of observed behavioural or psychiatric disorder ('storm and stress'). A selection of the results are shown in tables 8.8 and 8.9, based on the random sample of 200.

Regarding the extent of conflicts, only about one parent in six reported any altercations or arguments with their children about when and where they went out, or about their choice of activities (table 8.8). About one parent in three however said they disapproved of their youngster's clothing or hairstyles. The great majority of parents approved of their children's friends, and nearly all had discussed with them their plans after leaving school. Rather more of the teenagers themselves reported having altercations with parents. However, only about one-third made any criticism of their mother or father during the interview; and only a small percentage expressed outright rejection of either parent.

By and large these results confirm that the average adolescent is not in a state of crisis and severe conflict with parents. Nevertheless, such conflict does characterize a minority (for example 9 per cent of girls expressed outright rejection of their father, table 8.8). These difficulties are much greater in the children with some behavioural or psychiatric disorder (the second subgroup). Altercations with parents, physical withdrawal of children from the rest of the family, and communication difficulties or problems parents had in 'getting through' to adolescents, were all some three times more common in this sample.

What about experiences of inner turmoil, sadness and misery? Only about one-fifth of the adolescents reported on the questionnaire that they often felt miserable or depressed; from the psychiatric interview, nearly a half were diagnosed as reporting miserable feelings, though a much smaller proportion actually looked sad in the interview (table 8.8). It would seem that severe clinical depression is rare, but that some degree of inner turmoil may well characterize many adolescents.

In making judgements about adolescence as a stage, it is obviously necessary to compare with other ages and stages of development. In the Isle of

Table 8.8 Percentages of parents and 14-year-old children in the Isle of Wight study reporting conflicts and feelings of inner turmoil (Rutter et al., 1976: based on the random sample of 200)

	Boys	Girls
Parental interview		
any altercation with parents	18	19
physical withdrawal	12	7
communication difficulties	24	9
Adolescent interview		
any altercation with parents	42	30
any criticism of mother	27	37
any criticism of father	32	31
any rejection of mother	3	2
any rejection of father	5	9
Often feel miserable or depressed (questionnaire)	21	23
Reported misery (psychiatric interview)	42	48
Observed sadness (psychiatric interview)	12	15

Source: Rutter et al., 1976: based on the random sample of 200

Wight study such comparisons were made for the prevalence of psychiatric disorder, as based on parental interview. Table 8.9 shows the rates of disorder for the teenagers at 14–15 years, for the same children at the age of 10, from a previous survey of psychiatric disorder, and for adults (the parents of the teenage sample). There is a rather modest peak in adolescence (though the adolescent interview data gave a slightly higher figure for disorder of 16.3 per cent at this age). Again, this suggests that adolescent turmoil is not a myth, but that it should not be over-exaggerated. As Rutter et al. (1976) conclude, 'adolescent turmoil is a fact, not a fiction, but its psychiatric importance has probably been over-estimated in the past'.

◄Adolescence in Different Cultures►►►

So far we have looked mainly at adolescents in modern Western societies. We have seen that the view of adolescence as a difficult period does have some validity, even if it has probably been exaggerated by some writers (perhaps especially by psychoanalytic or clinical authors, such as Blos or Erikson, who would have come into most contact with the minority of adolescents who are particularly disturbed). But are such difficulties an inevitable part of puberty, sexual maturity and gaining independence from parents, or merely a product of our particular kind of society, and the way we treat adolescents? Different cultures vary widely in the treatment of adolescents, as we have noted earlier in connection with puberty rites.

Table 8.9 Percentages of those interviewed in the Isle of Wight study having any psychiatric disorder, at different ages

	10 yr	14–15 yr	Adult (parent)
Males	12.7	13.2	7.6
Females	10.9	12.5	11.9

Source: Rutter et al., 1976

Margaret Mead and Samoa

One study has often been quoted to support the view that adolescence can be a tranquil and conflict-free period. This is Margaret Mead's book *Coming of Age in Samoa* (1928). In this, Mead described adolescence as 'the age of maximum ease', with 'an absence of psychological maladjustment'. Indeed, Samoan society as a whole was described as 'replete with easy solutions for all conflicts'. This picture of an island paradise was supported by drawing attention to two important differences between Samoan and American society at the time. The first related to the context of child-rearing. Compared with what, at its extreme at least, can be the oppressive and confining atmosphere of the Western nuclear family, the Samoans had a more open and extended family-rearing system, in which 'the child is given no sense of belonging to a small intimate biological family'. As a result, an adolescent who might be in disagreement with parents could easily go and stay with another relative. Human relationships were thus warm, but diffuse.

The second point related to methods of child-rearing. There was little physical punishment of children by parents, and little repression or sense of guilt. Therefore, there was little for teenagers to rebel against. According to Mead, Samoan society 'never exerts sufficient repression to call forth a significant rebellion from the individual'. There was 'no room for guilt'. In particular, there was no guilt about sexual behaviour and experimentation before marriage. According to Mead, adolescents had 'the sunniest and easiest attitudes towards sex', and promiscuity and free love were the norm in the adolescent period.

Samoan society would thus seem to be about as different from the 'storm and stress' model of adolescence as one could imagine. Mead's work, and that of other anthropologists such as Ruth Benedict, suggested that the adolescent experience was entirely a matter of social structure and cultural pressures. The biological impact of puberty was of little consequence. As Franz Boas, the eminent anthropologist who supervised Mead's work in Samoa, put it: 'much of what we ascribe to human nature is no more than a reaction to the restraints put upon us by our civilisation'.

Mead's work was influential for a long time, but not all writers on Samoa agreed with her interpretations. These disagreements were publicized by Australian anthropologist Derek Freeman (1983, 1996), and he argued that Mead's methodology was poor and that she had simply found what she was looking for. The study was Mead's first (in a long and distinguished career) and at the age of 23 (as Mead herself said) she did not 'really know much about fieldwork'. Although Mead reported that she had spent 9 months in Samoa, 'speaking the language and living in the conditions in which they lived', she only spent six weeks learning Samoan, and only three months on her study of adolescence. She did not live in the native way, but stayed with the only white family on Ta'u, the island where her interviews were carried out. Thus, it is not clear how much trust or rapport she had with the adolescents whom she interviewed (often about very personal matters such as sexual experience). Mead interviewed 50 girls and young women, but only half of these (aged 14–20) were past puberty. In fact only 11 of these reported having heterosexual experience. Thus, Freeman suggested that Mead was selective in the way she interpreted her results, and was also misled by some female adolescents who, taking advantage of her naïvety and poor understanding of the language, fooled her about the extent of their sexual adventures. One elderly Samoan lady, Fa'apua'a Fa'amu, who had known Mead well, testified to Freeman of just such hoaxing in a 1987 interview.

Freeman states that both earlier and later studies of Samoa give a different overall picture from Mead's. Recent studies (and reports by older Samoans of their society in the 1920s) suggest that family bonds are strong, that physical punishment is used, that brides are expected to be virgins (in one survey Freeman found that about three-quarters are), and that strong emotions including sexual jealousy and competitiveness are common.

Not all researchers agree with all Freeman's conclusions. He bases many of his contentions on his own work in Samoa in the 1940s and the 1960s; yet, due to the influence of Christian missionaries and American military bases, Samoan society may have changed greatly even since the 1920s. A partial defence of Mead's work has been published by Cote (1992). But Freeman's criticisms are sufficient to bring a verdict of 'not proven' against Mead's Samoan evidence. The picture of an adolescent paradise may have been more a wish-fulfilment dream, than a reality.

Broad and narrow socialization

Arnett (1992) has drawn attention to the trend in Western societies for adolescents to be over-represented in categories of what he calls 'reckless behaviour'; primary components of which are having sex without contraception; delinquency and crime; illegal drug use; and driving at high speeds and while drunk. While reviewing evidence that these may be influenced by hormonal changes, cognitive factors such as adolescent egocentrism, and peer influences, he also draws attention to marked cultural differences. He summarizes this in terms of a distinction between narrow and broad socialization patterns.

Arnett argues that narrow socialization is characterized by firm expectations of, and restrictions on, personal (including adolescent) behaviour. He argues that this will be typical of smaller societies, usually pre-industrial, in which neighbours know each other. Family, peers and community (and the mass media, if present) will all tend to act to reduce reckless behaviour, though at the expense of producing conformity and reducing independence and creativity.

By contrast, broad socialization is characterized by few personal restrictions. There are more expectations of self-expression and autonomy. Arnett argues that this will be typical of modern Western societies, with large diverse communities. There is less conformity and more creativity, but also more reckless behaviour. An example of a study in this framework, carried out in Denmark, is given in box 8.2.

Arnett does not make judgements about which system is better. Each has costs and benefits. Some societies are clearly in transition; Russia, the Eastern European countries and to some extent China, for example, are relaxing personal restrictions but with consequent increases in delinquency and sexual experimentation, often in adolescents.

◀**Further Reading**▶ ▶

M. Tanner 1973: Growing up, *Scientific American*, gives a succinct overview of the physical aspects of adolescence. More detail is available in Tanner's books (e.g. 1978: *Fetus into Man*, Cambridge, MA: Harvard University Press; 1981: *A History of the Study of Human Growth*, Cambridge: Cambridge University Press) and in H. Katchadourian 1977: *The Biology of Adolescence*, San Francisco: Freeman.

A good general overview is J. C. Coleman and L. Hendry 1990 (2nd edn): *The Nature of Adolescence*, London: Routledge. For work on identity, see J. Kroger 1996 (2nd edn): *Identity in Adolescence*, London: Routledge. For a collection of recent work on parent and peer relations, see R. Montemayor, G. R. Adams and T. P. Gullota (eds) 1994: *Personal Relationships during Adolescence*, Thousand Oaks and London: Sage. M. Rutter and D. J. Smith (eds) 1995: *Psychosocial Disorders in Young People: Time Trends and Their Causes*, London: Wiley, looks further at why psychosocial disorders such as crime, drug abuse and depression may be higher in adolescence.

◀**Discussion Points**▶ ▶

1 Does the biological phenomenon of puberty have any direct psychological effects?
2 Is there an 'identity crisis' at adolescence?
3 How have attitudes to sexual behaviour changed over the past 50 years? Why might this have happened?
4 Why might parent–child closeness change during adolescence?
5 Is adolescence inevitably a period of 'storm and stress'?

Box 8.1
Unravelling girls' delinquency: biological, dispositional and contextual contributions to adolescent misbehaviour

This study in New Zealand aimed to examine whether early maturation in girls was related to delinquency, as in the Swedish study of Magnusson et al. (1985); and whether such a link was related to dispositional factors (childhood history of externalizing problems), and contextual factors (single- or mixed-sex secondary school).

This kind of study aims at delineating developmental pathways; and for this, a longitudinal design is essential. The researchers drew on data from the Dunedin Multidisciplinary Health and Development Study, which sampled all children born in Dunedin, NZ, between 1 April 1972 and 31 March 1973; the children were followed up at 3, 5, 7, 9, 11, 13 and 15 years of age. Of 1,139 eligible children, 1,037 were assessed at 3 years, of whom 501 were girls; 415 girls were re-assessed at age 13 and 474 at age 15. Of these, 279 lived in the city of Otago and their data was used in this study, which also took account of schooling. Single-sex schools are still common in New Zealand, unlike many other industrial countries, and 165 girls entered all-girl secondary schools at age 13, while 132 entered mixed-sex schools.

Three pupil self-report questionnaires provided data relevant to this study. At 13, girls filled in an Early Delinquency scale which measured whether they had engaged in activities such as breaking windows, getting drunk, making prank telephone calls, stealing from pupils at school. They also filled in a Familiarity with Delinquent Peers scale, which measured whether their friends, or other kids they knew, did these behaviours. At 15, the girls filled in a Delinquency scale which measured whether they had engaged in activities such as shoplifting, car theft, smoking marijuana, using weapons.

To examine effects of maturational timing, the researchers used self-reports of menarche to divide their sample into: early maturers (those reaching menarche before 12 years 6 months; 30% of sample), on-time (12 years 6 months to 13 years 6 months; 40% of sample) and late maturers (after 13 years 6 months; 30% of sample).

The results are shown in box table 8.1.1. Considering the aims of the study, it does confirm that early maturing girls are more at risk. Effects of maturational timing are significant for all three of the measures used.

However this effect is a complex one. For one thing, it interacts with context, in the sense of type of school. For the Familiarity with Delinquent Peers measure, there is a statistically significant effect, with more evidence of familiarity with other girls' delinquency in the mixed-sex schools than in the

Box Table 8.1.1 Rates for early delinquency, familiarity with delinquent peers, and delinquency, at ages 13 and 15, by onset of physical maturation

		Early maturers	On-time maturers	Late maturers
Age 13	All girl	2.0	2.5	1.3
Early delinquency	Mixed sex	4.3	2.4	1.2
Age 13	All girl	14.1	13.7	12.1
Delinquent peers	Mixed sex	19.3	17.0	13.6
Age 15	All girl	1.8	2.5	1.5
Delinquency	Mixed sex	3.2	3.5	1.3

Source: Adapted from Caspi et al., 1993

same-sex schools; and this effect is largest for early-maturing girls. This interaction effect is statistically significant for the Early Delinquency measure, which confirms that early maturing girls are more at risk of being delinquent themselves, but only in mixed-sex schools. The effect is not significant for the Delinquency at age 15 measure, where it seems that both early and on-time maturers are scoring higher than late maturers. The authors suggest that by this time, the on-time maturers have 'caught up' with the early maturers so far as delinquency is concerned.

In addition, the researchers examined what they called dispositional factors, measured here as parent and teacher ratings of externalizing (e.g. aggressive) behaviour problems at age 9. They found that familiarity with peers was especially important in predicting delinquency, for early-maturing girls without an earlier history of externalizing problems.

In interpreting these results, the authors argue that (as Magnusson et al., 1985, found), early-maturing girls are likely to associate with older peers, who are more into norm-breaking activities. Also, such peer pressures may be particularly strong in mixed-sex schools, with higher delinquency rates among boys, and possibly greater opportunities for observing or engaging in delinquent activities. These effects of peers were particularly strong for early-maturing girls with no earlier history of externalizing problems. Probably, those who did have an earlier history of externalizing problems were already familiar with delinquent acts by age 13 and did not need peer familiarity to get into such activities.

The New Zealand context provided an unusual opportunity to show the effects of single-sex versus mixed-sex secondary schooling. The researchers were aware that school differences might reflect differences in families due to parental choice of school; however, they found no differences between the school samples in parental values, or in behaviour problems at age 9. There was a trend for higher-social-class parents to choose all-girl schools, so social class was taken account of in the statistical analyses.

The study shows the power of a longitudinal design with a large, representative sample. Dropout rates were not large. There is a reliance on self-report measures, which characterizes much work on antisocial behaviour (see also box 4.2), due to the difficulties of getting valid alternative measures on a large scale. This is a sophisticated quantitative study; the use of more qualitative methods (for example, in-depth interviews with some early and late maturers) might throw even more light onto the processes involved.

Based on material from A. Caspi, D. Lynam, T. E. Moffitt and P. A. Silva 1993: *Developmental Psychology*, 29, 19–30.

Box 8.2
Cultural bases of risk behaviour:
Danish adolescents

In this study, risk behaviour (similar to, but wider than, reckless behaviour or delinquency) was assessed in 1,053 Danish adolescents. The authors wished to assess absolute levels of types of risk behaviour, and also see how these varied by community size and family type. In addition, they made comparisons with similar behaviours in the USA.

Like most Western societies, Denmark tends to what Arnett calls 'broad socialization', with few restrictions on adolescent behaviour; however, car driving is not permitted until 18 (and per capita, car ownership is about one-half of US levels). There is much better provision for cyclists than in many countries such as the USA or even the UK. Sex education including knowledge of contraception is provided in schools before adolescence.

Denmark has a rather homogeneous population of about 5 million. One million live in Copenhagen; there are three cities of 100,000–150,000, including Odense; and about four-fifths of the population live in small cities (population less than 50,000). The researchers chose three schools/colleges each, in

Box Table 8.2.1 Prevalence (at least once during last year) of risk behaviours, in male (M) and female (F) Danish adolescents

		12–13 yrs	14–15 yrs	16–17 yrs	18–20 yrs
Drink/cycling	M	18	56	77	76
	F	13	52	61	63
Drink/car driving	M	0	0	7	15
	F	0	0	2	8
Sex without	M	4	4	25	42
contraception	F	2	12	20	34
Sex with	M	2	14	53	65
contraception	F	3	15	43	75
Marijuana use	M	12	22	33	32
	F	10	13	22	24
Cigarette dependency	M	6	18	23	19
(20 days in last	F	5	18	18	33
month)					
Cocaine use	M	2	0	0	1
	F	0	0	1	2
Shoplifting	M	14	21	25	17
	F	5	16	14	11
Vandalism	M	18	38	33	34
	F	5	12	14	10

Source: Adapted from J. Arnett and L. Balle-Jensen, 1993

Copenhagen, Odense and Varde, a small town. Risk behaviours were measured by a short self-report questionnaire on the frequency of engaging in a variety of risk activities over the past year; participation rates were 99 per cent. Family measures were taken using a Family Relationships questionnaire.

A sample of the results, broken down by age and sex, is given in box table 8.2.1. There are low rates of driving a car while drunk, but much higher rates of riding a bicycle while drunk. Rates of sex without contraception are quite considerable in older adolescence, although less than rates with contraception (included not as a risk behaviour, but for comparison); in fact, those who engaged in sex with contraception were also more likely to do so without contraception. Marijuana use and cigarette dependency were fairly frequent, but use of cocaine or other drugs was very rare. All these risk behaviours increased with age; but shoplifting and vandalism peaked in the 16–17-year period. Generally,

risk-taking behaviours were less frequent in girls, with the exception of sexual behaviours, and cigarette dependence.

Family influences did not appear to be very strong in this study. There were few differences between intact and divorced or lone-parent families, for example; and no effects of parental strictness. However, lower parental monitoring did predict to increased drink/cycling and marijuana use and cigarette dependency; and poorer family relationships generally did predict to greater risk of shoplifting and vandalism.

Many types of risk behaviour were greatest in Copenhagen (large city) compared with the smaller communities; for example, sex without contraception, cigarette dependency and marijuana use, and shoplifting; however, vandalism was more frequent in Odense (mid-size city).

Drawing comparison with US studies, the authors conclude that rates of sex without contraception are somewhat similar; but since teenage pregnancy rates are much lower in Denmark, this may reflect occasional lapses in the Danish adolescents rather than a consistent pattern. The low rates of drink/driving (but high rates of drink/cycling) can be related to legal restrictions and cultural opportunities. Surprisingly, the authors do not comment on the very low rates of hard drug use; they do comment that cigarette dependency is higher than in US studies, perhaps because of more intensive media anti-smoking campaigns in the US.

This study, cross-sectional in design, does potentially confound historical factors with what are apparently age changes (in box table 8.2.1, for example); but it could be argued that historical changes might not be very large over the eight-year period which represents the total age range in the study, at least compared with the size of age changes obtained. The data on risk behaviour and on family factors are all obtained from adolescent self-report, as is quite common in research of this kind; but other sources of data could help validate the conclusions. A strength of the study is the way it takes account of the social and legal context of the country of study, Denmark, and contrasts it with much more widely studied adolescent populations in the USA.

Based on material in J. Arnett and L. Balle-Jensen 1993: *Child Development*, 64, 1842–59.

Part Three   Children's Developing Minds

9 Perception

The sensory capacities of very young babies have long posed many questions for psychologists. What can a newborn infant perceive? How early does she begin to interpret the stimuli which surround her? And how active a part does the infant herself play in the process? To what extent can environmental influences modify perceptual development? These are but some of the intriguing issues.

Psychologists make an important distinction between sensation and perception. 'Sensation' refers to the process through which information about the environment is picked up by sensory receptors and transmitted to the brain. It is known that infants have certain sensory abilities at birth because they respond to light, sound, smell, touch and taste. 'Perception' refers to the interpretation by the brain of this sensory input. It is through perception that we gain knowledge about the events, objects and people who surround us. As Gibson and Spelke (1983, p. 2) wrote, '[perception] is the beginning of knowing, and so is an essential part of cognition'.

As adults we can discriminate speech from birdsong, or a distant tree from a nearby flower. But can infants, with their limited experience, understand the variety of stimuli which their sensory receptors detect? Are they born with certain perceptual capacities or must these be acquired through learning and experience?

The debate about the relative influence of heredity and environment in perception has a long history. Empiricists, following the tradition of the philosopher John Locke (1690), argued that the infant was a 'tabula rasa', a blank slate, upon which experiences were imprinted. For example, the psychologist William James (1890) is famous for his assertion that, to the infant, sensory inputs become fused into 'one blooming, buzzing confusion' and that it is only later, through experience, that the child can discriminate amongst them. In other words, children's ability to perceive develops as the result of a long learning process.

A contrasting view was proposed by the nativists, who claimed that many perceptual abilities were present at birth. Philosophers such as Descartes (1638) and Kant (1781) argued that infants' capacity to perceive space, for example, was innate. Later, psychologists of the Gestalt school (in the early twentieth century) lent support to the idea that certain perceptual abilities were present at birth because of the structural characteristics of the nervous system. Furthermore, they argued that the infant, far from being a tabula rasa, actively tried to create order and organization in her perceptual world.

In recent years experimental psychologists have been able to make an important contribution to our knowledge of perceptual development in the infant. Researchers have found that babies are born with a wider range of perceptual capabilities than the empiricists had suggested, and that their capacity to learn from experience is greater than the nativists allowed. The evidence we have of infants' perceptual competence must be balanced against the mistakes which young infants make, revealing the long learning process that has to be undertaken during the early years.

The neonate (newborn infant) possesses some capacity for exploring events and objects in her world (Mehler and Dupoux, 1994). This is enough to form the basis for a long process of gaining understanding about the environment. Through exploration, infants discover both about invariant aspects of their surroundings, and about the properties of objects and people under different conditions. Exploration of the environment appears to be directed from the start, but as the child grows this exploration becomes more systematic and focused, and the child learns more about the structure of the world around her.

◄Methods for Studying Infants' Perception►►

It is not easy to work with young infants, because they cannot tell you what they are thinking, and therefore what they know has to be inferred from their behaviour. But as an infant's repertoire of behaviours is very limited re-searchers have had to invent ingenious techniques for measuring their per-ceptual abilities. We will explain some of these before describing the results from specific studies.

Preference technique   In this procedure a researcher presents two stimuli to an infant at the same time – for example these might be two pictures (A and B). The researcher can then measure how long the infant looks at each picture. If, over a period of time, the infant looks at each picture equally it may be because she does not differentiate between them. If she looks at A more than B it can be inferred that she 'prefers' A and two conclusions follow from this. First, that the infant can in fact distinguish between the two pictures (having a preference is indicative of discriminating between the two stimuli). Second, that for some reason, the infant finds A to be the more

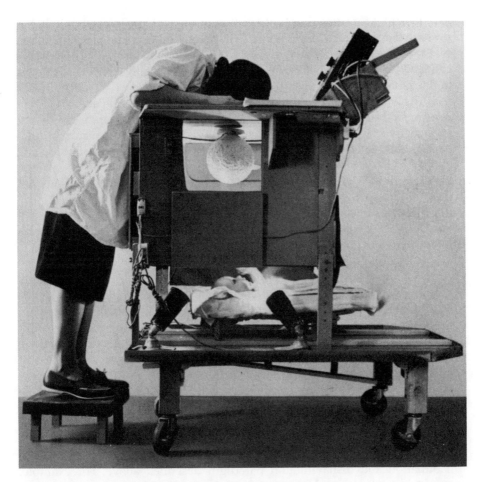

Plate 9.1 The 'looking chamber' used by Fantz (from Fantz, 1961).

stimulating picture to look at, and whatever infants find particularly stimulating may give us clues about which aspects of the environment are contributing to their development.

The preference technique is a comparatively easy technique to employ if accurate measures of the infant's looking can be made. The early research which employed this technique was based on an observer watching the infant's face and measuring how long she looked at a stimulus (see plate 9.1). With the advent of sophisticated video film and other technology it is now possible to record infants' gaze perfectly accurately and, if necessary, an infant's eye fixations can also be recorded. This means that researchers can measure not only how long an infant looks at a stimulus but also which parts of the stimulus an infant focuses on.

Habituation Another method involves habituation and dishabituation to a stimulus. For example if an infant is shown an interesting stimulus (A) she may look at it for some time, but eventually she will lose interest in it. If A is presented again and again it is likely that each time it is presented the infant will spend less and less time looking at it (she habituates to it). Then, if A is changed for a different stimulus (B) she is likely to show a renewed interest in this novel stimulus and start looking at it for some time (she dishabituates to it). This pattern of habituation and dishabituation can be exploited by a researcher. For example, suppose you want to know if an infant can distinguish between two very similar pictures. You could show her picture A until she has habituated to it. Then show her picture B. If she does not start looking at B it is as if she treats it as A (which she's already lost interest in). It can then be inferred that she cannot distinguish B from A. If, however, the infant does start looking at B, it can be assumed, from this dishabituation, that she can discriminate between A and B. This technique is effective for finding out just how large or small a difference there needs to be between two stimuli for an infant to detect the difference between them.

Conditioning   Infants will learn to carry out behaviours if those behaviours are reinforced, and this is called conditioning. For example, Bower (1965) conditioned infants to turn their head to one side by 'rewarding' the infant every time she did so (see box 9.1). The reward in this case was an adult popping up into the infant's line of sight and playing peek-a-boo (something which infants like!). At the start of such an experiment, the adult has to wait until the infant naturally moves her head to one side, and then give a peek-a-boo response. If the adult does this every time the infant turns her head, the infant will learn to make the head movement each time she wants to get the peek-a-boo response. In Bower's experiment he conditioned infants' head turning as part of an investigation of infants' visual perception (see box 9.1). Other experimenters have used infants' responses in a manner similar to the habituation and dishabituation paradigm described above. For example, suppose an infant is sucking on a teat, if she increases her sucking rate above the usual rate this can be rewarded by presenting a stimulus (e.g. a sound A). The infant will learn that every time she increases her sucking rate she can get to hear the sound. For as long as the sound remains an interesting stimulus the infant is likely to go on sucking to hear it. However, there will come a point when the infant's interest in the sound declines and she no longer sucks so frequently (she has habituated to it). At that point the experimenter can alter the sound (to sound B). If the infant does not increase sucking it can be assumed that she does not differentiate between A and B, but if she does increase sucking (i.e. dishabituates) when she first hears B then it can be inferred that she treats B as a different sound from A. In this way researchers can find out how well infants distinguish between different stimuli.

As well as observable behaviours, like looking, sucking or head turning, other less obvious responses can also be measured. In particular, researchers have measured changes in infants' heart rate. If infants are surprised or upset their heart rate increases; if they are focusing or attending to a stimulus their heart rate tends to slow down. To use the example of differentiating sounds again, an infant hearing sound A for the first time may show a decline in heart rate (assuming that A is not such a frightening noise that the infant's heart rate increases rapidly). After having heard sound A several times, she will habituate to it and then the researcher can present sound B. If the infant's heart rate slows down at the sound of B it indicates dishabituation, which can be taken as evidence that the infant distinguishes between sounds A and B.

Infants' preferences, habituation and conditioning are all important in their own right. Preferences indicate those aspects of the environment which the infant finds most stimulating at the time. Habituation is important because it means that an infant will not just concentrate on one object, but after a time will lose interest in that object and therefore seek out new stimuli. Habituation is, in effect, a constant encouragement to explore new things. Conditioning allows an infant to have some control over her environment, by turning her head she can make an adult appear to play peek-a-boo, by sucking harder on a teat, she can hear an attractive sound, and these responses reflect infants' understanding of patterns and relationships within the world and are the first signs of learning.

It should be added that none of the above methods can be used without difficulty. Very young children are hard to work with, they may be easily distracted, they may become upset, or they may even fall asleep during an experiment! Apart from these problems researchers may sometimes find it difficult to measure or interpret the sort of infant behaviours (like head turning, or heart rate change) which are fundamental to the investigation of perceptual abilities. Nonetheless, the invention of different experimental techniques permits researchers to approach each question about perceptual development in several ways, and if the results from experiments using different techniques are all similar it gives us confidence in the reliability of those results.

◀Visual Perception▶ ▶ ▶

Investigating infants' perception

The visual abilities of a newborn infant are very different from those of an adult. For example, a newborn infant has much poorer visual acuity. Visual acuity is a measure of how well an individual can detect visual detail. A person can be asked to look at a visual display made up of vertical black and white lines (of equal width) and then the lines can be made progressively narrower. There will come a point when people can no longer distinguish the lines as separate, and the display will just appear as a grey image. Newborn infants can only detect the separation of the lines if they are about 30 times wider than the minimum width that adults can detect (Atkinson and Braddick, 1981). Although children's acuity does improve rapidly, their limited acuity in the early months means that young children view a world which is more fuzzy and blurred than an adult's.

The vision of a newborn infant is also limited in other ways. For example, infants younger than 2 months cannot track a moving object very smoothly, instead they tend to follow a moving object by making a series of jerky

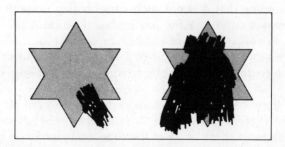

Figure 9.1 Visual scanning of a geometrical figure by 1- and 2-month-old children (from Shaffer, 1985).

eye-movements (Aslin, 1981). To take in the whole of an object it is usually necessary to scan across the object, but infants may have less effective scanning abilities. Salapatek (1975) investigated the eye movements of young infants as they scanned geometric shapes such as triangles, circles and squares. He found that at one month of age infants tended to focus on a single feature, or limited number of features, in the shape (for example, just part of the boundary of the shape – see figure 9.1). By two months of age infants have adopted more comprehensive scanning strategies.

Newborn infants can probably distinguish between some colours, for example between colours like red, green and white (e.g. Adams, 1989), and by four months of age children may have colour vision which is similar to adults' (Teller and Bornstein, 1987). In summary, young infants have a functional and effective visual system, but the quality of their vision, at least in the first few weeks and months of life, is poorer than adults' vision. To illustrate visual development we will examine two areas of research in some detail: these are pattern perception, and especially the perception of the human face, and the perception of space, especially depth perception and size constancy of objects at varying distances.

Pattern perception

Fantz and Miranda (1975) showed patterns to infants who were less than 1 week old, and found that they had a preference for patterns which had curved edges rather than straight edges (see upper two rows of figure 9.2). However, this preference disappeared if the patterns were placed in a surround (see lower two rows of figure 9.2). This may be because, as we mentioned above, infants prefer to look at the edges of figures or shapes. In other words, if there are curves within a pattern they will attract less attention than when the shape itself is curved.

Other researchers have found that children, at least after the age of about 4 months, prefer patterns that are symmetrical rather than ones that are not symmetrical (Bornstein, Ferdinandsen and Gross, 1981). Fantz (1961) found that infants as young as 2 days could discriminate between patterned and unpatterned shapes. For example, they preferred striped, bulls-eye or

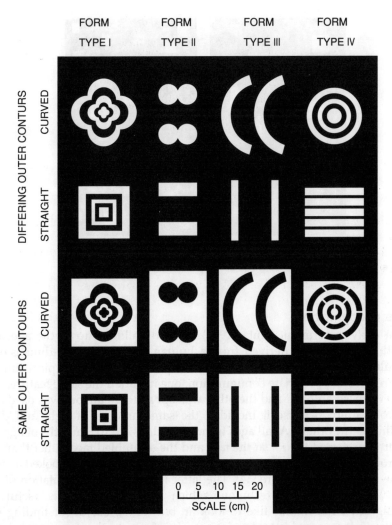

Figure 9.2   The stimulus pairs (presented in left–right arrangements rather than up–down as pictured). Upper four pairs were constructed of white cutouts (or white and black for Type I) glued to plaques matching the blue felt lining the test chamber. Bottom four pairs have reversed figure-ground brightness on white cards mounted on the plaques. From Fantz and Miranda (1975).

checker-board patterns to plain discs or squares. In another experiment, Fantz and Fagan (1975) showed 1- and 2-month-old children two stimuli which each had identical amounts of light and dark areas on them, but differed in the complexity of their patterns (see figure 9.3). The 1-month-old infants preferred the less complex stimuli (with eight 1-inch squares), and the 2-month-old infants preferred the more complex pattern (with 32 smaller squares).

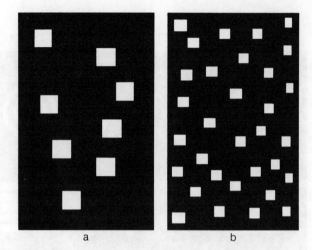

a   b

Figure 9.3   Stimuli similar to those used by Fantz and Fagan.

Face recognition

In an early experiment Fantz (1961) showed children up to the age of 6 months three stimuli derived from a human face. These two-dimensional stimuli are illustrated in figure 9.4. One pattern included typical human features in an appropriate configuration, one included the same features but these were 'scrambled' and the other was not a face at all, but was used as a control pattern because it included the same amount of light and dark shading as the others. At all ages from a few days old to 6 months of age the children preferred to look at the face and the scrambled face rather than the control stimulus, but there was no difference in how long they looked at each of the two faces (see figure 9.4). The latter result reveals a limitation of the study. The 'preference' technique which Fantz developed is useful for finding out what infants like to look at, but not so useful for finding out whether infants are able to discriminate. If infants do show a preference for one stimulus then it must mean that they can discriminate between that stimulus and another, but a lack of preference (as between real and scrambled faces) does not necessarily mean the infant does not discriminate between them – she might just find both equally interesting.

Do the results from Fantz's (1961) experiment indicate that children have an early, or even innate, preference for looking at faces? Fantz implied that it did and wrote: 'The degree of preference for the "real" face to the other one was not large, but it was consistent among individual infants. The experiment suggested that there is an unlearned primitive meaning in the form perception of infants' (p. 70). Fantz went on to speculate that the infant's interest in pattern was related to the social uses which vision has for the child. The human face could have an intrinsic interest for the infant with its changing expressions and contours and this interest would be adaptive in facilitating the development of attachment relationships (see chapter 3).

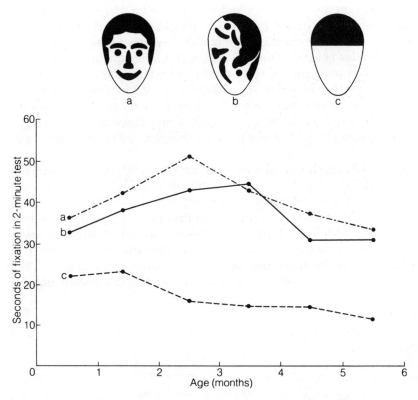

Figure 9.4 Average time scores of infants' visual fixation when presented with three face-shaped objects paired in all the possible combinations (from Fantz, 1961).

There are, however, several difficulties in interpreting the results from Fantz's (1961) experiment. We saw earlier that, at least after a certain age, infants prefer to look at more complex patterns. Both the face and the scrambled face were more complex than the control stimuli and if infants preferred these simply because they were more complex this would limit any inferences about children's recognition of faces. We also noted that young infants prefer symmetrical to asymmetrical non-facial patterns, and if, as Fantz suggested, the infants did prefer the real face to the scrambled face, this may only have been because the real face was symmetrical and the scrambled face was not. Both Fantz and other researchers realized the problems in interpreting the results of this original study, and designed later experiments to overcome its limitations.

Maurer and Barrera (1981) used both the preference technique and the habituation technique to find out which of three face-like stimuli infants preferred. These are shown in figure 9.5, one was a natural face, the second a symmetrical scrambled face, the third an asymmetrical scrambled face; all had the same facial features, and thus the same brightness and contour information.

In the first experiment Maurer and Barrera used a preference technique somewhat similar to that of Fantz, with babies aged 1 month and 2 months. But rather than pairing stimuli, as Fantz did, they timed how long an infant fixated a stimulus before looking away. The mean fixation times over many trials are shown in figure 9.5. For 1-month-old infants there was no difference in how long they looked at any of the stimuli. At 2 months, however, the natural face was looked at for longer. The preference for just the natural face shows that by two months of age, at least, a preference for faces involves something more than the fact that faces are complex and symmetrical visual stimuli.

In a second experiment Maurer and Barrera (1981) looked further at whether the infants could actually discriminate amongst the stimuli which they did not show a preference for, namely all the stimuli at 1 month of age, and the two scrambled faces at 2 months of age. To do this they used the habituation technique. First, they presented an infant with the asymmetrical scrambled face pattern many times, until fixation time was less than half what it was at the beginning (i.e. the infant had habituated to it). Then, they presented one of the other stimuli to find out if infants dishabituated to it.

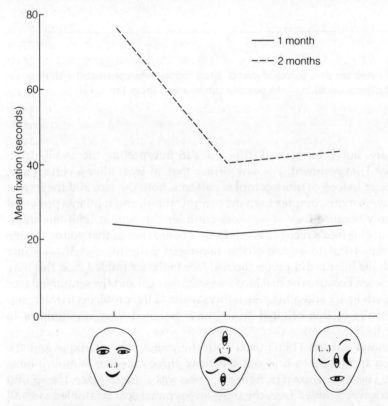

Figure 9.5   The mean fixation time on each stimulus by infants (from Maurer and Barrera, 1981).

This did not happen with the 1-month-olds, who did not look for any longer at the new stimuli. However, the 2-month-olds did. Of 18 infants tested, 17 looked longer at the natural face and 16 looked longer at the symmetrical scrambled face, compared with the asymmetrical scrambled face to which they had been habituated. (In addition, most looked longest at the natural face.) This result confirms that infants who are a month old neither discriminate nor prefer any of the stimulus patterns; at two months they discriminate all three, though they only significantly prefer the natural face.

The difference between 1- and 2-month-old infants was also found in eye-movement studies. Maurer and Salapatek (1976) recorded the eye-movements of infants aged 1 and 2 months as they scanned drawings of real faces. One-month-old infants tended to scan only a small part of the face, usually at its boundaries, but 2-month-old infants were more likely to scan the internal aspects of the face and focused on features such as the nose, the mouth and particularly the eyes. Maurer and Salapatek concluded that the younger infants scanned faces in the same way as they scanned geometrical forms, i.e. by focusing mainly on the edges, and therefore they responded as they would to a non-social stimulus.

The studies by Maurer and colleagues are a good example of how studies using different techniques (preference, habituation and eye-movement detection) can produce converging evidence to answer a psychological question – in this case about young children's perception. Taken together these studies of face recognition indicate that infants do not have an innate preference for face-like stimuli, but do show a preference for faces as they become able to distinguish faces from non-faces at about two months of age.

However, other researchers have found, using different techniques, that there may be face recognition earlier than two months of age. Goren, Sarty and Wu (1975) showed newborn infants a face or a scrambled face, which were moved in front of the infant. The infants followed the realistic looking face further than the scrambled face, and Goren et al. concluded that even very young children had some ability to distinguish between faces and non-faces. Other researchers have also found that slightly older children, at one month of age, were more likely to track a moving face than a moving non-face (see Johnson and Morton, 1991). It is therefore possible that, under some conditions, infants can recognize faces at a very early age.

In the period from 3 to 6 months infants show an increasing ability to discriminate between and respond to different facial patterns. Barrera and Maurer (1981) found that by the age of 3 months children could discriminate a smiling face from a frowning face (see figure 9.6). This ability is based on more than just distinguishing facial expressions, but probably also reflects an understanding of what the expressions indicate, because Serrano, Iglesias and Loeches (1995) found that infants, from the age of 4 months, made appropriate responses to different expressions (e.g. made more approaching movements and smiles to a picture of a happy face, and more avoidance responses and frowning to a picture of an angry face). Furthermore, Samuels

and Ewy (1985) found that babies at 3 months preferred attractive to unat-
tractive faces and that these preferences correspond to adults' judgements of
attractiveness. They suggested that some kind of aesthetic sensibility to the
attractiveness or otherwise of a human face begins early in life.

One topic which has received much investigation is when infants can first
recognize familiar faces. Field, Woodson, Greenberg and Cohen (1982), using the live faces of mothers and strangers, found that infants who were less
than 2 days old preferred to look at their mother's face than a stranger's face.
However, there may be reasons other than face recognition for why infants
can identify their own mothers. One possibility is that the infants were using
olfactory cues – because very young infants can distinguish the odour of
their mother (Porter, Makin, Davis and Christensen, 1992). Another alternative explanation would be that compared with strangers, the mothers in
Field et al.'s experiment may have produced expressions which were more
stimulating as they interacted with their own infants, and therefore the
infants' preference was a preference for an expression rather than an indication of recognition. Even if the infants in Field et al.'s study had identified
their own mother, this might have been on the basis of some single salient
feature (such as hairline or hair colour). If so it might be exaggerating infants'
abilities to suggest that they recognized a face when they were relying on
rather gross cues to identify their mother.

To overcome these difficulties, Walton, Bower and Bower (1992) carried
out an experiment similar to Field et al.'s, but they videotaped the faces of
mothers and other females. All the adults maintained a neutral expression,
and then Walton et al. selected pairs of similar looking females (i.e. with
same eye and hair colour, complexion and hairstyle). One of the pair was the
infant's own mother. Using this procedure meant that olfactory cues were
not present, expressions were constant and gross features could not be used
as cues. Infants were from 1 to 4 days old when they were shown the

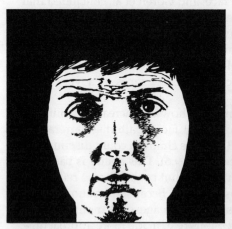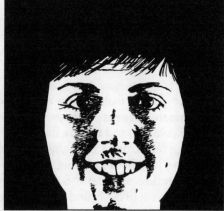

Figure 9.6   Stimuli of a frowning and a smiling face, such as those used by Barrera and
Maurer (1981).

videotapes. The infant was first shown one face and if they sucked on a teat the face remained on the screen; if they did not suck, the second face appeared (and remained on the screen as long as the infants sucked, otherwise the first face reappeared). In this way the infant could control the picture they were looking at. Walton et al. measured the number of times that infants sucked while keeping their mother's face visible and how often they sucked to keep the stranger's face in view. Eleven out of 12 infants in the study sucked more to see their mother's face. This result confirms the earlier research and shows that even very young infants have the ability to start distinguishing their mother from other people.

The investigation of pattern and face recognition is a good example of how researchers have generated progressively more sophisticated and carefully controlled experiments to find out about young children's perceptual abilities. Such experiments have demonstrated how children first perceive, scan and identify images and the development of their ability to distinguish faces from non-faces, familiar faces from unfamiliar ones, and different types of expressions. There is still a great deal that we do not know about infants' pattern perception, but the ingenuity of, and the results from, the existing research have provided a framework for future research.

◀Spatial Perception and Depth Perception▶▶▶

As a person or object moves relative to the viewer, the visual size, shape and colour information it projects on the eye will change. Yet we perceive a given object as the same, even though its apparent size, shape and colour change in this way. These effects are called perceptual 'constancies'. For example, shape constancy refers to the fact that we see the shape of an object as the same even when its orientation changes. Slater and Morison (1985) suggested that infants might have some shape constancy from birth. They showed newborn infants a shape until they had habituated to it. Then the infants were shown the same shape at a novel angle, but they did not dishabituate to it. The infants' lack of interest in the shape when it was presented from a different angle suggests that they did not think of the shape at a different angle as a new shape; in other words, they had shape constancy.

Size constancy can be illustrated with the following example. If we observe a car driving away from us along a road, the image of the car on the retina becomes smaller but we do not perceive the car as getting smaller. We perceive that the car remains the same size, but is actually getting further away. To perceive this way is to display 'size constancy'; in other words, we understand that the size of an object remains constant even though the object may be at a different distance. This is an observation that seems obvious to the adult, but does the infant have the same knowledge at birth or must she learn to respond to the appropriate cues? An experiment into size constancy was carried out by Bower (1965), and is described in detail in box 9.1. Bower found that infants as young as 6–12 weeks demonstrated size constancy by responding to the real size of a cube rather than the size of its retinal image.

In similar, more recent studies researchers have shown that infants might have size constancy from birth (Slater, Mattock and Brown, 1990).

Bower (1965) also investigated the cues that infants used to gauge the distance of the object. Understanding the distance or depth of objects is important – for example, if an infant wants to reach for an object she has to judge how far away it is. Several kinds of cues can be used to estimate distance or depth. They include: (i) texture gradients, because patterns become more closely spaced and less definite, the further away they are; (ii) motion parallax – as we move, nearer objects seem to move in an opposite direction relative to more distant objects (like trees against the moon, as we walk through a wood); and (iii) retinal disparity – each eye has a slightly different view of the world (as you can see if you close one eye, then the other) and this disparity is greater for nearer objects. The results of Bower's experiment are summarized in box 9.1.

At what age does this capacity to perceive distance appear? Bower (1972) suggested that it might be present from or soon after birth. He showed two objects to infants who were less than two weeks old. One object was just out of the infants' reach, and the other was twice as far away, but it was also twice the size of the first object. The reason for this set up was that both objects produced an image of the same size on the retina (and therefore size of retinal image could not be a reason for discriminating between the objects). Bower found that infants tried to reach the near object much more often than they tried to reach for the far object. As reaching was directed mainly to the object which could nearly be touched, and the further object was ignored, Bower argued that the infants had an appreciation of distance.

In another study of distance, Bower, Broughton and Moore (1970) investigated the responses of 6- to 20-day-old infants to a cube which 'loomed' towards their face. Bower et al. found that as the object came close to the infants, they showed movements such as moving their heads back, throwing up their arms and opening their eyes very wide. Bower interpreted these responses as defensive movements, which indicated that the infants did have the capacity to perceive distance and the approach of an object (the cube). However, a criticism of this interpretation is that the infants may only have been tracking the top edge of the object, which appeared higher as the object approached. If they were tracking the top edge this would cause the infant to lift her head up, but as infants do not have good motor control over their head movements there would be a point when their head tipped backward and when this happened the infants would raise their arms. In other words, the infants' movements might have been defensive responses as Bower suggested, or they might have been the result of tracking just the edge of the object. Nanez (1988) clarified earlier results by carrying out similar experiments with objects that appeared, on a screen, to be looming towards an infant. Nanez measured what part of the screen the infants were looking at and found that they actually focused on the centre of the looming object and not on its top edge. If this is the case, then infants' reactions to looming objects are defensive ones, which indicates that they really do see the object as one coming towards them.

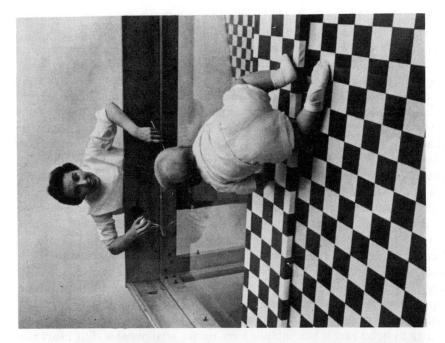

Plate 9.2 A mother encourages a child to venture over the 'visual cliff' (from Gibson and Walk, 1960).

An early study that succeeded in showing depth perception in infants was the ingenious 'visual cliff' experiment by Gibson and Walk (1960). They used a glass table with a checker-board pattern underneath the glass; there was a central platform and on the shallow side of this the pattern was immediately below the glass; at the other, deep, side the pattern was several feet below the glass (see plate 9.2). Gibson and Walk argued that if an infant had no depth perception she would readily crawl over the 'deep side' of the table; if she did have depth perception, she might be unwilling to go over the edge. The children were 6 to 14 months of age, that is they were old enough to crawl. Gibson and Walk placed children on the central platform and observed which way they moved. The children were happy to crawl on the shallow side of the table but would not crawl over the 'cliff' even when encouraged to do so by their mothers.

Although Gibson and Walk's (1960) result demonstrated depth perception in children from 6 months of age, their experiment depended on children crawling (or not crawling) over different sides of the visual cliff. As younger children are not able to crawl, later researchers considered other measures to find out if younger children had depth perception. Campos, Langer and Krowitz (1970) placed 2-month-old infants on the deep and shallow sides of the visual cliff, and measured their heart rate. There was no change in heart rate when infants were on the shallow side, but heart rate decreased when infants were on the deep side. It is difficult to interpret this finding, because if the infants recognized that they were over the deep side it might have been expected that heart rate would increase (reflecting surprise or fear). A decrease in heart rate is usually interpreted as increased attention. The fact that there was a change in heart rate on both sides of the cliff indicates that the children noticed that there was a difference between the sides, but whether they actually perceived the depth remains an open question.

As the examples in this section have shown, it is possible that very young infants may have size and shape constancy, and from studies of infants' reaching, and their reactions to looming objects, it may be that they have some understanding of distance.

A further source of sensory information about objects comes from auditory cues, and we consider these in the next section.

◀Auditory Perception▶▶▶

For adults, vision is the most important of the senses. For young infants, this may not be so. Relative to adults, the auditory acuity of newborn infants is much better than their visual acuity, for example, newborns will turn their heads towards a sound, which suggests they can locate sounds very soon after birth. Here we shall look especially at infants' responses to voices and speech sounds, since these are important auditory stimuli for the development of both attachment relationships (chapter 3) and language (chapter 10).

To find out when infants can first discriminate the mother's voice from that of others Mills and Melhuish (1974) used a procedure similar to the one we described earlier in connection with Walton et al.'s (1992) face recognition study. By sucking on a teat an infant could hear either their own mother's voice or the voice of a stranger. Infants aged 3 to 4 weeks old sucked more to hear their mother's voice. In a similar study, DeCasper and Fifer (1980) found such a discrimination during the first 1 or 2 days of life. As this was after only about 12 hours of postnatal contact with the mother it suggests very rapid learning after birth. Alternatively, there is evidence that some learning may be possible before birth. For example, DeCasper and Spence (1986) asked mothers to read a story out loud twice a day for 6 weeks before they gave birth. At 2 days old their infants were tested with that story and a new story and DeCasper and Spence found that infants sucked more to hear the story that they had been exposed to before birth (even when the story was read by a stranger) – it is possible that some aspects of the rhythm or pacing of the story were recognized by the infants. This is good evidence that prenatal experiences may be learnt.

Other studies have indicated very early responses to the speech-like nature of sounds; for example, infants prefer patterned sounds, at the frequency range of human speech, to monotones. Condon and Sander (1974) made observations of very fine synchronization between the sound patterns of adult speech and the body movements of newborn infants. Even as young as two days, infants matched the movements of their hands, legs, heads and elbows to the structure of spoken language. The synchronization did not occur in response to tapping sounds or random vowel sounds but seemed to be specifically elicited by speech sounds.

There is also evidence that young infants can distinguish speech sounds in the same way as adults. For example, speech sounds like 'ba' and 'pa' are part of a continuum in the sense that by a series of gradual changes 'ba' can be changed into 'pa', and this implies that there will be a range in the middle of this continuum where it is difficult to distinguish between the two sounds. However, this is not the case, because adults do not hear a range of sounds, rather there is a point on the spectrum and before that point adults perceive a sound as a 'ba' and after that point they perceive it as a 'pa'. For this reason the perception of these consonants is referred to as 'categorical perception' to reflect the fact that we only hear such sounds in either one or other category.

Several researchers have shown that, like adults, infants also have categorical perception of consonants (see Eimas, Miller and Jusczyk, 1987). For example, Kuhl (1985) trained 6-month-old infants to turn their heads towards a loudspeaker whenever contrasting vowel sounds interrupted background noise (a colourful toy appeared on top of the loudspeaker to reward successful responses). The infants were able to identify the vowel 'i' (as in 'peep') against a background noise of 'o' (as in 'pop'), and these vowels were heard in a variety of voices and intonations. Success averaged 80 per cent. Even with less clear-cut differences like 'a' and 'o', infants were successful 67 per cent of the time. Kuhl concluded that infants are sensitive to the acoustic

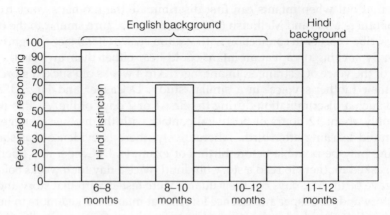

Figure 9.7   The decline in unused perceptual abilities among infants from English backgrounds compared with those from Hindi backgrounds (adapted from Eimas, 1985).

dimensions of speech long before they understand language. As Eimas (1985, p. 34) put it, young children are 'richly endowed with innate perceptual mechanisms, well adapted to the characteristics of human language, that prepare them for the linguistic world they will encounter'.

What is particularly interesting is that infants in different cultures (who therefore have exposure to different languages) can make the same sound discriminations. However, some sound contrasts may not actually be used in the infant's native language and adults speaking that language may have more difficulty distinguishing particular sound contrasts than infants. For example, Japanese adults find it difficult to distinguish 'r' and 'l' even though Japanese infants are sensitive to differences between these consonants. One question is, when do infants lose the ability to discriminate sounds which are not part of their own language? This was investigated by Werker and Tees (1985) who found that 6- to 8-month-old infants from an English-speaking community could distinguish consonantal contrasts in Hindi. But by 12 months of age the same infants could no longer detect the differences. By comparison, Hindi infants retained their ability to perceive the consonantal contrasts that occurred in their own language (see figure 9.7). These findings suggest that infants are born with the underpinnings of language, but without the reinforcing experience of actually hearing particular sound contrasts, the ability to distinguish certain sounds becomes more effortful and is then effectively lost during the first year of life. In other words, the perceptual abilities that infants are born with are modified by the environment in which the child develops.

◀Intersensory Perception▶▶▶

So far we have examined visual and auditory perception separately. In everyday life, however, it is unusual to receive perceptual information from one source only. Normally we co-ordinate information from a number of senses – vision, audition, touch, taste and smell. We see a bus approaching and hear its engine sound getting louder; we see, taste and smell our food as we eat. This co-ordination of information from different sensory modalities is called 'intersensory perception'.

Adults use their knowledge of intersensory perception in a number of ways. For example, it can be used to direct a person's attention. The increasing sound of the engine round the corner from the bus-stop results in a visual search for the approaching bus. Also it means that an object familiar in one sensory mode may be recognized when presented in another mode. As adults, we can often recognize an object by touch which previously we have only identified visually. This ability is called 'cross-modal perception'.

But do infants understand these intersensory relationships? When does stimulation in one sensory mode lead to exploratory searching or expectation in another? At what point do infants become capable of cross-modal perception? Put another way, are the neonate's senses integrated at birth and differentiated through learning and experience, or are they separate at birth and only later integrated?

How can these questions be investigated? Auditory–visual co-ordination is often investigated by showing infants two visible events, and then presenting the sound from just one of the events, to find out if the infant will look at the more appropriate visual event (see plate 9.3). For example, Spelke (1976) showed 4-month-olds two films, at the same time. One film included percussion music (tambourines, wooden blocks and so on) and the other showed a game of peek-a-boo. While the infants were watching the films

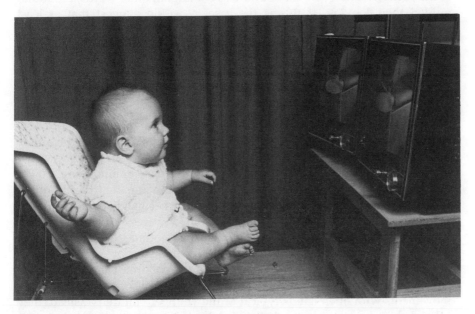

Plate 9.3   One infant experiences two visual inputs.

the sound track from one of the films was played (from a speaker placed at an equal distance from both screens). Spelke found that the infants looked longer at the film that corresponded to the sound track that was being played, and this finding indicated auditory–visual co-ordination by at least 4 months. In a similar experiment Spelke (1981) found that if a 3- or 4-month-old infant could see both her mother and father, and hear a tape-recorded voice of one of them, the infant would look at the parent whose voice she heard.

Another way of investigating auditory–visual co-ordination is to produce situations of intersensory incongruity – clashes between information from two sensory modalities – and then observe how infants respond. Aronson and Rosenbloom (1971) examined the effects of incongruities between vision and audition on infants' behaviour. Three-week-old infants were seated so that they could see their mothers through a soundproof screen but only hear them through two loudspeakers. When the two speakers were equally loud, the mother's voice was perceived as coming from the mother's mouth, as would be expected. But when the speakers were imbalanced there was a separation of sight and sound, with the mother's voice appearing to come from the left or right. When this happened the infants were very upset, suggesting that even in the first few weeks of life infants expect there to be co-ordination between auditory and visual stimuli. These results are, however, controversial because other researchers have not been able to replicate them (McGurk and Lewis, 1974).

Is there any other evidence that very young infants have intersensory co-ordination? Castillo and Butterworth (1981) placed visible patterns to the left and right of newborn infants, and played a sound which came from only one of the patterns. They found that the infants looked more at the pattern from where the sound was coming. In other words, the sound guided their looking. If this is the case, it would suggest that at least some intersensory co-ordination is present from birth. But as we have seen, matching sounds to events or voices to faces may well be a later development. In other words, there is evidence for intersensory co-ordination at birth (in Castillo and Butterworth's experiment) but infants probably have to learn about other aspects of intersensory co-ordination from experience.

Other researchers have examined the co-ordination of vision and touch. Bower, Broughton and Moore (1970) showed infants an object which they could easily reach. But the object was in fact a 'virtual object', that is, a visual illusion. When the infant reached out for it, there was nothing there. Bower et al. argued that, if the baby expected to touch an apparently solid object which she saw, she should show surprise when her hands passed through it. Younger infants in this study, aged from one week to 6 months old, were extremely upset when their hands grasped nothing, despite a number of attempts to take hold of the object. Older infants, however, showed a different pattern of behaviour. At 6 months the children were still startled by the virtual object, but quickly stopped making the grasping movements with open hands typical of the younger children. Instead, they rubbed their hands or banged their heads as if trying to verify that their hands were still in working order! These responses were usually followed by exploratory visual behaviour, e.g. swaying their heads as if to check normal motion parallax. After that, the infants would stop reaching; they seemed to realize that this virtual object did not have normal properties and saw no need to continue their efforts, unlike the younger children.

To Bower, the results of this experiment suggested that younger babies have an integrated awareness, responding with all sensory modalities at once to a stimulus; by 6 months, however, vision and touch have become differentiated modalities. Bower's results seem to indicate a high level of intersensory competence amongst babies, but again we cannot be absolutely certain about this conclusion. Other experimenters have not been able to replicate Bower's findings; for example, Gordon and Yonas (1976) reported that 5-month-old infants made fingering movements but gave no indication of emotional upset when they reached out for a virtual object.

A related line of research has focused on cross-modal perception. Researchers have looked to see whether an object that is known already through one modality can be recognized when it can only be sensed in another modality. One study suggests that this is possible very early in life. Meltzoff and Borton (1979) found that one-month-old infants showed visual preference for an object which they had only previously experienced by touch. An object (either a smooth sphere or a nubbed sphere) was placed directly into the mouth so that the infants could not see it. When larger versions of these objects were later presented to the infants visually, they showed a clear preference for the object they had mouthed (i.e. the infants who had sucked on the smooth sphere, spent more time looking at the visually presented smooth sphere). Meltzoff and Borton interpreted this to mean that the infants could co-ordinate information gained through touch with visual information.

Given what we said earlier in this chapter about habituation and dishabituation, it might be thought a little surprising that Meltzoff and Moore interpreted infants looking at the same object as they had sucked on as evidence for cross-modal transfer. After all, it might have been thought that if infants had had experience of the smooth sphere (from sucking) they would have habituated to it and would have been more inclined to look at the nubbed sphere when it was presented visually because it was a new object. However, this pattern of behaviour does not apply in cross-modal studies. Rather, infants show a preference for the object that they have experienced previously. It seems that the greatest interest is generated by experiencing a previously known object but in a novel way.

As might by now be expected from the reservations we made in relation to other studies with very young children, the results from Meltzoff and Borton's experiment have not always been found by later researchers (Rose and Ruff, 1987). As in other areas of early perception we are left with the likelihood that infants do have abilities (such as cross-modal matching) from an early age, but we have to be cautious in interpreting results from what are still only a small number of experiments with very young infants.

◀Environmental Influences▶▶▶

We have seen that some aspects of visual perception might be present very early on in life. These could be described as 'innate', or more correctly as 'highly canalized' processes (see chapter 2). However, we know from a variety of sources of evidence that environmental influences are also important for the way in which perceptual abilities develop. We will look mainly at evidence from experiments, with non-human species, which have manipulated the visual environment in which an animal is raised.

An early series of studies was carried out by Riesen (1950). He reared a number of young chimpanzees with bandages over their eyes or (on finding that the chimpanzees removed the bandages) in a completely darkened room. He found that when reared in this way, and tested at 16 months of age, chimpanzees were visually incompetent. Although their pupils were sensitive to light, and they were startled by sudden changes of illumination, they did not respond to approaching objects or visually track moving objects in a systematic way. In fact, they showed little response to objects (such as a feeding bottle) unless touched by them.

In part, these deficits were found to be due to deterioration or degeneration of the optic nerve and retinal cells. Such degeneration was irreversible if the dark experience lasted more than about 7 months. When chimpanzees were reared with diffuse, unpatterned light, however, this seemed to avoid physiological deterioration of the retina; yet the difficulties in visually recognizing objects remained. Improvement in this area was very slow to develop. Such difficulties seemed to be similar to those of humans who had been operated on for congenital cataracts.

This work led researchers to investigate which visual inputs were important for certain visual abilities, and whether there were critical or sensitive periods (see chapters 2 and 16) for such input. As an example of how this research has developed, we will consider work on binocular vision.

Critical periods in the development of binocular vision

Many visual cortical cells respond binocularly, that is, they will fire if a visual stimulus is shown to either eye. However, this is not so if one eye is covered or occluded early in life. In such circumstances most cells will only fire in response to stimuli presented to the non-deprived eye. This was shown to be the case for kittens in an experiment by Weisel and Hubel (1963). They covered one eye on each of several kittens, soon after birth, for periods of 2 or 3 months. After this period the kittens had defective vision in the deprived eye, and recordings from the visual cortex showed that very few cortical cells would respond binocularly. Subsequent research has shown that there is a critical period between about 3 weeks and 3 months after birth for binocular connections to be made in the kitten's visual cortex. Subsequent experience cannot reverse the effects of deprivation through this period. A similar phenomenon has been found in monkeys, though with a critical period extending up to about 18 months.

What relevance does this have for human infants? The parallels seem to be quite close. Banks, Aslin and Letson (1975) carried out a study with 24 human participants who had suffered abnormal binocular experience due to squint in childhood, which was later corrected. The degree of binocularity was assessed in these people by means of the tilt after-effect. This visual illusion is shown in figure 9.8. Staring between the tilted gratings and then between the vertical gratings leads to the latter being perceived as tilted in opposite directions. Banks et al. asked participants to stare at the tilted gratings with one eye, then at the vertical gratings with the other eye. The amount of transfer of the after-effect from one eye to the other (called interocular transfer) was used as a measure of binocularity.

Of 12 participants with congenital squint (i.e. with onset at or near birth), six had had surgery between the ages of 14 and 30 months. These people had

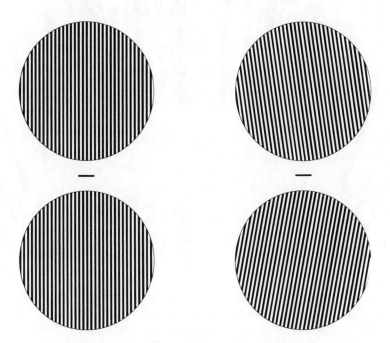

Figure 9.8 Demonstration of the tilt after-effect. Stare at the horizontal line between the two gratings on the right for one minute, allowing the eyes to wander along the line. Then quickly transfer fixation to the line between the two left-hand gratings. Instead of appearing vertical they will briefly appear to be tilted in opposite directions to each other (from Mitchell, 1978).

levels of interocular transfer not greatly below those of normal persons. The other six had not had surgery until between the ages of 4 years and 20 years. None of these people showed any appreciable interocular transfer. These results suggest that there may be a critical period before about 3 or 4 years in human infants for the development of binocular vision.

For a true critical period the length of deprivation is not as important as the stage of development in which it occurs. Banks et al. (1975) checked that this was the case. Some of their other participants had a late onset of squint: several had squint diagnosed at between 2 years and 7 years of age, but were not operated on until 2 or 3 years later. Nonetheless, these individuals achieved reasonably good levels of binocularity. Even though these people had abnormal binocular experience for several years, it could be corrected successfully because the period of abnormal vision was not during the critical period. The identification of a critical period for binocularity has important practical implications: early corrective surgery is important for

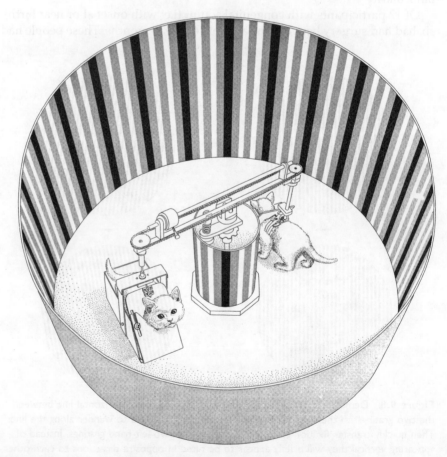

Figure 9.9 Active and passive kittens in the Held and Hein experiment (from Held, 1965).

congenital cases of squint, but is not so urgent when the squint is of late onset.

Depth perception and the effects of movement

Held and Hein (1963) argued, from research with kittens, that active rather than passive experience was essential for the development of depth perception. They reared kittens in the dark for 8–12 weeks and then the kittens were given 3 hours a day in a lighted environment as shown in figure 9.9. The environment consisted of a cylindrical container with vertical stripes. One active kitten moved around, while the other, passive, kitten was in a holder and pulled around by the movements of the first kitten. After about 10 days of this, the kittens were tested for visually guided behaviour. In general, the active kittens showed evidence of depth perception at this point; the passive kittens did not and required some further experience of running around in a normal environment before their visually guided behaviour recovered.

Held and Hein (1963) argued that for each pair of kittens the two animals had experienced similar visual input, but had differed in activity. They argued that active movement in a visual environment, together with sensory feedback accompanying this movement, was important in perceptual adaptation. However, they may have been wrong in assuming that the pairs of kittens had equivalent visual experience. The passive kittens might have dozed off more, or paid less attention to the visual environment. Subsequent research by Walk (1981) found that kittens that were constrained in their movements, but had interesting visual stimuli to watch (such as toy cars moving on a racetrack), showed good depth perception. Thus attention, rather than activity, may have been the crucial variable in Held and Hein's results. Studies of human infants who have been restricted in motor activity in the early years of life (for example, infants reared on cradleboards; or thalidomide victims without limbs) have not found deficits in depth perception, which would also suggest that activity may not be as crucial as Held and Hein believed.

Effect of the visual environment

We know that in adult cats some cells in the cortex respond mainly to bar-like stimuli at a certain orientation. However, the response of these cells may be only weakly specified at birth and the nature of the early visual environment may affect how the responsiveness of such cells develops. This was shown for kittens in an experiment by Blakemore and Cooper (1970) who found that rearing kittens in an environment which consisted of just horizontal contours resulted in the kittens detecting horizontal contours better than vertical contours. The reverse was also the case; if kittens were reared in an environment of vertical contours they were better at detecting vertical contours than horizontal ones. Blakemore and Cooper's experiment is described in box 9.2. Later work has confirmed the general nature of their findings, even though some details are disputed. It seems that, in both the cat and the monkey, the development of cells that fire to certain visual stimuli is facilitated if such stimuli are experienced early in life.

Further Reading

J. G. Bremner 1994 (2nd edn): *Infancy*, Oxford: Blackwell Publishers, is a very good and clearly written source on perceptual development, and on all other aspects of early development.

A. Fogel 1997 (3rd edn): *Infancy, Infant, Family and Society*, Saint Paul: West, is a really comprehensive book on all aspects of infant development. Unlike most books, which consider development topic by topic, Fogel describes development month by month and provides a summary of what infants have achieved in any one period. Each period includes a section on the development of perceptual abilities.

J. H. Flavell, P. H. Miller and S. A. Miller 1993 (3rd edn): *Cognitive Development*, Englewood Cliffs, NJ: Prentice-Hall, is a good textbook on all aspects of cognitive development with some very good sections on perceptual development; particularly good for highlighting the importance of specific studies.

R. Rosser 1994: *Cognitive Development. Psychological and Biological Perspectives*, Boston: Allyn and Bacon, is another good textbook with a major section on perceptual development.

◄Discussion Points►►►

1   Discuss some of the difficulties of working with very young children and explain how researchers have attempted to overcome those difficulties.
2   Is the infant well adapted for the world into which she is born? Discuss with reference to infants' perceptual abilities during the first 6 months of life.
3   How early does a young child recognize faces? Discuss the evidence to support your answer.
4   Can infants integrate information from different sensory modalities?

Box 9.1
Stimulus variables determining space perception in infants

The aim of Bower's study was to assess the age at which infants show size constancy (perceiving an object at varying distances as the same, even though it projects different sizes of retinal image).

Bower used a procedure in which he rewarded infants aged between 40 and 60 days for turning their heads to one side. The reward was a peek-a-boo response by an adult who popped up in front of the infant and then disappeared again (see box figure 9.1.1). The adult only gave the peek-a-boo response if the infant turned her head to the left,

and the adult knew when this happened because the action of turning operated a sensitive pressure switch on a pad behind the infant's head. As we saw in chapter 3, infants enjoy contingent responses like an adult playing peek-a-boo, and therefore they learn to make head turns to get the adult's response.

Once Bower had firmly established the head-turning response, he changed the procedure slightly. Sometimes a 30-cm cube was placed at 1-metre distance from the infant. The infant only

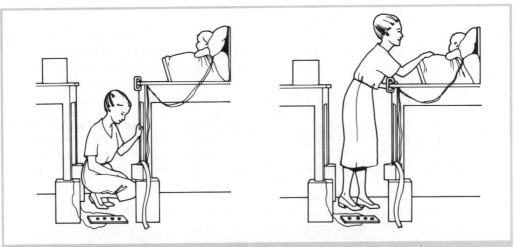

Box Figure 9.1.1   The apparatus used in Bower's experiment (from Bower, 1982).

received the reward (the peek-a-boo response) if she turned her head when the cube was present. In this way infants learnt to make a head turn only when they saw the cube at that distance.

Bower then presented four stimuli (in a counter-balanced order) for four 30-second periods each. The four stimuli were:

1   The original 30-cm cube on which the infant had been rewarded, or 'conditioned', placed 1 m away.
2   The same 30-cm cube placed 3 m away.
3   A 90-cm cube placed 1 m away.
4   The 90-cm cube placed 3 m away.

As box table 9.1.1 shows, stimulus 4 (the 90-cm cube) projected the same size image onto the infant's retina as stimulus 1 (the original 30-cm cube).

Bower thought that if infants do not have size constancy or depth perception, they would continue to display head-turning when they could see stimulus 4, because it projected the same retinal image as stimulus 1.

If, however, infants possess size constancy or depth perception they would turn their heads when they could see stimulus 2 (which was the same object as stimulus 1), or stimulus 3 (which was at the same distance as stimulus 1), but not when they saw stimulus 4 (which was a different object, at a different distance).

Nine infants were tested. The results are presented in box table 9.1.1 (top line) and show that

stimulus 2 and stimulus 3 each elicited two to three times as many responses as stimulus 4. In other words, infants were affected by the real distance or size of the object, and did not seem to use the size of the retinal image as a guide.

What cues might the babies have been using to gauge the depth (distance) of the stimuli? We saw in this chapter that possible cues include texture gradients, motion parallax and retinal disparity. Bower (1965, 1966) conducted further studies to investigate these potential cues, using three new conditions based on the first experiment. Nine infants were included in each condition. In one of the new conditions Bower covered one eye of each infant with a patch; this prevented them using retinal disparity as a cue. In another, he projected slides of cubes rather than putting real cubes in front of the infant; this removed both retinal disparity and motion parallax as cues. In a third condition, infants wore stereoscopic goggles and viewed projected stereograms; this removed motion parallax but not the other cues. The cues that infants could use to gauge depth in each condition, and Bower's results, are shown in box table 9.1.1.

It can be seen that when only texture gradient cues were available (the projected slides condition), infants responded to retinal size and not to real size or distance. This means that the infants could not use texture gradient cues as a guide to distance. The best performance, equal to that of the original group, was achieved by infants with a patch over one eye. If they could not use texture gradients (as we have just concluded) then they must have been using motion parallax. They did not need retinal disparity cues for depth perception. However, the results of the group viewing projected stereograms (who could not use motion parallax but could use retinal disparity) were intermediate between the results for the other two groups, from which it can be inferred that infants may make limited use of retinal disparity in depth perception.

Bower concluded that infants of 6 to 8 weeks have some depth perception and size constancy, and that this depends primarily on motion parallax, to some extent aided by retinal disparity. Texture gradients did not seem to be used as a cue.

This study has an experimental design with the different conditions as the independent variable,

and the head-turning response as the dependent variable. The ingenious arrangements allow strong conclusions to be drawn about infants' perceptual abilities. Working with infants so young is difficult because they can be fussy, fidgety or drowsy. Such difficulties can be made worse by requiring such young children to wear stereoscopic goggles! Getting a conditioned response from infants of this age is not easy. Behaviour can be difficult to interpret and studies difficult to repeat. Not surprisingly, some researchers have questioned the reliability of Bower's findings.

Based on material in T.G.R. Bower (1965): *Science*, 149, 88–9.

Box Table 9.1.1 Number of responses elicited by conditioned stimulus and three test stimuli when shown to babies aged six to eight weeks under four differenct conditions

	Stimulus 1 (conditioned)	Stimulus 2 (test)	Stimulus 3 (test)	Stimulus 4 (test)
Size of cube:	30 cm	same (30 cm)	different (90 cm)	different (30 cm)
Distance:	1 m	different (3 m)	same (1 m)	different (3 m)
Retinal image: Condition and cues available		different	different	same
Normal, i.e. with retinal disparity, texture gradients, and motion parallax,	98	58	54	22
Patch over one eye can use texture gradients; or motion parallax	101	60	53	22
Projected slides can only use texture gradients	94	52	44	96
Projected stereograms can use retinal disparity or texture gradients	94	44	40	32

Box 9.2
Development of the brain depends on the visual environment

Blakemore and Cooper (1970) investigated how the visual environment might affect both the development of cells in the visual cortex, and thus visually guided behaviour. They conducted an experiment with kittens.

The kittens were housed from birth in a completely dark room. From the age of 2 weeks each kitten was put into a special apparatus for 5 hours a day. This was a tall cylinder, without visible corners or edges, covered with high-contrast black-and-white stripes. The kitten was also prevented from seeing its own body by a wide black collar round its neck. Some kittens were put in cylinders with vertical stripes (an example is shown in box figure 9.2.1) and some were put in cylinders with horizontal stripes. The different rearing environments of the kittens constituted the independent variable of the experiment.

After 5 months of experience in these environments, all the kittens were put in a small, well-lit room containing tables and chairs for several hours a week. The experimenters then recorded the visu-

ally guided behaviour of the kittens in this new environment.

At first the kittens were visually inept. They did not show a startle response when an object was suddenly brought up close to their eyes, nor did they show visual placing (putting out their paws to land on when put down on a table top). However, after about 10 hours of normal visual experience these abilities improved. But other visually guided behaviour remained poor. The kittens used clumsy, jerky head movements in following objects, they tried to reach out for things which were well out of reach on the other side of the room, and often they bumped into table legs.

These deficits applied to all the kittens. In addition, it seemed that the kittens reared with vertical stripes were effectively blind to the horizontal contours in the room, and those reared with horizontal stripes were effectively blind to the vertical contours. As Blakemore and Cooper described it: 'The differences were most marked when two kittens, one horizontally and the other vertically

Box Figure 9.2.1   A kitten in a cylinder with vertical black-and-white stripes (from Blakemore and Cooper, 1970).

experienced, were tested simultaneously with a long black or white rod. If this was held vertically and shaken, the one cat would follow it, run to it and play with it. Now if it was held horizontally the other cat was attracted and its fellow completely ignored it.'

The visual-rearing environment had clearly affected the kittens' visual behaviour. An explanation for this became apparent when the experimenters looked at another dependent variable, the nature of cells in the visual cortex. When the kittens were 7.5 months old they were anaesthetized and recordings were made from single-nerve cells (neurons) in the primary visual cortex at the back of the brain. The researchers found that most of the cells were binocular, that is, they would fire to stimuli presented to either eye. However, in kittens that had been reared with vertical stripes, it was found that almost all the neurons responded most to stimuli that were at or near vertical, and none responded to horizontal stripes. The reverse was true for kittens reared with the horizontal stripes.

The vertically reared kitten may have been effectively blind to horizontal stimuli, because it lacked visual cortical neurons to respond to such stimuli (and vice versa for the horizontally reared kitten). In other words, the nature of the visual cortex had been changed by the rearing environment – visual neurons had developed to respond to the kinds of visual features encountered during early rearing.

Relatively little quantitative data was presented in the report, and not all the conclusions reached have been accepted. While Blakemore and Cooper claimed that the response of cortical cells was changed in response to the visual environment, another possibility is that cells not stimulated by the visual environment atrophied or decayed. This study has not always been replicated and although it is clear that the visual-rearing environment can have an effect on kittens, the details of this effect are still subject to debate.

Based on material in C. Blakemore and G. F. Cooper (1970): *Nature*, 228, 477–8.

10 **Language**

The relative speed with which children acquire the complex system of language is not yet fully understood. It may be that children are in some way programmed to learn language (canalized development, see chapter 2) but psychologists also emphasize the role of dialogue between child and significant others in the achievement of meaning. A number of questions have intrigued developmental psychologists. Do children go through identical stages as they learn to talk? Is there any connection between the non-verbal sounds and gestures which the baby produces and later speech? What part do adults play in creating a context in which child language will flourish? How important is it to examine the child's growing competence in a socially meaningful context? These and other issues will be explored in the following sections as we examine the sequences of language development through which children progress and the contexts where this happens. We will look at some research findings in the field and major theoretical explanations of the processes involved in learning language.

◀**Main Areas of Language Development**▶▶

There are four main areas of language competence which the child must acquire. These are the rules of sounds (phonology), grammar (syntax), meaning (semantics) and knowledge of social context (pragmatics).

Phonology is the system which governs the particular sounds (or phonemes) used in the language of a child's community. For example, an English speaker treats the sounds 'l' and 'r' as two separate phonemes; to a Japanese speaker they are one (p. 286). Scottish people use the speech sound 'ch' (as in 'loch'), which many English people cannot pronounce properly.

Syntax refers to the form in which words are combined to make grammatical sentences. The child progresses, for example, from saying 'Anna cup' to saying 'Anna please pass me that cup over there'.

Semantics refers to the meaning of words and utterances. Phonemes, which are by themselves meaningless, are combined to form morphemes, the smallest meaningful units of language. These may be whole words ('dog' in English, 'chien' in French) or grammatical markers, such as '-ed' at the end of a verb to make the past tense. The child learns that morphemes, words and longer utterances refer to events, people, objects, relationships, in short, that they convey meaning.

Pragmatics is knowledge about how language is used in different contexts. The young child must learn to adapt her language to the situation in which she finds herself. A toddler may shout out loudly in the restaurant, 'That man's greedy!': the sentence shows understanding of phonology, syntax and semantics, but lacks sensitivity to others. Engel (1994, pp. 36–7) gives an example of the use of pragmatics in which a 4-year-old demonstrates her awareness of the sensitivity which may be needed in order for her to address a question about social relationships:

> Stella, who is white, arrived at school one day and walked over to one of her teachers, Robert, a black man. She told him she had a story she wanted to tell him, but she was afraid it might upset him. He reassured her that it would not upset him, so she began: 'A long time ago, black people weren't allowed on the front of the bus. Does this upset you?' to which he replied, 'No, it doesn't upset me. So who was allowed to sit on the front of the bus?' She continued, 'Only white people were allowed on the bus.' Robert asked, 'And then what happened?' Stella answered: 'I don't know. I haven't heard the rest of the tape yet.'

Stella is puzzled by the different ways in which black and white people may be treated and would like to understand the issue more deeply; at the same time, she is aware that her questions may be upsetting to a black person. Robert, her teacher, acknowledges her tact and so enables her to explore a sensitive issue further.

◀ Sequences in Language Development ▶ ▶ ▶

There seem to be great similarities in all human societies in the sequence of language development, as children progressively master the rules of sounds (phonology), of grammar (syntax) and of meaning (semantics), and learn to combine words in ways which are acceptable and understandable (pragmatics) within their linguistic community. For example, whether the child speaks pidgin, dialect, patois, Japanese, French or English, he constructs a grammar with rules and strategies. Let us start with the newborn baby to see how this complex process of acquiring language begins.

Shared rhythms

In chapter 3 we saw how babies can pass on vital information about their needs to their parents through different patterns of crying. From around 1 month babies produce the vowel 'ooo', a sound which seems to grow out of pleasurable social interactions, especially out of the dialogues which occur spontaneously during normal caregiving activities like nappy-changing and bathing. This is the period of 'shared rhythms and regulations' (Kaye, 1984, p. 66) where the parent builds on the biological rhythms of the baby to

Table 10.1   Joey at four and one-half months: a face duet

Adult Perspective	Joey's Perspective
Joey is sitting in his mother's lap, facing her. She looks at him intently but with no expression on her face, as if she were preoccupied and absorbed in thought elsewhere. At first, he glances at the different parts of her face but finally looks into her eyes.	I enter the world of her face. Her face and its features are the sky, the clouds and the water. Her vitality and spirit are the air and the light. It is usually a riot of light and air at play. But this time when I enter, the world is still and dull. Neither the curving lines of her face nor its rounded volumes are moving. Where is she? Where has she gone? I am scared. I feel that dullness creeping into me. I search around for a point of life to escape to.
He and she remain locked in silent mutual gaze for a long moment. She finally breaks it by easing into a slight smile. Joey quickly leans forward and returns her smile. They smile together, or rather, they trade smiles back and forth several times.	I find it. All her life is concentrated into the softest and hardest points in the world – her eyes. They draw me in deep and deeper. They draw me into a distant world. Adrift in this world, I am rocked from side to side by the passing thoughts that ripple the surface of her eyes. I stare down into their depths. And there I feel running strong the invisible currents of her excitement. They churn up from those depths and tug at me. I call after them. I want to see her face again, alive. Gradually life flows back into her face. The sea and sky are transformed. The surface now shimmers with light. New spaces open out. Arcs rise and float. Volumes and planes begin their slower dance. Her face becomes a light breeze that reaches across to touch me. It caresses me. I quicken. My sails fill with her. The dance within me is set free.

Source: Adapted from Stern, 1990, pp. 57–9

develop a mutual 'dialogue' which will form the basis for the communication patterns which characterize the adult world.

Stern (1990) has collected detailed observational data on the interactions between caregiver and baby in the early months of the baby's life. These observations indicate that the interaction is distinctively different from typical adult–adult interaction. When adults interact with infants there is close proximity, an emphasis on exaggerated facial expressions, much repetition and more eye contact – the sort of interaction which might sometimes occur between adults when acting playfully towards one another or at points in the course of a very intimate relationship. Stern plots 'phrases of interaction' organized into 'runs' – sequences which have a common characteristic. Stern explains the rationale for this characteristic form of interaction as being one which ensures optimal attention on the part of the infant. The adult tries to make sure that the baby is neither bored nor over-aroused by engaging in a sort of 'dance' with the infant in which each trades similar responses back and forth. These exchanges are rhythmic and both partners contribute to the rhythm.

Stern (1990) has attempted to recreate the world of a baby, Joey, from 6 weeks to 4 years old. He does this in an original way, by describing events both from the adult's perspective, and also from the infant's point of view. You can see in table 10.1 that Stern has used images, metaphors, space and movement to capture the essence of Joey's non-verbal experience.

Babbling and echolalia

From 6 to 9 months, the baby produces more vowels and some consonants. She no longer confines herself to cries and cooing sounds. Echolalia is the frequent repetition of sounds – like 'dadadadad' or 'mummummummum' – in which the baby engages. She can also shout for attention or scream with rage; she spends time making noises when alone. During this stage infants begin to develop a whole range of behaviours some of which are directed only at familiar people. For example, certain gestures, facial expressions and sounds seem to be reserved only for the mother, or primary caregiver (see chapter 3).

There is still disagreement among researchers about the extent to which babbling and later speech are related to one another. It would seem, however, that babies' vocalizations at this stage have some of the phonetic characteristics of speech and that there is a process of continuity in the ways in which vocal abilities develop. (For a useful discussion on the origins and significance of babbling see Messer, 1994, pp. 84–7.) In any event, parents tend to believe that their babies' babbling is an attempt to communicate meaningfully and seem to spend a lot of time guessing at the intentions which underlie the baby's actions and sounds. The fact that they often go beyond the actual meaning of the baby's actions (as far as we can determine) plays a crucial part in the parents' integration of the young child into their social system, and provides an early example of scaffolding (see chapter 12). It is certainly clear that long before the first words appear the baby shows signs of understanding some of what is said to him. This

Plate 10.1   A mother and her 9-month-old baby engage in 'turn-taking' during their 'conversation'; although he cannot talk, he responds to her with speech-like rhythms, gestures and facial expressions.

capacity to share the adult's intentions has been called 'a shared memory' (Kaye, 1984, p. 67).

First words and sentences

It is easy to miss the first words a baby utters since they are often sounds not to be found in the dictionary! However, they can be considered as words if the child uses them consistently in the presence of a particular object or situation (Bates, Bretherton and Snyder, 1988). One 12-month-old baby, for example, said 'da' every time he pointed at something which he wanted, and 'oof' whenever he saw animals.

These first words have the function of naming or labelling the people and objects in the child's environment. But they also condense meaning. 'Milk' can mean 'I want milk' or 'My milk is spilt'. Even though the child can only say one word at a time, variations in context, intonation and gesture can convey a richer meaning. Single words used in this way are known as holophrases since the one word can be interpreted as expressing a whole idea.

It can take 3 or 4 months after the emergence of the first words before vocabulary increases very much, but after that the acquisition of new words is rapid. Vocabulary typically grows from around 20 words at 18 months to around 200 words at 21 months. New words are mainly object names ('daddy', 'car', 'cat') but also include action names ('look', 'gone'), state names ('red', 'lovely', 'sore') and some 'function' words referring to types of events ('there', 'more', 'bye-bye'). The vast majority of object names refer to objects which the child is able to manipulate (e.g. shoes, toys, foodstuffs, etc.) or which are spontaneously dynamic (e.g. people, animals, vehicles, etc.) (Nelson, 1981).

At around 18 months the child starts to combine single words into two-word sentences. Of course single-word utterances continue to be used for some time, but they gradually give way to more complex word combinations. The child's first sentences are often described as telegraphic speech, i.e. speech in which the meaning is highly condensed. 'Ben shoe' means 'That is Ben's shoe' or 'Put on my shoe'. The child may also have a characteristic way of asking for more information – 'Who dat?' or of making observations – 'Mummy gone'; 'Sammy here', often repeated.

From 2 to 3 years

By 24 to 27 months the child is regularly producing three- and four-word utterances. There are many sentences which are in a strict sense 'ungrammatical' but which reveal that the child is in fact using grammatical rules of syntax. These errors are 'logical errors'. The child will produce sentences like: 'Mouses gone away' in which the normal rule for plurals is extended to exceptions like 'mouse'. These 'errors' are made because the child is applying a basic set of rules (in this case, adding -s to make a noun plural). Idiosyncratic words are also common. For example, one child called a chocolate biscuit a 'choskit', a word which he had invented himself. Grammatical rules are applied to such words; for example the plural is formed by adding 's' – choskits.

After the three- and four-word linking stage, there is a rapid increase in use of grammatical rules. Prepositions and irregular verb endings appear. Now the child can begin to re-order the words of a sentence, for example to make questions or negative statements. Thus, 'John is swimming?' becomes 'Is John swimming?' 'Wh-' questions are formed, though often at first in an unorthodox form – 'Where my glove?' or 'Why John is eating?' in which the 'wh-' form is just tacked on to the beginning of the sentence. The negative is used more, though also in unusual forms, such as 'Not my daddy work'; 'I no want it'; 'Not shut door, no!' In these sentences, 'no' or 'not' is put in to express negation. Later, the child will re-order the sentence in a more 'adult' way, e.g. 'My daddy not working'.

Children at this age show a great interest in rhymes and will sing songs they have learned, though sometimes in a distorted form. Imaginative play, too, reflects developing language (see chapter 6). Conversations acted out in play or commentaries which accompany actions contribute greatly to the expression of ideas and experience. Pre-sleep monologues (table 10.2) may be important for the processing of interpersonal experiences and their subsequent organization in memory. Schank (1982) and Nelson (1989) argued that autobiographical memories are processed, reprocessed and cross-indexed

Table 10.2 Pre-sleep monologues

Weir (1962) studied her child Anthony as he talked himself to sleep each night between the ages of 28 and 80 months (see also chapter 6). The monologues which she recorded took the form of social exchanges even though he was alone. Anthony asked questions, responded to an imaginary companion, invented words and created rhythmical songs. It seems that his language served three purposes. First he seemed to be practising new words and grammar forms which he had recently learned. Secondly, he was playing with sounds for their own sake and creating poetic rhythms. Thirdly, he seemed to be trying to make sense of his world by ordering events in a systematic way. Here is an example of one of Anthony's monologues; another is given on p. 177.

That's for he
Mamamama with Daddy
Milk for Daddy
OK
Daddy dance
Daddy dance
Hi Daddy
Only Anthony
Daddy dance
Daddy dance
Daddy give it
Daddy not for Anthony
   (Weir, 1962, pp. 138–9)

Weir argues that Anthony is practising language as well as trying to make sense of the non-linguistic world of which he is a part – the sharing of his attachment between Mama and Daddy is one theme, his offer of milk 'for Daddy' another. The second example shows sound play with no clear meaning at all.

Bink
Let Bobo bink
Bink ben bink

Blue kink.

You will notice the use of rhyming and alliteration, a skill which will have implications for the future process of learning to read (Weir, 1962, p. 105).

into a system of interlinked schema categories which retain aspects of the structure of the experienced event in terms of time, space, movement and causality. These become 'scripts' (for example, the script of putting a doll to bed or the script of a mealtime routine).

A study by Bruner and Lucariello (1989) of the monologues of Emmy as she talked herself to sleep between the ages of 21 months and 3 years gives insight into the process of organizing information into such meaningful units. Emmy would often repeat the stories and add her own predictions and inferences. As the analysis of the tapes suggests, Emmy was actively constructing experience, not simply reflecting it.

From 3 to 4 years

The 3-year-old's speech is largely understandable to adults, even outside the family. Her vocabulary is now around 1,000 words, length and complexity of utterances has increased, and she can carry on reasonable conversations, though these still tend to be rooted in the immediate present.

By 3 years children begin to use complex sentences containing relative clauses. Sentences like 'See the car that I got' appear before 'The car that I got is a red one'. The second sentence is more difficult for children since the relative clause 'that I got' is embedded. By the time a child enters school she can understand and express complex sentences and her use of language is very similar to that of an adult. She can also adjust her speech in a number of ways to suit listeners of different ages with whom she is communicating. Despite these skills, however, the child is still perfecting various linguistic systems, such as pronouns and auxiliary, passive and irregular verbs. She will still produce logical errors like: 'That one's the bestest'. Some specific aspects of syntax continue to pose difficulties. In general, however, by the time children enter school their language use is correct, and their basic sentence types are similar to those used by adults.

The emergence of narrative

Bruner (1990) suggests that we learn about the physical world by devising paradigms or models which are logical and rule-bound, whereas we come to understand the cultural world in a more personal, dynamic way – by, for example, telling stories. Bruner argues that not only do children devise narratives as a way of understanding their own experiences but they also use narrature as a medium for communicating to others what these experiences mean.

Of course, children do not rely only on stories to learn about the world; nor do they communicate only in narrative form. But many researchers have argued that the narrative form plays a key part in the development of children's capacity to make sense of events in their lives and to evoke meanings. Their narratives may be elusive and fragmentary in nature but are still a rich source of insight into the child's mind. One opportunity, common in the pre-school years, to practise the skills of story-telling comes through sociodramatic play (chapter 6). Scarlett and Wolf (1979) showed that, whereas children under the age of 3 demonstrate play which is mainly carried out by actions, by the time the children are ready to enter first school at 5, the meaning of their stories is much more likely to be expressed in linguistic ways – through the recounting of a narrative, through the dialogue of the characters in the story, and through communications which reveal a growing sense of audience.

Scarlett and Wolf (see table 10.1) concluded that the emergence of the different types of story language and the resolution of problems within the story itself are major advances which preschool children make as they gradually free themselves from concrete props and actions and rely more on

Table 10.3 Stories told by one child at different ages

Age (yr. mth)	Story	Commentary
2.10	C. picks up the dragon prop and makes a hissing noise while having the dragon's mouth touch the king's crown. The dragon touches the queen and goes on to the forest where he touches, while hissing, the prince and all the animals. The story ends when the dragon knocks over the trees and the castle, all the while saying 'Bang!'	The meaning of the story depends almost entirely on the actions. The hissing sounds and bangs only embellish what is being enacted
3.3	C. uses a toy lion, man and house. While putting the man outside the house facing a window, she says, 'Him looks in window'. Next, putting the lion in the house, she says, 'This one's in'. Finally, putting the lion on its side, C. says 'Him lay down'	Language is emerging as an important aspect of the story presentation. The language outlines the basic structure of events in the story. Notice that the action is all in the present
3.8	C. takes the dragon and says, 'He's gonna killed them'. She then has the dragon fly up to the king and queen and knock them off the turret. She then says, 'And the dragon killed them'. C. then has the dragon knock over all the other props	The narrative refers to past enactments and forecasts future events. This time-split gives the story some independence from the immediate actions
3.11	C. moves the dragon towards the king and queen. C. says, 'He huffed and puffed and he blew, then the king and queen runned [C. moves king and queen to the forest]. Then he goes to the forest [C. moves the dragon to the forest] and scares the prince so he [the prince] goes home' [C. moves the prince to the castle]	Story language goes beyond the action. This is shown when C. conveys information which is not obvious from the enactment. This gives C. freedom to express feelings and intentions on the part of her characters. Without her narrative, we could not understand why the royal family move between castle and forest
4.00	C. makes a purple elephant walk up to and stand outside a toy house containing a girl prop. Without moving the props, C. says, 'And he [the elephant] says there's no one there. And he says, 'Knock, knock, knock! Who's there?' Then C. says for the girl prop, 'No-one', 'no one who?' [speaking for the elephant] 'There's not a little girl who lives here' [speaking for the little girl]	C. begins to speak for the characters so the language tells far more than the action. The dramatic speech and the voice intonations (deep for the elephant, squeaky for the girl) carry the meaning of the story event. Without changes in the props, the story moves on

Source: Adapted from Scarlett and Wolf, 1979

the language itself. In addition, the children are becoming aware of the pragmatics of language – the rules which govern the most effective ways of communicating with others. Many contemporary researchers into reading argue that we need to build on this spontaneous creation of narrative if we are to sustain children's interest in actually reading stories for themselves (Engel, 1994; Root, 1986). The experience of being read to by adults and taking part in mutual story-telling during the preschool years creates conditions that facilitate the transition to independent reading by the child (plate 10.2).

Re-telling stories can enable children to become familiar with the convention of written stories, thus providing motivation and a framework for help with reading. Wade (1984) suggests that parents have a crucial part to play in the period before the child begins to read by making stories an enjoyable, shared experience. He describes the role of turn-taking, sharing and empathizing in this experience and argues that these form a natural basis for later learning experiences, including reading. The narrative process which began in the preschool years can be fostered by sensitive parents and teachers and harnessed to the emerging skills of writing.

Plate 10.2 The child's interest in books develops throughout the preschool years; parents and other adults have a key role to play in facilitating pre-reading skills.

◀Pre-reading and Pre-writing Skills▶▶▶

By 6 or 7 years of age most children have begun the process of learning to read and write. Obviously some perceptual skills are needed, but other aspects of language development in the preschool years may also be important or necessary if a child is to become a proficient reader and writer a few years later. These are called 'pre-reading skills' and 'pre-writing skills'. As well as the usual skills of perception and discrimination, these include the understanding of reading conventions and the concept of story, and the awareness of rhyming and alliteration. From an early age the child can be helped to develop these skills.

When a child begins to read and write he needs to consider visual information as well as the sound and sense of words. During the preschool years the child's perceptual skills can be sharpened by encouraging him to observe specific aspects of his environment. Training in visual discrimination can be done in an enjoyable way through games; for example, jigsaws, picture-matching games, exercises in grading shapes and objects by size or by colour, or the experience of noticing differences and similarities between objects can give the child useful preparation for discriminating among words and letters. It is also useful if the child understands concepts of 'up', 'down', 'forwards' and 'backwards' (Gardner, 1980).

Bryant and Bradley (1985) and Bryant, MacLean and Bradley (1990) argue that young children's awareness of rhyming and alliteration indicates a skill in analysing the constituent sounds of words, which is essential for learning to read. Young children usually respond with delight to nursery rhymes such as 'Ring a ring o' roses' which contain rhyming ('Roses' and 'posies') and alliteration (the recurrence of the letter 'r' in 'ring a ring o' roses' and 'p' in 'a pocket full of posies') and will often create their own rhymes, as we saw in the rhyming couplets created by 3-year-olds (Chukovsky, 1963) and the alliteration in some of the presleep monologues produced by 2-year-old Anthony (Weir, 1962).

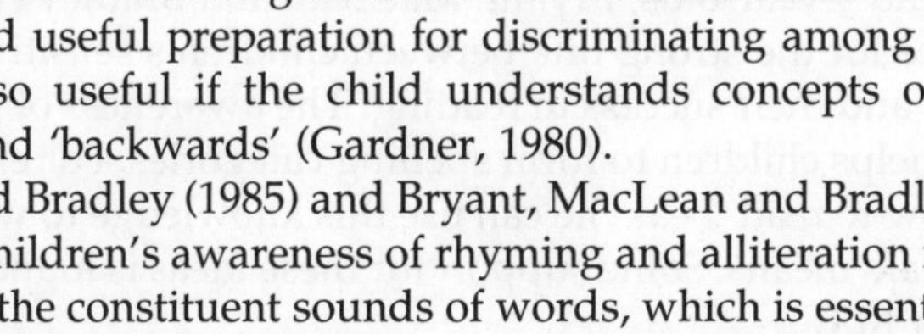

oiA

ᴅAiOA i OAi

Figure 10.1 Writing by Javier, aged 5 years 5 months. Top row, 'Gatito' (little cat); bottom row, 'Gatitos' (three little cats in the picture). He explains as he is writing: 'One little cat' (the first three letters); 'the little cats here' (six letters); 'another cat' (the three remaining letters). You can see that the plural is obtained by repeating the original word as many times as there are cats to be represented (adapted from Ferreiro, 1985).

Bryant and Bradley (1985, pp. 47–8) quote (from Chukovsky) jingles by 3-year-olds which also demonstrate the children's ability to change words to suit the rules of rhyme:

> The red house
> Made of strouss
> The duckling and the big goose
> Sat on the broken sail-oose.

They argue that 'all these children know a great deal about how to spot the common sounds in different words. Children show this every time that they produce rhyme.' In the process of becoming familiar with rhymes and alliteration they are also developing an awareness of speech sounds which will have an influence on their later ability to read and spell. Bryant and Bradley hypothesize a direct link between sensitivity to sounds (as shown in responses to rhyming and alliteration games) and competence in learning to read. The backward reader is likely to be a child who has not developed this skill in detecting speech sounds during the preschool years. In a longitudinal study of 65 3- and 4-year-olds, Bryant, MacLean and Bradley (1990) provide further evidence for the strong link between children's sensitivity to rhyme and alliteration and their success in reading. The awareness of rhyme, argue these authors, helps children to form spelling categories. For example, if the child knows how to read 'beak' he can use this knowledge to work out what a new word 'peak' means. Some support for these ideas is found in the study reported in box 10.1.

◀Dyslexia▶ ▶

Developmental dyslexia is an important topic, because it is the most common of the developmental disorders, with an estimated incidence rate of 5 per cent in the Western world (Badian, 1984). Children with dyslexia are identified in school when they fail to learn to read. The traditional definition of dyslexia is that provided by the World Federation of Neurology (1968): a disorder in children who, despite conventional classroom experience, fail to attain the language skills of reading, writing and spelling commensurate with their intellectual abilities. These children seem to be as intelligent as the other children in their class, and therefore it is a surprise to both their teachers and their parents when they show these unexpected difficulties. However, any more careful analysis of the development of a dyslexic child typically shows a range of differences in their language development. Many, for example, will have had some form of speech therapy in the preschool period. Others may show subtle impairments in their speech, ranging from mislabelling to mispronunciation to word-finding difficulties. In a particularly sensitive analysis of the dyslexic syndrome, Miles (1982, 1993) describes problems in repetition of polysyllabic words, in acquiring familiar sequences, such as the months of the year, in correctly labelling left and right, and learning tables, as well as the characteristic problems in reading and spelling. The problems of dyslexia interest a wide range of researchers, because it seems that whichever area of research you are interested in, dyslexics show intriguing deficits in just that area.

Explanations of dyslexia

The phonological deficit hypothesis suggests that dyslexic children for some reason have particular difficulty with the sounds of words, so that when they try to link the phoneme (the sound 'sss') to the grapheme (the letter squiggle 's') they make mistakes. Children who are going to have difficulties of this type can be identified preschool by their problems in rhyming and alliteration (see box 10.1). These children seem to have missed the stage of playing with words, which seems to come naturally to most children. Later on, they may have problems in segmenting a word, that is breaking it down into sounds. By the late 1980s, the phonological deficit hypothesis had become the dominant explanation for the difficulties dyslexic children suffer in reading and spelling, largely based on the work of researchers such as Bradley and Bryant (1985).

More recently, Nicolson and Fawcett (1990, 1996) suggest that the key to the dyslexic deficit seems to be early problems in articulation, which has been found to be significantly slower and more error prone in dyslexia (Snowling, Goulandris, Bowlby and Howell, 1986). It may be that in the early stages of speech, dyslexic children are simply less efficient at repeating

Plate 10.3 Testing for dyslexia.

words correctly. These articulation difficulties lead to problems in basic phonological skills such as segmentation, which impacts on the development of grapheme–phoneme conversion skills, leading to reading difficulties. Reading and spelling are the most severely impaired skills in dyslexia, because not only does a dyslexic child have problems in acquiring the basic building blocks, such as the grapheme/phoneme correspondence, they also have problems in becoming expert in these skills. This leads to problems in identifying whole words, or noting the sequences of letters that traditionally occur together (these are known as orthographic regularities). The result is that at each stage dyslexics are investing too many resources in just coping with the basics, which leaves them less spare capacity for acquiring new information. Nicolson and Fawcett are hopeful that early screening tests (Fawcett and Nicolson, 1996) will allow many dyslexic children and those with more generalized difficulties to receive the help they need before they fail. They are currently working on a series of computer programs to help the teacher with component reading skills. Early identification and appropriate support should allow children with dyslexia to progress through the education system at a normal rate, thus limiting the impact of dyslexia on children's development. It should then be possible for dyslexic children to express their strengths, without being hampered by their weaknesses.

◀Theories of Language Development▶▶▶

Our review of sequences in language development has outlined the remarkable achievements that can be made during the preschool years. The child masters the phonology of her language. She has acquired grammatical morphemes (e.g. pluralizing nouns or adding modifiers such as '-ed' to verbs to indicate past tense) and learned how to produce declarative statements (e.g. 'I have a cup'), 'why-' questions (e.g. 'Where is my cup?' or 'Why is my cup on the floor?') and the negative ('I do not have a cup'). Sentences have become more complex and relative clauses appear ('The cup, which is on the table, is red'). Semantic development has progressed in that children can express quite subtle meanings in their language. Their skill as tellers of stories, jokes and riddles is increasing as they realize the layers of meaning embedded in language. The pragmatics of communication have improved and there is growing awareness that they need to adapt language to particular contexts and adjust speech to suit the requirements of different people.

How does the child achieve this? As yet, there is no one theory which successfully encompasses all aspects of language development. Explanations, as opposed to description, of the course of language development vary in emphasis. For a time, the principles of learning theory seemed to provide a logical explanation with an emphasis on reinforcement and imitation; while other theorists have suggested that there is a biological basis for language acquisition with innate mechanisms underlying it. Piagetians emphasize the importance of cognitive development. Still others take the interactionist approach and argue that the development of linguistic competence needs to be studied within its social context. We will consider each of these broad approaches in turn.

The role of reinforcement and imitation

Skinner (1957) argued that children acquire language because adults reinforce correct usage. The baby's random coos and babbling sounds are progressively shaped into words by adults rewarding those which are most 'word-like'. Later the adults reinforce word combinations into sentences. Successive approximations are rewarded or reinforced until finally the child's language is similar to the adult's. Other learning theorists suggested that imitation also plays an important part in language acquisition (Bandura, 1971).

At face value this explanation sounds plausible. The environment must be responsible for differences in learning one language or another, or one particular dialect. How else can we explain why one child speaks Russian and another Japanese, or why 'I were stood there while six' is said by one speaker and 'I was standing there until six o'clock' by another? But the empirical evidence suggests that the process is more complicated. Brown, Cazden and Bellugi (1969), tape-recording mothers talking to their young children, found that as far as syntax was concerned there was very little evidence that mothers shaped their children's grammar. Statements like, 'Want milk' or 'Ben cup' were accepted. For the most part mothers corrected the content of what their children said rather than the grammatical structure. Thus they only corrected sentences which were untrue. For example, if the child said, 'That pig' (indicating a sheep), the mother would say, 'No, that's a sheep'. If the child said 'That sheep' the mother might then say, 'Yes'.

Findings like these gave no support for reinforcement or reward as an explanation for syntactic acquisition. What about the role of imitation? Clearly it must have some effect on language acquisition since children learn the same language and accent as members of their social group. They often learn new words by reproducing the words of other people. Furthermore, in terms of sheer quality of language, it has been found that children whose mothers talk a lot to them have larger vocabularies than those whose mothers do not (Clarke-Stewart, 1973).

Nelson et al. (1973), investigating the impact of different kinds of adult feedback on children's grammatical constructions, compared the effects of expanding children's incomplete sentences (that is, putting them in their complete form) and recasting them (that is, keeping the topic the same but giving the child a new way of talking about it). For example:

Child's incomplete   *Adult expansion*   *Adult recasting*
sentence
Doggy eat   Doggy is eating   What is the doggy eating?

Children whose sentences were recast performed better in a sentence imitation task than children whose sentences were only expanded. Furthermore, the children whose utterances were recast used more complex grammatical forms in their spontaneous speech than those whose sentences were simply expanded. An even more specific effect was found when an experimenter recast children's utterances into questions or into complex verb constructions: each treatment group showed growth in the use of negative 'wh-' questions or complex verb constructions depending on the type of adult intervention. Box 10.2 gives the details of this study.

More recently, social learning theory has contributed to the debate. Moerke (1991) proposes a skill learning model based on an integration of learning theory (operant conditioning), social learning theory and aspects of Piaget's cognitive developmental theory. He uses the idea that language depends on continuous feedback cycles within which the 'trainer' – usually the parent – invites a response from the child and then provides feedback. Moerke provides many examples of this kind of learning interaction with the parent.

The innate basis of language

By contrast, other theorists focus on the universal properties of language, pointing out that the sequences of language acquisition are broadly similar in all societies; language occurs in all human cultures, and all languages have certain features in common (Chomsky, 1965; McNeill, 1970).

The essence of Chomsky's argument is that the relationship between speech sounds and meaning is not a simple one of association (as the behaviourist school of psychology and the learning theory approach suggested). Instead, we need to distinguish between the surface structure of the language and its deep structure, that is, between the arrangement of words in the utterance and the logical, grammatical relationships among the elements in that utterance. The connection between the two is specified by the transformational procedures or rules of grammar. Different languages use different transformational rules but the universal features are to be found in deep structure.

Chomsky proposed that humans have an innate 'language acquisition device' (LAD), without which language could not develop. The LAD is so constructed that it can 'perceive' regularities in the utterances which the child hears. The LAD generates hypotheses about these regularities (for example, that the plural is formed by adding -s to the noun). These are then tested against new utterances and so come to be rejected or accepted as appropriate. The LAD can acquire any language and faced with the utterances of a particular language, it develops a grammar. To do so, however, one must suppose that all human language (and hence too the LAD) must share some common, universal constraints as to the types of language that may occur.

Chomsky stresses the tacit knowledge which we all have of the structure of language even though we may not be able to describe the structures using the language of linguistics experts. Even young children have a tacit knowledge. By 5 years most children – whatever their background or culture – have a good grasp of the basic rules of their language. So who teaches them? Not the parents – most are not professional linguists. Chomsky proposes that it must be because of innate knowledge. This theory, then, encompasses not just specific languages but the general form of human language, and proposes that 'the theory of grammar and its universal constraints describes the internal structure of LAD, and, thus, of children' (McNeill, 1970, p. 151). The ability to infer such transformational rules from surface structure utterances was, Chomsky and McNeill both thought, embodied in the LAD.

Chomsky's theory of transformational, generative grammar provided the impetus for a great deal of research into child language. His own work investigated grammars in which deep structure or 'meaning' had transformational rules applied to it in order to change it to a surface or spoken utterance. This he called 'generative grammar' because the application of rules generates actual sentences. Chomsky's research focused on examples of child grammars; he argued that the child was involved in the creative process of generating language, as utterances like 'Two sheeps' or 'All done milk' seemed to show.

The picture becomes clearer when children produce sentences. Brown and Fraser (1963), studying telegraphic speech in children, concluded that the utterances could all be classified as grammatical sentences from which certain words had been omitted. For example, 'Mummy hair' only omitted the possessive inflection ('Mummy's hair'); 'chair broken' was an acceptable sentence if 'is' was added. Similarly, McNeill (1966) noted other grammatical relationships in the telegraphic speech of young children. Ordering was important in the structure of children's speech even though it was not in direct imitation of the order of adult language. The child might say 'Me want that coat', but phrases like 'Want that coat me' did not appear. Brown and Bellugi (1964) analysed the early speech of two children, Adam and Eve, and noted the over-generalization of inflections described earlier. For example, the use of -s to form plurals was observed as 'deers', 'sheeps', 'knifes', 'tooths'. Use of -ed to form past tense was observed as 'comed', 'doed', 'growed', 'hurted', 'swimmed', 'caughted', 'drinked'.

The child's innate propensity to use rules, argued Brown and Bellugi, led to 'errors' from which the linguist can infer the grammar being used. The incorrect grammatical constructions made by Adam and Eve did not come from adult models; it seemed that the children had produced them themselves on the basis of simple grammatical 'hypotheses'. This would be consistent with the LAD theory.

Linguistic research has also investigated transformational rules in child language. We will look at one kind of transformation, the question. Table 10.5 gives examples of a child using telegraphic speech and shows the gradual development of the correct form of question. This is one type of transformation; there are many others (e.g. use of the past tense, the negative, the use of plurals) which also seem to demonstrate that the child, from an early age, acts as though she expected language to be governed by a set of rules.

The analysis of children's utterances in terms of deep structure, surface structure and the transformational rules which relate the two (Brown, 1973; Slobin, 1973; McNeill, 1970) has greatly enriched our understanding of early

Table 10.4   Stages in the development of question forms

Ages for Adam	Questions	Commentary
28 months	Sit chair? Ball go?	Expressed by intonation only
	What that? Where mummy go? What mummy doing?	The child has developed a routine form of the question
38 months	Will you help me? Does the kitty stand up?	The child has developed the use of *auxiliary verbs*
	What I did yesterday? Why the Christmas tree going? How he can be a doctor?	For questions expecting the answer yes or no, there is inversion of the verb but not for 'what' and 'why' questions
42 months	Are you thirsty? Why can't we find it?	Inversion of the verb in 'why' questions
	I have two turn, huh? We're playing, huh? That's funny, isn't it?	Development of 'tag' questions, e.g. tags on 'huh?' at the end of a sentence
	Why can't they put on their swimming suits?	Later, inversion of auxiliary verbs appears too

Source: Adapted from Cazden, 1972

language development. Children's language does seem to be governed by rules and does seem to develop in a systematic way. Children do seem to progress through similar stages in the acquisition of language. However, many contemporary psychologists question the notion of an inborn LAD which operates most efficiently during a critical period between birth and puberty.

Chomsky himself has revised his views on transformational grammar. In a later version of his theory (Chomsky, 1986), he proposes Principles and Parameters Theory (PPT), in which he adds to his concept of deep and surface structures the idea of processes through which the child must pass in order to achieve grammatical utterances. He still holds to the assumption that humans have an innate capacity for language but puts more emphasis on the recent formulation of his theory, on the psychological processes of learning different kinds of grammatical structure. As with the earlier version, it is difficult to test PPT theory formally. (For a detailed exposition and critique of PPT, we recommend Messer, 1994, chapters 10 and 11.)

Pinker (1994), in *The Language Instinct*, provides compelling evidence for the innate basis of language. He argues (p. 32) that 'complex language is universal because *children actually reinvent it*, generation after generation – not because they are taught, not because they are generally smart, not because it is useful to them, but because they just can't help it'. As one source of evidence for this view, Pinker indicates how pidgin languages have been transformed – by children learning and changing them – into full languages. He cites research (Bickerton, 1990) into the pidgin language developed by labourers who were imported into the sugar plantations in Hawaii around the turn of this century. These people came from China, Japan, Korea, Portugal, the Philippines and Puerto Rico, and developed a pidgin in order to communicate with one another. Typically, this pidgin did not have the usual grammatical structures; it had 'no consistent word order, no prefixes or suffixes, no tense or other temporal and logical markers, no structure more complex than a simple clause, and no consistent way to indicate who did what to whom' (Pinker, p. 34). He quotes examples from two speakers (p. 33):

Speaker 1: Me cape buy, me check make.
Speaker 2: Good dis one. Kaukau any-kin' dis one. Pilipine islan' no good. No mo money.

The meaning intended by these pidgin speakers is as follows:

Speaker 1: He bought my coffee; he made me out a cheque.
Speaker 2: It's better here than in the Philippines; here you can get all kinds of food, but over there there isn't any money to buy food with.

Pinker points out that, in each case, the meaning has to be filled in by the listener since pidgin does not have the grammatical resources to convey complex messages. But for the children who grew up in Hawaii it was a totally different matter. Their language – which is now called Hawaiian Creole – was grammatical, since it contained auxiliaries, prepositions, case markers and relative pronouns, despite the fact that they had been exposed only to the pidgin of their parents. Here are some examples (p. 34) each followed by a 'translation':

Speaker 4: Da firs japani came ran away from japan come.
'The first Japanese who arrived ran away from Japan to here.'

Speaker 5: Some filipino wok o'he-ah dey wen' couple ye-ahs in filipin islan'.
'Some Filipinos who worked over here went back to the Philippines for a couple of years.'

Bickerton concluded that creoles like Hawaiian Creole, which have been formed from unrelated language mixtures, have strong similarities which support the concept of a basic common grammar.

Similar insights come from research into sign language (Kegl and Lopez, 1990). In Nicaragua deaf children were not introduced to any form of sign language other than the basic signs which their families had separately devised to communicate with one another. After 1979, special schools for the deaf were founded in which the teachers tried to teach the children to lip-read, with small success. At the same time, and spontaneously, the children were devising their own sign language based on the signs which they had each individually developed within the family – a form of pidgin which linguists have named Lenguaje de Signos Nicaraguense (LSN). Over time, this has developed into a creole created by the younger children who had been exposed to the pidgin of the older children in the school. This is now known as Idioma de Signos Nicaraguense (ISN) and has become a standardized language with grammatical devices absent in LSN. The new language is so sophisticated that a dictionary of its signs is soon to be published. The children use ISN to tell one another stories, make jokes and plays on words, and share experiences in their linguistic community. Kegl and Lopez point out that the older students, who had entered school in their teens, failed to achieve the level of fluency that was obtained by the younger children, who had gained exposure to one another and had signed to one another at an earlier age. Kegl (now Shepard-Kegl) and Lopez suggest that this is clear evidence of the claim that language has universal rules. (The concept of sensitive periods here is also discussed in chapter 16.)

What are these universal characteristics of language? First they refer to phonological aspects of language, since every language has consonants, vowels and a syllabic structure. They also apply to syntax. All languages have sentences, noun phrases, verb phrases and a grammatical structure underlying them. Chomsky (1965) argued that there are deep structures and surface structures in all languages as well as rules of transformation which connect the two. The surface structure – that is the ordering of words in a sentence – can vary but still reflect the same deep structure, that is the underlying meaning. For example:

The dog bit the man.
The man was bitten by the dog.

These two sentences have the same deep structure in the sense that they are about the same occurrence, but the surface ordering of words is different. The relationship between deep and surface structures is achieved through the rules of transformation. These rules make the connection between sound and meaning in a language. Table 10.5 shows sentences which, by contrast, show differences in deep structure but a similar surface structure.

We understand that, although the three sentences have the same surface structures, different relationships among the words are implied and thus different meanings. Finally, some sentences can have two meanings: for example, 'The peasants are revolting'. It is the rules of transformation which enable us to understand whether the peasants 'are in revolt' or 'revolt us'. As McNeill (1970) writes: 'Every sentence, however simple, has some kind of underlying structure related to some kind of surface structure by means of certain transformations.'

Table 10.5 Examples of sentences with similar surface structure but a different deep structure

Sentence	Paraphrase	Non-paraphrase
They are buying glasses	–	–
They are drinking glasses	They are glasses to use for drinking	They are glasses that drink
They are drinking companions	They are companions that drink	They are companions to use for drinking

Source: McNeill, 1970

Language and cognition: a Piagetian perspective

As we have seen, Chomsky and his colleagues suggested that the child has an innate knowledge of the basic rules and constraints of language, and of her community. But some psychologists have suggested that the rule-bound nature of children's speech arises not so much from an innate LAD as from the child's prelinguistic knowledge, since the child, it is argued, already has some ability to categorize her world even before she can communicate with others in language. We turn now to an examination of three aspects of this approach – the relationship between language and cognition, the relationship between language and social interaction, and the study of adult–child (A–C) speech.

Here the investigator focuses back on the precursors of early language, for example, gestures, facial expression, actions. This approach moves its emphasis away from grammatical competence to the study of understanding and communication. As we see in chapter 11, Piaget claims that during the first 2 years of life the child's intellectual skills do not rely on symbols, such as words and images, but are rooted in sensori-motor experiences, such as seeing, hearing and touching. Symbolic actions do not appear until the end of the sensori-motor period. Although interactionists would accept that children develop a system of rules, they would not accept that the rules grow out of an innate LAD but rather that they come from a much wider cognitive system. Children talk alike because they share many similar experiences and their language is facilitated by the sensori-motor schemas of early infancy. This hypothesis – called the 'cognition hypothesis' (Cromer, 1974) – states that:

(i)   we understand and use particular linguistic structures only when our cognitive abilities enable us to do so (for example, the child can gesture that he wants an apple before he uses the holophrase 'Apple');

(ii) even once our cognitive abilities allow us to grasp an idea, we may say it in a less complex way because we have not yet acquired the grammatical rule for expressing it freely. Thus the child may not be able to say 'Have you looked?' but he can express the same meaning in the less complex sentence 'Did you look yet?'

What Piagetians are suggesting is that children form schemas to explain events in their lives and only then talk about them. Language development reflects the stages of cognitive development through which the child is progressing. They agree with other theorists that, as children develop intellectually, they produce more elaborate sentences, which are expanded by the adults and older children who are close to them. Out of these interactions arise even more sophisticated utterances which in turn prompt a more complex response from others in the child's environment. This is a reciprocal relationship, in which the child plays an active part. However, the child is not applying an innate LAD to the talk which he hears. Instead, his understanding arises out of his existing knowledge of the world.

Many observations support this interactionist approach. In chapter 11, we examine Piaget's work on the object concept, which shows that by the end of the first year the child understands that objects exist independently of herself, whether in her sight or not. In Piaget's view, the child needs to have this sense of object permanence before she can begin to understand that words can represent things. Observations of first words show that children usually focus on familiar actions or objects. In this way, they are using words to express aspects of their environment which they already understand non-verbally, and there seem to be regularities in the ways in which children combine their early one- and two-word utterances with gestures or with knowledge of the context in which the word occurs.

This cognitive approach to children's language development was very influential in the 1970s, until some psychologists began to suggest that it gave a rather narrow view of the child. It ignored, for example, the child's social skills and the effect of the social environment on a child's capacity to learn. It is this shift of emphasis towards the child as communicator in a social world that we will consider next.

Language and social interaction

Piaget's theory emphasizes the child's knowledge of the world as a precursor of language and demonstrates the role of language in representing objects and events in the child's physical world. A second interactionist approach places greater emphasis on the child's early experiences of communicating and interacting socially with the people in her surroundings; the baby masters a social world on to which she later 'maps' language.

But how does this happen? One powerful factor according to this theory is the adults' tendency to give meaning to the sounds and utterances of infants. As we have seen (Snow, 1977), observations of parents interacting with very young babies indicate that burps, gurgles and grunts are interpreted as expressions of intention and feeling on the part of the baby: 'You really enjoyed that, didn't you?', or 'Will you please make up your mind?' Many infants experience extensive verbal exchanges with their mothers, during which the mother actively interprets, comments upon, extends, repeats and sometimes misinterprets what the child has said, in a 'conversational' format.

Another important development, according to this viewpoint, is the development of joint attention, and mutual understanding of gestures. As early as 6 months, infants will follow the mother's gaze to see what she is looking at (Butterworth, 1987); and by 9 or 10 months, they will start pointing at objects in a communicative way. It is communicative because the infant clearly wants to direct the mother's attention to the object, and is not satisfied until this is achieved. Non-verbally, it is the equivalent of saying 'look at this!' A good response of the adult is to name the object or say something about it.

By this age, too, reaching for objects changes and becomes more social. At 6 months, a baby reaching is really trying to get the object herself. By 9 months, she may make a more ritualized gesture of reaching, and look at the mother. This is the non-verbal equivalent of 'give me this!' At about this age infants will show or give objects to a parent or adult, as well.

The crucial development at this age, shortly before first words appear, is joint attention; both adult and infant are jointly giving their attention to a particular object, and are communicating about this by shared understanding of gestures such as looking, pointing, reaching and showing. The adult often names the object in these situations; and one can see that it is a relatively small step for the infant to start naming objects also. In this view, joint attention, together with the experience of turn-taking or 'conversational' formats of interaction, are crucial precursors of early language development.

The psycholinguist's emphasis on grammar obscures the function which these interactions have in preparing the infant for language. Infants and adults together create a range of formats, that is, habitual exchanges, which form the basis for interpreting what both parent and child mean. In the course of these dialogues or pre-speech 'conversations', the child is developing skills which are 'as essential to speaking and understanding language as the mastery of grammar is supposed to be'. Furthermore, the skills are extended by ritualized games such as peek-a-boo, and joint picture-book reading.

Bruner (1983) calls these interactive precursors and later supports for language the Language Acquisition Support System (LASS). These social formats or rituals, and experience of social reciprocity, are important parts of the environmental context which structures the child's understanding of the world and hence her early language utterances. The distinctions between subject and object, or between nouns and verbs, for example, may be facilitated in this way. In fact, Bruner argues, adult conversation would be impossible if this prior shared meaning and reciprocity between speakers had not been established.

This sociocognitive perspective traces the child's competence in language back to her experience as a communicator in the pre-verbal stage – a time when the responsiveness of adults is a key factor. It considers both social and cognitive functioning, with particular reference to the adult's sensitivity to the child's early capacity to perceive and understand experiences. Where infants do not experience this reciprocity and shared social interaction, or where the parents fail to give feedback to the baby's early vocalizations and gestures (as happens with children reared in restricted environments), then later linguistic development is likely to suffer.

Adult–Child speech

Research into Adult–Child (A–C) speech gives a third perspective on the interactionist stance. In the 1960s it was believed that A–C speech to children (motherese, as it was called then) was similar to that between adults. Chomsky (1965) took this position, indicating that language acquisition was very difficult – too difficult for the young child to do unless some innate capacity were present. But empirical research since that time has indicated that A–C speech is distinctively different from Adult–Adult (A–A) speech.

Mothers typically use the simplest speech with infants of 8-12 months (Stern et al., 1983). This could be because prior to this age children cannot understand the content of speech but after this age they are more able to deal with increasingly complex material. Adults also adjust their speech to the cognitive ability of the child, whether it is first or later born and whether siblings are present. Messer (1994) argues that adults do in fact modify their speech when talking to young children, as we saw in the work of Snow (1977). The most commonly used measure of grammatical complexity has been the mean length of utterance (MLU). Messer shows that when you compare A–C speech with A–A speech there are very clear differences (see table 10.6).

A–C (Adult–Child) speech has a higher pitch, a greater range of pitch and is simpler in meaning. The mean length of utterance (MLU) is shorter; A–C speech is also simpler, for example, through number of verbs or conjunctions per utterance. It is also more likely to be in the present tense. It is easier to process; it is slower; it has more repetitions and an exaggerated form. It is more likely to concern events that are happening in the here and now, contains more concrete nouns, uses proper names rather than pronouns. It will also use special words like 'tummy', 'poo', 'dummy', 'doggy'.

Table 10.6   A comparison of Adult–Child (A–C) speech with Adult–Adult (A–A) speech

SYNTAX	A–C speech	A–A speech
Mean length of utterance (MLU)	3.7 words	8.5 words
Verbs per utterance	0	81.5
Percentage of utterances with conjunctions (e.g. 'since', because', 'then')	20%	70%
Percentage of pauses at end of sentence	75%	51%
Speed, words per minute	70	132

Source: Adapted from Messer, 1994, p. 221

Babies indicate soon after birth that they prefer A–C speech to the Adult–Adult speech they hear. (See also chapters 2 and 9 on neonatal perceptual abilities.) Why is this? Before infants are able to speak or even to respond to words, they seem to be able to respond to the sound patterns – or 'prosodic' characteristics – of speech. This refers to the general pattern of sound, which is not related to individual words. Stern et al. (1983) identified a number of distinctive prosodic patterns in speech to infants. For example, when infants were inattentive, parents would typically raise the pitch of their voice; so a form of bell-shaped pitch contours – a pattern of rising and falling pitch – took place as a means of capturing and then maintaining the infant's attention.

Papousek et al. (1987) found that A–C speech has the following kinds of melodic units: level, rising, falling, U-shaped, bell-shaped or complex sinusoidal. These were found across three languages – English, Mandarin and German. They suggest that these melodic units may be universal patterns of pre-linguistic communication. They are used in consistent ways in a culture and, in addition, are attuned to the perceptual preferences and abilities of infants (see chapter 9 on perception). Papousek, Papousek and Symmes (1991) found that Chinese mothers use similar melodic contours, suggesting that there are universal patterns across languages and cultures which parents use to communicate with their infants. They are also present in SES blacks in the USA, and in non-Western cultures, e.g. the Kaluli of New Guinea (Schieffelin and Ochs, 1983).

It would appear that the prosodic contours enable infants to understand the intent of speech before they can identify the meaning of individual words. In addition, they must identify individual words in the speech which they hear before they can produce words themselves. But how do they reach the point where, like adults, they can distinguish individual words in the speech which they hear? Gleitman and Wanner (1982) suggested that infants are predisposed to attend to smaller segments of speech (such as stressed syllables) and that this is how they eventually identify words. First of all they identify whole utterances by 'silences before and after them, suprasegmental contour, the melody of the utterance and its rhythm' (Messer, 1994, p. 79). At the same time as the infants begin to segment or split an utterance into smaller units the mothers also stress words in their speech in ways which help the infants to locate them in speech – for example by stressing the ones which are especially important or by speaking loudly at particular points in the 'conversation'.

Some support for this idea comes from a study by Messer (1981) of the amplitude of words in mothers' speech to 14-month-old infants. He found that labels for objects were more likely than any other word class to be the loudest in an utterance. This emphasis, on the part of the mothers, clearly helps infants to identify the words for everyday objects in the child's world. These labels also occurred more frequently in the last position in an utterance and therefore were more likely to be remembered.

Such findings have been confirmed by Fernald and Mazzie (1991). They found that mothers consistently gave new words prominence when reading a story to an infant of 14 months. Again these new words were more likely to be positioned at the end of the utterance and be spoken with more emphasis. This suggests that there are a number of strategies which infants use to identify certain words but also that the mother provides useful cues which help the infant to identify important words.

The issue of the value and nature of this special A–C talk remains controversial. Some researchers argue that the sentences which parents use to children are 'finely-tuned' to the child's needs as a learner (e.g. Furrow et al., 1979); others disagree (e.g. Gleitman et al., 1984). A number of questions remain unanswered. How short should the mother's MLU ideally be, for example? No-one has suggested that mothers should speak in one-word utterances! One theory might be that optimal MLU should be longer, but only a bit longer, than child MLU, through a process of scaffolding. This would predict a positive correlation between maternal MLU and child MLU, but in fact Furrow et al. (1979) report a negative correlation. Some of the conflicting results may be due to the different age levels of the children and the fact that sample sizes tend to be small. The controversy can only be resolved by further analyses of real conversations carried out in naturalistic settings, preferably on representative samples of children.

Researchers have also explored the ways in which social interaction between adults and children reflects cultural attitudes and beliefs about children. The child-rearing practices in Samoa, for example, are quite different from the child-centred ways of Western culture. There society is stratified according to rank and the methods of child-rearing reflect the social levels. Children are not treated as partners in dialogue but are spoken 'at' through songs or rhythmical vocalizations. Speech is loud and sharp, and is not simplified by adults as appears to be the case in the A–C speech of the West. The onus is on the child to make himself clear to the adult – no allowance is made. If the utterances are not intelligible then adults do not respond to them.

Schieffelin (1990) reports on the Kaluli of Papua New Guinea who develop language despite the fact that mothers and babies do not appear to engage in mutual eye-contact as is customary in Western society. In this society conversation is given a high status. However, the Kaluli do not talk at any length about their feelings. Kaluli mothers usually put babies in such a position as to be seen by others and to see others, but they do not engage in mutual gaze. Although Kaluli mothers are very attentive to their infants, they do not seem to view them as conversational partners, so they are rarely addressed except to call them by name or in the use of expressive vocalizations. When the babies are 6–12 months old adults begin to speak to them using short utterances. Teaching is done by giving the child a model utterance and then instructing the child to repeat it. When an adult talks to an infant, the mothers reply on the part of their infants in a high-pitched child-like voice. Such exchanges seem to be designed to foster certain social relationships rather than to teach language.

Work with blind children, who also learn to speak without mutual eye-gaze and peek-a-boo games, indicates that joint attention seems to develop whatever the means of achieving it may be. Blind babies obviously do not 'look', but they learn how to direct their parents' attention and may even use the word 'look'. Transcripts of Kaluli children and parents talking indicate that they also develop mutual points of focus. It could be that interactions between adults and babies do not occur according to one particular biologically designed choreography (Schieffelin and Ochs, 1988, p. 127) but it does happen in all these different environments.

Summary

Research into Adult–Child (A–C) speech (see box 10.2) indicates that adults' and peers' feedback plays an important role in children's language learning, but that the principles of reinforcement and imitation are not in themselves sufficient to explain how the process occurs.

As the painstaking analysis of real-life conversations between parents and their children has shown, children do not directly imitate adult language and adults do not normally use reinforcement techniques to teach their children to speak. Rather, infants are given speech by adults which has the intent of the speech clearly marked so that, by the age of 12 months, they can respond to patterns in an appropriate way – e.g. they look when there is rising intonation. There are various explanations about how infants are able not only to respond to intonation but also to identify individual words. In A–C speech individual words seem to be emphasized in certain ways and this can help the young child.

The presence of involved adults and children who use a form of A–C speech closely adapted to the child's level, and who recast sentences in a form to which the child has access, seems to provide an environment in which language will flourish.

◀Further Reading▶▶

A useful book, which shows how the study of children's talk gives us rich insights into the ways in which they understand their social world, is C. Garvey 1984: *Children's Talk*, London: Fontana. Garvey discusses turn-taking in conversation and shows how young children learn to adapt their speech to different social contexts.

D. Stern 1990: *Diary of a Baby*, Harmondsworth: Penguin, takes everyday interactions and describes them from the two perspectives of adult and child. This is a highly original attempt to enter the inner world of the baby.

For more advanced reading, D. Messer 1994: *The Development of Communication from Social Interaction to Language*, Chichester: Wiley, describes the development of communication and language from birth to 3 years. He discusses a number of research traditions in the field, notably those which emphasize language as an innate process and those which stress language as the outcome of learning.

For reference, J. Rosenblith 1992: *In the Beginning: Development from Conception to Age Two*, London: Sage, gives an exhaustive review of research into the early years of the child and provides a scholarly synthesis of current thinking in the field. A clear introduction to Chomsky's ideas is provided by J. Lyons 1985: *Chomsky*, London: Fontana.

On the subject of story development, S. Engel 1994: *The Stories Children Tell*, New York: W. H. Freeman, argues that through hearing and telling stories children are enabled to understand more deeply the people and events in their lives. She examines language use, the development of the concept of story and the ways in which parents and teachers can nurture the child's narrative voice.

D. Wood 1988: *How Children Think and Learn*, Oxford: Blackwell (chapter 4, 'Language and learning'), describes competing views on the relationship between language, learning and educational achievement.

S. Pinker 1994: *The Language Instinct*, London: Allen Lane, Penguin Press, argues persuasively that language is an instinct. The book is scholarly but also immensely readable and draws on research from a wide range of sources.

◀ Discussion Points ▶ ▶ ▶

1   What is the developmental importance of pre-linguistic communication between adult and baby?
2   Discuss how research findings on A–C speech can help parents to talk more effectively with their young children.
3   How important is it to take semantic (or meaning) aspects into account when examining the language of young children?
4   Does the study of child grammar in the preschool years help us to understand the process through which children acquire language?
5   Evaluate the belief that language development is an innately guided process.

Box 10.1
Categorizing sounds and learning to read: a causal connection

The investigators in this study wished to test the hypothesis that the child's experience of categorizing sounds, as in rhyming and alliteration, has a considerable effect on later success in learning to read and spell. To do this, they used two methods – a large-scale correlational study, and a small-scale experimental study.

The correlational study started with 118 4-year-olds and 285 5-year-olds. None could yet read. The children were tested on their ability to categorize sounds, by detecting the odd word out, i.e. the one that did not share a common sound, in a series of words. This common sound could be at the end of the word (e.g. bun, hut, gun, sun), the middle (e.g. hug, pig, dig, wig) or the beginning (bud, bun, bus, rug). Where it came at the end or the middle of the word, the task was to spot words which rhymed. Where it came at the beginning of the word, the children's awareness of alliteration was tested.

In addition, each child was given a test of verbal

intelligence (the English Picture Vocabulary Test, or EPVT), and a memory test. Four years later, when the children were 8 or 9 years old, Bradley and Bryant gave them standardized tests of reading and spelling. They also tested their IQ, using the WISC-R, and their mathematical ability on a standardized test. (By this time, 368 of the original 403 children remained in the project sample.)

There were high correlations between the initial sound categorization scores (at ages 4–5 years) and the children's reading and spelling scores 4 years later (box table 10.1.1). This in itself does not prove the hypothesis that the ability to categorize sounds has a causal connection with reading success. Some third factor might lie behind both abilities. For example, general intelligence, or perhaps memory for words, might help in both. However, as can be seen in box table 10.1.1, the correlations of reading and spelling scores with sound categorization are a bit higher than with the EPVT or memory scores. This means that while intelligence and memory may explain some of the association between sound categorization and reading and spelling, it is unlikely that they can explain all of it.

To provide more definite evidence for the causal relationship which this suggested, the investigators carried out a training study with an experimental design (a field experiment, see chapter 1), using 65 children from the larger sample. They were selected from those whose original scores on sound categorization were at least two standard deviations below the mean.

Two experimental groups received training in sound categorization skills for 40 individual sessions over 2 years. In Group 1 ($n = 13$) coloured pictures of familiar objects were used to teach the children that the same word could share common beginning (hen, hat), common middle (hen, pet) and common end (hen, man) sounds with other words. This training experience was purely concerned with increasing awareness of rhyming and alliteration. For Group 2 ($n = 13$), in addition to the rhyming and alliteration training, the children were shown plastic letters and taught how to identify the sounds which the names of the pictures had in common with particular letters ('c' for 'cat' and 'cup'). The relationship between common sounds and letters of the alphabet which represented them was made clear (plate 10.1.1).

Two control groups were also used. Group 3 ($n = 26$) were taught over the same period of time to categorize the same pictures in a conceptual way (e.g. hen and bat are animals: hen and pig are farm animals) but received no tuition in sound categorization. Group 4 ($n = 13$) received no training at all. All four groups were matched for age, initial EPVT scores and initial scores on sound categorization. The results are shown in box table 10.1.2. Group 1, the experimental group which had been trained on sound categorization only, was ahead of Group 3 (the group trained to categorize conceptually) by 3–4 months in reading and spelling levels. The second experimental group, Group 2, which had been trained on sound categorization and alphabetic letters as well, performed best of all in reading and spelling. The authors conclude that not only does

Box Table 10.1.1   Correlations between initial sound categorization, EVPT and memory scores, and final reading and spelling levels

| | | Initial scores | | | | |
| | | Sound categorization | | EPVT | | Memory | |
Age (yr)	4	5	4	5	4	5
Final reading score (Schonell test)	0.57	0.44	0.52	0.39	0.40	0.22
Final spelling score (Schonell test)	0.48	0.44	0.33	0.31	0.33	0.22

Source: Bradley and Bryant, 1983

Box Plate 10.1.1 Children receiving training in sound categorization skills: (a) selecting pictures with names which have common sounds (e.g. bat, mat, hat); (b) identifying sounds with the aid of plastic letters.

training in sound categorization have an influence on reading and spelling, but that if it is combined with alphabetic teaching, it will be even more effective. They also argue that the effect is specific to reading and spelling since the differences among the four groups in scores in the mathematics test were considerably smaller and not statistically significant.

The drawbacks of this training study are that the numbers in the experimental groups are small, and some differences are not statistically significant (for example, the scores for Group 1 in themselves do not differ significantly from those in Group 3). Also,

Box Table 10.1.2   Mean final reading, spelling and mathematics levels, and intelligence test scores, in groups from the training study

	Experimental groups		Control groups		Significance of group differences
	1	2	3	4	
Reading age in months (Schonell test)	92.2	97.0	88.5	84.5	$p < 0.01$
Spelling age in months (Schonell test)	86.0	98.8	81.8	75.2	$p < 0.001$
Mathematics score	91.3	91.1	88.0	84.1	n.s.
Final IQ (WISC-R)	97.2	101.2	103.0	100.2	n.s.

Source: Adapted from Bradley and Bryant, 1983

as the investigators point out, we do not know how well such experimental results would generalize to a wider spectrum of children in real-life teaching conditions.

This is where the strength of combining two methods comes in. The original correlational study strongly suggests that the relationship between sound categorization skills and later reading and spelling abilities is an ecologically valid one. Taken together, these results provide strong evidence for a moderate degree of causal influence along the lines the investigators hypothesized. The educa-tional implications are considered further in P. Bryant and L. Bradley 1985: *Children's Reading Problems*, Oxford: Basil Blackwell, and in P. Bryant, M. MacLean and L. Bradley 1990: Rhyme, language and children's reading, *Applied Psycholinguistics*, 11, 237–52. In view of the large number of children who do experience reading difficulties, this study offers practical guidelines for identifying specific problem areas and intervening to overcome them.

Based on material in L. Bradley and P. E. Bryant 1983: *Nature*, 301, 419–21.

Box 10.2
Facilitating children's syntax development

Nelson had already shown (Nelson et al., 1973) that the recasting of children's incomplete sen-tences by adults had a positive effect on both performance on a sentence-imitation task, and complexity of grammar use in spontaneous speech. In this experiment he aimed to discover whether these effects were specific. Would children whose utterances were recast into complex questions show improvement in the use of question forms? Would children whose utterances were recast into sentences that contained complex verbs show greater use of verbs? To answer these questions he devised an experimental intervention study.

His sample was 12 children (six boys and six girls), aged 28–29 months, who all lacked two cate-gories of syntactic structures in their spontaneous speech. These were complex questions and com-plex verbs of the type given below:

Complex questions

1   Tag questions   For example 'I changed them round, didn't I?' where 'didn't I?' is tagged on to the end of a statement.

2   'Wh-' negative   Negative questions beginning
    question   with 'what', 'why', 'where',

'who', etc., e.g. 'Why can't I go?'

3   Other negative questions   For example, 'Doesn't it hurt?' or 'It won't fit?'

Complex verbs

1   Single verbs in future or conditional tense   For example, 'He will help me' or 'He would help me'.

2   Sentences in which two verbs were used   For example, 'He will run and jump' or 'The bear ate the girls who visited'.

Two one-hour sessions with each child were taped to determine initial language levels. Assignment of children in groups was based on mean length of utterance (MLU) in words. Three boys and three girls were assigned to an intervention schedule focused on complex questions; the remaining six children were assigned to receive an intervention designed to facilitate the use of complex verbs. Each

group had an average MLU of 3.69 words per utterance (range 3.09–4.29). Both groups were closely comparable in terms of the presence or absence of complex verbs and complex questions in their spontaneous speech during these two sessions.

Five 1-hour sessions of intervention were scheduled for each child. Three women were the experimenters, each one working with four children (two assigned to question intervention and two to verb intervention).

In question intervention sessions the experimenter frequently recast the child's sentences in the form of tag or negative questions. For example, when one child said, 'You can't get in', the researcher replied, 'No, I can't get in, can I?' If recastings did not come readily, the experimenter constructed new examples. When one child said, 'And you're a girl', the experimenter replied, 'Right! And aren't you a little girl?'

Similarly in verb intervention sessions both recastings and new constructions were used. If the child said, 'Where it go?', the adult replied, 'It will

Box Table 10.2.1   Type of sentence structure used by each participant (numbered) after intervention but not prior to intervention

Sentence type	Question intervention						Verb intervention					
	1	2	3	4	5	6	1	2	3	4	5	6
Tag questions	+		+	+	+							+
'Wh–' negative questions			+									
Other negative questions		+										
Future tense (one verb)						+				+		
Conditional tense (one verb)						+	+	+				+
Future tense (two verbs)						+	+				+
Conditional tense (two verbs)						+					
Past tense (two verbs)						+		+	+			+

Note: Sign tests show the results to be significant ($p < 0.01$) for both question and verb intervention. MLU for both groups was not affected. Examples of sentences with complex questions or verb structures which appeared after intervention are given in the text.

go there'. When one child said, 'I got it, I reached it', the adult said, 'You got under the bed and reached it'.

The children's utterances during the fourth and fifth sessions (the last two intervention sessions) were recorded. Each child's transcript was scored for presence or absence of sentences containing complex questions or complex verbs, using the measures shown in box table 10.2.1. Analysis of the data revealed clear-cut effects of the interventions. Complex questions, which had been lacking before intervention, were used by all six children in the question intervention group; only one of the children in this group (subject 6) also showed use of complex verbs. The opposite pattern held for the acquisition of new verb forms. All the children in the verb intervention group used complex verbs which they had not expressed before intervention; only one (subject 6) also used new complex questions. Sign tests showed the results to be significant for both question and verb intervention. MLU was not affected for either group.

Nelson concluded that this experiment increases our understanding of how children get information from adults about syntax. In comparing the experimenters' recasting with normal parental responses, he noted that in real life adults do use negative and tag questions, and complex verbs when they talk to their children, but they do not use them frequently. So why did recastings of children's sentences have the effect shown by this experiment?

Nelson suggested that the experimental recasting probably drew the child's attention to the new forms. The experience of hearing complex questions and verbs was not a wholly new one to the child but the researchers, by reworking the child's own sentences, pointed attention to a more complex form which was close to the child's existing language use and which made immediate sense to the child. The experimenter's response to 'Donkey ran' of 'The donkey did run didn't he?' was more complex but also entirely appropriate in a playful, conversational content. The child was thus able to make a direct comparison between her own utterances and the sentence structure of the adult's reply. The introduction of new grammatical forms which are still closely tied to the child's language use thus seems to be one way of extending language development.

Based on material in K. Nelson 1977: *Developmental Psychology*, 13, 101–7.

11 Cognition: Piaget's Theory

Jean Piaget (1896–1980) was born in Neuchâtel, Switzerland. At an early age he showed a keen interest in observing animals in their natural environment. At the age of 10 he published his first article, a description of an albino sparrow which he had observed in the park; before he was 18 years old, journals had accepted several of his papers on the subject of molluscs. During his adolescent years a second major intellectual interest grew from his study of philosophy, in particular the branch of philosophy concerned with knowledge – 'epistemology'. His undergraduate studies, however, were in the field of biology and his doctoral dissertation was on molluscs.

Piaget then worked for a period at Bleuler's psychiatric clinic in Zurich where he became interested in psychoanalysis. As a result, he went to the Sorbonne University in Paris in 1919 to study clinical psychology. Here he could also pursue his continuing interest in epistemology. While in Paris, he worked at the Binet Laboratory with Theodore Simon on the standardization of intelligence tests (see chapter 15). Although his task was to examine children's correct responses to test items, Piaget became much more interested in the mistakes the children made and in the mental processes they brought to bear on these test items. Binet was a French psychologist who had pioneered studies of children's thinking, and his method of observing children in their natural settings was one which Piaget followed himself when he left the Binet Laboratory to begin his own research programme.

Piaget saw that through the discipline of psychology he had an opportunity to forge links between epistemology and biology. By integrating the disciplines of psychology, biology and epistemology, Piaget aimed to develop a scientific approach to the understanding of knowledge – the nature

Plate 11.1   Jean Piaget in 1936 (courtesy of the Archives J. J. Rousseau).

of knowledge and the ways in which an individual acquires knowledge. Although the quantitative methods of the French intelligence testers did not appeal to Piaget, he was strongly influenced by the developmental work of Binet. As a result, he integrated his experiences of psychiatric work in Bleuler's clinic with the questioning and observational strategies which he had learned from Binet. Out of this fusion emerged the 'clinical interview' – an open-ended, conversational technique for eliciting children's thinking processes. His interest was in the child's own judgements and explanations. He was not testing a particular hypothesis, but rather looking for an explanation of how the child comes to understand his or her world. The method is not easy, and Piaget's researchers were trained for a year before they actually collected data. They learned the art of asking the right questions and testing the truth of what the children said.

Piaget's life was devoted to the search for the mechanisms of biological adaptation on the one hand, and the analysis of logical thought on the other. He wrote more than 50 books and hundreds of articles, revising many of his early ideas in later life. In essence Piaget's theory is concerned with the human need to discover and to acquire deeper knowledge and understanding. Piaget's prolific output of ideas suggests that he was constantly constructing and reconstructing his theoretical system, but this, as we shall see, was quite consistent with his philosophy of knowledge.

The main theme of Piaget's theory was that adaptation is based on the achievement of a successful equilibrium in the interactions between the organism and the environment. This concept grew out of his early interest in biology, and near the end of his life he wrote in the foreword to the anthology of his writings by Gruber and Vonèche (1977, p. xi) that he had always viewed the mechanisms of biological adaptation as the source for epistemology, that is, for knowledge itself. In Piaget's view, the individual is always in the process of reconstructing reality: the only way in which we come to have knowledge of our world is through a process of continual construction of it. There is no point at which we can say 'I have arrived. I know'; there is always something else ahead:

> In epistemology . . . I am happy with what I have been able to glimpse, although very conscious of the gaps to be filled. (Piaget, 1977, p. xi)

In this chapter we will describe the model of cognitive structure developed by Piaget. We will also take notice of modifications and reinterpretations which subsequent researchers have made to Piaget's ideas. Although many aspects of Piaget's theory are now questioned, no one denies the valuable contribution he made to our understanding of the thinking processes of both children and adults.

Piaget argued that in order to understand how children think we have to look at the qualitative development of their ability to solve problems. Let us look at two examples of children's thinking. The first example is taken from one of Piaget's dialogues with a 7-year-old:

Adult: Does the moon move or not?
Child: When we go, it goes.
Adult: What makes it move?
Child: We do.
Adult: How?
Child: When we walk. It goes by itself.

(Piaget, 1929, pp. 146–7)

From this, and many similar observations, Piaget described a period during childhood which was characterized by egocentrism. Because the moon appears to move with the child, she concludes that it does indeed do so. But later, with the growth of logic, she makes a shift from her own egocentric perspective and learns to distinguish what she sees from what she knows. Gruber and Vonèche (1977, p. xix) quote an observation by Anne Roe of a child – later to become a scientist – as he tackled this problem. He sent his little brother down to the garden to find out what each of them saw when one of them was moving and the other standing still. What was self-evident to the younger child – that the moon moved with him – was seen by the older boy as an inconsistency which could be solved by logic.

The second example is adapted from Piaget's research into children's understanding of quantity. Suppose John, aged 4, and Mary, aged 7, are given a problem. Two glasses, A and B, are of equal capacity but glass A is short and wide and glass B is tall and narrow (see figure 11.1). Glass A is filled to a certain height and the children are each asked, separately, to pour liquid into glass B so that it contains the same amount as glass A. In spite of the striking difference in the proportions of the two containers, John cannot grasp that the smaller diameter of glass B requires a higher level of liquid. To Mary, John's response is incredibly stupid: of course you have to add more to glass B. From Piaget's perspective both responses are revealing. John cannot 'see' that the liquid in A and the liquid in B are not equal, since he is using a qualitatively different kind of reasoning, not yet having the mental operations (or schemas) that will enable him to understand conservation. Mary finds it difficult to understand why John cannot see his mistake.

Piaget proposed that the essence of knowledge is activity. This may refer to the infant directly manipulating objects and so learning about their properties; it may refer to a child pouring liquid from one glass to another to find out which has more in it; or it may refer to the adolescent forming hypotheses in order to solve a scientific problem. In all these examples, the child is learning through action, whether physical (e.g. exploring a wooden brick) or mental (e.g. thinking of different outcomes and what they mean). Piaget's emphasis on activity was important in stimulating the child-centred approach to education, because he believed that in order to learn, children not only need to manipulate objects; they also need to manipulate ideas. We discuss the educational implications of Piaget's theory later in this chapter.

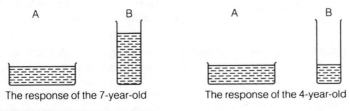

The response of the 7-year-old   The response of the 4-year-old

Figure 11.1   The conservation of liquid.

◀Underlying Assumptions: Structure and Organization▶▶▶

Using observations, dialogues and small-scale experiments, Piaget suggested that children progress through a series of stages in their thinking each of which corresponds to broad changes in the structure or logic of their intelligence (see table 11.1). Piaget called the main stages of development the sensori-motor, pre-operational, concrete operational and formal operational stages and emphasized that they occur in that order.

Piaget's structures are sets of mental operations which can be applied to objects, beliefs, ideas or anything in the child's world. Such a mental operation is called a *schema* (plural, schemas or schemata). The schemas are seen as evolving structures, in other words, structures which grow and change from one stage to the next. We will look at each stage in detail in the next section, but before we do so, we need to look at Piaget's concepts of the unchanging (or 'invariant', to use his term) aspects of thought; that is, those broad

Table 11.1 The stages of intellectual development according to Piaget

Stage	Age (yr)	Characteristics
Sensori-motor	0–2	The baby knows about the world through actions and sensory information. She learns to differentiate herself from the environment; the child begins to understand causality in time and space; and the capacity to form internal mental representations emerges.
Pre-operational	2–7	Through the symbolic use of language and intuitive problem-solving; the child begins to understand about classification of objects. But children's thinking is characterized by egocentrism, focusing on just one aspect of a task and lack of operations like compensation and reversibility. By the end of this stage, children can take another's perspective and can understand the conservation of number.
Concrete operational	7–12	The child understands conservation of mass, length, weight and volume; she can more easily take the perspective of others; can classify and order, as well as organize objects into series. The child is still tied to the immediate experience but within these limitations can perform logical mental operations.
Formal operational	12	Abstract reasoning begins. The child can now manipulate ideas in her mind as well as actual objects and people; she can speculate about the possible; she is able to reason deductively, and formulate and test hypotheses.

characteristics of intelligent activity which remain the same at all ages. These are the organization of schemas and their *adaptation* through *assimilation* and *accommodation*.

Organization   Piaget used this term to refer to the inborn capacity to co-ordinate existing cognitive structures, or schemas, and combine them into more complex systems. For example, the infant of 3 months has learned to combine looking and grasping with the earlier reflex of sucking. She can do all three together when feeding, an ability which the newborn baby did not have. Or at the age of 2 Ben has learned to climb downstairs, to carry objects without dropping them and to open doors. He can combine all three operations to deliver a newspaper to his grandmother in the basement flat. In other words, each separate operation combines into a new action which is more complex than the sum of the parts.

Organization also grows in complexity as the schemas become more elaborate. Piaget described the development of a particular action schema in his son Laurent as he attempted to strike a hanging object. At first Laurent only made random movements towards the object, but by the age of 6 months the movements had become deliberate and well directed. As Piaget described it, by 6 months Laurent possessed the mental structure which guided the action involved in hitting a toy. He had also learned to accommodate his actions to the weight, size and shape of the toy and its distance from him.

This leads us to the other invariant function identified by Piaget – *adaptation*. By adaptation he means the striving of the organism for balance (or equilibrium) with the environment, which is achieved through the complementary processes of assimilation and accommodation. Through *assimilation* the child 'takes in' a new experience and fits it into an existing schema. For example, a child may have learnt the words 'dog' and 'car'. For a while all animals are called 'dogs' (i.e. different animals taken into a schema related to the child's understanding of dog), or all four-wheeled vehicles might be considered as 'cars'. This process is balanced by *accommodation*, in which the child adjusts an existing schema to fit in with the nature of the environment. From experience, the child begins to perceive that cats can be distinguished from dogs (and he or she may develop different schemas for these two types of animals) and that cars can be discriminated from other vehicles.

Through the twin processes of assimilation and accommodation the child achieves a new state of equilibrium. This equilibrium, however, is not permanent. The balance will soon be upset as the child assimilates further new experiences or accommodates his existing schemas to another new idea. In a sense, equilibrium only prepares the child for disequilibrium, that is further learning and adaptation; the two cannot be thought of separately. Assimilation helps the child to consolidate mental structures; accommodation results in growth and change. All adaptation contains components of both processes. If accommodation occurred without assimilation, the result would be disorganized, unpredictable behaviour; by contrast, assimilation without accommodation would lead to rigid and unchanging behaviour patterns. The striving for balance between assimilation and accommodation results in the child's intrinsic motivation to learn, says Piaget, and when new experiences are close to the child's capacity to respond, then conditions are at their best for change and growth to occur.

◀The Stages of Cognitive Development▶▶▶

Piaget considered intellectual development to be a continuous process of assimilation and accommodation. Although we go on here to describe the four stages he identified, there is no sharp dividing line between each. The order of stages is the same for all children, but the ages at which they are achieved may vary from one child to another.

Table 11.2 Substages of the sensori-motor period according to Piaget

Substage	Age (mth)	Characteristics
Reflex activity	0–1	The infant practises the innate reflexes, e.g. sucking, looking. Behaviour largely, but not entirely, assimilative.
Primary circular reactions	1–4	The behaviour is primary in the sense that it is basically made up of reflexes or motor responses; it is circular in the sense that the child repeats it. The primary circular reactions centre on the baby's own body. There appears to be no differentiation between self and outside world.
Secondary circular reactions	4–10	The infant now focuses on objects rather than on her own body. She begins to make interesting things happen, e.g. moving a hanging toy by hitting it. She has begun to change her surroundings intentionally.
Co-ordination of secondary circular reactions	10–12	She begins to combine schemas in order to achieve goals, or to solve problems in new situations. For example, she will use the hitting schema in order to knock down a barrier between herself and a toy.
Tertiary circular reactions	12–18	She actively uses trial and error methods to learn about objects. Increased mobility enables her to experiment and explore. Learns new ways of solving problems and discovers more about the properties of the environment.
Internal representation	18–24	The beginning of mental action, and insightful solutions to problems. Objects and people can be represented symbolically; behaviour can be imitated from previous observations.

◄The Sensori-motor Stage►►►

During the sensori-motor stage the child changes from a newborn, who focuses almost entirely on immediate sensory and motor experiences, to a toddler who possesses a rudimentary capacity for thinking. Piaget described in detail the process by which this occurs, by carefully documenting his own children's behaviour. On the basis of such observations, carried out over the first 2 years of life, Piaget divided the sensori-motor period into six substages (see table 11.2).

The first stage, *reflex activity*, included the reflexive behaviours and spontaneous rhythmic activity with which the infant was born. Piaget called the second substage *primary circular reactions*. His use of the term 'circular' was to emphasize the way that children will repeat an activity, especially one which is pleasing or satisfying (e.g. thumb sucking), and the term 'primary' refers to simple behaviours which are derived from the reflexes of the first period (e.g. thumb sucking develops as the thumb is assimilated into a schema based on the innate suckling reflex).

Secondary circular reactions again refer to the child's willingness to repeat actions, but the word 'secondary' points to behaviours which are the child's own. In other words, she is not limited to just repeating actions based on early reflexes, but having initiated new actions can repeat these if they are satisfying. At the same time, such actions tend to be directed outside the child (unlike simple actions like thumb sucking) and are aimed at influencing the environment around her. This is Piaget's description of his daughter Jacqueline at 5 months of age kicking her legs (in itself a primary circular reaction) in what becomes a secondary circular reaction as the leg movement is not just repeated for itself, but is initiated in the presence of a doll.

> Jacqueline looks at a doll attached to a string which is stretched from the hood to the handle of the cradle. The doll is at approximately the same level as the child's feet. Jacqueline moves her feet and finally strikes the doll, whose movement she immediately notices . . . The activity of the feet grows increasingly regular whereas Jacqueline's eyes are fixed on the doll. Moreover, when I remove the doll Jacqueline occupies herself quite differently; when I replace it, after a moment, she immediately starts to move her legs again. (Piaget, 1936, p. 182)

In behaving as she did Jacqueline seemed to have established a general relation between her movement and the doll's and was engaged in a secondary circular reaction.

Co-ordination of secondary circular reactions   As the word co-ordination implies, it is in this substage that children start to combine different behavioural schemas. In the following extract Piaget describes how his daughter (aged 8 months) combines several schemas, such as 'sucking an object' and 'grasping an object' in a series of co-ordinated actions when playing with a new object.

> Jacqueline grasps an unfamiliar cigarette case which I present to her. At
> first she examines it very attentively, turns it over, then holds it in both
> hands while making the sound *apff* (a kind of hiss which she usually
> makes in the presence of people). After that she rubs it against the
> wicker of her cradle then draws herself up while looking at it, then
> swings it above her and finally puts it into her mouth. (Piaget, 1936, p.
> 284)

Jacqueline's behaviour illustrates how a new object is assimilated to various existing schemas in the fourth substage. In the following stage, that of *tertiary circular reactions*, children's behaviours become more flexible and when they repeat actions they may do so with variations which can lead to new results. By repeating actions with variations children are, in effect, accommodating established schemas to new situations and needs.

The final substage of the sensori-motor period is called the substage of *internal representation*. Internal representation refers to the child's achievement of mental representation. In previous substages the child has interacted with the world via her physical motor schema; in other words, she has acted directly on the world. But by the final substage she can act indirectly on the world because she has a mental representation of the world. This means that instead of just manipulating the world around her directly she can also manipulate her mental representation of the world; i.e., she can think and plan. What evidence did Piaget put forward to demonstrate that children have achieved mental representations by the end of the sensori-motor period?

He pointed out that by this substage children have a full concept of *object permanence*. Piaget noticed that very young infants ignored even attractive objects once they were out of sight. For example, if an infant was reaching for a toy, but then the toy was covered with a cloth, the infant would immediately lose interest in it, she would not attempt to search for it and might just look away. According to Piaget it was only in the later substages that children demonstrated an awareness (by searching and trying to retrieve the object) that the object was permanently present even if it was temporarily out of sight. Searching for an object which cannot be seen directly implies that the child has a memory of the object, i.e. a mental representation of it.

Piaget suggested that it was only towards the end of the sensori-motor period that children demonstrated novel patterns of behaviour in response to a problem. For example, if children want to reach for a toy, but there is another object between them and the toy, younger children might just try to reach the toy directly. It may be that in the course of trying to reach the toy they happen to knock the object out of the way and succeed in reaching the toy itself, but this is best described as 'trial and error' performance. A child in the later substages of the sensori-motor period might solve the problem not by reaching for the toy immediately but by first removing the object and then getting the toy easily. If a child carries out such structured behaviour it implies that she was able to plan ahead and to plan ahead indicates that she had a mental representation of what she was going to do.

Piaget gave an example of planned behaviour by Jacqueline at 20 months. She is trying to solve the problem of opening a door while carrying two blades of grass at the same time.

> She stretches out her right hand towards the knob but sees that she cannot turn it without letting go of the grass. She puts the grass on the floor, opens the door, picks up the grass again and enters. But when she wants to leave the room things become complicated. She puts the grass on the floor and grasps the door knob. But then she perceives that in pulling the door towards her she will simultaneously chase away the grass which she placed between the door and the threshold. She therefore picks it up in order to put it outside the door's zone of movement. (Piaget, 1936, pp. 376–7)

Jacqueline solved the problem of the grass and the door before she opened the door. In other words, she must have had a mental representation of the problem, which permitted her to work out the solution before she acted.

A third line of evidence for mental representations comes from Piaget's observations of *deferred imitation*. This is when children carry out a behaviour which is copying other behaviour which they have seen some time before. Piaget provides a good example of this:

> At 16 months Jacqueline had a visit from a little boy of 18 months who she used to see from time to time, and who, in the course of the afternoon, got into a terrible temper. He screamed as he tried to get out of a playpen and pushed it backward, stamping his feet. Jacqueline stood watching him in amazement, never having witnessed such a scene before. The next day, she herself screamed in her playpen and tried to move it, stamping her foot lightly several times in succession. (Piaget, 1951, p. 63)

If Jacqueline was able to imitate the little boy's behaviour a day later she must have retained an image of his behaviour; in other words, she had a mental representation of what she had seen from the day before, and that representation provided the basis for her own copy of the temper tantrum.

In summary, during the sensori-motor period the child progresses from very simple and limited reflex behaviours at birth, to complex behaviours at the end of the period. The more complex behaviours depend on the progressive combination and elaboration of schema, but are, at first, limited to direct interaction with the world – hence the name Piaget gave to this whole period because he thought of the child developing through her sensori-motor interaction with the environment. It is only towards the end of the period that the child is freed from immediate interaction by developing the ability to mentally represent her world. With this ability the child can then manipulate her mental images (or symbols) of her world; in other words, she can act on her thoughts about the world as well as on the world itself.

◀Reinterpretations of Piaget: the Sensori-motor Stage▶▶▶

Piaget's observations of babies during this first stage have been largely confirmed by subsequent researchers, but he may have under-estimated children's mental capacity to organize the sensory and motor information they take in. Several investigators have shown that children have abilities and concepts earlier than Piaget thought.

Bower (1982) examined Piaget's hypothesis that young children did not have an appreciation of objects if they were out of sight. Children a few months old were shown an object, then a screen was moved across in front of the object, and finally, the screen was moved back to its original position. There were two conditions in the experiment, in one condition when the screen was moved back the object was still in place, but in the second condition the object had been removed and there was only an empty space. The children's heart rate was monitored to measure changes which reflected surprise. According to Piaget young children do not retain information about objects which are no longer present, and if this is the case there would be no reason for them to expect an object behind the screen when it was moved back. In other words, children should not show any reaction in the second condition. However, Bower found that children showed more surprise in the second condition than in the first condition. Bower inferred that the children's reaction was because they *had* expected the object to re-appear. If so, this would be evidence that young children retained an image or representation of the object in their head, and this could be interpreted as children having a concept of object permanence at an earlier age than Piaget suggested.

In another experiment, Baillargeon and DeVos (1991) showed 3-month-old children objects which moved behind a screen and then re-appeared from the other side of the screen. The upper half of the screen had a window in it. In one condition children saw a short object move behind the screen. The object was below the level of the window in the screen and therefore it was not visible again until it had passed all the way behind the screen. In a second condition a tall object was moved behind the screen. This object was large enough to be seen through the window as it passed behind the screen. However, Baillargeon and DeVos created an 'impossible event' by passing the tall object all the way behind the screen but without it appearing through the window. Infants showed more interest by looking longer at the event when it included the tall object than when it included the short object. Baillargeon and DeVos argued that this was because the children had expected the tall object to appear in the window. If so, this would be further evidence that young children are aware of the continued existence of objects even when they have been out of view. The results from Bower (1982) and from Baillargeon and DeVos (1991) indicate that children have some understanding of object permanence earlier than Piaget suggested.

Other researchers have considered Piaget's conclusion that it is only towards the end of the sensori-motor period that children demonstrate planned actions which reflect their ability to form a mental representation of the event. Willatts (1989) placed an attractive toy out of reach of 9-month-old children. The toy was placed on a cloth (and therefore children could pull the cloth to move the toy closer), but the children could not reach the cloth directly because Willatts placed a light barrier between the child and the cloth (and therefore they had to move the barrier to reach the cloth). Willatts found that children were able to get the toy by carrying out the appropriate series of actions – first moving the barrier, and then pulling the cloth to bring the toy within reach. Most importantly, many of the children carried out these actions on the first occasion they were faced with the problem, and did not need to go through a period of 'trial and error', learning to work out how to get the toy. If children at this age can demonstrate novel, planned actions, it can be inferred from such behaviour that they are operating on a mental representation of the world which they can use to organize their behaviour before carrying it out. This is earlier than Piaget suggested.

Piaget pointed out that deferred imitation was evidence that children must have a memory representation of what they had seen at an earlier time. Infants can imitate facial expressions from birth (Meltzoff and Moore, 1983), but this type of imitation is performed while the stimulus being imitated is present (in other words, there is no need to store a memory of the stimulus). According to Paiget imitation based on stored representations only develops towards the end of the sensori-motor period. However, Meltzoff and Moore (1994) showed that 6-week-old children could imitate a behaviour a day after they had seen the original behaviour. In Meltzoff and Moore's study some children saw an adult make a facial gesture (for example, stick out her tongue) and others just saw the adult's face while she maintained a neutral expression. The following day all the children saw the same adult again, but on this occasion she maintained a passive face. Compared with children who had not seen any gesture, the children who had seen the tongue protrusion gesture the day before were more likely to make tongue protrusions to the adult the second time they saw her. Meltzoff and Moore argued that to do this the 6-week-old children must have had a memory representation of the gesture. If so, this is evidence of mental representations at a much earlier age than Piaget proposed.

◀The Pre-operational Stage▶▶▶

Piaget divided this stage into the pre-conceptual period (2–4 years) and the intuitive period (4–7 years).

The pre-conceptual period   The pre-conceptual period builds on the capacity for internal, or symbolic, thought which has developed in the sensori-motor period. In the pre-conceptual period there is a rapid increase in children's language which, in Piaget's view, results from the development of symbolic thought. Piaget differs from other theorists who argue that thought grows out of linguistic competence. However, as we saw in chapter 10, Piaget maintained that thought arises out of action and this idea is supported by research into the cognitive abilities of deaf children who, despite limitations in language, are able to reason and solve problems. Piaget argued that thought shapes language far more than language shapes thought, at least during the pre-conceptual period. Symbolic thought is also expressed in imaginative play (see chapter 6).

Despite the rapid development of children's thinking and language in the pre-conceptual period Piaget identified two limitations in the child's abilities at this stage – *animism* and *egocentrism*. Piaget noted that children at this stage may attribute feelings and intentions to inanimate objects: the moon follows them, teddy has a sore head, the table can kick them. Piaget called this animistic thinking.

According to Piaget, the pre-operational child is still centred in her own perspective and finds it difficult to understand that other people can look at things differently. Piaget called this 'self-centred' view of the world egocentrism. Egocentric thinking occurs because of the child's view that the universe is centred on herself. She finds it hard to 'decentre', that is, to take the perspective of another person. The following dialogue illustrates a 3-year-old child's difficulty in taking the perspective of another:

Adult: Have you any brothers or sisters?
John: Yes, a brother.
Adult: What is his name?
John: Sammy.
Adult: Does Sammy have a brother?
John: No.

John's inability to decentre makes it hard for him to realize that from Sammy's perspective, he himself is a brother.

One of Piaget's most famous experiments, and one which he described as reflecting egocentric thought, is the three mountains experiment (see figure 11.2). Piaget and Inhelder (1956) asked children between the ages of 4 and 12 years to say how a doll, placed in various positions, would view an array of three mountains from different perspectives. For example, in figure 11.2, a child might be asked to sit at position A, and a doll would be placed at one of the other positions (B, C, or D). Then the child would be asked to choose, from a set of different views of the model, the view that the doll could see. When 4- and 5-year-old children were asked to do this task they often chose the view that they themselves could see (rather than the doll's view) and it was not until 8 or 9 years of age that children could confidently work out the doll's view. Piaget interpreted this result as an example of young children's egocentricity – that they could not decentre from their own view to work out the doll's view. However, several criticisms have been made of the three mountains task. Some researchers have pointed out that it is a particularly unusual task to use with young children who might not have much familiarity with model mountain landscapes (see Donaldson, 1978). When the materials are made more familiar and the task is made less arbitrary even young children can work out the perspective of

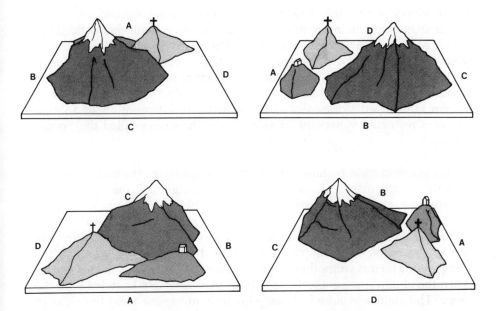

Figure 11.2   The model of the mountain range used by Piaget and Inhelder viewed from four different sides.

another character in the scene (see Borke's, 1975, study described in box 11.1).

Piaget used the three mountains task to investigate spatial perspective taking, but there are also other kinds of perspective-taking skills, some involving empathy with other people's feelings and some involving the ability to know what other people are thinking (see also chapter 13). The context within which these perspective-taking skills are expressed is an important factor, and Piaget may well have under-estimated the ability of the pre-conceptual child in this area. Let us look first at a study that investigated the child's ability to respond empathically to the feelings of another.

Borke (1971) found that children as young as 3 or 4 years are aware of other people's feelings and can take the perspective of others. Using a series of short stories she asked children between 3 and 8 years to indicate how the child in each story felt by selecting a picture of a 'sad', 'happy', 'angry' or 'afraid' face. Even 3-year-olds showed that they could empathize with the feelings of another child in some situations, a result which challenges Piaget's position that the child between the ages of 2 and 7 years is primarily egocentric. Young children could, it seemed, show awareness that 'other people have feelings and that these feelings vary according to the situation in which the individual finds herself' (Borke, 1971, p. 269).

Borke's study was open to the criticism that it did not differentiate clearly enough between the child's own response to the situation in the story and that of the character. Most children are happy at birthday parties (the scene of one story), so the child might be giving her own (egocentric) viewpoint rather than empathizing with the child in the story. With this criticism in mind, Mossler, Marvin and Greenberg (1976) investigated the ability of young children to take the perspective of another person using a task based on the notion of a secret. They tested 80 children ranging in age from 2 to 6 years, who were tested at home with their mothers. The children were shown videotaped stories and asked to make an inference about another person's restricted viewpoint. Here is one of the stories called the 'cookie story':

> A 5-year-old child is shown sitting at a kitchen table. The child stands up and walks over to his/her mother. In the sound track, the child asks, 'Mummy, can I have a cookie?' and the mother replies. 'Sure.'

Each child was shown one of the videotapes while their own mother was out of the room. Then the children watched the videotape again in the company of their own mothers, but this time the sound was turned down. Then the children were questioned about their mother's knowledge of the story. The child was asked, 'Does your mummy know what the child in the cookie story wanted?' The answers were scored as egocentric (if the child thought that her mother would have the same knowledge of the story that she herself had from watching it before) or non-egocentric (if the child said that her mother did not know what the child in the cookie story wanted).

There were developmental differences in perspective taking. Two-year-olds and all but one of the 3-year-olds gave egocentric answers. However, nearly all of the children aged 4 years or older gave non-egocentric answers, and Mossler et al. (1976) therefore concluded that children from this age could engage in conceptual perspective taking.

Piaget had suggested that the ability to make inferences about another person's thoughts, feelings and motives does not appear until about the age of 7 years, but studies such as these by Borke (1971) and by Mossler et al. (1976) suggest that Piaget's results could have been caused by using tasks, like the three mountains task, that were too far removed from the child's everyday experience.

The intuitive period   Piaget suggested that there was a further shift in think-ing at about the age of 4 years, and that it is at about this time that a child begins to develop the mental operations of ordering, classifying and quanti-fying in a more systematic way. Piaget applied the term *intuitive* to this period because even though a child can carry out such operations she is largely unaware of the principles that underlie the operations and cannot explain why she has done them, nor can she carry them out in a fully satisfactory way.

If a pre-operational child is asked to arrange sticks in a certain order, this poses difficulties. Piaget gave children ten sticks of different sizes from A (the shortest) to J (the longest), arranged randomly on a table. The child was asked to seriate them, that is to put them in order of length. Some pre-

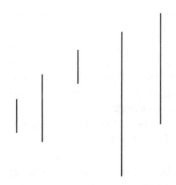

Figure 11.3   The pre-operational child's ordering of different-sized sticks. One arrangement in which the child has solved the problem of seriation by ignoring the length of the sticks.

operational children could not do the task at all; some arranged a few correctly, but could not sustain the complete ordering; others would put all the small ones in a group and all the larger ones in another; another more advanced response was to arrange the sticks so that the tops of the sticks were in the correct order even though the bottoms were not (see figure 11.3). In short, the child at this stage is not capable of ordering more than a very few objects.

Piaget found that pre-operational children also have difficulty with class inclusion tasks. These are tasks that involve part–whole relations. Suppose a child is given a box that contains 18 brown beads and two white beads; all the beads are wooden. When asked 'Are there more brown beads than wooden beads?', the pre-operational child will typically reply that there are more brown beads. According to Piaget the child finds it hard to consider the class of 'all beads' at the same time as considering the subset of beads, the class of 'brown beads'.

Such findings tend to be true of all children in the pre-operational stage, irrespective of their cultural background. Investigators found that Thai and Malaysian children gave responses very similar to Swiss children and in the same sequence of development. Here a Thai boy, shown a bunch of seven roses and two lotus, states that there are more roses than flowers when prompted by the standard Piagetian questions:

Child: More roses.
Experimenter: More than what?
Child: More than flowers.
Experimenter: What are the flowers?
Child: Roses.
Experimenter: Are there any others?
Child: There are.
Experimenter: What?
Child: Lotus.

Experimenter: So in this bunch which is more roses or flowers?
Child: More roses.

(Ginsburg and Opper, 1979, pp. 130–1)

One aspect of the pre-operational child's thinking processes which has been extensively investigated is what Piaget called *conservation*. Conservation refers to a person's understanding that superficial changes in the appearance of a quantity do not mean that there has been any fundamental change in that quantity. For example, if you have ten dolls standing in a line, and then you re-arrange them so that they are standing in a circle, this does not mean that there has been any alteration in the number of dolls. If nothing is added or subtracted from a quantity then it remains the same (i.e. it is conserved).

Piaget discovered that a pre-operational child finds it hard to understand that if an object is changed in shape or appearance its qualities remain the same, for example its weight, or volume. There is a series of conservation tests; examples are given in figure 11.4 and plate 11.2. If a child is given two identical balls of clay and asked if they have the same amount of clay in them, she will agree that they have. But if one ball is rolled into a sausage shape, the child will say that one or other of the balls is larger. When asked why, she will say 'Because it is larger'. Piaget suggested that a child has difficulty in a task like this because she can only focus on one attribute at a time (for example, the length of the clay sausage in figure 11.4b). To appreciate that the sausage of clay has the same amount of clay as the ball means understanding that the greater length of the sausage is *compensated* for by the smaller cross-section of the sausage. Piaget said that pre-operational children cannot apply principles like compensation.

If the row of sweets in figure 11.4a is made longer by spreading them out, the pre-operational child thinks that there are now more sweets. She thinks that when the appearance of the row alters, the number of objects in it changes. In other words she does not realize that the greater length of the row of sweets is compensated for by the greater distance between the sweets.

Compensation is only one of several processes which can help children overcome changes in appearance. Another process is *reversibility*. This means that children could think of 'reversing' the change they have seen. For example, if children imagine the sausage of clay being rolled back into a ball, or the row of sweets being pushed back together, they may realize that once the change has been reversed the quantity of an object or the number of items in the row is the same as it was before. According to Piaget, pre-operational children lack the thought processes needed to apply principles like compensation and reversibility, and for that reason they have difficulty in conservation tasks. In the next stage of development, the concrete operational stage, children have achieved the necessary logical thought processes which give them the ability to use appropriate principles and deal with conservation and other problem-solving tasks easily.

(a)

(b)

Plate 11.2 A 4-year-old puzzles over Piaget's conservation of number experiments; he says that the rows are equal in number in arrangement (a), but not in arrangement (b) 'because they're all bunched together here'.

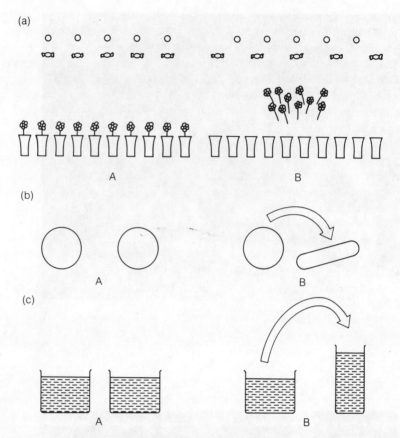

Figure 11.4   Some tests of conservation: (a) two tests of conservation of number; (b) conservation of mass; (c) conservation of quantity.

◀Reinterpretations of Piaget: the Pre-operational Stage▶▶▶

We have seen how Piaget claims that the pre-operational child cannot cope with tasks like part–whole relations or conservation, because they lack the logical thought processes to apply principles like compensation. However, other researchers have pointed out that children's lack of success in some tasks may be due to factors other than ones associated with logical processes.

Piaget found that pre-operational children had difficulty with *transitive inferences*. He showed children two rods A and B. Rod A was longer than rod B. Then he put rod A away and showed the children rods B and C. Rod B was longer than rod C. Then he asked children which rod was longer A or C? Young children find such questions difficult and Piaget suggested that they cannot make logical inferences of the nature: if A is longer than B and B is longer than C, then A must be longer than C.

Bryant and Trabasso (1971) also considered transitive inference tasks. They wondered if children's difficulties were less to do with making an inference and more to do with remembering all the information in the task. For children to make a correct response they not only have to make the inference they also have to remember the lengths of all the rods they have seen, and it is possible that young children, who have limited working-memory capacity (see chapter 12), were unable to retain in memory all the information they needed for the task. Bryant and Trabasso investigated transitive inferences using a task similar to Piaget's original task, but before asking the children to carry out the task itself, they trained them to remember the lengths of the rods. Obviously they did not train them using rods A and C together, but the children were trained on the other comparisons they needed to remember (i.e. that A was longer than B and that B was longer than C). Only when Bryant and Trabasso were satisfied that the children knew all the relevant information were they asked the test question. Children succeeded well in this version of the task – in fact Bryant and Trabasso used more than just two pairs of rods, but as long as the children had encoded all the relevant information about the lengths of the rods they could make inferences without difficulty.

The pre-operational child seems unable to understand the relationship between the whole and the part in class inclusion tasks, and will happily state that there are more brown beads than wooden beads in a box of brown and white wooden beads 'because there are only two white ones'. However, some researchers have pointed out that the questions that children are asked in such studies are unusual, for example it is not often in everyday conversation that we ask questions like: 'Are there more brown beads or more wooden beads?'

Even slight variations in the wording of the questions which may help to clarify the meaning of the question can have positive effects on the child's performance. McGarrigle (quoted in Donaldson, 1978) showed children four toy cows, three black and one white, all lying asleep on their sides. If the children were asked 'Are there more black cows or more cows?' (as in the standard Piagetian experiment) they tended not to answer correctly. If the question was rephrased 'Are there more black cows or more sleeping cows?', pre-operational children were more likely to respond correctly. McGarrigle found that in a group of children aged 6 years 25 per cent answered the standard Piagetian question correctly. When it was rephrased, 48 per cent of the children were correct, a significant difference. In other words, some of the difficulty was in the wording of the question rather than just an inability to understand part–whole relations in such class inclusion tasks.

McGarrigle and Donaldson (1974) questioned Piaget's interpretation of the conservation experiments and considered whether the form of questioning influenced children's responses. By introducing a character called 'Naughty Teddy' who muddled up the experimental displays 'accidentally', McGarrigle and Donaldson found that many more 4- to 6-year-old children were capable of conserving than in the classical Piagetian condition (see box 11.2).

Donaldson (1978) suggested an alternative explanation for young children's failure to conserve. She argued that children build up a model of the world by formulating hypotheses which help them anticipate future events on the basis of past experience. The child, therefore, has expectations about any situation. The child's interpretation of the words she hears is influenced by the expectations she brings to the situation. When the experimenter clearly points out the change in the array of counters (figure 11.4a), it is probably quite logical for the child to think that there is some link between that action (changing the display) and the next question ('Are there more counters or are they both the same?'). Why should an adult ask them such a question if there hasn't actually been a change? Donaldson's point is that we normally interact within a context, and that children may interpret questions in terms of expected contexts, rather than focus on the precise wording of the question.

Piaget was right to point out difficulties that pre-operational children have with conservation and other reason tasks. But researchers since Piaget have found that, given appropriate wording and context, young children seem capable of demonstrating at least some of the abilities which Piaget thought only developed later. In the right social context, the child emerges as a more competent being than Piaget's work would suggest (see chapter 14).

◄The Concrete Operational Stage►►►

From about the age of 7 years children's thinking processes change again as they develop a new set of strategies which Piaget calls *concrete operations*. These strategies are called 'concrete' because children can only apply them to immediately present objects. Nonetheless, thinking becomes much more flexible in the concrete operational period because children no longer have a tendency just to focus on one aspect of a problem, rather they are able to consider different aspects of a task at the same time. They have processes like compensation, and other processes like reversibility. For these reasons children succeed on conservation tasks. For example, when the round ball of clay is transformed into a sausage shape, children in the concrete operational stage will say, 'It's longer but it's thinner' or 'If you change it back, it will be the same'. Conservation of number is achieved first (about 5 or 6 years), then conservation of weight (around 7 or 8 years), but conservation of volume is fully understood at 10 or 11 years. Operations like addition and subtraction, multiplication and division become easier. Another major shift comes in the concrete operational child's ability to classify and order, and, in particular, to understand the principle of class inclusion which the pre-operational child found so difficult.

The ability to consider different aspects of a situation at the same time enables a child to perform successfully in perspective-taking tasks. For example, in the three mountains task a child can consider that she has one view of the model and that someone else can have a different view.

There are still some limitations on thinking, because children are reliant on the immediate environment and have difficulty with abstract ideas. Take the following question: 'Edith is fairer than Susan. Edith is darker than Lily. Who is the darkest?' This is a difficult problem for concrete operational children, yet faced with dolls to rank in order, children would solve the problem immediately. What children at this stage cannot do is speculate abstractly. Abstract reasoning is not found until the child has reached the stage of formal operations.

◄Reinterpretations of Piaget: the Concrete Operational Stage►►►

Many of Piaget's observations about the concrete operational stage have been broadly confirmed by subsequent research. Tomlinson-Keasey (1978), for example, has noted that conservation of number, weight and volume are acquired in the order stated by Piaget. Although Piaget had noted that related concepts may develop at different times he gave no explanation for it.

As in the previous stage, children's performance in the concrete operational period may be influenced by the context of the task. In some contexts children in the concrete operational stage may demonstrate more advanced reasoning than would typically be expected of children in that stage. For example, Jahoda (1983) showed that 9-year-olds in Harare, Zimbabwe, had more advanced understanding of economic principles than British 9-year-olds. The Harare children, who were involved in their parents' small businesses, had a strong motivation to understand the principles of profit and loss. Jahoda set up a mock shop and played a shopping game with the children. The British 9-year-olds could not explain about the functioning of a shop, did not understand that a shopkeeper buys for less than he sells, and did not know that some of the profit has to be set aside for purchase of new goods. The Harare children, by contrast, had mastered the concept of profit and understood about trading strategies. These abstract principles had been grasped by the children as a direct outcome of their own active participation in the running of a business. Jahoda's experiment, like Donaldson's studies (1978), indicated the important function of context in the cognitive development of children, and we discuss this issue – how children learn to make sense of the world in a shared, social context – in chapter 14.

◄The Formal Operational Stage►►►

We have seen that during the period of concrete operations the child is able to reason in terms of objects (e.g. classes of objects, relations between objects) when the objects are present. However, Piaget argued that it is only during the period of formal operations that young people are able to reason hypothetically.

Young people no longer depend on the 'concrete' existence of things in the real world. Instead, it is possible to reason in terms of verbally stated hypotheses, to consider the logical relations among several possibilities or to deduce conclusions from abstract statements. For example, consider the syllogism 'all green birds have two heads'; 'I have a green bird at home called Charlie'; 'How many heads does Charlie have?' The young person who has reached formal operational thinking will give the answer which is correct by abstract logic: 'two heads'. Children in the previous, concrete operational stage will usually not get beyond protesting about the absurdity of the premise.

Young people are also better at solving problems by considering all possible answers in a systematic manner. If asked to make up all the possible words from the letters A, S, E, T, M, a person at the formal

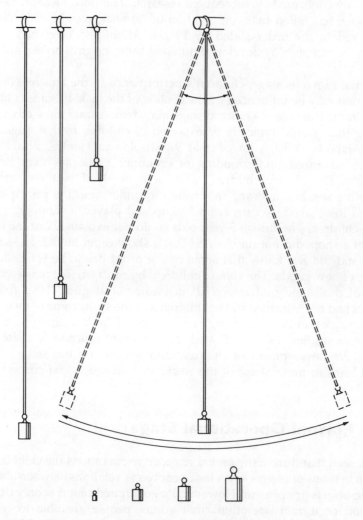

Figure 11.5 The pendulum problem (from Inhelder and Piaget, 1958).

operational level can do this in a logically ordered way, for example by considering first all combinations of two letters AS, AE, AT and so on, checking whether such combinations are words, and then going on to consider three-letter combinations, and so on. In earlier stages children attempt tasks like this in an unsystematic and disorganized way.

Inhelder and Piaget (1958) described the process of logical reasoning used by young people when presented with a number of natural science experiments. An example of one of their tasks – the pendulum task – is shown in figure 11.5. The person is given a string, which can be shortened or lengthened, and a set of weights, and is asked to find out what determines the speed of swing of the pendulum: possible factors are the length of the string, the weight at the end of the string, the height of the release point and the force of the push. In this problem the materials are concretely in front of the person, but the reasoning, to be successful, involves formal operations: a systematic consideration of the various possibilities, the formulation of hypotheses (e.g. 'what would happen if I tried a heavier weight?'), and logical deductions from the results of trials with different combinations of materials. Other tasks considered by Inhelder and Piaget included determining the flexibility of metal rods, balancing different weights around a fulcrum, and predicting chemical reactions. These tasks mimic the processes of scientific inquiry and Piaget would have said that formal scientific reasoning is one of the most important characteristics of formal operational thinking.

From his original work, carried out in schools in Geneva, Piaget claimed that formal operational thinking was a characteristic stage which children or young people reached between the ages of 11 and 15 years, having previously gone through the earlier stages of development.

Reinterpretations of Piaget: the Formal Operational Stage ▶▶▶

Piaget's claim has been modified by more recent research. Work carried out in Britain and the USA has found that the achievement of formal operational thinking is more gradual and haphazard than Piaget assumed. It may be dependent on the nature of the task and is often limited to certain domains.

Shayer et al. (1976; Shayer and Wylam, 1978) gave problems such as the pendulum task (see figure 11.5) to a large number of British schoolchildren. Their results (see figure 11.6) showed that by 16 years of age only about 30 per cent of young people had achieved 'early formal operations'. In a study in the USA, Martorano (1977) gave ten of Piaget's formal operational tasks to girls and young women aged 12–18 years. At 18 years success on the different tasks varied from 15 per cent to 95 per cent; but only two children out of 20 succeeded on all ten tasks. On the one hand, young people's success on one or two tasks might indicate some formal operational reasoning, but their failure on other tasks demonstrates that such reasoning might be limited to certain tasks or contexts. It may only be much later

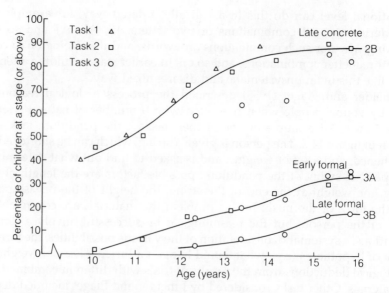

Figure 11.6   Proportion of boys at different Piagetian stages as assessed by three tasks (from Shayer and Wylam, 1978).

that young people can apply formal reasoning across a range of problem tasks.

The results described above are from experiments carried out in Western urban societies, where scientific, logical, and thus formal operational, thought is fostered in secondary schooling. Some researchers have found that in non-literate societies there is a delay of formal operational thinking, or even an absence in adults. So can formal operational thought really be considered a proper developmental stage? This problem was discussed by Piaget (1972). He considered three possibilities. One was that everyone proceeded through the same stages, but at different speeds depending on the amount of cognitive and social stimulation they received. Thus, in poor environments formal operations might be delayed to between 15 and 20 years, or 'perhaps in extremely disadvantageous conditions, such a type of thought will never really take shape' (1972, p. 7). A second possibility was that aptitudes became more diversified with age, so that abilities in older children could not be considered within one single general framework such as formal operations; in other words, 'our fourth period can no longer be characterized as a proper stage' (p. 9). A final possibility, which Piaget favoured, was a combination of the previous two; 'all normal subjects attain the stage of formal operations or structuring if not between 11–12 to 14–15 years, in any case between 15 and 20 years. However, they reach this stage in different areas according to their aptitudes and their professional specializations (advanced studies or different types of apprenticeships for the various trades)' (p. 10). This third possibility is consistent with evidence that secondary schooling does promote formal operational thinking in natural science tasks, while allowing also that non-literate persons may well use

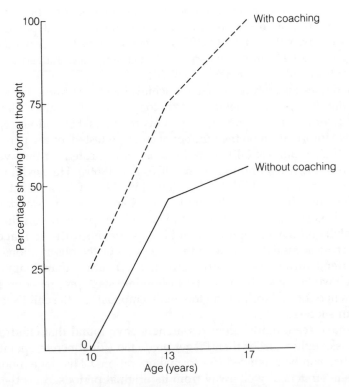

Figure 11.7 Levels of availability of formal thought. Percentage of adolescents showing formal thought, with and without coaching (from Danner and Day, 1977).

formal operational thought in domains familiar in their culture (for example, Blurton Jones and Konner, 1976, found that Kalahari bushpeople use hypothetical and logical reasoning in hunting and tracking animals).

Several researchers have shown that formal thinking can be trained. Figure 11.7 shows the results of a study by Danner and Day (1977). They coached students aged 10 years, 13 years and 17 years in three formal operational tasks. As would be expected, training only had a limited effect at 10 years, but it had marked effects at 17 years. In summary, it seems that the period from 11 to 15 years signals the start of the possibility of formal operational thought, rather than its achievement. Formal operational thought is only used some of the time in certain domains we are familiar with, are trained in or which are important to us. Often formal thinking is not used. After all, we all know of areas of life where we should have thought things out logically, but in retrospect realize we did not do so.

◄Piaget's Theory: an Overview►►►

Piaget's theory was elaborated over many decades throughout his long life. At first, it was slow to make an impact in the UK and the USA, but by the

1950s and 1960s its ambitious, embracing framework for understanding cognitive growth was becoming the accepted and dominant paradigm in cognitive development. Since the 1970s Piaget's theory has received extensive evaluation, such that many aspects of his theory, and indeed its whole basis, have been subject to major criticisms.

No one denies the stature of Piaget's achievement, beginning his work as he did in the 1920s, when scientific psychology was in its infancy. However, several objections have been raised as to his methods. He seldom reported quantitative information on the number of children tested, or the percentage who passed a certain test (although this was compensated for by investigators who replicated his findings in the 1950s and 1960s). He used a flexible method of interviewing children, the 'clinical method', which meant that he adapted his procedure to suit the child rather than following a standardized approach. This has advantages, but it puts a heavy premium on the interviewer's skill and makes replication of his experiments difficult. Piaget also relied on cross-sectional data (with the exception of the observations of his own children, during the sensori-motor period) rather than longitudinal data, which would have given a better insight into stage progressions. Piaget has also been criticized for putting too much emphasis on the child's failures rather than successes.

As we have seen, more recent researchers have found that children can perform tasks either earlier than Piaget predicted (for concrete operations), or only later than he predicted (for formal operations). His stage model has clearly been 'stretched' well away from its original periods. So is the stage model still useful? It may only be appropriate if certain abilities go hand in hand, linked by similar processes of thinking. For example, concrete operational thought might occur earlier and still be a stage, but only if the various aspects (conservation, classification, seriation, decline of egocentrism) still remain linked together. Unfortunately, the evidence for this kind of linkage is not strong, for either concrete or formal operations. For example, different measures of egocentrism do not correlate together strongly (Ford, 1979). Also, Piaget himself admitted that formal operational thought is achieved in a limited, patchy way. Only for the sensori-motor period (which seems to be a much more canalized or maturational process, see chapter 2) does the stage model hold up reasonably well. However, some researchers (called 'neo-Piagetians') have taken the framework proposed by Piaget, and rather than describing different stages in terms of different reasoning abilities they have tried to explain the stages with reference to the development of children's information-processing abilities and limitations. The latter approach will be described in chapter 12.

◀Educational Implications▶▶▶

Whatever its shortcomings, Piaget's approach provided the most comprehensive account of cognitive growth ever put forward and it has had considerable implications for education, most notably for child-centred learning methods in nursery and infant schools, for mathematics curricula in primary schools, and for science curricula at the secondary-school level.

Piaget argued that young children think quite differently from the adult and view the world from a qualitatively different perspective. It follows that a teacher must make a strong effort to adapt to the child and not assume that what is appropriate for adult learning is necessarily right for the child. At the heart of this child-centred approach to education lies the idea of active learning. From the Piagetian standpoint, children learn from actions rather than from passive observations; for example, telling a child about the properties of materials is less effective than creating an environment in which the child is free to explore, touch, manipulate and experiment. A teacher must recognize that each child needs to construct knowledge for him or herself, and that active learning results in deeper understanding.

How can the teacher promote active learning on the part of the pupil? First, it is the child rather than the teacher who initiates the activity. This does not mean that the children are free to do anything they want, but rather that a teacher sets tasks which are finely adjusted to the needs of their pupils and which, as a result, are intrinsically motivating to young learners. Second, a teacher is concerned with process rather than end-product. For example, nursery-school classrooms provide children with play materials which encourage their learning, e.g. climbing frames, which provide the opportunity for knowledge about the spatial properties of objects; small toys, which encourage the practice of sorting, grading and counting; play areas, like the Wendy House, where children can develop role-taking skills through imaginative play; and materials like water, sand, bricks and crayons which help children make their own constructions and create symbolic representations of the objects and people in their lives.

From these varied experiences the child constructs knowledge and understanding for herself. A teacher's role is to create the conditions in which this learning may best take place, since the aim of education is to encourage the child to ask questions, try out experiments and speculate, rather than accept information unthinkingly. From this it follows that a teacher should be interested in the reasoning behind the answer that a child gives to a question rather than just in the correct answer. Conversely, mistakes should not be penalized but treated as responses that can give a teacher insights into the child's thinking processes at that time.

The idea of active learning has meant a radical change in attitudes towards education. A teacher's role is not to impart information, because in Piaget's view, knowledge is not something to be transmitted from an expert teacher to an inexpert pupil. It is the child, according to Piaget, who sets the pace. A teacher's part in the educational process is to create situations which challenge the child to ask questions, to form hypotheses and to discover new concepts. A teacher is the guide in the child's process of discovery, and the curriculum should be adapted to each child's individual needs and intellectual level.

In mathematics and science lessons at primary school, children are helped to make the transition from pre-operational thinking to concrete operations through carefully arranged sequences of experiences which develop an understanding, for example, of class inclusion, conservation, and perspective taking. At a later period a teacher can encourage practical and experimental work before moving on to abstract deductive reasoning. In this way, a teacher can provide the conditions which are appropriate for the transition from concrete operational thinking to the stage of formal operations. The post-Piagetian research into formal operational thought (see above) also has strong implications for teaching, especially science teaching, in secondary schools. Tasks used in teaching can be analysed for the logical abilities that are required to fulfil them, and the tasks can then be adjusted to the age and expected abilities of the children who will use them.

Ideally, much of this learning should be individualized in view of the wide range of activities and interests which appear in any class of children. However, Piaget did not ignore the importance of social interaction in the learning process. Through interaction with peers, the child is also enabled to move out of an egocentric viewpoint (see also chapter 14). This occurs through co-operation with others, arguments and discussions. By listening to other children's opinions, having one's own view challenged and experiencing through others' reactions the illogicality of certain concepts, the child learns about perspectives other than her own. Communication of ideas to others also helps a child to sharpen concepts by finding the appropriate words. Piaget recognized the social value of interaction and viewed it as an important factor in cognitive growth.

◀Further Reading▶▶▶

H. Ginsburg and S. Opper 1979: *Piaget's Theory of Intellectual Development: an Introduction*, Englewood Cliffs, NJ: Prentice Hall, is an excellent exposition of Piaget's ideas which provides a detailed commentary on his theory and many extracts which give the flavour of Piaget's style.

P. H. Miller 1993 (3rd edn): *Theories of Developmental Psychology*, New York: Freeman, has a major chapter with a very clear summary of Piaget's theory, probably the most accessible introduction to his theory. Other chapters in the book consider and compare different developmental theories.

M. A. Boden 1979: *Piaget*, London: Fontana, provides a biographical account of Paiget's research and discusses the biological and philosophical issues which influenced Piaget. It makes links between Piaget's ideas and current work on artificial intelligence.

J. G. Bremner 1994 (2nd edn): *Infancy*, Oxford: Blackwell Publishers, focuses on infancy; it has a good chapter on the sensori-motor period, and includes a summary of the most important post-Piagetian research with infants.

M. Donaldson 1978: *Children's Minds*, London: Fontana, is a very readable book. Donaldson is critical of Piaget's research and argues forcefully that he underestimated the logical powers of young children. She also summarizes many of the studies which have demonstrated young children's abilities.

◄Discussion Points►►►

1 What does Piaget mean by egocentrism? How have his ideas on egocentrism been challenged?
2 Did Piaget under-estimate children's abilities in the pre-operational stage of development?
3 Discuss ways in which Piaget seems to have misjudged the age at which formal operations are acquired. Illustrate with examples from your own experience.
4 What are the implications of Piaget's theory for education? Discuss in relation to your own educational experiences.

Box 11.1
Piaget's mountains revisited: changes in the egocentric landscape

Borke questioned the appropriateness for young children of Piaget's three mountains task (described on p. 344). She thought it possible that aspects of the task not related to perspective taking might have adversely affected the children's performance. These aspects included the following possibilities. First, viewing a mountain scene from different angles may not have been an interesting or motivating problem for young children. Second, Piaget had asked children to select pictures of the doll's views and young children might have had difficulty with such a response. Third, because the task was so unusual children may have performed poorly because they were unfamiliar with the nature of the task and Borke considered whether some initial practice and familiarity with the task might improve performance. With those points in mind, Borke repeated the basic design of Piaget and Inhelder's experiment but changed the content of the task, avoided the use of pictures and gave children some initial practice. She used four three-dimensional displays: these were a practice display and three experimental displays (box figure 11.1.1).

Borke's participants were eight 3-year-old children and 14 4-year-old children attending a day nursery. Grover, a character from the popular children's television programme *Sesame Street*, was used instead of Piaget's doll. Each display had two identical scenes, one for the child to look at, and

the other for Grover to drive around. The children were tested individually. Each was first shown the practice display, a large fire engine. An exact duplicate of the fire engine appeared on a revolving turntable to the left of the child. Borke then told the child that Grover was going to play a game: 'He will drive his car along the road. Sometimes Grover likes to stop and look out of his car. Now the fire engine on this other table turns so you can look at it from any side. When Grover stops to look out of his car, I want you to turn the scene that moves so you are looking at it in the same way Grover is.' Then Borke parked Grover in turn at each of the three sides which presented a view different from the child's view.

If necessary, Borke helped the children to move their turntable to the correct position and also walked the child round to where Grover was to show how Grover saw things. Only after this practice period was the child ready to move on to the experiment itself. Here the procedure was the same, except that no help was given by the experimenter. Each child was shown the three experimental displays one at a time (see box figure 11.1.1). Grover drove round his display, and, when he stopped, the children rotated the replica displays on their turntables to give Grover's point of view.

The analysis of responses showed statistically

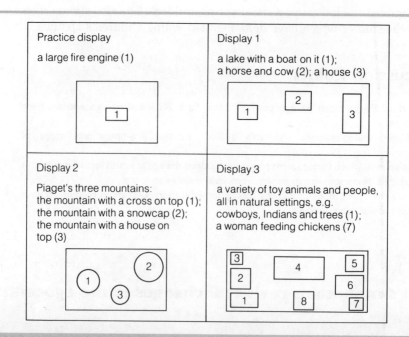

Box Figure 11.1.1 A schematic view of Borke's four three-dimensional displays viewed from above (based on H. Borke (1975), *Developmental Psychology*, 11, 240–3).

significant differences in the children's perceptual role-taking ability on the three displays. Using analysis of variance, it was found that the difference was significant at $p < 0.001$. All subjects showed a good ability to take Grover's perspective for Display 1 (3- and 4-year-olds were correct 80 per cent of the time) and Display 3 (3-year-olds were correct 79 per cent of the time and 4-year-olds, 93 per cent). For Display 2, however (the three mountains task), the 3-year-olds were correct only 42 per cent of the time and 4-year-olds 67 per cent of the time. As far as errors went, there were no significant differences in the children's responses for any of the three positions – 31 per cent of errors were egocentric (i.e. took the child's perspective rather than Grover's) and the rest were random.

Borke demonstrated clearly that the task itself had a crucial influence on the perspective-taking skills of young children. When toys which are interesting to the children were used, even a complex problem like taking Grover's perspective in Display 3 could be solved by a high proportion of 3- and 4-year-olds after a brief practice session. Furthermore, asking the children to rotate a turntable with

a replica of the scene presented much less difficulty for young children than selecting a picture, as Piaget and Inhelder had asked their participants to do.

Faced with the more difficult display similar to that which Piaget and Inhelder had used, the children seemed to fall back on their egocentric perspective rather more, even though they still performed at above chance levels.

Borke's conclusion was that the potential for understanding another's viewpoint is already present in children as young as 3 and 4 years of age – a strong challenge to Piaget's assertions that children of this age are egocentric and incapable of taking the viewpoint of others. It would seem that young children make egocentric responses when they misunderstand the task, but given the right conditions show that they are quite capable of working out another's viewpoint.

Further confirmation of these results comes from Hughes's study reported by Donaldson (1978), in which children were asked to hide a little boy doll from two toy police officers – a task which required understanding what each of the police officers could see and then hiding the little boy so that neither of them could see him. Three-year-olds succeeded at this perspective-taking task because, in Hughes's opinion, the task 'made sense' to them in a way that the three mountains test did not. There is no obvious reason for working out another person's view of a group of mountains, but the reasons for hiding from police officers are clear, even to children as young as three!

Based on material in H. Borke 1975: *Developmental Psychology*, 11, 240–3.

Box 11.2
Conservation accidents

McGarrigle and Donaldson set out to discover whether children as young as 4 to 6 years could succeed at conservation tasks when a different procedure from Piaget's was used. Altogether 80 children, aged between 4 years 2 months and 6 years 3 months, were tested in two situations involving conservation of number (equal and unequal) and two situations involving conservation of length (equal and unequal). Each child performed each conservation task under two conditions:

IT intentional transformation, when the transformation of materials was clearly intended by the experimenter.

AT accidental transformation, when the materials were disarranged 'accidentally' by a mischievous teddy bear.

The children were divided into two groups of 40, each balanced for age and sex. Group 1 made all their conservation judgements in the AT condition before encountering the IT condition. Group 2 made all their conservation judgements in the IT condition before the AT condition. Within each of the two groups, half of the children were given the number conservation task first and half were given the length conservation task first (thus counterbalancing for the order of the tasks).

In the number equal situation, four red and four white counters were arranged in a one-to-one correspondence into two rows of equal length (see box figure 11.2.1).

Transformation occurred when the counters of one row were moved until they touched one another. In the IT condition, the experimenter did this deliberately. In the AT condition, 'Naughty Teddy' swooped over the counters and pushed them together; the child, who had already been warned that Teddy might 'mess up the toys', helped to put Teddy back in its place. Before and after the transformation the child was asked: 'Is there more here or more here, or are they both the same number?'

In the number unequal situation, rows of four and five counters were used and the child was asked: 'Which is the one with more – this one, or this one?' (box figure 11.2.2). A similar procedure was carried out for the conservation of length, using lengths of black and red string. In this study the independent variables are the equal and unequal conditions, the IT and AT conditions, and the order of presentation of IT and AT (Groups 1 and 2). The dependent variable is the number of correct responses.

As can be seen in box table 11.1.1, the largest effect is between the IT and AT conditions.

Before transformation   After transformation

Box Figure 11.2.1 Transformation of counters in the number equal situation, either intentionally or accidentally.

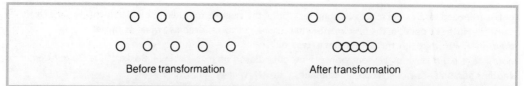

Box Figure 11.2.2 Transformation of counters in the number unequal situation, either intentionally or accidentally.

Correct responses were more frequent when the transformation was accidental: 72 per cent of the responses were correct when the display was moved accidentally, whereas only 34 per cent were correct in the intentional transformation condition (which corresponded to the normal Piagetian procedure). There was little difference between the equal and unequal conditions; this was found in both the conditions that investigated conservation of number (using counters) and those that investigated conservation of length (using pieces of string).

However, the order in which the displays were presented did have an influence on the children's responses. When the authors compared performance in the AT condition of Group 2 (where IT came first) with that in Group 1, the difference was significant ($p < 0.05$). In other words, if the children were given the 'Naughty Teddy' task first and then the traditional task second, they performed significantly better than the children who did the tasks in the reverse order.

McGarrigle and Donaldson concluded that the experimenter's behaviour towards the task materials can influence the interpretation a child makes of the situation because the child will be trying to make sense of the situation, and to understand what the experimenter wants. Unless the setting is considered, the child's ability to conserve may be greatly under-estimated – something which traditional tests of conservation seem to do. The traditional experiments in number conservation seem to make the child think that a real change in the materials has taken place – why else would an adult alter something? If the context is changed to one in which no importance is attached to the change (because they are simply messed up by a 'Naughty Teddy' who is only playing about), the child's ability to conserve improves markedly. This result indicates that how a child interprets the social setting of the conservation experiments may be an important factor in whether or not the child demonstrates the ability to conserve. As McGarrigle and Donaldson conclude:

> It is possible that the achievements of the concrete operational stage are as much a reflection of the child's increasing independence from features of the interactional setting as they are evidence of the development of a logical competence. (p. 349)

It should be noted that although this experiment has been widely cited to support the view that Piaget under-estimated the abilities of pre-

Box Table 11.2.1 Total of correct responses given by Groups 1 and 2 under AT and IT conditions

	Group 1 (n = 40)		Group 2 (n = 40)	
	AT then IT		IT then AT	
Number equal	32	19	14	22
Number unequal	36	18	13	22
Length equal	34	15	8	24
Length unequal	37	12	9	23
	139	64	44	91

operational children, subsequent investigators have not always replicated McGarrigle and Donaldson's main findings (see Eames, Shorrocks and Tomlinson, 1990).

Based on material in J. McGarrigle and M. Donaldson 1974: *Cognition*, 3, 341–50.

12 Cognition: the Information Processing Approach

In the previous chapters we discussed the theories put forward by Piaget and by Vygotsky to describe the development of children's thinking. Some of Piaget's work was re-evaluated by researchers like Donaldson (1978) and her colleagues who found that children can be successful in problem-solving tasks (based on Piaget's original tasks) at an earlier age than Piaget suggested. As Donaldson and others have argued, there may be many factors associated with a task that can influence performance on that task, including the language used in the instructions, the context of the information which is used in the experiment, and the familiarity of the materials (see chapter 11).

Other researchers have pointed out how other factors in experiments could also influence children's success. As Bryant and Trabasso (1971) found in their study of transitive inferences (see chapter 11), children may have difficulty with the task, not because they are incapable of making the appropriate inferences to solve the problem (as Piaget had suggested), but because they do not always remember the information required to make the inferences. Once the experimental procedure was changed and children were given the opportunity to learn all the information they needed before making an inference they were much more successful. Many factors associated with the presentation of a task will influence the way that children perform the task.

The discovery that often minor changes in experimental materials and procedures can affect children's performance is important for several reasons. First, it has made researchers very aware that what might be thought of as quite superficial changes (e.g. in the way that a question is phrased) may have a significant impact on the way that children interpret a task. Second, knowing that factors associated with the presentation of a task influence children's success can highlight some important aspects of cognitive development – it tells us that compared with older children, young children may be more dependent on the context of the task, or more dependent on the clarity of the instructions if they are to succeed in solving a problem. Third, if children can succeed on some tasks earlier than Piaget predicted it influences how we interpret his theory.

However, as Piaget himself emphasized, describing development means more than just describing task factors, it means understanding the *cognitive* factors which influence the way that children approach problem-solving tasks. As we saw in chapter 11, Piaget described children's intellectual development in terms of their ability to apply processes (like 'compensation' and 'reversibility') in progressively more effective ways. Other researchers have also investigated the mental processes associated with cognitive development, but rather than following Piaget's description of mental operations, they have used the *information processing approach* to describe the development of cognitive abilities.

One of the first models of information processing was put forward by Atkinson and Shiffrin (1968) who described cognitive processing in terms of three memory stores, and control processes which operate on those stores (see figure 12.1). This model emphasized the flow of information through or between the different components. Any information in the environment which is attended to will be encoded via the *sensory register*. This will encode what is seen, heard or otherwise sensed, in full, but only for a very brief period of time before the information decays or is overwritten by new information coming into the sensory register. Some of the information from the sensory store may be selected for processing in *short-term memory*.

Atkinson and Shiffrin's model of short-term memory was of a store which could only retain a limited number of 'units' of information, but more recent theorists have placed less emphasis on the 'capacity' of short-term memory and more emphasis on short-term memory as the conscious part of information processing which is constrained by the number and the processes being carried out at the same time (Baddeley, 1992). Processes will vary, depending on how well practised they are. For example, a novice car driver may need all her attention just to drive the car, but for an experienced driver many aspects of driving are automatic and require little active thought – this will leave the experienced driver with available cognitive resources (perhaps to listen to the car radio and carry out a conversation at the same time as driving). In other words, some processes (if they are relatively unpractised) may require a lot of capacity, but others (which are well learnt and automatic) may make little demand on capacity. This emphasis on processing capacity has led to the original term short-term memory being replaced by the term *working memory*.

How information is processed in working memory will determine whether it is transferred into long-term memory. Long-term memory is unlimited and retains information indefinitely, and information from that store can be retrieved and re-entered into working memory. Information can be processed by various control mechanisms as it flows through

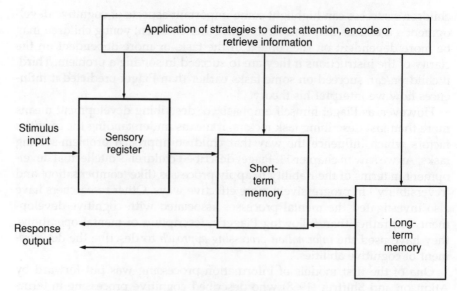

Figure 12.1 Application of strategies to direct attention, encode or retrieve information (adapted from Atkinson and Shiffrin, 1968).

the system, and such mechanisms include strategies for retaining information in working memory – these are called *encoding strategies*. We will discuss how children develop effective encoding strategies later in this chapter.

To provide an example of the flow of information through the different components, think about glancing at the front page of a newspaper for a moment and then closing your eyes. You might, very briefly in the sensory register, retain an image of the whole page, but only that part of the page which is specifically attended to (e.g. the headline) will be transferred to working memory. The headline will only be kept in working memory if it is actively processed – for instance, you may need to keep repeating the headline to retain it in working memory; or you may link the words in the headline with some information you already know in long-term memory. Such strategies increase the likelihood that the headline will be transferred to long-term memory. If some time later you want to recall the headline you may be able to retrieve the words directly from long-term memory, or you may find that you cannot immediately remember them and you may need to find some way of recalling them. You might, for example, try to think what the headline was about, or what you associated it with when you first encoded it. The latter processes are referred to as *retrieval strategies* and we will describe some of these later in the chapter.

Processing information is subject to many limitations. Only a small proportion of all the information we perceive is attended to and processed, and apart from attentional limitations there are also processing limitations. For example, few adults could calculate a mathematical problem like

$(123 \times 456)/78$ in their working memory. That is not because adults do not know the appropriate rules for multiplication and division, it is simply because the complexity of the calculation will exceed the processing space available in working memory. However, most adults can solve $(12 \times 34)/5$ without using a calculator, because the figures in the problem and the calculation itself can be held in working memory. But children have more limited processing abilities than adults and therefore, even if they understand multiplication and division, they may not find it possible to solve $(12 \times 34)/$ 5 by mental arithmetic.

Models such as Atkinson and Shiffrin's provided the basis for describing cognitive development in terms of the components within the information processing models. For example, Brainerd (1983) considered how limitations in different components might affect children's performance in problem-solving tasks. Brainerd discussed five aspects of information processing limitations in working memory:

Encoding limitations Children may not encode the appropriate information about a problem. In a problem like $(12 \times 34)/5$, a child might not encode the multiplication symbol correctly, and so add the figures in the bracket rather than multiply them. Brainerd pointed out that failure in some Piagetian problem-solving tasks (e.g. those that involve part–whole relationships – see chapter 11) may be because when children listen to the question in that task they fail to encode the crucial information about the required comparison.

Computational limitations Children may encode all the relevant information about a problem and retain it in working memory, but they may not have appropriate strategies in long-term memory that they can apply to the encoded information. For example, they may not be able to solve the mathematical problem because they do not know a procedure for multiplying two-digit numbers.

Retrieval limitations Children may have the necessary strategies in long-term memory but when they try to retrieve the strategy from their long-term store they retrieve an inappropriate strategy. For example instead of retrieving the procedures for multiplication they retrieve, in error, the procedures for division.

Storage limitations Children may have encoded all the information, and have retrieved the appropriate strategies from long-term memory, but they may not be able to retain all the relevant information in working memory while they carry out the calculation. For example, as children calculate (12×34) they may forget the information relating to the rest of the equation and be unable to complete the problem.

Work-space limitations As working memory is limited children will only be able to retain a few items of information at the same time. For example, if a mathematical problem only involves two digits and one calculation

(4 + 5) this may all be held in working memory. If the problem is $(1 + 9 - 2 - 8 + 5 - 7 + 3 - 6 - 4 + 11 - 3 + 9)$ it may be that the calculation is possible, but there will not be enough space in working memory to retain all the digits.

After a consideration of these limitations Brainerd (1983) investigated Piaget and Inhelder's (1951) 'probability judgement' task. In one version of this problem 4- and 5-year-old children were shown ten tokens – seven of the tokens had a picture of a rabbit on them and three had a picture of a horse. All the tokens were placed in an opaque bag, which was shaken, and then the experimenter pulled out one of the tokens and held it in his hand so that the child could not see it. Children were asked to predict the picture on the token in the experimenter's hand. After one trial the token was replaced in the bag (without the child seeing it) and then the procedure was repeated for another four trials.

The best way to be correct in this task is always to predict that the token which will be pulled out is the one which occurs most frequently in the bag (i.e. rabbit), but Piaget and Inhelder found that young children were poor at this task – children did not consistently predict the picture with the higher frequency. Brainerd carried out a series of trials to find out why children had difficulty, and found that on the first trial the majority of children predicted that the token taken out of the bag would have a rabbit on it – in other words most of the children realized the need to choose the more frequent picture (and if they knew this they did not have an encoding problem). However, on the remaining four trials the children did not go on predicting the rabbit tokens (e.g. after the first trial they might just predict the horse and rabbit tokens alternately).

Brainerd's first hypothesis was that the children had *storage limitations* so that by the second and later trials the children had forgotten the frequency of the pictures in the bag and were simply guessing. Therefore, in a further experiment Brainerd placed a second set of seven tokens with rabbits and three tokens with horses on the table in front of the child throughout the experiment, to help children retain the relative frequency of the tokens. However, children's performance did not change (they still did poorly after the first trial). As there was no need to store information about the frequency of the tokens (because that information was always in front of them) Brainerd assumed that it was something other than storage limitations which was the cause of the children's difficulty.

Brainerd therefore considered what was different between the first (often successful) trial and the later (unsuccessful) trials. He thought that *after* the first trial the most recent information in children's working memory was their own response to the previous trial, and that this might have been influencing their predictions – for example, on the second trial children remembered that they had said rabbit (or horse) on the first trial and in recalling that response some children went on to repeat that response, and some decided to say the alternate response. In other words, they based their later predictions on the recall of their previous response, and this strategy was not related to the crucial information about the relative frequency of the tokens. Brainerd called this a *retrieval problem* because the children were retrieving the wrong information (their own previous response) as the basis for their predictions and ignoring the frequency information. When Brainerd changed the experimental procedure so that the most recent item in working memory (before the children made a prediction) was information about token frequency the children were successful on all the trials.

We have described Brainerd's (1983) studies in some detail because they illustrate how a model of information processing can provide the stimulus for a series of studies which do not just identify whether children succeed or fail a task at a certain age, but can explain why children have difficulty with a task. In the case of the probability task, Brainerd's first studies supported Piaget and Inhelder's (1951) conclusion that young children were poor at the task, but by generating a series of hypotheses based on a theoretical model Brainerd was able to go beyond the initial findings, identify children's retrieval difficulties and then demonstrate that when these difficulties were overcome children could perform successfully. This latter finding leads to a very different conclusion about children's ability and illustrates the need to have a specific model of the processes which may be involved in a task.

The information processing approach implies that children's cognitive abilities develop in three possible ways. First, the 'size' of components like working memory may increase so that with increasing age children may develop more 'slots' in memory which means that more items of information can be stored at the same time (Kail, 1990). Second, as children get older they may become more efficient at processing items of information, and increased efficiency will mean that there are less demands on working memory and therefore the free capacity can be used for processing more information at the same time (Case, 1985). Third, it is possible that both size and processing efficiency develop during childhood.

Case (1978, 1985), like Piaget, thought that cognitive development could be interpreted as a series of stages. But unlike Piaget (who described stages in the development of children's logical thinking and reasoning – see chapter 11), Case described children's stage-like performance on particular problem-solving tasks in information processing terms (and for this reason Case is sometimes referred to as a 'neo-Piagetian'). This can be exemplified by Case's analysis of Noelting's (1980) orange juice problem (see figure 12.2).

In Noelting's problem children are shown two sets of glasses. In each set some of the glasses contain orange juice and some contain water.

A   B

Figure 12.2 Example of juice problem (based on Noelting, 1980).

Children are also shown two empty jugs and told that the contents of one of the sets of glasses will be poured into one jug, and the other set will be poured into the second jug. The children are then asked which of the two jugs will taste more strongly of juice. For example, in figure 12.2 one set of glasses includes a glass of orange juice and a glass of water; and the second set includes two glasses of orange juice and three of water. Children have to compare the proportion of orange juice in each set and (if they do this correctly) say that the first jug would taste more strongly of orange. Noelting described children's performance in terms of four age-related strategies:

3- to 4-year-olds only considered whether orange was present or absent in each set. They could only succeed if one set of glasses had some orange in it and the other did not. If both sets included glasses of orange they would say that both jugs would taste more strongly of orange juice.

5- to 6-year-olds chose the set which had more glasses of orange (so, in the example in figure 12.2 they would make an incorrect prediction).

7- to 8-year-olds compared the number of glasses of water and orange in each set, and if one set had more glasses of orange than glasses of water said that the jug receiving that set would taste more strongly of juice. If both or neither sets had more glasses of orange, the children simply guessed.

9- to 10-year-olds were able to use an appropriate strategy to select the correct set of glasses (e.g. by subtracting the number of glasses with water from the number with orange and choosing the set with the larger remainder).

Each of the strategies described above takes into account an additional aspect of the task, and therefore the later strategies can be applied successfully to a larger number of different problems. Case (1978) suggested that information processing limitations restricted younger children to the less effective strategies. For example, the strategy used by the 3- and 4-year-olds can be described in the following terms:

Look for orange juice in one set of glasses. If there is orange juice say 'that set will taste more strongly of juice', If there is no orange juice say 'that it won't taste of juice'.

This strategy only requires a minimum of information in working memory (the colour of the glasses in the set). Then children can turn to the other set of glasses and repeat the strategy:

Look for orange juice in the other set of glasses. If there is orange juice say 'that set will taste more strongly of juice', If there is no orange juice say 'that set won't taste of juice'.

Again this only requires one item of information (the colour of the glasses) in working memory. Of course, this is not a very effective strategy because, as we have pointed out, it sometimes leads children to make apparently contradictory responses such as that both jugs will taste more strongly of orange juice.

The strategy used by 5- and 6-year-olds requires the children to count the number of glasses of juice in one set (and retain this number in working

Figure 12.3   Pairs of houses used by Vurpillot (1968). Children were asked whether the houses in each pair were the same or different.

memory); then count the number of glasses of orange in the other set (and retain this number in working memory); then compare the two numbers and predict that the set with the greater number will taste more strongly of orange. In other words, to complete this strategy children need to hold two items (the numbers) in working memory, as well as having the processing space to carry out the comparison of these items. The other two strategies, used by older children, each require increasing amounts of working memory capacity for completion.

Case (1985) has analysed the strategies required in a large number of Piagetian and other problem-solving tasks and has concluded that one of the main constraints on children's performance is their information processing capacity. Other factors will also influence children's cognitive development, which we will discuss later, but if a particular problem-solving strategy requires more processing capacity than a child has available it will be difficult for the child to apply that strategy.

Noelting's (1980) analysis of the orange juice problem focused on the strategies that children used in attempting to solve the problem. Many such analyses are carried out after an experimenter has collected data, because then the experimenter can look for patterns in the children's performance (when they were correct, when they were incorrect, the type of errors they made, and so on). Having analysed the performance, an experimenter can often suggest the likely strategies that children bring to the problem. An alternative way of investigating children's strategies was used by Siegler (1976, 1978) and is described in box 12.1.

Attention   It is a truism that for any information to be processed at all, it must be attended to in the first instance. One difference between young children and older children is in the ability to identify the most crucial aspects of a task and pay attention to those aspects. Vurpillot (1968) demonstrated differences in the attentional strategies of children between 3 and 9 years of age. Vurpillot showed the children drawings of two houses and each house had six windows (see figure 12.3). Some pairs of houses were identical, but other pairs of houses had different windows (e.g. in one house a specific window might have a blind, but the corresponding window in the other house might have curtains). Children were asked to look at the drawings and say whether the two houses were the same or different.

The most appropriate strategy in this task was to look at a window in one house and then check that the corresponding window in the other house was the same, and to continue this until either a difference was found, or all six windows in each house had been examined and it could be concluded that there were no differences. While the children were looking at the houses Vurpillot recorded their eye-movements, and found that all the children aged 5 years or below, only examined a few windows, and made few comparisons between corresponding windows. As a result the younger children often incorrectly concluded that the houses were the same because they had not detected differences in unchecked windows. Children from the age of 6 years were more likely to examine pairs of windows, and between 6 and 9 years of age the children used this strategy more effectively, by considering all windows exhaustively.

◀Memory Development▶▶▶

The word 'strategy' is used in two ways, either to refer to the strategies used in specific problem-solving tasks (like Noelting's juice problem) or to refer to general strategies which can be applied across a range of different tasks. Such general strategies include memory strategies like *encoding* and *retrieval* strategies.

Encoding strategies

Rehearsal   This refers to the mental repetition of information. For example, if you want to remember a telephone number you can repeat it to yourself until you have a chance to write it down. To investigate children's use of rehearsal, Flavell, Beach and Chinsky (1966) showed groups of 20, 5-, 7- and 10-year-olds a set of seven pictures. The experimenters pointed to some of the pictures and told the children that they should try to remember those specific pictures. Then 15 seconds later the children were asked to say, aloud, all the pictures they could recall. During the 15-second interval the children were observed by a lip-reader to assess what they might be saying to themselves while waiting to recall the pictures. Only two of the 5-year-olds repeated the pictures to themselves, but more than half the 7-year-olds and nearly all the 10-year-olds could be seen repeating the pictures.

When young children begin to use rehearsal they may not use it as effectively as older children or adults. Ornstein, Naus and Liberty (1975) asked 7-year-olds and adults to remember a list of words, which were presented at the rate of one every 5 seconds. During this task participants were asked to say what they were thinking while they tried to remember the words. Ornstein et al. found a difference in the way that the children and adults rehearsed the words. The children's rehearsal was sometimes limited to repeating a word when it was presented, and then repeating the next word and so on. The adults grouped a number of words and rehearsed these as a group. For example, imagine a list made up of the words 'cat ... dog ... house ... car ...'. Children might try to remember this list by saying 'cat, cat, cat' and then 'dog, dog, dog' as each word is presented. In contrast adults might begin by saying 'cat, cat, cat,' and then after the presentation of the second word say 'cat, dog, cat, dog' and then 'cat, dog, house' and so on. The latter procedure is a more effective way of encoding the list, but it depends not only on the use of rehearsal but also on an awareness of the benefits of organizing (or 'chunking') information together to increase the likelihood of remembering it.

Organization   Grouping information together is another aspect of encoding. If information is linked together it may be encoded more effectively than unlinked information, and this effect will be greater when the information can be linked in a meaningful way. Like rehearsal, the realization that organizing information into meaningful chunks aids encoding is a gradual development. Moely, Olson, Halwes and Flavell (1969) showed children a set of pictures which were laid out in front of them in no particular order. Within the set of pictures there were several showing animals, several showing pieces of furniture and so on. The children were asked to learn the names of all the pictures and were told that they could rearrange the pictures if they thought that would help them to remember the pictures. Moely et al. found that it was only after the age of 10 years that children realized the usefulness of rearranging the pictures into categories so that they could learn all the animals as a group, and then all the furniture as a group, and so on with the other groups of items. Children younger than 10 years do show evidence of organizing material which has to be remembered, but often they do so in only a partially effective way – for example, organizing a list of items is achieved best if all the items can be grouped into a small number of categories, but young children may use a large number of categories, and have several 'categories' which only include a single item.

Elaboration   Grouping will benefit from another encoding strategy, called elaboration. Elaboration means making associations between items to help recall them better. For example, to remember that two words like 'fish' and 'hat' occur together in a list of items, they could be linked together in several ways. One way would be to include them in a sentence like 'the fish put her hat on', and another way would be to form a mental image of a fish wearing a hat. In general, the more unusual the image that is generated the more likely the information will be remembered. Foley, Wilder, McCall and Van Vorst (1993) suggested images to 6- and 9-year-olds to help them remember pairs of words like 'ant' and 'comb'. At both ages the children recalled the words better if they thought of images like 'the large black ant was using a comb to fix its hair' than if they thought of images like 'the black ant crawled in and out of the teeth of the comb'.

Pressley and Levin (1980) found that 6-year-olds could be taught how to use images to remember words, but children of this age did not spontaneously think of the images when they were later asked to recall the words – they had to be reminded that it was useful to think of the image they had formed earlier. In contrast, 11-year-olds were not only able to form images to combine words, but at recall they were able to use the images without being prompted to do so. In another experiment, Buckhalt, Mahoney and Paris (1976) found that when children first used elaborative strategies they tended to use less effective elaborations than older children. Buckhalt et al. asked children to think of ways to remember pairs of words like 'broom' and 'lady' and found that younger children used what might be called 'static' elaborations like 'the lady had a broom', but older children were more likely to use 'active' elaborations like 'the lady flew on the broom on Hallowe'en'. The latter are often more effective because they generate a more memorable and distinctive image.

Retrieval strategies

Adults are familiar with the feeling of knowing something but not being able to recall it immediately, and most adults have learnt ways to retrieve information from long-term memory. For instance, when trying to recall the name of a person, it is useful to go through the letters of the alphabet and sometimes the initial letter of the name will trigger the rest of the person's name. As with encoding strategies the use of retrieval strategies is an ability which develops gradually. In one study of retrieval strategies Kreutzer, Leonard and Flavell (1975) told 5- and 10-year-old children a story about a boy who wanted to remember which Christmas he was given a puppy, and then they were asked what the boy could do to remember the correct Christmas. Possible ways to do this include working out the age of the dog, thinking about other presents received at the same time as the puppy, or going back from the most recent Christmas to each previous Christmas in turn until the one when the puppy was received. All the 10-year-olds were able to suggest at least one appropriate retrieval strategy, but only about half the 5-year-olds were able to do so.

In another study of retrieval strategies Kobasigawa (1974) showed 6-, 8- and 11-year-olds a set of 24 pictures. The pictures showed items from eight different categories (for example, toys, musical instruments, vehicles or playground equipment). Children were shown all 24 pictures and asked to learn them, and at the same time they were shown eight cue cards which reflected the categories (for example the cue cards showed a play pen, music book, street and park). Later the children were shown (just) the cue cards and asked to recall as many of the original pictures as they could. Only a third of the 6-year-olds spontaneously used the cue cards as an aid, but the majority of the older groups did so, and what was of particular interest was how the children used the cues. The 6- and 8-year-olds who used the cues did so by looking at a cue card and recalling one of its associated small pictures, and then they moved on to the next cue card. In contrast, 11-year-olds looked at a cue card and tried to recall as many associated pictures as possible before moving on to the next cue. In this way the oldest children were able to recall the majority of the small pictures effectively.

◄How do Memory Strategies Develop?►►►

As shown by the research into different strategies, children do not simply change from not using a strategy to using it, rather there is a gradual progression in how effectively children apply that strategy. As described above, Flavell et al. (1966) showed that children used rehearsal spontaneously after about the age of 7 years. Keeney, Cannizzo and Flavell (1967) found that younger children could in fact use rehearsal if they were prompted to do so. Keeney et al. identified 6-year-olds who did not use rehearsal, and then prompted them to use this strategy – they were told to keep whispering the names of the items to themselves until they needed to recall them. After this instruction the majority of the children were able to use rehearsal effectively, but they only did so in tasks when they were explicitly prompted to do so by the experimenters.

Why should children who are capable of using a strategy not employ it when it would be appropriate? Kennedy and Miller (1976) investigated this in an experiment with two groups of children (who did not use rehearsal spontaneously) who were asked to remember the names of pictures. Children in one group were just prompted to use rehearsal, but children in the other group were given feedback about their performance – they were told that when they used rehearsal they remembered the names better. Later, Kennedy and Miller gave both groups further memory tests for which rehearsal was an appropriate strategy. Only the group which had been given feedback about their performance continued to use rehearsal in the later tests. One implication of this result is that even when children can use rehearsal they fail to do so because they do not realize that it will be beneficial; only after they are given feedback which makes it explicit that using the rehearsal improves their recall do they realize the usefulness of the strategy. An awareness of one's own memory performance and the ability to apply strategies in appropriate contexts is an aspect of metacognition and will be discussed below.

We can see from the results of these experiments that the development of memory strategies is gradual; even when children have realized the need to apply a strategy they may at first use it only in a limited way. This is a common finding that applies to most strategies and as we have seen, when grouping information children may not use the most effective categories; when using elaboration they may only link items in a static way; and when they have cues for retrieving information they may only use them in a limited way. Children may also vary in how consistently they apply a strategy. For example, McGilly and Siegler (1989) gave children several similar memory problems in the course of an experiment, and found that rather than applying the same strategy to all these problems some children used different strategies each time. Even when children begin to use a strategy which is appropriate to learning material in a memory task, their recall of the material may only be slightly improved – it may be that the processing effort of using a novel strategy is such that it leaves little processing capacity to actually learn the material. The use of memory strategies in more sophisticated ways may be a gradual development over several years (see Miller, 1994) and will depend on several factors including children's processing capacity and their knowledge (which we discuss later).

◀Metacognition▶▶▶

Metacognition refers to a person's awareness of his or her own cognitive abilities and limitations. For example, most adults know that their memory span is six or seven items and that they may be able to hold that many items in working memory. Adults also know that to retain information for more than a short time it is necessary to process that information in such a way that it is retained in long-term memory. An awareness of one's own memory capacity and processes is an understanding which has to develop.

Awareness of capacity Flavell, Friedrichs and Hoyt (1970) showed children cards with up to ten pictures on them, and asked them how many pictures they thought they could remember. The children were later given a test to find out how many pictures they could actually remember. Young children were unrealistic in the number they said that they would remember. Four- and 5-year-olds actually recalled only three or four pictures, but thought they would be able to recall at least eight pictures. It was only after about the age of 9 years that the majority of children made accurate predictions about the number of items they were likely to remember.

How do children develop a better understanding of their own memory capacity? They may learn from experience. Kail (1990) cited a study by Markman who showed 5-year-olds a set of items, asked the children how many they thought they could remember, and then tested their actual recall. Markman repeated this procedure several times with the same children and found that with repeated testing they became more realistic about how many items they could remember. Children may also learn about memory by considering how well other people can recall information. For example, Yussen and Levy (1975) asked 4- and 8-year-olds to estimate how many items they could remember (from a large number of items that they were shown). The children were also told what an average child of their own age would be able to recall, and this information helped the 8-year-olds to make realistic estimates about their own ability. The information had little effect on the 4-year-olds who may not have realized that knowing how other 4-year-olds performed had implications for their own performance.

Awareness of strategies Children must also become aware of the usefulness of memory strategies and which ones are the most appropriate for a particular task. Kreutzer, Leonard and Flavell (1975) asked 5-, 6-, 8- and 10-year-olds how they would remember to take their skates to school. The suggested strategies could be divided into several categories – using the skates as a direct reminder (e.g. putting them with other things to be taken to school); using an external aid (e.g. writing a note and putting it where it would be seen); relying on someone else's memory (e.g. asking parents to remind them); or just relying on their own memories. The older children were able to suggest more types of strategy, and were more likely to suggest the reliable ones.

◀Knowledge and Memory Development▶▶▶

An important aspect of memory development is the knowledge that children can bring to bear on a memory task – knowledge here does not just mean a knowledge of memory strategies, but children's general knowledge and experience. As children learn more, they can build up a rich information base and hence new information can be linked to the known information in a more meaningful and effective way. In other words, as children know more they should become better at processing and encoding novel information which can be related to pre-existing knowledge.

The importance of knowledge was demonstrated in a study by Chi (1978) who compared the memory of children who were experienced chess players with the memory of adults who knew how to play chess but were not particularly proficient. Both the children and the adults were asked to carry out two memory tasks; in one they were asked to learn lists of ten digits, and in the other they were asked to memorize chess board positions with an average of 22 pieces. The adults were better at remembering the digits, but the children performed much better at learning the chess positions. It is unusual for children to perform better than adults in a memory task, and Chi argued that the children's greater knowledge of chess contributed to their performance. As they were familiar with chess positions it may have been easier for them to 'chunk' groups of pieces into meaningful patterns and encode them more effectively than the less-experienced adult chess players. This advantage only applied to learning chess positions and indicated the importance of having an established knowledge base which was directly relevant to the task.

Other studies have also demonstrated that if people have established information in a particular domain of knowledge it is easier for them to encode new information related to that domain. Spilich, Vesonder, Chiesi and Voss (1979) described an invented baseball game to two groups of students. One group was knowledgeable about baseball and the other was not. The knowledgeable group recalled more details about the game. In a similar experiment with children, Schneider and Bjorklund (1992) divided a number of 7- to 9-year-olds into a group who knew a lot about soccer and a group who only knew a little. The children were asked to learn two sets of drawings. One set included drawings of items that were related to soccer and the other set included unrelated items. There was no difference between the two groups in their recall of unrelated items, but the group who knew more about soccer were better at remembering the lists of related items. These experiments demonstrated how relevant knowledge can increase the likelihood of information being learnt successfully.

The relationship between knowledge and memory strategies is not straightforward. Some researchers have argued that having good knowledge of an area can contribute to recall of information from that area, because it allows a child to recognize and understand the information more readily so that more capacity remains in working memory for generating memory strategies (Bjorklund, 1989). In contrast, other researchers have suggested that when children recognize that they have only limited knowledge of material which is to be learnt, this realization will trigger the use of more deliberate memory strategies to compensate for learning material which is not easily encoded (Alexander and Schwanenflugel, 1994).

◀Constructive Memory and Knowledge Structures▶▶▶

Constructive memory refers to a person's ability to infer, extrapolate or invent information which might never have been directly experienced. If people listen to sentences like 'the box is to the right of the tree' and 'the chair is on top of the box', and then, later, they are given several similar sentences and asked to say which ones they heard previously, they may be convinced that a sentence like 'the chair is to the right of the tree' is one they heard before. From the original information people may infer the scene being described and then come to believe that a sentence which includes information that corresponds to the inferred scene must be a sentence which they had heard previously. In this example constructive memory leads to an incorrect inference.

Brown, Smiley and Lawton (1978) showed that children also make false inferences. They told 7- and 12-year-olds a story about an invented group of people called the Targa. All the children heard the same story but half were told that the Targa were Eskimos and half were told that the Targa lived in the desert. Later, the children were asked to re-tell the story from memory. Brown et al. examined the recalled stories for intrusions which were related to assumptions about where the Targa lived. For example, the original story included a reference to bad weather, and some of the children who thought that the Targa lived in desert areas recalled this reference as a mention of hot conditions, and some of the children who thought the Targa were Eskimos recalled it as a reference to cold weather. The older children made many more of this type of error than the younger children. Brown et al. suggested that the intrusions were due to the children introducing information from knowledge they already had about Eskimos or desert people, and the larger number of intrusions by the older children reflected their greater knowledge of such cultures.

Constructive memory is related to 'scripts' and 'schemas'. The term script was used by Schank and Abelson (1977) to describe a sequence of actions which are appropriate within a particular context and lead to a specific goal. For example, you might have a script for going to a restaurant and this would include an expected sequence of actions involving specific aspects of the restaurant. The script would include sequences for entering (locating a table, sitting down, etc.); ordering (reading the menu, speaking to the waiter, etc.); eating (being served, eating courses in expected sequence, etc.); and leaving (paying the bill, leaving a tip, etc.). Each part of the script can be thought of as a 'slot' which needs to be filled, with both obligatory and optional actions. For example, it would be obligatory to order before eating, but leaving a tip might depend on how much you liked the service. Adults may have any number of scripts relating to different events. They are important because without generalized script knowledge it would be difficult to function in new contexts. When we go into almost any new restaurant most of what happens can be predicted from a script derived from previous visits to other restaurants.

Do children structure their knowledge of the world as scripts? Nelson and Gruendel (1986) investigated eight preschool children's scripts by asking them what happened in different eating contexts (at lunch in their day-care centre, eating dinner at home and going to McDonald's). Most of the children mentioned the same actions for each event, and focused on main actions. For example, children typically said they ate food, but did not usually specify what they ate – in other words they reported the events as if they had an 'open slot' which could be filled with more specific information if that was required. All the children reported, without error, the sequence of actions involved in eating a meal, with the significant exception that children reported paying for food at McDonald's after eating it. This error suggests that children were referring to script-based knowledge about what it means to go out for food – at nearly all restaurants, payment is made at the end of a meal, but the procedure at McDonald's is an exception. On the one hand, children's ability to develop scripts is important in structuring their experience in such a way that they can use and adapt their knowledge of previous events to make sense of similar but novel events. On the other hand, a dependence on script-based knowledge can lead to inaccurate assumptions when recalling information, if specific events do not correspond to the script (as in the McDonald's example). With age and experience children's scripts become more elaborate, and they become better at distinguishing specific events from generalized script knowledge.

A schema is similar to a script because it refers to an organized grouping of knowledge, but unlike a script, the term schema denotes what is known (for example) about a scene, or a place, or an object. A schema can generate expectations about what a scene should include. For instance, a schema for a kitchen might include 'slots' for sink, cooker, refrigerator, table and so on. Even young children can have established schemas for objects or places which are well-known. Blades and Banham (1990) asked children to learn a realistic model of a kitchen. The model included ten items of typical kitchen furniture, but it did not include a cooker. When the children had learnt the model layout all the items were removed and placed in a box with an additional ten items of toy furniture (for example, a bed, an armchair, book shelves). These additional items included a cooker. The children were asked to use the box of toy furniture to reconstruct the model kitchen from memory as accurately as possible. The reconstruction was generally accurate, and very few of the children included non-kitchen items in their models. However, 60 per cent of the children did include the cooker in their reconstructions. Blades and Banham suggested that the inclusion of the cooker indicated that children's reconstructions were based not only on recall of the model they had learnt, but also on their knowledge, or schema, about kitchens in general.

Generating schemas and scripts is an important way to represent knowledge and to use that knowledge effectively to make inferences and predictions about the world. However, in using schema-based knowledge it is also important to retain flexibility because there may sometimes be exceptions to the schema (e.g. paying for food before eating it at McDonald's, or kitchens without cookers) and this flexibility may only develop with age and experience (Nelson, 1986). As Kail (1990) says: 'Knowledge is a double-edged sword. On the one hand, knowledge allows us to understand novel versions of familiar experiences (e.g. going to a restaurant) that would be completely uninterpretable if knowledge consisted only of specific previous experiences. On the other hand, knowledge does so at the cost of introducing some distortions into our perception of experiences and our later recall of those experiences' (p. 95).

Summary

In the previous sections we described some examples of use of the information processing approach to the study of children's cognitive development. The emphasis of this approach is on the mechanisms which children bring to bear in any task, coupled with an appreciation of the limitations which might affect children's performance. The information processing approach includes detailed studies of children's performance in specific tasks (see box 12.1) as well as investigating the more general processes (such as memory strategies) which might be applied across a range of different tasks. Researchers in the information processing tradition attempt to explain developmental change with reference to a number of interrelated and inseparable factors – these include the changing capacity of the child's processing abilities as they mature; changes in children's ability to focus attention; the development of memory strategies; the ability to apply progressively more sophisticated strategies in specific tasks; the growth of children's structured knowledge; and children's increasing awareness of their own abilities (i.e. their metacognitive ability).

◀Children's Eyewitness Research▶▶▶

Much of the research into children's memory has focused on the development of memory capacity and strategies. Such research can be carried out successfully using well-established and appropriate paradigms – for example, asking children to learn lists of words, remember the names of pictures or recall stories they have heard. However, in the last few years researchers have investigated memory development in the context of children's ability to give accurate testimony about events that they have witnessed. These investigations have been driven by the fact that more, and younger, children are taking part in court proceedings. One of the reasons for children's greater involvement in courts has been the growing realization about the frequency of child abuse and the need to bring abusers to court. The nature of child abuse often means that the child himself or herself may be the only witness that the prosecution can call on for evidence (Perry and Wrightsman, 1991).

In the past, children were rarely called upon to be witnesses, because there was a general belief that children would be unreliable when giving testimony. Several different and influential arguments contributed to this belief. Freud reported that, during therapy, a number of his adult patients claimed to have been abused when they were children. Although Freud at first accepted such accounts as accurate descriptions of what had happened during childhood, he later decided that such claims were fantasies invented by his patients. Freud's belief that adults invented fantasies about early sexual experience became a key part of his psychoanalytic theory (see Masson, 1992). His belief that people invent traumatic events was frequently cited as evidence that adults' or children's reports of abuse could not be accepted as reliable.

Other researchers argued that children were too suggestible to be accurate witnesses. Varendonck (1911) investigated children's suggestibility after the murder of a young girl in Belgium in 1910. The police had arrested a man on the basis of testimony provided by a 9-year-old friend of the girl. The friend described the man in detail and claimed that she saw him take the murdered girl into a wood. However, this testimony was given the day after the murder; when the friend had been questioned on the day the girl disappeared the friend had not mentioned seeing a man at all. Varendonck was concerned that the friend's statement might have been suggested to her. He therefore carried out several experiments with children of a similar age. In one experiment he tested a total of 58 children aged between 7 and 9 years. He went into their classrooms and, referring to a teacher (Monsieur Th.) who was not present but with whom the children were familiar, simply wrote a question on the blackboard: 'What colour is Monsieur Th.'s moustache?' Fifty-one of the children gave a colour, only seven either gave no answer or realized that the teacher did not have a moustache at all!

In other experiments Varendonck (1911) asked 8-year-olds to name a man who had visited the school earlier in the day. A few of the children named the man without further prompting, and when Varendonck asked the others, who had made no response 'Wasn't it Monsieur M. who came to me?' nearly all agreed. Under further questioning some children went on to describe what Monsieur M. said and did. However, no one had visited the school earlier in the day. On the basis of these findings Varendonck argued that young children were too suggestible to be regarded as credible witnesses, and his experiments contributed to the acquittal of the man accused of murder. Varendonck concluded his argument with the words 'When are we going to give up, in all civilised countries, listening to children in courts of law?' (1911, p. 136). These studies and several similar ones meant that courts of law did give up listening to children for many years (see Ceci and Bruck, 1993).

Only comparatively recently have researchers considered how well children recall real-life events. Marin, Holmes, Guth and Kovac (1979) tested the recall of 6-, 9-, and 13-year-olds, and adults for a brief staged incident (an argument between two people). A few minutes later participants were given an unexpected recall test and were asked to recall as much as they could about the incident, answer 20 objective questions about it, and then pick out a photograph (from a set of six) of one of the people who took part in the argument.

In free recall the youngest children gave little information about the event (only one or two items), but there was an age-related increase in the number of items of information recalled (the adults mentioned seven or eight items). However, the youngest participants made virtually no errors in free recall, but on average the adults gave approximately one incorrect item of information in free recall. In other words, the children said little but what they did say was usually accurate. The most important, and surprising result, was that there was no difference between the groups for the objective questions – all groups answered three-quarters of the questions correctly. Nor were there any age differences for the photograph recognition task.

The results from Marin et al.'s (1979) experiment demonstrated that children could be as accurate as adults in reporting information about an event, at least when answering specific objective questions about it. This finding contradicted the earlier assumptions that children would be poor eyewitnesses. However, Marin et al.'s experiment was limited. Participants were only exposed to a brief incident lasting a few seconds. Also, Marin et al. only asked a single misleading question (and found that about half of each age group answered it correctly), but it is likely that most eyewitnesses are exposed to many misleading or suggestive questions, and as early researchers (e.g. Varendonck, 1911) have shown, it may be suggestive questions which highlight age-related differences.

Nonetheless, Marin et al.'s study was an important stimulus for later experiments, most of which confirmed Marin et al.'s original findings. One such experiment was by Goodman and Reed (1986) who used a more elaborate event, and then asked children both objective questions and suggestive questions about it. Children were as accurate as adults on the objective questions (supporting the results from Marin et al.), but more likely than adults to be misled by suggestive questions (supporting the earlier research into children's suggestibility). The Goodman and Reed experiment is described in detail in box 12.2.

The cognitive interview

Marin et al. (1979) found that children were unlikely to offer much information in free recall, even when they knew a lot about the event as demonstrated by their responses to objective questions. Objective questions can only be asked if the interviewer already knows about the event. If the interviewer does not know about the event it is often difficult to ask objective questions because many questions involve assumptions, in other words they become suggestive questions and, as many researchers have demonstrated, children may be misled by such questions. To elicit information from witnesses about events, without asking direct questions, researchers have developed an interview procedure referred to as the 'cognitive interview' (Fisher and Geiselman, 1992).

The interview procedure relies on established cognitive principles to maximize what witnesses recall. These include asking a witness to reconstruct the original context of the event by describing the scene and how they felt at the time, encouraging the witness to report as much as possible, even if some details are only partially remembered or thought not to be important, re-telling the event in a different order (e.g. from the last thing which happened to the first), and asking the witness to report the events from different perspectives (e.g. by describing what someone else who was involved would have seen and heard). The witness might also be encouraged to use specific retrieval techniques – for example, associating memories (e.g. 'Did the man's face remind you of anyone you knew?') or, if trying to recall an overheard name or word, thinking of similar words or going through the alphabet to trigger recall of the name when the initial letter of the name is reached. Compared with a standard interview (in which witnesses are just asked to recall as much as they can) the cognitive interview can be a successful way to elicit additional information from adults without increasing the amount of inaccurate information reported (Fisher and McCauley, 1995).

The same effect has been found when using the cognitive interview procedure with children (e.g. McCauley and Fisher, 1995). But many researchers have found that, with children, the improvement in their recall is often much less than the improvement found with adults. This may not be surprising because, as discussed earlier in this chapter, children may have less well-developed memory strategies and less understanding of their own abilities than adults. In other words, some of the techniques employed in the cognitive interview may be less applicable for children. Nonetheless, the research into the cognitive interview provides a good example of how an understanding of cognitive processes, and an awareness of how children's memory abilities develop, can have important practical implications.

Children's suggestibility

Goodman and Reed's (1986) result that children were more suggestible than adults has been found by most other researchers who have included misleading questions in interviews with children. There may be several reasons why children are more suggestible, and in a review of the relevant research Ceci and Bruck (1993) suggested several cognitive mechanisms which might account for the effect of misleading questions. If information about an event (e.g. that a man wore a brown shirt) has only been encoded weakly, when a witness is given a misleading suggestion in the course of an interview (e.g. 'The man was wearing a red shirt wasn't he?') the latter information may overwrite the earlier, weakly encoded information. Warren, Hulse-Trotter and Tubbs (1991) found that if some aspects of an event were only weakly encoded it was those aspects which were most open to suggestive questioning. If children encode some aspects of an event less well than adults then they may be more likely than adults to be misled by later suggestions. If some information was never encoded at all there may simply be 'gaps' in memory which may be filled with the information implied by a suggestive question. It is likely that young children encode less about an event than adults encode (see Vurpillot's 1968 experiment) and therefore they may have more gaps which are susceptible to later suggestions.

If a child has certain knowledge of some facts it is unlikely that they will be misled – children are unlikely to be persuaded that their own name is something different. As we described in the previous section, even young children develop knowledge schemas, and suggestibility and schemas may interact in two different ways. When children do have schema-based knowledge of an event, but are inflexible in their use of a schema (Nelson, 1986), it might be easier to mislead them about an event which they witnessed when the suggested information corresponds to what they expected to happen rather than what actually happened. On the other hand, when young children do not have schema-based knowledge of an event they may be better at reporting what they actually saw than adults who draw false inferences. Lindberg (1991) showed 8-year-olds, 11-year-olds and adults a film of students working in a classroom. The film included scenes in which one student (innocently) asked another student for the time. After the participants had seen the film Lindberg told them that the film included scenes of cheating. When they were then asked what they had seen in the film the 11-year-olds and the adults interpreted incidents like asking the time as acts of cheating, but the 8-year-olds described the same incidents (correctly) as one student simply checking the time. Lindberg suggested that 8-year-olds probably did not have a script for cheating and without knowing that asking the time could be a pretext for cheating they were less likely to be misled by Lindberg's suggestion about what they had seen.

As well as cognitive factors there will be other factors associated with the conduct of an interview which may influence children's suggestibility. These will include factors like the perceived authority of the interviewer. If a parent, teacher or police officer makes a suggestion a child may feel under greater pressure to go along with the suggestion than if it comes from a less authoritative person (Perry and Wrightsman, 1991). The style of the interviewer may also affect children's suggestibility. For example, Goodman, Rudy, Bottoms and Aman (1990) compared 4-year-olds' and 7-year-olds' responses to misleading questions which were given by either a 'nice' interviewer who created an atmosphere of support and encouragement during questioning or a 'neutral' interviewer who remained detached. Seven-year-olds were not influenced by the style of the interviewer, but the younger children were less likely to give incorrect answers to misleading questions from the 'nice' interviewer. In another study, Moston (1987) considered the effect of asking 6-year-olds the same question more than once. The first time they were asked the question about an event 60 per cent of the children's answers were correct, but when the question was repeated only 39 per cent of the responses were correct. This may not be surprising if children assume that being asked a question more than once implies that the first answer was wrong. After all, teachers and parents do not usually ask a question more than once if they receive an adequate answer the first time.

Children's suggestibility is an important area of research because the results from this research have crucial implications for assessing the credibility of child witnesses and formulating policy about the way that children should be interviewed. As we have seen, many factors can contribute to children's suggestibility, and in practice all or most of these may be operating, but as yet, researchers have only considered the different factors in isolation and little is known about the combined effect of such factors in actual interviews (see Ceci and Bruck, 1993).

The effects of stress on children's recall

If children are witnesses they may be reporting events which were stressful and stress may influence memory in either a negative or a positive way (Baddeley, 1993). It is possible that an event which is stressful or frightening will be recalled more vividly than more mundane events, or alternatively, as Freud suggested, an unpleasant experience might be repressed or lost because it is too stressful to hold in conscious memory.

Researchers are limited in how much they can investigate this issue, because it is clearly inappropriate to place experimental participants under stress just to find out how stress might affect their recall of an event. Nonetheless, some researchers have taken advantage of 'naturally' occurring stressful experiences to find out how well children remember unpleasant or traumatic events. Goodman, Hepps and Reed (1986) compared two groups of children, aged between 3 and 7 years. Both groups visited a clinic, the 'high-stress' group were taken to the clinic to have a blood sample taken, and the 'low-stress' group went through the same procedure but instead of a blood sample they had a washable transfer placed on their arm. A few days later the children were questioned about the visit and both groups had good recall of the events which had happened at the clinic, and there was no difference between the groups – the children in the high-stress group recalled as much as the other children.

In a similar experiment, Saywitz, Goodman, Nicholas and Moan (1991) investigated how well 5- and 7-year-olds recalled a visit to a clinic which involved them being examined by a doctor who asked the children to undress for a physical examination. Half the children (in the low-stress group) were given an examination of their spine by a doctor who only touched them on their back, and half (in the high-stress group) were given a physical examination which involved touching genital areas. Then, a week later, the children were interviewed about what had happened. In free recall there was no difference between the 5-year-olds in the low- and high-stress groups, both groups recalled a similar amount of correct information. However, in free recall the 7-year-olds in the high-stress group offered less information about the event than the 7-year-olds in the low-stress group. Nonetheless, when these children were asked specific questions about what had happened they correctly answered questions about where they had been touched. The older children may have been more hesitant in spontaneously revealing what had happened, but this was not because they had forgotten the stressful information, as they were able to report the event accurately when specifically asked about it. Not surprisingly, children may be less willing to report information which is distressing, but this only points to the need for sensitive interviewing techniques.

Children may experience stress not only at the time of witnessing an event, but also at the time of re-telling it, especially if they have to appear in an open court. In an experiment by Saywitz and Nathanson (1993) 8- to 10-

year-old children witnessed a staged event and then half the children were interviewed on their own by an interviewer in a room at their school, and the other half were interviewed in a full mock courtroom (in a university law school) with actors representing all the key court figures as well as jurors and spectators. The children in the court condition found the experience more stressful than those who were interviewed in the classroom. Most importantly, the children in school recalled more correct information about the event than the children in court, and the children in school were less likely to make errors in response to misleading questions. In this experiment it was clear that stress at the time of recall had a negative effect on children's performance as witnesses.

Summary

Research into children's ability as witnesses is important for what it can reveal about memory in everyday contexts and it is also important because of the implications it has for talking to and interviewing children who have been involved in events which might become the focus of legal proceedings (Dent and Flin, 1992; Goodman and Bottoms, 1993). The results from the research have already made a significant contribution to the treatment of children in courts. For example, in the UK there are now carefully constructed guidelines about the initial interviewing of children who may later have to appear in court (HMSO, 1992) and the frequent publication of psychological research in legal and other journals has meant that all those involved in the interviewing of children are more aware of the issues relating to the development of children's memory abilities.

◄Further Reading►►

R. Kail 1990 (3rd edn): *The Development of Memory in Children*, New York: Freeman, is an excellent and very readable introduction to all aspects of children's memory development. Kail includes a brief introduction to research into eyewitness memory.

S. Meadows 1993: *The Child as Thinker. The Development and Acquisition of Cognition in Childhood*, London: Routledge, is an extensive text book, with very fluent discussions of all the factors which contribute to children's cognitive development.

P. H. Miller 1993 (3rd edn): *Theories of Developmental Psychology*, New York: Freeman, takes a slightly different approach from most books by focusing on theories rather than specific research results. For this reason, the book has the best description of different approaches to child development including very clear comparisons between, for example, Piaget's theory and information processing approaches.

R. S. Siegler 1991 (2nd edn): *Children's Thinking*, Englewood Cliffs, NJ: Prentice Hall, provides a good coverage of cognitive development. The text is very clear, but a little more detailed and advanced than the preceding references.

J. H. Flavell, P. H. Miller and S. A. Miller 1993 (3rd edn): *Cognitive Development*, Englewood Cliffs, NJ: Prentice Hall, is a specialized and detailed book. Research results are often referred to briefly and the authors assume that the reader will already have some knowledge of the field. Nonetheless, it is an important book with particularly good discussions of the major issues in cognitive development.

S. Goodman and B. L. Bottoms (eds) 1993: *Child Victims, Child Witnesses. Understanding and Improving Testimony*, New York: Guilford Press, is a very good collection of papers which cover most aspects of the psychological research into children's eyewitness memory.

S. J. Ceci and M. Bruck 1995: *Jeopardy in the Courtroom. A Scientific Analysis of Children's Testimony*, Washington: American Psychological Association, is a good review of research into children's suggestibility which integrates the empirical findings from psychological studies with extensive examples of courtroom practice.

H. Dent and R. Flin (eds) 1992: *Children as Witnesses*, Chichester: Wiley, is a collection of papers which covers both psychological and legal topics. Many of these are written with reference to legal practice in the UK.

N. W. Perry and L. S. Wrightsman 1991: *The Child Witness. Legal Issues and Dilemmas*, Newbury Park, CA: Sage, is written from a legal rather than a psychological perspective, but does provide a good review of the psychological research into children's memory and is particularly good in drawing out the implications of this research for courtroom practice.

◀ Discussion Points ▶ ▶ ▶

1 Compare the stage theories put forward by Piaget, and by neo-Piagetians like Case.
2 Discuss what it means to describe development in terms of the progressive improvement of problem-solving and memory strategies.
3 Why is memory development such a gradual process?
4 How does research into children's eyewitness memory differ from earlier research into memory development?
5 Why are children suggestible in interviews?

Box 12.1
The origins of scientific reasoning

Siegler (1976) investigated the strategies which children used in Inhelder and Piaget's balance scale problem. In this task children were shown a balance scale with four equally spaced pegs on either side of the fulcrum (see box figure 12.1.1). A number of weights (each of the same value) were placed on some of the pegs. While the weights were placed the balance was held in place by a wedge. Then the child was asked to predict which side of the balance would go down, or whether it would remain in balance if the wedge was removed.

Rather than test children with the balance scale and then interpret their performance in terms of the strategies which they might have used, Siegler first considered what strategies were possible, and only then did he test children. Siegler's (1976)

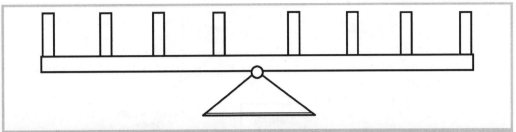

Box Figure 12.1.1   Redrawn and based on R. S. Siegler (1976), Three aspects of cognitive development, *Cognitive Psychology*, 8, 481–520.

methodology involved four steps. First, he considered the dimensions of the balance scale problem and the potential strategies which could be used to solve it. Second, he designed a set of tasks. Third, he predicted how a child who used a specific strategy would perform on the set of tasks. Fourth, he used the set of tasks to test a large number of children at different ages to establish developmental differences in the way they approached the task.

Strategies

According to Siegler there were four strategies which children might use (and there was also the possibility that they would have no strategy at all and simply guess the answer):

No strategy (i.e. just guess)
Strategy I: If there are a different number, then say 'the side with more weights will go down'. If the number of weights is the same on both sides, then say 'the scale will balance'. (This strategy

considers only the number of weights on either side of the fulcrum and ignores the distance of the weights.)
Strategy II: If there are a different number, then say 'the side with more weights will go down'. If the number of weights is the same on both sides, then say 'the side with the weights furthest from the fulcrum will go down'.
Strategy III: If the number of weights and the distance of the weights from the fulcrum on both sides are equal, then predict that the scale will balance. If both sides have the same number of weights then consider the distance of the weights and say that 'the side with weights furthest from the fulcrum will go down'. If both sides have weights at equal distance from the fulcrum, then say 'the side with the greater number of weights will go down'. If one side has more weights and the other side has weights at a greater distance from the fulcrum, then guess.
Strategy IV: Follow Strategy III, unless one side has

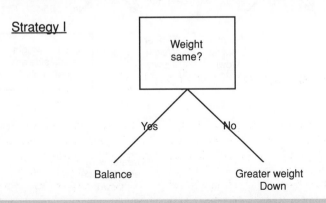

Box Figure 12.1.2a   Strategy I – redrawn and based on R. S. Siegler (1976), Three aspects of cognitive development, *Cognitive Psychology*, 8, 481–520.

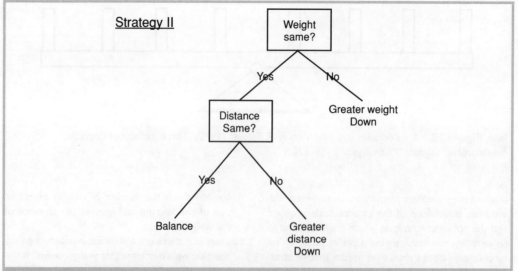

Box Figure 12.1.2b   Strategy II – redrawn and based on R. S. Siegler (1976), Three aspects of cognitive development, *Cognitive Psychology*, 8, 481–520.

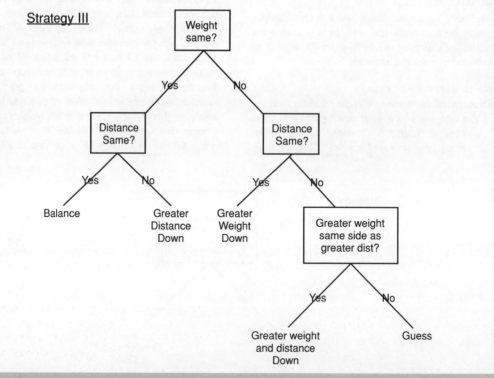

Box Figure 12.1.2c   Strategy III – redrawn and based on R. S. Siegler (1976), Three aspects of cognitive development, *Cognitive Psychology*, 8, 481–520.

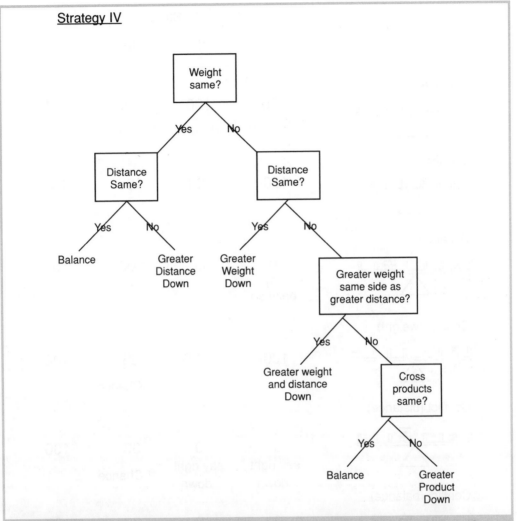

Box Figure 12.1.2d   Strategy IV – redrawn and based on R. S. Siegler (1976), Three aspects of cognitive development, *Cognitive Psychology*, 8, 481–520.

more weights and one has weights at a greater distance from the fulcrum. In this case, calculate torques by multiplying weights times distance. Then predict that the side with the greater torque will go down.

These strategies are shown diagrammatically in box figure 12.1.2. As can be seen particularly well from these diagrams, each strategy incorporates the preceding strategy. In other words, each strategy is like the preceding one, but with additional components, which contribute to progressively more accurate solutions to the balance problem.

Designing the tasks

Having described the possible strategies, Siegler then generated a set of different balance weight problems (these problems are shown in box figure 12.1.3):

1 Balance problems have the same configuration of weights on either side of the fulcrum.
2 Weight problems have unequal number of weights, but at the same distance on either side of the fulcrum.
3 Distance problems have equal number of weights on both sides, but at different distances.

	Strategy			
	I	II	III	IV
Balance	100	100	100	100
Weight	100	100	100	100
Distance	0 say balance	100	100	100
Conflict (weight)	100	100	33 Chance	100
Conflict (distance)	0 say right down	0 say right down	33 Chance	100
Conflict (balance)	0 say right down	0 say right down	33 Chance	100

Box Figure 12.1.3   Figures in each column are the percentage of correct answers expected when each strategy is applied to each problem. Redrawn and adapted from R. S. Siegler (1976), Three aspects of cognitive development, *Cognitive Psychology*, 8, 481–520.

4   Conflict-weight problems: one side has more weights, and the other side has weights further from the fulcrum. The side with the greater number of weights goes down.

5   Conflict-distance problems: one side has more weights, and the other side has weights further from the fulcrum. The side with the greater distance goes down.

6   Conflict-balance problems: one side has more weights, and the other side has weights further from the fulcrum. The two sides balance.

Predicting performance

Box figure 12.1.3 also describes the answer that you would expect a child to give to that problem if she was using one of the four strategies. For example, if a child is applying Strategy I to the balance, weight and conflict-weight problems she will give correct answers each time. However, if she uses Strategy I with distance problems, conflict-distance and conflict-balance problems, not only will she be wrong but it is possible to predict her incorrect answer. With the set of tasks designed by Siegler, the use of each strategy will generate a different pattern of responses. In other words, if children are given a set of tasks, it is then possible to identify the strategy that they are using from the pattern of their answers.

An intriguing aspect of box figure 12.1.3 is that on conflict-weight problems, children who use Strategy III will perform worse than children who use the less sophisticated Strategy I. It is not often in developmental psychology that children using a less advanced problem-solving strategy are predicted to perform better than children using a more complete strategy.

Testing children

Siegler asked 5- to 17-year-olds to carry out balance scale problems (like the ones described

above) and he found that most of them consistently used one of the expected strategies. Five-year-olds usually used Strategy I, 9-year-olds used Strategy II or III, and older children used Strategy III. Very few children used Strategy IV. Siegler also found that 5-year-olds (who nearly always used Strategy I) were correct on 89 per cent of the conflict-weight problems, but the 17-year-olds (who generally used Strategy III) were only correct on 51 per cent of these problems. These findings support Siegler's predictions about the use of the strategies he had described.

Siegler's approach provides a good example of how cognitive development can be investigated in a rigorous manner which involves the generation of hypothetical models (in this case the description of possible strategies prior to the experiment) and the use of specific predictions (in this example, the expected performance of children) which can then be empirically tested.

Based on material in R. S. Siegler 1976: Three aspects of cognitive development, *Cognitive Psychology*, 8, 481–520.

Box 12.2
Age differences in eyewitness testimony

Goodman and Reed (1986) were some of the first researchers to carry out an extensive study of children's eyewitness memory. Groups of children and adults took part in an event and were later asked questions, in several different ways, to find out how much of the event they could remember. The participants included groups of 3-year-olds, 6-year-olds and adults. All the participants were told that the experiment was about motor skills (i.e. physical movement). They were introduced to a confederate of the experimenters who asked the participants to copy him performing a series of arm movements.

Then, about 4 days later, participants took part in a second session in which they were told that the real purpose of the experiment concerned their memory, and they were first asked a series of questions about what happened in the first session.

There were 17 objective questions (e.g. 'What colour was the man's hair?' or 'Did the man have a ring on?') and four suggestive questions (e.g. 'The man was wearing a sweater wasn't he?' or 'Was the man wearing a watch on his right or left hand?'). Participants were then asked for free recall – i.e. they were asked to say everything they could remember about the event, and were given general prompts like 'What did the man look like?' 'What was in the room?' 'Anything else?' Following the free recall participants were given an identification task. They were presented with five pictures and asked to say whether the confederate's picture was among the photographs and, if so, to point him out.

The mean number of objective and suggestive questions answered by each group is shown in box table 12.2.1. There was no difference in the accuracy of adults and 6-year-olds on the objective

Box Table 12.2.1   Mean number of correct answers to objective and subjective questions

Type of questions	Age		
	3 years	6 years	Adult
Objective (out of 17)	10.0	11.8	12.6
Subjective (out of 4)	1.4	2.2	3.1

questions, but both groups gave more correct answers than 3-year-olds. For the subjective questions 3-year-olds were more likely to be misled than 6-year-olds who were more likely to be misled than the adults.

Participants' free recall was scored for the number of correct items of information. The mean number of items recalled by the 3-year-olds was 0.8, for the 6-year-olds it was 5.5, and for adults, 17.7. The adults recalled more information than 6-year-olds who recalled more than 3-year-olds. Goodman and Reed also considered intrusion errors (i.e. when participants reported events which did not happen). The adults made a mean of 2.3 intrusion errors, which was more than either of the two groups of children (6-year-olds made 0.9 and 3-year-olds made 0.6).

On the identification task 74 per cent of adults made correct identifications as did 95 per cent of the 6-year-olds, and both these groups were better than the 3-year-olds (38 per cent correct).

There are several important results in this experiment. The children, especially the 3-year-olds, offered little information in free recall. It was only the adults who gave much detail about the first session (though they also added more incorrect information). However, the limited responses of the children in free recall did not reflect a lack of knowledge because 6-year-olds answered specific, objective, questions as well as adults did. This indicates that young children can often provide reliable testimony, at least when asked questions which can be answered with yes/no or one-word responses. Although the 3-year-olds did not do as well as the older groups, they were still able to answer more than half the objective questions accurately. In other words, the children generally had good recall of the event, and were also good at the identification task. Nonetheless, there were important differences between the groups with the suggestive questions, because the children were more likely to be misled by this type of question.

This pattern of responses has been found in other studies (see Goodman and Bottoms, 1993). It indicates that children can often be relied on when reporting events which they have seen or in which they have been involved, but they may be particularly vulnerable to misleading questions.

Based on material in G. S. Goodman and R. S. Reed 1986: *Law and Human Behavior*, 10, 317–32.

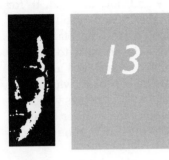

13 Children's Understanding of Mind

In chapter 2 we discussed the possible evolution of 'mindreading' in primates. As Byrne and Whiten (1987) argued, there are some observations of chimpanzees which are most easily interpreted as examples of deliberately deceptive behaviour. The presence of deceptive behaviour in other primates is the best evidence we have that some animals may be able to take into account the beliefs of others. Deception means altering the beliefs of others. In the example given on p. 49 one chimpanzee did not immediately go to some food which was available, but rather acted as if the food was not there at all. This was because a second chimpanzee was nearby who would have made an attempt to grab the food for himself. The first chimpanzee was, in effect, generating a false belief in the mind of the second chimpanzee, and this implies that the first chimpanzee had some understanding that the beliefs of the other chimpanzee could be manipulated. Put simply, the first chimpanzee understood that the other chimpanzee had a mind.

This chapter will concentrate on children's understanding of the mind. With a few exceptions (discussed later in the chapter) we assume that all adults have an awareness that other people have minds. It is basic to our everyday human understanding that both ourselves and others have beliefs. We know this in many ways: we know that we ourselves have beliefs about the world, that our beliefs change, that they might be wrong, and that what we say and what we do are based on our beliefs. We can also assume that other people have beliefs; they can tell us those beliefs directly or we can work out their beliefs indirectly from the way they behave.

Understanding that most individual behaviour is based on individuals' beliefs about the world is not just a useful facet of human knowledge, it is vital if we are to make sense of what others say and how they act. If, for example, we know that there is some chocolate in the kitchen cupboard (and nowhere else in the house) but a friend goes to look for the chocolate on the dining-room table, our friend's behaviour would make no sense to us at all if we could not interpret it in terms of what our friend believed about the world. We would assume that she thought that the chocolate was on the table, because we know that she has a mind which includes beliefs which, as in this case, might be wrong. If we did not take into account her beliefs it would be very difficult to explain why she went to the dining room (except as some form of random behaviour).

Having an understanding of other people as people who have desires, beliefs and their own interpretations of the world is often referred to as having a 'theory of mind' – calling it a 'theory' stresses two aspects of understanding about the mental world. First, we cannot directly see or touch the mind, and therefore we have to infer (or theorize) about others' mental states from what they say or the way they behave. Second, a theory is usually a complex interconnected set of ideas, and an adult's understanding of the mental world, taking into account emotions, desires, pretence, deception, beliefs and different perspectives of the world, is certainly a rich and complementary set of concepts, which it might be appropriate to call a 'theory'. However, the phrase 'theory of mind' is also troublesome, because it cannot be defined with precision (how much knowledge about the mind do you have to have for a theory of mind?), and although some researchers argue explicitly that the development of understanding the mind is similar to the development of theories in science, other researchers are against drawing too close an analogy between the development of understanding minds and the development of scientific theories (Russell, 1992).

What does it mean to have an understanding of the mind? The mind can be considered in different ways. We understand that we have emotions and feelings (e.g. we can feel happy or sad) and that we have desires (I want some chocolate) and that desires and feelings are related (I will be happy if I find some chocolate). We realize that the mind includes knowledge (I know what chocolate is, I know where it is); that we can think about information (I am thinking about chocolate); that there is a difference between thoughts and real things (you can only touch or eat real chocolate); and that we have beliefs about the state of the world (I believe that the chocolate is in the cupboard). Adults also have an appreciation of some aspects of how the mind can be used – for example in learning new information, or using mnemonics (see discussion of metacognition in chapter 12); and we know that knowledge is derived from particular sources, for example, if I see the chocolate in the cupboard then I know where it is and that my knowledge is derived from looking.

One of the most important aspects of understanding the mind is the realization that just as I have a mind so do other people. They too have feelings, desires and beliefs and just as I behave on the basis of my beliefs about the world, so do they. One of the most crucial points about understanding other people's minds is the realization that they may have beliefs that differ from our own. To put this another way – a person's set of beliefs about the world can be referred to as their (mental) representation of the world. Different people may represent the world in different ways; I believe the chocolate is in the cupboard, but my friend believes it is on the table. It is possible that we are both wrong about these beliefs (perhaps unknown to either of us someone has come along and eaten all the chocolate), but we cannot both be right about the same block of chocolate. If I'm right and the chocolate still is in the cupboard, then my friend's belief is incorrect and she has a false belief about the world.

◄The False Belief Task►►►

Do children, like adults, appreciate that other people can have false beliefs? In an influential experiment Wimmer and Perner (1983) investigated this question (see box 13.1). They used models to act out a story about a little boy called Maxi who put some chocolate in a blue cupboard. Then Maxi left the room, and while he was out of the room the children saw Maxi's mother transfer the chocolate to a green cupboard. The children were asked to predict where Maxi would look for the chocolate when he came back into the room. Four-year-olds usually said that he would look in the green cupboard. From an adult point of view this is a very surprising response because, of course, Maxi could not possibly know that the chocolate had been moved. We can infer from such a result that young children do not understand that Maxi's beliefs about the world are different from how the world really is, and that he will act on the basis of his beliefs and not on the actual state of the world.

This was a very important result because it indicated that young children's reasoning about other people's behaviour may be quite different from the assumptions that adults make about other people's behaviour. The discovery of such a major developmental difference generated a wealth of research into how children think about the mind and the relationship between mind and behaviour.

Wimmer and Perner's (1983) task is referred to as a 'false belief' task because Maxi's belief that the chocolate is in the blue cupboard is an incorrect belief after the chocolate is moved. Some researchers questioned the length of Wimmer and Perner's (1983) story, and suggested that children may have had difficulty with the amount of information they needed to consider to fully understand the story. Therefore, other researchers (Baron-Cohen, Leslie and Frith, 1985) reduced the complexity of the story, with a version called the Sally–Anne task (see figure 13.1). In this version, children are shown two dolls, Sally (who has a basket) and Anne (who has a box). Sally puts a marble in her basket and then leaves. While she is absent Anne takes the marble from the basket and puts it in the box. Sally returns and children are asked 'Where will Sally look for her marble?' The typical result from this task is that 4-year-olds realize that Sally will look in the basket, 3-year-olds say that she will look in the box. In other words, with this briefer version of the false belief task children perform correctly at a slightly earlier age, but 3-year-olds seem unable to understand how Sally will act. Indeed Wimmer and Perner (1983) found that by altering the story about Maxi and the chocolate, so that some features of the story were more salient, 4-year-olds could succeed, but 3-year-olds remained unable to work out what Maxi would do (see box 13.1).

Other false belief tasks, such as the 'Smarties task', have produced the

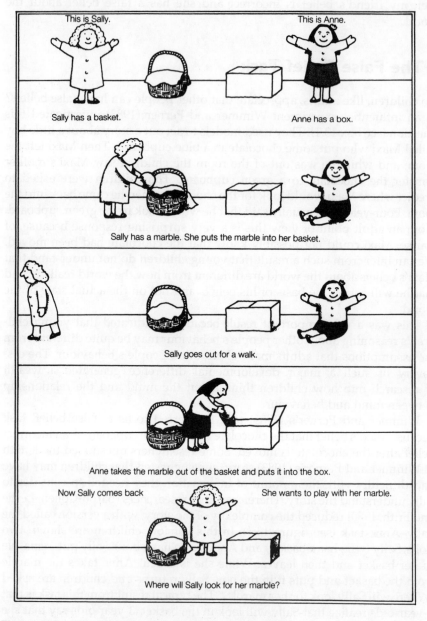

Figure 13.1   The Sally–Anne experiment (from Frith, 1989).

same result (Perner, Leekam and Wimmer, 1987). In the Smarties task children are shown a closed tube of Smarties and asked to say what is in the tube. Children nearly always say 'Smarties' or 'sweets'. Then the lid is taken off and the children are shown that the tube actually contains pencils. After this the lid is replaced and children are asked what one of their friends will think is in the tube: 'When X [friend's name] comes in I'm going to show her this tube. What will X think is in the tube?' The correct answer is Smarties, and although this is the most common answer given by 4-year-olds, younger children answer that their friend will say there are pencils in the tube. Children can also be asked what they thought was in the tube before it was opened. Four-year-olds give the correct answer ('Smarties'), but 3-year-olds say (incorrectly) that they thought there were pencils in it. In other words, 3-year-olds also lack insight into their own mind – they do not acknowledge that at an earlier time they believed that there were Smarties in the tube.

It is clear from experiments like these that children, before the age of about 4 years, have difficulty understanding that another person can have a false belief about the world. They respond as if Sally (in the Sally–Anne task) or their friend (in the Smarties task) will know what the actual state of the world is, even though they could not possibly know this. However, even if 3-year-olds fail the false belief task it does not mean that they know nothing at all about the mind, and in the next section we will give examples of the research into very young children's understanding of the mind.

◀Children's Knowledge of Mind before about Four Years of Age▶▶▶

Distinguishing mental states in language

From about 2 years of age children start to use words which refer for internal states of perception or emotion – words like 'want', 'see', 'look', 'taste' (see chapter 5) – and by the age of 3 years children also use cognitive terms like 'know', 'think' and 'remember'. When children use such words spontaneously it may be difficult to work out whether they use them to refer to mental states or whether they are being used in a more casual manner (for example, adults say 'you know' or 'know what' without any implication that the word 'know' refers to a mental state).

Shatz, Wellman and Silber (1983) examined 3-year-old children's spontaneous use of mental terms and to avoid instances of casual use they focused on utterances which included a contrasting use of terms. The statements collected by Shatz et al. included ones like:

'I thought it was an alligator. Now I know it's a crocodile.'
'I was teasing you. I was pretending 'cept you didn't know that.'
'I thought there wasn't any socks [in the drawer], 'cept when I looked I saw them. I didn't know you got them.'

In these examples children spontaneously contrasted reality and a belief – for example, in the first, the belief was that an animal was an alligator, the reality was that it was a crocodile. Shatz et al. inferred from such examples that the children could distinguish between mental states and external reality.

In another study, Wellman and Estes (1986) showed 3-year-olds two story characters and the children were told that character A had a biscuit, and that character B was, for example, thinking about a biscuit. The children were then asked which of the two biscuits (the physical one or the mental one) could be touched, be seen by the character, or be seen by another character. Different stories were used so that several contrasts could be made between the physical object (with character A) and the same object which character B was thinking about, or dreaming about, or remembering, or pretending about. Wellman and Estes found three-quarters of the children's judgements accurately reflected the distinction between physical and mental entities.

Understanding the relationship between seeing and knowing

Children from the age of 2 years have some understanding of the relationship between seeing and knowing. For example, Lempers, Flavell and Flavell (1977) asked 2-year-olds to show another person a picture which was glued to the inside bottom of a box. The children realized the need to angle the box so that the other person could see into it. Children of the same age also appreciated that if a person had their hands over their eyes it was necessary to move their hands if they were to see a picture, and by the age of 3 years children understood that if they hide something from another person that person will not be able to see it. In other words, by 3 years of age children realize something of the relationship between seeing an object and knowing about that object.

Three-year-olds also understand that different people may have a different view of the same object. For example, Masangkay et al. (1974) used a card with a cat drawn on one side and a dog drawn on the other. The card was placed with one side facing the child and the other facing the experimenter, and children were asked what each person could see. Three-year-olds realized that the experimenter saw a different picture from the one they were looking at. More than this, children of this age are aware that if people see something they will know about it, if they do not see something they will be unaware of. For example, if an object is hidden in a box, 3-year-olds understand that if person A has looked into the box she will know what is in it and if person B has not looked into the box she will not know its contents (Hogrefe, Wimmer and Perner, 1986). The results of these experiments show that young children appreciate that different people can have different knowledge about the world.

However, it is not until about 4 years of age that children realize that people may have different views of the *same* object. Masangkay et al. (1974) had a child (aged 3 to 5 years) sit opposite an experimenter, and between the two of them was a picture showing the side view of a turtle. The experimenter explained that when the turtle appeared as if it was standing on its feet, it was the right way up and when it appeared as if it was on its back, it was 'upside down'. The picture was placed flat on the table and children were asked which of the two views they saw and which the experimenter saw. All the children were correct in describing their own view of the turtle, but only a third of the 3-year-olds could describe the experimenter's view, and it was not until 4 years of age that children understood that their view and the experimenter's were different. This is an important realization, because it means that, at least in perspective-taking tasks, children by the age of 4 can recognize that the same object can be thought about in different ways.

Understanding the appearance–reality distinction

Most adults know that a realistic-looking apple which is made of wax is not a real apple, and they can distinguish what it looks like – an apple (its appearance), from what it is – wax (the reality). In other words, they realize that the *same* person can think about an object in different ways – they can represent the same object as fruit and as wax. However, young children have difficulty in tasks which involve distinguishing appearance and reality – for example, Flavell, Green and Flavell (1986) showed children a sponge which looked like a rock. The children were shown it from a distance (when it could be interpreted as a rock) and then they had an opportunity to feel it, and discovered that it was a sponge. Then they were asked two questions: 'What does it look like?' (the correct answer was, of course, a rock) and 'What is it really and truly?' (a sponge). Three-year-olds had difficulty in this task; once they had found out that it was a sponge they tended to answer 'sponge' to both questions.

The 3-year-olds had difficulty considering two (contradictory) representations of the object at the same time; as Flavell (1988, p. 246) said: 'they do not clearly understand that even though something may be only one way out there in the world, it can be more than one way up here in our heads, in our mental representations of it'. In other words, at the age of 3 years children do not realize that the appearance of an object is only a representation (which can be changed), instead they only consider one interpretation of the object – what they know it to be. It is only after about the age of 4 years that children begin to appreciate that an object can be represented as both what it looks like and what it is, and this also indicates an awareness that at least one of the representations is false (as when the sponge is represented as a rock).

Predicting behaviour

Two-year-olds understand that people have desires, and that these can influence the way they behave. Wellman (1990) told children a story about a character called Sam who wanted to find his rabbit so he could take it to school. The children were told that the rabbit could be hiding in one of two locations, and they saw Sam going to one of the two locations. At that location Sam either found his rabbit (the desired object) or he found a dog. After Sam had looked in one location, the children were asked 'Will he look in the other place, or will he go to school?' Two-year-olds answered correctly if Sam found the rabbit that he would then go to school, and if he found the dog that he would go on searching. In other words, they predicted what Sam would do from what they knew about his desires.

By the age of 3 years children understand that people not only have desires, they also have beliefs about the world. Wellman (1990) showed 3-year-olds two locations (for example, a shelf and a toy box), and the children were shown that there were books on the shelf and in the box. Then a character was introduced: 'This is Amy. Amy thinks there are books only on the shelf; she doesn't think there are books in the toy box. Amy wants some books. Where will Amy look for books?' (The children could have answered 'shelf, or 'toy box', or both places.) Two-thirds of the responses made by the children were correct – they realized that Amy's beliefs would lead to her looking for the books on the shelf.

In this last experiment Amy had a true belief about the world – she thought that there were books on the shelf, and there were books in that place, and 3-year-olds appreciated the relationship between a true belief and behaviour. However, as we saw in the previous section, 3-year-olds cannot predict someone else's behaviour when that person has a false belief (as in the Sally–Anne or Smarties tasks).

◀Children's Knowledge of Mind after about Four Years of Age▶▶▶

The results from experiments with false belief tasks, which we described earlier, showed that after about 4 years of age children realize that another person can have inaccurate beliefs about the world. Put another way, they realize that people's representation of the world does not necessarily coincide with the state of the world. Understanding the distinction between a mental representation and reality is a very important realization, but it is not the end point of children's insights into the mind.

The false belief task involves a 'first order' belief (e.g. I think that Sally thinks that the marble is in the basket). A 'second order belief' is one that involves understanding that someone else can have beliefs about a third person – for example, I think that Jack thinks that Jill thinks that the marble is in the basket. Children's understanding of second order false belief was investigated by Perner and Wimmer (1985) who told children a story about John and Mary who are playing in a park. They see an ice-cream man at the park. Mary wants to buy an ice-cream, but has no money, so she goes home to get some money. John goes home for his lunch. The ice-cream man leaves the park, and goes to the school. Mary is on her way back to the park with some money when she sees the ice-cream man going to the school. She asks him where he is going and says she will follow him to buy an ice-cream at the school. John finishes his lunch and goes to Mary's house. When he gets there Mary's mother says that Mary has gone to buy an ice-cream. John leaves Mary's house to look for her. At the end of the story children were asked 'Where does John think that Mary went to buy an ice-cream?' Wimmer and

Perner found that children only succeeded on this type of task after about the age of 6 years (in other words, about 2 years later than they succeeded on first order belief tasks like the Sally–Anne task).

Even though children understand about false beliefs in tasks like the Sally–Anne and Smarties tasks, it may be slightly later that they apply similar understanding in other contexts. In chapter 5 we discussed a study by Harris (1989) in which children were told about Ellie the elephant who only liked to drink Coke. Ellie was given a can of Coke which, unknown to her, had been filled with milk (which she did not like). Children were asked how Ellie would feel when she received the can (and before she had drunk from it). Although the 4-year-olds realized that Ellie did not know what was in the can, when the children were asked how she would feel, most of them said that she would feel sad. It was only after 5 years of age that children realized that Ellie would feel happy when she was given the can of Coke. In other words, understanding the relationship between false belief and emotion (e.g. in Harris's experiment) may be a slightly later development than understanding the relationship between false belief and behaviour (as in the Sally–Anne task).

False belief and deception

Once children realize that people can have false beliefs, they can also become aware of the possibility of deceptive behaviour. Deception involves planting a false belief in another person's mind (see the examples of chimpanzee deception in chapter 2), and obviously this is only possible if you realize that other people can have false beliefs! Peskin (cited by Perner, 1991) investigated young children's ability to deceive another person. Three-, 4- and 5-year-olds were shown four stickers and each child was told that she could have the one she liked best. But the children were also told that two puppet characters would each be allowed to choose a sticker before the child could take the one she wanted. Children were told that one puppet was friendly, and would never take a sticker that the child wanted, but the other puppet was mean and always wanted the same sticker that the child wanted.

After the child had said which sticker she wanted, the friendly puppet came, and before choosing, the friendly puppet asked the child which sticker she wanted. Nearly all the children, truthfully, pointed out the one they preferred and the friendly puppet chose a different one. Then the mean puppet arrived and also asked the child which she wanted. Nearly all the 3- and 4-year-olds pointed out the one they wanted and the mean puppet took it. Most of the 5-year-olds pointed to a sticker they did not want. This result could be taken as evidence that the younger children did not have any understanding of how to deceive the mean puppet – they did not seem to realize that by telling the puppet a lie they could instil a false belief in the puppet so that he would not take the sticker they wanted.

What is particularly interesting about Peskin's experiment is that after the first trial (that we have just described) Peskin gave the children a further four trials using the same procedure. Not surprisingly the 5-year-olds were as good in the later trials as they were in the first trial. The 4-year-olds showed a rapid improvement in performance – by their second trial half of them realized the need, when the mean puppet was around, to point to a sticker other than their preferred one. Presumably these children's rapid learning was based on an awareness that others can have a false belief. However, the 3-year-olds did not improve; even by the fifth trial nearly all of them continued to point to the sticker they wanted and every time the mean puppet took it from them. Despite the children's dismay and frustration and despite the repeated trials, it appeared that the 3-year-olds had no way of deceiving the mean puppet – they did not realize that they could generate a false belief in the mean puppet by pointing to a sticker they did not want.

Some researchers have argued that there are examples of deception by 3-year-olds that show that children of this age do attempt to manipulate the beliefs of another. For example, in chapter 5 we described an experiment by Lewis et al. (1989) in which children peeked at a toy they were not supposed to look at. Most of the children who peeked later told an adult they had not done so, and some of the children who lied did so with positive facial expressions. As we suggested in chapter 5, the results from Lewis et al.'s study might indicate that at 3 years of age children realize the need to encourage a false belief in the mind of someone else. However, such an interpretation is at odds with the poor performance of the 3-year-olds in Peskin's experiment. Exactly when young children can deceive others, and whether some early deceptive behaviours indicate an understanding of false belief, is an area of some debate (see Mitchell, 1997).

Theories about the Development of Understanding the Mind ▶ ▶ ▶

Several theories have been put forward to explain how children develop an understanding of their own and other people's minds. We will only mention these briefly to give an indication of the different approaches which researchers have taken. We described a couple of Wellman's (1990) experiments earlier, and on the basis of such studies he suggested that children's understanding develops in three phases. Two-year-olds have a 'theory' based on 'desire psychology' – they assume that people's desires influence their behaviour. For example in the experiment with Sam looking for his rabbit, Sam's behaviour (searching) is determined by his desire (to take the rabbit to school).

By the age of 3, children have a 'theory' based on 'belief–desire psychology' – they take into account not only a person's desires, but also their beliefs about the world. For example, in the experiment with Amy looking for some books, 3-year-olds realize that, although there are books in two places, if Amy only knows that they are in one place she will go there. This means that 3-year-olds are able to take Amy's beliefs into account – they can predict her behaviour on the basis of Amy's representation of the world. However, Amy had a true belief about the world – her representation reflected the actual state of the world. Wellman (1990) suggested that 3-year-olds may think of beliefs as a 'copy' of the world, they do not realize that a belief is not a copy but an interpretation of the world. It is only at about 4 years of age that children adopt a theory that includes the crucial realization that beliefs are interpretations, and like all interpretations they may be inaccurate (like Sally's belief, in the Sally–Anne task).

Wellman (1990) referred to children's understanding as involving progressively more sophisticated 'theories' about the mind. Put another way, they are developing a 'theory of mind'. By describing development in this way Wellman made an explicit comparison between children's developing understanding and the way that scientific theories develop. A scientist tries to understand a large number of facts or events by proposing a theory which explains the relationships between those facts, and then on the basis of that theory the scientist can predict the existence of other facts or relationships. Wellman suggested that in the same way that a scientist uses a theory to explain the world around her, so a child (who sees and experiences a constant stream of information about others' actions and behaviours) also tries to make sense of all this information by establishing a 'theory'. At first this may be quite a simple theory (e.g. one based on 'desire psychology'). Such a theory may explain some behaviours but as the child comes across examples of behaviour that cannot be explained simply from knowing a person's desires, she will be forced to consider a more elaborate theory (e.g. one based on belief–desire psychology). This shift in theories is rather like a scientist considering new facts which do not fit into an already established scientific theory – at a point when the old theory no longer helps understand the new facts, the scientist has to develop a new theory.

Wellman (1990) suggested that children's understanding of the mind progresses through several theory changes between the ages of 2 and 4 years. Support for the theory view of children's development comes from research that has shown that children achieve success on several different tasks at roughly the same age (see Astington, 1994). For example, children's appreciation of the distinction between appearance and reality (that the same person can have two representations of the same object), children's understanding of the relationship between what is seen and what is known (that two people's views – i.e. their representations – of the same object can be different) and children's awareness of false belief (that different people can have different representations of the world) are all achieved at about the same time. That children start to succeed on a variety of different tasks at the same age can be taken as evidence that there has been a significant underlying change in their thought which is influencing their understanding of a number of related mental concepts – and such a change might well be described as a shift in their 'theory' about the mind.

Rather than postulating several phases, Perner (1991) put great emphasis on the major change which occurs at about 4 years when children can understand false belief. He argued that the most important aspect of understanding the mind occurs when a child has acquired the concept of 'metarepresentation'. This means an understanding of the distinction between what is being referred to (the referent) and what it is represented as.

For example, consider a photograph (i.e. a representation) of a pyramid. If the photograph is taken from the ground the pyramid will be represented by a triangular shape, if taken from a plane flying directly above the pyramid it will be represented as a rectangular shape, if taken from a satellite it will be represented as a dot. These are all representations of the pyramid, but they are not copies of the pyramid. To think of representations simply as copies of reality is to misunderstand the nature of representations. It is only when you understand that representations are not copies of reality that you have the concept of metarepresentation. So that when a 4-year-old succeeds on a false belief task like the Maxi task she can make the distinction between *what* is represented (chocolate in location A) and *how* it is represented (by Maxi, as chocolate in location B).

As Perner (1991) pointed out, having the concept of metarepresentation, at about the age of 4 years, is a major achievement. Perner said that younger children can, of course, understand a lot about minds (see the examples we gave in the previous section) but he argued that they can do so without an understanding of the nature of mental representations (see Perner, 1991). In other words, Perner put most emphasis on a major change in children's representational thinking at 4 years of age.

Leslie (1987) also used the word 'metarepresentation' but in a very different way from Perner (1991). Leslie used the word in relation to young children's pretend play. Leslie pointed out that children start to demonstrate pretend play from about 18 months of age (see chapter 6) and he also noted that pretend play should actually be very confusing for a child who is still learning to categorize objects. For example, suppose a child has learnt that yellow curved fruits are called bananas and that mechanical instruments you put to your ear are called telephones. Children do not usually mistake bananas for telephones or vice versa. However, in pretend play the child herself or someone else (e.g. her mother) might pick up a banana, put it against her ear and pretend to be using it as a telephone. It might be expected that re-labelling the banana as a telephone has every potential to disrupt a child's categorization of objects. But this does not happen, young children are quite happy to pretend that a banana is a telephone, or a block of wood with wheels is a car, and they do not then get so confused that they start calling all bananas 'telephones' or all blocks of wood 'cars'.

In considering why children can indulge in pretend play without getting confused, Leslie (1987) suggested that children must have two types of representations when they indulge in pretend play. One is a primary representation (thinking about the banana as a banana) and the other is a secondary representation. The latter is the child's re-representation of the primary representation (so that the banana is also thought of as a telephone). Leslie called these secondary representations 'metarepresentations'. He also pointed out that in pretend play with others, young children interact with what other children are pretending (and not what they are actually doing). Children's ability to co-ordinate pretend play implies that they understand what is in the mind of the children with whom they are playing.

If young children can represent representations, and have some insight into others' minds, this might be thought of as a good basis for developing a fuller understanding of other minds. But it is at least 2 years between the beginning of pretend play and succeeding on a false belief task. This is a surprisingly long time if the representational abilities proposed by Leslie (1987) really are the foundation for later understanding of minds. For this reason, several researchers have argued that pretend play is not dependent on representational abilities at all, and suggested that children can pretend by acting out behaviours. They can act out picking up a banana or talking into it, because that is what they would do with a telephone. In other words, the pretence is based on applying well-known actions to an object, and to do this children do not necessarily need to have a representation of the banana as a telephone, all they need to do is think about all the actions they would use with a telephone and apply those to the banana (see Lillard, 1993; Perner, 1991).

Wellman (1990), Perner (1991) and Leslie (1987) all suggested that the children's understanding of mind is based on the development of their representational abilities. In contrast, Harris (1989, 1991) suggested that children can understand others' minds without necessarily understanding that others have mental representations, instead children could use a process that Harris called 'simulation'. In chapter 5 we discussed Harris's description of how children might develop an understanding of emotions. He pointed out that young children know about their own emotions and that they have the ability to pretend. With this knowledge and ability they can project emotions onto others (e.g. if they have felt upset when they have fallen down, then in doll play they can pretend that the doll feels upset when it has fallen down). In the same way, children can project emotions and explanations for those emotions onto other people (see chapter 5).

Harris (1991) argued that by simulation children can work out, not only other people's emotions, but also their desires and beliefs. It is worth noting, that adults probably use simulation all the time to imagine other people's feelings and behaviour. For example, if you hear that a friend has just passed an important examination, you may well be able to imagine your friend's emotions – how she felt immediately before and after she received the result; and her behaviour – what she will do and what plans she can make now that she knows that she has passed. This simulation can be achieved by considering how you felt and behaved in a similar situation and applying that information to your friend. In the same way, a child faced with the Sally–Anne task could imagine what she herself would think and do if she was Sally, and then work out what actions and consequences would follow.

To a greater or lesser degree, all the theories put forward to describe the development of children's understanding of mind refer to children's reasoning. For example, in Wellman's (1990) account children develop theories by reasoning from their experience of others' behaviour and in Harris's (1991) simulation theory it is explicit that children reason from their own beliefs to the actions of another person. It is, of course, axiomatic that any problem-solving task involves reasoning, and in many areas of cognitive development researchers have tried to describe the reasoning and strategies that children apply in problem-solving (see chapter 12).

However, much of the research into children's understanding of mind has concentrated on what children can do at particular ages (see Wellman, 1990, and Perner, 1991). In particular, some researchers have concentrated on the false belief task to find out if children might be able to succeed on this task before the age of 4 years. Some have found that if the questions in false belief tasks are made more specific, younger children can sometimes succeed on the task (Lewis and Osborne, 1990), and other changes in the procedure can also contribute to younger children's success (e.g. Freeman, Lewis and Doherty, 1991; Mitchell and Lacohee, 1991; Mitchell, 1996). This focus on when children can succeed on various tasks is important, because if we can say that 3-year-olds succeed on task A (which involves components x and y) but they fail on task B (which involves components x, y, and z), we can infer that 3-year-olds have some difficulty with component z.

In contrast to this approach other researchers have focused less on the nature of the tasks, and more on the reasoning that might be needed to succeed in them. For example, Riggs, Peterson, Robinson and Mitchell (in press) considered the reasoning that might be involved in a typical false belief task. They suggested that in tasks like the Maxi task (see box 13.1) children have to engage in reasoning that is called 'counterfactual reasoning'. This refers to reasoning that is based on a state of the world that is not in fact the case. The child has to imagine how something might be (chocolate in blue cupboard) had some event not occurred (mother moved it to green cupboard) – this is, in effect, imagining a non-existent state of the world. Then the child has to work out where Maxi will look.

Riggs et al. (in press) tested children who were just 4 years of age. The children were told the following story: Maxi and his mother put chocolate in the cupboard, Maxi goes to school, mother uses some of the chocolate to make a cake, and puts the remaining chocolate in the fridge, then Maxi comes home. Children were asked two questions about the story. One was the typical question in false belief tasks: 'Where does Maxi think the chocolate is?' – in such tasks it has been assumed that a correct answer to this question depends on understanding Maxi's mental representation (i.e. his false belief). The other question was a reasoning question: 'If mum had not made a cake, where would the chocolate be?' – the answer to this question depends on the hypothesized reasoning that is needed in the false belief task *but* does not involve any understanding of false belief or mental representations.

Nearly all the children who answered the false belief question correctly answered the reasoning question correctly, and nearly all the children who failed the false belief question also failed the reasoning question. All the children who failed the false belief question said that Maxi would think the chocolate was in the fridge, and all the children who failed the reasoning question said that the chocolate would be in the fridge. In other words, irrespective of whether the question involved understanding a mental representation or not, the children performed in the same way. From this result Riggs et al. (in press) concluded that children's performance in false belief tasks may be due, not to their understanding (or lack of understanding) of mental representation, but rather to their ability (or lack of ability) to reason about the task.

On the one hand, Riggs et al.'s (in press) finding casts doubt on how much the false belief task is testing children's knowledge of representation at all. On the other hand, it will require much more research into children's reasoning to explain why children's performance on the false belief task corresponds to their performance on other tasks, like the appearance reality task. As we discussed earlier, tasks like the appearance reality task have also been assumed to depend on children's understanding of mental representation. Therefore, in the current state of the research we have evidence for age-related improvement across a range of tasks that all seem to involve understanding mental representations, but the results from studies such as Riggs et al. are also making researchers aware that performance on these tasks may be dependent on children's ability to reason as much as on their understanding of representations.

◀ Do Children with Autism Lack an Understanding of Others' Minds? ▶ ▶ ▶

Autism was first described by Kanner (1943) and Asperger (1944) who both (independently) used the term 'autism' to label a disorder that they described in children who usually, but not always, had a low IQ. Kanner described two main features in the children he saw. One is 'autistic aloneness', which refers to children's inability to relate to others – for example, they make little physical contact with parents, make little eye contact, prefer to be alone and prefer playing with objects to playing with people. The second feature is a 'desire for sameness', because children often become very upset by changes in their surroundings or routine (for example, they may insist on always having the same furniture arrangement in a room, or want the same food every dinner time).

Kanner also discussed several secondary features in the children he examined. These include difficulties with language; children with autism might have a good vocabulary, but may use language without meaning, may use correct language but in inappropriate contexts and may demonstrate 'echolalia' (repeating what another speaker has just said). Children with autism also lack spontaneous activities, they have repetitious behaviours, restricted interests, and sometimes have an obsessive interest in what most people might think are obscure activities. They may also be over-sensitive to particular stimuli, reacting excessively to noises or to particular objects.

Contemporary diagnosis of people with autism is based on the criteria described in DSM-IV (the 'Diagnostic and statistical manual of mental disorders, fourth edition' of the American Psychiatric Association, 1994), which stresses three fundamental impairments:

qualitative impairments in social interaction (e.g. impairment of non-verbal behaviours, such as a lack of eye-to-eye contact, or a failure to develop peer relations).

qualitative impairments in communication (e.g. delay in the development of language, or a lack of varied, spontaneous make-believe play).

restricted repetitive and stereotyped patterns of behaviour, interests and activities (e.g. an inflexible adherence to specific routines and rituals which have no practical function).

One other feature of autism is that people often show 'islets of ability', this means that in contrast with their generally poor performance in most areas, they may be as good if not better than normal people on specific tasks. For example, people with autism often have very good rote memory, and good performance on some spatial tasks (like doing jigsaws, or finding a hidden shape in a complex pattern).

Autism affects about four or five people in 10,000, and although all people who are diagnosed as having autism will have the impairments we described above, they may have them to a greater or lesser degree. Some people with autism may have very severe learning difficulties, but others, who may have average levels of intelligence, may be able to function with some independence.

The challenge for any researcher investigating autism is trying to explain how one syndrome can lead to the specific combination of impairments which typify a person with autism (lack of socialization, communication and imagination); how different people with autism can be affected in markedly different ways; and how it is that people with autism can sometimes have better than average abilities in one or two areas (the 'islets of ability').

Several theories have been put forward to explain autism (see Frith, 1989; Happé, 1994) but most of these theories only explained a small part of the pattern of impairments which are seen in people with autism. Then researchers began to consider whether people with autism had an understanding of minds, using the same types of experiment which had been used to investigate normal children's understanding. Baron-Cohen et al. (1985) were the first to do this using the Sally–Anne false belief task. They tested children with autism who had a mental age of over 4 years – because it is about this age that normal children succeed on false belief tasks. They also tested a group of normal children aged 4 years and a group of children with Down's syndrome with a mental age of 4 years or more. It was important to include the latter group because if the children with autism had been poorer than the normal children, they might have been poorer for many reasons (e.g. not understanding the instructions), but if they were poorer than children with Down's syndrome (who also have learning difficulties) then it could be assumed that any differences between the children with autism and children with Down's syndrome were due to factors in the task. (For an explanation of the need for matched groups in experiments that include children with autism, see box 13.2.)

Baron-Cohen et al. (1985) found that more than 80 per cent of the normal children and the children with Down's syndrome succeeded on the Sally–Anne task, but only 20 per cent of the children with autism were successful. Failure on the task was unlikely to be due to learning difficulties in general (otherwise the children with Down's syndrome would have failed as well), but it seemed to be specific to the group with autism. Perner, Frith, Leslie and Leekam (1989) also tested children with autism using the Smarties false belief task with similar results – most of the children failed the task.

Children with autism also have difficulty in other tasks which require an appreciation of another's false belief. Baron-Cohen, Leslie and Frith (1986) showed children with autism sets of four pictures each of which made a story (see figure 13.2). One type of story was called a 'mechanical' story because the action in the story did not involve any people:

Picture 1: shows a balloon leaving a person's hand
Picture 2: the balloon in the air
Picture 3: the balloon near a tree
Picture 4: the balloon bursts on the tree

Another type was called 'behavioural' stories because they included people but did not require any understanding of what the people were thinking:

Picture 1: shows a girl walking in a street
Picture 2: the girl goes into a sweet shop
Picture 3: the girl buys sweets at the counter
Picture 4: she leaves the shop with a bag of sweets

The third type of story required an understanding of the beliefs of the characters in the pictures:

Picture 1: shows a boy putting a sweet into a box
Picture 2: the boy leaves the room, to play soccer outside
Picture 3: mother takes the sweet out of the box and eats it
Picture 4: the boy comes back to the box and looks surprised

The children were given the pictures in a mixed-up order, and were asked to put them in an appropriate sequence, and they were asked to explain what was happening in the story. The children with autism were able to order and describe the events in both the mechanical and the behavioural stories, but they were poor at understanding the mentalistic stories – they put the pictures in a jumbled order and only reported what they could see in them, they did not refer to the 'mentalistic' aspect of the story (for example in the story about the boy and the chocolate, they could not explain why the boy was surprised when he found that the box was empty).

We said earlier that having an understanding of another person's mind is essential if you want to deceive them by giving them a false belief. If children with autism have difficulty understanding others' minds, how well can they deceive others? This was examined by Sodian and Frith (1992) who showed children a box, which contained a sweet, and the children were told about a robber puppet (who would take the sweet). They were also told that the robber was lazy and would not try to open the box if it was locked. In the 'sabotage' condition of the experiment children could decide whether to leave the box open or to lock it when they were told that the robber was coming. In the 'deception' condition children were not able to lock the box, but before the robber reached the box he asked the child whether the box was open or locked (and therefore the children could deceive him by saying that the box was locked).

In the sabotage condition the children were, in effect, manipulating the robber's *behaviour* (by locking the box so that he could not look in it). In the deception condition they were manipulating the robber's *beliefs* (by telling him that the box was locked). Children with autism were successful in the sabotage condition, but failed to think of ways to deceive the robber in the other condition. Even though they understood the task and were motivated to stop the robber getting the sweet (as demonstrated by their success in the sabotage condition) they were unable to manipulate the robber's belief in the

A mechanical story

A behavioural story

A mentalistic story

Figure 13.2   Three types of picture sequence.

deception condition. This again demonstrated the difficulty children with autism have in a task which depends on understanding the mind of someone else.

These studies have shown that children with autism have difficulty in tasks that involve mental representations, but is this specific to understanding mental representations or do children with autism have a difficulty understanding all types of representations? There are several 'non-mental' representations of the world: maps represent the landscape; drawings and photographs represent scenes in the world. As we pointed out before, all these represent the world in a (single) specific way, and they may often no longer portray the world in its current state. For example, a map of a city might have been an accurate representation of that city when it was drawn, but if several buildings are pulled down the map is then a 'false' representation of the world. If children with autism have a general difficulty with representations then it would be predicted that they will have difficulty understanding the nature of pictures and photographs and other such representations.

Leslie and Thaiss (1992) investigated this issue. They tested normal children and children with autism using a false belief task (a test of understanding a mental representation) and a 'false' photograph task (a test of understanding a non-mental representation). Leslie and Thaiss's procedure and findings are described in box 13.2, and it was clear that although the children with autism performed poorly in the false belief task, they performed very well in the false photograph task. This would suggest that children with autism have a specific deficit in understanding *mental* representations.

How Far can a Deficit in Understanding Mental Representations Contribute to an Explanation of Autism? ▶ ▶ ▶

One problem for any explanation of autism based on children's lack of understanding of mental representations is the fact that in most studies a proportion of children with autism succeed on false belief tasks (e.g. in Baron-Cohen et al., 1985; in Leslie and Thaiss, 1992 – see box 13.2). If a failure to understand minds is not a universal deficit in autism any explanation based on understanding minds is very much weakened. However, even though some people with autism can pass a first order false belief task like the Sally–Anne task, when the same people are given a second order false belief task, like John and Mary in the park (see p. 404) they rarely succeed (Baron-Cohen, 1989). It seems that some people with autism may be able to pass first order tasks but the fact that they fail second order tasks suggests that they do not have a secure understanding of others' minds, and it is possible that they succeed on first order tasks using strategies that do not necessarily include an understanding of mental states (see Happé, 1994).

If people with autism do not have an understanding of minds, does this explain the impairments seen in autism? Major social impairments might be expected in people who do not realize that other people have thoughts and beliefs about the world, and that people's behaviour is based on those beliefs. A failure to understand that people have independent beliefs, and a failure to appreciate that people's beliefs may not coincide with reality, must make it very difficult to interpret why other people act as they do, and this will limit effective social understanding. It will also make it difficult to communicate, because people with autism will not realize that what a speaker says is a statement based on the speaker's thoughts, and requires interpretation. Being unable to interpret what people do and what they say, may lead to a world in which many things appear to be, at best puzzling and confusing, and at worst, arbitrary and disturbing. In such a world it would not be surprising if people with autism insist on sameness and routine, because at least in this way, some sense of consistency and predictability might be maintained.

The finding that people with autism have a deficit in understanding of minds has been a major discovery. It has led to the recognition of many, previously unrecognized, aspects of the autistic syndrome, it has stimulated much new and original research into autism, and it goes part of the way to explaining some of the impairments, especially social ones, that typify autism. However, a deficit in understanding minds does not help us to understand all the impairments associated with autism. For example, it is not obvious how specific language problems (e.g. echolalia), obsessive behaviours or 'islets of ability' could be linked to a lack of understanding minds.

Other hypotheses have also been put forward to explain the difficulty that people with autism have in tasks like the false belief task. Hughes and Russell (1993) suggested that people with autism are unable to 'disengage from an object'. They argued that when children with autism fail false belief tasks like the Sally–Anne task by saying that Sally will look for her marble in the box (where the marble actually is, even though Sally does not know that), they do so because they are unable to overcome the salience of knowing that the marble *is* in the box. In other words, the salience of the fact that the marble is in the box overwhelms children's ability to ignore the marble's actual position and consider where it was before (in Sally's basket). In other words, children with autism do not fail the Sally–Anne task because they do not understand Sally's mind, rather they fail because they cannot ignore the information they have about the marble's position. To demonstrate this possibility Hughes and Russell used what they called a 'windows task'.

In the windows task children were shown two boxes, and each box had a window in one side so that the children could see inside. One box had a sweet in it, and children were told that if they pointed to the *empty* box they would win the sweet. They were then given 20 trials. Children with autism were poor at this task, and half the children persisted in pointing to the box with the sweet on every trial (and therefore they never received a sweet at all). Hughes and Russell (1993) argued that the children were unable to ignore the presence of the sweet and could not inhibit themselves pointing to it, even though they 'lost' the sweet every time.

Hughes and Russell's (1993) results support the hypothesis that children with autism are unable to disengage from an object. However, this is not the case in all tasks. For example, in the photograph task used by Leslie and Thaiss (1992) – see box 13.2 – children watched as a photograph was taken of Polly the horse sitting on a box. Then Polly was moved and a toy mouse was placed on the box. The children were asked who was sitting on the box in the photograph. Even though the children with autism could see the mouse on the box in front of them, they all correctly realized that the photograph showed Polly. In other words, they were capable of ignoring the scene they could see – they did not say that the photograph showed the mouse on the box, and this result does not support the hypothesis that children are 'unable to disengage from the object' as Hughes and Russell suggested. Nonetheless, the difficulty that children with autism have with the windows task points to an impairment which needs to be explained for a full understanding of autism (see Ozonoff, Rogers and Pennington, 1991).

Unlike Hughes and Russell (1993) other researchers accept that the poor performance of children with autism on false belief tasks does reflect a deficit in their understanding of mind, but do not accept that this is a core impairment in autism. Instead, they have argued that there are more fundamental impairments and that failure to understand others' minds stems from these other impairments. For example, on p. 408 we described Leslie's (1987) analysis of pretend play. One of the defining features of autism is a lack of imaginative or pretend play; although normal children are capable of pretend play by 2 years of age, children with autism rarely engage in pretend play. According to Leslie pretend play depends on children's ability to metarepresent (in his use of the term), which involves forming representations of representations. A similar process might apply in false belief tasks (where the child has to represent Sally's representation). In other words, there may be a fundamental deficit in metarepresentational abilities underlying both pretence and understanding minds.

Baron-Cohen (1995) has also suggested a fundamental deficit. He described a 'shared attention mechanism' which combines information about your own direction of gaze and another person's direction of gaze. This includes information like: I see that X sees the object; X sees that I see the object. For example: I see that Mummy sees a toy; Mummy sees that I see the toy. Baron-Cohen suggested that the shared attention mechanism allows a child to work out whether she and someone else are both looking at the same thing. Such a mechanism would also mean that a child could understand the perceptual mental state of another person (i.e. that Mummy sees the toy). More than this, a child may also be able to interpret another's look in terms of desire – for example, young normal children know that if someone is looking at one of four blocks of chocolate, she wants that particular block (Baron-Cohen et al., 1995). Baron-Cohen argued that from an early understanding about gaze a young normal child can gain insights into another's mental state, and that these insights are the foundation for children's later understanding of mind.

Baron-Cohen et al. (1994; cited in Baron-Cohen, 1995) screened 16,000 infants at the age of 18 months using tests of shared attention and pretend play. Seventeen of the children showed no evidence of either shared attention or pretend play, and most of these children were later diagnosed as having autism. Baron-Cohen et al. (1995) found that in contrast to normal children, when children with autism saw someone looking at one of four blocks of chocolate they did not realize that it was that block which the person wanted. Taken together the results from these two studies showed that children with autism lack shared attention and the ability to interpret the direction of gaze of another person, and Baron-Cohen argued that the lack of a shared attention mechanism in children with autism may explain the later deficit in their understanding of mind.

The research into how children develop an understanding of another person's mind has become a large and important area of developmental research. The discovery that normal 3-year-olds have difficulty understanding the concept of mind has stimulated many new studies, and led to the generation of radical new theories about early cognitive development. The equally important discovery that many children and adults with autism also lack insight into others' minds has provoked many new directions of research into autism and stimulated a new look at the causes and development of autism.

◀Further Reading▶▶▶

P. Mitchell 1997: *Introduction to Theory of Mind*, London: Arnold, is an excellent description of the empirical research into children's understanding of mind, covers the research with non-human species and has sections on autism, and on deceptive behaviour. Despite the title, Mitchell goes beyond just an introduction and provides a very clearly written summary of the empirical research. P. Mitchell 1996: *Acquiring a Conception of Mind. A Review of Psychological Research and Theory*, Hove: Erlbaum, is a more advanced book than the above, which goes into more detail about the different theoretical approaches in this area and provides a very good review of the field.

J. W. Astington 1994: *The Child's Discovery of the Mind*, London: Fontana, is another good book. It covers rather less than Mitchell (1996) and has less detail about particular studies, but does take a more theoretical approach, with particularly good summaries of the positions taken by different researchers in this field.

F. Happé 1994: *Autism. An Introduction to Psychological Theory*, London: University College London Press, gives a very clear discussion of autism, including a good assessment of the contribution that theory of mind research has made in the understanding of autism, with summaries of other theories as well.

U. Frith 1989: *Autism. Explaining the Enigma*, Oxford: Blackwell, is still a good introduction to autism, but now a little dated.

◄Discussion Points►►►

1 What does it mean to say that a child has an understanding of others' minds?
2 Why is the false belief task important?
3 How much has the research into children's conception of mind contributed to an understanding of autism?
4 Compare the way that understanding the mind has been investigated in children with the way that it has been investigated in non-human primates (see chapter 2).

Box 13.1
Beliefs about beliefs: representations and constraining function of wrong beliefs in young children's understanding of deception

Wimmer and Perner carried out the first investigation of children's understanding of false belief. In this study children heard a story about a boy (Maxi) who was looking for some chocolate. The children knew where the chocolate actually was, but they were told that Maxi thought the chocolate was in another place. The children were asked to predict where Maxi would look for the chocolate, and the key aspect of the experiment was whether children would predict that Maxi would look for the chocolate where they knew it was or where he thought it was. Of course, this is not a difficult task for most adults who reason that Maxi can only look for the chocolate in the place where he believes it to be (i.e. that people's behaviour is based on what they believe about the world rather than how the world really is). Wimmer and Perner wanted to find out if children would also reason in the same way. They tested three groups of 12 children, aged 4, 6 and 8 years, in Austria.

The children were told a story, which was also acted out in front of them using three differently coloured matchboxes which were glued high up on a model wall, and paper cut outs for the characters. The story was given in two versions. One was called the co-operative story (because one character offers to help Maxi find the chocolate) and one was called the competitive version, because another character may take the chocolate from Maxi.

The story was as follows (taken from Wimmer and Perner, 1983, where it was translated into English):

Mother returns from her shopping trip. She brought chocolate for a cake. Maxi may help her put away the things. He asks her: 'Where should I put the chocolate?' 'In the blue cupboard' says the mother.

'Wait I'll lift you up there, because you are too small.'

Mother lifts him up. Maxi puts the chocolate into the blue cupboard. [A toy chocolate is put into the blue matchbox.] Maxi remembers exactly where he put the chocolate so that he can come back and get some later. He loves chocolate. Then he leaves for the playground. [The boy doll is removed.] Mother starts to prepare the cake and takes the chocolate out of the blue cupboard. She grates a bit into the dough and then she does *not* put it back into the *blue but* into the *green* cupboard. [Toy chocolate is thereby transferred from the blue to the green matchbox.] Now she realizes that she forgot to buy eggs. So she goes to her neighbour for some eggs. There comes Maxi back from the playground, hungry, and he wants to get some chocolate. [Boy doll reappears.] He still remembers where he had put the chocolate.

Children were then asked the 'belief' question: 'Where will Maxi look for the chocolate?', and had to indicate one of the three matchboxes.

Then in the co-operative story children were told: 'OK, there he'll look, but he is too small to reach up there. Here comes Grandpa and Maxi says: dear Grandpa, please could you help me get the chocolate from the cupboard?' Grandpa asks 'Which cupboard?'

The children were then asked the 'utterance' question: 'Where will Maxi say the chocolate is?', and had to indicate one of the matchboxes.

In the competitive story children were told: 'However, before Maxi gets a chance to get at the chocolate his big brother comes into the kitchen. He, too, is looking for the chocolate. He asks Maxi where the chocolate is. 'Good grief,' thinks Maxi, 'now big brother wants to eat up all the chocolate. I will tell him something completely wrong so that he won't find it, for sure.'

As with the co-operative story the children were then asked an 'utterance' question: 'Where will Maxi say the chocolate is?', and had to indicate one of the matchboxes.

Then, to make sure that the children had paid attention to the story, the children were asked two questions. First, to check that they had not forgotten where the chocolate actually was, they were asked the 'reality' question: 'Where is the chocolate really?'

Second, to check that they also remembered where the chocolate had been put, they were asked the 'memory' question: 'Do you remember where Maxi put the chocolate in the beginning?'

There was also a second story, with the same structure as this one, that was set in a nursery-school room where a little girl hid her favourite book. While she was out of the room the caretaker moved it to a different place. In the co-operative version, when the girl came back into the room, she offered to show the book to her friend. In the other version another child was competing for the

book and the girl tried to mislead him. The questions paralleled the ones in the Maxi story.

Each child heard both stories, and box table 13.1.1 shows the number of children who gave correct answers to the belief question 'Where will Maxi look for the chocolate?' (or 'Where will the little girl look for the book?'). The children could have been correct for both stories, for one, or for neither.

As shown in the table, the two older age groups were generally successful, but the 4-year-olds did comparatively poorly. It was important to be sure that the younger children's poor performance was not simply due to them forgetting information from the story. When Wimmer and Perner examined the children who gave incorrect answers to the belief question they found that 100 per cent gave correct responses to the reality question and 80 per cent gave correct responses to the memory question. In other words, all the children had paid attention to the stories and remembered the details. Therefore, the 4-year-olds' poor performance was not likely to be due to task factors, it was more likely that they only had a limited understanding that Maxi might hold an incorrect belief about the location of the chocolate.

Of the children who were correct on the belief question (predicting where Maxi would look for the chocolate, or where the girl would look for the book) in the co-operative versions, 85 per cent gave appropriate answers to the utterance question (e.g. they said that Maxi would tell Grandpa that the chocolate was in the blue cupboard). Similarly, of the children who were correct on the belief question in the competitive versions, 82 per cent gave an appropriate answer to the utterance question (e.g. they said that Maxi would tell his brother that the chocolate was not in the blue cupboard, but in one of the others).

Box Table 13.1.1 Number of children giving correct answers to the belief questions

Age	Number of correct answers		
	2	1	0
4 years	4	2	6
6 years	11	0	1
8 years	11	1	0

In response to the utterance questions, in both versions of the story, children who were incorrect on the belief question (and said that Maxi would look for the chocolate in the green cupboard) tended to indicate the green cupboard. For example, in the co-operative version they said that Maxi would tell Grandpa that the chocolate was where it actually was; and in the competitive version they also said that Maxi would tell his brother where the chocolate really was. These responses were inappropriate given Maxi's false belief, and even if these children thought that Maxi would know that the chocolate was in the green cupboard, it was rather ineffective to tell his brother where he thought the chocolate was if he wanted to stop his brother getting it. In other words, these children did not seem to understand how to deceive the brother.

Wimmer and Perner went on to rule out some of the possible reasons why the youngest children gave inappropriate replies to the belief question. They thought that because the children had seen the toy chocolate put in the green box and it was still there when they were asked the questions, the knowledge of where the chocolate was may have encouraged inappropriate responses from the 4-year olds. One possibility was that the 4-year-olds were responding without much reflection and simply pointing to where they knew the chocolate was. Wimmer and Perner also suggested another possibility – that Maxi's belief, 'the chocolate is in the blue cupboard', might have been overridden by the child's own, similar, knowledge that 'the chocolate is in the green cupboard', and that this effect was less likely to apply to the older children. (For similar arguments about the dominance of knowledge in false belief tasks, see Hughes and Russell's experiment discussed in this chapter, and for other arguments about children's limited information processing in problem-solving tasks, see Brainerd's experiments described in chapter 12.)

Therefore, in a second experiment, Wimmer and Perner introduced two new conditions (as well as the one they had used in the first experiment). Hence there were three conditions:

1 'Displaced' condition – this was the same as in the first experiment – children saw the chocolate moved from the blue to the green cupboard.
2 'Stop and think displaced' condition – to reduce the possibility of unconsidered responses the children were told, before the belief question, to pause and think carefully before they answered.
3 'Disappear' condition – the children were told that the chocolate was all used up in the baking (in other words, it no longer existed in any cupboard).

Both the chocolate story and the book story were modified as necessary. Wimmer and Perner tested 20 3-year-olds, 42 4-year-olds and 30 5-year-olds. Table box 13.1.2 shows the number of children in each condition answering the belief question correctly (as there were two stories children could

Box Table 13.1.2 Number of children in each condition answering the belief questions correctly

Age	Condition	No. of children	Number correct		
			2	1	0
3 years	2. Stop & think displaced	10	0	0	10
	3. Disappear	10	0	3	7
4 years	1. Displaced	14	6	1	7
	2. Stop & think displaced	14	4	2	8
	3. Disappear	14	11	0	3
5 years	1. Displaced	10	5	0	5
	2. Stop & think displaced	10	10	0	0
	3. Disappear	10	10	0	0

have been right on both, one or neither). Wimmer and Perner did not report any results for 3-year-olds in the displaced condition and presumably they did not test such young children in this condition on the assumption that they were unlikely to succeed if most of the 4-year-olds in the first experiment had failed in this condition.

As can be seen in the table, 5-year-olds were always correct in conditions two and three, though they were poorer in the original task. Four-year-olds also did well in condition three. In other words, the older children in this experiment performed best in the 'disappear' condition, and this supported Wimmer and Perner's suggestion that some of the 4-year-olds in the first experiment may have had difficulty because of the continuing presence of the chocolate. However, the 3-year-olds performed poorly irrespective of condition and there was no evidence that this age group could appreciate Maxi's false belief. Most of these children gave no response at all to the belief question (or because they had seen the experimenter remove the toy chocolate in the course of telling the story, they suggested that Maxi would look behind the model for it!).

Taken together these experiments demonstrated that young children had difficulty ascribing a false belief to another person. In particular, 3-year-olds were unable to appreciate Maxi's false belief even in the 'disappear' condition of the second experiment, when there was little direct conflict between Maxi's belief (chocolate in cupboard) and their own knowledge (chocolate disappeared).

Wimmer and Perner's experiment has been criticized because of the length of the story, and the amount of information children had to remember to understand it. Although 4-year-olds performed poorly in Wimmer and Perner's first experiment other researchers have shown that when the task is presented in the context of a briefer story (as in the Sally–Anne task described on p. 413), 4-year-olds can give appropriate answers to belief questions.

Based on H. Wimmer and J. Perner 1983: *Cognition*, 13, 103–28.

Box 13.2
Domain specificity in conceptual development: neuropsychological evidence from autism

Several experiments have shown that people with autism often have difficulty appreciating that other people behave on the basis of their beliefs about the world (Baron-Cohen et al., 1985; Perner et al., 1989). A belief about the world is usually referred to as a representation, and we all have a mental representation of the world derived from our knowledge and experience of the world. Most adults also realize that other people may have different representations from our own, and that both ourselves and other people may have a representation of the world which is inaccurate, but this realization often seems to be lacking in people with autism.

Leslie and Thaiss pointed out that as well as mental representations there are other types of representations (pictures, photographs, maps and so on). If children with autism are impaired in their understanding of mental representations are they also impaired in understanding other forms of representation?

In any experiment with people with learning difficulties it is very important to find an appropriate control group. If, for example, children aged 12 years were compared with normal children aged 12 years, it is likely that on almost any cognitive measure the normal children would preform better than the children with autism, because the normal children would have a mental age which was approximately the same as their chronological age, but the children with autism would have a much lower mental age. Discovering that a group of children with a normal mental age performed better than a group of children with a comparatively low mental age would not be very surprising or informative.

Therefore, to measure the abilities of children with autism, it is usual to compare them with other children who have the same mental age (but who do not have the diagnosis of autism). For example, if a group of children with autism who have a mental age of 6 years are compared with a group of normal children who also have a mental age of 6 years, and the children with autism perform more poorly than the normal children on a task, it can be assumed that their poorer performance is due to their autism.

(However, a note of caution should be added here, in such an experiment it would be likely that the chronological age of the normal children would be about 6 years of age, but the children with autism might (say) have a chronological age of 12 years. In other words, there may be a large difference in the actual age, and therefore the experience of the two groups. To overcome this, some researchers have compared children with autism with children with other learning difficulties. In this way it is possible, for example, to find a group of children with autism with an average chronological age of 12 years and an average mental age of 6 years; and a group of children with learning difficulties who also have an average chronological age of 12 years and an average mental age of 6 years. If both groups carry out the same test, and the children with autism perform less well then the children with learning difficulties it can be inferred that the deficit in the performance of the children with autism is due to some factor associated with autism, because other factors, like chronological and mental age, are the same for both groups.)

Leslie and Frith compared 15 children with autism with 20 normal children who had a similar average mental age. The details of the children are given in table box 13.2.1. All the children were given two tasks. In one task children's understanding of mental representations was tested by asking them about a false belief. In the other task their understanding of a non-mental representation (a photograph) was tested by asking them about the content of the photograph.

The false belief task was based on the Smarties task (see p. 414). The children were shown a Smarties box and asked what it contained. All the children said 'Smarties'. The top was then removed and the child was shown that the box actually contained a pencil. The pencil was then replaced in the box and the top put back. The child was then asked 'Now [name of child's friend] has not seen this box before. When I show this box to [name of friend] before I take the top off – what will [name of friend] say is in here?

The children were also asked a 'reality' question: 'What is really in here?', to check that they remembered what was actually in the box.

The photograph task involved a story about three puppets and a toy box. A cat puppet took a photograph of Polly the horse puppet while Polly was sitting on the toy box. After the photograph was taken it was placed faced down (without the child seeing it). Then Polly was moved from the toy box and a mouse puppet put in Polly's place. The child was then asked the photograph question: 'In the photograph who is sitting on the toy box?'

The child was also asked a 'memory' question; 'Who was sitting on the toy box when the cat took the photograph?' and a 'reality' question: 'Who is sitting on the toy box now?' to check that they had remembered all the story details.

Four of the children with autism and three of the normal children failed one or both of the memory and reality questions and were excluded from the analysis.

Table box 13.2.2 shows the percentage of children in each group who gave a correct answer to the belief question in the Smarties task, and the percentage who gave a correct answer to the photograph question. There was a significant interac-

Box Table 13.2.1 Mean ages and age ranges of children in Leslie and Thaiss's (1992) experiment

	Chronological age	Mental age
Children with autism	Mean 12:0 Range 7:10 – 18:7	Mean 6:3 Range 4:4 – 14:5
Normal children	Mean 4:0 Range 3:8 – 4:5	Mean 4:5 Range 2:6 – 7:3

Box Table 13.2.2   Percentage of children in each group who were correct in the false belief and photograph tasks (from Leslie and Thaiss, 1992)

	False belief task	Photograph task
Children with autism	33%	100%
Normal children	75%	66%

tion in the performance of the children ($p < 0.001$). As can be seen in the table, the normal children performed similarly on both the false belief and the photograph task. In contrast, the children with autism performed poorly in the false belief task and were all correct in the photograph task. Their poor performance in the false belief task (a task which required an appreciation of someone else's mental representation) is typical of the findings from other researchers (see this chapter).

However, the children with autism had no difficulty in the photograph task. This means that any impairment that children with autism have in understanding representations does not extend to non-mental representations like photographs. In a second experiment Leslie and Thaiss carried out a similar study, but instead of showing children a photograph they showed them a map of a model room (and a sticker on the map marked the posi-

tion of a puppet character who later moved). The children were then asked where the character was sitting 'in the map' to test whether they realized that the map did not change even though the character had moved. As in the photograph task, the children with autism were much better in the map task than in a false belief task.

This experiment by Leslie and Thaiss (and similar studies with photographs by Leekam and Perner, 1991, and with drawings by Charman and Baron-Cohen, 1992) demonstrated that although children with autism have an impaired understanding of mental representations, they are not impaired in understanding non-mental representations, such as photographs and maps.

Based on A. M. Leslie and L. Thaiss 1992: *Cognition*, 43, 225–51.

14 Learning in a Social Context

◀The Challenge of Vygotsky▶▶▶

We saw in chapter 11 Piaget's account of how children develop as thinkers and learners. Essentially the Piagetian model shows us children as individual 'scientists' who formulate and test increasingly complex hypotheses about their world and about their own experiences and interactions. By and large, it is the inanimate world of objects which Piagetian psychologists have paid most attention to. But developmental psychologists have also explored the idea of the child as someone who negotiates meaning and understanding in a *social* context. Margaret Donaldson and her colleagues, for example, have demonstrated young children's competence at taking the perspective of another person in tasks which are socially meaningful to them (chapter 11). Developmental psychologists are also increasingly interested in the critical role that language plays in enabling children to enter into their culture (chapter 10). The child develops repertoires of shared meanings even before the emergence of language, starting with such phenomena as 'joint attention' (p. 321). But with language the child gains a much more powerful entry point into the images, metaphors and ways of interpreting events which are distinctive in her own culture. The point is that these are social representations which give to the child a framework for constructing knowledge.

A major challenge to Piaget's theory comes from this more recent emphasis, within the field of developmental psychology, on the intricate and reciprocal relationship between the individual person and the social context. One influential strand in this shift of perspective comes from Russian psychologists; in particular from the writings of Vygotsky (1896–1934), whose work was unknown in the West until it began to be translated in the 1960s and

1970s. Since then, there has been a huge upsurge of interest in his writings. In the past decade, he has become increasingly cited in the literature; there have been several new translations of his work and biographies written of his life. His ideas have influenced a growing number of empirical and theoretical studies, and are currently viewed as highly relevant to applied fields such as education.

Vygotsky (plate 14.1) created an ambitious model of cognition with a sociohistoric approach at its centre. He came from a Jewish family; his father was a bank official; and he was a brilliant student of law, literature and cultural studies at the University of Moscow, and at Shaniavskii People's University (an unofficial university that appeared in Moscow when the authorities expelled staff and students from Moscow University on suspicion of being involved in anti-tsarist activities). Like Piaget, he saw the child as an active constructor of knowledge and understanding. But he differed from Piaget in his emphasis on the role of direct intervention by more knowledgeable others in this learning process. Vygotsky argued that it is as a result of the social interactions between the growing child and other members of that child's community that the child acquires the 'tools' of thinking and learning. In fact, it is out of this co-operative process of engaging in mutual activities with more expert others that the child becomes more knowledgeable. Instruction, according to Vygotsky, is at the heart of learning.

During his short life, despite poor health, he worked intensely and productively. Yet much of his work was censored or simply hidden by his colleagues out of fear. *The Psychology of Art*, which led to the award of his Ph.D. in 1925, was not published even in Russian until 1965; *Thought and Language*, his best-known work, was first published in 1934 but was suppressed by the Stalinist authorities in 1936 and did not reappear until 1956.

Vygotsky's colleagues have been unforthcoming about his path through the stormy years of the Russian Revolution, but we have to remember how dangerous it was for social scientists during the Stalinist era to express views which did not conform to party doctrine. In the 1930s many eminent scholars and intellectuals were arrested, imprisoned or deported for their ideas. The very fact that Vygotsky had visited several European countries during the 1920s was sufficient grounds for suspicion, and we do know that for a period Vygotsky was disgraced for exploring the changing mentality of peasant farmers as they experienced collectivization. He and his colleagues worked constantly under this threat.

During this period, a reductionist model of mind predominated in Russia, as it did in the USA, and was derived from a distorted interpretation of the physiologist Pavlov's work (which Pavlov himself never endorsed). This was that higher mental processes, such as reasoning, and even consciousness itself, could be accounted for within the conditioned reflex approach. Vygotsky distanced himself from this dominant view:

> A human being is not at all a skin sack filled with reflexes, and the brain is not a hotel for a series of conditioned reflexes accidentally stopping in. (Vygotsky, quoted in Joravsky, 1989, p. 260)

Plate 14.1   L. S. Vygotsky.

By contrast, he argued that consciousness is central to the science of mind and that human beings are subject to 'dialectical interplay' between biological and cultural factors.

Vygotsky's psychology was consistent with Marxism, but it was far more sophisticated than the psychology favoured by Stalinist party ideologists. He had to tread a minefield and, for the most part, managed to avoid head-on conflict with the authorities while stating his own views with integrity:

> Our science will become Marxist to the degree that it will become true, scientific; and we will work precisely on that, its transformation into a

true science, not on its agreement with Marx's theory. (Vygotsky, quoted in Joravsky, 1989, p. 264)

It says a great deal for him that he was able to separate himself from the Stalinist pressure to reject 'bourgeois' aspects of science and to address himself to the study of the self-directed, conscious mind.

◀Individual Mental Functioning: its Sociocultural Origins▶▶▶

Whereas Piaget's view of the child's intellectual growth was as 'a manifestion of the child's largely unassisted activities' (Wood, 1988, p. 24), Vygotsky's view was quite different. From his perspective, we can only understand mental functioning in the individual if we take account of the social processes on which it is based:

> Children solve practical tasks with the help of their speech, as well as with their eyes and hands. This unity of perception, speech and action . . . constitutes the central subject matter for any analysis of the origins of uniquely human forms of behaviour. (Vygotsky, 1978, p. 26)

Vygotsky placed a greater emphasis on language than Piaget, but in addition he stressed that this process must also be seen in the context of the person's culture, and the tools and aids which exist in that culture.

The interactions between the individual child, the significant people in her immediate environment, and her culture can be represented diagrammatically (figure 14.1). From this diagram we can see that Vygotsky saw mental functioning as action, and argued that before this conscious, self-directed control develops, action is the way in which the child responds to the world. Furthermore, it is the process of turning round and reflecting on one's own thoughts, using language, that enables one to see things in a new way. Learning is achieved first through co-operation with others in a whole variety of social settings – with peers, teachers, parents and other people who are significant to the child, and secondly through the 'symbolic representatives' of the child's culture – through its art and language, through play and songs, through metaphors and models. In this two-way process, the child's development as a learner reflects her cultural experience; in turn, significant cultural experiences become internalized into the structure of the child's intellect. Vygotsky's theory stresses the role of interpersonal processes and the role of society in providing a framework within which the child's construction of meaning develops.

Vygotsky (1981, p. 163) stated that 'social relations or relations among people genetically underlie all higher functions and their relationships'. Wertsch and Tulviste (1996, p. 55), in their commentary on this statement, highlight the originality of Vygotsky's perspective by indicating that, in contemporary Western psychology, the terms 'cognition', 'memory' and

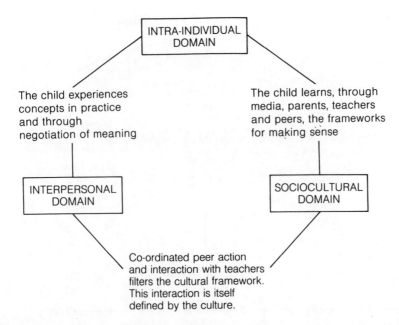

Figure 14.1 A model for the relationship between the intra-individual, interpersonal and social domains (adapted from Haste, 1987).

attention' are automatically assumed to be individual characteristics. We only place them in the social plane by adding markers such as 'socially shared' or 'socially distributed'.

The zone of proximal development (ZPD)

A central concept of Vygotsky's is the zone of proximal development, or ZPD, which provides an explanation for how the child learns with the help of others. The ZPD is the distance between the child's actual developmental level and his or her potential level of development under the guidance of more expert adults or in collaboration with more competent peers. To Vygotsky the child is initiated into the intellectual life of the community and learns by jointly constructing his or her understanding of issues and events in the world. Unlike Piaget, Vygotsky did not wait for the child to be 'ready'. Instead, he argued, children learn from other people who are more knowledgeable than themselves (figure 14.2).

How does this 'expert intervention' enable the child to learn? It should be at a level beyond the child's existing developmental level so that it provides some challenge; but not too far ahead, so that it is still comprehensible. This is then within the ZPD and the child can accomplish something he or she could not do alone, and learn from the experience. When the child's level of understanding is deliberately challenged (but not challenged too much), then he or she is more likely to learn new things effectively without experiencing failure. Instruction itself should be geared to the ZPD of the person receiving the instruction (Wertsch and Tulviste, 1996). The intervention is at

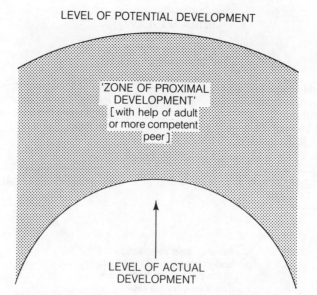

LEVEL OF POTENTIAL DEVELOPMENT

'ZONE OF PROXIMAL
DEVELOPMENT'
[with help of adult
or more competent
peer]

LEVEL OF ACTUAL
DEVELOPMENT

Figure 14.2   Vygotsky's concept of the zone of proximal development (ZPD).

its most effective when it is contingent upon the child's existing repertoire of skills and knowledge, that is, when it is within the ZPD. However, as we see in the section 'Implications for education' (p. 436), some social contexts are not conducive to learning and may even inhibit it, for example, where the teacher asks too many closed questions or where the child is in a group of domineering or intimidating peers.

The process of collaborating with another person who is more knowledgeable not only gives the child new information about a topic but also confirms those aspects of the issue which the child does understand. This co-operation between the child and more expert others helps the child to move on intellectually (Vygotsky, 1978; Wood, 1988).

An example from a contemporary description of a session in a nursery class will perhaps make this point clearer. The teacher, Mrs Morgan, has given the children a box of cardboard toilet-roll centres and invites them to explore the possibilities of this material. Amongst other things, some of the children spontaneously make sounds with their new-found toilet-roll trumpets. When she judges the moment to be right, Mrs Morgan intervenes to build on the children's ideas:

She stood back – she watched – she thought – and then acted in a manner which did not destroy the validity of the children's work, but contributed to it. She produced other cylindrical and tubular items which, in turn, produced new effects. The children who seemed keen on the sound idea sorted amongst the items – selected – tried out – rejected – found others – combined watering cans with tubes – plastic pipes and bowls of water – teapots with rubber hose. It looked rather chaotic, and sounded terrible, but the five children were feverishly excited. After ten minutes Mrs Morgan once again stepped into the situation together with her tape recorder, and a new event evolved. Listening – not just hearing, but really listening.

'What is this sound?'

'Who else thinks that's Till's cardboard tube we can hear?'

'Who thinks it is Robert's watering can with the tube on it?' 'Who would like me to play it again so we can listen more carefully?' Edward's device with the screwed up ball of paper squashed into the end of a washing machine hose was generally acclaimed to be the funniest, and Jo's the shrillest. Jill's was easily the longest sound, but it seemed impossible to agree as to whose was lowest . . . Gerald's offering was impossible to record due to the fact that he had gone outside and pushed his piece of plastic piping into the spout of the drainpipe. (Dixon, 1986, pp. 21–2)

What is happening in this short episode? For one thing, the children are discovering more about their own 'noise-making devices' by listening, sorting and categorizing the tape-recorded sounds. They build on the teacher's intervention and introduce objects and tubes for sound-making; for example, a drainpipe, hoses, bicycle pumps, ballpoint pens and straws all become wind instruments. The children exercise their own potentiality and desire to learn, but the teacher's sensitive intervention has played a significant part in the process. The children have been encouraged to look rather than simply see; to listen rather than simply hear; to feel rather than simply touch. The teacher is engaging with the children as they make sense of their experience, and it is through this interplay of words, actions and shared experiences that Mrs Morgan guides each child through his or her ZPD.

◀The Impact of Bruner▶ ▶

Vygotsky's ideas have been extensively developed and applied in educational settings by the American psychologist Jerome Bruner (plate 14.2). Bruner and his colleagues have proposed the concept of 'scaffolding' (Wood, Bruner and Ross, 1976). The term 'scaffolding' refers to the wide range of activities through which the adult, or the more expert peer, assists the learner to achieve goals which would otherwise be beyond them, for example by modelling an action, by suggesting a strategy for solving a problem or by structuring the learning into manageable parts. Scaffolding does not imply a rigid structure or a didactic teaching method but rather a flexible and child-centred supportive strategy which supports the child in learning new things and which enables the child to have a sounding board for action. As the child becomes more independent in the mastery of a new skill, the adult is able gradually to remove the scaffolding until the child no longer needs it.

Plate 14.2   Professor Jerome Bruner.

The idea of scaffolding is, of course, a metaphor, since the more expert adult or peer does not literally build a structure of scaffolding to support the child. Although it evokes a powerful visual image, it is no more than a metaphor and does not in itself explain the processes through which the child internalizes new learning (Daniels, 1996, p. 270). However, the concept of scaffolding has been extremely useful to educators in giving a theoretical justification for methods which structure learning without being unnecessarily didactic, and in exploring the area which covers the distance between learning with adult support and performing without help, that is the ZPD.

Central to Bruner's thinking is the conviction that the process of learning is the same whether we are talking about the pioneer at the frontier of knowledge or the child engaged in making a construction of wooden blocks:

> If one respects the ways of thought of the growing child, if one is courteous enough to translate material into his logical forms and challenging enough to tempt him to advance, then it is possible to introduce

him at an early age to the ideas and styles that in later life make an educated man. We might ask, as a criterion for any subject taught in primary school, whether, when fully developed, it is worth an adult's knowing, and whether having known it as a child makes a person a better adult. If the answer to both questions is negative or ambiguous, then the material is cluttering the curriculum. (Bruner, 1963, p. 52)

Bruner described the child's cognitive development as made up of distinct ways of representing the world. The earliest to appear is the *enactive* mode of representation, in which the child represents the world through action. Events are portrayed through appropriate motor responses (e.g. building with bricks, riding a bicycle). Between the ages of 2 and 6 years the child begins to represent the world through images or spatial schemas. Bruner called this the *iconic* mode of representation, which enables children to use images to stand for objects. Last and most important to emerge is the *symbolic* mode of representation which, appearing at around the age of 7 years, frees children from the immediate context and enables them to symbolize (Bruner, 1966). Children at this stage are beginning to be able to 'go beyond the information given' and represent their world symbolically. This ability to symbolize, depending to a large extent on language, is at the heart of the child's capacity to think abstractly and to make knowledge her own.

These modes of representation lie at the heart of Bruner's concept of the *spiral curriculum*. By this Bruner means that the principles of a subject come to be understood by the person at increasingly sophisticated levels. He was not happy with the Piagetian view that educators should wait for the child to be ready to learn. Instead he proposed a much more active policy of intervention. He is famous for his dictum that 'any subject can be taught effectively in some intellectually honest form to any child at any stage of development' (Bruner, 1963, p. 33). The idea behind this statement is that true knowledge arises out of a process of deepening understanding. Ideas, Bruner claimed, need to be 'revisited'. Bruner's concept of the spiral curriculum implied that even quite young children can grasp ideas in an intuitive way which they can return to later at progressively more complex levels of difficulty. For example, children can intuitively understand the concept of tragedy as represented in story or myth. As adults they will understand the concept in a more abstract way. Each level of understanding is valid; each can be taught in a way which is intellectually honest. In fact, he argued, the school curriculum should be built around the important issues and values of society.

Bruner argued forcefully that educators need to be concerned with the role of structure in learning. Teachers must address the issue of enabling students to grasp the structure of a discipline rather than simply mastering facts. The structure of a body of knowledge is as important as its mode of representation. By structure he means the principles and concepts of a discipline – relative and related to the needs of the learner. The mastery of structure gives the learner purpose and direction; it is a process which enables the child to go beyond the information given in order to generate ideas of her own. Bruner also stressed the need to encourage students to make links and to understand relationships between and across subjects. Curriculum planning should be concerned to enhance learning as an active and problem-solving process.

◀Language and Thought▶▶

As we have seen, Vygotsky's model proposed not only the idea of an individual functioning in his own immediate social context (for example, in the family or social group) but also the idea that the human mind itself 'extends beyond the skin' (Wertsch and Tulviste, 1996, p. 60) and is inherently social. This view suggests that all human functioning is by its nature sociocultural in the sense that it incorporates socially evolved and socially organized cultural tools, such as language, systems for counting, works of art, diagrams, maps, signs and models. These systems become part of the shared knowledge of a culture. For example, theoretical knowedge which has become part of everyday knowledge can be seen among young people who know enough about electronics to build themselves a sound system, or who have the mechanical knowledge to repair their motorbikes (Hedegaard, 1996).

This view has strong implications for education and differs quite sharply both from the child-centred model of education, which sprang from Piaget's theory, and from traditional, didactic models of education. From the Vygotskian standpoint children do not operate in isolation but make knowledge their own in a community of others who share a common culture. Language plays a key part in this process. Vygotsky suggested that it was through speech – which had been formed through the processes of social interaction as outlined above – that the child developed as a thinker and learner.

Vygotsky argued that language reflects our culture and its forms, whether in academic texts, professional practice, the arts, folklore or customs. The person as a conscious thoughtful being could accomplish very little without the aids and tools which are provided by his or her history and culture. Piaget, by contrast, had not stressed the importance of language as the principal source of cognitive development. Piaget, as discussed in chapter 11, maintained that language was strongly influenced by the underlying cognitive structures in the child. We have already examined one of his major theoretical constructs – egocentrism. Piaget made extensive observations of children at the Rousseau Institute in Geneva and, on that basis, concluded that up to half of the utterances made by children under the age of 7 years are examples of egocentric speech; in other words, they show no sign that the children have attempted to communicate with another person or adapted their speech so that another might understand it. Piaget observed further that young children often did not seem to care whether anyone else could understand them or not. He noticed that young children would often talk at length to themselves while engaged in solitary activity; these monologues were like commentaries on the children's own actions rather than forms of communication. They might also carry out collective monologues where children were close to one another and spoke in pairs or a group, but where the utterances were not made in response to other children's speech.

Piaget interpreted this behaviour as a sign of the child's inability to take account of the perspective of another, and argued that, with maturity, the child comes to decentre and also becomes more logical. She is then able to take the perspective of others and engage in socially meaningful verbal exchanges. This process of decentration, according to Piaget, unfolds between the ages of 4 and 7 (see also chapter 10). By 7 the child's speech would become more fully socialized. Vygotsky's view was quite different. He did not accept that the young child's language is largely egocentric and that monologues have no part to play in cognitive development.

The monologues of younger children were to Vygotsky highly social and represented the transition from language as a tool for regulating action and communicating needs, to language as a tool for thought (see also chapter 10). In fact, he argued that the monologues show children's development in their capacity – already socially formed – to regulate their own activities. The monologues, as a form of communication with the self, help children to plan and organize their behaviour. Three-year-old Ben, for example, talks to himself as he cuts out a paper figure:

> Now I'm going to make a man. Cut round here. This is his magic wand. He's a wizard now. Oops! Too far. Oh! Start again.

Vygotsky suggested that monologues become internalized at around 7 years to become inner speech – the dialogue with ourselves in which we all engage – which becomes thought. You may even still experience a tendency to revert to *externalized* monologues when tasks are too challenging, for

Table 14.1   The contrasting views of Piaget and Vygotsky on preschoolers' private speech

Piaget's model	Vygotsky's model
Repetition: the child merely repeats sounds	*Social dialogue* between adult and child: children and adults engage in joint activities, e.g. peek-a-boo play
Monologue: the child alone speaks to herself as if she were thinking aloud	*Monologues or overt inner speech:* these are internalized to regulate a child's activity, and originate from social dialogues
Collective monologue: the child uses monologue in social settings but does not take the listeners' viewpoint into consideration. True dialogue does not emerge until around age 7	*Inner speech:* utterances internalized in private speech to guide behaviour. Inner speech is internalized by the end of the preschool period

example, talking yourself through a difficult problem ('Now how do I open this door now that the high-tech new lock has been installed?') or commenting on your lack of expertise ('Stupid! Try turning the key the other way!' or 'I'd better ring the locksmith.')! Vygotsky's and Piaget's contrasting views are summarized in table 14.1.

In Vygotsky's words, language reflects 'the organizing consciousness of the whole culture' (see figure 14.1). He argued that the child's development as a thinker arises both from the dialogue with parents and other adult carers, and in relation to the wider society of which the parents are a part. His perspective encompasses the use of language as a framework for thought and the use of language as a representation of the culture. The two are inextricably intertwined. This is a fundamental point of disagreement between Vygotskian and Piagetian thinking and many developmental psychologists have become increasingly critical of the lack of emphasis on social and cultural context in Piaget's model, with its concentration on the child as an individual progressing through developmental stages. The debate continues in the field of academic developmental psychology but it is of more than academic significance. There are important practical implications for the ways in which we educate our children.

◀Implications for Education▶ ▶ ▶

The teacher in the Piagetian tradition is a facilitator who provides the right materials for the child's level of development and helps the child to 'discover' by herself, through the conflict between her existing schemas and the evidence facing her. The teacher does not confront the child with these discrepancies but stands back and allows the child to find out for herself. The view of Vygotsky and of Bruner is that the adult and child can work together to construct new schemas, and that the intervention by the more expert adult is positively helpful in moving the child's thinking on. The adult's expertise should be actively harnessed to the child's level of competence and to the ZPD. Concepts are 'jointly constructed through interaction with those who already embody them, together with the ways of doing and thinking that are cultural practices, recreated with children through processes of formal and informal teaching' (Wood, 1988, p. 195). It is important, from this standpoint, to give help to the child which is contingent on her failure to give a correct response. If the child succeeds, it is important to give less help. The more the teacher's behaviour is contingent on the child's behaviour in these sorts of ways the more able the child becomes to work independently.

Even if children do not properly understand something, they may know enough for the adult to be able to direct them to a relevant activity. If this activity is within the ZDP, then, as we have seen, the scaffolding function supports the young learners. 'Contingent control helps to ensure that the demands placed on the child are likely neither to be too complex, producing defeat, nor too simple, generating boredom or distraction' (Wood, 1988, p. 201). In fact, the commentary from more expert people helps the child integrate existing knowledge into a wider framework. Thus it supports existing understanding while giving the opportunity to branch out into new regions.

Children may also need help in having their attention directed towards significant features of a task or a situation, when, left alone, they might not make the right connections. The interventions by the knowledgeable adult give the child a structure within which to formulate meaning. By helping the young learner to use language as an instrument of thought, the adult frees the child from the world of immediate perceptions and enables her to 'go beyond the information given'.

Bruner pointed out that the invention of 'schooling' itself has had a great impact on the nature of thinking since schooling creates particular ways of looking at problems and of acting on the world. Teachers are not, he argues, simply handing on knowledge but actively recreating distinctive ways of thinking. This can be enabling or inhibiting. Donaldson's research has shown how children's will to learn may be unwittingly crushed by the educational experience. Competence, where not recognized or fostered, can wither. Failure to scaffold on the part of teachers, failure to build on the knowledge which the child brings to the classroom, may well lead the child to learn to fail in school settings. In box 14.2, for example, we see that Brazilian street children are more expert at mathematical calculation in the market place than in the classroom.

There are some similarities here with Piaget's theory (chapter 11). Both Bruner and Piaget view action as important in cognitive development. There are also similarities in the ways in which the two psychologists consider that abstract thinking grows out of action and perception. Both would agree that competence in any area of knowledge must be rooted in active experience and concrete mental operations. Where the two theorists differ, and where Bruner has been greatly influenced by the work of Vygotsky, is first in the part in which language and interpersonal communication play a role in the process; and secondly in the need for active intervention by expert adults (or more knowledgeable peers) at a suitable level (as in the spiral curriculum) so enabling the child to develop as a thinker and problem solver. Like Vygotsky, Bruner argues that instruction is an essential part of learning.

Adults as Tutors: Experimental Studies of Scaffolding

Vygotsky's *Thought and Language* was not translated into English until 1962. Bruner (1986, p. 72) describes how he welcomed the invitation to write an introduction to the book and how he read the ongoing translation with 'astonishment'. Vygotsky's ideas on thought and speech as instruments for planning out action were in tune with Bruner's views. He was intrigued by Vygotsky's suggestion that society provides the tools which enable the child to become more advanced as a thinker. Bruner was especially interested in the concept of the ZPD and the role which other people play in helping the child to learn and reflect on things. Bruner called this help 'the loan of consciousness'.

However, Vygotsky had not actually spelt out in any detail how the more expert adult might 'lend' consciousness to the child who did not already have it. Bruner's metaphor of scaffolding is illuminative here. Imagine the tutor has erected scaffolding which could help the child to climb to a higher level of understanding. To be more effective, scaffolding has to be constructed so that the child is not asked to climb too much at once. It has to take account not only of the child's existing level, but of how far she can progress with help; essentially the idea of Vygotsky's ZPD.

Bruner and his colleagues initiated a number of research studies to investigate the role of scaffolding in learning. For example, Wood, Bruner and Ross (1976) decided to look at what happens when a tutor tries to pass on her knowledge to a child. Scaffolding, they concluded, has distinctive aspects:

Recruitment The tutor's first task is to engage the interest of the child and encourage the child to tackle the requirements of the task.

Reduction of degrees of freedom The tutor has to simplify the task by reducing the number of acts needed to arrive at a solution. The learner needs to be able to see whether he has achieved a fit with task requirements or not.

Direction maintenance The tutor needs to keep the child's motivation up. Initially the child will be looking to the tutor for encouragement; eventually the solution of the problem should become interesting in its own right.

Marking critical features A tutor highlights features of the task that are relevant. This gives information about any discrepancies between what the child has produced and what he would recognize as a correct production.

Demonstration Modelling solutions to the task involves completion of a task or explanation of a solution already partly done by the young learner. The aim is that the learner will imitate this back in a better form.

(Adapted from D. Wood, J. S. Bruner and G. Ross, 1976, p. 98)

Details of an experimental study by these researchers are given in box 12.1. Here the tutor acknowledged the ZPD by being aware of what the children could recognize and then guiding them towards what they could do on their own. This kind of tutoring skill can in itself be learned. It is a skill which demands that the tutor act contingently upon the child's abilities.

◀ Adults as Tutors: the Family and Community Context ▶ ▶

Scaffolding appears in a whole variety of forms. Parents do it routinely through the rituals and games which are part of normal adult–child interaction (see chapter 8) and clearly language plays a critical part in the scaffolding process. It may appear when the parent responds to the child's first attempts at speech (see the section on Adult–Child speech in chapter 10). We might see it when the adult, closely in tune with the child's ongoing monologues, helps to solve a problem. We might see it when the child, frustrated by inability to convey the excitement of a new experience, is guided by the adult to use appropriate words and images.

Wertsch et al. (1980) investigated the role of parents in guiding 2-, 3- and 4-year-olds through the ZPD by means of spontaneous scaffolding of the children's activities. The preschoolers and their mothers were asked to build a replica of a model truck, using pieces of different colours and shapes. The researchers found that when the mother checked the colour, shape or position of a piece against the original model truck, the children would look too. This happened in over 90 per cent of the instances. This phenomenon was age related and the frequency of mother-guided looks declined with the age of the children.

Dunn (1984) describes the scaffolding process in operation when mothers in her study structured the feeling states of 2-year-olds, so giving the child a framework for interpreting emotions (see chapter 3). Butterworth's (1987) studies highlight the scaffolding processes at work when the mother builds on the infant's capacity to adjust his or her own line of gaze to that of the mother, by commenting on the object of joint attention; and through the enjoyable experience of turn-taking in ritual language games and rhymes (see chapter 10).

Greenfield and Lave (1982) observed how Zinacanteco Mexican women scaffolded the weaving skills of young girls who were 'apprenticed' to them to learn their traditional craft. Initially the girls spent up to 50 per cent of their time watching the skilled weavers; the next step was to work co-operatively with the women, under their close guidance; finally, they were able to take responsibility for their own work. At each stage of the process, however, the teachers adjusted the level of difficulty and structured the amount of help they gave so that the girls learned an increasing repertoire of weaving skills.

These examples, commonplace in family and community life, show the collaborative nature of the learning process and suggest that language, foremost among the social representations, provides a framework within which the growing child comes to interpret and understand experience.

◀Working in the ZPD: the School Context▶▶▶

Child-initiated encounters upon which the teacher can be immediately contingent are difficult to establish and sustain in the classroom. There is less opportunity for exploratory activity in which the teacher can find out the individual child's ZPD. Ideally what the adult seeks to 'show and tell' children should be contingent on what they know already. In sharp contrast to the home, however, teachers are much more likely to control the learners and to ask questions which require a specific answer. Wood (1988) argues that this kind of questioning strategy is counter-productive and all too frequently only serves to highlight children's *lack* of knowledge. So how can the teacher, managing a class of 30 pupils, create conditions in which to become more aware of each child's existing thoughts and tentative ideas on a topic and then respond to them contingently?

Hedegaard (1996) describes a teaching experiment based on the methodology developed by Leontiev (1981) and other followers of Vygotsky. From this perspective, the children's understanding grows out of the process of making the shift from *actions*, through *symbolization*, to *formulation*. Action involves direct exploration of the subject through research based on, for example, observation in the field, at the museum or through film. Symbolization is achieved once the children are able to find ways of representing relationships among things which they have observed; this may be done by means of charts, drawings or models of their research findings. Formulation of broader principles comes when the children can clearly state principles which go beyond the specific subjects of their research. At each stage, the concept of the ZPD provides an essential framework for evaluating children's development as thinkers.

Hedegaard's longitudinal study involved teaching a class of Danish children, from third through to fifth grade in elementary school, a method for integrating three distinct but related areas of the curriculum – evolution of species, origin of man and historical change in societies. In order to achieve this aim, she and the teachers in the project designed carefully structured learning experiences to give the children the 'tools' to tackle questions like: 'How can an animal population adapt to changes in its habitat while many individual animals do not succeed in managing this adaptation and so die?' As an abstract question this would be difficult for elementary-school children to answer. But, claimed Hedegaard, if the problem is presented through the direct study of, say, the polar bear and how it adapts to its Arctic surroundings, children can use this information first to symbolize adaptations of the polar bear and later, on the basis of other similarly concrete studies, to formulate broader laws about survival and change in a whole species. Hedegaard proposed that theoretical knowledge has a 'tool character'; the initial models proposed by the children may become the tools which guide the next stage of the inquiry. By the direct experience of finding contradictions in their active modelling of the problem area under study, pupils' concepts become richer and clearer.

The teachers' method of deliberately working within the ZPD built on shared, concrete activities using whole-class dialogue, co-operative group work and collective problem-solving tasks. At the heart of the method was the tool of research activity, which in turn led to a critical appraisal on the part of the children of the models which they themselves had constructed. These intellectual tools were then applied to other learning situations which the children encountered.

Hedegaard's results demonstrated that teachers can successfully work with the ZPD in a whole-class context. The children developed a qualitative change in their interest in the subject matter and in the methods used to discover new things. They showed loss of interest in specific animals when they became too familiar and shifted instead to an interest in general formulation of models applicable in a more general way to the issue of animals' adaptation to living conditions. They also developed a critical interest in the teaching methods as they related to problem identification and solution. Overall, the children demonstrated a shift in interest from the concrete to an interest in general principles which might, in turn, be applied to new concrete situations. Significantly, she found that fast learners were stimulated by the approach; but that the less able children, too, maintained interest and motivation.

◀The Role of Peers as Tutors▶▶▶

We have seen how teachers can use Vygotskian principles in whole-class settings. Are there ways in which peers might also play a part in scaffolding one another's learning? Slavin, a proponent of co-operative learning, asserts that:

> Under the right motivational conditions, peers can and, more important, will provide explanations in one another's proximal zones of development and will engage in the kind of cognitive conflict needed for disequilibration and cognitive growth. (Slavin, 1987, p. 1166)

Group learning environments, if properly structured, encourage questioning, evaluating, and constructive criticism, leading to restructuring of knowledge. For example, in these learning settings a child may need to explain something to another, defend his or her own viewpoint, engage in debate or analyse a disagreement. This can result in learning with understanding, and, many proponents claim, in fundamental cognitive restructuring.

Co-operative group work (CGW) in the classroom (Cowie, Smith, Boulton and Laver, 1994) can offer one effective method for enabling children in the role of experts to act contingently upon one another, so guiding their peers through the ZPD. For example, the Jigsaw method (Aronson, 1978) is designed in such a way that children work interdependently by splitting a task into four or five sections. Each pupil has access to only part of the material to be mastered and must work with others to fit together all the pieces of the 'Jigsaw'. The pupils work in groups where they become expert in one section; the expert pupils then return to their home groups where they tutor other members of their team in the material which they have mastered.

Bennett and Dunne (1992) investigated the effect of three types of grouping arrangement (one of which was Jigsaw) on primary-school children's talk. They noted an increase in the quality of children's language and thinking when they were given the opportunity to work in small, interactive co-operative groups. The children who participated in co-operative group work showed less concern for status, less competitiveness and were significantly more likely to express evidence of logical thinking. This was particularly so when the children were encouraged to engage in an exchange of views, often conflicting, and to explore a range of possible perspectives. Even the most stilted discussions, write Bennett and Dunne, were characterized by talk in abstract modes rarely found in individualized work.

Such possibilities do depend on structuring the learning environment correctly, and not all social interaction in co-operative learning leads to cognitive growth. Slavin (1987) emphasizes the importance of motivation, and encourages inter-group competition in learning. Brown and Palenscar (1989) suggest that the effect of collaboration depends on key factors such as the initial ability of the child and the child's social status in the peer group. They argue that co-operative learning will be most helpful to a child who has only a partial grasp of the situation, and who, while not overruled by another more dominant child, is faced with a view that not only conflicts with theirs but is also one they can take seriously. Cowie, Smith, Boulton and Laver (1994) show the positive influence of co-operative group work on the quality of social relationships in the classroom but also provide evidence of the disruptive effect which domi- neering or bullying behaviour can have on small group work (see also chapter 4).

There is a growing literature on peer-tutoring (Topping, 1988) in the learning process. Here the expert tutor is a fellow pupil. Foot, Morgan and Shute (1990) stress the appropriateness of Vygotsky's model in explaining how peer-tutoring works. One child (the tutor) is more knowledgeable than the other (the tutee) and each is aware of the distinctiveness of their roles as expert and novice; it is clear to each child that the aim is for the expert to impart his or her knowledge to the novice. However, the 'expert' is not likely to be that much ahead of the 'novice', and so more readily appreciates the latter's difficulties and thus can scaffold effectively within the latter's ZDP. Peer-tutoring provides a good example of interaction as a necessary condi- tion for cognitive growth since it is through the processes which are involved in this interaction between tutor and tutee that the less expert child masters a new skill. Note that it is not simply the encounter between child and child that brings about the change but the impact of communication and instruc- tion from the more capable peer. Learning occurs when this joint intellectual activity becomes internalized. The instruction is effective when it is slightly ahead of the tutee's actual level and when the assistance from the peer tutor lies within the ZDP.

Advances in technology also offer support to the model of instruction outlined in this chapter. The recent development of computer-assisted learn- ing (CAL) enables teachers to harness the educational potentialities of com- puters to the specific needs of the child. The computer can present a series of information and tasks to the child. In intelligent tutoring systems, the stu- dent does not just go through a rigid linear sequence of tasks, but (depending on his or her prior responses) is taken down a branching route suited to the student's ability; for example being given more detailed help or prompts when required. Also computers can increase opportunities for socially inter- active learning. Pupils, knowledgeable in this area, often become a valued resource in the classroom, thus also increasing the opportunities for genuine peer-tutoring. Crook (1994) discusses the role of scaffolding in CAL. The pupil's experience, he argues, takes place in a socially organized context. We should not forget that computers are configured by programmers and designed for a schedule determined by teachers and administrators – features which are socially constituted! The child's encounters with the computer can be extremely collaborative with a high degree of participation by the child and contingent responses by the computer program. When children work together in CAL there is a great deal of collaboration and jointly co-ordinated problem-solving in which the novice (or less expert child) witnesses and takes part in more advanced strategies for achieving goals. This learning takes place on an inter-individual plane (see figure 12.1) and is an example of socially shared cognition.

◀ Is a Synthesis Possible? ▶ ▶ ▶

As we have seen, there are a number of ways in which Piaget's and Vygotsky's theories differ. They have contrasting views on language and thought. Piaget argues that thinking develops out of action rather than out of language. Language does not create thought but enables it to emerge. Before the age of around 7, that is before the onset of concrete operations, the child, in Piaget's view, is unable to think or discuss things rationally. Preschoolers' language and thought is primarily egocentric since the child is unable to enter into the perspective of another person. Children do not enter into discussions with one another since there is no real reciprocity or attempt at mutual understanding.

Vygotsky, by contrast, did not view children's speech as egocentric but as highly social. Vygotsky saw the collective monologues in which preschoolers typically engage as representing a transition between the communicative function of language and its function as a tool of thought, that is between the social and the intellectual. The child who talks to herself, then, is involved in a process of regulating and planning ongoing activity. This overt commentary will later be internalized as inner speech or thought. Vygotsky proposed that language arises out of social interaction.

With regard to learning and thinking, Piaget claimed that children pass through a series of stages of intellectual development before they are able to reason and think logically. Teaching, from this standpoint, is only effective if the child is 'ready' to assimilate the new idea or experience. Conflicting viewpoints can lead to cognitive change through the twin processes of assimilation and accommodation. Piaget emphasized the key part of action for the child's learning. Vygotsky agreed that action underlined thinking and learning but placed much more emphasis on the role of language, and of direct intervention and help by others more skilled in a task. However, it is sometimes overlooked that Piaget too valued peer interactions as playing a significant part in facilitating children's intellectual development (see also chapter 7).

Developmental psychologists (e.g. Slavin, 1987) have begun to examine ways in which the insights from both Piaget's and Vygotsky's perspectives might be synthesized. Piagetian researchers such as Doise and Mugny (1984) have also documented the types of co-operative context in which children progress in their understanding. Conflict of views and perspectives can encourage children to rethink (see also box 7.2). Doise and Mugny have shown that children working in pairs or in small groups come to solve problems more effectively than when they work alone. The reason seems to be that it is through social interaction that they come to see the solution. When the child encounters conflicting views this stimulates internal disequilibrium which the child is motivated to resolve. The social process of negotiating with peers erects a 'scaffold' which helps each child to reconstruct his or her ideas. This interpretation by Doise and Mugny starts from a Piagetian standpoint but takes account of the social context of peer interaction within which the child operates.

There are some disadvantages in working collaboratively in a team. Foot et al. (1990), despite their sympathy with the Vygotskian perspective, found that friendship groupings were not always the most productive and that in those settings there were more opportunities for being 'off-task'. Other researchers into co-operative learning (Slavin, 1987) have also identified 'free-riders' who allow fellow group members to do all their work for them! Cowie, Smith, Boulton and Laver (1994) found wide differences in the capacity which children in three multi-ethnic classrooms had to work co-operatively with one another, and suggested that children worked best in groups where there was a positive climate of mutual regard. However, they also noted the huge difficulties facing teachers in trying to achieve this goal. It would appear that the dynamics of the group or of the whole class must be taken into account. This is an issue which faces both Piagetians and Vygotskians. There would seem to be a case for a fuller integration of developmental and social theories.

◄Further Reading►►►

R. van der Veer and J. Valsiner 1991: *Understanding Vygotsky: a Quest for Synthesis*, Oxford: Basil Blackwell, give a comprehensive and critical account of Vygotsky's life and work with an analysis of the social context in which he developed his ideas. D. Joravsky 1989: *Russian Psychology*, Oxford: Blackwell, gives a fascinating and very detailed historical analysis of the social and political context in which Russian psychologists, including Vygotsky, developed their theories of the human mind. An accessible introduction to Vygotsky's ideas with topical research studies and recommendations for further reading is H. Daniels (ed.) 1996: *An Introduction to Vygotsky*, London: Routledge. Daniels's book also contains a useful review (chapter 2) on the implications of Vygotsky's ideas for current thinking in psychology and education: J. Wertsch and P. Tulviste 'L. S. Vygotsky and contemporary developmental psychology'. For a clear introduction to Vygotsky try F. Newman and L. Holzman 1993: *Lev Vygotsky: Revolutionary Scientist*, London: Routledge. For a scholarly and insightful psychological analysis of Vygotsky's cultural-historical approach to human development read J. Wertsch 1985: *Vygotsky and the Social Formation of Mind*, Cambridge, MA: Harvard University Press. For another overview see A. Kozulin 1990:

Vygotsky's Psychology: A Biography of Ideas, New York and London: Harvester-Wheatsheaf.

J. Piaget 1959: *The Language and Thought of the Child*, London: Routledge and Kegan Paul, was originally written in 1923. It contains his ideas on children's egocentric speech, which Vygotsky disagrees with in L. Vygotsky 1962: *Thought and Language*, Cambridge, MA: MIT Press. This actually dates from 1934, and was the first of Vygotsky's writings to be widely available in English (though in truncated form).

D. Wood 1988: *How Children Think and Learn*, Oxford: Blackwell, compares Piaget's ideas with those of Bruner and Vygotsky. He also considers practical implications for teachers and gives useful perspectives on the emergence of the mathematical mind and the literate mind.

M. Richards and P. Light (eds) 1986: *Children of Social Worlds*, Cambridge: Polity Press in association with Blackwell, looks at children's development through the process of communication with others. The authors are strongly critical of the individualistic approach to the study of child development. They also look at ways in which children come to understand social phenomena such as the threat of nuclear war.

◀Discussion Points▶▶▶

1 Vygotsky argued that instruction is at the heart of developing and internalizing new ideas. How can the adult most effectively help children to do this?
2 Think of the strategies which teachers might use to scaffold children's learning in the classroom. Can you think of examples from your own experience as a student?
3 Bruner claimed that 'any subject can be taught in some intellectually honest form to any child at any stage of development' (Bruner, 1963, p. 33). Do you agree? For example, how could you teach a 10-year-old about developmental psychology?
4 How do the views of Piaget and Vygotsky differ? In what ways might they be reconciled?
5 Does language structure our thinking, or thinking structure our language?

Box 14.1
The role of tutoring in problem-solving

This study aimed to investigate the nature of the tutorial role of the adult expert in helping the less expert child to solve a problem. The tutor was to teach 3-, 4- and 5-year-old children to build a three-dimensional structure, a task which on their own they would not have been able to do. The researchers proposed that, in order to benefit from help, the learner has to be able to recognize a solution before he is able to produce a good strategy for solving the problem alone. The investigators, therefore, were looking at the behaviour which young children engage in when they are trying to identify the nature of the problem; and they were also interested in the way in which the adult tutor 'scaffolded' the children's steps towards the completion of the task. The method was observational. They were not testing a hypothesis about the tutoring process, but giving a systematic description of children's responses to different kinds of help from the adult tutor.

Thirty children were equally divided into groups of 3-, 4- and 5-year-olds; the age groups contained

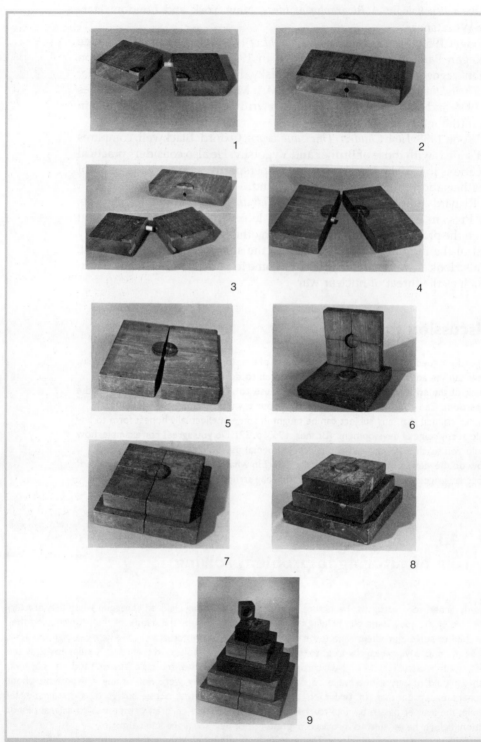

Box Figure 14.1.1 Stages in the construction of a pyramid. Source: D. Wood (1988), *How Children Think and Learn*, Oxford: Blackwell (p. 68, figure 3.3).

equal numbers of boys and girls. The researchers had designed a task which, in their view, would be interesting and challenging to young children. David Wood had designed a wooden toy consisting of 21 blocks which combined to form a pyramid 9 inches high on a 9-inch square base. The pyramid had six levels. The top block was a solid square with a circular depression in its bottom. The other five layers were composed of four equal-sized blocks made up of two interlocking pairs. Each pair fitted together by a hole and peg system. Each four-block layer had a round depression in its base and a matched elevation on top. These could only be formed by putting the pairs together in the correct orientation. (See box figure 14.1.1.)

It was agreed in advance that the tutor, Gail Ross, working with individual 3-, 4- and 5-year-olds, was to allow the children (here referred to as 'he' or 'they') to do as much as possible by themselves. When she had to intervene she would do so verbally before she demonstrated what to do. She was 'led' by each child in the sense that his success or failure at the task determined the next level of instruction.

After the initial period of free play with the jumbled blocks, the tutor began to show the child how to connect a pair. If he succeeded in doing this spontaneously, then she would invite him to 'make some more like that one'. The tutor then began to respond systematically to three types of response from the child. The tutor's interventions were classified into three categories:

1   Direct interventions, e.g. joining and positioning two blocks to make a pair; if the child ignored

her and continued with play then she would join two blocks to form a correct pair.
2   Verbal corrections, e.g. 'Does this (a mismatched construction) look like this (a matched one)?' If the child picked up the blocks which she had assembled and manipulated them then she would verbally tell the child that the pieces were not correctly joined.
3   General verbal direction to remind the child of the task requirements, e.g. 'Can you make any more like this?' If the child tried to do something with the blocks (e.g. putting pegs into holes) similar to the tutor but had overlooked an aspect, she would ask him to compare his with hers.

Box table 14.1.1 shows that there were significant age-related differences in the amount and type of help which the children required. The 5-year-olds received significantly less help than the 4-year-olds ($p < 0.05$) and the 3-year-olds ($p < 0.05$). If we look at the ratio of 'showing' and 'telling' we can see that both 5-year-olds ($p < 0.002$) and 4-year-olds ($p < 0.0002$) received significantly higher proportions of verbal assistance than the 3-year-olds.

Box table 14.1.1 shows that the main kind of interaction between tutor and 4-year-olds was verbal. As the researchers point out, 'with the youngest ones, the tutor is principally concerned with luring them into the task either by demonstrating it or by providing tempting material. Consequently, the tutor intervenes directly twice as often with the 3-year-olds as with the 4-year-olds, and four times more often than with the eldest group. The tutor, then, is both intervening more and being ignored

Box Table 14.1.1   Median instances of direct interventions, verbal corrections and general verbal directions

	Age		
	3	**4**	**5**
Direct intervention	12.0	6.0	3.0
Verbal corrections	3.0	5.0	4.5
Verbal directions	5.0	8.0	3.0
Total verbal intervention	8.0	13.0	7.5
Total help received	20.0	19.0	10.5
Ratio: $\dfrac{\text{'show'}}{\text{'tell'}}$	$\dfrac{12.0}{8.0} = 1.5$	$\dfrac{6.0}{13.0} = 0.46$	$\dfrac{3.0}{7.5} = 0.40$

Box Table 14.1.2 Relative successes of each group with 'showing' and 'telling'

	Age		
	3	4	5
Showing succeeds	40%	63%	80%
Telling succeeds	18%	40%	57%

more when working with 3-year-olds than with older children.' So the tutor seems to be principally a lure to the younger children but takes on the role of 'verbal prodder and corrector' for 4-year-olds. When we come to the 5-year-olds, the median number of tutorial interventions drops by half. The tutor seems to have become a 'confirmer or checker of constructions' since the children are clearly aware of the point of the task. For older children verbal interventions are more successful (box table 14.2.2).

This experiment demonstrates the function of scaffolding. The youngest children in this study can recognize a correct solution but they have to be induced to try the task in order to learn through recognition. These children had other ideas about what to do with the blocks. The tutor had a hard task in keeping the goal before their eyes. By the age of 4, the children now know about constructing, so the role of the tutor has changed. She now has to help them recognize the discrepancy between what the task requires and what they have achieved so far. This shifts the balance from showing to telling. The 5-year-old needs the tutor in a still different way. He knows what he wants to do and only asks for help when he is having problems or needs to check on a particular construction. The tutor is becoming superfluous. The child is becoming self-controlling and can do the task on his own.

What can these results tell us about the effect which adult help can have on the child's capacity to solve a problem? The results suggest that the tutor became 'consciousness for two' (Bruner, 1986, p. 75) for the children she tutored. She directed their attention to the task, kept them on task, kept the segments of the task appropriate to the child's capacity, she set things up so that the child could recognize a solution before he could solve the problem or even understand a verbal explanation of it. She operated within the ZPD which existed between what children can recognize when shown the way and what they can do on their own. She did what the child could not do, but she then enabled the child to do with her what he could not do alone.

As the children acquired mastery of the task requirements, they became able to be self-regulating. At this point the tutor handed over those parts of the task where she was no longer needed. This demonstrated the transactional nature of the learning process. The study provides in microcosm an illustration of the way in which the adult can help the child through the ZPD.

One of the limitations of this study was that, whilst identifying tutoring functions, it had little to say about the actual processes (e.g. when and how each function should be realized). In part, the notion of contingent control of learning was an attempt to specify at least some aspects of the processes involved. The next step would be an examination of how the tutor could learn to do it most effectively. Case studies documenting in detail the interactions which take place between tutor and child would make a useful complement to this kind of study. In fact, it is instructive to look at Wells (1985) in the analysis of pupil–teacher talk to see examples of good and bad practice.

Based on material in D. Wood, J. S. Bruner and G. Ross 1976: *Journal of Child Psychology and Psychiatry*, 17, 89–100.

Box 14.2
Mathematics in the streets and in schools

Problem-solving in the street market is significantly superior to that carried out with paper and pencil. This was the conclusion of Nunes and her colleagues, using a research method combining participant observation and the Piagetian clinical method, in their study which demonstrated that youngsters who work on the streets have developed computational strategies which are different from those who are taught in schools. These young people performed better in problems which were embedded in real-life contexts than they did when asked to solve context-free problems involving the same numbers and mathematical operations.

Nunes and her colleagues carried out this research in Recife, Brazil, among the children of street vendors who often helped out their parents from the age of 8 years onwards. Young people may also develop their own small businesses selling peanuts, pop-corn or coconut milk. As part of this work, the children have to be able to carry out mathematical problem-solving, usually mentally, involving addition (4 coconuts and 12 lemons cost x + y), multiplication (one coconut costs x; 4 coconuts cost 4x), subtraction (500 cruzeiros minus the purchase price = the amount of change to be given) and, less frequently, division (where a customer wants a fraction of a unit, such as 0.5 kilo of oranges).

In the study there were four boys and one girl, age range 9–15, with a mean age of 11.2. All were from poor backgrounds. They were recruited to the study from street-corner stalls where they were working with their parents or alone. Test items were posed by the researchers posing as customers in the course of a normal transaction. At the end of the informal test, the children were asked to take part in a formal test a week later administered by the same researcher. There were 99 questions in the formal test and 63 questions in the informal test. The order of testing was the same for all participants.

The informal test

This was carried out in Portuguese in the naturalistic setting of the street-corner market. A researcher, posing as a customer, asked the children successive questions about potential purchases. The responses were written down by another researcher. After receiving the answer, the researcher asked the child how they had solved the problem. Here is an example of an informal test taken by M., a 12-year-old vendor:

Researcher: How much is one coconut?
M.: 35.
Researcher: I'd like ten. How much is that?
M. (pause): Three will be 105; with three more, that will be 210. (Pause) I need four more. That is ... (pause) ... 315 ... I think it is 350.

M. has solved the problem in the following way:

(a) 35×10
(b) 35×3 (a sum which he probably already knew)
(c) $105 + 105$
(d) $210 + 105$
(e) $315 + 35$
(f) $3 + 3 + 3 + 1$

Even though he had been taught in school that to multiply any number by 10 you simply add a zero to the right of that number, M. used a different problem-solving routine.

The formal test

After the test in a naturalistic setting, participants were invited to take part in the second part of the study. This took place on the street corner or at the child's home. The items for the formal test were devised on the basis of the problems which the child had successfully solved in the naturalistic context. These test items were presented as 38 mathematical problems dictated to the child (e.g. 105 + 105) and 61 word problems (e.g. Mary bought x bananas; each banana cost y; how much did she pay altogether). In either case, the child solved problems involving the same numbers as those which were used in the informal test. The children were given paper and pencil, and were encouraged to use them if they wished. When the problems were solved mentally, the child was still asked to write down the answer. Only one of the children refused to do this on the grounds that he did not know how to write.

As you can see in box table 14.2.1, problems which were embedded in the context of the street market were much more easily solved than those which were context-free. In the informal test, 98.2 per cent of the 63 problems presented were correctly solved. By contrast, in the formal test, word problems (which provided some context) were correctly answered in 73.7 per cent of cases; mathematical problems with no context were solved in only 36.8 per cent of cases. The frequency of correct answers for each child was converted into scores from 1 to 10 reflecting the percentage of correct answers. A two-way analysis of variance of score ranks compared the scores of each participant in the three types of testing situation. The scores differ significantly across conditions ($X^2 = 6.4$, $p = 0.039$). Mann-Whitney U's were calculated. The children performed better on the informal test than on the formal test ($U = 0$, $p < 0.05$).

How can we interpret these results? One possible explanation is that errors in the formal test were related to the transformations that had been performed on the informal test problems in order to construct the formal test. But when the researchers tested this hypothesis by separating items which had been changed by inverting the operation or changing the decimal point from those which remained identical to their informal test equivalents they found no significant difference between the rates of correct response in each of these conditions.

A second explanation is that the children were still 'concrete' thinkers. This meant that in their natural setting they could solve problems about coconuts and lemons because these items were physically present in front of them. But the researchers rejected this interpretation on the grounds that the presence of the food items in itself does not make a mathematical calculation any easier. In any case, the children carried out the calculations mentally, without external memory aids in the form of coconuts!

A third interpretation was confirmed by a qualitative analysis of the interview protocols. This analysis suggested that the children were using different routines in each of the two situations. In the context of the street market, they were using 'convenient groups'; in the formal context, they were using school-based routines. Let's look again at how 12-year-old M. solved the same problem in informal and formal contexts.

Informal test
Researcher: I'm going to take four coconuts. How much is that?
M.:   Three will be 105, plus 30, that's 135 ... one coconut is 35 ... that is ... 140!

Formal test
M. (asked to solve 35×4):   4 times 5 is 20, carry the 2; 2 plus 3 is 5, times 4 is 20.
Written answer: 200.

Here are two examples from MD, aged 9 years:

Informal test
Researcher: OK, I'll take three coconuts (at the price of Cr$40.00 each). How much is that?

Box Table 14.2.1   Test results in three conditions: each participant's score is the percentage of correct items divided by 10 (adapted from Nunes et al., 1985)

Child	Informal test Score	Formal test Score
M	10	2.5
P	8.9	3.7
Pi	10	5.0
MD	10	1.0
S	10	8.3

MD (without gestures calculates out loud): 40, 80, 120.

Formal test
MD solves the problem 40 × 3 and obtains 70. *She says:* 'Lower the zero; 4 and 3 is 7.'

Informal test
Researcher: I'll take 12 lemons (1 lemon is Cr$5.00).
MD: 10, 20, 30, 40, 50, 60 (while separating out two lemons at a time).

Formal test
In solving 12 × 5 she proceeds by lowering first the 2, then the 5 and the 1, obtaining 152. She explains this to the researcher when she is finished.

When solving the informal test items, the children relied on mental calculations closely linked to the quantities which they were dealing with. The strategy for dealing with multiplication was a form of successive additions. When the addition became too difficult, the child would 'decompose' a quantity into 10s and units. But in the formal tests, the children would try, unsuccessfully, to use school-based routines in which mistakes were frequent. They did not show any sign of checking the final answer in order to assess whether it was a reasonable answer.

The researchers conclude that thinking which is sustained by daily 'common sense' can be at a higher level than thinking out of context. They are, therefore, critical of teaching mathematical operations in a disembedded form before they are applied to real world problems. In many of the cases which they observed, the school-based routines actually seemed to interfere with the successful solution of the problem. Even when the answers were absurd, children would not notice.

They do not conclude that teachers should allow children to develop their own strategies independently of conventional systems devised in our culture! However, they point out that the mathematics taught in school has the potential to serve 'as an "amplifier" of thought processes' (Bruner, 1971). They recommend that schools should develop methods in which mathematical systems are introduced to children in ways which allow them to be sustained by common sense, rooted in everyday contexts. This study has demonstrated that children have the potential for devising their own efficient routines which have little to do with the formal procedures of school.

Based on material in T. Nunes Carraher, D. W. Carraher and A. D. Schliemann 1985: *British Journal of Developmental Psychology*, 3, 21–9.

15 Intelligence and Attainment

As we saw in previous chapters, psychologists studying cognitive development have been interested in the processes of intellectual growth, but a rather different tradition has been the 'psychometric' one. In this tradition psychologists have devised tests to measure a person's ability with an emphasis on comparing individuals' performance in a way that can be quantified – usually people are given a 'score' to indicate their performance on a test. The most well-known tests of ability are 'intelligence' tests.

◀The Development of Intelligence Tests▶▶

The first tests

Galton, in England, in the 1880s was the first to attempt the scientific measurement of intelligence with a series of tests which included both physical measures like the strength of hand squeeze or the capacity of the lungs and behavioural measures like reaction time tests (e.g. how quickly a person could make a response after they heard a sound). Galton believed that intelligence was an underlying trait that would influence a person's performance on all tasks. In other words, if someone had more intelligence than someone else they would generally be better on all tests whatever the type of test. Galton also believed that there would be a relationship between a person's status (i.e. their rank in society) and their performance on his tests. But he failed to find such a relationship, and when other researchers compared how well college students performed on Galton's tests and how well they performed academically they too found little relationship between the tests and academic achievement (e.g. Wissler, 1901).

Early in the twentieth century, two French psychologists, Binet and Simon (1905), published tests which, they claimed, could identify children who were failing to make progress within the normal school system. Their aim was to identify such children so that they could be removed from the over-crowded French schools and be given special education. The battery of tests which Binet and Simon had devised represented the kinds of abilities which, in their view, children typically used during the school years. The tests included word definitions, comprehension tests, tests of reasoning and knowledge of numbers. Binet and Simon spent a long time in schools using different tests with students who had a range of ability to find out which tests distinguished between younger and older children and between good and poor learners. The latter were defined by teachers – in other words, Binet and Simon selected tests on which children who were rated as bright by their teachers did well, and on which children who were considered less able did poorly. Therefore the selection of the original tests by Binet and Simon was

Table 15.1 Items used in the 1905 Binet–Simon scale

1	Follows a moving object with the eyes
2	Grasps a small object that is touched
3	Grasps a small object that is seen
4	Recognizes the difference between a square of chocolate and a square of wood
5	Finds and eats a square of chocolate wrapped in paper
6	Executes simple commands and imitates simple gestures
7	Points to familiar objects (e.g. 'show me the cup')
8	Points to objects represented in pictures (e.g. 'put your finger on the window')
9	Names objects in pictures
10	Compares two lines of markedly unequal length
11	Repeats three spoken digits
12	Compares two weights
13	Shows susceptibility to suggestion
14	Defines common words by function
15	Repeats a sentence of fifteen words
16	Tells how two common objects are different (e.g. paper and cardboard)
17	Names from memory as many as possible of 13 objects displayed on a board
18	Reproduces from memory two designs shown for ten seconds
19	Repeats a series of more than three digits
20	Tells how two common objects are alike (e.g. butterfly and flea)
21	Compares two lines of slightly unequal length
22	Compares five blocks to put them in order of weight
23	Indicates which of the previous five weights the examiner has removed
24	Produces rhymes for given words
25	Word completion test
26	Puts three nouns in a sentence (e.g. Paris, river, fortune)
27	Answers a given set of 25 comprehension questions
28	Reverses the hands of a clock
29	After paper folding and cutting, draws the form of the resulting holes
30	Distinguishes abstract words (e.g. boredom and weariness)

based on purely practical considerations – the tests which most effectively differentiated between good and poor students.

Once Binet and Simon (1905) had identified the 30 most effective tests they listed them in order of difficulty (see table 15.1). For example, a younger child might be able to repeat three numbers; an older child would not only be able to do this but could also repeat a sentence with fifteen words in it. Any particular child would then attempt test items of increasing difficulty until he or she consistently failed them, at which point the tester could calculate the child's mental level. The average 5-year-old, for example, would complete test items at the 5-year-old level; a less able 5-year-old might fail to solve test problems beyond the 4-year-old level, and would be said to have a mental level of four.

The use of Binet and Simon's ordered series of tests (or 'scale') was an effective way of measuring children's abilities: it was simple to administer, it could be used by teachers, it made it easy to compare different children, and it was successful. Not surprisingly, given the reasons behind the choice of tests, if a child did well on the Binet–Simon scale she was likely to be successful academically, if a child did poorly on the scale she was likely to have difficulties in school. In other words, the test was an effective way of identifying those children who might be in need of extra help.

Revisions of the Binet–Simon scale

After Binet and Simon had produced their scale of items for measuring mental age, it was adapted by Terman at Stanford University in California, for use in the USA. Terman increased the number of tests to 90, and the new version, called the Stanford–Binet Intelligence Scale, was introduced in 1916.

In this new scale were two main types of test item – verbal and non-verbal. Verbal tests relied on language abilities, e.g. general knowledge, comprehension, understanding similarities between things, vocabulary. Non-verbal or performance tests aimed to measure the child's perceptual skills and non-verbal reasoning, such as the ability to arrange pictures in a logical sequence to make a coherent story, to copy designs using a set of coloured blocks or assemble pieces of a jigsaw-type puzzle into the right arrangement as quickly as possible.

One of the limitations of the original Binet–Simon scale was the way it led to a comparison between a child's mental level as tested on the scale and his or her chronological age. For example, if a child aged 7 years performed at the level expected of a 4-year-old it could be said that the 7-year-old was retarded by 3 years. And, if a child aged 12 years performed at the level of a 9-year-old then she also would be classified as retarded by 3 years. However, a 3-year delay at the age of 7 years might be very different in its implications from the same length of delay at 12 years. A better measure of the ability of a child can be calculated by taking a ratio of mental level to chronological age. This gives the child's mental age as a fraction, and Terman suggested multiplying the fraction by 100 and describing the result as the 'Intelligence Quotient' (or IQ):

$$\frac{\text{Mental age}}{\text{Chronological age}} \times 100 = \text{IQ}$$

This change was introduced with the first Stanford–Binet scale. The average child's IQ by this calculation is 100 and the IQs of children above or below the average can be calculated accordingly. The numerical scores of the IQ were less cumbersome than the original age scores and made it possible to make direct comparisons between the intellectual capability of individuals, even at different ages. The IQ assessment also made it easier to calculate correlations between intelligence and other variables. Nonetheless, the idea of labelling people with an 'IQ' has always been controversial. Binet had died before the use of IQ was introduced, but Simon described the concept of IQ as a betrayal of his and Binet's original objectives in assessing children (Gregory, 1992). From a scale which had been intended to identify children who needed special education, the scale had become a way of to make comparisons between all people and rank them according to 'IQ'.

The Stanford–Binet scale has undergone many revisions, and its most recent form, the fourth edition, is still used today (Thorndike, Hagen and Sattler, 1985). The scale now consists of 15 sub-tests, though not all would be used with younger children because some would be too difficult for them. The sub-tests can be scored individually, or they can be grouped to give measures of different abilities (e.g. verbal reasoning), or they can be combined in total to give an overall measure of intelligence (see table 15.2 – the examples in this table are similar but not identical to the actual test items). One of the differences between the Stanford–Binet and other tests of general intelligence is the emphasis placed on short-term memory as an important component of intelligence.

Each time a scale is revised it is important to 'standardize' the new version. For example, the fourth edition of the Stanford–Binet was tested on over 5,000 people from 2 to 24 years of age. Before choosing these people, the United States Census was used to make sure that the individuals in the sample were representative of the age, sex, ethnic background, community size and geographic region of the whole country. In this way the results from the sample could be considered as representative of all the people who might be tested on the scale. Scales designed for use in particular countries or with particular age groups also have to be standardized on appropriate samples from those countries or age groups.

It is important that intelligence scales are tested on large samples, because IQ is no longer calculated by the MA/CA formula. Rather a person's performance on an intelligence scale is compared to the distribution, the performance of everyone else of the same age on the same scale. Intelligence scales are designed so that at each age the average performance of all people of that age will be a score of 100. For example, if several thousand 10-year-olds were assessed using the Stanford–Binet scale, their average score would be 100, and the scores of all the children would be normally distributed. This means that there will be a large number scoring 100, and only a slightly smaller number scoring 99 (or 101) with slightly fewer scoring 98 (or 102),

Table 15.2   Items similar to those used in the Stanford–Binet Intelligence Scale

Verbal reasoning

Vocabulary: the child is asked to name pictures of objects and give the meaning of words which increase in difficulty – 'What is an apple?' 'What is harmony?'

Comprehension: the child is asked questions that test practical and social judgement: 'What is the thing to do if you are lost in a strange city?' 'What should you do if a child younger than you hits you?'

Absurdities: the child is asked to say what is silly about a picture in which the characters are doing something odd like sunbathing in the rain.

Verbal relations: the child is asked to say why one of four items is different from the rest: 'How are a horse, a cow and a sheep different from a dog?'

Abstract and visual reasoning

Pattern analysis: the child has to place pre-cut forms into a form board or copy patterns by putting together blocks.

Copying: copying a design with paper and pencil.

Matrices: the child is asked to select an item (a design or an object) which completes a given set of items.

Paper folding: the child is shown a folded piece of paper and shown several possible examples of what it would look like if it was unfolded. The child has to choose the correct one.

Quantitative reasoning

Arithmetic: the child is given a series of arithmetical problems to solve

Number series: the child is given a sequence and asked to say which number should come next: '1, 2, 4, 7, 11, 16, 22, . . .'

Equations: the child is asked to re-arrange an equation which has been mixed up: 2 3 4 10–x =

Tests of short-term memory

Memory for beads: the child is shown a photograph of several beads (in different shapes and colours) for five seconds. She must then reproduce the order of beads, from memory, with real beads.

Memory for sentences: the child must repeat, exactly, a sentence they have heard.

Memory for digits: the child is asked to repeat a series of numbers, either forwards or backwards, e.g. 4–7–3–8–5–9.

Memory for objects: the child is shown several pictures of objects (at the rate of one every second). Then she is shown a larger set of pictures and asked to point to just the pictures she saw presented (and in the same order).

Other items

Missing parts: the child is asked to say what is missing in a picture: e.g. a drawing of a table showing the table without a leg.

Spatial: the child traces a path through a maze.

slightly fewer again with a score of 97 (or 103) and so on with only very small numbers of children having particularly low or high scores.

Intelligence scales are also designed so that the distribution of scores at each age follows the same pattern. If the mean score is 100 then 34 per cent of scores will fall between 85 and 100 and 34 per cent will be between 100 and 115. Fourteen per cent will fall between 70 and 85, and 14 per cent between 115 and 130. Two per cent will fall between 55 and 70, and 2 per cent between 130 and 145. In this way a child's score can be compared easily with the expected scores for the whole of his or her age group.

The Stanford–Binet test is still in use, but one of the tests most commonly used nowadays was designed by Wechsler. His first test, for adults in 1939, was based on other tests which existed at the time (including the Stanford–Binet). Since then it has been revised many times and a children's version of the scale was first produced in 1949. The most recent versions of the scales are:

for adults (16–74 years): *Wechsler Adult Intelligence Scale – Revised UK Edition (WAIS-R.[UK])* (Wechsler, 1986).

for children (6–16 years): *Wechsler Intelligence Scale for Children – Third UK Edition (WISC-III[UK])* (Wechsler, 1992).

for young children (3–7 years): *Wechsler Pre-school and Primary Scale of Intelligence – Revised UK Edition (WPPSI-R.[UK])* (Wechsler, 1990).

Examples of the type of items in the WISC are given in table 15.3.

As well as the Stanford–Binet and the Wechsler scales there are other tests which include similar batteries of tests. For example, the British Ability Scales (Elliot, Murray and Pearson, 1983) is a battery of 24 tests grouped into tests of reasoning, information processing speed, spatial imagery, perceptual matching, short-term memory, spelling and the application of knowledge (e.g. naming objects or giving word definitions).

Intelligence scales like the Stanford–Binet and the Wechsler scales are to some extent dependent on verbal abilities. Not only are there specific items that test children's performance in various verbal tests (like 'vocabulary' or 'similarities') but of course the instructions and many of the children's responses also depend on verbal abilities. Tests with a large verbal component may under-estimate the intellectual capacity of children who speak a different dialect, or for whom the language of the test is not their mother tongue; furthermore, some backgrounds do not stress the language skills measured by intelligence tests. Thus, children who have language difficulties or who come from another cultural background may be at a disadvantage when taking the test.

Tests like the Stanford–Binet and the Wechsler scales are individually administered (see plate 15.1). However, for reasons of speed and efficiency, psychologists have devised tests that can be given to groups of people. While individual tests are mainly used in clinical settings for help in the diagnosis of learning difficulties, group tests can be used for selection purposes in education or at work. Correlations between performance on individually administered tests and on group tests are fairly high and it is felt that they are

Table 15.3 Items similar to those used in the Wechsler Intelligence Scale for Children

Information:	the child is asked a series of general knowledge questions
Comprehension:	the child explains why certain courses of action are appropriate: 'What should you do if you break a friend's toy by mistake?'
Similarities:	the child is asked to say in what way two things are alike, e.g. a pear and a plum
Vocabulary:	the child is asked to define words of increasing difficulty
Picture arrangement:	the child is shown a series of cartoon pictures which are out of order and asked to arrange them correctly
Picture completion:	the child is asked to say which part is missing in a picture; a dog with one ear, a cup with no handle
Block design:	the child is shown blocks which have some sides all white, some all red and some half white and half red; the child is asked to reproduce a series of designs using first four blocks and later nine blocks
Object assembly:	the child has to assemble a jigsaw of parts into a whole shape; e.g. six pieces into the shape of a dog
Digit span:	the child is asked to repeat a series of numbers which increase in length, either in the same order or backwards
Arithmetic:	the child answers a series of arithmetical problems
Coding:	the child matches symbols with numbers according to a given key. For example, on the key, number 1 may be symbolized by †; number 2 by ¶, and so on. The child is given a random list of numbers and against each number has to write down its corresponding symbol
Mazes:	the child traces routes in a series of mazes
Symbol search:	the child is shown rows of abstract shapes. In some rows all the shapes are different, in some the same shape occurs more than once, and the child has to distinguish between the two types of rows

each measuring the same kinds of ability. However, the group test has certain disadvantages. The examiner may not notice signs of anxiety in the testee which would be more obvious in a one-to-one testing situation, and after the test has begun there is no opportunity for the psychologist to reassure the candidate. People with language difficulties or people for whom English is a second language are at a disadvantage since they may find it hard to read the instructions for each item.

One example of a test which can be administered to a group is Raven's Progressive Matrices (e.g. Raven, 1986). This test also has the advantage that it requires little specific verbal ability – the way that a person completes the test can, if necessary, be demonstrated with examples which avoid verbal instructions, and the tests do not depend on people giving verbal responses. Raven's Progressive Matrices are available in three different versions (for

Plate 15.1   A preschool child is tested on one of the subscales of the WPPSI.

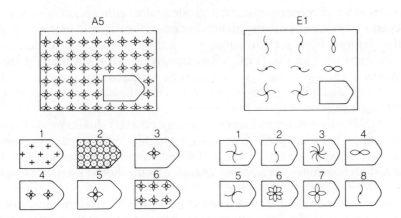

Figure 15.1   Sample items from the *Progressive Matrices* (from Raven, 1958).

different levels of ability), but the principle behind each test is the same. A person is shown a 'matrix' of nine patterns, with one of the patterns missing (see figure 15.1). Below the matrix there is a selection of different patterns and the person is asked to choose the one that they think best fits the missing piece in the matrix. The test is called 'progressive' because a person completes a number of different matrices which are presented one at a time, in a booklet, in order of increasing difficulty. A person's performance on Raven's Progressive Matrices correlates with their performance on other intelligence tests.

◀Reliability and Validity▶▶▶

All tests of intelligences should meet several criteria if they are to be effective ways of measuring a person's ability:

Reliability

A test must be 'reliable'. This means that each time a person takes a test they should achieve the same result. For example, if someone is given an intelligence scale one day and then the same scale on the next day, it is essential the person's level of performance is the same both times. Of course, there is a difficulty in checking reliability in this way because if someone has done a test once it is likely that practice and familiarity will lead to better performance the second time. One way round this problem is to give a person half the test (perhaps alternate questions from it) on one occasion and the other half of the test on a second occasion. The person should have the same level of performance on both halves of the test. The most frequently used intelligence scales like the Stanford–Binet and the Wechsler scales have very high levels of reliability.

Validity

Concurrent validity means assessing a scale against either another scale or an independent measure of performance. For example, if a child performed well on the Stanford–Binet scale it would be expected that the same child would also preform well on the WISC. Alternatively, if a teacher thought that a child was at the top of the class it would be expected that the child would have one of the highest levels of performance in the class when tested with an intelligence scale.

Predictive validity means that performance on a test should predict future performance. For example, if a child scores highly on an intelligence test, it would be expected that the child will do well academically. Similarly, the level a student achieves in a college entrance exam should predict the grade they achieve at the end of college.

Content validity (which is also called face validity) refers to how appropriate a test is. For example, if you wanted to test a person's driving ability it would be appropriate to test how well she actually drove a car on the road and how well she answered questions about driving. It would not be appropriate to test that person's short-term memory or vocabulary. This example makes content validity appear rather obvious, and for many practical abilities (like driving) it is not difficult to see the relationship between the test and what it is measuring. However, as we will explain later, intelligence is not easy to define, and the content validity of a test depends on what the test designers believe intelligence to be. If you believe that intelligence is mainly about how accurately you process and remember information you might include several measures of short-term memory, comprehension and general knowledge. If you think that intelligence is about how well a person adapts to the world around her you might want to include tests of social and practical skills.

Content validity is difficult to define if there is no common agreement on the meaning of a construct. Although many researchers have considered that tests of memory, reasoning, and knowledge are appropriate ways to measure intelligence, other researchers have developed concepts of intelligence that include skills and abilities which are not directly tested by the more established intelligence scales. We will discuss the different concepts of intelligence in a later section.

◀The Early Uses of Intelligence Tests▶▶▶

The Binet–Simon scale was initially used simply to differentiate between average children and children with learning difficulties who might be in need of special education. However, during the First World War, when large numbers of people were being assigned into categories to meet the requirements of different work roles, there was a proliferation of intelligence testing (Gregory, 1992). After the war, large industrial companies also demanded batteries of tests which could measure specific aptitudes in skills such as engineering, typing, dressmaking. This type of selection procedure, it was claimed, provided an effective means of assigning individuals to occupations appropriate to their abilities. In the UK, Cyril Burt was one of the first psychologists in the National Institute of Industrial Psychology. Burt was committed to the idea that intelligence was innate, static throughout a person's lifetime and measurable using intelligence tests.

Burt proposed that intelligence tests also be used in schools with the aim of providing all children with an education appropriate to their level of mental ability. He argued that in any group of normal children, the variations in mental ability would be so wide as to make it impossible to teach them all at the same level. Since he had observed that the gap between bright and dull children became even wider at the secondary school, he recommended the organization of school classes on the basis of mental ability rather than chronological age. It was this view that the individual should be assigned a place in society according to his or her (innate) intellectual ability which was to have far-reaching effects on the educational system in Britain (Broadfoot, 1996). In his day Burt was highly respected as an educational psychologist, although he is now largely discredited because of his fraudulent research into the heritability of intelligence (Hearnshaw, 1979).

In the early days of intelligence testing it was believed that intelligence tests were objective and accurate means of assessing mental ability. The tests appeared to offer a fairer measure of the potential ability of children from differing backgrounds than did conventional examinations and school reports, and they were thought to be less susceptible to social biases which might affect teachers' evaluations. Unfortunately, because of Burt's strong assumption that intelligence tests measure 'innate ability', insufficient consideration was given to the way that a child's environment might also influence her test performance.

What then were the implications of the psychometric approach for educational practice? If, as Burt and many psychometrists believed, intelligence is an innate, stable factor, it would follow logically that once suitable measures had been devised, children could be grouped according to ability levels for educational purposes. In the years following the First World War, when the Hadow Report (1926) recommended the establishment of secondary education for all children after 11 years, current psychological thinking had a very strong influence. Previously the majority of children had remained at the same elementary school until they were old enough to leave; only those bright enough to win a scholarship at 11 went on to 'grammar' schools. The Hadow Report suggested that for all children there should be a change of school at the age of 11 and that there should be a range of post-elementary schools available – 'technical', non-selective 'modern' schools and traditional grammar schools. To assign each child to the appropriate school, some form of assessment had to take place, and by the late 1930s it was standard practice to select children on the basis of the 11-plus examination, which tested attainment in English and arithmetic, and performance on an intelligence test.

By the end of the Second World War, attitudes were changing again. A Labour government came to power with a large majority and popular support for an attack on inequality in society. IQ tests themselves were coming to be seen as a less objective measure of mental ability than the psychologists claimed. There was also a greater awareness of the detrimental effects which selection and streaming could have on children, and the way in which the selective system discriminated against children from under-privileged backgrounds. However, despite the reaction against selection at 11, the tripartite secondary system and streaming in schools, the Labour government did not make the establishment of a comprehensive system of secondary education a high priority. The 1944 Education Act aimed to provide equality of opportunity for all children 'according to age, aptitude and ability', but it left the implementation of this policy to local education authorities. Official sanction had been given to egalitarianism, but so firmly entrenched was the selective system that the change to a comprehensive system of secondary education was only a very gradual one (Broadfoot, 1996).

The original intelligence scales were designed primarily to meet educational needs (e.g. to distinguish children who had difficulties, or to allocate children to different streams within a school) and, therefore, they focused on tasks that related to knowledge, reasoning and memory. However, more recent researchers have argued that such tasks may only reflect a rather narrow concept of intelligence, and that many other aspects of a person's abilities should be taken into account when assessing intelligence. We will discuss different concepts of intelligence in the following section.

◀Concepts of Intelligence▶ ▶ ▶

As we pointed out earlier, Galton who was the first to invent intelligence tests believed that intelligence was a general ability that would be reflected in any test or task undertaken by an individual. The implication of Galton's view is that any test that produces differences in individual performance could be used as an intelligence test. Some tests (e.g. stating your name) are unlikely to produce many individual differences but many others (like vocabulary tests) result in a range of performance and might therefore be used to compare people. Other researchers also came to the conclusion that intelligence was an underlying trait which affected performance across all the tasks used in typical intelligence scales. For example, Spearman (1904) found that there were correlations between children's performance on different academic tests. Spearman (1927) found the same when he gave adults, with a range of different mental abilities, tests, i.e. those who did better than others on one test also tended to do better on other tests. From this Spearman concluded that there was probably a single factor, which he labelled 'g' (for 'general' intelligence) which influenced a person's performance on all tests. Vernon (1950) agreed with Spearman that general intelligence was important, but also pointed out that performance on groups of tests might correlate quite highly. For example, a child's performance on tests of spelling, vocabulary and reading might correlate quite highly with each other, and the same child might perform differently on tests of drawing, solving mazes and jigsaw construction, but the latter would also correlate well with each other. This led Vernon to propose that, as well as general intelligence, there were more specific factors (what he called 'verbal-educational ability' and 'spatial-mechanical ability') which also accounted for intelligent performance on tasks related to those factors.

Galton, Spearman and Vernon (as well as Burt) were all British psychologists and can be seen in the tradition of researchers who put most emphasis on a single general intelligence permeating an individual's performance. In contrast, many American psychologists emphasized the independence of the different factors that might make up a person's intelligence. Thurstone (1931), for example, suggested that there were seven factors that accounted for performance on the type of tests found in traditional intelligence scales. Thurstone called these 'primary mental abilities' and labelled them 'verbal meaning' (e.g. vocabulary and comprehension), 'word fluency' (e.g. speed of naming all the words in a category, like all the animal names beginning with 'c'), 'numerical reasoning' (e.g. mental arithmetic), 'spatial ability' (e.g. imagining what objects will look like after they are rotated), 'perceptual speed' (e.g. being able to quickly check through lists of items for a specific target item), 'memory' (e.g. recall of words or sentences) and 'inductive reasoning' (e.g. completing number series). This 'group factor' approach has the implication that a child might perform differently on different sets of items; for example, a child might have very good memory and verbal meaning but average numerical reasoning, and poor spatial ability. This means that children cannot easily be assessed in terms of general intelligence, rather, they may perform differently across a range of tasks.

Gardner (1983) proposed a more radical view of intelligence. He proposed a theory of 'multiple intelligences' and suggested that there were six distinct kinds of intelligence – linguistic, logical-mathematical, spatial, musical, body-kinesthetic and personal. The first three are already familiar from our discussion of intelligence scales, but the last three constitute a marked departure in thinking about intelligence. Musical intelligence refers to the abilities to comprehend and play or compose music. Body-kinesthetic intelligence refers to bodily control and grace of movement as shown, for example, in athletics, dance or skating. Personal intelligence refers to an awareness of one's own behaviour and that of others, and this is related to social and interpersonal skills and to role-taking ability (see chapters 5 and 11). By putting forward the theory of multiple intelligences, Gardner was effectively criticizing the use of conventional intelligence scales which do not measure abilities like musical, athletic or social skills.

Other researchers have also pointed out that conceptions of intelligence based only on academic abilities are too narrow and that other aspects of human performance must be taken into account to provide a full picture of intelligent behaviour. Sternberg, Conway, Ketron and Bernstein (1981) asked a number of people to give examples of what they thought of as intelligent or unintelligent behaviour (see box 15.1). Sternberg et al. collected 250 different types of intelligent behaviour, and classified these under different headings. What was notable about the behaviours which Sternberg et al. collected was that people included many aspects of practical and social behaviour in their examples of intelligent behaviours. Although researchers like Gardner (1983) pointed out the importance of social intelligence, other theorists had not included such behaviours under the heading of intelligence. Sternberg (1985) proposed a triarchic theory of intelligence which recognized the importance of social and practical skills as well as purely academic ones.

Sternberg's (1985) triarchic theory was so called because it consisted of three subtheories. One was called the 'experiential subtheory', and this emphasized how effectively a person learns new skills. For instance, many skills (e.g. driving a car) become automatic, that is they do not require much conscious attention, and an experienced driver can not only drive but hold a conversation at the same time. Sternberg pointed out that how quickly someone achieves task automaticity could be a reflection of their intelligence. For instance, a person might be able to achieve automaticity in a task after so many hours of experience. Another person might also achieve automaticity but only after twice as much experience. Such differences are not examined by conventional intelligence scales but may be important. Vygotsky (see chapter 14) made a similar point when he criticized testing children's intelligence. He argued that finding out that one child scored the same as another on an intelligence scale might not mean very much unless there were also other measures of the children's potential to learn – one child might progress faster than another if they were better able to gain from their environment and the support they received from others. However, assessing how quickly and how well a person achieves automaticity on a task and assessing a child's potential to learn are both very difficult measurements. In practice it is unlikely that a convenient and realistic test of such abilities could be devised. As it is, most intelligence scales include novel tasks and measure a child's reasoning and knowledge at one point in time – they do not measure a child's ability to learn from practice or experience.

Sternberg (1985) called another subtheory the 'contextual subtheory', which referred to the way that people interact with their environment (e.g. in school, at home, with their families, with friends and so on). Sternberg pointed out that people can adapt themselves to the environment they find themselves in at the time, or they can try to change their environment, or they can select an alternative environment. Much of what Sternberg says applies more to adults than children, nonetheless the idea of adapting to an environment is important at all ages (e.g. children who adapt most success- fully to school may do better academically).

The contextual subtheory has important implications for measuring intel- ligence, because Sternberg (1985) suggested that this aspect of intelligence is best measured with tests of practical and social skills. Practical measures might include sets of tests that, for example, include filling in forms, reading street maps, understanding bus and railway timetables, following technical instructions and so on. Measures of social skills might include tests of how well a person interprets non-verbal information. For example, Sternberg took photographs, in the street, of couples standing together; sometimes the couples were genuine couples, but at other times they were two strangers who had been asked to stand together just for the purpose of the photograph. Sternberg then used the photographs as a test to find out if people could work out, from just looking at the photographs, which couples were 'genu- ine' and which were 'fake'. Such tests of practical and social intelligence have been designed primarily for adults, but they are mentioned here because they highlight how the concept of intelligence has been broadened and extended by researchers like Sternberg. As yet, little emphasis is placed on the measurement of children's abilities in social and practical contexts.

The other subtheory was called the 'componential subtheory' and was concerned with the information processing aspects of tasks typically used in tests of intelligence. For example, Sternberg and Rifkin (1979) analysed the components required for the picture in analogy tasks shown in figure 15.2. They suggested that one way to solve the task involved six components: *encoding* (e.g. considering the type of hat, footwear, clothing, etc. of all five figures); *inference* (this involves working out the changes needed to make A into B, e.g. changing A's hat to match B's hat); *mapping* (comparing A and C, e.g. in this example noting that they have the same hat but all their other features are different); *application* (applying the changes worked out by the inference component to C, e.g. changing C's hat, to produce an 'ideal' answer for the analogy, and then the ideal answer can be compared with the two alternatives and the appropriate figure selected); *justification* (if neither of the given figures matches, choosing the better one and justifying this choice); and *respond* (giving the answer).

Figure 15.2   Typical analogies used in the experiments. Schematic-picture analogies were used in Experiment 1 (Sternberg and Rifkin, 1979).

The analysis we have described is not the only way to solve the problem in figure 15.2 – in this example one of the given figures is the correct match and therefore there is no need for the justification component. Sternberg (1985) made the point that if such a task was included in an intelligence scale, a person's answer would be scored as correct or incorrect without any reference to how they reached their answer, but Sternberg and Rifkin (1979) found that adults and children approached the picture analogy in a different way. At the encoding stage adults attended to all the information in the picture (i.e. all the features of the figures) before applying the other components, and at this stage they were actually slower than 10-year-olds. The children, probably because of limited working memory capacity (see chapter 12), may only have encoded one or two features before moving on to the other components. The latter would either result in more errors, or mean that sometimes the children had to return to the encoding process again to consider other features. Analysing such tasks provides a greater insight into children's approach to the problem than simply scoring them as right or wrong on the basis of their final response.

Sternberg's (1985) triarchic theory is the most ambitious theory of intelligence; however, the three subtheories are not very well integrated into the whole and this weakens the attempt to bring all the different aspects of intelligence together. Nonetheless, Sternberg demonstrated how extensive a description of intelligence needs to be if it is to encompass all the contemporary ideas and concepts about intelligence.

Some researchers have been particularly interested in the 'cognitive style' of a person, i.e. the characteristic way in which he or she approaches the world. Guilford (1967) viewed cognitive style on a dimension called convergence/divergence thinking. A converger is good at dealing with problems that require one correct answer and will tend not to go beyond the information given, and therefore can cope well with the kinds of tasks that are commonly presented in intelligence scales. By contrast, divergers are in their element with open-ended situations that call for a variety of responses involving fluency, flexibility, originality and elaboration of ideas.

Several tests of divergent thinking have been devised (Torrance, 1972). One, for example, is the 'uses of objects' test in which a child is asked to think of as many alternative uses of common objects as possible (e.g. uses for a brick, for a paper clip or for a cardboard box). Responses are scored for

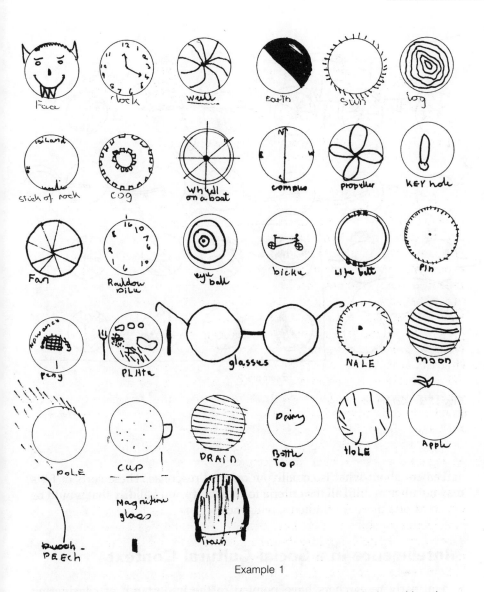

Example 1

Figure 15.3   Circle test: children are given a page of circles and asked to add to them in any way they like. Responses are scored for fluency, flexibility and originality. Some children treat each circle separately (example 1); others combine the circles into larger pictures (example 2). (Figure continued on p. 468.)

fluency and originality. Another example is the 'circles' test, shown in figure 15.3 – in this test children are given a sheet of paper with unfilled circles and asked to complete them in any way they like. Some children tend to fill in each circle separately (see figure 15.3, example 1), but others are much more imaginative in the way they use the sheet (see example 2). However, a major limitation with any such test is the difficulty of scoring it, and the lack of

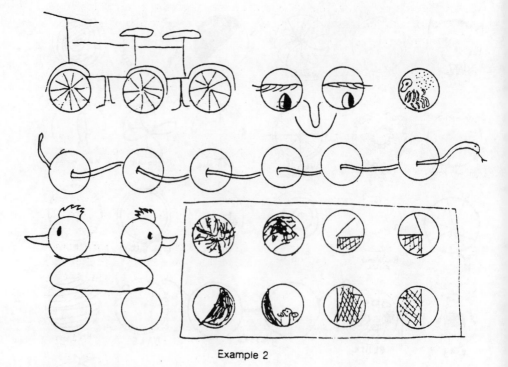

Example 2

Fig. 15.3   *Continued*

agreement about what is actually an original response. These sorts of tests may not always fulfil all the criteria for reliability and validity that would be expected of a more traditional intelligence scale.

◀Intelligence in a Social-Cultural Context▶▶▶

Several early researchers have pointed to the importance of considering intelligence in the context of the real world. For example, Binet and Simon (1916) defined intelligence as below:

> It seems to us that in intelligence there is a fundamental faculty, the impairment or the lack of which is of the utmost importance for practical life. This faculty is judgement, otherwise called good sense, practical sense, initiative, the faculty of adapting oneself to circumstances. To judge well, to reason well, these are the essential activities of intelligence. (Binet and Simon, 1916)

and Wechsler (1944) said:

Intelligence is the aggregate or global capacity of the individual to act purposefully, to think rationally, and to deal effectively with his environment.

However, despite these descriptions of intelligence, it is only comparatively recently, in the work of psychologists like Sternberg (1985), which we described earlier, that specific emphasis has been placed on the context of intelligent behaviour.

Contextualists take the view that intelligence must be defined within a particular cultural context and that comparisons across cultures can only be made with caution. Berry (1984) argued that it is important to define intelligence in terms of 'cognitive competence' which is needed in a particular culture, and that psychologists should take local conceptions of intelligence into account when they design tests (figure 15.4). For example, the ability to construct and use a bow and arrow is irrelevant for most people in our society, but such skills may well be of prime importance among hunter-gatherers. Intelligence scales that have been validated in a technologically advanced society would not assess skills like using a bow and arrow, but it cannot be concluded that the hunter-gatherers are less intelligent.

Clearly the constructs of intelligence will vary across cultures. Some cultures (e.g. Western industrial societies) place most emphasis on the intelligence 'within' an individual, but other cultures have conceptualized intelligence more in terms of the relationship between the individual and society. Wober (1974), in Uganda, found that 'intelligence' referred to shared knowledge and wisdom, and in particular the way an individual acted to the benefit of his or her community. Serpell (1977), in Zambia, asked adults to explain why particular children could be labelled intelligent. The adults not only referred to the children being clever (i.e. having good mental abilities) but also said that intelligent children were ones who were obedient, who could be trusted to follow instructions, and who had respect for their elders. These descriptions of intelligence place far more importance on social behaviour and responsibility, than do the traditional Western descriptions of intelligence.

Sternberg (1985) argued that it is far more useful to see intelligence as being embedded in a particular context than as a static quality possessed by an individual; what is important is the relative emphasis that different cultures place upon certain skills at different historical times. For example, skills needed for reading are present in individuals from pre-literate societies but are not developed and are thus not important until literacy becomes widespread. Within modern Western society, in the past decade or so, children have gained familiarity with computers both for academic work and for recreation, and interacting with a computer may depend more on visual, auditory and manual aspects of intelligence, which are skills that are not so readily measured by traditional intelligence tests. In other words, the contextualist view emphasizes a malleable concept of intelligence which can accommodate to such changes over space and time.

'YOU CAN'T BUILD A HUT, YOU DON'T KNOW HOW TO FIND EDIBLE ROOTS AND YOU KNOW NOTHING ABOUT PREDICTING THE WEATHER. IN OTHER WORDS, YOU DO TERRIBLY ON OUR I.Q. TEST."

Figure 15.4   Intelligence needs to be seen in its cultural context (from Current Contents, 1981).

◄Savants►►►

Savants are individuals who usually have a generally low score as measured on traditional intelligence scales but may have one, or very rarely, two, exceptional abilities. For this reason, such people used to be referred to as 'idiots savants'. Howe and Smith (1988) described the case of 'Dave' who was 14 years of age when they investigated his abilities. His IQ was about 50, and at the age of 14 years his reading skills were only the equivalent of a 6-year-old. He was withdrawn, solitary, rarely talked, and was generally un-communicative in response to questions. However, he could remember any dates which he was told, and could recall the birthdays of all the people he knew. Dave knew the number of days in a week and in a month but could not say the number of months in a year. Nonetheless, when asked questions like 'On what day of the week is the 9th September 1999?', he could nearly always give a correct answer for any year in the range 1900–2000. He was also accurate at answering questions like 'In what years does the 9th October fall on a Wednesday?', often giving a list of several years when this occurred. Howe and Smith were unable to explain how Dave achieved such remarkable calendar calculations.

Savants are also known with other outstanding skills, and Howe (1989) has described examples of savants with exceptional memories, mathematical abilities, musical abilities or drawing skills. The pattern of abilities found in savants is not easy to explain. As we discussed earlier some researchers conceptualized intelligence as a general trait which influences most aspects of a person's performance; however, savants are people with low intelligence but with one outstanding ability, and such a pattern may be easier to consider in the context of theories put forward by researchers like Gardner (1983) who suggested that different 'intelligences' may be independent abilities – a person can be poor in one area of skill but excellent in another domain.

◄ The Use of Intelligence Tests ►►►

Despite concerns about the content validity of traditional intelligence scales, they are still used frequently, because they are one way to find out about a child's strengths and weaknesses. Over and above just measuring a child's performance, many educational psychologists treat intelligence tests like a clinical interview in which they can gain insights into the child's personality, self-image, attention-span and motivation as well as level of intelligence. Thus, in the hands of an experienced clinician, a test can be of important diagnostic value. From this point of view, intelligence scales can be useful. They can be used to identify children with particularly low levels of ability who may need special help and schooling (which was Binet's original intention in designing tests); they can be used to identify gifted children who may also need special educational provision; and they can also be used to identify distinctive patterns of performance. For example, adults with dyslexia (see chapter 10) often have a pattern of performance on the WAIS that is called the 'ACID' profile – this means that they have below average scores on four tests on this scale – i.e. Arithmetic, Coding, Information and Digit span tests (these are similar but more advanced versions of the tests described in table 15.3), but they may have average or above average scores on the other tests. This particular profile is typical of adults who have dyslexia.

Children with learning difficulties

In assessing children who perform poorly in school, educational psychologists would rely only partly on the results from an intelligence test and would also try to assess children in the context of their home background, their medical history of life events and in relation to the problems which the children might be experiencing. For example, if a child has had prolonged periods of illness or experienced a traumatic event such as the loss of a parent, then these circumstances are taken into account when assessing the child's level of attainment.

Some learning difficulties have been ascribed to general intellectual impairment. Others, however, may be due to an unstimulating or stressful home background, to emotional disturbance, to a physical condition, to poor diet or to a combination of factors and therefore psychologists may use methods of assessment that best identify such potential problems. In addition to intelligence scales, many other measures can be used; for example, naturalistic observation of the child's behaviour as recorded by parents and teachers can lead to a greater understanding of the child's difficulties. Social assessment can also be helpful to indicate a child's communicative abilities, social skills and emotional adjustment. Psychologists can also use attainment tests to measure performance in specific areas, such as mathematics and reading, and diagnostic tests can help to unravel the reasons for a child's poor performance. We will say more about attainment tests later in this chapter.

Gifted children

A child may be described as 'gifted' who is outstanding in either a general domain (such as exceptional performance on an intelligence test) or a specific area of ability, such as music, or sport (Radford, 1990). The borderline between gifted children and others is not clearly defined, and different researchers have used different levels of performance on intelligence scales to define a gifted child as one with an IQ of more than 120, more than 130 or more than 140. Children with such high scores are rare: only 1 in 10 children have scores over 120; 1 in 40 have scores over 130; 1 in 200 have scores over 140; and 1 in 1000 have a score over 150.

The most famous investigation of giftedness is Terman's (1925–59) study (at Stanford University in California) which began in 1921 with children aged about 10 years. Terman defined gifted as referring to children with IQ scores about or above 140 (on the Stanford–Binet scale) and all the children in his sample had scores of between 130 and 190. The children were followed up for most of their lives and Terman published regular reports about their achievement. Physical health and growth were superior from birth on, they walked and talked early, and the children excelled in reading, language and general knowledge.

A follow-up in 1947 when the children's average age was 35 indicated that the initial level of intelligence had been maintained. Sixty-eight per cent had graduated from college, and many had been outstanding in their professions; for example, they had produced a large number of publications and patents. In 1959 another follow-up indicated that they had continued to maintain their high achievements in occupational level; 71 per cent were in professional, semi-professional or managerial positions compared with 14 per cent of the Californian population as a whole, and their average income was higher than that of the average college graduate.

Terman's study showed that gifted children are, perhaps not surprisingly, very likely to become successful adults. However, one limitation of Terman's study should be noted. The children in his sample were selected partly on the basis of teachers' ratings and in this way home background factors may have been confounded with his criterion of high intelligence; for instance, working class and ethnic minority children may have been under-represented from the start of the study. In other words, the children in the sample may have had advantageous social environments and home upbringings, and some of their success may have been due as much to these factors as to their higher IQ levels.

Most of the subjects in Terman's sample appeared to be well-integrated, healthy and well-adjusted individuals. However, some researchers have pointed out the problems and difficulties which gifted children can face. For example, Gross (1993) described the case of Ian who, at the age of five years, hated school, was uncontrollable in class, was aggressive towards other children, and was to be referred to a special school for behaviourally disturbed children. As part of the referral process, Ian was assessed by an educational psychologist who tested him on the Stanford–Binet scale, and found that he had an IQ of over 170; he also had the reading age of a 12-year-old. The psychologist suggested that any behavioural problems were most likely the result of frustration. When measured at the age of 9, Ian's IQ was about 200 (put another way, he had the mental age of an 18-year-old), and yet his school insisted that he undertook the curriculum designed for 9-year-olds. Clearly, this was inappropriate, and Gross argued that such exceptional children should be given special consideration and support. Other researchers (e.g. Freeman, 1980) who have investigated gifted children have come to different conclusions about the causes of their behavioural difficulties and the way that they should be treated (see box 15.2).

◀Attainment Tests▶▶▶

Measures of intelligence usually include tests which are unfamiliar to the person taking the test – in other words the test designers are attempting to measure the performance of a person on tests which are novel and which have not been practised. In contrast, tests of attainment measure what a person has achieved after specific training. Examples of attainment tests include school examinations, driving tests, examinations for music, tests of sporting achievement and so on. Such measures have a variety of purposes (Gipps and Stobart, 1993) and we will give examples of the different ways that educational tests can be used.

Certification and selection   Passing an examination is an indication that a person has achieved a specified level of competence. Examinations were first introduced in Britain in 1815 for doctors, and were later also used by other professions (e.g. solicitors and accountants) to determine entry into the profession. They were also used from the mid-nineteenth century to assess candidates for the Civil Service, and for university entrance. These examinations were meant to be a way of giving more (middle-class) people access to the professions or university, because previously such opportunities had been based on family background or payment. The early professional examinations were all written ones and established the tradition of written school and university examinations. The use of tests for selection at all ages and levels is one of the main perceived uses of examinations, and earlier we discussed the use of the 11-plus examination for selection to secondary school. Presently in the British educational system, performance in GCSE examinations at 16 determines the opportunity to study for A-levels, and they in turn determine access to higher education.

Motivation   Assessment is a way to motivate children to be successful. At a minimum, examinations focus attention on hard work and channel behaviour into what is educationally and socially desirable. But more than this, assessment may be seen as both intrinsically rewarding (because children learn as they prepare for tests) and externally rewarding (if success in an examination gives access to the next step on the educational ladder). At all stages children can be given feedback, which should contribute to both their learning and their motivation to improve.

Record keeping   All assessment (e.g. examinations or teachers' judgements) can contribute to a record of a child's performance. This can be used to check on a child's progress, and is particularly important if a child is having difficulties, as the course and extent of those difficulties can be identified.

Screening and diagnostic assessment   Screening means that all the children at a certain age or level are given the same test, or set of tests, to identify any who might be in need of special help. Once a child who needs special help has been identified he or she can be given diagnostic tests to find out about his or her particular weaknesses. For example, if a child is poor at reading, diagnostic tests of reading can be used to discover the specific reading disabilities that she may have. Measures used for screening are usually standardized tests

Standardized tests   There are a wide range of tests designed to measure attainment in reading, verbal reasoning, English, numeracy and comprehension, and so on. Standardized tests (like intelligence scales) have been pretested on large numbers of children in order to eliminate badly worded questions or items that fail to discriminate between different children. The instructions for administering the tests are also standard so that all children take the test under the same conditions. As such tests have been used on large numbers of children, the test designers can state how an average child at any given age should perform on the test, and this enables a teacher to make a meaningful assessment of an individual child's performance in comparison with other children of the same age. Performance on many attainment tests correlates quite highly with IQ, but the primary function of an attainment test is to measure achievement within a particular subject area rather than general intelligence.

Criterion-referenced tests   These are tests that measure whether a child can achieve a specified level of performance on a task. For example, a teacher might want to know whether a child understood how to do long division, and might set the criterion of understanding as successfully solving 20 long division problems. A criterion-referenced test is different from a standardized test (which is based on comparisons between children of the same age) because set criteria are given. For example, a driving test is a criterion-referenced test because a person either meets the requirements of the test and passes, or does not meet them and fails. In other words, you either pass or fail; the test is the same whatever your age. If all driving test candidates met the required criteria then 100 per cent could pass the test. In contrast, on a standardized test 50 per cent of children at any age are below the average score and 50 per cent are above that score. An argument in favour of criterion-referenced tests is that they may be more motivating than other tests, because children can take a criterion-referenced test at their own pace – the 'principle of readiness' refers to the strategy of only entering children for a test when they are likely to succeed on it.

Curriculum control and school evaluation   One use of assessment is to determine what is taught in schools. If children are to take a particular examination, the school syllabus must include the appropriate teaching needed for that examination. More explicitly, following the 1988 Education Reform Act in the UK, a National Curriculum was introduced that included specific attainment targets. Pupils are assessed at the ages of 7, 11, 14 and 16 years of age using tests which are the same nationally. These are criterion-referenced tests because, ideally, all children, at each age, should have achieved the knowledge and ability to succeed on them. The use of common tests for all pupils can provide important information about the progress of individual children, and at the same time both teachers and schools can be assessed in terms of their pupils' performance (Gipps and Stobart, 1993). However, a major concern in the use of national assessment tests is whether they might be biased against particular groups of pupils – for example that one or other gender, or that children from minority ethnic groups might be disadvantaged by the tests (see Gipps and Murphy, 1994).

◀Conclusions▶▶▶

Intelligence and attainment tests are useful for assessing an individual child. This can often be of great importance for identifying children who are exceptional (in terms of either learning difficulties or giftedness), or in identifying a particular child's strengths and weaknesses. However, the results from all tests should be treated with caution, because both intelligence scales and attainment tests are designed for specific educational purposes. They may often be effective for the very specific purposes for which they were designed, but a child's performance on a single test should not lead to any more extensive assumptions about that child's ability. For example, a child's performance on an intelligence test may be helpful to an educational psychologist who needs to assess that child, but as we pointed out in the section on concepts of intelligence, the 'intelligence' measured by a traditional intelligence scale may not reflect the whole range of behaviours and abilities which go together to make up an intelligent individual. While there is so little agreement about the nature of intelligence, any measures of it have to be considered with reservation.

◀Further Reading▶ ▶ ▶

K. Richardson 1991: *Understanding Intelligence*, Buckingham: Open University Press, is a good introduction to the discussion about what intelligence is, and the theories and concepts underlying intelligence testing.

R. J. Gregory 1992: *Psychological Testing. History, Principles and Applications*, Boston: Allyn and Bacon, is an encyclopaedic book which describes development of intelligence testing and has a section describing every major psychological test. Invaluable if you want a clear and critical description of any available intelligence test.

C. Gipps and G. Stobart 1993 (2nd edn): *Assessment. A Teacher's Guide to the Issues*, London: Hodder and Stoughton, is a good introduction to the different types and purposes of attainment tests. C. Gipps and P. Murphy 1994: *A Fair Test? Assessment, Achievement and Equity*, Buckingham: Open University Press, provide a critical review of assessment in the UK, including a good discussion of ethnic and gender bias in tests, and a detailed review of the development of assessment within the National Curriculum.

A note about intelligence and attainment tests. Many intelligence and attainment tests can be purchased; however, the publishers of tests only sell them to registered users. Before registering a user the publishers require evidence of the user's qualifications, and in addition, for specific tests they may require evidence that a user has been on an appropriate course for training in the use of that test. These procedures are followed to ensure that tests are used responsibly and correctly, and that both test material and test results are always kept confidential.

◀Discussion Points▶ ▶ ▶

1 What does 'intelligence' mean?
2 Is an individual's 'intelligence' a single trait or is it made up of many different abilities?
3 What implications do recent concepts of intelligence have for how we measure people's intelligence?
4 Do school and college examinations measure intelligence?
5 What purposes do attainment tests serve?

Box 15.1
People's conceptions of intelligence

Sternberg et al. asked 186 people to list behaviours that they thought were characteristic of 'intelligence', 'academic intelligence', 'everyday intelligence' and 'unintelligence'. The people included 61 studying in a Yale college library, 63 waiting for trains and 62 shoppers at a supermarket. In total they collected 250 different behaviours which included 170 examples of intelligent behaviours and 80 examples of unintelligent behaviours.

Sternberg et al. then found two further groups of people. One group of 'laypersons' recruited through newspaper advertisements, and one group of 'experts' all of whom had higher degrees in psychology and were carrying out research in universities. These groups were given questionnaires which included the list of 250 behaviours and they were asked to rate each behaviour, on a 1 (low) to 9 (high) scale, according to how important they thought that behaviour was in defining the concept of an ideally (a) intelligent person, (b) academically intelligent person and (c) an everyday intelligent person.

The experts' view of an ideally intelligent person could be divided into three factors that Sternberg et al. labelled as verbal intelligence, problem-solving ability and practical intelligence. The first factor included behaviours like: 'displays a good vocabulary', 'reads with high comprehension', 'displays curiosity' and 'is intellectually curious'. The second factor included behaviours such as 'able to apply knowledge to problems at hand', 'makes good decisions', 'poses problems in an optimal way' and 'displays common sense'. The third factor included behaviours like 'sizes up situations well', 'determines how to achieve goals', 'displays awareness of the world around him or herself' and 'displays interest in the world at large'.

Laypersons' views of an ideally intelligent person could also be divided into three main factors that were labelled practical problem-solving ability, verbal ability and social competence. Although there was an overlap with the experts' views, there was also an important difference because laypersons put more emphasis on social competence, a category that included behaviours such as 'accepts others for what they are', 'admits mistakes' and 'is on time for appointments'.

Experts' views of academic intelligence were divided into three factors: problem-solving ability, verbal ability and motivation. Clearly there was an overlap between their views of ideal intelligence and ideal academic intelligence, but with the difference that experts also stressed motivation in the context of academic intelligence. This was a factor that included behaviours like, 'displays dedication and motivation in chosen pursuits', 'gets involved in what he or she is doing', 'studies hard' and 'is persistent'. The laypersons' view of academic intelligence was slightly different because they included behaviours linked to verbal ability, problem-solving ability and social competence, rather than motivation.

For everyday intelligence the experts' views could be divided into three factors: practical problem-solving ability, practical adaptive behaviour and social competence. The laypersons' description of everyday intelligence included four factors. The first two were the same as the first two factors proposed by the experts, but laypersons also thought that character and an interest in learning and culture were important.

As all the participants were asked to describe types of intelligence it is not surprising that there were many similarities in the patterns that Sternberg et al. identified. Nonetheless, there were also differences both in the way that the same groups described different types of intelligence and between the groups. These differences reflect the difficulty of describing intelligence with any brief or single definition of the term. What is most noticeable about Sternberg et al.'s data is the very large number of behaviours that people were willing to include as examples of intelligent behaviour. As Sternberg et al. say in summing up their results, no one theory of intelligence is likely 'to do justice to the full scope of intelligence' (1981, p. 55).

Based on R. J. Sternberg, B. E. Conway, J. L. Ketron and M. Bernstein 1981: *Journal of Personality and Social Psychology*, 41, 37–55.

Box 15.2
Giftedness in a social context

The definition of giftedness varies across cultures and throughout history and cannot be viewed apart from its social context. Thus argued Joan Freeman in the introduction to the Gulbenkian Research Project on gifted children which she directed. Her aim was to discover whether the experience of being labelled as 'gifted' had any behavioural effects on children. She was also interested in the part played by parents and teachers in the emotional development of high-ability children. Specifically, she investigated a prevailing view that gifted children may be emotionally disturbed at home or at school because their intellectual maturity makes them out of tune with others in their environment. Accordingly, she asked three research questions:

1 Are children identified by parents as 'gifted' different from other children not so identified?
2 Are the home backgrounds of children identified as gifted by their parents different from those not so identified?
3 Do gifted children suffer from emotional problems when receiving non-specialist education?

Freeman's sample consisted of three groups with 70 children in each, ranging in age from 5 to 16 years. The Target Group (T) was a sample of children selected from the records of the National Association for Gifted Children (NAGC), in other words, children whose parents had identified them as being of high ability.

Control Group 1 (C1) was a sample of children who were matched with the above children for ability (as measured by the Raven's Progressive Matrices), age, sex and school. The essential difference was that these children were not in the NAGC.

Control Group 2 (C2) was a sample of children of normal ability matched with C1 for age, sex and school class so that they differed only in ability. In this way, each target child was matched with two control children in different ways – one for high ability but not in the NAGC (C1) and one of normal ability (C2).

The children were given a battery of tests covering intelligence (Stanford–Binet), and social adjust-

ment (Bristol Social Adjustment Guide); interviews were carried out with parents (at home) and teachers (at school) about the children's behaviour, their own attitudes to education and views on how educational aims are achieved; in addition, the home background of the children was assessed.

There were differences in intelligence between the target group and control groups C1 and C2. The T and C1 children had been accurately matched for intelligence on the Raven's Matrices Test but when Stanford–Binet scores were compared, they were found to be significantly different (see box table 15.2.1). Freeman explained these differences as follows. The Raven's Matrices Test is non-verbal and so more 'culture-free' than a verbal test; furthermore, it does not discriminate finely amongst children at upper levels of ability. The Stanford–Binet test, by contrast, does give a more precise assessment at higher levels of intelligence and measures many learned abilities that would put children from privileged, educationally stimulating homes at an advantage.

Interviews with the parents suggested behaviour differences between the T group and groups C1 and C2. The target children were rated as more 'difficult', 'sensitive', 'emotional' and as having 'few friends'. Parents described them as 'very emotional' five times as often as controls and as 'feeling different' 17 times as often as controls. Similarly, teachers' ratings on individual items on the Bristol Social Adjustment Guides indicated that the target children had more problems in making friends and were more likely to be either withdrawn or aggressive in the classroom (see box table 15.2.2).

From home interviews, Freeman observed that the target children were more likely to have unusual backgrounds, e.g. were adopted, came from families where the parents were divorced or separated, or were from single-parent families. For example, one-parent families were found seven times as often in T as in C groups. The target children's mothers were more frequently well-educated but were also discontented about their own achievements. This was surprising since many of these mothers had successful professional or managerial careers (53 per cent compared with 33 per cent in

Box Table 15.2.1   Raven's Matrices scores and Stanford–Binet IQs of target (T) and control (C) children

Test	IQ	T	C1	C2
Raven's Matrices	mean	34.5	34.6	28.8
	s.d.	12.9	11.5	11.6
Stanford–Binet	mean	147.1	134.3	119.2
	s.d.	17.4	7.1	16.1

Box Table 15.2.2   Percentage of children in each group getting high scores from teacher's ratings on items from the Bristol Social Adjustment Guide

	T	C1	C2	Significance level
Peer maladaptiveness (problems making friends)	29	14	9	$p < 0.01$
Withdrawal (being socially withdrawn)	23	10	10	$p < 0.01$
Hostility (aggressive/over-reacting)	39	17	13	$p < 0.01$

C1 and C2). The homes of the target children were very stimulating and parents encouraged their children's education and attainment. However, this involvement at times took the form of an 'intense pursuit of culture' which in the view of Freeman put some pressure on the children.

What might cause the adjustment problems of the target group of children? To find out whether the emotional difficulties were due to intelligence or to other factors, Freeman compared the highest IQ children from the whole sample (i.e. children with IQs of 141 or more from both target and control groups) with the rest. The features which had distinguished the target groups from the controls were rarely those which distinguished high IQ children from the rest. In fact, Freeman found no evidence to suggest that problems arose simply from being highly intelligent, but rather that it arose from the way in which giftedness was handled. For example, signs of unhappiness, such as finding it difficult to make friends, did not feature in the list of behaviours that could be identified with high IQ. Although T group parents frequently reported that their children were difficult because they were gifted, Freeman's results did not support such a viewpoint.

Freeman suggested that the T group parents had

joined the NAGC not only because their children were gifted but because they were difficult. The problems, she suggested, stemmed from parental expectations and handling of these bright children. The parents of the target children were more likely to be dissatisfied with school, but this Freeman saw as being related to the parents' ambitions for their children rather than the children's giftedness by itself. Her overall conclusion was that she could see no good reason for segregating gifted children from normal children. Those gifted children who did have problems were also found to have a number of disturbing environmental pressures, such as intense parental pressure, which seemed to be more responsible for the difficulties than giftedness by itself.

This is a challenging study which is unfortunately weakened by the IQ differences between T and C1 children, and Freeman's view that the act of labelling a bright child as 'gifted' can have negative effects on the child's behaviour remains controversial. For an alternative view about the behaviours and needs of gifted children see Gross (1993).

Based on material by J. Freeman 1980: in R. Povey (ed.), *Educating the Gifted Child*, London: Harper and Row.

16 The Social Context: Deprivation and Enrichment

In this final chapter we look at disadvantage, deprivation and enrichment and the part played by families, by schools and by society itself in the linguistic development and academic attainment of children, with particular emphasis on those from less advantaged environments. The primary focus of the chapter will be to examine the effect which living in disadvantaged conditions has on the growth of the child. We will also consider the concepts of deprivation and enrichment. There are ethical considerations to take into account when undertaking the study of deprivation since children cannot, of course, be deliberately deprived of essential experiences. So, as you will see, the research studies tend to be carried out in naturalistic settings in circumstances which were occurring anyway. This makes for particular problems in research design. By contrast, it is ethically permissible to provide enrichment for children in conditions of adversity, and we will review studies, both experimental and in naturalistic settings, which attempt to evaluate the effect on children of ameliorating the conditions of their lives.

Why are some children at a disadvantage in society? How significant a factor is social class or membership of an ethnic minority? What effects does poverty have on a child's intellectual development? Can schools compensate for deprivation in the home? How does the wider culture shape the direction of a child's aspirations and achievements? None of the answers is simple since these questions concern the complex interaction of many factors, from the parent–child relationship to the social context within which the child develops.

In trying to answer them, it may help to consider Bronfenbrenner's ecological model of human development, summarized in chapter 1 (see figure

1.3). In advocating this model, Bronfenbrenner is warning of the dangers of focusing on the individual without taking into account the context within which he or she exists or the processes of interaction through which the behaviour of individuals in a particular system evolves. He is arguing that when psychologists try to understand the many factors influencing development, they should use methods which are ecologically valid (chapter 1). They should be aware of the effects on the participant of their removal from their natural environment to a strange setting (for example, a university laboratory or a psychological testing room). It is useful to bear Bronfenbrenner's ideas in mind as you consider the issues raised in this chapter. But first, let us look at the idea of disadvantage itself.

◀The Concept of Disadvantage▶▶▶

We have all had unfavourable experiences which we would say 'put us at a disadvantage' in some way, perhaps socially or intellectually. To the psychologist, however, disadvantage usually means a relatively enduring condition that results in lower academic achievement at school and reduced opportunities in the wider society; this tends to refer to social or cultural characteristics, for example being a member of an ethnic minority group, living in an inner city area or having a low income. Passow (1970, p. 16) defined the disadvantaged child as one who 'because of social or cultural characteristics, for example social class, race, ethnic origin, poverty, sex, geographical location, etc. comes into the school system with knowledge, skills and attitudes which impede learning'. Wedge and Essen (1982, p. 11) defined the disadvantaged as 'that group of children who failed to thrive, who failed to mature as much or as quickly physically, or who have failed to achieve as well in school as other British children'. Important social factors which served to identify such children included family composition (a large number of children in the family, or only one parent figure), low income and poor housing. Each of these factors was related to poor physical and academic development and less acceptable behaviour.

Historically, this concern coincides with the advent of a universal free education system and the corresponding philosophy of 'equality of opportunity' which arose in most Western societies, including Britain and the USA, in the years following the Second World War. As the Newsom Report (1963) put it, 'all children should have an equal opportunity of acquiring intelligence, and developing their talents and abilities to the full'. It was assumed by many that this would also result in an equality of achievement amongst different social class and racial groups. Yet, surveys consistently show that children from lower social class groups and ethnic minorities, and those experiencing adverse social conditions, such as those described by, for example, Wedge and Essen, have on average achieved poorly in the school system (Coleman et al., 1966, table 16.7).

We begin with an example of extreme disadvantage in order to highlight the dire circumstances in which some young people are forced to live. Huggins, Mesquita and de Castro (1996) began their research when they

Table 16.1   Average under-achievement, in grades (years), of different groups of American children in standardized scores of verbal ability and mathematics, from the Coleman Report of 1966

	Verbal ability	Mathematics		Verbal ability	Mathematics
White children, western cities	0.5	0.8	Mexican/American children	3.5	4.1
White children, rural south	1.5	1.4	Puerto Rican children	3.6	4.8
Black children, NE cities	3.2	5.2	Indian American children	3.5	3.9
Black children, rural south	5.2	6.2	Oriental-American children	1.6	0.9

Note: White children from north-east urban communities are taken as the standard

worked in shelters and on street programmes for impoverished youth in São Paulo, Rio de Janeiro and Recife; their statistical data were gathered from Brazilian morgue and police records, newspaper archives and work with children's rights groups. They discovered that the official statistics greatly under-estimated (in fact, by nearly 50%) the actual number of youth homicides in Brazil. The authors discovered that between 1988 and 1991, alone, more than 7,000 poor children and adolescents were murdered in Brazil, mostly by strangers, who were on- and off-duty police, citizen 'justice-makers', death-squad exterminators and private security police; most of the murderers received a fee for their services and the vast majority were never identified or prosecuted. In July 1991, the going rate for killing a street youth was half-a-month's adult minimum wage. The authors estimated that, in 1993 in Brazil's four biggest cities, up to five youths were murdered each day; 80 per cent of these victims were aged between 15 and 17.

> Ethnicity structures the probability of being among Brazil's poorest and of having to live on the streets, and influences who among poor youth are bearers of multiple social stigmas, since they are both poor and black. And where goods, services and justice are allocated and awarded according to a group's relative class and color, the blackest poor youth are in a highly disadvantaged position – excluded economically, socially and civically. (Huggins, Mesquita and de Castro, 1996, p. 95)

At this time of life, more privileged young people are given opportunities to engage in studies and to prepare for life in their society. By contrast, hard-core street youths devote most of their time trying to survive harsh conditions by day and by night, with a constant requirement to maintain vigilance against danger. This study identifies particular conditions which transform certain types of Brazilian young people into 'social problems' or even 'non-persons'.

Ethnic minority groups

Earlier reports in the UK (Rampton Report, 1981; Commission for Racial Equality, 1988; Eggleston, Dunn and Anjali, 1986; Swann Report, 1985) provided large-scale statistical evidence about the educational under-achievement of ethnic minority groups in the UK. The reports looked at examination results, and destinations, of school leavers from schools with high concentrations of ethnic minority children. All the reports recommended that it is the responsibility of schools to give their pupils, regardless of gender, class or ethnic background, the confidence and the ability to have an equal opportunity in society.

A more recent report (HMSO, 1996, quoted by Brindle, 1996) indicates that blacks and Asians in Britain are still at a social disadvantage in the UK. In education, Asian children do better at GCSEs than all other groups, including whites. At age 18, 65 per cent of Indians, 61 per cent of Pakistanis and Bangladeshis, 72 per cent of other Asians and 50 per cent of blacks are still in full-time education, compared with 38 per cent of whites. However, unemployment is far higher among all minority groups than among whites. Black and Asian/Bangladeshi people in particular have jobless rates three times as high as whites. Average rates of hourly pay are £4.78 for Pakistani/Bangladeshi women compared with £6.59 for white women; average rates of hourly pay are £6.87 for Pakistani/Bangladeshi men compared with £8.34 for white men.

One American study gives intriguing evidence of the vital part which can be played by the families themselves in ensuring that their children achieve well in the educational system. Caplan, Choy and Whitmore (1992) reviewed key factors which, in their view, contributed to the outstanding academic achievement of refugee children in their study. During the 1970s and 1980s many Vietnamese and Lao people sought a new life in the USA. The children of these families had lost months or years of formal schooling, they lived in relocation camps and had suffered trauma and disruption as they escaped from SE Asia. They had little knowledge of English and had experienced extreme poverty and material hardship. The researchers surveyed 6,750 members of refugee families and, from this larger group, selected a random sample of 200 nuclear families and their 536 children of school age; 27 per cent of the families had 4 or more children, a factor not usually associated with high academic achievement. At the time of the study, the children had been in the USA for an average of three and a half years. All attended schools in low-income, inner city areas, not known for their scholastic success. The children did outstandingly well in their academic grades, since their mean grade point average was B; 27 per cent had an A; 52 per cent had a B; 17 per cent had a C; and only 4 per cent were below C. As expected, their grades in English and liberal arts were unexceptional. But in maths and science almost half had A scores; another third earned Bs. These grades were matched by test scores on the California

Achievement Test, which indicated that they out-performed 54 per cent of all students taking the test, placing them just above the national average. These achievements held for the majority of the children, not just a few gifted individuals.

The researchers explored aspects of the family context which might be encouraging the high academic achievement of these children. They found through interviews conducted in the language of the families that in the evenings the whole family would typically collaborate on the children's homework. The children spent an average of 3 hours and 10 minutes each evening on their homework. (American students spend on average only 1 hour and 30 minutes each day.) The parents were usually unable to engage in the content of the homework, but they set standards and goals for each evening and took responsibility for the household chores so that the children could get on with their studies.

> After dinner, the table is cleared, and homework begins. The older children, both male and female, help their younger siblings. Indeed, they seem to learn as much from teaching as from being taught. It is reasonable to suppose that a great amount of learning goes on at these times – in terms of skills, habits, attitudes and expectations as well as the content of a subject. The younger children, in particular, are taught not only subject matter but how to learn. Such sibling involvement demonstrates how a large family can encourage and enhance academic success. The familial setting appears to make the children feel at home in school and, consequently, perform well there. (Caplan, Choy and Whitmore, 1992, pp. 21–2)

In addition, the parents read regularly to their children, either in English or in their own language, and it seemed to be the experience of reading which strengthened emotional ties between parent and child, strengthened cultural understanding of traditions, and transmitted the wisdom of the culture through stories. Not only that, the experience was enjoyable and shared with all members of the family.

Caplan, Choy and Whitmore concluded that the parents had carried their cultural heritage with them to the USA and handed it down to their children. This meant that the families were securely linked to their own past as well as to the realities of the present and the possibilites of the future in a new environment.

This study explored the role of the family in the academic performance of Indochinese children from refugee families, and the results firmly confirm the need for close integration between home and school, the importance of familial commitment to education, and the need for the creation of an environment which is conducive to learning. Yet we cannot expect the families to do all this by themselves; nor do the authors of this paper suggest this. Families need acknowledgement of what they are doing and some sense that their own experiences are valued within the school system. Studies like these can help us identify some of the cultural components which contribute to the academic success or failure of children in order to give educators insights into the processes at work and the ways in which they can encourage these processes.

◀Causes of Educational Disadvantage▶▶▶

In the 1960s and early 1970s many psychologists and educational researchers thought that the reasons for the relative failure in school of children from lower social class groups, and ethnic minorities, must lie in psychological factors such as the quality of parent–child language in the home, or parental attitudes to school. It was felt that parents of these children did not provide the intellectual stimulation which children needed. In the UK the Newsom Report (1963) identified linguistic disadvantage in some home backgrounds; the abilities of boys and girls, it stated, were often unrealized because of their 'inadequate powers of speech'. These ideas came to be known as the 'deficit' model, which places blame on the home for failing to give an adequate socialization experience for the children; as a result children have poor language skills, and/or inadequate intellectual skills to cope at school.

In the UK the National Child Development Study, a longitudinal study of all children born in one week of March 1958, found that social class was a strong predictor of school achievement in reading and arithmetic. The children were the subjects of a socio-medical survey soon after birth. At 7, 11 and 16 years, detailed information was obtained about the children's educational progress, psychological development and home circumstances.

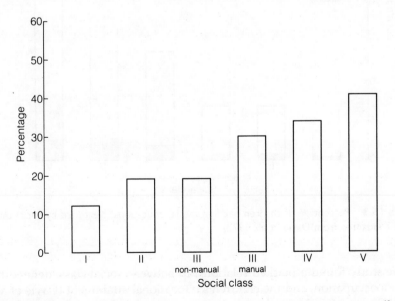

Figure 16.1   Percentage of children with 'poor' problem arithmetic test scores (0–3) at age 7 (adapted from Davie et al., 1972).

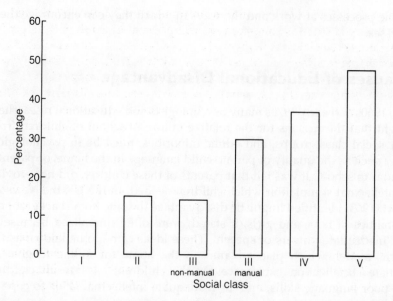

Figure 16.2   Percentage of children with 'poor' Southgate reading test scores (0–20) at age 7 (adapted from Davie et al., 1972).

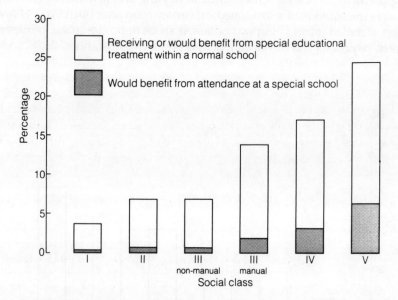

Figure 16.3   Percentage of children needing special educational treatment by social class at age 7 (adapted from Davie et al., 1972).

The study found a marked relationship between social class, defined by father's occupation, and the children's educational attainment (Davie et al., 1972). Figure 16.1 shows the percentages by social class of those children from the cohort who performed badly on a test of arithmetic at the age of 7.

It shows that 41 per cent of children from unskilled families (social class V) had a poor test score as compared with 12 per cent of children from professional families (social class I). Figure 16.2 shows a similar pattern of scores on the Southgate reading test: 48 per cent of children from social class V made low scores compared with 8 per cent of children from social class I. If the criterion of poor reading is made more stringent, the disparity is much larger. The chances of a social class V child being a non-reader are 15 times greater than those of a social class I child. Teachers were also asked to say whether the children would benefit from special educational treatment. Figure 16.3 shows that around 25 per cent of children from social class V were said to be receiving or in need of specialist teaching; only 3 per cent of children in social class I fell into this category. The gap between children of different social class backgrounds remained at the age of 11, as can be seen from the reading scores presented in table 16.2.

The term 'cultural deprivation' became popular in this period to describe what was thought of as a lack of 'cultural' stimulation in the homes of 'deprived' children. Such a perspective led naturally to the idea of programmes of 'enrichment' or of 'compensatory education' to remove these children's supposed psychological deficits.

We shall examine the effects of such enriched environments or compensatory education shortly. In certain circumstances, for example institutional rearing, enrichment programmes can have very substantial effects. However, the outcome of compensatory education programmes has seemed more modest, at least at first. The apparent failure of these programmes to remove educational disadvantage led to explanations other than the deficit model being seriously considered.

Advocates of an alternative approach, known as the 'difference' model, argue that schools are essentially white, middle-class institutions in terms of their values, the language used by teachers and the content of courses. Hence, children from different backgrounds achieve less well. Difference theorists would wish to see greater tolerance of the values, attitudes and behaviour which the children bring to school from their home background;

Table 16.2 Evidence of academic under-achievement by young black students (Rampton Report, 1981)

	Asians	Afro-Caribbeans	All other leavers	All school leavers in England
Five or more passes at 'O' level or CSE Grade I	18%	3%	16%	21%
One or more 'A' level passes	13%	2%	12%	13%
Went to university	3%	1%	3%	5%
n =	527	799	4,852	693,840

Source: Rampton Report, 1981

or even separate kinds of schooling for ethnic minorities. For example, Labov (1969) demonstrated the verbal skills which American ghetto children can display in the right context, but also argued that educators seldom value or encourage the non-standard English of inner city children.

Another approach is something of a compromise between the deficit and the difference positions. This emphasizes the 'social disadvantage' of lower social class and ethnic minority groups. Usually, such families have lower income, poor housing and more difficult family circumstances. These factors may be responsible for some real deficits in children's development, which may then show up in psychological or educational tests but which are not primarily psychological in origin. In common with difference theorists, this perspective would not expect too much from compensatory education programmes which did not deal with social and material inequalities. Moreover, such deficits produced by the culture might be exaggerated by actual discrimination against lower class or ethnic minority children in schools, as difference theories suggest.

From a very different and controversial standpoint it has been argued that children from lower social class backgrounds or from certain ethnic minorities have, on average, genetically lower potential for intelligence and hence for education. One well-known proponent of this view is Arthur Jensen (1969). This hypothesis naturally raises considerable indignation amongst members of minority groups. Although its supporters argue that it is scientifically valid to present it as a hypothesis, to advance it seems insensitive to the prolonged injustice and discrimination suffered by many ethnic minority groups in Britain and the USA.

Much of the early research on race and intelligence was biased and unsound (see Gould, 1981, and chapter 1), while more recent research is against the hypothesis. For example, Scarr and Weinberg (1976) studied 130 black children adopted by middle-class white families in the USA. These children achieved comparable levels of intellectual achievement to adopted white children in similar families. These and other studies (Scarr, 1984) suggest strongly that, while individual differences in intellectual ability may indeed be partly genetic in origin, racial differences in intelligence test scores are overwhelmingly due to environmental factors. Whether these environmental factors are best seen as due to psychological deficits in the home environment, educational prejudice against cultural/subcultural differences, or the consequence of social and material disadvantage is still actively under debate.

◀The Effects of Severe Deprivation and Institutional Rearing▶▶▶

The deficit model of disadvantage supposes that some children experience a deprived or impoverished rearing environment. This is contentious as applied to the homes of lower social class or ethnic minority children. However, it is not contentious in certain extreme circumstances. These include the experience of children reared in orphanages or children's homes in the years before and soon after the Second World War. As we also saw in chapter 3, at that time children's institutions provided little stimulation of any kind. The children had few toys or playthings, little conversation with staff, and experienced extreme multiple caregiving. As a result, institutionally reared children scored very poorly on tests of cognitive or linguistic development, as well as showing problems in later social adjustment. It was the work of Bowlby and other psychologists which drew attention to these consequences of institutional rearing, and hence led to great improvements in the quality of the institutional environment. The success of these efforts was one factor contributing to the broad popularity of the deficit model in the 1960s, and the enthusiasm for compensatory education and enrichment programmes.

At around the same time, Spitz (1946) noted that infants in institutions fared very badly in comparison with infants reared at home. They were under-weight, reached developmental milestones later, and were more vulnerable to illness.

Two early studies showed dramatically the effects that could be achieved by enriching the environment for institutionally reared children. Skeels and Dye (1939) chanced to notice the effect of environmental change on two apparently retarded children who had been transferred at 18 months from an orphanage to the women's ward in an institution for the mentally retarded, with an associated school. Their new environment was in fact an enriched one in comparison with the orphanage. Both staff and patients lavished attention and affection on them, played with them and took them on outings, and the children were given a much more stimulating experience than they had had previously. The gains were dramatic and after 15 months of this experience the children were considered to be within the normal range of intelligence. Children who had remained in the unstimulating environment of the orphanage did not make progress in this way.

Skodak and Skeels (1945) then carried out a more systematic longitudinal study in which 13 mentally retarded infants from the orphanage were transferred in the same way as the earlier two. The infants were aged 11–21 months, and had a mean IQ of 64. Again the children made dramatic gains; after an average of 19 months' stay their mean IQ was 92. By the age of 3 or 4 most were adopted by families and went on to attend normal school. A similar, control group of 12 children who stayed in the orphanage, however, actually decreased in IQ from a mean of 87 to 61 over this period. More than 20 years later, a follow-up study (Skeels, 1966) indicated that the gains made by the experimental group of children were lasting. They had obtained significantly more grades at school than the control group, four had attended college, and one had graduated and then gone on to achieve a Ph.D.; they had formed stable partnerships, and had a varied range of occupations (e.g. teacher, beautician, airline stewardess, sales manager). In the control group, all but one were in unskilled occupations, were unemployed or still living in the institution. These dramatic findings suggested that intervention at an early age had crucial effects on later educational and vocational success.

Kirk (1958) advised caution in interpreting Skeels and Skodak's results. Was it the intervention alone which had the effect, or was it the long-term stimulation and care from the adopted families? Kirk followed groups of retarded children during the preschool and first school years. Twenty-eight of his sample were given an enriched preschool experience in the community; 15 remained within the institution but attended an institution nursery school; 12 in a different institution had no preschool education. In terms of intellectual level the community preschool group made an average gain of 12 IQ points, the institution preschool group made an average gain of 10 IQ points, while the institution control group had an average loss of 6–7 IQ points. However, some of the differences became smaller after the children had entered school. Much of the intervention effect 'wore off' or 'washed out' after the experimental period was over. The reason for this could have been acceleration on the part of the control children once they experienced the stimulation of school, or deceleration on the part of the experimental children once their enriched experience was over. The Kirk experiment suggested that early intervention could have immediate effects, but needed to be reinforced by a continuing experience of enrichment, warmth and stimulation (like that of the adopted children in Skeels and Skodak's study) if the gains were to be permanent.

Although these studies have been criticized for their small number of participants, possible lack of random assignment to experimental and control groups, and the diversity of the sample, the striking results provide a strong indication that environmental stimulation can undo at least some of the negative effects of deprivation. Later studies in different cultures tell a very similar story. Dennis (1973; 1982) carried out a series of studies in the Crèche, a Lebanese orphanage run by French nuns. The children were fed and kept clean, but were given very little intellectual stimulation; the ratio of caregivers to children was 1–10; the babies were kept in cribs with white sheets round them; if they cried, no-one came; the caregivers rarely talked to them. As you would expect, the children were very delayed in terms of locomotor, intellectual and linguistic development. The children stayed in the Crèche until the age of 6 when boys and girls were transferred to separate institutions. The girls went to an orphanage where the emphasis was on domestic work and where again the environment was extremely unstimulating; many of them were destined to work as caregivers in the Crèche. By the age of 16, the girls had an average IQ of 50. By contrast, the boys went to an orphanage where the emphasis was on giving them a much wider range of skills to equip them for work in the outside world; they were also taken on outings. By the age of 15, their average IQ was 80.

Dennis also investigated the intellectual development of those children from the Crèche who were adopted, following a change in legislation in the Lebanon in the 1950s. He found that children who were adopted by the age of 2 years regained normal IQs, even though their average IQ at the time of adoption was 50. However, Crèche children who were adopted at a later age were less likely to 'catch up' intellectually. He observed that, after adoption, the children gained 1 year of mental age with each year of chronological age. But the older children had suffered more deficit in terms of mental retardation. For example, a 4-year-old with an IQ of 50 has a mental age of 2 years; an 8-year-old with an IQ of 50 has a mental age of 4 years. By 12 years of age, the 4-year-old had 8 years of normal growth; but the 8-year-old had only 4 additional years of normal growth. Dennis concluded that deprivation during the first 2 years of life can be overcome if the later environment is normal, and suggested that his results indicated that if there was a critical period for intellectual development it would be later – between 2 and 8 years.

Kagan (1976) confirmed Dennis's conclusion that deprivation in infancy does not necessarily have permanent effects. He studied children in an isolated Guatemalan community where the custom was to keep babies in an extremely unstimulating environment until they could walk, at around 13–16 months. There seemed to be very little verbal stimulation; the babies slept a lot; there were no toys or other objects to play with; the babies lived in a state of near darkness for most of the time. Kagan found that, at the age of 1 year, these babies were 3–4 months delayed in comparison with American babies of the same age. They were passive, uncommunicative, did not appear to be alert, and rarely smiled. However, when they were followed up in late childhood and early adolescence, the children were found to be normal on a range of cognitive and social tasks. It must be remembered, however, that these children had formed a close one-to-one relationship with their mothers and so were not emotionally deprived as the orphanage children at the Crèche were.

There have also been some case studies of the effects of extreme deprivation and neglect on young children. There have, for example, been anecdotal accounts of 'wild children', that is children discovered in the wild with apparently no form of human contact. When rescued, these children tended to display behaviour more characteristic of animals, such as running on all fours, and this led some to believe that the children had survived through being reared by and among animals. Such cases are often inadequately documented. Whatever the circumstances of their rearing, the prognosis for wild children has been poor. Their linguistic and cognitive attainment has tended to remain low, and their social behaviour strange. However, we cannot be sure that such children were normal when they were abandoned by their parents, and some investigators have suggested that wild children may have been psychotic or retarded in the first instance.

We do have a few more reliable case studies of children who have been reared in conditions of extreme deprivation in their own homes and who have subsequently been rescued. These accounts can help answer the question of how far an enriched environment can compensate for the effects of very severe neglect in the early years.

Koluchova's (1972) case study of Czechoslovakian twins born in 1960 gives evidence to support the argument that these effects need not be irreversible. The twins' mother died when they were born and they spent the next 11 months in an institution where they were said to be making normal progress. The father then took them back into his home but, on his remarriage, they were again put into care until the new household was formed. From around the age of 18 months until 7 years the twins lived with their father and his new wife. However, the stepmother kept them in conditions

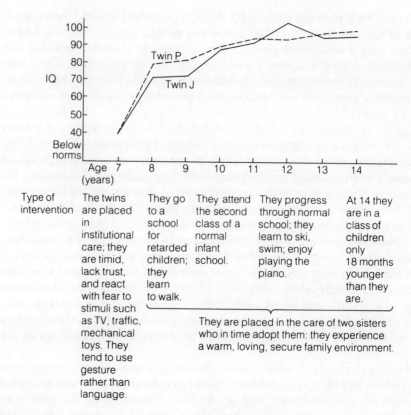

Figure 16.4   Changes in the IQ score of the Koluchova twins, measured by the WISC, after intervention began.

of extreme deprivation. She forbade her own children to talk to the twins and denied them any affection herself. They spent their time either in a bare, unheated room apart from the rest of the family or, as a punishment, were locked in the cellar. They never went out, and lacked proper food, exercise and any kind of intellectual or social stimulation apart from what they could provide for themselves. The neighbours did not know of their existence but from time to time heard strange, animal-like sounds coming from the cellar. By the age of 7, when the authorities became aware of the twins' existence, they had the appearance of 3-year-olds; they could hardly walk because of rickets, they could not play, their speech was very poor and they relied mainly on gestures to communicate. On their discovery, they were removed from the family and placed in a home for preschool children.

They had experienced such severe emotional, intellectual and social deprivation that the prognosis seemed very poor, but once placed in a supportive environment, they began to make remarkable gains. After a year they were ready to be placed in a school for mentally retarded children. There they made such progress that they were transferred the next year to the second class of a normal infant school. At the same time, they were placed in the care of two sisters who gave them the emotional security and intellectual stimulation that had been so lacking in their own family environment. As a result, in the next 15 months, the twins' mental age increased by 3 years, showing clearly how the environmental change had compensated for early neglect. A follow-up found the twins completely normal in their language development at the age of 14; school performance was good and motivation high.

They were now functioning at an average academic level in a class of children who were only 18 months younger than they. They were socially adjusted and had realistic aspirations to go on to take a vocational training. Figure 16.4 indicates the intellectual progress made by the twins from 3 months after intervention began. Prior to that, Koluchova had estimated their intelligence to be around an IQ of 40, although no formal assessment was possible because of their unfamiliarity with any of the tasks that appear in intelligence tests.

Koluchova's study indicates how removal from an extremely impoverished environment can reverse the effects of deprivation. It could be argued of course that the success of the intervention was only possible because the twins had experienced some normal nurturing in the first few months of their lives; in addition, they were not totally isolated since they had the support of one another. Finally, the twins were discovered when they were still relatively young. A less favourable outcome was found in another case study, that of a girl called 'Genie', where two of these ameliorative factors were absent (Curtiss, 1977).

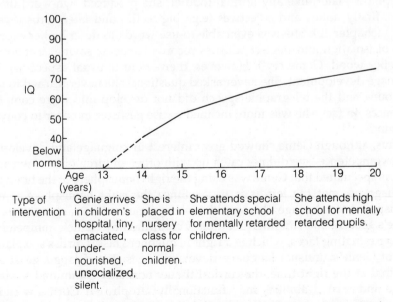

Figure 16.5 Changes in Genie's IQ scores, measured by the Leiter International Performance Scale (a non-verbal test), after intervention began.

Genie's isolation was even more extreme than that of the Czechoslovakian twins and lasted for a longer period of time. From the age of 20 months until she was 13 years old she was imprisoned alone in a darkened room. By day she was tied to an infant potty chair in such a way that she could only move her hands and feet; at night, she was put in a sleeping bag and further restrained by a sort of wire straitjacket. She was beaten by her father if she made any sound and he forbade other members of the family to speak to her. She lived in an almost silent world deprived of warmth, proper nourishment and normal human contact. She was kept in these conditions until her mother, who was partially blind and dominated by Genie's father, finally escaped with her. At this point, Genie could not walk, she was emaciated, weighing only 59 pounds, she spent much of her time spitting and salivating, and was virtually silent apart from the occasional whimper. When tested soon after admission to hospital, she was functioning at the level of a 1-year-old.

Curtiss (1977), a graduate student of linguistics at the time, has given a moving and detailed account of Genie's development after she was taken into care. Despite the terrible conditions she had endured, Genie did respond to treatment. She soon learned to walk. Her level of intellectual functioning (measured by a non-verbal intelligence test developed for use with deaf children) increased (see figure 16.5) and in some perceptual tasks, such as the Mooney Faces Test, which required subjects to distinguish between real and distorted faces, she performed well above average. She also became able to form relationships with other people.

In the area of language, however, Genie's development proved puzzling. During the first 7 months in care she learned to recognize a number of words and then began to speak. At first she produced one-word utterances like 'pillow'; later, like any normal toddler, she produced two-word utterances, firstly nouns and adjectives (e.g. 'big teeth') and later verbs ('want milk') (chapter 10). She was even able to use words to describe her experience of isolation and neglect (Curtiss records Genie as saying, 'Father hit arm. Big wood. Genie cry'). However, there were unusual aspects to her language development. She never asked questions, she never learned to use pronouns and the telegraphic speech did not develop into more complex sentences. In fact, she was more inclined to use gestures in order to convey meaning.

Thus, although Genie showed great interest in language and developed some competence, she did not catch up with other children of her own age. Curtiss speculated that Genie was using the right hemisphere of the brain for language use not the left as is usual. Since the right hemisphere is not predisposed to language, this would explain some of the strange aspects of Genie's speech. Such an interpretation is confirmed by Genie's competence at discriminating faces, which is a right hemisphere task. Curtiss's explanation of Genie's unusual language development is that if language is not acquired at the right time, the cortical tissue 'normally committed for language and related abilities may functionally atrophy'. If Curtiss is right, Genie provides support for the idea that there is indeed a critical period for the development of left hemisphere functioning.

Some of the questions remain unanswered since all research into Genie's development stopped in 1978 when a court allowed her mother to become her legal guardian. At this point Genie's mother filed a lawsuit claiming that Curtiss and others had used Genie for their own personal gain (see Rymer, 1994).

Intervention did have a considerable impact on Genie's development, but apparently without such dramatic success as was obtained with the twins in Koluchova's study. A review of these and similar cases has been made by Skuse (1984). In general, it would seem that the results of these recent case studies of extreme deprivation, and the improvements made in institutional care of young children, point to the great positive benefits which intervention, based on knowledge of children's psychological needs, can have.

◀The Role of the Family and the Community▶▶▶

One of the factors implicated in producing the unstimulating environment of the orphanages of the 1930s was the lack of linguistic stimulation. Infants were largely left to their own devices, with little interaction or conversation with staff or caregivers. Yet, as we saw in chapter 10, there is a large body of evidence to suggest that children's language flourishes in an environment where adults and siblings use rich, varied language themselves, and where they respond with sensitivity to the language which the child produces.

Some deficit theorists have extended this finding to suggest that children in lower social class or ethnic minority groups have also been deprived of an adequate linguistic environment in the home. If so, this might explain their later educational disadvantage. One of the early theorists of this kind was Basil Bernstein, who examined social class differences in the speech of London children.

Bernstein (1962) proposed a distinction between two kinds of conversational language, or code: these are a public language, or 'restricted code', and

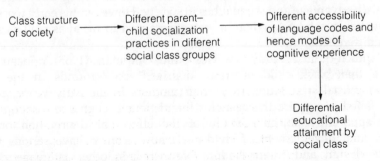

Figure 16.6   Schematic diagram of Bernstein's early model.

a formal language, or 'elaborated code'. The restricted code is colloquial and context-dependent. Phrases such as 'Do as I tell you', 'Lay off that', 'It's only natural, isn't it?' or you wouldn't believe it' are given as examples. These are idiomatic phrases of a fairly simple grammatical type which can be understood in context but not fully out of context (for example, with 'Do as I tell you' we have no idea, out of context, what the child is being asked to do).

By contrast, an elaborated code is more formal and context-independent. The meaning is made explicit for the other person, rather than aspects of meaning being taken for granted. Sentences such as 'I've asked you not to put dirty hands in your mouth since it may make you sick', or 'I know many children are brought up to like sweets, but I believe you can educate them to prefer other more healthy foods', might be examples of elaborated code. You know what the person is meaning, without being present. The sentences also tend to be more complex.

Bernstein proposed that children from middle-class backgrounds could use either restricted or elaborated codes, depending on which was most appropriate in the circumstances; but that children from working-class backgrounds could only use the restricted code. The restricted code had disadvantages, in that it 'limits the range of behaviour and learning', and leads to 'a low level of conceptualization – an orientation to a low order of causality, a lack of interest in processes'. This could contribute to the educational disadvantage of lower class children in school (see figure 16.6).

Bernstein (1971) also distinguished between 'person-orientated' and 'position-orientated' communications. A person-orientated message uses personal appeal, such as 'I know you don't like kissing grandpa, but he is unwell, and he is very fond of you, and it makes him happy'. A position-orientated message appeals to status roles of a general kind, such as 'I don't want none of your nonsense; children kiss their grandpa'. Bernstein thought the latter to be more characteristic of traditional working-class families.

This and other research suggested that any differences in the language of middle-class and working-class children in Britain are not so much a matter of competence (the deficit model) as one of contexts in which particular kinds of language may be used, contexts that are facilitating or threatening to the child (the difference model). In later writings, Bernstein himself went some way to agreeing with this view, thus modifying aspects of his early theories. He also has more recently laid greater stress on the direct effects of social disadvantage and inequalities in society. However, his early work was influential in the USA, where it was generalized to racial as well as social class differences.

A much-quoted study by Hess and Shipman (1965) appeared to prove that black children from 'deprived' backgrounds in the USA lacked crucial stimulation from their mothers in the early years so that they failed to acquire the basis for linguistic and cognitive development. This apparently objective study of the effects of deprivation on the intellectual development of children is now seen to have serious flaws in its design and interpretation. Nevertheless, other language deficit theorists (e.g. Bereiter and Engelmann, 1966) have written about children from ghetto backgrounds as if they had virtually no language which could be of use outside their local environment, and attributed difficulties in reading and writing to the children's deficient, non-standard version of English. As Pinker (1994) observes, if only the psychologists had actually listened to the spontaneous conversations of family members they would have discovered that everyday black American culture is highly verbal, and that black street youths place a high value on linguistic virtuosity.

The inadequacy of this sort of conceptualization of lower-class black children in the USA was vividly demonstrated by William Labov (1969). He recorded the spontaneous language of black children aged 8–17 years in a ghetto area in Harlem, New York. Many of the boys were gang members, most were failures at school. Labov used black interviewers. Two examples of transcripts follow. In the first, the interviewer Clarence Robins (C. R.) is talking to an 8-year-old called Leon.

C. R.: What if you saw somebody kickin' somebody else on the ground, or was using a stick, what would you do if you saw that?
Leon: Mmmmm.
C. R.: If it was supposed to be a fair fight.
Leon: I don't know.
C. R.: You don't know? Would you do anything . . . huh? I can't hear you.
Leon: No.
C. R.: Did you ever see somebody get beat up real bad?
Leon: . . . Nope???
C. R.: Well – uh – did you ever get into a fight with a guy?
Leon: Nope.
C. R.: That was bigger than you?
Leon: Nope.
C. R.: You never been in a fight?
Leon: Nope.
C. R.: Nobody ever pick on you?
Leon: Nope.
C. R.: Nobody ever hit you?
Leon: Nope.
C. R.: How come?
Leon: Ah 'on' know.
C. R.: Didn't you ever hit somebody?
Leon: Nope.
C. R. [incredulous]: You never hit nobody?
Leon: Mmm.
C. R.: Aww, ba-a-a-be, you ain't going to tell me that.
(Labov, 1969, pp. 200–1)

Although the interviewer is also a black person raised in Harlem, in the formal interview situation he elicits very little from Leon. Is Leon 'deprived of language', or just clamming up in this context? The following extract proves it is the latter.

C. R.:   Is there anybody who says *your mamma drink pee?*
Leon [rapidly and breathlessly]:   Yee-ah!
Greg: Yup!
Leon: And your father eat doo-doo for breakfast!
C. R.:   Ohhh!! [laughs]
Leon: And they say *your father – your father eat doo-doo for dinner!*
Greg: When they sound on me, I say CBM.
C. R.:   What that mean?
Leon: Congo-booger-snatch! [laughs]
Greg: Congo-booger-snatch! [laughs]
Greg: And sometimes I'll curse with BB.
C. R.:   What that?
Greg: Black boy! [Leon – crunching on potato chips] Oh that's a MBB.
C. R.:   MBB. Whats that?
Greg: 'Merican Black Boy!
C. R.:   Ohh . . .
Greg: Anyway, 'Mericans is same like white people, right?
Leon: And they talk about Allah.
C. R.:   Oh yeah?
Greg: Yeah.
C. R.:   What they say about Allah?
Leon: Allah – Allah is God.
Greg: Allah –
C. R.:   And what else?
Leon: I don't know the res'.
Greg: Allah i – Allah is God, Allah is the only God, Allah –
Leon: Allah is the son of God.
Greg: But can he make magic?
Leon: Nope.
Greg: I know who can make magic.
C. R.:   Who can?
Leon: The God, the real one.

(Labov, 1969, p. 201)

Clarence Robins changed the context here by bringing along potato chips, by inviting along Leon's friend Gregory, by sitting down in Leon's room, and introducing taboo words and topics. Leon is transformed from a suspicious non-verbal child into one who is actively competing to speak. From this example it is also apparent that Leon is using a distinct dialect of 'non-standard English' (or NSE) which is different from standard English (SE). NSE used by black American children differs from SE in systematic ways, for example copula deletion (omission of 'is' or 'are'), and the use of double negatives (see table 16.3). These are surface structure differences which reflect a similar deep structure of meaning (see p. 314, chapter 10). There is nothing inferior in these features, and many languages use them. For example, the double negative is used in French (e.g. 'il ne comprend rien').

Table 16.3 Some differences between non-standard English (NSE) used by black Americans and standard English (SE)

	NSE	SE
Copula deletion	You crazy	You are crazy
	They mine	They are mine
Double negative	You ain't going to no heaven	You are not going to any heaven
	Don't nobody know it's really a God	Nobody knows that there really is a God
	He don't know nothing	He doesn't know anything

Labov thus stressed 'difference', rather than 'deficit' in analysing the language of children from disadvantaged backgrounds. Lower-class black children acquire NSE at home and with peers, but are faced with SE at school or in psychological test situations. There is no intrinsic deficit in NSE, but its difference from the SE required in the school, and the biased attitude of educators to NSE, puts lower-class black children at a disadvantage. In fact, when Labov examined the percentage of grammatical sentences in tape recordings of speech in a range of social contexts, he found that the great majority of sentences in casual speech were grammatical, whatever the social setting. The highest percentage of ungrammatical sentences – that is those where there were broken-off fragments of sentences, slips of the tongue, tongue-tied humming and hawing – was found in the proceedings of learned academic conferences (quoted in Pinker, 1994, p. 31)!

Criticism of the deficit model also comes from a study by Wells (1983) on social class differences in the UK. He collected a large amount of data in naturalistic settings at home and in school of children's conversations both with adults and with other children. He was especially interested in differences between talk at home and at school, aiming to investigate the claim that 'a major cause of differential success is the difference between children in their ability to meet the linguistic expectations of the classroom as a result of their preschool linguistic experience at home' (p. 127). His Bristol Longitudinal Study followed a representative sample of children through the preschool years into infant school with recordings of the children's spontaneous talk in the two contexts of home and school. Wells found that there were very few homes which did not provide richer opportunities than are found at school for learning through interaction with adults. Wells concluded that it is simply false to suggest that working-class children are linguistically 'disadvantaged'; his observations did not identify clear-cut social class differences in the use of language by parents and their children. He stressed the need for teachers to provide opportunities for children to continue the process of learning through the active conversation which had typically been their experience in the preschool years.

◀Compensatory Education Programmes in the USA▶▶▶

As we have seen, in the later 1960s, a deficit or cultural deprivation model became the most accepted hypothesis to explain the educational disadvantage and under-achievement of lower social class and ethnic minority children. The early work of Bernstein, and Hess and Shipman, combined with what psychologists had found out about the successful consequences of early intervention with children reared in orphanages, suggested that the answer to this deficit was early intervention with disadvantaged children, particularly focusing on their language where much of the supposed deficit was thought to be located. This led to a large number of programmes of compensatory education for preschool children in the USA (and also in the UK, see below).

One of the earliest examples, in Illinois, USA, was a highly structured language programme for 4-year-old black children devised by Bereiter and Engelmann (1966). This aimed to teach English to non-standard English speakers as if it were a foreign language, by drilling and repetition. Bereiter and Engelmann thought that 'the language of culturally deprived children is not merely an underdeveloped version of Standard English, but is a basically non-logical mode of expressive behavior'. The viewpoint has since been exposed by Labov, and other difference theorists, as biased and completely insensitive to the different features of black American culture or dialect (cf. examples on pp. 497–8 above).

Another early example was the work of Blank and Solomon (1969). They did not require the children in their programmes to speak standard English, nor did they use drilling or repetition. Instead, 'a specialised language program was devised to facilitate abstract thinking in young deprived children through short, individual tutoring sessions on a daily basis'. They involved the children in conversations that arose naturally out of the child's own interests and experiences. Blank and Solomon found that children experiencing this programme increased in terms of IQ scores more than did control children, which suggested the programme was having some benefit, and subsequently the Blank language programmes were quite widely used.

Following the apparent success of these kinds of compensatory education programmes, a massive policy of intervention occurred in the USA with 'Project Head Start'. This started in the summer of 1965 and built up over the next few years until millions of preschool children across the USA had participated in some form of Head Start programme. The general goal was to give 'deprived' children a head start in schools by some form of early intervention to stimulate cognitive and linguistic development. Up to the 1960s, nursery schools had tended to be more orientated towards the needs of the middle-class child. Much of the emphasis was on social and emotional development through free play, and unstructured imaginative activities. Preschool programmes of compensatory education, by contrast, aimed directly to prepare children for entry into infant school and to give them skills which, it was felt, their homes had failed to provide. Programmes were often based on the assumption that the children's language was deficient, that they lacked cognitive strategies appropriate for school learning, and that their parents used ineffective modes of control. However, no detailed syllabus was laid down and the exact nature and length of programmes varied widely.

◄Compensatory Education in the UK►►►

The Plowden Report of 1967 advocated a policy of positive discrimination in favour of children from poor areas throughout Britain, through the provision of more resources, more teachers and better school buildings. These areas were to be designated 'Educational Priority Areas' (EPAs). In response to the recommendations of the Plowden Report, Halsey (1972) mounted a large project, the Educational Priority Area Project, to initiate and evaluate compensatory education programmes in exceptionally deprived communities in London, Birmingham, Liverpool, Yorkshire and Dundee. Each area formulated its own programme within the wider framework of the Project in order to take account of the particular needs of the region. Halsey's overall conclusion was a positive one. He argued that the concept of Educational Priority Areas was a useful one which enabled positive discrimination to be made in favour of underprivileged children. He advocated the use of structured programmes which were flexible enough to accommodate to local needs and he recommended the development of community schools as one means of bridging the gap between home and school. Although he did not claim that programmes like his could fully compensate for deprived social conditions, he argued that education could play an important role in extending young children's cognitive and linguistic abilities.

◄Compensatory Programmes Evaluated►►►

Some of the early evaluation studies showed disappointing results for the compensatory programmes. The first national evaluation of Project Head Start was carried out in 1969 in Ohio University by the Westinghouse Learning Corporation. This research study showed that the intervention programmes had very little, if any, effect on the children who had taken part. Any benefits seemed to be very transient, disappearing after a year or so at school. Some psychologists, such as Arthur Jensen (1969), took this to confirm their view that children from poor families had inherited low academic ability which no amount of compensatory education could make up for. Others thought there should be more intervention. This might mean more intensive intervention, involving parent as well as child education; or starting intervention earlier; or following intervention through into the early school years. At an extreme, this might virtually involve removing a young child from a 'deficient' home environment. Yet others – the difference theorists – argued that the whole premise of intervention was biased or racist. As

Baratz and Baratz (1970, p. 43) put it, 'Head Start has failed because its goal is to correct a deficit that simply does not exist'. By now the ignorance and insensitivity which many white researchers had shown to black culture and to the thoughts and feelings of black mothers and children had become more obvious. Baratz and Baratz claimed that the 'Head Start programs may inadvertently advocate the annihilation of a cultural system which is barely considered or understood by most social scientists'.

However, the Ohio–Westinghouse study took place only 5 years after Project Head Start began. By 1976, researchers who were following the long-term effects of intervention programmes began to report encouraging results. One major research project (Lazar and Darlington, 1982) was a collaborative study in which 11 preschool research teams came together to pool their results for a group named the Consortium for Longitudinal Studies. Each researcher had independently designed and carried out preschool programmes in the 1960s; the children who had participated, mainly black children from low-income families, were followed up in 1976 when their ages ranged from 9 to 19.

For example, one project, organized by Weikart et al. (1970) in Ypsilanti, Michigan, involved 123 children from low-waged black families. Half of them, selected at random, experienced an intervention programme; the other half, the control group, had no preschool educational provision. The programme children spent 12.5 hours per week for 2 years in a special preschool intervention programme which stressed active learning and a great deal of communication between child and adults and between child and child. There were also home visits by the teachers.

The results for IQ scores from the project and later follow-ups are shown in table 16.4. The programme group children showed an initial increase (more than the control group) in the year or so immediately following the intervention, but through the middle school years this showed a familiar falling-off or wash-out effect. However, some long-term effects of the intervention were found in other areas. By the age of 15, the programme group scored on average 8 per cent higher on reading, arithmetic and language tests than the control group. By the end of high school, only 19 per cent of the programme children had been placed in remedial classes compared with 39 per cent in the control group. Socially too there were effects. The programme

Table 16.4 Changes in IQ with age, for programme and control group children, in Weikart's preschool programme

	Pretest	3	4	5	6	7	8	9	10	14
Programme group	79.6	79.9	92.7	94.1	91.3	91.7	88.1	87.7	85.0	81.0
Control group	78.5	79.6	81.7	83.2	86.3	87.1	86.9	86.8	84.6	80.7

Source: Lazar and Darlington, 1982

youngsters were less likely to be delinquent (36 per cent as compared with 42 per cent of the control group). Ten per cent of the programme group went on to college but none of the control group did. These findings were fairly typical of the other ten projects in the survey. However, the most recent follow-up of the children, who are now in their late 20s, has shown some dramatic results (Weikart, 1996). At the age of 27, 95 per cent of the original study participants were interviewed and additional data were gathered from their school, social services and arrest records. There were significant differences between experimental and control groups. By the age of 27, only one-fifth as many programme members as non-programme members had been arrested five or more times (7% v. 35%) and only one-third as many were arrested for drug dealing. Those who had experienced the programme were four times as likely to earn $2,000 per month as non-programme members; they were three times as likely to own their own homes and to own a second car. One-third more than no-programme members had graduated from high school; they were also significantly more likely to be literate and to score more highly on achievement tests.

Weikart (1996, p. 120) concludes that the evidence gives very strong support for the effectiveness of preschool interventions and argues that the benefits are long-term because they:

- empower children by enabling them to initiate and carry out their own learning activities and to make independent decisions;
- empower parents, by involving them in ongoing relationships as full partners with teachers in supporting their children's development;
- empower teachers by providing them with systematic in-service training, supportive curriculum supervision, and observational tools to assess children's development.

As discussed in box 16.2, the Consortium for Longitudinal Studies concluded that early intervention programmes could have significant, long-term effects (Lazar and Darlington, 1982). The interpretation of achievement test scores was difficult because of variability in the tests themselves. However, the authors reported some evidence that children who had experienced early intervention performed better on school attainment tests than controls. But perhaps more important were the non-cognitive differences – the changes in attitudes towards themselves as learners, in aspirations and beliefs in their own competence (box 16.2).

A continuing debate

The apparent failure of Project Head Start around 1970 led many workers, such as Baratz and Baratz, to reject the idea of compensatory education and to replace the deficit model with the difference model. The deficit theorists had certainly been naïve in their assumptions. Nevertheless, the difference model too may be naïve if taken to the extreme of supposing that all kinds of rearing conditions are equally valid. Poor material conditions, inadequate housing, and poverty, may well affect the quality of a child's development.

Lower social class groups, and many ethnic minorities, tend to suffer from these material and social disadvantages, as well as possible prejudice or bias within and outside the educational system.

In a review of American compensatory education programmes, Bronfenbrenner (1979) argued that the best schemes are those that involve the families, since those that focus on the child alone tend to have only short-term effects. If the parents are involved throughout, they can sustain the effects after the programme is over. He recommends child-care education for young people before they become parents, and support for them once the children are born, as well as a network of community support services amongst parents and other members of the community. However, he concluded that programmes of compensatory education are not effective for the most deprived groups if they concentrate only on the parent–child relationship. He calls also for intervention at other levels (see figure 1.3) to alleviate the desperate conditions in which some families are forced to live. Removal of educational disadvantage requires that the families themselves have adequate health care, reasonable housing, enough food and a sufficient income. Programmes of compensatory education cannot by themselves undo the inequalities that continue to exist in our society, and should not replace efforts to tackle poverty and racial prejudice.

More recent research shows that material disadvantage, and discrimination in the educational system, remain convincing explanations of much educational under-achievement. There is plenty of evidence to show that poor children perform less well at school than children from better-off families, are less healthy and have a narrower range of opportunities in later life. As we saw earlier, reports from the National Child Development Study (Wedge and Essen, 1982) defined social disadvantage in terms of adverse family composition, poor housing and low income. Children experiencing all three of these were defined as 'disadvantaged' in their analyses. Figure 16.7 shows the populations of children experiencing each of these three kinds of adversities separately, and those defined as disadvantaged, at ages 11 and 16. The number of children included in all three categories amounted to 4.5 per cent at age 11. At 16, the figure was 2.9 per cent. This means that amongst all 16-year-olds in Britain in 1974, there were 46,000 who were socially disadvantaged by these criteria.

These children had more difficulties than ordinary children; besides their poor housing and income, the fathers were more likely to be unemployed, and both parents were more likely to be chronically sick. In school these children were less motivated; at 16 only 41 per cent hoped to continue their education as compared with 71 per cent of their peers. Teachers were asked to say whether the 16-year-olds in the survey were able to do all the calculations normally required of an everyday shopper, and whether they were able to read well enough to cope with everyday needs. Again, the largest proportion of those unable to do these tasks were pupils from disadvantaged homes (figure 16.8).

Was the poor attainment solely attributable to home conditions? Wedge and Essen argue that 'the particularly poor exam records of the disadvantaged could to quite a large extent be attributed to the tendency to enter them

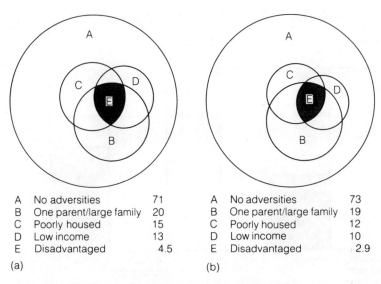

		(a)				(b)
A	No adversities	71		A	No adversities	73
B	One parent/large family	20		B	One parent/large family	19
C	Poorly housed	15		C	Poorly housed	12
D	Low income	13		D	Low income	10
E	Disadvantaged	4.5		E	Disadvantaged	2.9

Figure 16.7   An analysis of social adversities among British children at (a) age 11 and (b) age 16 in percentages (from Wedge and Essen, 1982).

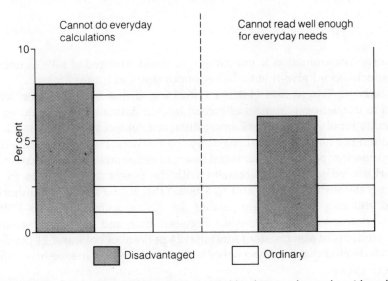

Figure 16.8   Percentage of 16-year-olds assessed by their teacher to be without basic arithmetic and reading skills (from Wedge and Essen, 1982).

for fewer exams, and not necessarily to their performance in those exams'. Figure 16.9 shows that disadvantaged children, even when they scored in the top range on attainment tests in reading and mathematics, were less likely to be entered for examinations in English and mathematics than others in their year group with similar scores. The authors recommended a policy

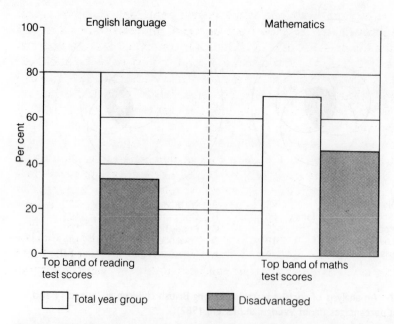

Figure 16.9   Entry for 'O' level examinations among children with the same range of scores in reading and mathematics (from Wedge and Essen, 1982).

of positive discrimination to encourage the disadvantaged to take examinations which would give them a better opportunity in future life.

A study by Troyna and Hatcher (1992) found that black children were subject to frequent experiences of racism in their daily lives. The children in their study reported that racist name-calling or references to their skin colour were often not noticed or challenged by the teachers. Furthermore, the discrimination was part of a wider racial discrimination endemic in the community, which led to a disillusionment with the power of authorities to do anything about the problem and to a belief that if you appeal to authority figures you may well end up getting the blame yourself. Kelly's (1988) investigation into the relationship between race and friendship among school students in Manchester found that 24 per cent of boys and 21 per cent of girls indicated that they had never been friends with someone of a different racial group.

In another study, of young white single mothers aged between 17 and 23 years who had black children and who were in therapy (Banks, 1996), the most common theme was the experience of isolation from both black and white communities; this was demonstrated by the community at large, by the women's own families and by the former partners. The women were more anxious and depressed than average. Many revealed that they had not anticipated the difficulties of becoming the parent of a black child, who would 'become a living visual indication of their personal affiliation and sexual activities with a black man' (ibid., p. 20). The women had experienced name-calling by both black and white people, intimidation, rejection and social disapproval, and the experience of sexual innuendoes by black and white men in the presence of the children was common. Banks argued that the extent of the prejudice and discrimination experienced by children and their families must not be under-estimated if we are to devise effective strategies for helping such families to challenge racism when they encounter it and for helping professionals and community leaders to consider ways of enabling a change in attitude to take place.

A dilemma facing educators is that if the curriculum is changed to accommodate to issues arising in the home and in the community, there is no guarantee that what is taught will still be valued by society, e.g. by employers or examining boards. However, we know that there is a danger that a *laissez-faire* attitude may block the avenues that help children from disadvantaged backgrounds gain access to mainstream culture. By failing to take action, educators help to perpetuate injustice in our society. Clearly this is a topic in which the values of society and the political possibilities of the times must be considered together with our psychological knowledge of the processes of children's development.

Reason to hope?

It seems then that deprivation and disadvantage arise out of a complex interaction among ecological, cultural, historical, demographic and psychological risk factors. Given that there are so many varied factors and given the different theories and explanations offered for disadvantage, it may be thought to be unrealistic to expect an easy solution to such a complex problem. So is there any reason to hope that as a society we can create better conditions for the children of the future? One line of inquiry might by through the study of those children and families who, against all the odds, overcome incredible hardships and achieve intellectual and social goals which could not have been predicted. We know, for example, that children who have experienced bad parenting do not necessarily mature into adults who lack parenting skills. Street children do not necessarily stay on the street. Children born into poor families can make good. History does not need to repeat itself.

Psychologists have recently begun to address the concept of resilience. Fonagy et al. (1994, p. 232), in a useful review, reflects that, 'although resilience must be specific to particular risks which may seem to have little in common (economic deprivation, parental divorce, nuclear disasters, maltreatment, forest fires, parental delinquency or psychopathology, institutionalization), the indicators of resilience which emerge from studies have a reassuring predictability about them'. These include higher SES, being female if prepubescent, male after that, having no organic deficits, having an easy temperament, being young at the time of the trauma, having an absence of early losses or separations. Fonagy et al. point out too that there are certain environmental circumstances which can protect a child from adversity. These include: competent parenting, a warm relationship with at least one parent, the availability of social support from a spouse or other close family member in adult life, a network of informal relationships, educational experience, involvement with religion and faith. The individual characteristics of resilient children include: high IQ, superior coping styles, task-related self-efficacy, autonomy, a sense of self-worth, interpersonal awareness and empathy, capacity to plan, a sense of humour. Rutter (1990) points out that resilience is more usefully thought of as a process which is part of a complex social system at a particular point in time.

One key factor in all of this may be the capacity on the part of children and their parents to develop a reflective stance on themselves and their circumstances. A second may be the development of political awareness (see box 16.1). Children who live in impoverished conditions are strongly affected by them, even if they have the qualities of resilience and the opportunities to rise above them. But rescuing them is not enough. The environmental conditions need to be changed in order to offer to all children the opportunity to realize their potential. This surely is a fundamental human right. We should not wait until their presence becomes a threat to society so that severe steps are taken to coerce or restrain them (or even to kill them). We should not wait until their presence on the streets and in the inner city slums occurs in such numbers that they are a threat. We know enough from the literature to understand that there are ways in which we can give respect, initiative, autonomy, opportunity to disadvantaged children and families.

◄Further Reading► ►

R. Davie, N. Butler and H. Goldstein 1972: *From Birth to Seven*, London: Longman (National Children's Bureau), is the report of the National Child Development Study at the first follow-up of the 1958 'cohort' at the age of 7. There are many useful analyses of educational attainment, health and environmental conditions in different sectors of British society. A very readable account of the impact of disadvantage is P. Wedge and J. Essen 1982: *Children in Adversity*, London: Pan Books. This looks at the experiences of the same sample of children up to the age of 16, and in particular the consequences of living in disadvantaged circumstances. It is a disturbing book with important implications for educational policy and practice.

A collection of useful articles can be found in A. M. Clarke and A. D. B. Clarke 1976: *Early Experience: Myth and Evidence*, London: Open Books. The authors challenge the belief that the early years have an irreversible effect on later development. The book includes chapters on the effects of parent–child separation, the effects of institutionalization on children's cognitive development, and the case study of severe deprivation of the Czech twins. For a detailed account of the Genie case, see M. Pines 1981: The civilizing of Genie, *Psychology Today*, 15 (September), 28–34. This describes the effects that an intensive programme of intervention had on the social, intellectual and linguistic development of Genie. A number of important theoretical and practical issues are raised about deprivation and the extent to which its effects can be reversed. See also R. Rymer (1994) *Genie: a Scientific Tragedy*, Harmondsworth: Penguin, where you can read about the professional rivalries among the scientists who studied Genie's progress.

◀Discussion Points▶▶▶

1 Discuss the meaning of the terms 'disadvantage', 'deficit' and 'difference' in explaining educational under-achievement.
2 How useful is the concept of 'resilience'?
3 Consider the problems involved in evaluating the effects of a programme of compensatory education. How would you attempt to do this?
4 'Black students and their parents have academic aspirations and ambitions which are not being met by the present educational system' (Eggleston, 1985). Discuss how educators might change this state of affairs.
5 What effects do family composition, poor housing and low income have on a child's school performance, and why?

Box 16.1
Children and political violence: an overview

Do children suffer psychological changes as a result of growing up in regions where there is ongoing violent conflict? In a special section of the *International Journal of Behavioural Development* devoted to the impact of political violence on children's psychological development, Ed Cairns reviews four empirical studies which represent the geographical areas most researched – the Middle East, Northern Ireland and South Africa. He asks the following questions. Should researchers focus on the stresses which children face as a result of political violence or should the emphasis be on the resilience which children so often demonstrate? Cairns explores the view that the impact of political violence may not be as dramatic as some outside observers might predict but also considers the need to look at individual reactions to danger and violence both in the wider social context and with regard to longer-term political and historical perspectives.

Kostelny and Garbarino documented the dangers faced by Palestinian children for whom experiences with violence were a part of everyday life. They found that the younger children (aged 6–9) appeared to be more negatively affected with regard to personality and behavioural changes than older children and youth (aged 12–15). They noted the impact on young people of the community's ideology, which made them articulate about social and political issues in their country and which also acted as a protection against the stresses of experiencing violence. They concluded that political con-

flict is a collective phenomenon and that it may not be enough to research the impact on individuals while ignoring the wider context in which the conflict takes place. Furthermore, the group aspect of political conflict often establishes close feelings of solidarity which act as strong buffers against stress. So researchers in this field are challenged to find innovative ways of observing individuals in a particular social setting with a particular ideological belief system.

Liddell and her colleagues observed levels of aggressiveness among 5-year-old children from four communities in South Africa. Contrary to expectation, they found that, while children from violent communities were involved in aggressive behaviour, the context and nature of the aggression was broadly similar to that observed in less violent communities. But there was an interaction effect. Children's rates of involvement with aggression were influenced by their contact with older boys and men, which seemed to take place indirectly through modelling and imitation rather than through direct involvement in fights. The researchers conclude that it is the combination of community and child-related variables that explains the children's involvement in aggression. Young children's tendency to be involved in aggressive episodes was related to their contact with older males and this relationship was more marked the more violent the community. The researchers raise the question of direct versus indirect effects and suggest that children may become more aggressive in violent circumstances through the impact of ongoing violence on their families or on other significant people in their community.

Reick's study highlighted the fact that there may be more value for researchers to examine the long-term, subtle effects on children rather than the short-term effects which are more obvious because of their dramatic nature. She investigated the frequency of emotional problems amongst a sample of 5–16-year-old children of survivors of the Holocaust and found that they did not demonstrate any more difficulties than did controls. She found no evidence of excessive psychopathology in this sample of young people, contrary to the predictions of some earlier clinical work. She explored the idea that there may be a form of adaptation or resilience in the children of survivors, which suggests some impact of stress on later facility for coping.

Toner's study in Northern Ireland pointed to the changing aspects of a politically violent situation which need to be taken account of by researchers, and he contrasted 'inside' and 'outside' perspectives. His study of reconciliation programmes indicated that, while individual children might be helped, such interventions did little to change intergroup attitudes. He argued that there is an urgent need for researchers from a range of disciplines to develop valid methods which allow comparisons to be made among different regions around the world so that we can know more precisely what are the best ways of overcoming intergroup conflict.

Cairns overviews the main issues which seem to have emerged from this work.

(i)   He suggests that social scientists need a more flexible theory to guide their understanding of the interface between shared group identities and political ideologies on the one hand, and individual behaviour and beliefs on the other. In this way he asks researchers to cross traditional divisions among disciplines (for example, sociology, history, political science) and within the discipline of psychology itself (for example, between social and developmental psychology) in order to take account of political, economic and ethnic factors in the communities which they investigate.

(ii) He indicates that researchers in this field often face danger to themselves and pressures from various groups to report 'the truth' in particular ways. This means that research designs are not always as rigorous as they might otherwise be. As a result, researchers in the area of political violence may be less likely to secure funding or to be published in international journals. The outcome is that research in this area can be small-scale and consequently limited in time and place. If it is only published in local journals, the findings may not be disseminated to fellow researchers in other parts of the world, and so valuable insights and observations are lost.

(iii) He concludes that there is great need for longitudinal studies with a cross-cultural dimension if we are to do more than document atrocities and actually work towards well-evaluated interventions which may have an impact on the cycle of political violence. This research also offers a unique opportunity to observe resilience and coping strategies among young people exposed to unacceptably high levels of societal violence.

Based on material in E. Cairns 1994: *International Journal of Behavioral Development*, 17 (4), 669–74.

Box 16.2
Lasting effects of early education: a report from the Consortium of Longitudinal Studies

Lazar and Darlington attempted an impartial evaluation of the longer-term effectiveness of 11 compensatory education programmes. The individual projects differed; six had used preschool centres, two were home-based and three combined the two methods. The programmes also varied in the content of their curriculum. But what they had in common was that all were concerned with the acquisition of basic cognitive concepts and many stressed language development. All were well-designed studies which had compared the programme children with a control group, and which tested the children before, during and after the intervention began. As many as possible of the children (about three-quarters of the original samples) were traced, assessed on a range of educational and psychological tests, and both they and their families were interviewed. Four main sets of dependent variables were examined:

1   School competence: e.g. whether the child had ever been assigned to a remedial class, or retained in grade (held back to repeat a year in school).
2   Developed abilities: performance in IQ tests and standardized tests of achievement in reading and mathematics.
3   The children's attitudes and values: their self-concept, achievement orientation, and aspirations and attitudes towards education and a career.
4   Impact on family: the effect which participation in an intervention programme had had on the families, how the parents thought about children and what their aspirations were for their children.

Two samples of results are shown in box tables 16.2.1 and 16.2.2. (The number of projects varies, as not all the original projects had data on all the dependent variables.) Box table 16.2.1 shows that in seven out of eight projects fewer programme children were ever held back a year in school, compared with control children. Box table 16.2.2 shows that in six out of six projects more programme children gave achievement-related reasons for being proud of themselves in interview.

These tables show the strength of combining the results of independent studies. Most of the comparisons for individual studies are not statistically significant, but the pooled data are significant and the consistency of individual studies is convincing.

The overall conclusion was that these intervention programmes did have an effect in the long-term on the capacity of low-income children to meet school requirements. Other significant findings were that those who had experienced a programme of compensatory education were significantly less likely to be assigned to special education. Scores on intelligence tests did improve among the programme groups but the differences between the programme and control groups became insignificant over time (see table 16.5).

However, the authors reported some evidence that programme children performed better at

Box Table 16.2.1   Percentage of students retained in grade, in programme versus control groups from eight early intervention programmes

Location of programme	Programme group	Control group	Significance level
North Central Florida	27.6	28.6	n.s.
Tennessee	52.9	68.8	n.s.
New York	24.1	44.7	$p < 0.01$
Ypsilanti, Michigan	4.0	14.9	n.s.
Philadelphia	42.9	51.6	n.s.
Long Island, NY	12.9	18.8	n.s.
Louisville, Kentucky	7.8	0.0	n.s.
New Haven, Connecticut	26.6	32.3	n.s.
Median all projects	25.4	30.5	$p < 0.05$

Source: Lazar and Darlington, 1982

Box Table 16.2.2   Percentage of students giving achievement-related reasons for being proud of themselves, in programme versus control groups from six early intervention programmes

Location of programme	Programme group	Control group	Significance level
North Central Florida	88.2	76.5	n.s.
Tennessee	75.8	52.9	n.s.
Ypsilanti, Michigan	86.2	77.1	n.s.
Philadelphia	65.7	60.0	n.s.
Louisville, Kentucky	78.9	71.9	n.s.
Harlem, NY	77.8	52.4	$p < 0.05$
Median all projects	78.4	66.0	$p < 0.01$

Source: Lazar and Darlington, 1982

mathematics than at reading in relation to controls. More striking were the differences in attitudes towards education. In all groups, children's aspirations far exceeded those of their parents; but the programme children were significantly more likely than controls to give reasons related to school success when asked to describe ways in which they felt proud of themselves. The parents too seemed to have changed as a result of the programmes. Mothers of the programme group children were more likely to report higher educational aspirations for their children than control mothers, and they also reported more satisfaction with their children's performance at school. Interestingly, the authors did not find any significant differences in the long-term effects of early intervention programmes among subgroups of their samples. There was no difference reported between boys and girls, between single-parent families and two-parent families, nor did family size appear to be a significant factor.

The long-term effects of intervention programmes were found to be not so much on developed abilities (academic test achievement) as on school competence, attitudes and values. The authors conclude that there may be 'mutual rein-

forcement processes' in that children who take part in early intervention programmes may raise their mothers' expectations of them. The mothers' encouragement may in turn spur them on and furthermore, positive attitudes towards school are rewarded by teachers. Thus, they argue, high quality programmes can be effective for a number of different types of low-income families. The benefits are measurable; some of the qualitative changes are harder to assess objectively but can be inferred from interview material and from self-evaluation reports.

The quality of the Consortium report rests on the quality of data from the individual projects. The main reservation here is that not all the investigators were truly able to assign children randomly to programme or control groups. Thus (to varying degrees) some of the projects are best described as quasi-experiments rather than true experiments (chapter 1). Nevertheless, the findings rank among the most important and substantial in the area of compensatory education and early intervention.

Based on material in I. Lazar and R. Darlington 1982: *Monographs of the Society for Research in Child Development*, 47 (2–3).

Appendix A
Ethical Principles for Conducting Research with Human Participants

1 Introduction

1.1 The principles given below are intended to apply to research with human participants. Principles of conduct in professional practice are to be found in the Society's Code of Conduct and in the advisory documents prepared by the Divisions, Sections and Special Groups of the Society.

1.2 Participants in psychological research should have confidence in the investigators. Good psychological research is possible only if there is mutual respect and confidence between investigators and participants. Psychological investigators are potentially interested in all aspects of human behaviour and conscious experience. However, for ethical reasons, some areas of human experience and behaviour may be beyond the reach of experiment, observation or other form of

This statement was approved by the Council of the British Psychological Society in February 1990. Further copies may be obtained from the British Psychological Society, St Andrews House, 48 Princess Road East, Leicester LE1 7DR.

psychological investigation. Ethical guidelines are necessary to clarify the conditions under which psychological research is acceptable.

1.3   The principles given below supplement for researchers with human participants the general ethical principles of members of the Society as stated in the British Psychological Society's Code of Conduct (1985). Members of the British Psychological Society are expected to abide by both the Code of Conduct and the fuller principles expressed here. Members should also draw the principles to the attention of research colleagues who are not members of the Society. Members should encourage colleagues to adopt them and ensure that they are followed by all researchers whom they supervise (e.g. research assistants, postgraduate, undergraduate, A-level and GCSE students).

1.4   In recent years, there has been an increase in legal actions by members of the general public against professionals for alleged misconduct. Researchers must recognize the possibility of such legal action if they infringe the rights and dignity of participants in their research.

2   General

2.1   In all circumstances, investigators must consider the ethical implications and psychological consequences for the participants in their research. The essential principle is that the investigation should be considered from the standpoint of all participants; foreseeable threats to their psychological well-being, health, values or dignity should be eliminated. Investigators should recognize that, in our multi-cultural and multi-ethnic society and where investigations involve individuals of different ages, gender and social background, the investigators may not have sufficient knowledge of the implications of an investigation for the participants. It should be borne in mind that the best judges of whether an investigation will cause offence may be members of the population from which the participants in the research are to be drawn.

3   Consent

3.1   Whenever possible, the investigator should inform all participants of the objectives of the investigation. The investigator should inform the participants of all aspects of the research or intervention that might reasonably be expected to influence willingness to participate. The investigator should, normally, explain all other aspects of the research or intervention about which the participants enquire. Failure to make full disclosure prior to obtaining informed consent requires additional safeguards to protect the welfare and dignity of the participants (see section 4).

3.2   Research with children or with participants who have impairments that will limit understanding and/or communication such that they are unable to give their real consent requires special safeguarding procedures.

3.3 Where possible, the real consent of children and of adults with impairments in understanding or communication should be obtained. In addition, where research involves all persons under sixteen years of age, consent should be obtained from parents or from those *in loco parentis*.

3.4 Where real consent cannot be obtained from adults with impairments in understanding or communication, wherever possible the investigator should consult a person well-placed to appreciate the participant's reaction, such as a member of the person's family, and must obtain the disinterested approval of the research from independent advisors.

3.5 When research is being conducted with detained persons, particular care should be taken over informed consent, paying attention to the special circumstances which may affect the person's ability to give free informed consent.

3.6 Investigators should realize that they are often in a position of authority or influence over participants who may be their students, employees or clients. This relationship must not be allowed to pressurize the participants to take part in, or remain in, an investigation.

3.7 The payment of participants must not be used to induce them to risk harm beyond that which they risk without payment in their normal lifestyle.

3.8 If harm, unusual discomfort, or other negative consequences for the individual's future life might occur, the investigator must obtain the disinterested approval of independent advisors, inform the participants, and obtain informed, real consent from each of them.

3.9 In longitudinal research, consent may need to be obtained on more than one occasion.

4 Deception

4.1 The withholding of information or the misleading of participants is unacceptable if the participants are typically likely to object or show unease once debriefed. Where this is in any doubt, appropriate consultation must precede the investigation. Consultation is best carried out with individuals who share the social and cultural background of the participants in the research, but the advice of ethics committees or experienced and disinterested colleagues may be sufficient.

4.2 Intentional deception of the participants over the purpose and general nature of the investigation should be avoided whenever possible. Participants should never be deliberately misled without extremely strong scientific or medical justification. Even then there should be strict controls and the disinterested approval of independent advisors.

4.3 It may be impossible to study some psychological processes without withholding information about the true object of the study or deliberately misleading the participants. Before conducing such a study, the investigator has a special responsibility to (a) determine that alternative procedures avoiding concealment or deception are not available; (b) ensure that the participants are provided with sufficient information at the earliest stage; and (c) consult appropriately upon the way that the withholding of information or deliberate deception will be received.

5 Debriefing

5.1   In studies where the participants are aware that they have taken part in an investigation, when the data have been collected, the investigator should provide the participants with any necessary information to complete their understanding of the nature of the research. The investigator should discuss with the participants their experience of the research in order to monitor any unforeseen negative effects or misconceptions.

5.2   Debriefing does not provide a justification for unethical aspects of an investigation.

5.3   Some effects which may be produced by an experiment will not be negated by a verbal description following the research. Investigators have a responsibility to ensure that participants receive any necessary debriefing in the form of active intervention before they leave the research setting.

6 Withdrawal from the investigation

6.1   At the onset of the investigation investigators should make plain to participants their right to withdraw from the research at any time, irrespective of whether or not payment or other inducement has been offered. It is recognized that this may be difficult in certain observational or organizational settings, but nevertheless the investigator must attempt to ensure that participants (including children) know of their right to withdraw. When testing children, avoidance of the testing situation may be taken as evidence of failure to consent to the procedure and should be acknowledged.

6.2   In the light of experience of the investigation, or as a result of debriefing, the participant has the right to withdraw retrospectively any consent given, and to require that their own data, including recordings, be destroyed.

7 Confidentiality

7.1   Subject to the requirements of legislation, including the Data Protection Act, information obtained about a participant during an investigation is confidential unless otherwise agreed in advance. Investigators who are put under pressure to disclose confidential information should draw this point to the attention of those exerting such pressure. Participants in psychological research have a right to expect that information they provide will be treated confidentially and, if published, will not be identifiable as theirs. In the event that confidentiality and/or anonymity cannot be guaranteed, the participant must be warned of this in advance of agreeing to participate.

8   Protection of participants

8.1   Investigators have a primary responsibility to protect participants from physical and mental harm during the investigation. Normally, the risk of harm must be no greater than in ordinary life, i.e. participants should not be exposed to risks greater than or additional to those encountered in their normal lifestyles. Where the risk of harm is greater than in ordinary life the provisions of 3.8 should apply. Participants must be asked about any factors in the procedure that might create a risk, such as pre-existing medical conditions, and must be advised of any special action they should take to avoid risk.

8.2   Participants should be informed of procedures for contacting the investigator within a reasonable time period following participation should stress, potential harm, or related questions or concern arise despite the precautions required by these Principles. Where research procedures might result in undesirable consequences for participants, the investigator has the responsibility to detect and remove or correct these consequences.

8.3   Where research may involve behaviour or experiences that participants may regard as personal and private the participants must be protected from stress by all appropriate measures, including the assurance that answers to personal questions need not be given. There should be no concealment or deception when seeking information that might encroach on privacy.

8.4   In research involving children, great caution should be exercised when discussing the results with parents, teachers or others *in loco parentis*, since evaluative statements may carry unintended weight.

9   Observational research

9.1   Studies based upon observation must respect the privacy and psychological well-being of the individuals studied. Unless those observed give their consent to being observed, observational research is only acceptable in situations where those observed would expect to be observed by strangers. Additionally, particular account should be taken of local cultural values and of the possibility of intruding upon the privacy of individuals who, even while in a normally public space, may believe they are unobserved.

10   Giving advice

10.1   During research, an investigator may obtain evidence of psychological or physical problems of which a participant is, apparently, unaware. In such a case, the investigator has a responsibility to inform the participant if the investigator believes that by not doing so the participant's future well-being may be endangered.

10.2   If, in the normal course of psychological research, or as a result of problems detected as in 10.1, a participant solicits advice concerning educational, personality, behavioural or health issues, caution should be exercised. If the issue is serious and the investigator is not qualified to offer assistance, the appropriate source of professional advice should be recommended. Further details on the giving of advice will be found in the Society's Code of Conduct.

10.3   In some kinds of investigation the giving of advice is appropriate if this forms an intrinsic part of the research and has been agreed in advance.

11   Colleagues

11.1   Investigators share responsibility for the ethical treatment of research participants with their collaborators, assistants, students and employees. A psychologist who believes that another psychologist or investigator may be conducting research that is not in accordance with the principles above should encourage that investigator to re-evaluate the research.

Appendix B
Careers in Psychology

Psychology can be studied for intrinsic interest or as part of the general educational process, especially at GSCE or AS and A level. It is also a component of training in many people-orientated professions such as teaching, social work, nursing and occupational therapy, speech therapy and management studies. There are a number of careers, however, for which further training in psychology is required, training at degree level and sometimes beyond. A very helpful booklet entitled 'How about Psychology? A guide to courses and careers' is published by the British Psychological Society, 48 Princess Road East, Leicester LE1 7DR. They also publish several other guides, including A. Gale 1990: *Thinking about Psychology?*, and a booklet, 'Career choices in Psychology: A guide to graduate opportunities'. All these, with other materials, are also provided in the BPS Careers Pack, suitable for schools and careers officers. Another useful book, A. Colman 1988: *What is Psychology? The inside story*, London: Hutchinson, provides a readable introduction to what psychology generally covers, as well as advice on careers.

Educational psychologists work with children of school age and their parents and teachers in cases where there are behavioural or emotional problems manifest at school. A degree in psychology and a postgraduate qualification in educational psychology are needed, as well as a teaching qualification and experience.

Clinical psychologists work in hospitals, clinics, or in the community, usually with mentally ill persons, or persons experiencing difficulties of a psychological nature. A good degree in psychology and a postgraduate qualification in clinical psychology are required.

Occupational psychologists work in industry or government, dealing with issues such as personnel selection, job design and the quality of the working environment. A degree in psychology is required, and a postgraduate qualification in occupational psychology is an asset.

Counselling psychologists work in hospitals, clinics, or in the community, usually with people experiencing psychological difficulties; counselling psychologists work through the relationship with the client, and counselling psychology can be viewed as the application of psychological principles to the practice of counselling. A degree in psychology and a postgraduate qualification in counselling psychology are required.

Prison psychologists work in prisons and detention centres. They are concerned with aspects of counselling and training of prison staff, and training and rehabilitation of offenders. A degree in psychology is required.

Research psychologists work in universities, government departments, or other organizations, on diverse aspects of psychological inquiry. A degree in psychology is required, and often a postgraduate research qualification such as a Ph.D.

Teaching in psychology is carried out at universities, institutes of higher education, further education colleges, schools and other educational centres. Would-be teachers require a degree in psychology.

Altogether there are some 5,000 professional psychologists currently employed in the UK. Only a small proportion of psychology graduates become professional psychologists, but many (more than a third) go into careers closely related to psychology, such as social work, teaching, nursing or counselling.

References

Aboud, F. 1988: *Children and Prejudice*. Oxford: Basil Blackwell.

Adams, R. J. 1989: Newborns' discrimination among mid- and long-wavelength stimuli. *Journal of Experimental Child Psychology*, 47, 130–41.

Ainsworth, M. D. S. 1967: *Infancy in Uganda: Infant Care and the Growth of Love*. Baltimore, MD: Johns Hopkins University Press.

Ainsworth, M. D. S. 1973: The development of mother–infant attachment. In B. M. Caldwell and H. N. Ricciutti (eds), *Review of Child Development Research*, vol. 3. Chicago: University of Chicago Press.

Ainsworth, M. D. S., Blehar, M. C., Waters, E. and Wall, S. 1978: *Patterns of Attachment*. Hillsdale, NJ: Erlbaum

Ainsworth, M. D. S. and Bowlby, J. 1991: An ethological approach to personality development. *American Psychologist*, 46, 333–41.

Alexander, J. M. and Schwanenflugel, P. J. 1994: Strategy regulation: The role of intelligence, metacognitive attributions, and knowledge base. *Developmental Psychology*, 30, 709–23.

American Psychiatric Association 1994: *Diagnostic and Statistical Manual of Mental Disorders*, Fourth edition. Washington, D.C.: American Psychiatric Association.

Anderson, J. W. 1972: Attachment behaviour out of doors. In N. Blurton Jones (ed.), *Ethological Studies of Child Behaviour*. Cambridge: Cambridge University Press.

Apgar, V. 1953: A proposal for a new method of evaluation of the newborn infant. *Anesthesiology and Analgesia*, 32, 260–7.

Appel, M. H. 1942: Aggressive behaviour of nursery school children and adult procedures in dealing with such behaviour. *Journal of Experimental Education*, 11, 185–99.

Archer, J. 1989: Childhood gender roles: structure and development. *The Psychologist*, 12, 367–70.

Archer, J. and Lloyd, B. 1986: *Sex and Gender* (2nd edn). Harmondsworth: Penguin.

Archer, S. L. 1982: The lower age boundaries of identity development. *Child Development*, 53, 155–6.

Aries, P. 1962: *Centuries of Childhood: A Social History of the Family*. New York: Vintage Books.

Arnett, J. 1992: Reckless behavior in adolescence: A developmental perspective. *Developmental Review*, 12, 339–73.

Aronson, E. 1978: *The Jigsaw Classroom*. Beverly Hills: Sage.

Aronson, E. and Rosenbloom, S. 1971: Space perception in early infancy: perception within a common auditory-visual space. *Science*, 172, 116.

Asher, S. R. and Coie, J. D. 1990: *Peer Rejection in Childhood*. Cambridge: Cambridge University Press.

Asher, S. R., Parkhurst, J. T., Hymel, S. and Williams, G. A. 1990: Peer rejection and loneliness in childhood. In S. R. Asher and J. D. Coie (eds), *Peer Rejection in Childhood*, pp. 253–73. Cambridge: Cambridge University Press.

Asher, S. R. and Wheeler, V. A. 1985: Children's loneliness: A comparison of rejected and neglected peer status. *Journal of Consulting and Clinical Psychology*, 53, 500–5.

Aslin, R. N. 1981: Development of smooth pursuit in human infants. In D. F. Fisher, R. A. Monty and J. W. Senders (eds), *Eye-Movements: Cognition and Visual Perception*. Hillsdale, NJ: Erlbaum.

Asperger, H. 1944: Die 'Autistischen Psychopathen' in Kindesalter. *Archiv für Psychiatrie und Nervenkrankheiten*, 117, 76–136.

Asquith, S. 1996: When children kill children. *Childhood*, 3, 1, 99–116.

Astington, J. W. 1994: *The Child's Discovery of the Mind*. London: Fontana.

Atkinson, J. and Braddick, O. J. 1981: Acuity, contrast sensitivity and accommodation in infancy. In R. N. Aslin, J. R. Roberts and M. R. Petersen (eds), *The Development of Perception: Psychobiological Perspectives, Vol. 2: The Visual System*. New York: Academic Press.

Atkinson, R. C. and Shiffrin, R. M. 1968: Human memory: A proposed system and its control processes. In K. W. Spence and J. T. Spence (eds), *Advances in the Psychology of Learning and Motivation*, vol. 2. New York: Academic Press.

Atkinson, R. L., Atkinson, R. C. and Hilgard, E. R. 1981: *Introduction to Psychology*, Eighth edition). New York: Harcourt, Brace, Jovanovich.

Aviezer, O., Van IJzendoorn, M. H., Sagi, A. and Schuengel, C. 1994: 'Children of the Dream' revisited: 70 years of collective early child care in Israeli Kibbutzim. *Psychological Bulletin*, 116, 99–116.

Azmitia, M. and Montgomery, R. 1993: Friendship, transactive dialogues, and the development of scientific reasoning. *Social Development*, 2, 202–21.

Baddeley, A. 1992: Working memory. *Science*, 255, 556–9.

Baddeley, A. 1993: *Your Memory: A User's Guide*, Second edition. Harmondsworth: Penguin.

Badian, N. A. 1984: Reading disability in an epidemiological context: Incidence and environmental correlates. *Journal of Learning Disabilities*, 17, 129–36.

Baillargeon, R. and DeVos, J. 1991: Object permanence in young infants: further evidence. *Child Development*, 62, 1227–46.

Baltes, P. B., Reese, H. W. and Lipsitt, L. P. 1980: Life-span developmental psychology. *Annual Review of Psychology*, 31, 65–110.

Bandura, A. 1969: Social learning theory of identificatory processes. In D. A. Goslin (ed.), *Handbook of Socialization Theory and Research*. Chicago: Rand McNally.

Bandura, A. 1971: An analysis of modeling processes. In A. Bandura (ed.), *Psychological Modeling*. New York: Lieber-Atherton.

Banks, M. H. and Ullah, P. 1986: *Youth Unemployment in the 1980s: a Psychological Analysis*. London: Croom Helm.

Banks, M. S., Aslin, R. N. and Letson, R. D. 1975: Sensitive period for the development of human binocular vision. *Science*, 190, 675–7.

Banks, N. 1996: Young single mothers with black children in therapy. *Clinical Child Psychology and Psychiatry*, 1, 1, 19–28.

Baratz, S. S. and Baratz, J. C. 1970: Early childhood intervention: the social science base of institutional racism. *Harvard Educational Review*, 40, 29–50.

Barkow, J. 1989: *Darwin, Sex and Status*. Toronto: University of Toronto Press.

Baron-Cohen, S. 1989: The autistic child's theory of mind: a case of specific developmental delay. *Journal of Child Psychology and Psychiatry*, 30, 285–97.

Baron-Cohen, S. 1995: *Mindblindness: An Essay on Autism and Theory of Mind*. Cambridge, MA: MIT Press.

Baron-Cohen, S., Campbell, R., Karmiloff-Smith, A., Grant, J. and Walker, J. 1995: Are children with autism blind to the mentalistic significance of the eyes? *British Journal of Developmental Psychology*, 13, 379–98.

Baron-Cohen, S., Leslie, A. M. and Frith, U. 1985: Does the autistic child have a 'theory of mind'? *Cognition*, 21, 37–46.

Baron-Cohen, S., Leslie, A. and Frith, U. 1986: Mechanical, behavioral and intentional understanding of picture stories in autistic children. *British Journal of Developmental Psychology*, 4, 113–25.

Barrera, M. and Maurer, D. 1981: The perception of facial expressions by the three-month-old infant. *Child Development*, 52, 203–6.

Barry, H. III., Bacon, M. K. and Child, I. L. 1957: A cross-cultural survey of some sex differences in socialization. *Journal of Abnormal and Social Psychology*, 55, 327–32.

Bar-Tal, D., Raviv, A. and Goldberg, M. 1982: Helping behavior among preschool children: an observational study. *Child Development*, 53, 396–402.

Bates, E., Bretherton, I. and Snyder, L. 1988: *From First Words to Grammar: Individual Differences and Dissociable Mechanisms*. Cambridge: Cambridge University Press.

Bateson, P. P. G. 1982: Preference for cousins in Japanese quail. *Nature*, 295, 236–7.

Baumrind, D. 1967: Child care practices anteceding three patterns of preschool behavior. *Genetic Psychology Monographs*, 75, 43–88.

Baumrind, D. 1980: New directions in socialization research. *American Psychologist*, 35, 639–52.

Baumrind, D. 1993: The average expectable environment is not good enough: a response to Scarr. *Child Development*, 64, 1299–1317.

Baydar, N. and Brooks-Gunn, J. 1991: Effects of maternal employment and child-care arrangements on preschoolers' cognitive and behavioral outcomes. *Developmental Psychology*, 27, 932–45.

Belsky, J. 1984: The determinants of parenting: a process model. *Child Development*, 55, 83–96.

Belsky, J. 1988: Infant day care and socioemotional development: the United States. *Journal of Child Psychology and Psychiatry*, 29, 397–406.

Belsky, J. and Steinberg, L. D. 1978: The effects of day care: a critical review. *Child Development*, 49, 929–49.

Bem, S. L. 1975: Sex role adaptability: one consequence of psychological androgyny. *Journal of Personality and Social Psychology*, 31, 634–43.

Bem, S. L. 1989: Genital knowledge and gender constancy in preschool children. *Child Development*, 60, 649–62.

Ben Shaul, D. M. 1962: The composition of the milk of wild animals. *International Zoo Yearbook*, 4, 333–42.

Bennett, N. and Dunne, E. 1992: *Managing Classroom Groups*. Hemel Hempstead: Simon and Schuster.

Bereiter, C. and Engelmann, S. 1966: *Teaching Disadvantaged Children In the Preschool*. New York: Prentice-Hall.

Bergen, D. 1990: Young children's humour at home and school. Paper given at Eighth International Conference on Humour, Sheffield.

Berndt, T. J. 1982: The features and effects of friendship in early adolescence. *Child Development*, 53, 1447–60.

Berndt, T. J. and Keefe, K. 1995: Friends' influence on adolescents' adjustment to school. *Child Development*, 66, 1312–29.

Bernstein, B. 1962: Social class, linguistic codes and grammatical elements. *Language and Speech*, 5, 31–46.

Bernstein, B. 1971: A socio-linguistic approach to socialization: with some reference to educability. In D. Hymes and J. J. Gumperz (eds), *Directions in Sociolinguistics*. New York: Holt, Rinehart and Winston.

Berry, J. W. 1984: Towards a universal psychology of competence. *International Journal of Psychology*, 19, 335–61.

Best, D. L., Williams, J. E., Cloud, L. M., Davis, S. W., Robertson, L. S., Edwards, J. R., Giles, H. and Fowles, J. 1977: Development of sex-trait stereotypes among young children in the United States, England and Ireland. *Child Development*, 48, 1375–84.

Bickerton, D. 1990: *Language and Species*. Chicago: University of Chicago Press.

Bigelow, B. J. and La Gaipa, J. J. 1980: The development of friendship values and choice. In H. C. Foot, A. J. Chapman and J. R. Smith (eds), *Friendship and Social Relations in Children*. Chichester: Wiley.

Binet, A. and Simon, T. 1905: New methods for diagnosis of the intellectual level of subnormals. *L'Année Psychologique*, 14, 1–90.

Binet, A. and Simon, T. 1916: *The Development of Intelligence in Children*. Baltimore, MD: Williams and Wilkins.

Bjorklund, D. F. 1989: *Children's Thinking: Developmental Function and Individual Differences*. Pacific Grove, CA: Brooks/Cole.

Bjorkqvist, K., Lagerspetz, K. M. J. and Kaukainen, A. 1992: Do girls manipulate and boys fight? Developmental trends in regard to direct and indirect aggression. *Aggressive Behavior*, 18, 117–27.

Blakemore, C. and Cooper, C. R. 1970: Development of the brain depends on the visual environment. *Nature*, 228, 477–8.

Blank, M. and Solomon, F. 1969: How shall the disadvantaged child be taught? *Child Development*, 40, 47–61.

Blos, P. 1962: *On Adolescence*. London: Collier-Macmillan.

Blurton Jones, N. 1967: An ethological study of some aspects of social behaviour of children in nursery school. In D. Morris (ed.), *Primate Ethology*. London: Weidenfeld and Nicolson.

Blurton Jones, N. G. and Konner, M. J. 1973: Sex differences in behaviour of London and Bushmen children. In R. P. Michael and J. H. Crook (eds), *Comparative Ecology and Behaviour of Primates*. London and New York: Academic Press.

Blurton Jones, N. G. and Konner, M. J. 1976: Bushmen knowledge of animal behavior. In R. B. Lee and I. De Vore (eds), *Kalahari Hunter-Gatherers*. Cambridge, MA: Harvard University Press.

Borke, H. 1971: Interpersonal perception of young children: egocentrism or empathy? *Developmental Psychology*, 5, 263–9.

Borke, H. 1975: Piaget's mountains revisited: Changes in the egocentric landscape. *Developmental Psychology*, 11, 240–3.

Bornstein, M. H., Ferdinandsen, K. and Gross, C. G. 1981: Perception of symmetry in infancy. *Developmental Psychology*, 17, 82–6.

Bornstein, M. H., Gaughran, J. M. and Segui, I. 1991: Multimethod assessment of infant temperament: mother questionnaire and mother and observer reports evaluated and compared at five months using the Infant Temperament Measure. *International Journal of Behavioral Development*, 14, 131–51.

Boulton, M. J. 1992: Rough physical play in adolescents: does it serve a dominance function? *Early Education and Development*, 3, 312–33.

Boulton, M. J. and Smith, P. K. 1991: Ethnic and gender partner and activity preferences in mixed-race schools in the UK; playground observations. In C. H. Hart (ed.), *Children in Playgrounds*. New York: SUNY Press.

Boulton, M. J. and Smith, P. K. 1994: Bully/victim problems in middle-school children: stability, self-perceived competence, peer perceptions and peer acceptance. *British Journal of Developmental Psychology*, 12, 315–29.

Boulton, M. J. and Smith, P. K. 1996: Liking and peer perceptions among Asian and White British children. *Journal of Social and Personal Relationships*, 13, 163–77.

Bower, T. G. R. 1965: Stimulus variables determining space perception in infants. *Science*, 149, 88–9.

Bower, T. G. R. 1966: The visual world of infants. *Scientific American*, 215, 80–92.

Bower, T. G. R. 1972: Object perception in infancy. *Perception*, 2, 411–18.

Bower, T. G. R. 1982: *Development in Infancy*, Second edition. San Francisco: W. H. Freeman.

Bower, T. G. R., Broughton, J. M. and Moore, M. K. 1970: Infant responses to moving objects: an indicator of response to distal variables. *Perception and Psychophysics*, 8, 51–3.

Bowlby, J. 1953: *Child Care and the Growth of Love*. Harmondsworth: Penguin.

Bowlby, J. 1969: *Attachment and Loss, Vol. 1, Attachment*. London: Hogarth Press.

Bowlby, J. 1988: *A Secure Base: Clinical Applications of Attachment Theory*. London: Routledge.

Bradley, L. and Bryant, P. E. 1985: *Rhyme and Reason in Reading and Spelling*. International Academy for Research in Learning Disabilities series. Michigan: University of Michigan Press.

Brainerd, C. J. 1983: Working memory systems and cognitive development. In C. J. Brainerd (ed.), *Recent Advances in Cognitive Developmental Theory*. New York: Springer-Verlag.

Breakwell, G. M. and Fife-Schaw, C. 1992: Sexual activities and preferences in a United Kingdom sample of 16 to 20 year olds. *Archives of Sexual Behavior*, 21, 271–93.

Bremner, J. G. 1994: *Infancy*. Second edition. Oxford: Blackwell.

Bretherton, I. 1992: The origins of attachment theory: John Bowlby and Mary Ainsworth. *Developmental Psychology*, 28, 759–75.

Bretherton, I. and Waters, E. (eds) 1985: Growing points of attachment theory and research. *Monographs of the Society for Research in Child Development*, 50, nos 1–2.

Bretherton, I., Fritz, J., Zahn-Waxler, C. and Ridgeway, D. 1986: Learning to talk about emotions; a functionalist perspective. *Child Development*, 57, 529–48.

Brindle, D. 1996: Blacks and Asians at a social disadvantage. *Guardian*, 8 August, p. 9.

British Psychological Society 1990: Psychologists and child sexual abuse. *The Psychologist*, 3, 344–8.

Broadfoot, P. M. 1996: *Education, Assessment and Society*. Buckingham: Open University Press.

Bronfenbrenner, U. 1979: *The Ecology of Human Development*. Cambridge, MA: Harvard University Press.

Brooks-Gunn, J. and Lewis, M. 1981: Infant social perception: responses to pictures of parents and strangers. *Developmental Psychology*, 17, 647–9.

Brown, A. L. and Palenscar, A. S. 1989: Guided, cooperative learning and individual knowledge acquisition. In L. B. Resnick (ed.), *Knowing, Learning and Instruction*. Hillsdale, NJ: Lawrence Erlbaum.

Brown, A. L., Smiley, S. S. and Lawton, S. Q. C. 1978: Intrusion of a thematic idea in children's comprehension and retention of stories. *Child Development*, 48, 1454–66.

Brown, G. W. and Harris, T. 1978: *Social Origins of Depression: A Study of Psychiatric Disorders in Women*. London: Tavistock.

Brown, R. 1973: *A First Language*. Cambridge, MA: Harvard University Press.

Brown, R. and Bellugi, U. 1964: Three processes in the child's acquisition of syntax. In E. H. Lennenberg (ed.), *New Directions in the Study of Language*. Cambridge, MA: MIT Press.

Brown, R., Cazden, C. and Bellugi, U. 1969: The child's grammar from I–III. In J. P. Hill (ed.), *Minnesota Symposia on Child Psychology*, vol. 2. Minneapolis: University of Minnesota Press.

Brown, R. and Fraser, C. 1963: The acquisition of syntax. In C. N. Cofer and B. Musgrave (eds), *Verbal Behavior and Learning: Problems and Processes*, pp. 158–201. New York: McGraw-Hill.

Browne, K. 1989: The naturalistic context of family violence and child abuse. In J. Archer and K. Browne (eds), *Human Aggression: Naturalistic Approaches*. London: Routledge.

Bruner, J. S. 1963: *The Process of Education*. New York: Vintage Books.

Bruner, J. S. 1966: On cognitive growth. In J. S. Bruner, R. R. Oliver and P. M. Greenheld (eds), *Studies in Cognitive Growth*. New York: Wiley.

Bruner, J. S. 1971: *The Relevance of Education*. New York: Norton.

Bruner, J. S. 1972: The nature and uses of immaturity. *American Psychologist*, 27, 687–708.

Bruner, J. S. 1983: *Child's Talk*. New York: Norton.

Bruner, J. S. 1986: *Actual Minds: Possible Worlds*. Cambridge, MA: Harvard University Press.

Bruner, J. S. 1990: *Acts of Meaning*. Cambridge, MA: Harvard University Press.

Bruner, J. S. and Lucariello, J. 1989: Monologue as narrative recreation of the world. In K. Nelson (ed.), *Narratives from the Crib*. Cambridge, MA: Harvard University Press.

Bruner, J. S. and Sherwood, V. 1976: Peekaboo and the learning of rule structures. In J. S. Bruner, A. Jolly and K. Sylva (eds), *Play: its Role in Development and Evolution*. Harmondsworth: Penguin.

Bryant, B., Harris, M. and Newton, D. 1980: *Children and Minders*. London: Grant McIntyre.

Bryant, P. and Bradley, L. 1985: *Children's Reading Problems*. Oxford: Basil Blackwell.

Bryant, P. E., MacLean, M. and Bradley, L. 1990: Rhyme, language and children's reading. *Applied Psycholinguistics*, 11, 3, 237–52.

Bryant, P. E. and Trabasso, T. 1971: Transitive inferences and memory in young children. *Nature*, 232, 456–8.

Buchanan, C. M., Eccles, J. S. and Becker, J. B. 1992: Are adolescents the victims of raging hormones: evidence for activational effects of hormones on moods and behavior at adolescence. *Psychological Bulletin*, 111, 62–107.

Buckhalt, J. A., Mahoney, G. J. and Paris, S. G. 1976: Efficiency of self-generated elaborations by EMR and nonretarded children. *American Journal of Mental Deficiency*, 81, 93–6.

Buis, J. M. and Thompson, D. N. 1989: Imaginary audience and personal fable: a brief review. *Adolescence*, 24, 773–81.

Bukowski, W. M., Hoza, B. and Boivin, M. 1994: Measuring friendship quality during pre- and early adolescence: the development and psychometric properties of the Friendship Qualities Scale. *Journal of Social and Personal Relationships*, 11, 471–84.

Bullough, V. L. 1981: Age at menarche: a misunderstanding. *Science*, 213, 365–6.

Burman, E. 1996: International Children's Rights Legislation. *Childhood*, 3, 45–66.

Buss, D. M. and Schmitt, D. P. 1993: Sexual strategies theory: an evolutionary perspective on human mating. *Psychological Review*, 100, 204–32.

Butterworth, G. 1987: Some benefits of egocentrism. In J. S. Bruner and H. Haste (eds), *Making Sense*. London: Methuen.

Byrne, R. and Whiten, A. 1987: The thinking primate's guide to deception. *New Scientist*, 116, 54–6.

Byrne, R. W. and Whiten, A. (eds) 1988: *Machiavellian Intelligence: Social Expertise and the Evolution of Intellect in Monkeys, Apes, and Humans*. Oxford: Clarendon Press.

Cairns, R. B., Cairns, B. D., Neckerman, H. J., Gest, S. D. and Gariepy, J. L. 1988: Social networks and aggressive behavior. Peer acceptance or peer rejection? *Developmental Psychology*, 24, 815–23.

Cairns, R. B., Leung, M-C., Buchanan, L. and Cairns, B. D. 1995: Friendships and social networks in childhood and adolescence: fluidity, reliability, and interrelations. *Child Development*, 66, 1330–45.

Call, J. and Tomasello, M. 1996: The role of humans in the cognitive development of apes. In A. E. Russon (ed.), *Reaching into Thought: Minds of the Great Apes*. Cambridge: Cambridge University Press.

Campos, J. J., Caplovitz, K. B., Lamb, M. E., Goldsmith, H. H. and Stenberg, C. 1983: Socioemotional development. In M. M. Haith and J. J. Campos (eds), *Handbook of Child Psychology: Vol. 2, Infancy and Developmental Psychobiology*. New York: Wiley.

Campos, J. J., Langer, A. and Krowitz, A. 1970: Cardiac responses on the visual cliff in prelocomotor human infants. *Science*, 170, 196–7.

Caplan, N., Choy, M. and Whitmore, J. 1992: Indochinese refugee families and academic achievement. *Scientific American*, 266, February, 18–24.

Carlsson-Paige, N. and Levin, D. E. 1987: *The War Play Dilemma: Balancing Needs and Values in the Early Childhood Classroom*. New York: Teachers College, Columbia University.

Carlsson-Paige, N. and Levin, D. E. 1990: *Who's Calling the Shots?: How to Respond Effectively to Children's Fascination with War Play and War Toys*. Philadelphia, PA: New Society Publishers.

Carr, R. 1994: Peer helping in Canada. *Peer Counselling Journal*, 11, 6–9.

Carr, W. 1991: Education for citizenship. *British Journal of Educational Studies*, 39, 373–85.

Case, R. 1978: Intellectual development from birth to adulthood: a neo-Piagetian interpretation. In R. S. Siegler (ed.), *Children's Thinking: What Develops?* Hillsdale, NJ: Erlbaum.

Case, R. 1985: *Intellectual Development: Birth to Adulthood*. New York: Academic Press.

Caspi, A., Henry, B., McGee, R. O., Moffitt, T. E. and Silva, P. A. 1995: Temperamental origins of child and adolescent behavior problems: from age three to age fifteen. *Child Development*, 66, 55–68.

Castillo, M. and Butterworth, G. E. 1981: Neonatal localisation of a sound in visual space. *Perception*, 10, 331–8.

Ceci, S. J. and Bruck, M. 1993: The suggestibility of the child witness: a historical review and synthesis. *Psychological Bulletin*, 113, 403–39.

Charman, T. and Baron-Cohen, S. 1992: Understanding drawings and beliefs: a further test of the metarepresentation theory of autism. *Journal of Child Psychology and Psychiatry*, 33, 1105–12.

Cherlin, A. J., Furstenberg, F. F. Jr., Chase-Lonsdale, P. L. Kiernan, K. E., Robins, P. K., Morrison, D. R. and Teitler, J. O. 1991: Longitudinal studies of effects of divorce on children in Great Britain and the United States. *Science*, 252, 1386–9.

Chi, M. T. H. 1978: Knowledge structures and memory development. In R. Siegler (ed.), *Children's Thinking: What Develops?* Hillsdale, NJ: Erlbaum.

Chomsky, C. 1969: *The Acquisition of Syntax in Children from 5 to 10*. Cambridge, MA: MIT Press.

Chomsky, N. 1959: Review of Skinner's Verbal Behaviour, *Language*, 35, 26–58.

Chomsky, N. 1965: *Aspects of a Theory of Syntax*. Cambridge, MA: MIT Press.

Chomsky, N. 1986: *Knowledge of Language*. New York: Praeger.

Christie, J. F. 1986: Training of symbolic play. In P. K. Smith (ed.), *Children's Play: Research Development and Practical Applications*. London: Gordon and Breach.

Chukovsky, K. 1963: *From Two to Five*. Berkeley and Los Angeles: University of California Press.

Cillessen, A. H. N., Van IJzendoorn, H. W., Van Lieshout, C. F. M. and Hartup, W. W. 1992: Heterogeneity among peer-rejected boys: subtypes and stabilities. *Child Development*, 63, 893–905.

Clark, A. H., Wyon, S. M. and Richards, M. P. M. 1969: Free-play in nursery school children. *Journal of Child Psychology and Psychiatry*, 10, 205–16.

Clarke, A. M. and Clarke, A. D. B. 1976: *Early Experience: Myth and Evidence*. London: Open Books.

Clarke, L. 1992: Children's family circumstances: recent trends in Great Britain. *European Journal of Population*, 8, 309–40.

Clarke-Stewart, A. 1973: Interactions between mothers and their young children: characteristics and consequences. *Monographs of the Society for Research in Child Development*, 38 (serial no. 153).

Clarke-Stewart, A. 1982: *Day Care*. Glasgow: Fontana.

Clarke-Stewart, A. 1989: Infant day care: maligned or malignant? *American Psychologist*, 44, 266–73.

Clarke-Stewart, K. A. 1991: A home is not a school. *Journal of Social Issues*, 47, 105–23.

Clifford, B. R., Gunter, B. and McAleer, J. 1995: *Program Evaluation, Comprehension and Impact*. Hillsdale, NJ: Erlbaum.

Cohen, L. J. and Campos, J. J. 1974: Father, mother and stranger as elicitors of attachment behaviour in infancy. *Developmental Psychology*, 10, 146–54.

Coie, J. D. and Dodge, K. A. 1983: Continuities and changes in children's social status: A five-year longitudinal study. *Merrill-Palmer Quarterly*, 29, 261–82.

Coie, J. D. and Krehbiel, G. 1984: Effects of academic tutoring on the social status of low-achieving, socially rejected children. *Child Development*, 55, 1465–78.

Colby, A., Kohlberg, L., Gibbs, J. and Lieberman, M. 1983: A longitudinal study of moral judgement. *Monographs of the Society for Research in Child Development*, 48, nos 1–2.

Cole, P. M. 1986: Children's spontaneous control of facial expression. *Child Development*, 57, 1309–21.

Coleman, J. C. 1980: *The Nature of Adolescence*. London: Methuen.

Coleman, J. C. and Hendry, L. 1990: *The Nature of Adolescence*, Second edition. London: Routledge.

Coleman, J. S. 1961: *The Adolescent Society*. London: Collier-Macmillan.

Coleman, J. S., Campbell, E. Q., Hobson, C. J., McPortland, J., Wood, A. M., Weinfield, F. D. and York, R. L. 1966: *Equality of Educational Opportunity*. Washington, D.C.: Government Printing Office.

Collaer, M. L. and Hines, M. 1995: Human behavioral sex differences: a role for gonadal hormones during early development? *Psychological Bulletin*, 118, 55–107.

Collins, W. A., Sobol, B. L. and Westby, S. 1981: Effects of adults' commentary on children's comprehension and inferences about a televised aggressive portrayal. *Child Development*, 52, 158–63.

Commission for Racial Equality. 1988: *Learning in Terror: A Survey of Racial Harassment in Schools and Colleges.* London: CRE.

Condon, W. D. and Sander, L. W. 1974: Neonate movement is synchronized with adult speech: interactional participation and language acquisition. *Science*, 183, 99–101.

Conger, J. J. 1977: *Adolescence and Youth*, Second edition. New York: Harper and Row.

Connolly, J. A. and Doyle, A. B. 1984: Relation of social fantasy play to social competence in preschoolers. *Developmental Psychology*, 20, 797–806.

Cook, T. D. and Campbell, D. T. 1979: *Quasi-experimentation.* Chicago: Rand McNally.

Costabile, A., Genta, M. L., Zucchini, E., Smith, P. K. and Harker, R. 1992: Attitudes of parents towards war play in young children. *Early Education and Development*, 3, 356–69.

Costabile, A., Smith, P. K., Matheson, L., Aston, J., Hunter, T. and Boulton, M. 1991: Cross-national comparison of how children distinguish serious and playful fighting. *Developmental Psychology*, 27, 881–7.

Cote, J. 1992: Was Mead wrong about coming of age in Samoa? An analysis of the Mead/Freeman controversy for scholars of adolescence and human development. *Journal of Youth and Adolescence*, 21, 499–527.

Cote, J. E. and Levine, C. 1988: A critical examination of the ego identity status paradigm. *Developmental Review*, 8, 147–84.

Cowan, F. M. and Johnson, A. M. 1993: HIV, AIDS and adolescents. *ACPP Review & Newsletter*, 15, 49–54.

Cowen, E. L., Pederson, A., Babigian, H., Izzo, L. D. and Trost, M. A. 1973: Long-term follow-up of early detected vulnerable children. *Journal of Consulting and Clinical Psychology*, 41, 438–46.

Cowie, H. and Rudduck, J. 1988: *Cooperative Group Work: School and Classroom Studies.* London: British Petroleum Educational Services.

Cowie, H. and Sharp, S. 1996: *Peer Counselling in Schools: a Time to Listen.* London: David Fulton.

Cowie, H., Smith, P. K., Boulton, M. and Laver, R. 1994: *Cooperation in the Multi-ethnic Classroom.* London: David Fulton.

Creighton, S. J. and Noyes, P. 1989: *Child Abuse Trends in England and Wales 1983–1987.* London: NSPCC.

Crick, N. R. and Dodge, K. 1994: A review and reformulation of social-information-processing mechanisms in children's social adjustment. *Psychological Bulletin*, 115, 74–101.

Crick, N. R., and Grotpeter, J. K. 1995: Relational aggression, gender, and social-psychological adjustment. *Child Development*, 66, 710–22.

Crittenden, P. M. 1988: Distorted patterns of relationship in maltreating families: the role of internal representation models. *Journal of Reproductive and Infant Psychology*, 6, 183–99.

Crook, C. 1994: *Computers and the Collaborative Experience of Learning.* London: Routledge.

Cullingford, C. 1984: *Children and Television.* Aldershot: Gower.

Cummings, E. M., Iannotti, R. J. and Zahn-Waxler, C. 1985: Influence of conflict between adults on the emotions and aggression of young children. *Developmental Psychology*, 21, 495–507.

Cummings, E. M., Iannotti, R. J. and Zahn-Waxler, C. 1989: Aggression between peers in early childhood: individual continuity and developmental change. *Child Development*, 60, 887–95.

Curtiss, S. 1977: *Genie: a Psycholinguistic Study of a Modern-day 'Wild Child'*. New York: Academic Press.

Daly, M. and Wilson, M. I. 1982: Whom are newborn babies said to resemble? *Ethology and Sociobiology*, 3, 69–78.

Daly, M. and Wilson, M. 1996: Violence against stepchildren. *Current Directions in Psychological Science*, 5, 77–81.

Damon, W. 1977: *The Social World of the Child*. San Francisco: Jossey-Bass.

Daniels, H. (ed.) 1996: *An Introduction to Vygotsky*. London: Routledge.

Danner, F. W. and Day, M. C. 1977: Eliciting formal operations. *Child Development*, 48, 1600–6.

Dansky, J. L. 1985: Questioning 'A paradigm questioned': a commentary on Simon and Smith. *Merrill-Palmer Quarterly*, 31, 279–84.

Darling, N. and Steinberg, L. 1993: Parenting style as context: an integrative model. *Psychological Bulletin*, 113, 487–96.

Darwin C. 1877: A biographical sketch of an infant. *Mind*, 2, 285–94.

Davey, A. 1983: *Learning to be Prejudiced; Growing Up in Multi-ethnic Britain*. London: Edward Arnold.

Davie, R. 1973: Eleven years of childhood. *Statistical News*, 22, 14–18.

Davie, R., Butler, N. and Goldstein, H. 1972: *From Birth to Seven* (Second Report of the National Child Development Study). London: Longman and National Children's Bureau.

Davies, G. 1988: Use of video in child abuse trials. *The Psychologist*, 10, 20–2.

Davies, G. and Cummings, E. M. 1994: Marital conflict and child adjustment. *Psychological Bulletin*, 116, 387–411.

Davis, L. S. 1984: Alarm calling in Richardson's group squirrels (Spermophilus Richardsonii). *Zeitschrift für Tierpsychologie*, 66, 152–64.

DeCasper, A. J. and Fifer, W. P. 1980: Of human bonding: newborns prefer their mothers' voices. *Science*, 208, 1174–6.

DeCasper, A. J. and Spence, M. J. 1986: Prenatal maternal speech influences newborn's perception of speech sounds. *Infant Behavior and Development*, 9, 133–50.

Dekovic, M. and Janssens, J. M. A. M. 1992: Parents' child-rearing style and child's sociometric status. *Developmental Psychology*, 28, 925–32.

Dennis, W. 1973: *Children of the Creche*. New York: Appleton-Century-Crofts.

Dent, H. and Flin, R. (eds) 1992: *Children as Witnesses*. Chichester: Wiley.

Department of the Environment. 1973: Children at Play. *Design Bulletin*, 27. London: HMSO.

Dias, M. G. and Harris, P. 1988: The effect of make-believe play on deductive reasoning. *British Journal of Developmental Psychology*, 6, 207–21.

Dias, M. G. and Harris, P. 1990: The influence of the imagination on reasoning by young children. *British Journal of Developmental Psychology*, 8, 305–18.

Dishion, T., Andrews, D. W. and Crosby, L. 1995: Antisocial boys and their friends in early adolescence: relationship characteristics, quality, and interactional process. *Child Development*, 88, 139–51.

Dixon, P. 1986: *The Silver Toilet Roll*. Winchester: Cheriton Books.

Dodge, K. A., Pettit, G. S., McClaskey, C. L. and Brown, M. M. 1986: Social competence in children. *Monographs of the Society for Research in Child Development*, 51, 2.

Dodge, K. A., Schlundt, D. C., Shocken, I. and Delugach, J. D. 1983: Social competence and children's sociometric status: the role of peer group entry strategies. *Merrill-Palmer Quarterly*, 29, 309–36.

Doise, W. 1990: The development of individual competencies through social interaction. In H. Foot, M. Morgan and R. Shute (eds), *Children Helping Children*. Chichester: John Wiley.

Donaldson, M. 1978: *Childrens' Minds*. London: Fontana.

Douglas, J. W. B. 1975: Early hospital admissions and later disturbances of behaviour and learning. *Developmental Medicine and Child Neurology*, 17, 456–80.

Douglas, J. W. B. and Ross, J. M. 1964: Age of puberty related to educational ability, attainment and school leaving age. *Journal of Child Psychology and Psychiatry*, 5, 185–96.

Douvan, E. 1979: Sex role learning. In J. C. Coleman (ed.), *The School Years*. London: Methuen.

Douvan, E. and Adelson, J. 1966: *The Adolescent Experience*. New York: Wiley.

Drumm, P., Gardner, B. T. and Gardner, R. A. 1986: Vocal and gestural responses to announcements and events by cross-fostered chimpanzees. *American Journal of Psychology*, 99, 1–30.

Dunn, J. 1984: *Sisters and Brothers*. London: Fontana.

Dunn, J. 1988: *The Beginnings of Social Understanding*. Oxford: Basil Blackwell.

Dunn, J. 1995: Studying relationships and social understanding. In P. Barnes (ed.), *Personal, Social and Emotional Development of Children*. Oxford: Basil Blackwell, in association with the Open University.

Dunn, J., Brown, J. R. and Beardsall, L. 1991: Family talk about emotions, and children's later understanding of others' emotions. *Developmental Psychology*, 27, 448–55.

Dunn, J. and Kendrick, C. 1982: *Siblings: Love, Envy and Understanding*. Oxford: Basil Blackwell.

Dunphy, D. C. 1963: The social structure of urban adolescent peer groups. *Sociometry*, 26, 230–46.

Durkin, K. 1985: *Television, Sex Roles and Children*. Milton Keynes: Open University Press.

Durkin, K. 1995: *Developmental Social Psychology*. Oxford: Blackwell Publishers.

Dyson-Hudson, N. 1963: Karimojong age system. *Ethnology*, 3, 353–401.

Eames, D., Shorrocks, D. and Tomlinson, P. 1990: Naughty animals or naughty experimenters? Conservation accidents revisited with video-simulated commentary. *British Journal of Developmental Psychology*, 8, 25–37.

Edwards, C. P. and Lewis, M. 1979: Young children's concepts of social relations: social functions and social objects. In M. Lewis and L. A. Rosenblum (eds), *The Child and its Family*. New York: Plenum Press.

Eggleston, J., Dunn, D. and Anjali, M. 1986: *Education for Some: The Educational and Vocational Experiences of 15–18-year-old Members of Minority Ethnic Groups*. Stoke-on-Trent: Trentham Books.

Eibl-Eibesfeldt, I. 1971: *Love and Hate*. London: Methuen.

Eibl-Eibesfeldt, I. 1972: Similarities and differences between cultures in expressive movements. In R. A. Hinde (ed.), *Non-Verbal Communication*. Cambridge: Cambridge University Press.

Eibl-Eibesfeldt, I. 1989: *Human Ethology*. New York: Aldine de Gruyter.

Eifermann, R. 1970: Level of children's play as expressed in group size. *British Journal of Educational Psychology*, 40, 161–70.

Eimas, P. 1985: The perception of speech in early infancy. *Scientific American*, 252, no. 1.

Eimas, P. D., Miller, J. L. and Jusczyk, P. 1987: On infant perception and the acquisition of language. In S. Harnad (ed.), *Categorical Perception*. Cambridge: Cambridge University Press.

Eisenberg, N. 1983: Children's differentiations among potential recipients of aid. *Child Development*, 54, 594–602.

Eisenberg, N. and Mussen, P. 1989: *The Roots of Pro-social Behaviour in Children*. Cambridge: Cambridge University Press.

Eisenberg-Berg, N. and Hand, M. 1979: The relationship of preschoolers' reasoning about prosocial moral conflict to prosocial behaviour. *Child Development*, 50, 356–63.

Elkind, D. 1967: Egocentrism in adolescence. *Child Development*, 38, 1025–34.

Elliot, C. D., Murray, D. J. and Pearson, L. S. 1983: *British Ability Scales (BAS)*. Windsor: NFER-Nelson.

Emmerich W., Goldman, K. S., Kirsh, B. and Sharabany, R. 1976: Development of gender constancy in disadvantaged children. Unpublished report, Educational Testing Service, Princeton, NJ.

Engel, S. 1994: *The Stories Children Tell*. New York: Freeman.

Engestrom, Y. 1996: Non scolae sed vitae discimus. In H. Daniels (ed.), *An Introduction to Vygotsky*. London: Routledge.

Erikson, E. 1968: *Identity: Youth and Crisis*. London: Faber.

Eron, L. D. 1987: The development of aggressive behavior from the perspective of a developing behaviorism. *American Psychologist*, 42, 435–42.

Espin, O. M., Stewart, A. J. and Gomez, C. A. 1990: Letters from V: Adolescent personality development in sociohistorical context. *Journal of Personality*, 58, 347–64.

Fagan, R. M. 1974: Selective and evolutionary aspects of animal play. *American Naturalist*, 108, 850–8.

Fagot, B. I. 1978: The influence of sex of child on parental reactions to toddler children. *Child Development*, 49, 459–65.

Fagot, B. I. 1985: Beyond the reinforcement principle: another step toward understanding sex role development. *Developmental Psychology*, 21, 1097–104.

Falbo, T. and Polit, D. F. 1986: Quantitative review of the only child literature: research evidence and theory development. *Psychological Bulletin*, 100, 176–89.

Fantz, R. L. 1961: The origin of form perception. *Scientific American*, 204 (May), 66–72.

Fantz, R. L. and Fagan, J. F. 1975: Visual attention to size and number of pattern details by term and pre-term infants during the first six months. *Child Development*, 46, 3–18.

Fantz, R. L. and Miranda, S. B. 1975: Newborn infant attention to form of contour. *Child Development*, 46, 224–8.

Farrell, C. 1978: *My Mother Said*. London: Routledge and Kegan Paul.

Farrington, D. P. 1990: Childhood aggression and adult violence: early precursors and later-life outcomes. In D. J. Pepler and K. H. Rubin (eds), *The Development of Childhood Aggression*. Hillsdale, NJ: Erlbaum.

Fawcett, A. J. and Nicolson, R. I. 1996: Impaired performance of children with dyslexia on a range of cerebellar tasks. *Annals of Dyslexia*, 46, 259–83.

Fein, G. G. 1975: A transformational analysis of pretending. *Developmental Psychology*, 77, 291–6.

Feinman, S. 1982: Social referencing in infancy. *Merill-Palmer Quarterly*, 28, 445–70.

Feiring, C., Lewis, M. and Starr, M. D. 1984: Indirect effects and infants' reaction to strangers. *Developmental Psychology*, 20, 485–91.

Fenson, L. and Schnell, R. E. 1986: The origins of exploratory play. In P. K. Smith (ed.), *Children's Play: Research Developments and Practical Applications*. London: Gordon and Breach.

Fernald, A. and Mazzie, C. 1991: Prosody and focus in speech to infants and adults. *Developmental Psychology*, 27, 209–21.

Ferreiro, E. 1985: Literacy development: a psychogenic perspective. In D. Olson, N. Torrance and A. Hildyard (eds), *Literacy, Language and Learning*. Cambridge: Cambridge University Press.

Ferri, E. 1984: *Stepchildren: a National Study*. London: NFER-Nelson.

Field, T. 1984: Separation stress of young children transferring to new school. *Developmental Psychology*, 20, 786–92.

Field, T., Woodson, R., Greenberg, R. and Cohen, D. 1982: Discrimination and imitation of Facial expression by neonates. *Science*, 218, 179–81.

Fifer, W. P. and Moon, C. 1989: Psychobiology of newborn auditory preferences. *Seminars in Perinatology*, 13, 430–3.

Finkelstein, N. W. and Haskins, R. 1983: Kindergarten children prefer same-color peers. *Child Development*, 54, 502–8.

Fishbein, H. D. 1976: *Education, Development, and Children's Learning*. Pacific Palisades, CA: Goodyear Publishing Company.

Fisher, R. P. and Geiselman, R. E. 1992: Memory-enhancing techniques for investigative interviewing. *The Cognitive Interview*. Springfield, IL: Charles Thomas.

Fisher, R. P. and McCauley, M. R. 1995: Improving eyewitness testimony with the cognitive interview. In M. S. Zaragoza, J. R. Graham, G. C. Hall, R. Hirschman and Y. S. Ben-Porath (eds), *Memory and Testimony in the Child Witness*. Thousand Oaks, CA: Sage.

Flavell, J. H. 1988: The development of children's knowledge about the mind: from cognitive correlations to mental representation. In J. W. Astington, P. L. Harris and D. R. Olson (eds), *Developing Theories of Mind*. Cambridge: Cambridge University Press.

Flavell, J. H., Beach, D. R. and Chinsky, J. M. 1966: Spontaneous verbal rehearsal in a memory task as a function of age. *Child Development*, 37, 283–99.

Flavell, J. H., Friedrichs, A. G. and Hoyt, J. D. 1970: Developmental changes in memorization processes. *Cognitive Psychology*, 1, 324–40.

Flavell, J. H., Green, F. L. and Flavell, E. R. 1986: Development of knowledge about the appearance–reality distinction. *Monographs of the Society for Research in Child Development*, 51, no. 212.

Flavell, J. H., Miller, P. H. and Miller, S. A. 1993: *Cognitive Development*, Third edition. Englewood Cliffs, NJ: Prentice-Hall.

Foley, M. A., Wilder, A., McCall, R. and Van Vorst, R. 1993: The consequences for recall of children's ability to generate interactive imagery in the absence of external supports. *Journal of Experimental Psychology*, 56, 173–200.

Fonagy, P., Steele, M., Steele, H., Higgitt, A. and Target, M. 1994: The theory and practice of resilience. *Journal of Child Psychology and Psychiatry*, 35, no. 2, 231–57.

Foot, H., Morgan, M. and Shute, R. (eds) 1990: *Children Helping Children*. Chichester: John Wiley.

Ford, M. E. 1979: The construct validity of egocentrism. *Psychological Bulletin*, 86, 1169–88.

Fox, N. 1977: Attachment of Kibbutz infants to mother and metapelet. *Child Development*, 48, 1228–39.

Fox, N. 1995: Of the way we were: Adult memories about attachment experiences and their role in determining infant-parent relationships: A commentary on van IJzendoorn (1995). *Psychological Bulletin*, 117, 404–10.

Fox, N., Kimmerly, N. L. and Schafer, W. D. 1991: Attachment to mother/ attachment to father: a meta-analysis. *Child Development*, 62, 210–25.

Freedman, J. L. 1984: Effect of television violence on aggressiveness. *Psychological Bulletin*, 96, 227–46.

Freeman, D. 1983: *Margaret Mead and Samoa: the Making and Unmaking of an Anthropological Myth*. Cambridge, MA: Harvard University Press.

Freeman, D. 1996: *Franz Boas and the Flower of Heaven: Coming of Age in Samoa and the Fateful Hoaxing of Margaret Mead*. Harmondsworth: Penguin.

Freeman, J. 1980: Giftedness in a social context. In R. Povey (ed.), *Educating the Gifted Child*. London: Harper and Row.

Freeman, N. H., Lewis, C. and Doherty, M. J. 1991: Preschoolers grasp of a desire for knowledge in false-belief prediction: practical intelligence and verbal report. *British Journal of Developmental Psychology*, 9, 139–57.

Friedrich, L. K. and Stein, A. H. 1973: Aggressive and prosocial television programs and the natural behavior of preschool children. *Monographs of the Society for Research in Child Development*, 38, no. 4.

Frisch, R. E. 1988: Fatness and fertility. *Scientific American*, March, 71–8.

Frith, U. 1989: *Autism: Explaining the Enigma*. Oxford: Basil Blackwell.

Froebel, F. 1906: *The Education of Man*. New York: Appleton.

Fuligni, A. J. and Eccles, J. S. 1993: Perceived parent–child relationships and early adolescents' orientation toward peers. *Developmental Psychology*, 29, 622–32.

Fundudis, T. 1989: Children's memory and the assessment of possible child sex abuse. *Journal of Child Psychology and Psychiatry*, 30, 337–46.

Furman, W., Rahe, D. F. and Hartup, W. W. 1979: Rehabilitation of socially withdrawn preschool children through mixed-age and same-age socialization. *Child Development*, 50, 915–22.

Furrow, D., Nelson, K. and Benedict, H. 1979: Mothers' speech to children and syntactic development: some simple relationships. *Journal of Child Language*, 6, 423–42.

Galambos, N. L. and Almeida, D. M. 1992: Does parent–adolescent conflict decrease in early adolescence? *Journal of Marriage and the Family*, 54, 737–47.

Gallup, G. G. Jr. 1982: Self-awareness and the emergence of mind in primates. *American Journal of Primatology*, 2, 237–48.

Ganchrow, J. R., Steiner, J. E., and Daher, M. 1983: Neonatal facial expressions in response to different qualities and intensities of gustatory stimuli. *Infant Behavior and Development*, 6, 473–84.

Garcia, J., Ervin, F. R. and Koelling, R. A. 1966: Learning with prolonged delay of reinforcement. *Psychonomic Science*, 5, 121–2.

Gardner, H. 1980: *Artful Scribbles*. London: Jill Norman.

Gardner, H. 1983: *Frames of Mind: the Theory of Multiple Intelligence*. New York: Basic Books.

Gardner, R. A. and Gardner, B. T. 1969: Teaching sign language to a chimpanzee. *Science*, 165, 664–72.

Garvey, C. 1977: *Play*. London: Fontana/Open Books.

Gelfand, D. M., Hartmann, D. P., Cromer, C. C., Smith, C. L. and Page, B. C. 1975: The effects of instructional prompts and praise on children's donation rates. *Child Development*, 46, 980–3.

Genta, M. L., Menesini, E., Fonzi, A., Costabile, A. and Smith, P. K. 1996: Bullies and victims in schools in central and southern Italy. *European Journal of Psychology of Education*, 11, 97–110.

Gibson, E. and Spelke, E. 1983: The development of perception. In P. Mussen (ed.), *Handbook of Child Psychology*, vol. III, New York: Wiley.

Gibson, E. J. and Walk, R. D. 1960: The 'visual cliff'. *Scientific American*, 202 (April), 64–71.

Gil, D. 1970: *Violence against Children*. Cambridge, MA: Harvard University Press.

Gilligan, C. 1982: *In a Different Voice: Psychological Theory and Women's Development*. Cambridge, MA: Harvard University Press.

Gilmartin, B. G. 1987: Peer group antecedents of severe love-shyness in males. *Journal of Personality*, 55, 467–89.

Ginsburg, H. and Opper, S. 1979: *Piaget's Theory of Intellectual Development: An Introduction*. Englewood Cliffs, NJ: Prentice-Hall.

Gipps, C. and Murphy, P. 1994: *A Fair Test? Assessment, Achievement and Equity*. Buckingham: Open University Press.

Gipps, C. and Stobart, G. 1993: *Assessment. A Teacher's Guide to the Issues*, Second edition. London: Hodder and Stoughton.

Glaser, D. and Collins, C. 1989: The response of young, non-sexually abused children to anatomically correct dolls. *Journal of Child Psychology and Psychiatry*, 30, 547–60.

Gleitman, L. R., Newport, E. and Gleitman, H. 1984: The current status of the motherese hypothesis. *Journal of Child Language*, 11, 43–79.

Gleitman, L. R. and Wanner, E. 1982: Language acquisition: The state of the state of the art. In E. Wanner and L. R. Gleitman (eds), *Language Acquisition: the State of the Art*. Cambridge: Cambridge University Press.

Goldberg, S. 1983: Parent–infant bonding: another look. *Child Development*, 54, 1355–82.

Goldfarb, W. 1947: Variations in adolescent adjustment of institutionally reared children. *American Journal of Orthopsychiatry*, 17, 449–57.

Goldman, R. and Goldman, J. 1982: *Children's Sexual Thinking*. London: Routledge and Kegan Paul.

Goldstein, J. H. 1994: Sex differences in toy play and use of video games. In J. H. Goldstein (ed.), *Toys, Play and Child Development*. Cambridge: Cambridge University Press.

Goldstein, J. H. 1995: Aggressive toy play. In A. D. Pellegrini (ed.), *The Future of Play Theory*. Albany, NY: SUNY Press.

Golombok, S. and Fivush, R. 1994: *Gender Development*. Cambridge: Cambridge University Press.

Goodman, G. S. and Bottoms, B. L. (eds) 1993: *Child Victims, Child Witnesses. Understanding and Improving Testimony*. New York: Guilford Press.

Goodman, G. S. and Reed, R. S. 1986: Age differences in eyewitness testimony. *Law and Human Behavior*, 10, 317–32.

Goodman, G. S., Hepps, D. and Reed, R. S. 1986: The child victim's testimony. In A. Haralambie (ed.), *New Issues for Child Advocates*. Phoenix, AZ: Arizona Association for Children.

Goodman, G. S., Rudy, L., Bottoms, B. and Aman, C. 1990: Children's concerns and memory: issues of ecological validity in the study of children's eyewitness testimony. In R. Fivush and J. Hudson (eds), *Knowing and Remembering in Young Children*. Cambridge: Cambridge University Press.

Gordon, F. and Yonas, A. 1976: Sensitivity to binocular depth information. *Journal of Experimental Child Psychology*, 22, 413–22.

Goren, C., Sarty, M. and Wu, P. 1975: Visual following and pattern discrimination of face-like stimuli by new born infants. *Pediatrics*, 56, 544–9.

Gottman, J. M. and Katz, L. F. 1989: Effects of marital discord on young children's peer interaction and health. *Developmental Psychology*, 25, 373–81.

Gould, S. J. 1981: *The Mismeasure of Man*. Harmondsworth: Penguin.

Greenberg, B. S. 1976: Viewing and listening: parameters among British youngsters. In R. Brown (ed.), *Children and Television*. London: Collier-Macmillan.

Greenfield, P. M. 1984: *Mind and Media: the Effects of Television, Video Games and Computers*. Aylesbury: Fontana.

Greenfield, P. M. and Lave, J. 1982: Cognitive aspects of informal education. In D. A. Wagner and H. W. Stevenson (eds), *Cultural Perspectives on Child Development*. San Francisco: W. H. Freeman.

Gregory, R. J. 1992: *Psychological Testing. History, Principles and Applications*. Boston: Allyn and Bacon.

Greif, E. B. and Ulman, K. J. 1982: The psychological impact of menarche on early adolescent females: a review of the literature. *Child Development*, 53, 1413–30.

Groos, K. 1898: *The Play of Animals*. New York: Appleton.

Groos, K. 1901: *The Play of Man*. London: William Heinemann.

Gross, M. U. M. 1993: *Exceptionally Gifted Children*. London: Routledge.

Grossman, K. E., Grossman, K., Huber, F. and Wartner, U. 1981: German children's behavior towards their mothers at 12 months and their fathers at 18 months in Ainsworth's 'strange situation'. *International Journal of Behavioral Development*, 4, 157–81.

Gruber, H. and Vonèche, J. J. 1977: *The Essential Piaget*. London: Routledge and Kegan Paul.

Grusec, J. E. 1982: The socialization of altruism. In N. Eisenberg (ed.), *The Development of Prosocial Behavior*. New York: Academic Press.

Grusec, J. E., Saas-Kortsaak, P. and Simutis, Z. M. 1978: The role of example and moral exhortation in the training of altruism. *Child Development*, 49, 920–3.

Gunter, B. and McAlean, J. 1997: *Children and Television: The One-Eyed Monster*, second edition. London: Routledge.

Gurney, R. M. 1980: The effects of unemployment on the psycho-social development of school-leavers. *Journal of Occupational Psychology*, 53, 205–13.

HMSO 1992: *Memorandum of Good Practice. On Video Recorded Interviews with Child Witnesses for Criminal Proceedings*. London: HMSO.

HMSO 1996: *Social Focus on Ethnic Minorities*. London: HMSO.

Hadow Report 1926: *The Education of the Adolescent*. London: HMSO.

Hadow Report 1931: *Primary Education*. London: HMSO.

Haight, W. L. and Miller, P. J. 1993: *Pretending at Home: Early Development in a Sociocultural Context*. Albany: SUNY Press.

Hall, G. S. 1908: *Adolescence*. New York: Appleton.

Halsey, A. H. 1972: *Educational Priority, Vol. I: E. P. A. Problems and Policies*. London: HMSO.

Hamilton, W. D. 1964: The genetical evolution of social behaviour. *Journal of Theoretical Biology*, 7, 1–52.

Hanawalt, B. A. 1992: Historical descriptions and prescriptions for adolescence. *Journal of Family History*, 17, 341–51.

Happé, F. 1994: *Autism. An Introduction to Psychological Theory*. London: University College London Press.

Hargreaves, D. 1967: *Social Relations in a Secondary School*. London: Routledge and Kegan Paul.

Hargreaves, D. and Colley, A. (eds) 1986: *The Psychology of Sex Roles*. London: Harper and Row.

Harlow, H. F. 1958: The nature of love. *American Psychologist*, 13, 673–85.

Harlow, H. F. and Harlow, M. 1969: Effects of various mother–infant relationships on rhesus monkey behaviours. In B. M. Foss (ed.), *Determinants of Infant Behaviour*, vol. 4. London: Methuen.

Harris, M. 1968: *The Rise of Anthropological Theory*. London: Routledge and Kegan Paul.

Harris, P. L. 1989: *Children and Emotion*. Oxford: Basil Blackwell.

Harris, P. L. 1991: The work of the imagination. In A. Whiten (ed.), *Natural Theories of*

Mind: Evolution, Development and Stimulation of Everyday Mindreading. Oxford: Blackwell.

Harter, S. 1985: *Manual for the Self-perception Profile for Children.* Denver, CO: University of Denver.

Hartup, W. W. 1996: The company they keep: friendships and their developmental significance. *Child Development*, 67, 1–13.

Haviland, J. M. and Lelwica, M. 1987: The induced affect response: 10-week-old infants' responses to three emotional expressions. *Developmental Psychology*, 23, 97–104.

Hayes, C. 1952: *The Ape in our House.* London: Gollancz.

Hayvren, M. and Hymel, S. 1984: Ethical issues in sociometric testing: impact of sociometric measures on interaction behavior. *Developmental Psychology*, 20, 844–9.

Hearnshaw, L. 1979: *Cyril Burt: Psychologist.* London: Hodder and Stoughton.

Hedegaard, M. 1996: The zone of proximal development as basis for instruction. In H. Daniels (ed.), *An Introduction to Vygotsky.* London: Routledge.

Held, R. 1965: Plasticity in sensory-motor systems. *Scientific American*, 213 (Nov.), 84–94.

Held, R. and Hein, A. 1963: Movement-produced stimulation in the development of visually guided behavior. *Journal of Comparative and Physiological Psychology*, 56, 872–6.

Hertz-Lazarowitz, R., Feitelson, D., Zahavi, S. and Hartup, W. W. 1981: Social interaction and social organisation of Israeli five-to-seven-year olds. *International Journal of Behavioral Development*, 4, 143–55.

Hertz-Lazarowitz, R. and Miller, N. 1992: *Interaction in Cooperative Groups.* Cambridge: Cambridge University Press.

Hess, R. D. and Shipman, V. C. 1965: Early experience and the socialization of cognitive modes in children. *Child Development*, 36, 869–86.

Hetherington, E. M. 1988: Family relations six years after divorce. In K. Pasley and M. Ihinger-Tallman (eds), *Remarriage and Stepparenting: Current Research and Theory.* New York: Guilford Press.

Hetherington, E. M. 1989: Coping with family transitions: winners, losers, and survivors. *Child Development*, 60, 1–14.

Hetherington, E. M., Cox, M. and Cox, R. 1982: Effects of divorce on parents and children. In M. Lamb (ed.), *Nontraditional Families.* Hillsdale, NJ: Erlbaum.

Hewlett, B. S. 1987: Intimate fathers: patterns of paternal holding among Aka pygmies. In M. Lamb (ed.), *The Father's Role: Cross-cultural Perspectives.* Hillsdale, NJ: Lawrence Erlbaum.

Himmelweit, H. T., Oppenheim, A. N. and Vince, P. 1958: *Television and the Child: an Empirical Study of the Effect of Television on the Young.* London: Oxford University Press.

Hinde, R. A. and Stevenson-Hinde, J. (eds) 1973: *Constraints on Learning: Limitations and Predispositions.* London and New York: Academic Press.

Hodges, J. and Tizard, B. 1989: IQ and behavioural adjustment of ex-institutional adolescents; and, Social and family relationships of ex-institutional adolescents. *Journal of Child Psychology and Psychiatry*, 30, 53–76; 77–98.

Hoffman, M. L. 1970: Moral development. In P. H. Mussen (ed.), *Carmichael's Manual of Child Psychology*, vol. 2. New York: Wiley.

Hooff, J. A. R. A. M. van 1972: A comparative approach to the phylogeny of laughter and smiling. In R. A. Hinde (ed.), *Non-Verbal Communication.* Cambridge: Cambridge University Press.

Hopkins, J. R. 1983: *Adolescence: The Transitional Years.* New York and London: Academic Press.

Howe, M. J. A. 1989: *Fragments of Genius. The Strange Feats of Idiot Savants*. London: Routledge.

Howe, M. J. A. and Smith, J. 1988: Calendar calculating in 'idiots savants': how do they do it? *British Journal of Developmental Psychology*, 79, 371–86.

Howes, C. and Matheson, C. C. 1992: Sequences in the development of competent play with peers: social and pretend play. *Developmental Psychology*, 28, 961–74.

Howes, C., Droege, K. and Matheson, C. C. 1994: Play and communicative processes within long- and short-term friendship dyads. *Journal of Social and Personal Relationships*, 11, 401–10.

Huggins, M., Mesquita, M. P. and de Castro, M. 1996: Exclusion, civic invisibility and impunity as explanations for youth murders in Brazil. *Childhood*, 3, no. 1, 77–98.

Hughes, C. H. and Russell, J. 1993: Autistic children's difficulty with mental disengagement from an object: its implications for theories of autism. *Developmental Psychology*, 29, 498–510.

Humphrey, N. 1984: *Consciousness Regained*. Oxford: Oxford University Press.

Hunter, F. T. 1984: Socializing procedures in parent–child and friendship relations during adolescence. *Developmental Psychology*, 20, 1092–9.

Hutt, C. 1966: Exploration and play in children. *Symposia of the Zoological Society of London*, 18, 61–87.

Hutt, C. 1970: Curiosity in young children. *Science Journal*, 6, 68–72.

Hutt, C. and Bhavnani, R. 1972: Predictions from play. *Nature*, 237, 171–2.

Hwang, P. 1987: The changing role of Swedish fathers. In M. Lamb (ed.), *The Father's Role: Cross-Cultural Perspectives*. Hillsdale, NJ: Lawrence Erlbaum.

Hwang, P., Broberg, A. and Lamb, B. 1990: Swedish childcare research. In E. Melhuish and P. Moss (eds), *Daycare for Young Children: International Perspectives*. London: Routledge.

Hymel, S. 1983: Preschool children's peer relations: issues in sociometric assessment. *Merrill-Palmer Quarterly*, 29, 237–60.

Inhelder, B. and Piaget, J. 1958 (1955): *The Growth of Logical Thinking from Childhood to Adolescence*. London: Routledge and Kegan Paul.

Isaacs, S. 1929: *The Nursery Years*. London: Routledge and Kegan Paul.

Izard, C. E., Hembree, E. A., and Huebner, R. R. 1987: Infants' emotion expressions to acute pain. *Developmental Psychology*, 23, 105–13.

Jackson, B. and Jackson, S. 1979: *Childminder: a Study in Action Research*. London: Routledge and Kegan Paul.

Jacobson, J. L. 1980: Cognitive determinants of wariness toward unfamiliar peers. *Developmental Psychology*, 16, 347–54.

Jahoda, G. 1983: European 'lag' in the development of an economic concept: a study in Zimbabwe. *British Journal of Developmental Psychology*, 1, 113–20.

James, W. 1890: *Principles of Psychology*. New York: Holt.

James, J., Charlton, T., Leo, E. and Indoe, D. 1991: A peer to listen. *Support for Learning*, 6, 4, 165–9.

Jarrold, C., Carruthers, P., Smith, P. K. and Boucher, J. 1994: Pretend play: is it metarepresentational? *Mind and Language*, 9, 445–68.

Jensen, A. R. 1969: How much can we boost IQ and scholastic achievement? *Harvard Educational Review*, 39, 449–83.

Jersild, A. T. and Markey, F. V. 1935: Conflicts between preschool children. *Child Development Monographs*, 21. Teachers College, Columbia University.

Johanson, D. C. and Edey, M. A. 1981: *Lucy: the Beginnings of Humankind*. London: Granada.

Johnson, C. L. 1983: A cultural analysis of the grandmother. *Research on Aging*, 5, 547–67.

Johnson, J. E., Ershler, J. and Lawton, J. T. 1982: Intellective correlates of preschoolers' spontaneous play. *Journal of Genetic Psychology*, 106, 115–22.

Johnson, M. H. and Morton, J. 1991: *Biology and Cognitive Development: the Case of Face Recognition*. Oxford: Blackwell.

Joravsky, D. 1989: *Russian Psychology*. Oxford: Basil Blackwell.

Kagan, J. 1976: Resilience and continuity in psychological development. In A. M. Clarke and A. D. B. Clarke (eds), *Early Experience: Myth and Evidence*. New York: Free Press.

Kail, R. 1990: *The Development of Memory in Children*, Third edition. New York: Freeman.

Kanner, L. 1943: Autistic disturbances of affective content. *Nervous Child*, 2, 217–50.

Karmiloff-Smith, A. 1995: The extraordinary cognitive journey from foetus through infancy. *Journal of Child Psychology and Psychiatry*, 36, 1293–313.

Karniol R. 1978: Children's use of intention cues in evaluating behavior. *Psychological Bulletin*, 85, 76–85.

Katchadourian, H. 1977: *The Biology of Adolescence*. San Francisco: W. H. Freeman.

Katz, L. F. and Gottman, J. M. 1993: Patterns of marital conflict predict children's internalising and externalising behaviors. *Developmental Psychology*, 29, 940–50.

Kaye, K. 1982: *The Mental and Social Life of Babies*. London: Harvester Press.

Kaye, K. and Marcus, J. 1978: Imitation over a series of trials without feedback: age six months. *Infant Behavior and Development*, 1, 141–55.

Kaye, K. and Marcus, J. 1981: Infant imitation: the sensorimotor agenda. *Developmental Psychology*, 17, 258–65.

Keenan, E. O. and Klein, E. 1975: Coherency in children's discourse. *Journal of Psycholinguistic Research*, 4, 365–80.

Keeney, T. J., Cannizzo, S. R. and Flavell, J. H. 1967: Spontaneous and induced verbal rehearsal in a recall task. *Child Development*, 38, 953–66.

Kegl, J. and Lopez, A. 1990: The deaf community in Nicaragua and their sign language(s). Unpublished paper cited in Pinker.

Kelly, E. 1988: Pupils, racial groups and behaviour in schools. In E. Kelly and T. Cohn (eds), *Racism in Schools*. Stoke-on-Trent: Trentham Books.

Kempe, C. H. 1980: Incest and other forms of sexual abuse. In C. H. Kempe and R. E. Helfer (eds), *The Battered Child*. Third edition. Chicago: Chicago University Press.

Kennedy, B. A. and Miller, D. J. 1976: Persistent use of verbal rehearsal as a function of information about its use. *Child Development*, 47, 566–9.

Kinsey, A. C., Pomeroy, W. B. and Martin, C. E. 1948: *Sexual Behavior in the Human Male*. Philadelphia: W. B. Saunders.

Kinsey, A. C., Pomeroy, W. B., Martin, C. E. and Gebherd, P. H. 1953: *Sexual Behavior in the Human Female*. Philadelphia: W. B. Saunders.

Kirk, S. A. 1958: *Early Education of the Mentally Retarded*. Urbana, IL: University of Illinois Press.

Klaus, M. H. and Kennell, J. H. 1976: *Maternal–Infant Bonding*. St Louis: Mosby.

Kline, S. 1995: The promotion and marketing of toys: time to rethink the paradox? In A. D. Pellegrini (ed.), *The Future of Play Theory*. Albany, NY: SUNY Press.

Klinnert, M. D. 1984: The regulation of infant behavior by maternal facial expression. *Infant Behavior and Development*, 7, 447–65.

Kobasigawa, A. 1974: Utilization of retrieval cues by children in recall. *Child Development*, 45, 127–34.

Kochenderfer, B. and Ladd, G. 1996: Peer victimisation: Cause or consequence of school maladjustment? *Child Development*, 67, 1305–17.

Kohlberg, L. 1966: A cognitive developmental analysis of children's sex role concepts and attitudes. In E. E. Maccoby (ed.), *The Development of Sex Differences*. Stanford, CA: Stanford University Press.

Kohlberg L. 1969: Stages and sequence: the cognitive-developmental approach to socialization. In D. A. Goslin (ed.), *Handbook of Socialization Theory and Research*. Chicago: Rand McNally.

Kohlberg, L. 1976: Moral stages and moralization: The cognitive-developmental approach. In T. Lickona (ed.), *Moral Development and Behavior*. New York: Holt, Rinehart and Winston.

Koluchova, J. 1972: Severe deprivation in twins: a case study. In A. M. Clarke and A. D. B. Clarke (eds), *Early Experience: Myth and Evidence*. London: Open Books.

Kramer, R. 1976: *Maria Montessori: a Biography*. Oxford: Basil Blackwell.

Krasnor, L. R. and Pepler, D. J. 1980: The study of children's play: some suggested future directions. In K. H. Rubin (ed.), *Children's Play*. San Francisco: Jossey-Bass.

Kreutzer, M. A., Leonard, C. and Flavell, J. H. 1975: An interview study of children's knowledge about memory. *Monographs of the Society for Research in Child Development*, 40, 1–58.

Kuczaj II, S. A. 1986: Language play. In P. K. Smith (ed.), *Children's Play: Research Developments and Practical Applications*. London: Gordon and Breach.

Kuhl, P. (1985) in Eimas, P. The perception of speech in early infancy. *Scientific American*, 252(1).

Kuhn, D., Nash, S. C., and Bruken, L. 1978: Sex role concepts of two- and three-year-olds. *Child Development*, 49, 445–51.

Kupersmidt, J. B., Coie, J. D. and Dodge, K. A. 1990: The role of poor peer relationships in the development of disorder. In S. R. Asher and J. D. Coie (eds), *Peer Rejection in Childhood*, pp. 274–305. Cambridge: Cambridge University Press.

Kurtines, W. and Greif, E. B. 1974: The development of moral thought: review and evaluation of Kohlberg's approach. *Psychological Bulletin*, 81, 453–70.

Labov, W. 1969: The logic of non-standard English. Reprinted in 1972: *Language in Education: a Source Book*. London and Boston: Routledge and Kegan Paul/Open University Press.

Ladd, G. W. 1981: Effectiveness of a social learning method for enhancing children's social interaction and peer acceptance. *Child Development*, 52, 171–8.

Ladd, G. W. 1983: Social networks of popular, average and rejected children in school settings. *Merrill-Palmer Quarterly*, 29, 283–307.

Lamb, M. E. 1987: Introduction: the emergent American father. In M. E. Lamb (ed.), *The Father's Role: Cross-cultural Perspectives*. Hillsdale, NJ: Lawrence Erlbaum.

Lamb, M. E., Easterbrooks, M. A. and Holden, G. W. 1980: Reinforcement and punishment among preschoolers: characteristics, effects and correlates. *Child Development*, 51, 1230–6.

Lamb, M. E., Thompson, R. A., Gardner, W. P., Charnov, E. L. and Estes, D. 1984: Security of infantile attachment as assessed in the 'strange situation': its study and biological interpretation. *Behavioural and Brain Sciences*, 7, 127–71.

Langlois, J. H. and Downs, A. C. 1980: Mothers, fathers, and peers as socialization agents of sex-typed play behaviors in young children. *Child Development*, 51, 1217–47.

Larsen, R. and Ham, M. 1993: Stress and 'Storm and Stress' in early adolescence: the relationship of negative events with dysphoric affect. *Developmental Psychology*, 29, 130–40.

Laursen, B. and Collins, W. A. 1994: Interpersonal conflict during adolescence. *Psychological Bulletin*, 115, 197–209.

Lawton, D. 1968: *Social Class, Language and Education*. London: Routledge and Kegan Paul.

Lazar, I. and Darlington, R. 1982: Lasting effects of early education. *Monographs of the Society for Research in Child Development*, 47, nos 2–3.

Leakey, R. E. and Lewin, R. 1977: *Origins*. London: Macdonald and Janes.

Leekam, S. and Perner, J. 1991: Does the autistic child have a metarepresentational deficit? *Cognition*, 40, 203–18.

Lefkowitz, M. M., Eron, L. D., Walder, L. O. and Huesmann, L. R. 1977: *Growing Up to be Violent*. New York and Oxford: Pergamon.

Lempers, J. D., Flavell, E. R. and Flavell, J. H. 1977: The development in very young children of tacit knowledge concerning visual perception. *Genetic Psychology Monographs*, 95, 3–53.

Leontiev, A. N. 1981: The problem of activity in psychology. In J. V. Wertsch (ed.), *The Concept of Activity in Soviet Psychology*, pp. 37–71. Armonk, NY: Sharpe.

Leslie, A. M. 1987: Pretence and representation: the origins of 'theory of mind'. *Psychological Review*, 94, 412–26.

Leslie, A. M. and Thaiss, L. 1992: Domain specificity in conceptual development: Neuropsychological evidence from autism. *Cognition*, 43, 225–51.

Leutenegger, W. 1981: Encephalization and obstetrics in primates with particular reference to human evolution. In E. Armstrong and D. Falk (eds), *Primate Brain Evolution: Methods and Concepts*. New York: Plenum.

Lever, J. 1978: Sex differences in the complexity of children's play and games. *American Sociological Review*, 43, 471–83.

Lewis, C. 1986: *Becoming a Father*. Milton Keynes: Open University Press.

Lewis, C. and Osborne, A. 1990: Three-year-olds' problems with false belief: conceptual deficit or linguistic artifact? *Child Development*, 61, 1514–19.

Lewis, M. and Brooks-Gunn, J. 1979: *Social Cognition and the Acquisition of Self*. New York: Plenum Press.

Lewis, M., Feiring, C., McGuffoy, C. and Jaskir, J. 1984: Predicting psychopathology in six-year-olds from early social relations. *Child Development*, 55, 123–36.

Lewis, M., Stanger, C. and Sullivan, M. W. 1989: Deception in 3-year-olds. *Developmental Psychology*, 25, 439–43.

Lewis, M., Young, G., Brooks, J. and Michalson, L. 1975: The beginning of friendship. In M. Lewis and L. Rosenblum (eds), *Friendship and Peer Relations*. New York: Wiley.

Liddiard, M. 1928: *The Mothercraft Manual*. London: Churchill.

Lillard, A. S. 1993: Pretend play skills and the child's theory of mind. *Child Development*, 64, 348–71.

Linaza, J. 1984: Piaget's marbles: the study of children's games and their knowledge of rules. *Oxford Review of Education*, 10, 271–4.

Lindberg, M. 1991: A taxonomy of suggestibility and eyewitness memory: age, memory process, and focus of analysis. In J. L. Doris (ed.), *The Suggestibility of Children's Recollections*. Washington, D. C.: American Psychological Association.

Lopatka, A. 1992: The rights of the child are universal: the perspective of the UN Convention on the Rights of the Child. In M. Freeman and P. Veerman (eds), *The Ideologies of Children's Rights*. Dordrecht: Martinus Nijhoff.

Lorenz, K. 1966: *On Aggression*. London: Methuen.

Lovejoy, C. O. 1981: The origin of man. *Science*, 211, 341–50.

Luepnitz, D. A. 1986: A comparison of maternal, paternal, and joint custody: understanding the varieties of post-divorce family life. *Journal of Divorce*, 9, 1–12.

Ma, L. 1989: Premarital sexual permissiveness of American and Chinese college students: a cross-cultural comparison. *Sociological Spectrum*, 9, 285–99.

Maccoby, E. E., and Jacklin, C. N. 1974: *The Psychology of Sex Differences*. Stanford, CA: Stanford University Press.

Maccoby, E. E. and Martin, J. A. 1983: Socialization in the context of the family: parent–child interaction. In P. H. Mussen (ed.), *Handbook of Child Psychology, Vol. 4: Socialization, Personality, and Social Development*. New York: Wiley.

MacDonald, C. D. and Cohen, R. 1995: Children's awareness of which peers like them and which peers dislike them. *Social Development*, 4, 182–93.

MacDonald, I. 1989: *Murder in the Playground*. London: Longsight Press.

MacDonald, K. 1992: Parent–child play: An evolutionary perspective. In K. MacDonald (ed.), *Parent–Child Play: Descriptions and Implications*. Albany, NY: SUNY Press.

Magnusson, D., Stattin, H. and Allen, V. L. 1985: Biological maturation and social development: a longitudinal study of some adjustment processes from mid-adolescence to adulthood. *Journal of Youth and Adolescence*, 14, 267–83.

Main, M. and Cassidy, J. 1988: Categories of response to reunion with the parent at age 6: predictable from infant attachment classifications and stable over a 1-month period. *Developmental Psychology*, 24, 415–26.

Main, M., Kaplan, N. and Cassidy, J. 1985: Security in infancy, childhood, and adult-hood: a move to the level of representation. In I. Bretherton and E. Waters (eds), Growing Points of Attachment Theory and Research. *Monographs of the Society for Research in Child Development*, 50, nos 1–2.

Malik, N. and Furman, W. 1993: Problems in children's peer relations: What can the clinician do? *Journal of Child Psychology and Psychiatry*, 34, 1303–26.

Malina, R. M. 1979: Secular changes in size and maturity: causes and effects. *Monographs of the Society for Research in Child Development*, 44, 59–102.

Malinosky-Rummell, R. and Hansen, D. J. 1993: Long-term consequences of child-hood physical abuse. *Psychological Bulletin*, 114, 68–79.

Mannarino, A. P. 1980: The development of children's friendships. In H. C. Foot, A. J. Chapman and J. R. Smith (eds), *Friendship and Social Relations in Children*. Chichester: Wiley.

Manning, K. and Sharp, A. 1977: *Structuring Play in the Early Years at School*. London: Ward Lock Educational.

Manning, M., Heron, J. and Marshall, T. 1978: Styles of hostility and social interac-tions at nursery, at school and at home: an extended study of children. In L. A. Hersov, M. Berger and D. Shaffer (eds), *Aggression and Anti-social Behaviour in Childhood and Adolescence*, pp. 29–58. Oxford: Pergamon.

Marcia, J. E. 1966: Development and validation of ego-identity status. *Journal of Personality and Social Psychology*, 3, 551–8.

Marcia, J. 1980: Identity in adolescence. In J. Adelson (ed.), *Handbook of Adolescent Psychology*. New York: Wiley.

Marin, B. V., Holmes, D. L., Guth, M. and Kovac, P. 1979: The potential of children as eyewitnesses: A comparison of children and adults on eyewitness tasks. *Law and Human Behavior*, 3, 295–305.

Martin, P. and Bateson, P. 1991: *Measuring Behaviour: an Introductory Guide*, Second edition. Cambridge: Cambridge University Press.

Martin, P. and Caro, T. M. 1985: On the functions of play and its role in behavioral development. In J. S. Rosenblatt, C. Beer, M. C. Bunsel and P. J. B. Slater (eds), *Advances in the Study of Behavior*, vol. 15. Orlando, FL: Academic Press.

Masangkay, Z. S., McCluskey, K. A., McIntyre, C. W., Sims-Knight, J., Vaughn, B. E. and Flavell, J. H. 1974: The early development of inferences about the visual percepts of others. *Child Development*, 45, 237–46.

Mason, D. and Frick, P. 1994: The heritability of antisocial behaviour. *Journal of Psychopathology and Behavior Assessment*, 16, 301–23.

Masson, J. 1992: *The Assault on Truth. Freud and Child Sexual Abuse*. London: Fontana.

Maurer, D. and Barrera, M. 1981: Infants' perceptions of natural and distorted arrangements of a schematic face. *Child Development*, 52, 196–202.

Maurer, D. and Salapatek P. 1976: Developmental changes in the scanning of faces by young infants. *Child Development*, 47, 523–7.

Mayall, B. and Petrie, P. 1977: *Minder, Mother and Child*. Windsor: NFER.

Mayall, B. and Petrie, P. 1983: *Childminding and Day Nurseries: What Kind of Care?* London: Heinemann Educational Books.

McCauley, M. R. and Fisher, R. P. 1995: Facilitating children's eyewitness recall with the revised cognitive interview. *Journal of Applied Psychology*, 80, 510–16.

McGarrigle, J. and Donaldson, M. 1974: Conservation accidents. *Cognition*, 3, 341–50.

McGhee, P. E. 1979: *Humor: Its Origin and Development*. San Francisco: Freeman.

McGilly, K. and Siegler, R. S. 1989: How children choose among serial recall strategies. *Child Development*, 55, 172–82.

McGuire, A. 1994: Helping behaviors in the natural environment: dimensions and correlates of helping. *Personality and Social Psychology Bulletin*, 20, 1, 45–56.

McGurk, H., Caplan, M., Hennessy, E. and Moss, P. 1993: Controversy, theory and social context in contemporary day care research. *Journal of Child Psychology and Psychiatry*, 34, 3–23.

McGurk, H. and Lewis, M. 1974: Space perception in early infancy: perception within a common auditory-visual space? *Science*, 186, 649–50.

McLoyd, V. C. 1982: Social class differences in sociodramatic play: a critical review. *Developmental Review*, 2, 1–30.

McLoyd, V. C. and Ratner, H. H. 1983: The effects of sex and toy characteristics on exploration in preschool children. *Journal of Genetic Psychology*, 142, 213–24.

McNeill, D. 1966: Developmental psycholinguistics. In F. Smith and G. A. Miller (eds), *The Genesis of Language*. Cambridge, MA: MIT Press.

McNeill, D. 1970: *The Acquisition of Language*. New York: Harper and Row.

Mead, M. 1928: *Coming of Age in Samoa*. New York: Morrow.

Mead, M. 1935: *Sex and Temperament in Three Primitive Societies*. New York: Morrow.

Mead, M. 1949: *Male and Female*. New York: Morrow.

Mehler, J. and Dupoux, E. 1994: *What Infants Know. The New Cognitive Science of Early Development*. Oxford: Blackwell.

Meilman, P. W. 1979: Cross-sectional age changes in ego identity status during adolescence. *Developmental Psychology*, 15, 230–1.

Melhuish, E. 1993: A measure of love? An overview of the assessment of attachment. *ACPP Review & Newsletter*, 15, 269–75.

Melhuish, E. C. 1990: Research on day care for young children in the United Kingdom. In E. C. Melhuish and P. Moss (eds), *Day Care for Young Children: International Perspectives*. London: Routledge.

Meltzoff, A. and Borton, R. 1979: Intermodal matching by human neonates. *Nature*, 282, 403–4.

Meltzoff, A. and Moore, M. 1983: Newborn infants imitate adult facial gestures. *Child Development*, 54, 702–9.

Meltzoff, A. N. and Moore, M. K. 1994: Imitation, memory, and the representation of persons. *Infant Behavior and Development*, 17, 83–99.

Messer, D. 1981: The identification of names in maternal speech to infants. *Journal of Psycholinguistic Research*, 10, 69–77.

Messer, D. 1994: *The Development of Communication from Social Interaction to Language*. Chichester: Wiley.

Meyrick, J. and Harris, R. 1994: Adolescent sexual behaviour, contraceptive use and pregnancy: a review. *ACPP Review & Newsletter*, 16, 245–51.

Miles, T. R. 1982: *The Bangor Dyslexia Test*. Cambridge: Learning Development Aids.

Miles T. R. 1993: *Dyslexia: the Pattern of Difficulties*. London: Whurr.

Miller, P. H. 1993: *Theories of Developmental Psychology*, Third edition. New York: Freeman.

Mills, M. and Melhuish, E. 1974: Recognition of mother's voice in early infancy. *Nature*, 252, 123–4.

Milner, D. 1983: *Children and Race: Ten Years On*. London: Ward Lock Educational.

Mischel, W. 1970: Sex-typing and socialization. In P. H. Mussen (ed.), *Carmichael's Manual of Child Psychology*, vol. 2, Third edition. New York: Wiley.

Mitchell, D. E. 1978: Effects of early visual experience on the development of certain perceptual abilities in animals and man. In R. D. Walk and H. L. Pick, Jr (eds), *Perception and Experience*, pp. 37–75. New York and London: Plenum Press.

Mitchell, P. 1996: *Acquiring a Conception of Mind. A Review of Psychological Research and Theory*. Hove: Erlbaum.

Mitchell, P. 1997: *Introduction to Theory of Mind*. London: Arnold.

Mitchell, P. and Lacohee, H. 1991: Children's early understanding of false belief. *Cognition*, 39, 439–54.

Mitchell, R. W. 1986: A framework for discussing deception. In R. W. Mitchell and N. S. Thompson (eds), *Deception: Perspectives on Human and Nonhuman Deceit*. New York: SUNY Press.

Miyake, K., Chen, S. J. and Campos, J. J. 1985: Infant temperament, mother's mode of interaction and attachment in Japan: an interim report. In I. Bretherton and E. Waters (eds), Growing Points of Attachment Theory and Research. *Monographs of the Society for Research in Child Development*, 50, 276–97.

Moely, B. E., Olson, F. A., Halwes, T. G. and Flavell, J. H. 1969: Production deficiency in young children's clustered recall. *Developmental Psychology*, 1, 26–34.

Moerke, E. L. 1991: Positive evidence for negative evidence. *First Language*, 11, 219–51.

Møller, H. 1985: Voice change in human biological development. *Journal of Interdisciplinary History*, 16, 239–53.

Møller, H. 1987: The accelerated development of youth: beard growth as a biological marker. *Comparative Study of Society and History*, 29, 748–62.

Money, J. and Ehrhardt, A. A. 1972: *Man and Woman, Boy and Girl*. Baltimore, MD: Johns Hopkins University Press.

Montagu, A. 1961: Neonatal and infant immaturity in man. *Journal of the American Medical Association*, 178, 56–7.

Montemayor, R. and Eisen, M. 1977: The development of self-conceptions from childhood to adolescence. *Developmental Psychology*, 13, 314–19.

Moss, P. 1987: *A Review of Childminding Research*. University of London: Thomas Coram Research Unit.

Mossler, D. G., Marvin, R. S. and Greenberg, M. T. 1976: Conceptual perspective taking in 2- to 6-year-old children. *Developmental Psychology*, 12, 85–6.

Moston, S. 1987: The suggestibility of children in interview studies. *First Language*, 7, 67–78.

Mueller, E. and Brenner, J. 1977: The origins of social skills and interaction among playgroup toddlers. *Child Development*, 48, 854–61.

Mussen, P. and Eisenberg-Berg, N. 1977: *Roots of Caring, Sharing and Helping*. San Francisco: W. H. Freeman.

Mussen, P. H. and Jones, M. C. 1957: Self-conceptions, motivations and interpersonal attitudes of late- and early-maturing boys. *Child Development*, 28, 243–56.

Myers, B. J. 1984: Mother–infant bonding: the status of this critical-period hypothesis. *Developmental Review*, 4, 240–74.

Nadel-Brulfert, J. and Baudonniere, P. M. 1982: The social function of reciprocal imitation in 2-year-old peers. *International Journal of Behavioural Development*, 5, 95–109

Nanez, J. E. 1988: Perception of impending collision in 3- to 6-week-old human infants. *Infant Behavior and Development*, 11, 447–63.

Nelson, K. 1981: Individual differences in language development: implications for language and development. *Developmental Psychology*, 17, 170–87.

Nelson, K. (ed.) 1986: *Event Knowledge. Structure and Function in Development*. Hillsdale, NJ: Lawrence Erlbaum.

Nelson, K. (ed.) 1989: *Narratives from the Crib*. Cambridge, MA: Harvard University Press.

Nelson, K., Carskaddon, G. and Bonvillian, J. D. 1973: Syntax acquisition: impact of experimental variation in adult verbal interaction with the child. *Child Development*, 44, 497–504.

Nelson, K. and Gruendel, J. 1986: Children's scripts. In K. Nelson (ed.), *Event Knowledge. Structure and Function in Development*. Hillsdale, NJ: Lawrence Erlbaum.

Newcomb, A. F. and Bagwell, C. L. 1995: Children's friendship relations: A meta-analytic review. *Psychological Bulletin*, 117, 306–47.

Newsom Report (Central Advisory Council for Education) 1963: *Half Our Future*. London: HMSO.

Newson, E. 1994: Video violence and the protection of children. *The Psychologist*, 7, 272–4.

Newson, J. and Newson, E. 1968: *Four Years Old in an Urban Community*. London: Allen and Unwin.

Nicolson, R. I. and Fawcett, A. J. 1990: Automaticity: A new framwork for dyslexia research? *Cognition*, 30, 159–82.

Nicolson, R. I. and Fawcett, A. J. 1996: *The Dyslexia Early Screening Test*. The Psychological Corporation, London.

Nishida, T. 1980: The leaf-clipping display: a newly-discovered expressive gesture in wild chimpanzees. *Journal of Human Evolution*, 9, 117–28.

Noelting, G. 1980: The development of proportional reasoning and the ratio concept. *Educational Studies in Mathematics*, 11, 217–53.

Novak, M. A. 1979: Social recovery of monkeys isolated for the first year of life: II. Long term assessment. *Developmental Psychology*, 15, 50–61.

O'Connell, A. N. 1976: The relationship between life style and identity synthesis and resynthesis in traditional, neo-traditional and non-traditional women. *Journal of Personality*, 4, 675–88.

O'Connor, R. D. 1972: Relative efficacy of modeling, shaping and the combined procedures for modification or social withdrawal. *Journal of Abnormal Psychology*, 79, 327–34.

Oden, S. and Asher, S. R. 1977: Coaching children in social skills for friendship making. *Child Development*, 48, 495–506.

Olweus, D. 1991: Bully/victim problems among schoolchildren: basic facts and effects of a school based intervention program. In K. Rubin and D. Pepler (eds), *The Development and Treatment of Childhood Aggression*. Hillsdale, NJ: Erlbaum.

O'Moore, A. M. 1989: Bullying in Britain and Ireland: an overview. In E. Roland and E. Munthe (eds), *Bullying: an International Perspective*. London: David Fulton.

Opie, I. and Opie, P. 1959: *The Lore and Language of School Children*. London: Oxford University Press.

Oppenheim, D., Sagi, A. and Lamb, M. E. 1988: Infant–adult attachments on the kibbutz and their relation to socioemotional development four years later. *Developmental Psychology*, 24, 427–33.

Ornstein, P. A., Naus, M. J. and Liberty, C. 1975: Rehearsal and organizational processes in children's memory. *Child Development*, 46, 818–30.

Ostersehlt, D. and Danker-Hopfe, H. 1991: Changes in age at menarche in Germany: evidence for a continuing decline. *American Journal of Human Biology*, 3, 647–54.

Overton, W. F. and Jackson, J. P. 1973: The representation of imagined objects in action sequences: a developmental study. *Child Development*, 44, 309–14.

Ozonoff, S., Rogers, S. J. and Pennington, B. F. 1991: Executive function deficits in high functioning autistic children: relationship to theory of mind. *Journal of Child Psychology and Psychiatry*, 32, 1081–106.

Packer, C. 1977: Reciprocal altruism in olive baboons. *Nature*, 265, 441–3.

Paikoff, R. L. and Brooks-Gunn, J. 1991: Do parent–child relationships change during puberty? *Psychological Bulletin*, 110, 47–66.

Papousek, M. 1989: Determinants of responsiveness to infant vocal expression of emotional state. *Infant Behavior and Development*, 12, 507–24.

Papousek, M., Papousek, H. and Haekel, M. 1987: Didactic adjustments in fathers' and mothers' speech to their three-month-old infants. *Journal of Psycholinguistic Research*, 16, 491–516.

Papousek, M., Papousek, H. and Symmes, D. 1991: The meanings of melodies in mothers in tone and stress languages. *Infant Behavior and Development*, 14, 415–40.

Parke, R. D. 1977: Some effects of punishment on children's behaviour – revisited. In E. M. Hetherington and R. D. Parke (eds), *Contemporary Readings in Child Psychology*. New York: McGraw-Hill.

Parker, J. G. and Asher, S. R. 1987: Peer relations and later personal adjustment: are low-accepted children at risk? *Psychological Bulletin*, 102, 357–89.

Parker, S. T. and Gibson, K. R. 1979: A developmental model for the evolution of language and intelligence in early hominids. *Behavioral and Brain Sciences*, 2, 367–408.

Parten, M. B. 1932: Social participation among preschool children. *Journal of Abnormal and Social Psychology*, 27, 243–69.

Partington, J. T. and Grant, C. 1984: Imaginary playmates and other useful fantasies. In P. K. Smith (ed.), *Play in Animals and Humans*. Oxford: Basil Blackwell.

Passow, A. H. 1970: *Deprivation and Disadvantage: Nature and Manifestations*. Hamburg: UNESCO Institute of Education.

Patterson, C. J. 1992: Children of lesbian and gay parents. *Child Development*, 63, 1025–42.

Patterson, C. J. 1995: Sexual orientation and human development: An overview. *Developmental Psychology*, 31, 3–11.

Patterson, F. G. 1978: The gestures of a gorilla: language acquisition in another pongid. *Brain and Language*, 5, 72–97.

Patterson, G. R., DeBaryshe, B. D. and Ramsey, E. 1989: A developmental perspective on antisocial behavior. *American Psychologist*, 44, 329–35.

Pellegrini, A. D. 1988: Elementary school children's rough-and-tumble play and social competence. *Developmental Psychology*, 24, 802–6.

Pellegrini, A. D. 1994: The rough play of adolescent boys of differing sociometric status. *International Journal of Behavioral Development*, 17, 525–40.

Peller, L. E. 1954: Libidinal phases, ego development and play. *Psychoanalytic Study of the Child*, 9, 178–98.

Perner, J. 1991: *Understanding the Representational Mind*. Cambridge, MA: MIT Press.

Perner, J., Frith, U., Leslie, A. M. and Leekam, S. R. 1989: Exploration of the autistic child's theory of mind: knowledge, belief and communication. *Child Development*, 60, 689–700.

Perner, J., Leekam, S. R. and Wimmer, H. 1987: Three-year-olds' difficulty with false belief: the case for a conceptual deficit. *British Journal of Developmental Psychology*, 5, 125–37.

Perner, J. and Wimmer, H. 1985: 'John thinks that Mary thinks that . . .': Attribution of second order beliefs by 5–10 year old children. *Journal of Experimental Child Psychology*, 39, 437–71.

Perry, N. W. and Wrightsman, L. S. 1991: *The Child Witness. Legal Issues and Dilemmas*. Newbury Park, CA: Sage.

Pfungst, O. 1911: *Clever Hans: a Contribution to Experimental Animal and Human Psychology*. New York: Holt.

Piaget, J. 1929: *The Child's Conception of the World*. New York: Harcourt Brace Jovanovich.

Piaget, J. 1932 (1977): *The Moral Judgement of the Child*. Harmondsworth: Penguin.

Piaget, J. 1936/1952: *The Origin of Intelligence in the Child*. London: Routledge and Kegan Paul.

Piaget, J. 1951: *Play, Dreams and Imitation in Childhood*. London: Routledge and Kegan Paul.

Piaget, J. 1966: Response to Brian Sutton-Smith. *Psychological Review*, 73, 111–12.

Piaget, J. 1972: Intellectual evolution from adolescence to adulthood. *Human Development*, 15, 1–12.

Piaget, J. and Inhelder, B. 1951: *La genèse de l'idée de hasard chez l'enfant*. Paris: Presses Universitaires de France.

Piaget, J. and Inhelder, B. 1956: *The Child's Conception of Space*. London: Routledge and Kegan Paul.

Pinker, S. 1994: *The Language Instinct*. London: Allen Lane.

Plomin, R. and Daniels, D. 1987: Why are children of the same family so different from each other? *Behavioural and Brain Sciences*, 10, 1–16.

Plomin, R., DeFries, J. C., Rutter, M. and McClearn, G. E. 1997: *Behavioral Genetics: A Primer*, Third edition. New York: W. H. Freeman.

Porter, R. H., Makin, J. W., Davis, L. B. and Christensen, K. M. 1992: Breast-fed infants respond to olfactory cues from their own mother and unfamiliar lactating females. *Infant Behavior and Development*, 15, 85–93.

Povinelli, D. J. and Eddy, T. J. 1996: What young chimpanzees know about seeing. *Monographs of the Society for Research in Child Development*, 61, 3, 1–152.

Powdermaker, H. 1933: *Life in Lesu*. New York: W. W. Norton.

Premack D. 1971: Language in chimpanzee? *Science*, 172, 808–22.

Pressley, M. and Levin, J. R. 1980: The development of mental imagery retrieval. *Child Development*, 61, 973–82.

Profet, M. 1992: Pregnancy sickness as adaptation: a deterrent to maternal ingestion of teratogens. In J. H. Barkow, L. Cosmides and J. Tooby (eds), *The Adapted Mind*, pp. 327–65. New York and Oxford: Oxford University Press.

Querleu, D., Lefebvre, C., Renard, X., Titran, M., Morillion, M. and Crepin, G. 1984: Réactivité du nouveau-né de moins de deux heures de vie à la voix maternelle. *Journal de Gynécologie, Obstrétrique et Biologie de la Réproduction*, 13, 125–34.

Quinton, D. and Rutter, M. 1976: Early hospital admissions and later disturbances of behaviour: an attempted replication of Douglas's findings. *Developmental Medicine and Child Neurology*, 18, 447–59.

Radford, J. 1990: *Child Prodigies and Exceptional Early Achievers*. Hemel Hempstead: Harvester Wheatsheaf.

Radin, N., Oyserman, D. and Benn, R. 1991: Grandfathers, teen mothers, and children under two. In P. K. Smith (ed.), *The Psychology of Grandparenthood: An International Perspective.* London: Routledge.

Rampton Report 1981: *West Indian Children in our Schools.* London: HMSO, Cmnd 8273.

Rauh, H., Rudinger, G., Bowman, T. G., Berry, P., Gunn, P. V. and Hayes, A. 1991: The development of Down's syndrome children. In M. E. Lamb and H. Keller (eds), *Infant Development: Perspectives from German-speaking Countries.* Hillsdale, NJ: Erlbaum.

Raven, J. C. 1958: *Standard Progressive Matrices.* London: H. K. Lewis & Co. Ltd.

Raven, J. C. 1986: *Raven's Progressive Matrices.* London: J. C. Raven.

Raven, M. 1981: Review: the effects of childminding: how much do we know? *Child: Care, Health and Development*, 7, 103–11.

Reinhold, R. 1979: Census finds unmarried couples have doubled from 1970 to 1978. *The New York Times*, 27 June, p. 1: B5.

Reiss, I. L. 1967: *The Social Context of Premarital Sexual Permissiveness.* New York: Holt, Rinehart and Winston.

Richards, M. P. M. 1994: The international year of the family: family research. *The Psychologist*, 8, 17–24.

Richardson, K. 1991: *Understanding Intelligence.* Buckingham: Open University Press.

Riesen, A. H. 1950: Arrested vision. *Scientific American*, 183 (July), 16–19.

Rigby, K. 1996: *Bullying in Schools and What to do About It.* Melbourne: Australian Council for Educational Research.

Riggs, K. J., Peterson, D. M., Robinson, E. J. and Mitchell, P. 1996: Are errors in false belief tasks symptomatic of a broader difficulty with counterfactuality? *Cognitive Development*, in press.

Robarchek, C. A. and Robarchek, C. J. 1992: Cultures of war and peace: a comparative study of Waorani and Semai. In J. Silverberg and J. P. Gray (eds), *Aggression and Peacefulness in Humans and other Primates.* New York: Oxford University Press.

Robson, C. 1983: *Experiment, Design and Statistics in Psychology*, Second edition. Harmondsworth: Penguin.

Robson, C. 1993: *Real World Research.* Oxford: Blackwell.

Roche, A. F. (ed.) 1979: Secular trends in human growth, maturation, and development. *Monographs of the Society for Research in Child Development*, 44 (3–4), Serial no. 179.

Rogers, M. J. and Tisak, M. 1996: Children's reasoning about responses to peer aggression. *Aggressive Behavior*, 22, 4, 259–69.

Roland, E. 1989: Bullying: the Scandinavian research tradition. In E. Roland and E. Munthe (eds), *Bullying: an International Perspective.* London: David Fulton.

Root, B. 1986: *Resources for Reading.* London: Macmillan.

Rose, S. A. and Ruff, H. A. 1987: Cross-modal abilities in human infants. In J. S. Osofsky (ed.), *Handbook of Infant Development*, Second edition. New York: Wiley.

Rose, S. R., Kamin L. J. and Lewontin, R. C. 1984: *Not in our Genes: Biology, Ideology and Human Nature.* Harmondsworth: Penguin.

Rosenblith, J. F. 1992: *In the Beginning: Development from Conception to Age Two*, Second edition. Newbury Park and London: Sage.

Rosser, R. 1994: *Cognitive Development. Psychological and Biological Perspectives.* Boston: Allyn and Bacon.

Rossi, A. H. and Rossi, P. H. 1991: *Of Human Bonding: Parent–Child Relations across the Life Course.* New York: de Gruyter.

Rubin, K. H. and Pepler, D. J. 1982: Children's play: Piaget's views reconsidered. *Contemporary Educational Psychology*, 7, 289–99.

Rubin, Z. 1980: *Children's Friendships*. Glasgow: Fontana.

Ruble, D. N., Balaban, T. and Cooper, J. 1981: Gender constancy and the effects of sex-typed televised toy commercials. *Child Development*, 52, 667–73.

Ruble, D. N. and Brooks-Gunn, J. 1982: The experience of menarche. *Child Development*, 53, 1557–66.

Russell, J. 1992: The 'theory-theory': So good they named it twice? *Cognitive Development*, 7, 485–519.

Rutter, M. 1981: *Maternal Deprivation Reassessed*, second edition. Harmondsworth: Penguin.

Rutter, M. 1990: Psychological resilience and protective mechanisms. In J. Rolf, A. S. Masters, D. Cicchetti, K. H. Neuchterlein and S. Weintraub (eds), *Risks and Protective Factors in the Development of Psychopathology*. New York: Cambridge University Press.

Rutter, M., Graham, P., Chadwick, O. and Yule, W. 1976: Adolescent turmoil: fact or fiction? *Journal of Child Psychology and Psychiatry*, 17, 35–56.

Rymer, R. 1994: *Genie: A Scientific Tragedy*. Harmondsworth: Penguin.

Sahlins, M. 1977: *The Use and Abuse of Biology*. London: Tavistock.

Salapatek, P. 1975: *Infant Perception from Sensation to Cognition*, vol. 1. New York: Academic Press.

Samuels, C. A. and Ewy, R. 1985: Aesthetic perception of faces during infancy. *British Journal of Developmental Psychology*, 3, 221–8.

Savage-Rumbaugh, E. S. and Rumbaugh, D. M. 1978: Symbolization, language and chimpanzees: a theoretical re-evaluation based on initial language acquisition processes in four young *Pan troglodytes*. *Brain and Language*, 6, 265–300.

Savin-Williams, R. C. 1976: An ethological study of dominance formation and maintenance in a group of human adolescents. *Child Development*, 47, 972–9.

Savin-Williams, R. C. 1980: Social interactions of adolescent females in natural groups. In H. C. Foot, A. J. Chapman and I. R. Smith (eds), *Friendship and Social Relations in Children*. Chichester: Wiley.

Savin-Williams, R. C. and Demo, D. H. 1984: Developmental change and stability in adolescent self-concept. *Developmental Psychology*, 20, 1100–10.

Saywitz, K. J., Goodman, G. S., Nicholas, E. and Moan, S. F. 1991: Children's memories of a physical examination involving genital touch: implications for reports of child sexual abuse. *Journal of Consulting and Clinical Psychology*, 59, 682–91.

Saywitz, K. J. and Nathanson, R. 1993: Children's testimony and their perceptions of stress in and out of the courtroom. *Child Abuse and Neglect*, 17, 613–22.

Scaife, M. and Bruner, J. S. 1975: The capacity for joint visual attention in the infant. *Nature*, 253, 265–6.

Scarlett, G. and Wolf, D. 1979: When it's only make-believe: the construction of a boundary between fantasy and reality in story-telling. In E. Winner and H. Gardner (eds), *Fact, Fiction and Fantasy in Childhood*. San Francisco: Jossey-Bass.

Scarr, S. 1984: *Race, Social Class, and Individual Differences in I.Q.* London: Lawrence Erlbaum.

Scarr, S. 1992: Developmental theories for the 1990s: Development and individual differences. *Child Development*, 63, 1–19.

Scarr, S. and Thompson, W. 1994: Effects of maternal employment and child-care arrangements on preschoolers' cognitive and behavioral outcomes. *Early Development & Parenting*, 3, 113–23.

Scarr, S. and Weinberg, R. A. 1976: IQ test performance of black children adopted by white families. *American Psychologist*, 31, 726–39.

Schafer, M. and Smith, P. K. 1996: Teachers' perceptions of play fighting and real fighting in primary school. *Educational Research*, 38, 173–81.

Schaffer, H. R. 1996: *Social Development*. Oxford: Blackwell Publishers.

Schaffer, H. R. and Emerson, P. E. 1964: The development of social attachments in infancy. *Monographs of the Society for Research in Child Development*, 28.

Schank, R. C. and Abelson, R. P. 1977: *Scripts, Plans, Goals and Understanding*. Hillsdale, NJ: Lawrence Erlbaum.

Schank, R. C. 1982: *Dynamic Memory: a Theory of Reminding and Learning in Computers and People*. Cambridge: Cambridge University Press.

Schieffelin, B. 1990: *The Give and Take of Everyday Life: Language Socialization of Kaluli Children*. Cambridge: Cambridge University Press.

Schieffelin, B. and Ochs, E. 1983: A cultural perspective on the transition from prelinguistic to linguistic communication. In R. M. Golinkoff (ed.), *The Transition from Prelinguistic to Linguistic Communication*, pp. 115–28. Hillsdale, NJ: Lawrence Erlbaum.

Schneider, W. and Bjorklund, D. E. 1992: Expertise, aptitude and strategic remembering. *Child Development*, 63, 461–73.

Schofield, J. W. and Francis, W. D. 1982: An observational study of peer interaction in racially mixed 'accelerated' classrooms. *Journal of Educational Psychology*, 74, 722–32.

Schofield, M. 1965: *The Sexual Behaviour of Young People*. London: Longmans.

Selman, R. L. and Jaquette, D. 1977: Stability and oscillation in interpersonal awareness: a clinical-developmental analysis. In C. B. Keasey (ed.), *The Nebraska Symposium on Motivation*, vol. 25. Lincoln: University of Nebraska Press.

Serbin, L. A., Tonick, I. J. and Sternglanz, S. H. 1977: Shaping cooperative cross-sex play. *Child Development*, 48, 924–9.

Serpell, R. 1977: Estimates of intelligence in a rural community of Eastern Zambia. In F. Okatcha (ed.), *Modern Psychology and Cultural Adaptation*. Nairobi: Swahili Language Consultants and Publishers.

Serrano, J. M., Iglesias, J. and Loeches, A. 1995: Infants' responses to adult static facial expressions. *Infant Behaviour and Development*, 18, 477–82.

Seyfarth, R. M. and Cheney, D. L. 1984: The natural vocalisations of non-human primates. *Trends in Neurosciences*, 7, 66–73.

Shaffer, D. R. 1985: *Developmental Psychology: Theory, Research and Applications*. Monterey, CA: Brooks/Cole.

Shahidullah, S. and Hepper, P. G. 1993a: The developmental origins of fetal responsiveness to an acoustic stimulus. *Journal of Reproductive and Infant Psychology*, 11, 135–42.

Shahidullah, S. and Hepper, P. G. 1993b: Prenatal hearing tests? *Journal of Reproductive and Infant Psychology*, 11, 143–6.

Shapiro, G. L. 1982: Sign acquisition in a home-reared/free-ranging orang-utan: comparisons with other signing apes. *American Journal of Primatology*, 3, 121–9.

Shatz, M., Wellman, H. M. and Silber, S. 1983: The acquisition of mental verbs: A systematic investigation of first references to mental state. *Cognition*, 14, 301–21.

Shayer, M., Kuchemann, D. E. and Wylam, H. 1976: The distribution of Piagetian stages of thinking in British middle and secondary school children. *British Journal of Educational Psychology*, 46, 164–73.

Shayer, M. and Wylam, H. 1978: The distribution of Piagetian stages of thinking in British middle and secondary school children: II. *British Journal of Educational Psychology*, 48, 62–70.

Siegler, R. S. 1976: Three aspects of cognitive development. *Cognitive Psychology*, 8, 481–520.

Siegler, R. S. 1978: The origins of scientific reasoning. In R. S. Siegler (ed.), *Children's Thinking: What Develops?* Hillsdale, NJ: Erlbaum.

Singer, D. G. and Singer, J. L. 1991: *The House of Make-Believe: Children's Play and the Developing Imagination*. Cambridge, MA: Harvard University Press.

Singer, E. 1992: *Childcare and the Psychology of Development*. London: Routledge.

Skeels, H. M. 1966: Adult status of children with contrasting early life experiences: a follow-up study. *Monographs of the Society for Research in Child Development*, 31, no. 3.

Skeels, H. and Dye, H. B. 1939: A study of the effects of differential stimulation on mentally retarded children. *Proceedings of the American Association of Mental Deficiency*, 44, 114–36.

Skinner, B. F. 1957: *Verbal Behavior*. New York: Appleton-Century-Crofts.

Skodak, M. and Skeels, H. M. 1945: A follow-up study of children in adoptive homes. *Journal of Genetic Psychology*, 66, 21–58.

Skuse, D. 1984: Extreme deprivation in early childhood – II. Theoretical issues and a comparative review. *Journal of Child Psychology and Psychiatry*, 25, 543–72.

Slater, A. M., Mattock, A. and Brown, E. 1990: Newborn infants' responses to retinal and real size. *Journal of Experimental Psychology*, 49, 314–22.

Slater, A. M. and Morison, V. 1985: Shape constancy and slant perception at birth. *Perception*, 14, 337–44.

Slavin, R. E. 1987: Developmental and motivational perspectives on cooperative learning: a reconciliation. *Child Development*, 58, 1161–7.

Slobin, D. I. 1973: Cognitive prerequisites for the development of grammar. In C. A. Ferguson and D. I. Slobin (eds), *Studies in Child Language Development*. New York: Holt Rinehart.

Sluckin, A. 1981: *Growing Up in the Playground: the Social Development of Children*. London: Routledge and Kegan Paul.

Sluckin, A. M. and Smith, P. K. 1977: Two approaches to the concept of dominance in preschool children. *Child Development*, 48, 917–23.

Smetana, J. G. 1981: Preschool children's conceptions of moral and social rules. *Child Development*, 52, 1333–6.

Smilansky, S. 1968: *The Effects of Sociodramatic Play on Disadvantaged Preschool Children*. New York: Wiley.

Smilansky, S. and Shefatya, L. 1990: *Facilitating Play: A Medium for Promoting Cognitive, Socio-Emotional and Academic Development in Young Children*. Gaithersburg, MD: Psychosocial and Educational Publications.

Smith, P. K. 1974: Ethological methods. In B. M. Foss (ed.), *New Perspectives in Child Development*. Harmondsworth: Penguin.

Smith, P. K. 1978: A longitudinal study of social participation in preschool children: solitary and parallel play reexamined. *Developmental Psychology*, 14, 517–23.

Smith, P. K. 1980: Shared care of young children: alternative models to monotropism. *Merrill-Palmer Quarterly*, 26, 371–89.

Smith, P. K. 1982: Does play matter? Functional and evolutionary aspects of animal and human play. *The Behavioral and Brain Sciences*, 4, 139–84.

Smith, P. K. 1986: Exploration, play and social development in boys and girls. In D. Hargreaves and A. Colley (eds), *The Psychology of Sex Roles*. London: Harper and Row.

Smith, P. K. 1991: The silent nightmare: bullying and victimisation in school peer group. *The Psychologist*, 4, 243–8.

Smith, P. K. 1994: The war play debate. In J. H. Goldstein (ed.), *Toys, Play and Child Development*. Cambridge: Cambridge University Press.

Smith, P. K. 1996: Language and the evolution of mindreading. In P. Carruthers and P. K. Smith (eds), *Theories of Theories of Mind*, pp. 344–54. Cambridge: Cambridge University Press.

Smith, P. K. and Sharp, S. (eds) 1994: *School Bullying: Insights and Perspectives*. London: Routledge.

Smith, P. K. and Simon, T. 1984: Object play, problem-solving and creativity in children. In P. K. Smith (ed.), *Play in Animals and Humans*. Oxford: Basil Blackwell.

Smith, P. K. and Sloboda, J. 1986: Individual consistency in infant–stranger encounters. *British Journal of Developmental Psychology*, 4, 83–91.

Smith, P. K. and Vollstedt, R. 1985: On defining play: an empirical study of the relationship between play and various play criteria. *Child Development*, 56, 1042–50.

Snarey, J. R. 1985: Cross-cultural universality of social-moral development: a critical review of Kohlbergian research. *Psychological Bulletin*, 97, 202–32.

Snow, C. 1977: The development of conversation between mothers and babies. *Journal of Child Language*, 4, 1–22.

Snowling, M., Goulandris, N., Bowlby, M. and Howell, P. 1986: Segmentation and speech perception in relation to reading skill: a developmental analysis. *Journal of Experimental Child Psychology*, 41, 489–507.

Sodian, B. and Frith, U. 1992: Deception and sabotage in autistic, retarded and normal children. *Journal of Child Psychology and Psychiatry*, 33, 591–605.

Sorce, J. F., Emde, R. N., Campos, J. J. and Klinnert, M. D. 1985: Maternal emotional signalling: its effects on the visual cliff behavior of 1-year-olds. *Developmental Psychology*, 21, 195–200.

Spaccerelli, S. 1994: Stress, appraisal, and coping in child sexual abuse: a theoretical and empirical review. *Psychological Bulletin*, 116, 340–62.

Spearman, C. 1904: 'General intelligence' objectively determined and measured. *American Journal of Psychology*, 15, 201–93.

Spearman, C. 1927: *The Abilities of Man: Their Nature and Measurement*. London: Macmillan.

Spelke, E. S. 1976: Infants' intermodal perception of events. *Cognitive Psychology*, 8, 553–60.

Spelke, E. 1981: The infant's acquisition of knowledge of bimodally specified events. *Journal of Experimental Child Psychology*, 31, 279–99.

Spence, J. T. and Helmreich, R. L. 1978: *Masculinity and Femininity: their Psychological Dimensions, Correlates and Antecedents*. Austin: University of Texas Press.

Spencer, H., 1878, 1898: *The Principles of Psychology*. New York: Appleton.

Spilich, G. J., Vesonder, G. T., Chiesi, H. L. and Voss, J. 1979: Text processing of domain related information for individuals with high and low domain knowledge. *Journal of Verbal Learning and Verbal Behavior*, 18, 275–90.

Spitz, R. A. 1946: Hospitalism: a follow-up report. *Psychoanalytic Study of the Child*, 2, 113–18.

Sprinthall, N., Hall, J. and Gerber, E. 1992: Peer counselling for middle school students experiencing family divorce: a deliberate psychological education model. *Elementary School Guidance and Counselling*, 26, 4, 279–94.

Sroufe, L. A. 1977: Wariness of strangers and the study of infant development. *Child Development*, 48, 731–46.

Steinberg, L. 1987: Impact of puberty on family relations: effects of pubertal status and pubertal timing. *Developmental Psychology*, 23, 451–60.

Steinberg, L. 1988: Reciprocal relation between parent–child distance and pubertal maturation. *Developmental Psychology*, 24, 122–8.

Steinberg, L., Lamborn, S. D., Dornbusch, S. M. and Darling, N. 1992: Impact of parenting practices on adolescent achievement: Authoritative parenting, school involvement, and encouragement to succeed. *Child Development*, 63, 1266–81.

Stern, D. N. 1990: *Diary of a Baby*. Harmondsworth: Penguin.

Stern, D. N., Spieker, S., Barnett, R. K. and MacKain, K. 1983: The prosody of maternal speech: infant age and context related changes. *Journal of Child Language*, 10, 1–15.

Sternberg, R. J. 1985: *Beyond IQ. A Triarchic Theory of Human Intelligence*. Cambridge: Cambridge University Press.

Sternberg, R. J., Conway, B. E., Ketron, J. L. and Bernstein, M. 1981: People's conceptions of intelligence. *Journal of Personality and Social Psychology*, 1, 37–55.

Sternberg, R. J. and Rifkin, B. 1979: The development of analogical reasoning processes. *Journal of Experimental Child Psychology*, 27, 195–232.

Sternglanz, S. H. and Serbin, L. 1974: Sex-role stereotyping in children's television programming. *Developmental Psychology*, 10, 710–15.

Sternglanz, S. H., Gray, J. L. and Murakami, M. 1977: Adult preference for infantile facial features: an ethological approach. *Animal Behaviour*, 25, 108–15.

Stewart, R. B. 1983: Sibling attachment relationships: child–infant interactions in the strange situation. *Developmental Psychology*, 19, 192–9.

St. James-Roberts, I. 1989: Persistent crying in infancy. *Journal of Child Psychology and Psychiatry*, 29, 21–42.

St. James-Roberts, I. and Wolke, D. 1984: Comparison of mothers' with trained observers' reports of neonatal behavioral style. *Infant Behavior and Development*, 7, 299–310.

Strayer, F. F. and Strayer, J. 1976: An ethological analysis of social agonism and dominance relations among preschool children. *Child Development*, 47, 980–9.

Sundet, J. M., Magnus, P., Kvalem, I. L., Samuelsen, S. O. and Bakketeig, L. S. 1992: Secular trends and sociodemographic regularities of coital debut age in Norway. *Archives of Sexual Behavior*, 21, 241–52.

Suomi, S. J. and Harlow, H. F. 1972: Social rehabilitation of isolate-reared monkeys. *Developmental Psychology*, 6, 487–96.

Sutton-Smith, B. 1966: Piaget on play: a critique. *Psychological Review*, 73, 104–10.

Sutton-Smith, B. 1967: The role of play in cognitive development. *Young Children*, 22, 361–70.

Sutton-Smith, B. 1986: *Toys as Culture*. New York: Gardner Press.

Sutton-Smith, B. 1988: War toys and childhood aggression. *Play and Culture*, 1, 57–69.

Swann Report 1985: *Education for All*. London: HMSO, Cmnd 9453.

Sylva, K. and Lunt, I. 1981: *Child Development: an Introductory Text*. Oxford: Basil Blackwell.

Sylva, K., Roy, C. and Painter, M. 1980: *Child Watching at Playgroup and Nursery School*. London: Grant McIntyre.

Symons, D. 1978: *Play and Aggression: a Study of Rhesus Monkeys*. New York: Columbia University Press.

Symons, D. 1979: *The Evolution of Human Sexuality*. New York and Oxford: Oxford University Press.

Takahashi, K. 1990: Are the key assumptions of the 'strange situation' procedure universal? A view from Japanese research. *Human Development*, 33, 23–30.

Takhvar, M. and Smith, P. K. 1990: A review and critique of Smilansky's classification scheme and the 'nested hierarchy' of play categories. *Journal of Research in Childhood Education*, 4, 112–22.

Tanner, J. M. 1962: *Growth at Adolescence*, Second edition. Oxford: Basil Blackwell.

Tanner, J. M. 1973: Growing Up. *Scientific American*, 229 (Sept.), 35–43.

Tattum, D. P. and Lane, D. A. 1989: *Bullying in Schools*. Stoke-on-Trent: Trentham Books.

Teller, D. Y. and Bornstein, M. H. 1987: Infant color vision and color perception. In P. Salapatek and L. Cohen (eds), *Handbook of Infant Perception: Vol. 1, From Sensation to Perception*. New York: Academic Press.

Terrace, H. S., Pettito, L., Sanders, R. J. and Bever, T. G. 1979: Can an ape create a sentence? *Science*, 206, 891–902.

Thomas, A. and Chess, S. 1977: *Temperament and Development*. New York: Brunner/Mazel.

Thompson, R. A., Tinsley, B. R., Scalora, M. J. and Parke, R. D. 1989: Grandparents' visitation rights: legalizing the ties that bind. *American Psychologist*, 44, 1217–22.

Thompson, S. K. 1975: Gender labels and early sex-role development. *Child Development*, 46, 339–47.

Thorndike, R., Hagen, E. and Sattler, J. 1985: Stanford–Binet Intelligence Scale: Fourth Edition SB-FE. Windsor: NFER-Nelson.

Thorpe, W. H. 1972: Vocal communication in birds. In R. A. Hinde (ed.), *Non-verbal Communication*. Cambridge: Cambridge University Press.

Thurstone, L. L. 1931: *Multiple Factor Analysis*. Chicago: University of Chicago Press.

Tinbergen, N. 1951: *The Study of Instinct*. Oxford: Clarendon Press.

Tinsley, B. J. and Parke, R. D. 1984: Grandparents as support and socialization agents. In M. Lewis (ed.), *Beyond the Dyad*. New York: Plenum.

Tizard, B. and Hodges, J. 1978: The effect of early institutional rearing on the development of eight-year-old children. *Journal of Child Psychology and Psychiatry*, 19, 99–118.

Tizard, B. and Phoenix, A. 1993: *Black, White or Mixed Race?* London: Routledge.

Tizard, B. and Rees, J. 1974: A comparison of the effects of adoption, restoration to the natural mother, and continued institutionalization on the cognitive development of 4-year-old children. *Child Development*, 45, 92–9.

Tizard, J. and Tizard, B. 1971: The social development of two-year-old children in residential nurseries. In H. R. Schaffer (ed.), *The Origins of Human Social Relations*. London: Academic Press.

Tomasello, M. 1996: Chimpanzee social cognition. *Monographs of the Society for Research in Child Development*, 61, no. 3, pp. 161–73.

Tomlinson-Keasey, C. 1978: The structure of concrete operational thought. *Child Development*, 50, 1153–63.

Topping, K. 1988: *The Peer Tutoring Handbook*. London: Croom Helm.

Torrance, E. P. 1972: Predictive validity of the Torrance Tests of Creative Thinking. *Journal of Creative Behaviour*, 6, 236–52.

Townsend, P. 1957: *The Family Life of Old People*. London: Routledge and Kegan Paul.

Tremblay-Leveau, H. and Nadel, J. 1996: Exclusion in triads: can it serve 'metacommunicative' knowledge in 11 and 24 months children? *British Journal of Developmental Psychology*, 14, 145–58.

Trevarthen, C. and Logotheti, K. 1989: Child in society, and society in children: the nature of basic trust. In S. Howell and R. Willis (eds), *Societies at Peace*. London: Routledge.

Trevathan, W. 1987: *Human Birth: an Evolutionary Perspective*. New York: Aldine de Gruyter.

Trivers, R. L. 1971: The evolution of reciprocal altruism. *Quarterly Review of Biology*, 46, 35–57.

Trivers, R. L. 1974: Parent–offspring conflict. *American Zoologist*, 14, 249–64.

Troyna, B. and Hatcher, R. 1992: *Racism in Children's Lives*. London: Routledge.

Turiel, E. 1983: *The Development of Social Knowledge: Morality and Convention*. Cambridge: Cambridge University Press.

Underwood, B. and Moore, B. S. 1982: The generality of altruism in children. In N. Eisenberg (ed.), *The Development of Prosocial Behavior*. New York: Academic Press.

Van Cantfort, T. E. and Rimpau, J. B. 1982: Sign language studies with children and chimpanzees. *Sign Language Studies*, 34, 15–72.

Van IJzendoorn, M. H. 1995: Adult attachment representations. *Psychological Bulletin*, 117, 387–403.

Van IJzendoorn, M. H. and Bakermans-Kranenburg, M. J. 1996: Attachment representations in mothers, fathers, adolescents and clinical groups: a meta-analytic search for normative data. *Journal of Consulting and Clinical Psychology*, 64, 8–21.

Van IJzendoorn, M. H. and Kroonenberg, P. M. 1988: Cross-cultural patterns of attachment: A meta-analysis of the Strange Situation. *Child Development*, 59, 147–56.

Van IJzendoorn, M. H., Juffer, F. and Duyvesteyn, M. G. C. 1995: Breaking the intergenerational cycle of insecure attachment: a review of the effects of attachment-based interventions on maternal sensitivity and infant security. *Journal of Child Psychology and Psychiatry*, 36, 225–48.

Varendonck, J. 1911: Les témoignages d'enfants dans un procès retentissant. *Archives de Psychologie*, 11, 129–71.

Vaughn, B. E. and Langlois, J. H. 1983: Physical attractiveness as a correlate of peer status and social competence in preschool children. *Developmental Psychology*, 19, 561–7.

Vernon, P. E. 1950: *The Structure of Human Abilities*. London: Methuen.

Vollmer, H. 1937: The grandmother: a problem in child rearing. *American Journal of Orthopsychiatry*, 7, 378–82.

Vurpillot, E. 1968: The development of scanning strategies and their relation to visual differentiation. *Journal of Experimental Child Psychology*, 6, 632–50.

Vygotsky, L. 1962 (1934): *Thought and Language*. Cambridge, MA: MIT Press.

Vygotsky, L. S. 1966 (1933): Play and its role in the mental development of the child. *Voprosy Psikhologii*, 12, 62–76.

Vygotsky, L. S. 1978: *Mind in Society*. Edited by M. Cole, V. John-Steiner, S. Scribner and E. Souberman. Cambridge, MA: Harvard University Press.

Vygotsky, L. S. 1981: The genesis of higher mental functions. In J. V. Wertsch (ed.), *The Concept of Activity in Soviet Psychology*. Armonk, NY: Sharpe.

Waddington, C. H. 1957: *The Strategy of the Genes*. London: Allen and Unwin.

Walk, R. D. 1981: *Perceptual Development*. Monterey, CA: Brooks/Cole.

Wallerstein, J. S. 1985: Children of divorce – emerging trends. *Psychiatric Clinics of North America*, 8, 837–55.

Wallerstein, J. S. 1987: Children of divorce: report of a ten-year follow-up of early latency-age children. *American Journal of Orthopsychiatry*, 57, 199–211.

Walton, G. E., Bower, N. J. A. and Bower, T. G. R. 1992: Recognition of familiar faces by newborns. *Infant Behaviour and Development*, 15, 265–9.

Warren, A. R., Hulse-Trotter, K. and Tubbs, E. 1991: Inducing resistance to suggestibility in children. *Law and Human Behavior*, 15, 273–85.

Waterman, A. S. 1982: Identity development from adolescence to adulthood: an extension of theory and a review of research. *Developmental Psychology*, 18, 341–58.

Waterman, A. S., Geary, P. S. and Waterman, C. K. 1974: Identity status of college students in occupational and ideological areas. *Developmental Psychology*, 10, 387–92.

Waterman, C. K. and Waterman, A. S. 1975: Fathers and sons: a study of ego identity across two generations. *Journal of Youth and Adolescence*, 4, 331–8.

Waters, E., Vaughn, B. E., Posada, G. and Kondo-Ikemura, K. 1995: Caregiving, cultural, and cognitive perspectives on secure-base behavior and working models. *Monographs of the Society for Research in Child Development*, 60, nos 2–3.

Watson, M. W. and Peng, Y. 1992: The relation between toy gun play and children's aggressive behavior. *Early Education and Development*, 3, 370–89.

Wechsler, D. 1944: *The Measurement of Adult Intelligence*, Third edition. Baltimore: Williams and Wilkins.

Wechsler, D. 1986: *Adult Intelligence Scale – Revised UK Edition (WAIS-R^{UK})*. London: Psychological Corporation.

Wechsler, D. 1990: *Wechsler Pre-school and Primary Scale of Intelligence – Revised UK Edition (WPPSI-R^{UK})*. London: Psychological Corporation.

Wechsler, D. 1992: *Intelligence Scale for Children – Third UK Edition (WISC-III^{UK})*. London: Psychological Corporation.

Wedge, P. and Essen, J. 1982: *Children in Adversity*. London: Pan.

Weikart, D., Deloria, D., Lawser, S. and Wiegerink, R. 1970: Longitudinal results of the Ypsilanti Perry preschool project. *Monographs of the High-Scope Educational Research Foundation*, No. 1.

Weikart, D. 1996: High quality pre-school programs found to improve adult status. *Childhood*, 3, 117–20.

Weinraub, M., Clemens, L. P., Sockloff, A., Ethridge, T., Gracely, E. and Myers, B. 1984: The development of sex role stereotypes in the third year: relationships to gender labeling, gender identity, sex-typed toy preference and family characteristics. *Child Development*, 55, 1493–503.

Weinraub, M. and Lewis, M. 1977: The determinants of children's responses to separation. *Monographs of the Society for Research in Child Development*, 42, 1–78.

Weir, R. 1962: *Language in the Crib*. The Hague: Mouton.

Weisel, T. N. and Hubel, D. H. 1963: Single-cell responses in striate cortex of kittens deprived of vision in one eye. *Journal of Neurophysiology*, 26, 1003–17.

Weisler, A. and McCall, R. B. 1976: Exploration and play. *American Psychologist*, 31, 492–508.

Weisner, T. S. and Gallimore, R. 1977: My brother's keeper: child and sibling caretaking. *Current Anthropology*, 18, 169–90.

Wellman, H. M. 1990: *The Child's Theory of Mind*. Cambridge, MA: MIT Press.

Wellman, H. M. and Estes, D. 1986: Early understanding of mental entities: a re-examination of childhood realism. *Child Development*, 57, 910–23.

Wells, C. G. 1983: Talking with children: the complementary roles of parents and teachers. In M. Donaldson (ed.), *Early Childhood Development and Education*. Oxford: Basil Blackwell.

Wells, C. G. 1985: *Language Development in the Preschool Years*. Cambridge: Cambridge University Press.

Werker, J. F. and Tees, R. C. 1985: Cross-language speech perceptions: evidence for perceptual reorganization during the first year of life. *Infant Behavior and Development*, 7, 49–63.

Wertsch, J. V., McNamee, G. D., McLane, J. B. and Budwig, N. A. 1980: The adult–child dyad as a problem-solving system. *Child Development*, 51, 1215–21.

Wertsch, J. V. and Tulviste, P. 1996: L. S. Vygotsky and contemporary developmental psychology. In H. Daniels (ed.), *An Introduction to Vygotsky*. London: Routledge.

Westcott, H., Davies, G. and Clifford, B. 1989: The use of anatomical dolls in child witness interviews. *Adoption and Fostering*, 13, 6–14.

Westin-Lindgren, G. 1982: Achievement and mental ability of physically late and early maturing school children related to their social background. *Journal of Child Psychology and Psychiatry*, 23, 407–20.

Whitbread, N. 1972: *The Evolution of the Nursery-Infant School*. London: Routledge and Kegan Paul.

Whiten, A. (ed.) 1991: *Natural Theories of Mind: Evolution, Development and Stimulation of Everyday Mindreading*. Oxford: Basil Blackwell.

Whiten, A. and Byrne, R. W. 1988: Tactical deception in primates. *Behavioral and Brain Sciences*, 11, 233–73.

Whiten, A. and Byrne, R. W. 1991: The emergence of metarepresentation in human ontogeny and primate phylogeny. In A. Whiten (ed.), *Natural Theories of Mind: Evolution, Development and Stimulation of Everyday Mindreading*. Oxford: Basil Blackwell.

Whiting, B. and Edwards, C. P. 1973: A cross-cultural analysis of sex differences in the behavior of children aged three through 11. *Journal of Social Psychology*, 91, 171–88.

Whiting, B. B. and Whiting, J. W. M. 1975: *Children of Six Cultures: a Psycho-cultural Analysis*. Cambridge, MA and London: Harvard University Press.

Whiting, J. W. M., Kluckhohn, C. and Anthony, A. 1958: The functions of male initiation ceremonies at puberty. In E. Maccoby, T. Newcomb and E. Hartley (eds), *Readings in Social Psychology*. New York: Holt.

Whitney, I. and Smith, P. K. 1993: A survey of the nature and extent of bully/victim problems in junior/middle and secondary schools. *Educational Research*, 35, 3–25.

Willatts, P. 1989: Development of problem solving in infancy. In A. Slater and G. Bremner (eds), *Infant Development*. Hillsdale, NJ: Lawrence Erlbaum.

Williams, B. and Gilmour, J. 1994: Sociometry and peer relations. *Journal of Child Psychology and Psychiatry*, 35, 997–1013.

Wilson, E. O. 1978: *On Human Nature*. Cambridge, MA: Harvard University Press.

Wimmer, H. and Perner, J. 1983: Beliefs about beliefs: representations and constraining function of wrong beliefs in young children's understanding of deception. *Cognition*, 13, 103–28.

Wissler, C. 1901: The correlation of mental and physical tests. *The Psychological Review, Monograph Supplement*, 3(6).

Wober, M. 1974: Towards an understanding of the Kiganda concept of intelligence. In J. W. Berry and P. Dasen (eds), *Culture and Cognition: Readings in Cross-cultural Psychology*. London: Methuen.

Wohlwill, J. F. 1984: Relationships between exploration and play. In T. D. Yawkey and A. D. Pellegrini (eds), *Child's Play: Developmental and Applied*. Hillsdale, NJ: Lawrence Erlbaum.

Wood, D. J. 1988: *How Children Think and Learn*. Oxford: Basil Blackwell.

Wood, D. J., Bruner, J. S. and Ross, G. 1976: The role of tutoring in problem-solving. *Journal of Child Psychology and Psychiatry*, 17, 89–100.

Woollett, A. and Phoenix, A. 1991: Psychological views of mothering. In A. Phoenix, A. Woollett and E. Lloyd (eds), *Motherhoods: Meanings, Practices and Ideologies*. London: Sage.

Wright, C. 1985: The influences of school processes on the educational opportunities of children of West Indian origin. *Multicultural Teaching*, 4.1, Autumn.

Wright, D. 1990: Towards an adequate coneption of early oral development. In P. Kutnick and C. Rogers (eds), *The Social Psychology of the Primary School*. London: Routledge.

Wright, J., Binney, V. and Smith, P. K. 1995: Security of attachment in 8–12-year-olds: a revised version of the Separation Anxiety Test, its psychometric properties and clinical interpretation. *Journal of Child Psychology and Psychiatry*, 36, 757–74.

Young, F. W. 1965: *Initiation Ceremonies: a Cross Cultural Study of Status Dramatization*. Indianapolis: Bobbs-Merrill.

Youniss, J. 1980: *Parents and Peers in Social Development*. Chicago: University of Chicago Press.

Yussen, S. R. and Levy, V. M. 1975: Developmental changes in predicting one's own span of short-term memory. *Journal of Experimental Child Psychology*, 19, 502–8.

Zahn-Waxler, C. and Radke-Yarrow, M. 1982: The development of altruism: alternative research strategies. In N. Eisenberg (ed.), *The Development of Prosocial Behaviour*. New York: Academic Press.

Zahn-Waxler, C., Radke-Yarrow, M. and King, R. A. 1979: Child rearing and children's prosocial initiations toward victims of distress. *Child Development*, 50, 319–30.

Zarbatany, L., Hartmann, D. P. and Gelfand, D. M. 1985: Why does children's generosity increase with age: susceptibility to experimenter influence or altruism? *Child Development*, 56, 746–56.

Index